Introduction to Learning and Behavior

Third Edition

RUSSELL A. POWELL

Grant MacEwan College

DIANE G. SYMBALUK

Grant MacEwan College

P. LYNNE HONEY

Grant MacEwan College

WADSWORTH
CENGAGE Learning™

Australia • Brazil • Japan • Korea • Mexico • Singapore • Spain • United Kingdom • United States

WADSWORTH
CENGAGE Learning™

Introduction to Learning and Behavior, Third Edition
Russell A. Powell,
Diane G. Symbaluk
and P. Lynne Honey

Publisher: Michele Sordi

Assistant Editor: Rebecca Rosenberg

Editorial Assistant: Ryan Patrick

Technology Project Manager: Lauren Keyes

Executive Marketing Manager: Kim Russell

Marketing Communications Manager: Talia Wise

Project Manager, Editorial Production: Pat Waldo

Creative Director: Rob Hugel

Art Director: Vernon Boes

Print Buyer: Linda Hsu

Rights Acquisitions Account Manager, Text: Mollika Basu

Rights Acquisition Account Manager, Image: Deanna Ettinger

Text Researcher: Karyn Morrison

Photo Researcher: Terri Miller

Production Service: Deepti Narwat, International Typesetting and Composition

Text Designer: Brenda Duke

Copy Editor: Christianne Thillen

Cover Designer: Lisa Devenish

Cover Image: Alec Pytlowany/ Masterfile

Compositor: International Typesetting and Composition

For product information and technology assistance, contact us at **Cengage Learning Customer & Sales Support, 1-800-354-9706**

For permission to use material from this text or product, submit all requests online at **cengage.com/permissions**
Further permissions questions can be e-mailed to **permissionrequest@cengage.com**

Library of Congress Control Number: 2008922450

ISBN-13: 978-0-495-59528-1

ISBN-10: 0-495-59528-4

Wadsworth
10 Davis Drive
Belmont, CA 94002-3098
USA

Cengage Learning is a leading provider of customized learning solutions with office locations around the globe, including Singapore, the United Kingdom, Australia, Mexico, Brazil, and Japan. Locate your local office at **international.cengage.com/region**

Cengage Learning products are represented in Canada by Nelson Education, Ltd.

For your course and learning solutions, visit **academic.cengage.com**

Purchase any of our products at your local college store or at our preferred online store **www.ichapters.com**

Printed in Canada
1 2 3 4 5 6 7 12 11 10 09 08

To parents, mentors, and students who shaped our behavior so well as to make this book a reality.

Brief Contents

Contents

CHAPTER 2 Research Methods 50

CHAPTER 3 Elicited Behaviors and Classical Conditioning 91

CHAPTER 4 Classical Conditioning: Basic Phenomena and Various Complexities 128

CHAPTER 7 Schedules and Theories of Reinforcement 257

CHAPTER 8 Extinction and Stimulus Control 295

CHAPTER 9 Escape, Avoidance, and Punishment 339

CHAPTER 10 Choice, Matching, and Self-Control 379

CHAPTER 11 Biological Dispositions in Learning 421

CHAPTER 12 Observational Learning, Language, and Rule-Governed Behavior 457

Preface

"I wouldn't do this to my budgie," a student once muttered following a lecture in which I (the senior author of this text) had discussed the process of reinforcement. She apparently saw the use of reinforcement as manipulative and reprehensible. I can't remember how I responded (probably with something a bit more diplomatic than what follows), but I could have said that she actually does "this" to her budgie all the time and is simply not aware of it. Moreover, because she's not aware of it, she may be reinforcing her budgie's behavior quite erratically, with the result that the two of them are having a much less fulfilling relationship than they could be having. Unfortunately, this student's negative reaction to behavioral principles of conditioning is not uncommon, and most instructors who teach such courses can probably recount similar instances. Thus, one goal of this text is to help convince students that conditioning is not some dangerous form of manipulation, but rather a natural process that we do far better to understand and apply wisely than to ignore and apply carelessly.

Another opinion sometimes voiced is that the principles of conditioning, many of which have been derived from research with animals, are largely irrelevant to important aspects of human behavior. After all, how can studies of lever-pressing rats or key-pecking pigeons say anything meaningful about what truly matters to us? This was the very conclusion that I (the senior author again) came to when, as an undergraduate, I first encountered a demonstration of operant conditioning in my introductory psychology class. We were shown a film in which pigeons were taught to peck a little plastic disk (which I later learned is called a "response key") to earn food. The whole endeavor struck me as so completely artificial—not to mention mind-numbingly boring—that I couldn't understand why any psychologist would waste his or her time on it. Little did I know that some years later I would find myself sitting in a pigeon lab, thrilled that I had been given an opportunity to study something so interesting and important! What I had learned in the interim was that (1) you have to be careful what you criticize (fate has a way of making us pay for our arrogance) and (2) many of the principles derived from conditioning experiments with animals are among the most useful principles ever discovered by psychologists. Thus, a second goal of this text is to help convince students that the principles derived from behavioral research are far from irrelevant, and they often have useful and provocative things to say about human behavior.

An even more basic goal of this text is to provide students with a clear introduction to the basic principles of learning and behavior that would be both accessible and engaging, especially for those who may have had only limited prior exposure to these principles (such as in an introductory psychology course). Those students who later proceed to a higher-level course in the subject matter (one that might utilize, for example, Domjan's *The Principles of Learning and Behavior* or Lieberman's *Learning: Behavior and Cognition* as a text) will then have a solid foundation on which to build. Students who do not proceed to a higher-level course will nevertheless have gained an appreciation for the behavioral perspective and learned much that may be of relevance to their everyday lives and future careers.

Key Characteristics

The following summarizes some key characteristics of this text:

- **It emphasizes basic principles of learning and behavior rather than theory.** To the extent that theory is discussed, it is either because the theory itself has something meaningful and provocative to say about human behavior (e.g., melioration theory as discussed in Chapter 10) or because a simplified overview of certain theories (e.g., the Rescorla-Wagner theory, as presented in Chapter 5) can help prepare students for a more in-depth discussion of those theories in a higher-level course.
- **It attempts to strike an appropriate balance between basic research findings, many of which are derived from animal research, and the application of those findings to important and interesting aspects of human behavior.** Although many texts make this claim, we feel that this text represents a truly concerted effort in that direction. Wherever possible, examples from research paradigms with rats or pigeons are juxtaposed with everyday examples with humans. And although some of the applications to humans are highly speculative, they nevertheless represent the type of speculation that behaviorists themselves often engage in and that many students find entertaining and memorable.
- **Following from the above, this text is especially innovative in the many examples given of the application of behavioral principles to understanding certain aspects of romantic relationships.** In particular, scattered throughout the text are *Advice for the Lovelorn* columns in which hypothetical students are given behavioral-type advice concerning their relationship difficulties. Personal relationships are, of course, a key concern

for many students, who are often fascinated by the notion that behavioral principles may be helpful in understanding and resolving problematic relationships. These columns have thus proven to be an effective way to maintain student interest in the material, enhance their grasp of certain concepts, and provide them with a sense of what it means to think like a behaviorist. (Students are of course given due warning that the advice in these columns is quite speculative and not to be taken too seriously.)

- **This text contains numerous pedagogical features designed to facilitate students' ability to study and understand the material.** These features are described later in the section on learning aids.
- **The text contains many interesting and thought-provoking topics not normally found in textbooks on learning and behavior.** Many of these topics are presented in special boxed inserts entitled *And Furthermore*, which are intended to expand on material presented in the preceding section.

Changes to the Third Edition

Over the first two editions of this text, several professors have commented that this is the first textbook they have used that truly engages their students in the subject matter. Students likewise have almost overwhelmingly endorsed this text as one of the most interesting and student-friendly textbooks they have encountered. (In fact, the text is apparently also "bar-friendly." One of our students informed us that she regularly took it to the lounge where she waitressed and kept it on the counter to study from during her breaks. Patrons started passing it around, and it quickly became a big hit! "You should sell it to drinking establishments," the student commented, a suggestion that we have however declined to follow.) All of this feedback was, needless to say, very gratifying and confirms that we essentially fulfilled the goals we were trying to accomplish in the writing of this text.

Given the very positive feedback we have received to the first two editions, we did not undertake any radical changes to this third edition. Indeed, some major changes that we did propose for this third edition were soundly rejected by several reviewers, since it would have involved replacing material that they very much wanted to see remain. Hence, as with the second edition, many of the changes to this third edition have been directed mostly toward improving upon the present material, such as by clarifying concepts, adding examples, and tightening up definitions. Nevertheless, some significant changes have been made. For example, continuing a trend that started with the second edition, we have made a concerted effort to include more material on the contributions of evolutionary theory to behavior and learning. For example, Chapter 1 now contains an entire section on Darwin's theory of evolution as a contributing factor toward the rise of behaviorism, along with an extended discussion of the principle of natural selection. The recent trend toward considering and investigating evolutionary influences on behavior can be found in several other sections throughout the text, such as the inclusion of comparative control group designs in the discussion of research methods in Chapter 2 and the discussion of the evolutionary significance of sensitization and habituation in Chapter 3. Other significant changes to this edition include an expanded discussion of the compensatory-response model of conditioning in Chapter 5, especially as it applies to drug tolerance and addiction, with a more detailed and accurate presentation of the underlying process. The section on self-control in Chapter 10 has also been significantly altered. The various sections have been reorganized with *Mischel's delay of gratification paradigm* now presented before the *Ainslie-Rachlin model* (reviewers have told us that this sequence works better). As well, the hot–cool model that was added in the last edition has been dropped in favor of (what we have called) the *small-but-cumulative effects model*, which students are likely to find more engaging and applicable to understanding their own difficulties in self-control. The latter model follows more clearly from the Ainslie-Rachlin model (and, as we show, can even be considered an addition to it), and it is more congruent with the overarching theme of self-control as a temporal issue. Promoted most strongly by Malott (e.g., 1989), it is also a model that deserves more discussion in the research literature on self-control; giving it a distinctive title will hopefully assist in that process.

Probably the most significant change to this edition is the revised section on observational learning in Chapter 12, which now includes an extended, and timely, discussion of the relationship between exposure to media violence (including violent computer games) and aggression. Also included is a discussion of contagious behavior, generalized imitation, and an update on the controversy over the occurrence of "true imitation" in animals. Another new addition to this section is a discussion of whether animals sometimes engage in the act of "deliberately" teaching each other. To make room for this expanded discussion of observational learning, the section on acceptance and commitment therapy that was added in the second edition has now been dropped from this chapter. Most reviewers agreed with this exchange and regarded the revised chapter as considerably stronger than the previous version.

Learning Aids

This text contains many pedagogical features designed to facilitate students' reading and comprehension of the material. These include the following:

- **Quick Quizzes.** Scattered throughout each chapter are many fill-in-the-blank quizzes. The purpose of these quizzes is to help students actively work with the material as they read it. Although an early reviewer of the first edition commented that such frequent quizzing might frustrate students by interrupting their reading, actual use of the material in class revealed quite the opposite. Students uniformly commented that the quizzes were extremely beneficial in helping them engage with and process the material. They especially appreciated the *Quick Quizzes* embedded within sections that they perceived as quite technical, simply because the quizzes broke the material up into short chunks that they were better able to assimilate. Students therefore demanded more quizzes, not fewer, and the authors duly complied.

- **Study Questions.** A focused set of about 15 to 20 study questions is included at the end of each chapter. These study questions cover the most basic concepts discussed in that chapter. Because these questions are quite focused and require a relatively short answer—varying from a sentence to a paragraph in length—students are likely to incorporate them into their studying (as opposed to the standard, comprehensive list of learning objectives found in many texts, which many students unfortunately often ignore). Students can be further motivated to answer the study questions if instructors inform them that some of these questions may appear as short-answer items on exams. In fact, the senior author's own strategy is to utilize a random sample of these questions for weekly chapter tests. Students are required to answer five of the study questions, but do not know which five will be presented.
- **Concept Reviews.** Each chapter is followed by a concept review, which lists all key terms and definitions in the chapter. These key terms and definitions are then reiterated in the glossary at the end of the text.
- **Chapter Tests.** Each chapter ends with a chapter test, consisting mostly of fill-in-the-blank items. This test provides comprehensive coverage of the material presented in the chapter. It differs from the *Quick Quizzes* in that more items are of a conceptual, rather than factual, nature, thereby encouraging students to think more deeply about the material. These test items are numbered in random order, so that students can immediately look up the answer to any particular question without having to worry about inadvertently seeing the answer to the next question.
- **Opening Vignettes.** Each chapter begins with a chapter outline, followed by either a quotation or a vignette related to the material presented in that chapter. The vignettes usually consist of a short, fictional scenario illustrating a particular concept. The exact concept involved is not immediately revealed, however, thus encouraging students to actively ponder how the material they are reading may be related to the scenario. (An explanation of the concept each scenario is intended to illustrate can be found in the instructor's manual.)

Web Site Materials and Alternative Course Delivery

Accompanying this text is a well-designed student resource Web site that contains additional information, practice tests (including multiple-choice, short-answer, and fill-in-the-blank), answers to all *Quick Quiz* items in the text, and interesting Web links designed to enhance students' learning experience. This material will prove especially useful for instructors who are considering offering a learning and behavior course (especially a Web-based course) in a nonlecture, alternative delivery format. In fact, this text, with its many pedagogical features, was explicitly designed to function as a student-friendly, independent learning tool, and the senior author himself has used it as such for an independent study, computer-based, alternative delivery course.

Instructor's Manual

The instructor's manual includes a comprehensive test bank containing a large number of multiple-choice items per chapter, many of which are new or revised for this edition. Many of these items are conceptual in nature. They are organized by textbook headings and subheadings. A portion of the test bank items are drawn from the practice test items at the student resource Web site (and are clearly marked as such); thus, by including some of these items on exams and quizzes, instructors will be able to motivate students to access and work through these ancillary materials. The instructor's manual also contains answers to all of the *Quick Quiz* and study question items for each chapter, as well as a set of annotated Web links where students will find information of interest. In response to a clever suggestion from certain students and instructors, the manual also contains a description of how the *Advice for the Lovelorn* column can be adapted as a student assignment (along with additional examples of such columns that can be provided to students to facilitate their own efforts).

Computerized Test Bank

To ease the task of creating and generating tests, an electronic version of the test bank is available in either PC or Macintosh configuration. The program is user-friendly and allows instructors to insert their own questions. The test bank also contains a full listing of the end-of-chapter study questions, enabling instructors to easily generate a sample of these items for weekly quizzes or for inclusion as short-answer items on midterm and final exams.

Sniffy™ the Virtual Rat Lite, Version 2.0: An Available Option

Sniffy, the Virtual Rat Lite provides every student with hands-on experience in applying, either at home or in school, the principles of operant and classical conditioning. Sniffy is a computer-generated rat that can be taught to press a lever to earn food, a protocol that is then used to demonstrate many aspects of both operant and classical conditioning. Students purchasing Sniffy receive a laboratory manual with instructions, and a hybrid CD-ROM that operates on Mac OS Version 8.6 or later and Windows 95 SE, ME, 2000, or XP.

The Lite version of Sniffy includes 16 exercises that cover the essential phenomena of learning psychology. The stimulant operant phenomena covered include magazine training; shaping; primary and secondary reinforcement; variable-interval, variable-ratio, fixed-interval, and fixed-ratio schedule effects; and the partial-reinforcement effect. The classical conditioning phenomena covered include acquisition, extinction, and spontaneous recovery.

Students enjoy working with Sniffy and report that these exercises greatly enhance their understanding of the basic principles. We do not, of course, propose that Sniffy can fully substitute for the actual experience of working with live animals. Unfortunately, for various reasons, most institutions are no longer able to offer this valuable opportunity to their undergraduates. Sniffy was created precisely to fill this void. Additionally, some schools use Sniffy as a warm-up before allowing students to work with real animals. More information about *Sniffy, the Virtual Rat Lite, Version 2.0*, visit academic.cengage.com or obtain a 6-minute videotape by calling Wadsworth at 1-877-999-2350. Sniffy's creators discuss on the tape how they use Sniffy in their classes, and students describe their experiences working with Sniffy.

Acknowledgments

We wish to thank "Dr. Dee," Ally McBeal (who was all the rage on television when this text was first conceived), and all the other people (real and fictional) who inspired the *Advice to the Lovelorn* features. We also thank the following reviewers for their comments and suggestions, many of which we were able to incorporate and which have undoubtedly served to strengthen the text: Kevin Antshel, Le Moyne College; John Chelonis, State University of New York, Brockport; Eric Clapham, University of Nevada, Reno; Thomas Scott Critchfield, Illinois State University; Steven Dworkin, Jacksonville State University; Mirari Elcoro, West Virginia University; Renee Ha, University of Washington; Arthur Kennelly, Grossmont College; Neil Levens, University of South Carolina; Rebecca Newman-Gonchar, University of La Verne; Lesley Ricci, Northeastern University; Mary Shelton, Tennessee State University; James T. Todd, Eastern Michigan University; and Jane Vignovic, North Carolina State University. The improvements made in this third edition are largely a function of their helpful feedback and suggestions. Unfortunately, space limitations and conflicting requirements prevent us from incorporating all their suggestions. We especially wish to thank Dr. Todd Morris, who provided us with very lengthy and detailed feedback on several chapters in the first half of the text. His expertise on historical issues pertaining to behavior analysis was particularly appreciated (along with his wry sense of humor). Several changes in this edition are the direct the result of his input, although they represent only a fraction of his many suggestions, some of which we intend to seriously consider for the next edition.

In addition, we thank the great people at Wadsworth, including Michele Sordi, Rebecca Rosenberg, Ryan Patrick, Sara Swangard, Vernon Boes, and Pat Waldo, for all their support and hard work.

Finally, a very special thanks to Dr. Suzanne E. MacDonald, who served as a coauthor on earlier editions of the text and whose wonderfully engaging account of meeting the "wonderapes" of ape language research, Chantek and Kanzi, we have retained in Chapter 12.

Russ Powell
Diane Symbaluk
Lynne Honey

About the Authors

Russell A. Powell

Russ Powell completed his Ph.D. in psychology under the stimulating supervision of the late Frank Epling and his research partner, David Pierce, at the University of Alberta, and now serves as the Chair of the Department of Psychology at Grant MacEwan College, in Edmonton, Alberta. He has a wide range of academic experiences, the influence of which can be seen throughout this text. He has taught a variety of courses over the years, including social psychology, experimental psychology, and theories of personality. More importantly, he has almost 25 years of experience in teaching undergraduate students the basic course in principles of behavior. He was also the first instructor at Grant MacEwan College to develop and offer university-level courses in a nontraditional, alternative delivery format. In keeping with this diverse teaching background, Russ has also conducted research and published articles on such varied topics as operant conditioning, sleep paralysis nightmares, Freud criticism, and self-regulation (or self-control). He has also been involved in the ongoing controversy over the nature and causes of dissociative identity disorder, co-authoring articles that have appeared in the *Canadian Journal of Psychiatry* (Powell & Gee, 1999) and *Psychological Bulletin* (Lilienfeld et al., 1999).

Diane G. Symbaluk

Diane Symbaluk received her Ph.D. in sociology from the University of Alberta in 1997, with a specialization in criminology and social psychology. Much of her training, however, was in behavior analysis under the mentorship of David Pierce, Judy Cameron, and the late Frank Epling. She is currently a faculty member in the Department of Sociology at Grant MacEwan College in Edmonton, Alberta. Diane's student-centered approach to teaching is evident in her many publications, which include several study guides and resource manuals as well as Web-course tools and interactive Web sites. Her research background includes the investigation of self-control and impulsiveness in sex offenders, tendencies toward activity anorexia in male athletes (discussed in Chapter 11 of this text), and the effect of social modeling and self-efficacy on pain perception and tolerance. Her research publications include articles that have appeared in *Personality and Social Psychology Bulletin* (Symbaluk et al., 1997) and *Teaching of Psychology* (Symbaluk & Cameron, 1998).

P. Lynne Honey

Lynne Honey considers herself an "evolutionary behaviorist." She completed a Ph.D. in experimental psychology in B. G. Galef's lab at McMaster University, studying the role of social learning on alcohol consumption in rats. She has published a number of papers on this topic and considers social learning to be one of the most powerful adaptations available to our species and others. At McMaster, Lynne was inspired and influenced not only by her supervisor, a leading theorist in social learning, but also by the work of Shepard Siegel (on compensatory responses and conditioned drug tolerance) as well as Martin Daly and Margo Wilson (on evolution and human behavior). After completing a postdoctoral fellowship, Lynne joined the Department of Psychology at Grant MacEwan College, where she also serves as the advisor for honors students in psychology. Lynne is currently conducting research on human social behavior in an evolutionary context, including studies of dominance, attraction, and cooperation. In addition to these research interests, Lynne is a committed teacher and mentor to her students and on any given day you can find her in her office, the classroom or in the lab, chatting and working alongside students, trying to find new ways to demonstrate to them the beauty and elegance of the science of psychology.

CHAPTER 1

Introduction

CHAPTER OUTLINE

Historical Background

Aristotle: Empiricism and the Laws of Association

Descartes: Mind–Body Dualism and the Reflex

The British Empiricists

Structuralism: The Experimental Study of Human Consciousness

Functionalism: The Study of the Adaptive Mind

The Theory of Evolution: Humans as Animals

Behaviorism: The Study of Observable Behavior

Five Schools of Behaviorism

Watson's Methodological Behaviorism

Hull's Neobehaviorism

Tolman's Cognitive Behaviorism

Bandura's Social Learning Theory

Skinner's Radical Behaviorism

A review of Gerald Zuriff's Behaviorism: A Conceptual Reconstruction (1985) . . . begins with a story about two behaviorists. They make love and then one of them says, "That was fine for you. How was it for me?" The reviewer, P. N. Johnson-Laird, insists that [this story has a ring of truth about it]. Behaviorists are not supposed to have feelings, or at least to admit that they have them. Of the many ways in which behaviorism has been misunderstood for so many years, that is perhaps the commonest. . . . [In fact] how people feel is often as important as what they do.

B. F. SKINNER, 1989, p. 3

Of all contemporary psychologists, B. F. Skinner is perhaps the most honored and the most maligned, the most widely recognized and the most misrepresented, the most cited and the most misunderstood.

A. CHARLES CATANIA, 1988, p. 3

Imagine that while flipping through a new textbook you see that it spends a lot of time discussing experiments with rats and pigeons. Pretty boring, huh? But what if the principles of behavior discussed in those experiments could help you improve your study habits, understand your eating disorder, and overcome your fear of spiders? In fact, what if those same principles could help you improve your romantic relationships and be a more effective parent? Hmm, perhaps not so boring after all. Well, this book might be just such a book. Let's consider a few of these claims in more detail.

Improving study habits. Many of our behaviors, including study behaviors, are strongly influenced by their consequences. Chapter 6 discusses the basic processes by which consequences influence behavior, and Chapter 10 demonstrates how these processes can be directly applied to the development of self-control. As well, specific information about improving study habits through the use of "stimulus control" procedures can be found toward the end of Chapter 8.

Understanding eating disorders. Contrary to popular belief, eating disorders are not necessarily indicative of a psychological problem. For example, through a simple manipulation of a rat's feeding schedule, the rat can be induced to stop eating and to engage in extreme levels of exercise. Chapter 11 discusses how similar processes might account for the development of a clinical disorder in humans known as anorexia nervosa.

Overcoming fears and phobias. Whether you fear spiders, snakes, or exams, this textbook will provide you with insight into how these fears develop. You will learn how the principles of classical conditioning and negative reinforcement underlie many fears and anxieties, and how these same principles suggest effective means for treating problematic symptoms.

Improving relationships with others. In this text, we often use relationship issues to illustrate basic principles of learning and behavior. As well, each chapter contains an *Advice for the Lovelorn* column, in which relationship problems are discussed from a behavioral perspective. Although the advice given is necessarily speculative—and as such should not be taken too seriously—these columns highlight the manner in which behavioral principles have the potential to enrich our understanding of human relationships.

Raising children. Our students sometimes comment that "no one should be allowed to have children until they have taken a course like this." Although this is admittedly an exaggeration, it is nevertheless the case that many of the principles discussed in this text are directly applicable to many common parenting problems.

In general, a proper grounding in the basic principles of learning and behavior will help you understand why you behave the way you do and how your behavior can often be changed for the better. This knowledge can make you a better parent, a better teacher, and a better friend or partner. In a very real sense, the principles described in this text have the potential to enrich both your life and the lives of others—even though many of these principles have been derived from research with rats and pigeons!

Let's begin with a brief outline of what this textbook is about. Simply put, *behavior* is any activity of an organism that can be observed or somehow measured. As we will discuss in Chapter 2, the activity may be internal or external and may or may not be visible to others. *Learning* is a relatively permanent change in behavior that results from some type of experience. For example, reading this text is an example of a behavior, and any lasting change in your behavior as a result of reading this text (e.g., a change in your ability to speak knowledgeably about the subject matter) is an example of learning. Note that the change in behavior does not have to be immediate, and in some circumstances the change might not become evident until long after the experience has occurred.

This text emphasizes two fundamental processes of learning: classical and operant conditioning. Although these will be discussed in more detail later, a brief description of each is useful at this point. At its most basic level, *classical conditioning* (also known as Pavlovian or respondent conditioning) is the process by which certain inborn behaviors come to be produced in new situations. The behaviors involved are often what the average person regards as reflexive or "involuntary," such as sneezing in response to dust or salivating in response to food. A familiar example of classical conditioning, which is often presented in introductory psychology textbooks, is that of a dog learning to salivate in response to a bell that has been paired with food. This process can be diagrammed as follows:

Bell: Food → *Salivation*
Bell → *Salivation*

(See "Notation for Conditioning Diagrams" in the And Furthermore box.)

And Furthermore

Notation for Conditioning Diagrams

In this text, you will encounter many diagrams of conditioning procedures. In these diagrams, a colon separating two events indicates that the two events occur in sequence. For example, the term "Bell: Food" means that the sound of a bell is followed by the presentation of food. An arrow between two events also indicates that the two events occur in sequence, but with an emphasis on the fact that the first event *produces* or *causes* the second. For example, "Food → *Salivation*" means that the presentation of food causes the dog to salivate. Thus, with respect to a standard classical conditioning procedure, the term:

Bell: Food → *Salivation*

means that the bell is presented just before the food, and the food in turn causes salivation. This is followed by:

Bell → *Salivation*

which indicates that the presentation of the bell itself now causes the dog to salivate (because of the bell's previous association with food). For clarity, we usually italicize the behavior that is being conditioned (which is often called the "target behavior"). In writing out your notes, however, you may find it easier to indicate the target behavior by underlining it. For example:

Bell: Food → <u>Salivation</u>
Bell → <u>Salivation</u>

As you will learn in this text, classical conditioning underlies many of our emotional responses and contributes to the development of our likes and dislikes. It can even lead to the development of debilitating fears and powerful feelings of sexual attraction.

In contrast to classical conditioning, *operant conditioning* involves the strengthening or weakening of a behavior as a result of its consequences. The behaviors involved are often those that the average person usually regards as "voluntary" or goal directed. A common experimental example is that of a rat that has learned to press a lever to obtain food. This can be diagrammed as follows:

Lever press → **Food pellet**
The effect: Likelihood of lever pressing increases

Because the lever press produced a food pellet, the rat is subsequently more likely to press the lever again. In other words, the consequence of the behavior (the food pellet) has served to strengthen future occurrences of that behavior. Many of the behaviors that concern us each day are motivated by such consequences: We hit the remote button to turn on a favorite television show, compliment a loved one because it produces a smile, and study diligently to obtain a passing grade. The consequences can be either immediate, as in the first two examples, or delayed, as in the last example—though, as we will later discuss, the effect of delayed consequences on behavior can involve certain complexities. Because of its importance for humans, operant conditioning is the type of learning most strongly emphasized in this text.

Although the text concentrates on classical and operant conditioning, other types of behavioral processes are also discussed. For example, in *observational learning*, observation of a model's behavior facilitates the development of similar behavior in an observer. Certain types of non-learned, inherited behavior patterns, such as *fixed action patterns*, are also discussed, as is the effect of inherited dispositions in either facilitating or inhibiting certain types of learning. Let's begin, however, with a brief overview of the historical background to the study of learning and behavior.

QUICK QUIZ A

While reading the text, you will frequently encounter fill-in-the-blank quizzes like this one. Students report that these quizzes greatly facilitate the task of reading by breaking up the material into manageable chunks and encouraging them to be actively involved with the reading. For many of the items, we have provided helpful hints, usually in the form of the initial letter or two of the word that should be inserted into the blank. But we have not provided an answer key here, partly because most of the answers can be easily found in the text and partly because a certain amount of uncertainty can actually facilitate the process of learning (Schmidt & Bjork, 1992). Nevertheless, if you "just have to know" the answer to a particular item, the answers for all of the Quick Quiz items can be found at the textbook companion Web site at <http://www.academic.cengage.com/psychology/powell>.

1. The term *behavior* refers to any activity of an organism that can be o_____ or somehow m_____, whereas the term *learning* refers to a relatively p_____ change in what an organism does as a result of some type of ex_____.

2. In _____ conditioning, behaviors that the average person typically regards as (voluntary/involuntary) _____ come to be elicited in new situations.

3. In _____ conditioning, a behavior produces some type of consequence that strengthens or weakens its occurrence. Such behaviors are typically those that the average person perceives as v_____ or g_____ directed.

4. Feeling anxious as you enter a dentist's office is an example of a behavior that has most likely been learned through _____ conditioning.

5. Speaking with a loud voice in a noisy environment so that others will be able to hear you is an example of a behavior that has most likely been acquired through _____ conditioning.

6. According to the notational system to be used in this text, the term "A: B" means that event A (produces/is followed by) _____ event B, and the term "X → Y" means that event X (produces/is followed by) _____ event Y.

Historical Background

Just as it is impossible to outline all of the experiences that have made you who you are, it is impossible to outline all of the historical events that have contributed to the modern-day study of learning and behavior. Some particularly important contributions, however, are discussed in this section.

Aristotle: Empiricism and the Laws of Association

Aristotle was a Greek philosopher who lived between 384 and 322 B.C. Aristotle's teacher, Plato, believed that everything we know is inborn (which he conceived of as "residing in our soul"); thus, learning is simply a process of inner reflection to uncover the knowledge that already exists within. Aristotle, however, disagreed with Plato and argued that knowledge is not inborn but instead is acquired through experience.

Aristotle's disagreement with Plato is an early example of the classic debate of nativism versus empiricism, or nature versus nurture. The **nativist (nature)** perspective assumes that a person's abilities and behavioral tendencies are largely inborn, whereas the **empiricist (nurture)** perspective assumes that a person's abilities and tendencies are mostly learned. Plato is thus an early example of a nativist, and Aristotle is an early example of an empiricist.[1]

Aristotle also suggested that ideas come to be connected or associated with each other via four laws of association (well, actually three, but he also hinted at a fourth that later philosophers expanded upon).

1. **The Law of Similarity.** According to this law, events that are similar to each other are readily associated. For example, cars and trucks are readily associated because they are similar in appearance (wheels, doors, headlights, etc.) and function (both are used to carry passengers and materials along roadways). These similarities enable us to learn to view cars and trucks as instances of a larger category of objects known as automobiles.

2. **The Law of Contrast.** Just as events that are similar to each other are readily associated, so too events that are opposite from each other are readily associated. For example, on a word association test the word *black* often brings to mind the word *white*, and the word *tall* often brings to mind the word *short*. Likewise, the sight of your unwashed car readily reminds you of how nice it would look if you washed it, and an evening of work might remind you of how enjoyable it would be to spend the evening not working.

---

[1]In philosophy, the term *empiricism* usually refers to the mentalistic notion that *knowledge* can be gained only through sensory experience rather than through heredity or by pure reasoning. In psychology, the term has a slightly altered meaning, which is that *behavior* is the result of experience rather than heredity. But the word *empiricism* can also be used in a methodological sense to refer to the gathering of information through systematic observation and experimentation, as in, "behavioral psychology is an empirical approach to the study of behavior."

3. **The Law of Contiguity.** According to this law, events that occur in close proximity to each other in time or space are readily associated with each other (*contiguity* means "closeness"). For example, a child quickly learns to associate thunder and lightning because the sound of thunder soon follows the flash of lightning. Thunder and lightning are also usually perceived as coming from the same direction, meaning that there is a certain degree of spatial proximity between them. Imagine how difficult it would be to associate thunder and lightning if the thunder occurred several minutes after the lightning flash and was perceived to have arrived from a different direction.

4. **The Law of Frequency.** In addition to the three preceding laws, Aristotle mentioned a supplement to the law of contiguity, which holds that the more frequently two items occur together, the more strongly they are associated. You will more strongly associate a friend with a certain perfume the more frequently you smell that perfume upon meeting her. Likewise, you will more strongly associate a term (such as the law of frequency) with its definition the more frequently you practice saying that definition whenever you see the term (as when using flash cards to help memorize basic terminology).

Aristotle's laws of association are not merely of historical interest. As you will read later, *the laws of contiguity and frequency are still considered important aspects of learning.*

1. The nativist position, as exemplified by the Greek philosopher _____, emphasizes the role of (learning/heredity) _____.

2. The empiricist position, as exemplified by the Greek philosopher _____, emphasizes the role of (learning/heredity) _____.

3. Nativist is to (nature/nurture) _____ as empiricist is to (nature/nurture) _____.

4. The law of _____ states that we readily associate events that are opposite to each other, whereas the law of _____ states that we readily associate events that occur in close proximity to each other.

5. According to the law of _____, we readily associate events that resemble each other. According to the law of _____, the more often two events occur together, the stronger the association.

6. According to the law of _____, animals that have fur, four legs, a tail, and can bark should all quickly be perceived as belonging to the same species.

7. The fact that the words *full* and *empty* are readily associated with each other is an example of the law of _____.

8. According to the law of _____, the *more often* one practices a particular move in wrestling, the more likely one is to perform that move in a real match.

9. After once encountering a snake in her garage, Lisa is now quite nervous each time she is in the garage. This is an example of Aristotle's law of _____. This is also an example of (classical/operant) _____ conditioning.

René Descartes
(1596–1650)

© Bettman/CORBIS

Descartes: Mind–Body Dualism and the Reflex

René Descartes (1596–1650) is the French philosopher who wrote the famous line "I think, therefore I am." Fortunately for psychology, this was not his only contribution. In Descartes' time, many people assumed that human behavior was governed entirely by free will or "reason." Descartes disputed this notion and proposed a dualistic model of human nature. On the one hand, he claimed, we have a body that functions like a machine and produces involuntary, reflexive behaviors in response to external stimulation (such as sneezing in response to dust). On the other hand, we have a mind that has free will and produces behaviors that we regard as voluntary (such as choosing what to eat for dinner).

Thus, Descartes' notion of *mind–body dualism* holds that some human behaviors are reflexes that are automatically elicited by external stimulation, while other behaviors are freely chosen and controlled by the mind. Descartes also believed that only humans possess such a self-directing mind, while the behavior of nonhuman animals is entirely reflexive.

Descartes' dualistic view of human nature was a major step in the scientific study of learning and behavior because it suggested that at least some behaviors—namely, reflexive behaviors—are mechanistic and could therefore be scientifically investigated. It also suggested that the study of animal behavior might yield useful information about the reflexive aspects of human behavior.

The British Empiricists

Although Descartes believed that the human mind has free will, he also assumed, like Plato, that some of the ideas contained within it (e.g., the concepts of time and space) are inborn. This notion was disputed by a group of British philosophers, known as the *British empiricists,* who maintained that almost all knowledge is a function of experience. For example, John Locke (1632–1704) proposed that a newborn's mind is a *blank slate* (in Latin, *tabula rasa*) upon which environmental experiences are written—an empiricist concept that had earlier been promoted by Aristotle. The British empiricists also believed that the conscious mind is composed of a finite set of basic elements (specific colors, sounds, smells, etc.) that are combined through the principles of association into complex sensations and thought patterns—a sort of psychological version of the notion that all physical matter consists of various combinations of the basic elements.

1. Descartes' dualistic model proposed that human behavior has two aspects: an inv_____ aspect that functions like a machine and a v_____ aspect governed by f_____ w_____. By contrast, the behavior of animals was believed to be entirely (voluntary/involuntary) _____.

2. The British _____, such as John _____, maintained that knowledge was largely a function of experience and that the mind of a newborn infant is a (in Latin) t _____ r_____ (which means _____ _____).

3. They also perceived that the mind is composed of a finite set of basic _____ that are then combined through the principles of _____ to form our conscious experiences.

Structuralism: The Experimental Study of Human Consciousness

Edward B. Titchener
(1867-1927)

© Psychology Archives—The University of Akron

The British empiricists did not conduct any experiments to test the notion that the mind consists of various combinations of basic elements; their conclusions were instead based upon logical reasoning and the subjective examination of their own conscious experience. Realizing the deficiencies in this approach, the German philosopher Wilhelm Wundt (1832–1920) proposed using the scientific method to investigate the issue. This approach was strongly promoted by an American student of Wundt, Edward Titchener (1867–1927), and became known as structuralism. *Structuralism* holds that it is possible to determine the structure of the mind by identifying the basic elements that compose it.

Structuralists made great use of the method of *introspection,* in which the subject in an experiment attempts to accurately describe his or her conscious thoughts, emotions, and sensory experiences. To get a feel for how difficult this is, try to describe your conscious experience as you listen to the ticking of a clock (and just saying, "I'm bored" does not cut it). One thing you might report is that the ticks seem to have a certain rhythm, with a series of two or three clicks being clustered together. You might also report a slight feeling of tension (is it pleasant or unpleasant?) that builds or decreases during each series of ticks. As you can see, an accurate report of what we introspectively observe can be quite difficult.

Although this approach to psychology died out by the early 1900s (for reasons described shortly), its emphasis on systematic observation helped establish psychology as a scientific discipline. More importantly, its extreme emphasis on conscious experience as the proper subject matter for psychology resulted in a great deal of frustration and dissatisfaction—which laid the groundwork for the later establishment of a more objective approach to psychology known as behaviorism.

William James
(1842–1910)

Functionalism: The Study of the Adaptive Mind

William James (1842–1910), often regarded as the founder of American psychology, helped establish the approach to psychology known as functionalism. *Functionalism* assumes that the mind evolved to help us adapt to the world around us and that the focus of psychology should be the study of those adaptive processes. This proposition was partially derived from Darwin's theory of evolution, which proposes that adaptive characteristics that enable a species to survive and reproduce tend to increase in frequency across generations while nonadaptive characteristics tend to die out. Thus, according to a functionalist perspective, characteristics that are highly typical of a species, such as the characteristic of consciousness in humans, must have some type of adaptive value.

Rather than studying the structure of the mind, functionalists believed that psychologists should study the adaptive significance of the mind. Learning, as an adaptive process, was therefore a topic of great interest to the functionalists. Moreover, although functionalists still made use of introspection and emphasized the analysis of conscious experience (in this manner, being similar to the structuralists), they were not opposed to the study of animal behavior. Again following from Darwin, they believed that humans evolved in the same manner as other animals, and that much of what we learn from studying animals might therefore be of direct relevance to humans. Not surprisingly, two of the most important figures in the early history of behaviorism, E. B. Thorndike (discussed in Chapter 6) and John B. Watson (discussed later in this chapter), were students of functionalist psychologists.

QUICK QUIZ D

1. The (functionalist/structuralist) _____ approach held that the goal of psychology should be to identify the basic elements of the mind. The primary research method used for accomplishing this was the method of i_____.

2. Psychologists who adopted the (functionalist/structuralist) _____ approach to psychology emphasized the adaptive processes of the mind and were thus very interested in the study of learning.

3. The functionalist approach was strongly influenced by Darwin's theory of _____. As such, these psychologists viewed animal research as (relevant/irrelevant) _____ to the study of human behavior.

4. The functionalists were similar to the structuralists in that they still emphasized the study of c_____ experience. In doing so they often used the method of i_____.

5. William James was a (functionalist/structuralist) _____, and Edward Titchener was a _____.

The Theory of Evolution: Humans as Animals

As we have seen, the theory of evolution had a profound influence on the development of behaviorism, and it continues to influence it today. We should therefore take some time to discuss this theory more fully. Charles Darwin published the theory of evolution in 1859 in his book, *On the Origin of Species by Means of Natural Selection* (often simply called *The Origin of Species*). It describes how species, including humans, change across generations in response to environmental pressures. The basis of the theory is the principle of ***natural selection,*** which is the concept that individuals or species that are capable of adapting to environmental pressures are more likely to survive and reproduce than those that cannot adapt.

Charles Darwin
(1809–1882)

There are three main components to the principle of natural selection. The first is that *traits vary,* both within a species (e.g., some dogs are larger than other dogs) and between species (e.g., humans have a slower metabolism than do hummingbirds). The second is that *many traits are heritable,* meaning that they have a genetic basis and can be inherited by offspring. The third component of natural selection is that *organisms must compete for limited resources* (bearing in mind, however, that being an effective competitor might sometimes involve cooperation as much as conflict).

Now let us put all three of these ideas together. Some individuals will acquire more resources than others based on certain, inherited traits that give them an advantage. These individuals are therefore better able to survive—which, of course, is commonly referred to as "survival of the fittest." But here is where a lot of people misunderstand evolutionary theory. The real driving force behind evolution is not survival of the fittest, but the *reproductive advantage that accrues to those individuals possessing traits that are best suited to the environment.* In other words, successful individuals are more likely to have offspring who, when they inherit the successful traits from their parents, are also more likely to survive and reproduce. As this process continues through each succeeding generation, the proportion of individuals possessing the successful traits increases while the proportion of individuals possessing the unsuccessful traits decreases. At times, the changed population differs so much from the source population that it becomes a new species.

A trait that evolves as a result of natural selection is referred to as an ***evolutionary adaptation.*** We usually think of such adaptations as physical characteristics (e.g., the trunk of an elephant), but adaptations can also be behaviors. For example, as you will learn in Chapter 3, if you inadvertently place your hand over a flame, a *flexion reflex* will cause you automatically to pull your hand away from the damaging fire even before you consciously feel pain. You can imagine how a reflex like this would help an individual live long enough to reproduce, compared to an individual who lacked such reflexes.

A particularly important evolutionary adaptation, which is the focus of this text, is the ability to learn. From an evolutionary perspective, the ability to learn evolved because it conferred significant survival advantages to those who had this ability. Thus, the distinction between nature and nurture can be seen as extremely simplistic, since the ability to learn (nurture) is itself an inherited trait (nature).

In this text, you will learn about features of learning that are common across a wide variety of species. These common features suggest that the ancestors of these species faced similar environmental pressures that resulted in the evolution of such features. Nevertheless, you will also learn (especially in Chapter 11) about some differences in learning ability across species. From an evolutionary perspective, these differences indicate special selective pressures to which a certain species was exposed, which resulted in particular variations in learning ability.

As noted, Darwin's theory of evolution had a profound effect on the early development of behaviorism, especially through its influence on the functionalist school of psychology out of which behaviorism developed. It continues to have an effect through the increased attention given these days to the role of genetic factors in learning, and through the recent establishment of "evolutionary psychology" as a major area of specialization within psychology.

QUICK QUIZ E

1. A trait that has evolved through n_____ s_____ is called an ev_____ ad_____.

2. The three main components to the theory of natural selection are

a.

b.

c.

3. To say that a trait is h_____ means that it has a genetic basis and can be inherited by offspring.

4. The real driving force behind evolution is not survival of the fittest, but rather the r_____ advantage held by those individuals who possess adaptive traits.

5. Evolutionary theory illustrates that the n_____–n_____ debate is overly simplistic because the way that we learn is itself an _____ trait.

John B. Watson
(1878–1958)

Behaviorism: The Study of Observable Behavior

In 1913 a flamboyant young psychologist by the name of John B. Watson published a paper titled "Psychology as the Behaviorist Views It." In it, he lamented the lack of progress achieved by experimental psychologists up to that time, particularly the lack of findings that had any practical significance. A major difficulty, Watson believed, was the then-current emphasis on the study of conscious experience, especially as promoted by the structuralists. In particular, the method of introspection was proving to be highly unreliable. Researchers frequently failed to replicate each other's findings, which often led to bitter squabbles. Watson mockingly described the types of arguments that often ensued.

> If you fail to reproduce my findings, it is not due to some fault in your apparatus or in the control of your stimulus, but it is due to the fact that your introspection is untrained. . . . If you can't observe 3–9 states of clearness in attention, your introspection is poor. If, on the other hand, a feeling seems reasonably clear to you, your introspection is again faulty. You are seeing too much. Feelings are never clear. (Watson, 1913, p. 163)

The difficulty, of course, is that we are unable to directly observe another person's thoughts and feelings. We therefore have to make an *inference* that the person's verbal reports about those thoughts and feelings are accurate.[2] It is also the case that many of the questions being tackled by the structuralists were essentially unanswerable, such as whether sound has the quality of "extension in space" and whether there is a difference in "texture" between an imagined perception of an object and the actual perception of the object (Watson, 1913, p. 164). In a very real sense, experimental psychology seemed to be drowning in a sea of vaguely perceived images and difficult-to-describe mental events. Moreover, the notion that the proper subject matter of psychology was the study of consciousness was so strongly entrenched that it affected even those who studied animal behavior. As Watson exclaimed,

> On this view, after having determined our animal's ability to learn, the simplicity or complexity of its methods of learning, the effect of past habit upon present response . . . we should still feel that the task is unfinished and that the results are worthless, until we can interpret them by analogy in the light of consciousness. [In other words,] we feel forced to say something about the possible mental processes of the animal. (Watson, 1913, p. 160)

Watson reasoned that the only solution to this dilemma was to make psychology a purely "objective science" based solely on the study of directly observable behavior and the environmental events that surround it. All reference to internal processes, such as thoughts and feelings that could not

---

[2]An *inference* is a supposition or guess based on logical deduction rather than on observation. For example, if you describe a dream that you had last night to me, your report is based on your direct observation of a subjective experience. But if I accept that description (because there seems to be no reason for you to lie about it), I am making an inference that your report is accurate. Now suppose I interpret the dream as indicating that you have some unresolved, unconscious conflict, and you accept that interpretation as true. We are now both making an inference that this unconscious conflict exists, because neither you nor I have directly observed it. Needless to say, inferences about unconscious processes are even more problematic than inferences about conscious processes, because not even the person in whom the unconscious process exists is able to directly observe it.

be objectively measured by an outside observer, were to be stricken from analysis. By objectifying psychology in this manner, Watson hoped that psychology could then join the ranks of the *natural sciences*—biology, chemistry, and physics—which had traditionally emphasized the study of observable phenomena. In Watson's now-classic words,

> Psychology as the behaviorist views it is a purely objective experimental branch of natural science. Its theoretical goal is the prediction and control of behavior. Introspection forms no essential part of its methods, nor is the scientific value of its data dependent upon the readiness with which they lend themselves to interpretation in terms of consciousness. (Watson, 1913, p. 154)

Thus, as originally defined by Watson, **behaviorism** is a natural science approach to psychology that focuses on the study of environmental influences on observable behavior.

Watson also believed strongly in the value of animal research. In keeping with his functionalist background—in turn following from Darwin's theory of evolution—he believed that the principles governing the behavior of nonhuman species might also be relevant to the behavior of humans. Thus, traditional behavioral research is often conducted using nonhuman animals, primarily rats and pigeons. As many of the examples in this text illustrate, the results obtained from such research are often highly applicable to human behavior.

Behavioral psychology also adheres to the **law of parsimony,** which holds that simpler explanations for a phenomenon are generally preferable to more complex explanations. One version of this law—which strongly influenced Watson—is known as *Morgan's Canon* (*canon* means "principle"). Conway Lloyd Morgan was a 19th-century British physiologist/psychologist who became distressed about the manner in which many scientists of his era were attributing human characteristics to nonhuman animals. Morgan (1894) argued that, whenever possible, one should interpret an animal's behavior in terms of lower, more primitive processes (e.g., reflex or habit) rather than higher, more mentalistic processes (e.g., decision or imagination). Watson essentially took this one step further by arguing that psychologists should avoid interpreting even human behavior in terms of mentalistic processes.

It is worth noting that Watson was not the first psychologist to recommend a more objective, natural science approach to psychology. He reflected a growing sentiment among many researchers at that time that such a move was necessary. Watson's arguments, however, were the most clearly stated and therefore had a strong effect. Thus, while his 1913 paper (which later became known as the "Behaviorist Manifesto") did not have an immediate impact, its influence slowly grew until, by the 1920s, the behaviorist revolution was well under way. (For a brief discussion of Watson's personal life, see "John B. Watson: Behaviorism's Controversial Founder" in the And Furthermore box.)

And Furthermore

John B. Watson: Behaviorism's Controversial Founder

John B. Watson was a charismatic and aggressive individual and as such was perhaps ideally suited for lifting psychology out of the mentalistic quagmire in which it had become immersed. Unfortunately, those same traits led to a life of conflict. The most infamous story about Watson concerns the manner in which he was forced to resign from his university position. One commonly told version has it that he and a female student were caught conducting intimate experiments on human sexual responding, and he was forced to resign over the resultant scandal. There is, however, little evidence for this story (see Benjamin, Whitaker, Ramsey, & Zeve, 2007, for a description of how this rumor became established), and the real events appear to be as follows.

In 1920, at the height of his academic career, Watson began an affair with Rosalie Rayner, a graduate student whose family was both well connected and powerful. Catching wind of the affair, Watson's wife entered Rosalie's room during a social visit to the Rayners and stole the letters Watson had written to his young lover. Watson's wife then filed for divorce and used the letters to help win a lucrative settlement. Meanwhile, the university told Watson to end his affair with Rosalie. Watson refused and, when given an ultimatum, immediately tendered his resignation. Soon after, news of Watson's divorce and of the affair found its way into the national media, with one of Watson's love letters even appearing in several newspapers. In the space of a few months, his academic career was ruined.

Cast adrift, Watson married Rayner and obtained a job with a New York advertising firm. In his new position, he attempted to promote a more scientific approach to the discipline of advertising—though the extent to which he had any significant influence on the industry is questionable (Coon, 1994). He also continued to publish books and magazine articles promoting his behavioristic views. In fact, Watson was very much the pop psychologist of his era, much like the present-day Dr. Phil. Unfortunately, as with pop psychology today, some of his advice was based more on personal opinion than on well-established principles. For example, Watson believed that children should be trained to act like adults and even recommended giving them a handshake, rather than a hug or a kiss, when sending them to bed! In fact, the only time he ever showed affection to his own children was when his wife died in 1935. Teary eyed, Watson lightly put his arms around his children as he told them that their mother had passed away, then never again mentioned her name. Not surprisingly, his children retained bitter memories of their upbringing, and one son later committed suicide.

It has been suggested that Watson had an underlying fear of emotions, as though fearful of losing control. In his love relationships (and he had numerous affairs throughout his life) he was extremely impulsive and amorous; yet in a group setting he would reportedly flee the room when the discussion turned to emotional issues. Thus, although Watson's proposal to banish thoughts and feelings from psychology helped establish it as a more objective science, it may also have reflected some of his personal difficulties.

In his later years, Watson became something of a recluse, living in the country and raising animals. He had always been fond of animals—sometimes claiming that he preferred their company to that of humans—which may account for his early interest in animal research. He died in 1958 at the age of 80. (See Buckley, 1989, for a comprehensive biography of Watson.)

1. Watson noted that a major problem with the method of _____ was that the results obtained were often unreliable.

2. A basic problem with relying on someone's report about his or her thoughts and feelings is that we are making a(n) _____ that the report is accurate. This term is defined in the footnote as a supposition or guess based on logical d_____ rather than direct o_____.

3. The notion that the proper subject matter of psychology should be the study of consciousness was so strong that even those who studied _____ behavior felt compelled to make inferences about possible mental processes in their subjects.

4. Watson argued that psychology needed to become a n_____ science (like biology, chemistry, and physics) based solely on the study of directly ob_____ events.

5. According to the law of p_____, the (simpler/more complex) _____ explanation is generally the preferable explanation.

6. One version of the above law, known as _____ _____, holds that it is preferable to interpret animal behavior in terms of lower, more primitive processes, such as reflex or habit, than higher, more mentalistic processes, such as reasoning.

Five Schools of Behaviorism

Many people believe that behaviorism is some monolithic entity, with Watson's views being the same views held by other behaviorists. In fact, there are several schools of behaviorism, each based on a somewhat different set of assumptions about how best to study environmental influences on behavior. In this section, we describe five of these schools, beginning with Watson's original brand of behaviorism, which is sometimes referred to as methodological behaviorism (e.g., O'Donohue & Ferguson, 2001).[3]

Watson's Methodological Behaviorism

Among the most extreme versions of behaviorism is the one originally proposed by Watson. As previously noted, Watson believed that psychologists should study only publicly observable behavior. All reference to internal

---

[3]Be aware that the names of the different schools presented here are not at all standardized. For example, a quick search of scholarly postings on the Internet will soon reveal alternative names for Watson's approach, such as *classical behaviorism* and even *radical behaviorism* (which is usually reserved for Skinner's version of behaviorism). And the term *methodological behaviorism* is sometimes applied to any approach that rejects the value of data gathered through introspection, including many cognitive approaches to psychology. This inconsistency in terminology has arisen not only from the adoption of different labels by different writers but also from subtle commonalities and distinctions between the different schools of behaviorism, which are the subject of some debate among behaviorists and philosophers.

FIGURE 1.1   In methodological behaviorism, internal events, such as consciously perceived thoughts and feelings and unconscious drives and motives, are excluded from the analysis of behavior. Instead, one studies the direct relationship between changes in the environment and changes in observable behavior.

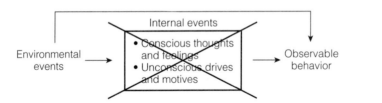

events—that is, events that can only be subjectively perceived (such as our inner thoughts and feelings) or that are assumed to exist on an unconscious level (e.g., a mother's unconscious hatred of her unwanted child)—were to be stricken from scientific analysis (see Figure 1.1).

Thus, ***methodological behaviorism*** asserts that, for methodological reasons, psychologists should study only those behaviors that can be directly observed. Subjectively perceived activities, such as thinking, are methodologically too difficult to assess to be of much use in a scientific analysis of behavior. Such activities can be included for analysis only if they can, in some way, be directly measured. Watson, for example, hypothesized that thinking involves minute movements of the vocal cords in the larynx—and he enjoyed goading his critics by referring to his own thoughts as "laryngeal activity" (Buckley, 1989). If this were true, and if such movements could be precisely measured, then the act of thinking could be subjected to scientific analysis. (As it turns out, laryngeal activity is not a reliable measure of thinking.)

It is important to emphasize that Watson's behavioristic proposal to ignore thoughts and feelings in scientific analysis was not simply an attempt to dehumanize people or to pretend that thoughts and feelings do not exist (whatever his own personal biases may have been); rather, it was in part a logical response to a crisis. If the discipline of psychology was to survive, it would need to break free from the extreme mentalism of the time and adopt a much different perspective. Watson's behavioral call to arms, though extreme, accomplished just that.

Nevertheless, it must be conceded that Watson's specific view of learning was rather mechanistic. Drawing from Pavlov's work on classical conditioning, he came to believe that all behavior, both animal and human, is essentially reflexive. He also believed that learning involves the development of a simple connection between an environmental event (the "stimulus") and a specific behavior (the "response"). Watson's theory of learning is therefore regarded as a type of ***S-R theory,*** in which learning is believed to involve the establishment of a connection between a specific stimulus (S) and a specific response (R). Complex behavior is presumed to involve extremely long chains of these S-R connections.

Over time, Watson also became something of an extremist regarding the nature–nurture issue. In his original 1913 article, he had emphasized the influence of *both* heredity and environment on behavior. In fact, he was one of the first individuals to systematically study inborn behavior patterns in animals (he spent several strenuous summers engaged in field research with a type of seabird). Later, however, following extensive observations of human infants, he came to the conclusion that humans inherit only a few fundamental reflexes along with three basic emotions (love, rage, and fear). Everything else, he believed, is learned. This led Watson, in 1930, to make one of his most famous claims:

> Give me a dozen healthy infants, well-formed, and my own specified world to bring them up in and I'll guarantee to take any one at random and train him to become any type of specialist I might select—doctor, lawyer, artist, merchant-chief, and, yes, even beggar-man and thief, regardless of his talents, penchants, tendencies, abilities, vocations, and race of his ancestors. (p. 104)

Unfortunately, many textbooks quote only this passage and omit the very next sentence, which reads, "I am going beyond my facts, but so have the advocates of the contrary and they have been doing it for many thousands of years" (p. 104). And this was precisely Watson's point: The supposition that a person's abilities are largely inherited has been strongly promoted throughout history (and has often been used to justify acts of discrimination and racism). Watson was one of the first to issue a strong challenge to this assumption, arguing instead that there is at least as much evidence suggesting that human abilities are mostly learned. For this reason, Watson's behavioral model became quite popular among the reformists of his day who were attempting to combat racism. (For some recent evidence on the importance of learning as opposed to heredity, see "Deliberate Practice and Expert Performance" in the And Furthermore box.)

As we previously noted, many people mistakenly equate behaviorism with Watson's rather extreme version. In fact, few behaviorists were this extreme; instead, they developed approaches that were considerably more moderate. One of the most influential of these was Hull's neobehaviorism, which we discuss next.[4]

---

[4]While reading about these different schools of behaviorism, bear in mind that behavioristic assumptions are just that—assumptions. They do not necessarily reflect some type of absolute truth, nor do they necessarily reflect the private beliefs of the scientist. Thus, one can adopt these assumptions as a useful way of looking at behavior without abandoning other assumptions, such as certain religious beliefs about the existence of free will. After all, even if free will does exist, the environment still has a major impact on our behavior, and it would be foolish for us not to learn the principles by which the environment influences behavior. In this regard, the first author recalls a seminary student he once taught who could always be seen carrying around his two favorite textbooks—his behavior analysis text and the Bible.

1. Watson's brand of behaviorism is often referred to as _____ behaviorism.

2. According to this type of behaviorism, psychologists should study only those behaviors that can be _____ _____.

3. Watson believed that all reference to _____ events should be eliminated from the study of behavior.

4. Watson's brand of behaviorism is a(n) ____-____ theory in that it hypothesizes that learning involves the formation of a direct connection between a st_____ and a r_____.

5. In his 1913 article on behaviorism, Watson emphasized the role of both h_____ and e_____ in the development of human behavior. In his later theorizing, however, he downplayed the role of _____.

6. In his later theorizing, Watson proposed that humans inherit (many/a few) _____ basic reflexes, along with three basic emotions: _____, _____, and _____.

Hull's Neobehaviorism

One of the first major challenges to methodological behaviorism came from Clark Hull (1884–1952), who claimed that Watson's rejection of unobservable events was scientifically unsound. Hull noted that both physicists and chemists make inferences about events that have never been directly observed but that can nevertheless be *operationalized* (that is, defined in such a way that they can be measured). For example, gravity cannot be directly observed, but its effect on falling objects can be precisely measured. Hull believed that it might likewise be useful for psychologists to infer the existence of internal events that might *mediate* (draw a connection) between the environment and behavior.

Clark L. Hull
(1884–1952)

© Psychology Archives—The University of Akron

The mediating events that Hull incorporated into his theory consisted largely of physiological-type reactions, for example, a "hunger drive" that can be operationalized as number of hours of food deprivation. Such mediating events are formally called *intervening variables*, meaning that they intervene between a cause (such as food deprivation) and an effect (such as speed of running toward food). Thus, Hull's *neobehaviorism* is a brand of behaviorism that utilizes intervening variables, in the form of hypothesized physiological processes, to help explain behavior (see Figure 1.2).

It is important to note that Hull's use of intervening variables did not mean that he advocated a return to mentalism. Like Watson, he strongly opposed the use of introspection as a scientific tool, believing that subjective experiences are too vague and unreliable to be of much use. Thus, whether the organism actually experienced a feeling of hunger was of no concern to him.

And Furthermore

Deliberate Practice and Expert Performance

Watson's emphasis on the importance of nurture over nature in determining human behavior is often viewed with a great deal of skepticism. This is especially the case when it comes to behaviors that are indicative of exceptional ability. Most people, including many psychologists (e.g., Gardner, 1993), assume that, unless a person is born with a certain amount of talent, there are limits in how far he or she will be able to progress in a particular endeavor. Indeed, the notion that a Babe Ruth, Albert Einstein, or Wolfgang Amadeus Mozart is to a large extent born, and not made, is part of the mystique surrounding these individuals.

But consider the following:

- Expert performers in almost all fields of endeavor, ranging from music to athletics to chess, require a minimum of 10 years of intensive training before achieving a high level of performance. Even Mozart, who started composing at age 4, did not compose world-class music until his late teens. (Mozart's father was also a professional musician who published the first book on violin instruction and provided his children with intensive musical training from an early age.)
- As an experiment, a Hungarian educator, Polgar, set out to systematically train his daughters to become expert chess players. All three daughters have achieved high rankings in international chess, and one daughter, Judit, became the youngest grand master ever at 15 years of age.
- The superlative abilities shown by experts are almost always specific to their field of endeavor. For example, chess experts have the ability to memorize the exact positions of all the chess pieces in a game after only a few seconds' glance at the chessboard. But they perform no better than non–chess players at memorizing chess pieces randomly distributed around the board in a non–game pattern. As well, their performance on standard memory tests is typically no better than that of the average person.
- Almost all of the remarkable feats displayed by *savants*—individuals of low intellectual ability who nevertheless possess some remarkable skill—have been taught to normal individuals. For example, the ability of some savants to name the day of the week for any arbitrary date (e.g., "What day of the week was June 30, 1854?") has been duplicated by ordinary college students after only a few weeks of training.
- Excellent musicians often have perfect pitch, which many people assume is something a person is born with. Researchers, however, have been able to systematically train this ability in some adults. More importantly, people who display perfect pitch have almost always had considerable exposure to music at an early age. This suggests that, as with language development, there may be a critical period in childhood during which perfect pitch can be more readily acquired.

Based on findings such as these, Ericsson, Krampe, and Tesch-Römer (1993; see also Ericsson & Charness, 1994) have argued that the most critical factor in determining expert performance is not innate ability but deliberate practice. Deliberate practice is practice that is not inherently enjoyable and does not involve mere repetition; it instead involves intense concentration and considerable effort with a view toward improving one's performance. More than any other variable, the accumulated amount of deliberate practice in an activity is strongly predictive of an individual's level of performance.

For example, Ericsson et al. (1993) compared student violinists who were the "best" with those who were merely "good" and with those who were in training to become music teachers. The best students had accumulated about 7,400 hours of deliberate practice by the age of 18 compared to 5,300 hours for the good students and 3,400 hours for the teachers-in-training. Such differences account for why elite performers so often report having begun their training at an early age. An early start allows one to begin accumulating the huge number of practice hours needed to out-perform others. Those who begin at a later age are simply unable to catch up.

Because deliberate practice is so effortful, the amount that can be tolerated each day is nec-essarily limited. For this reason, elite performers often practice about 4 hours per day. Ericsson et al. (1993), for example, found that the best violin students engaged in solitary practice (which was judged to be the most important type of practice) for approximately 3.5 hours per day, spread out across two to three sessions, each session lasting an average of 80 minutes. Note that this did not include time spent receiving instruction, giving performances, or playing for enjoyment. The students also devoted about 3.5 hours a day to rest and recreation and obtained more than average amounts of sleep.

Top-level performers in intellectual pursuits display similar characteristics. Novelists typi-cally write for about 3 to 4 hours each day, usually in the morning. Eminent scientists likewise write for a few hours each morning—the writing of articles arguably being the most important activity determining their success—and then devote the rest of the day to other duties. Skinner is especially instructive in this regard. In his later life, he would rise at midnight and write for 1 hour, then rise again at 5:00 A.M. and write for another 2 hours. The remainder of the morning was devoted to correspondence and other professional tasks, while much of the afternoon was devoted to recreational activities such as tinkering in his workshop and listening to music. He deliberately resisted any urge to engage in serious writing at other times of the day, feeling that this often resulted in poor-quality writing the next morning. The limited amount of writing he did each day was more than compensated for by the consistency with which he wrote, resulting in a steady stream of influential articles and books throughout his career (Bjork, 1993). Skinner (1987) recommended that students adopt a similar approach to improve the quality of their writing. Congruent with this, research has shown that effective college students are more likely to describe themselves as utilizing a *balanced* approach to studying, involving regular study ses-sions with frequent breaks, than a *driven* approach, involving minimal breaks and studying to the point of exhaustion (Bouvier & Powell, 2008).

Of course, Ericsson et al. (1993) do not completely discount the role of heredity in expert performance. Heredity might well affect the extent to which one becomes interested in an endeavor, as well as one's ability to endure the years of hard work needed to become an elite performer. Nevertheless, the obvious importance of deliberate practice suggests that we should not be too quick to discount our ability to acquire a certain skill. Although many of us might not have the desire, time, or resources to become elite athletes, excellent musicians, or famous scientists, this does not rule out the possibility of becoming better tennis players, learning how to play the guitar, or significantly improving our math skills. After all, the best evidence available suggests that it is largely a matter of practice. (See Ericsson, Charness, Feltovich, & Hoffman, 2006, for a recent comprehensive overview of scientific research on expert performance; see also Starkes & Ericsson, 2003, for an overview of research on expert performance in sports.)

FIGURE 1.2 In Hull's neobehaviorism, theorists make use of intervening variables, in the form of hypothesized physiological processes, to help explain the relationship between the environment and behavior.

What did concern him was whether the *concept of hunger*, as defined in some measurable way (such as number of hours of food deprivation), was scientifically useful and led to testable hypotheses.

Hull's theory was also a pure S–R theory because it assumed that learning consists of the establishment of connections between specific stimuli and specific responses. Thus, like Watson, he viewed behavior in a very mechanistic fashion. Lest this seem dehumanizing, recognize that it is not far removed from some modern-day cognitive approaches, which view humans as analogous to computers that process bits of information from the environment (input) to produce responses (output). This is actually quite similar to Hull's model of behavior: Specific stimuli (input) yield specific responses (output), with certain internal events mediating the process. In fact, some versions of modern-day cognitive psychology can even be considered an outgrowth of Hull's neobehaviorism.[5]

Hull was the most influential experimental psychologist of the 1940s and 1950s. Unfortunately, it turned out that major aspects of his theory (which are beyond the scope of this text) were very difficult to test. As well, the theory was highly mathematical and grew increasingly complex as equations were expanded and modified. Many of these modifications were forced on Hull by his critics, the most famous of whom was Edward C. Tolman. (For a major overview of Hull's theory, as well as to gain a sense of its complexity, see Hull, 1943.)

---

[5]Interestingly, people seem less critical of the cognitive information-processing approach to psychology, which draws an analogy between humans and computers, than they are of the traditional behavioral approach, which draws an analogy between humans and animals such as rats. Perhaps this is because we are impressed by the ability of computers to perform certain human-like tasks (e.g., play chess), and we are insulted by the notion that humans and rats have anything in common. Yet, outside their specialized abilities, computers are quite inferior to rats. Imagine, for example, that a man, a rat, and a computer are washed up on a deserted island. To the extent that the man emulates the rat (if he is capable of it), he will likely survive; to the extent that he emulates the computer, he will sit on the beach and rot. Rats have a marvelous ability to learn and adapt; present-day computers do not. Fortunately for us, humans are far more rat-like than computer-like.

1. Hull believed that it might be useful to incorporate internal events into one's theorizing so long as they can be op_____ by defining them in such a way that they can be measured.

2. In Hull's approach, the internal events he included were of hypothetical ph_____ processes.

3. Such internal events are called i_____ variables in that they are presumed to m_____ between the environment and behavior.

4. Hull's theory was a pure ____-___ theory in that it assumed that the process of learning involves the creation of connections between specific s_____ and specific r_____.

Tolman's Cognitive Behaviorism

Hull's S-R theory of learning is often categorized as a "molecular" theory because it viewed behavior as consisting of a long chain of specific responses connected to specific stimuli. Edward Tolman (1886–1959) disagreed with this approach and believed that it would be more useful to analyze behavior on a "molar" (i.e., broader) level. For example, he felt that we can understand a rat's behavior in a maze more accurately as a goal-directed attempt to obtain food than as a long chain of discrete stimulus-response connections that, in machine-like fashion, lead to food (e.g., Tolman, 1932). This molar approach to learning is similar to the gestalt approach to perception (Kohler, 1947), from which Tolman drew much of his inspiration. To the gestalt psychologists, perception is not simply the summation of different bits of conscious experience but is instead a

Edward C. Tolman
(1886–1959)

© Psychology Archives—The University of Akron

"holistic" process resulting in an organized, coherent, perceptual experience. We perceive a house as more than just a combination of bricks and boards; it is bricks and boards plus something more. As the famous gestalt saying goes, "the whole is more than the sum of the parts." Similarly, for Tolman, behavior was more than just a chain of discrete responses attached to discrete stimuli. It was instead an overall pattern of behavior directed toward particular outcomes, and it can be properly analyzed only on that level.

Although Tolman disagreed with much of Hull's theorizing, he did agree that intervening variables may be useful in a theory of learning (in fact, it was Tolman who first suggested this). However, while Hull's intervening variables were physiological-type processes like hunger and fatigue, Tolman's were considerably more mentalistic. The Tolmanian rat, as well as the Tolmanian person, was not simply motivated by drives and habits but also had "expectations" and "hypotheses." Thus, Tolman's *cognitive behaviorism* (sometimes called "purposive behaviorism") utilizes intervening variables, usually in the form of hypothesized cognitive processes, to help explain behavior (see Figure 1.3).

FIGURE 1.3 In Tolman's cognitive behaviorism, theorists make use of intervening variables, in the form of hypothesized cognitive processes, to help explain the relationship between environment and behavior.

Tolman's (1948) most famous intervening variable is the **cognitive map,** which is a mental representation of one's spatial surroundings. Evidence for this concept was derived from a study on "latent learning" by Tolman and Honzik (1930). This experiment was conducted in an attempt to disprove Hull's notion that behavior must be rewarded for learning to take place; that is, in the absence of some type of reward, nothing can be learned. To test this notion, Tolman and Honzik trained three groups of rats on a complex maze task (see Figure 1.4). The rats in a continuous-reward group always found food when they reached the goal box, but the rats in the two other groups found no food when they reached the goal box (they were simply removed

FIGURE 1.4 Maze used by Tolman and Honzik (1930) in their study of latent learning. (Adapted from Tolman, 1948).

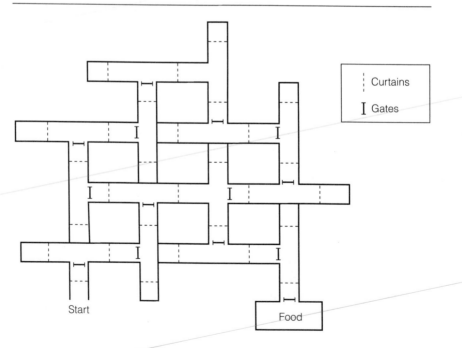

from the maze and then fed several hours later). Training proceeded at the rate of one trial per day for 10 consecutive days. As expected, the rewarded group learned to run quickly to the goal box, whereas the two nonrewarded groups took much longer to do so.

Following this initial phase of training, on day 11 of the study the rats in one of the nonrewarded groups also began receiving food when they reached the goal box. According to Hull, the rats in that group should only then have started to learn their way through the maze, which would have been demonstrated by a gradual improvement in their performance. What Tolman and Honzik found instead was a dramatic improvement in the rats' performance on the very next trial. In fact, on day 12 of the study, the newly rewarded group slightly outperformed the group that had been receiving a reward from the outset (see Figure 1.5).

FIGURE 1.5   Errors made by the different groups of rats in Tolman and Honzik's (1930) latent learning experiment. The vertical axis represents the average number of wrong turns the rats in each group made before reaching the goal box. Group NR are those rats that never received a reward for reaching the goal box. Group R are those rats that always received a reward for reaching the goal box. Group NR-R received no reward for the first 10 days of the study, then began receiving a reward on day 11. Note that this group was run for a few days longer than the other two groups to see if there would be any additional change in their performance. (Adapted from Tolman & Honzik, 1930; see also "How to Read Graphs" in the And Furthermore box.)

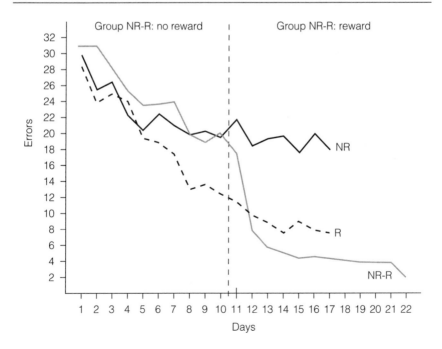

Tolman interpreted these results as indicating that the initially nonrewarded rats had in fact learned the maze during the first 10 trials of the experiment, and that they had learned it at least as well as the group that had been receiving food. He would later interpret these findings as indicating the development of a "cognitive map" (Tolman, 1948), which only became apparent when the rats finally began to receive food. Thus, this experiment is regarded as a classic demonstration of ***latent learning***, in which learning occurs despite the absence of any observable demonstration of learning and only becomes apparent under a different set of conditions. The experiment also demonstrates the distinction between *learning and performance*, because learning was apparently taking place even when the subjects showed no evidence of such learning in their performance at that time. (See, however, Jensen, 2006, for a more detailed exposition and critique of these findings and how they have been interpreted.)

Although Tolman believed that it was theoretically useful to incorporate cognitive variables, he remained, in many other ways, a standard behaviorist. For example, like Hull and Watson, he believed that introspective reports of thoughts and feelings are so unreliable as to be of little scientific value. He maintained that his own theoretical inferences about cognitive processes were based entirely on direct observations of behavior and were thus objectively based. Tolman once even apologized for the "shameful necessity" of having to discuss conscious experience in a text he was writing (Tolman, 1932)—a reflection perhaps of how frustrated psychologists had been by the old introspectionist approach. Like other behaviorists, Tolman also believed strongly in the usefulness of animal research for discovering basic processes of learning, and almost all of his research was conducted with rats.

Much of Tolman's research was directly aimed at refuting Hull's theory of learning. Hull was able, in increasingly complex ways, to modify his theory sufficiently to account for many of Tolman's findings.[6] As a result, during Tolman's life, his cognitive approach never achieved the same popularity as Hull's neobehavioral approach. With the advent of the cognitive revolution in psychology, however, many of Tolman's research methods and concepts

---

[6]Roughly speaking, Hull (1943) was able to account for the results of Tolman and Honzik's latent learning experiment by hypothesizing that the rats in the nonrewarded conditions found the mere act of being removed from the maze when they reached the empty goal box to be slightly rewarding. This slight reward was sufficient to ensure that the rats learned the pathway to the goal box, but not sufficient to motivate them to greatly reduce the number of errors they were making. Only when the incentive to get to the goal box was increased by the availability of food did the number of errors drop significantly and the degree of learning become evident. Alternatively, Jensen (2006) has recently pointed to evidence indicating that the rats in the nonrewarded group may have found the act of entering a blind alley punishing, thereby reducing their tendency to make incorrect responses. This would again argue against interpreting these particular results as strong evidence of latent learning.

P. BYRNES.

"Bathroom? Sure, it's just down the hall to the left, jog right, left, another left, straight past two more lefts, then right, and it's at the end of the third corridor on your right."

have been adopted by modern researchers. Cognitive behaviorism is now a flourishing field of study, and the study of cognitive processes in nonhuman animals is specifically known as "animal cognition" or "comparative cognition."

1. Tolman's approach is known as _____ behaviorism because it utilizes mentalistic concepts, such as "expectations," to explain behavior. This approach is also sometimes called p_____ behaviorism.

2. A _____ _____ is an internal representation of one's surroundings.

3. The experiment by Tolman and Honzik (1930) has traditionally been regarded as a demonstration of _____ learning, in which learning appears to take place in the absence of any reward. The experiment has also been regarded as a demonstration of the distinction between learning and _____ .

4. Tolman believed that introspectively observed thoughts and feelings are (useless/ useful) _____ in the analysis of behavior. As well, almost all of Tolman's research was conducted using _____ as subjects.

5. The modern-day study of cognitive processes in nonhuman animals is known as a_____ c_____ or com_____ c_____ .

And Furthermore

How to Read Graphs

A graph is a concise way of conveying information. It has two axes: the horizontal or x-axis, which is formally called the abscissa, and the vertical or y-axis, which is formally called the ordinate. The vertical axis is usually a measure of the target behavior in which we are interested; in Figure 1.5 this is the number of errors the rats made while running through a maze. The horizontal axis usually indicates some aspect of the experimental manipulation, in this case, the days on which the rats were run through the maze. The broken line between days 10 and 11 indicates that there was a change in conditions at this time, which is described by the labels on each side of the broken line (namely, that group NR-R switched from receiving no reward to receiving a reward). The three lines within the graph therefore indicate the average number of errors made by each group of rats on each day of the experiment.

Bandura's Social Learning Theory

© Linda A. Cicero/Stanford News Service

Albert Bandura
(b. 1925)

If Tolman's use of cognitive concepts seems to represent a partial return to mentalism, Albert Bandura's social learning theory is an even stronger step in that direction. The roots of social learning theory can be partially traced to Hull's neobehaviorism in that Bandura had considerable exposure to Hullian theorists during his graduate training. In addition, the term *social learning theory* was first used by followers of Hull who were attempting to apply Hullian concepts to human social behavior, particularly to the process of imitation (Miller & Dollard, 1941). Bandura was very much interested in imitation, which he referred to as observational learning, and he eventually became the dominant researcher in the field. His most famous investigations concern the influence of observational learning on aggressive behavior (Bandura, 1973).

Although Bandura's interests were partially influenced by Hullian psychologists, his interpretation of the learning process is more closely aligned with that of Tolman. Like Tolman, Bandura focuses on broad behavior patterns (i.e., he uses a molar approach) and emphasizes the distinction between learning and performance. He also gives internal events, such as expectations, a primary role in the learning process. Bandura's approach differs from that of Tolman, however, in that these internal events are viewed as more than just theoretically useful; they are viewed as actual events occurring within us that strongly influence our behavior. Additionally, these internal events include *self-referent thoughts* about our abilities and accomplishments, a distinctly

FIGURE 1.6   Bandura's model of reciprocal determinism, in which observable behavior, environmental events, and internal events are all viewed as interacting with each other.

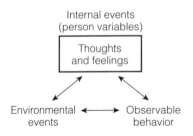

human form of cognition that Bandura believes has significant impact on our behavior. This means that, unlike the other behaviorists we have discussed, Bandura does not dismiss the value of introspectively observed, subjective experience in explaining behavior. Thus, *social learning theory* is a cognitive-behavioral approach that strongly emphasizes the importance of observational learning and cognitive variables in explaining human behavior (Bandura, 1977, 1997).[7]

Social learning theory also has a distinct view of determinism (the notion that each behavior has a cause). More specifically, Bandura has proposed the concept of *reciprocal determinism,* in which environmental events, observable behavior, and "person variables" (including thoughts and feelings) are seen as having a reciprocal influence on each other (see Figure 1.6). Reciprocal determinism can be contrasted with the deterministic models proposed by other behaviorists in which internal events, if they are included, simply mediate between the environment and behavior (Environment → Internal events → Behavior).

As an illustration of reciprocal determinism, imagine that you are out on a date with someone to whom you are very attracted. Trying to impress this individual, you start the evening off by telling a joke (thus, an aspect of your environment—namely, the person you are dating—has affected your behavior). Unfortunately, your off-color sense of humor is not appreciated, and your date reacts to the joke with a look of horror (your behavior has affected your environment). The look of horror in turn elicits feelings of anxiety (your environment has affected your feelings), which then causes you to stammer as you speak (your feelings have affected your behavior). Observing yourself stammer then leads you to conclude that your date must think you are an idiot (your behavior has affected your beliefs), which in turn leads you to interpret your date's smile as a smile of pity (your beliefs have affected the environment—or, more precisely, the environment as you

---

[7]Bandura (e.g., 1997) has more recently referred to this approach as "social-cognitive" theory, so as to emphasize the importance of cognitive variables.

perceive it). Needless to say, the evening turns out to be a complete disaster, with the environment, behavior, and person variables (thoughts and feelings) all interacting to conspire against you. (No wonder life is rough!)

Social learning theory has stimulated a lot of research, particularly in the area of observational learning. It has also stimulated the development of *cognitive-behavior therapy*, in which psychological disorders are treated by altering both environmental variables and cognitive processes. For example, a cognitive-behavioral treatment for an irrational fear of spiders might involve some type of safe exposure to spiders (an environmental manipulation) along with instructions to replace fearful thoughts with certain types of calming thoughts (a cognitive manipulation). Cognitive-behavioral treatments have become very popular in recent years. It (along with its cousin, animal cognition) has become a dominant force in behavioral psychology and is rivaled by only one other school of thought—B. F. Skinner's radical behaviorism.

1. Bandura's _____ _____ theory emphasizes the importance of o_____ learning and c_____ variables.

2. The concept of _____ _____ proposes that three variables: e_____, b_____, and p_____ variables, all interact with each other.

3. Bandura's work has influenced the development of a type of therapy known as _____-_____ therapy, in which an attempt is made to change behavior by altering both environmental and c_____ factors.

Skinner's Radical Behaviorism

© Yvonne Hemsey/ Getty Images

Burrhus Frederick Skinner
(1904–1990)

From Watson to Bandura, we see a steady increase in the use of internal events to help explain behavior. Not everyone has agreed with this trend. Burrhus Frederick Skinner argued for a return to a stricter form of behaviorism. Skinner's version of behaviorism, known as *radical behaviorism,* emphasizes the influence of the environment on overt behavior, rejects the use of internal events to explain behavior, and views thoughts and feelings as behaviors that themselves need to be explained. Thus, unlike Watson's methodological behaviorism, radical behaviorism does not completely reject the inclusion of internal events in a science of behavior; it merely rejects the use of these events as explanations for behavior (Skinner, 1953, 1974). We explain this notion more fully in the following section.

Skinner's View of Internal Events Skinner viewed internal events, such as sensing, thinking, and feeling, as "covert" or private behaviors that are subject to the same laws of learning as "overt" or publicly observable behaviors. Thus, internal events can be included in an analysis of behavior but only as behaviors that themselves need to be explained. For example, whereas a social learning theorist might say that a student studies because she *expects* that studying will result in a high mark, Skinner would say that both the act of studying and any thoughts about achieving a high mark by studying are the result of some experience, such as a history of doing well on exams when the student did study.

For several reasons, Skinner was loath to consider internal events as explanations for behavior. First, he agreed with Watson's concern that, since we do not have direct access to the internal events of others, we must rely on their verbal reports of such events. Our assessments of internal thoughts and feelings thus are often unreliable. Skinner further noted that such unreliability is to be expected, given the manner in which people learn to label their internal events. More specifically, young children need to be taught by their caretakers to describe their internal experiences. Because these caretakers (usually parents) cannot directly observe internal events in their children, they must infer their occurrence from the children's observable behaviors.

Consider, for example, the task of teaching a young boy to correctly label the feeling of pain. The parent must wait until the child is displaying some observable behavior that typically accompanies pain, such as crying in response to a stubbed toe. Based on this behavior, the parent then infers that the child is experiencing pain and says something like, "My, your toe must really hurt!" After a few experiences like this, the child will himself begin using the word *hurt* to describe what he is feeling in such circumstances.

Pain is probably one of the easier feelings to teach, given that the observable behaviors accompanying it are usually quite distinct (although even here, there may be considerable variability across individuals in the intensity of sensation required before something is called painful). Consider how much more difficult it is to teach a child to accurately describe subtle emotions such as contentment or discomfort, for which the observable behaviors are often much less distinct. Because the parents have less reliable information on which to base their inferences about such states, the labels they provide to the child are likely to be only crude approximations of the child's actual feelings. As a result, the labels people learn to use for describing their feelings may be only crude approximations of what they actually feel. For this reason, Skinner was uninterested in using a person's description of an internal emotional state as an explanation for behavior; he was, however, quite interested in how people come to label their internal experiences.

A second problem with using internal events to explain behavior is that it is often difficult to determine the actual relationship of thoughts and feelings to behavior. Do the thoughts and feelings precede the behavior, follow the behavior, or simply occur parallel to the behavior? Take, for example, the act of providing help in an emergency. Do you provide help because you feel concern for the person involved (Figure 1.7a)? Or do you provide help and feel concerned at the same time, with no necessary link between the two (Figure 1.7b)? After all, people often take action in an emergency quite quickly, without reflecting upon how they feel.

FIGURE 1.7 Three ways in which feelings of concern can be associated with the behavior of helping.

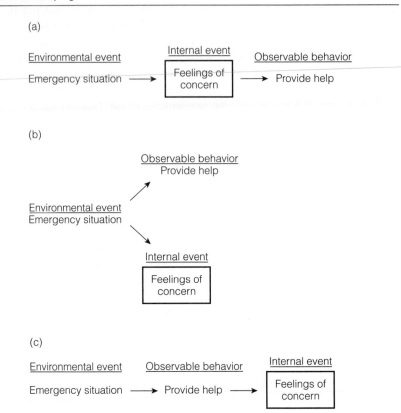

(a)

Environmental event   Internal event   Observable behavior

Emergency situation → [Feelings of concern] → Provide help

(b)

Observable behavior
Provide help

Environmental event
Emergency situation

Internal event
[Feelings of concern]

(c)

Environmental event   Observable behavior   Internal event

Emergency situation → Provide help → [Feelings of concern]

Or do your feelings of concern for someone sometimes arise after you have tried to help them (Figure 1.7c)? Lest this notion seem rather strange to you, consider that people's feelings about an event can often be altered simply by manipulating their behavior toward the event. For example, people can often be induced to change their opinion about a certain issue—such as whether capital punishment should be abolished—by asking them to write an essay promoting a certain point of view. If they do not already hold a strong opinion about that issue and do not feel that they are being forced to write the essay, they may alter their opinion to be consistent with what they have written (Cialdini, 1993). In similar fashion, the concern you feel for others might sometimes result from, or at least be strengthened by, the act of helping them.

A third difficulty with using internal events to explain behavior is that we do not have any means of directly changing these internal events. Our only means of changing both internal events and external behavior is to change some aspect of the environment. For example, if I instruct a client to think calm, relaxing thoughts whenever he or she is in an anxiety-arousing situation, and this effectively reduces the anxiety, a radical behaviorist would say that the effective treatment is not the calm, relaxing thoughts but the instructions I have given the person about thinking calm, relaxing thoughts. And since exposing the client to these instructions is really a manipulation of the client's environment, then it is really a change in the environment that is ultimately responsible for reducing the level of anxiety. Therefore, if changing the environment is the only manner in which behavior can be influenced, then why not emphasize the environment as the ultimate cause of behavior?

A fourth problem with using internal events to explain behavior is that (as with explanations based on instinct) such explanations are sometimes only pseudo explanations. For example, if I say that I "feel like going to the movies," am I referring to a bodily condition of some sort, or am I simply making a prediction about my future behavior? Perhaps all I am really saying is that I am quite likely to go to the movies under these particular circumstances (which may or may not include a certain bodily state), given that nothing prevents me from doing so. Thus, my "feeling" statement is much more a statement about potential behavior than about a bodily feeling of some sort. For this reason, saying that I am going to the movies because I "feel like going" is really no explanation at all.

For reasons such as these, Skinner rejected internal events as explanations for behavior; instead, he focused on the environment—in particular, the environmental consequences of our behavior—as the ultimate cause of both observable behavior and internal events. But neither did he believe that we are helpless pawns of our environment. He assumed that once we understand the manner in which the environment affects us, we can change the environment so that it will exert a more beneficial influence on our behavior. Skinner referred to this process as **countercontrol,** which is the deliberate manipulation of environmental events to alter their impact on our behavior. Nevertheless, in Skinner's view, even such acts of countercontrol can ultimately be traced to environmental influence. Suppose, for example, that Jamie decides to improve her study habits by rearranging her study environment. On one level of analysis, Jamie's decision is the cause of the improvement in her study habits. On another level, however, Jamie would not have decided to implement these changes unless she had first been exposed to information about their usefulness. The source of this information is an environmental influence and is, in Skinner's view, the ultimate cause of the improvement in Jamie's study habits.

Thus, Skinner might be seen as agreeing with some aspects of Bandura's notion of reciprocal determinism, in the sense that environmental events, internal events, and observable behavior are seen as capable of interacting with each other. Where Skinner differs, however, is in his assumption that the environment ultimately determines both external behavior and internal events. A diagrammatic depiction of Skinner's approach might therefore look something like that depicted in Figure 1.8. (See Skinner [1953, 1987, 1989] for a discussion of his perspective on private events; also see Anderson, Hawkins,

FIGURE 1.8 A diagrammatic representation of Skinner's view of the relationship between environmental events, internal events, and observable behavior. Although all three components are capable of influencing each other, the emphasis is on environmental events as the ultimate cause of both observable behavior and internal events (as indicated by the solid arrows).

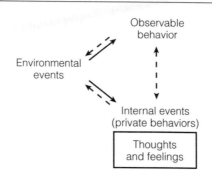

Freeman, and Scotti [2000] for the many issues involved in incorporating private events into a science of behavior.)

QUICK QUIZ K

1. Skinner's _____ behaviorism views both internal and external behaviors as resulting from e_____ influences.

2. Skinner views thoughts and feelings as pr_____ behaviors that themselves need to be explained.

3. In teaching children to label their thoughts and feelings, parents first have to make inf_____ about what the child is feeling.

4. In determining the relationship of thoughts and feelings to behavior, it is sometimes difficult to know if the internal event pr_____, f_____, or occurs pa_____ to the behavior.

5. Yet another issue with respect to using internal events to explain behavior is that we (can/cannot) _____ directly change such events.

6. Saying that you are feeling "happy" to explain why you are always smiling and laughing is, from Skinner's perspective, an example of using feelings as a ps_____ explanation for your behavior.

7. Altering the environment so as to control our own behavior is referred to as c_____. However, even this type of behavior is ultimately the result of some type of e_____ influence.

Skinner's Approach as Molar Although Skinner disagreed with Tolman about the value of using internal events to help explain behavior, he agreed with Tolman in emphasizing a molar rather than a molecular approach. Critics are thus incorrect in referring to Skinner as an S-R psychologist who held a mechanistic view of behavior. He did not believe, as Watson and Hull did, that all behaviors consist of long chains of S-R connections that propel the animal forward in a robotic, step-by-step fashion. Skinner (1938) instead believed that only reflexive behaviors—those that can be classically conditioned, such as salivating in response to food—are automatically elicited by the stimuli that precede them. Such behaviors need to be distinguished from operant behaviors—behaviors that are controlled by their consequences—which have a more flexible, less predictable quality to them. Therefore, for both Skinner and Tolman, the rat's behavior of running through the maze is an operant behavior that is controlled by the consequence of obtaining food in the goal box. The difference is that the Tolmanian rat is running through the maze because it *expects* that doing so will lead to food, whereas the Skinnerian rat is running through the maze because such behavior has *in the past* resulted in food. Tolman was comfortable with hypothesizing the existence of a mental event inside the animal to help explain its present behavior—a mental event that was, of course, based on the rat's past experience—whereas Skinner preferred to explain the behavior by simply referring to past experience.

Skinner's View of Genetic Factors   What about the role of genetic influences on behavior? In discussing these various schools of behaviorism, we have focused on the role of the environment; but we have done so simply because that is what behaviorists traditionally do—they study the effects of environmental experiences on behavior. Traditionally, they have left it to other disciplines, such as ethology (a subfield of zoology that studies instinctive behavior patterns in animals), to study the role of genetic factors in behavior. This does not mean that behaviorists discount the role of heredity. As we noted earlier, Darwin's theory of evolution played a strong role in the eventual establishment of behaviorism, and many behaviorists clearly recognize that heredity can profoundly influence animal and human behavior. Skinner (e.g., 1953, 1987, 1989), in fact, repeatedly acknowledged that behavior was fundamentally the result of the interaction between genes and the environment. Moreover, far from being dismayed by research indicating genetic limitations on operant conditioning (some of which is discussed in Chapter 11), Skinner (1987) was quite fascinated by it and even initiated some early research along these lines.

Skinner also noted that operant conditioning bears a striking resemblance to the evolutionary principle of natural selection. As earlier discussed, according to the principle of natural selection, members of a species that inherit certain adaptive characteristics are more likely to survive and propagate, thereby passing those characteristics on to their offspring. Thus, over many generations, the frequency of those adaptive characteristics within the population increases and becomes well established. In a similar fashion, according to the principle of operant conditioning, behaviors that lead to favorable outcomes are more likely to be repeated, whereas those that do not lead to favorable outcomes are less likely to be repeated. In other words, operant conditioning is sort of a mini-evolution in which behaviors that are adaptive (that lead to favorable consequences) increase in frequency while behaviors that are nonadaptive (that do not lead to favorable consequences) decrease in frequency. The processes of natural selection and operant conditioning are therefore very similar. The basic difference is that natural selection is concerned with the evolution of inherited characteristics within a species, whereas operant conditioning is concerned with the evolution of learned behavior patterns within an individual.

Skinner (1953) was more accepting of the effects of heredity on behavior than was Watson, but he nevertheless remained wary about placing too much emphasis on such factors. Genetic factors are largely unmodifiable, and to assume that a behavior pattern has a strong genetic basis is to assume also that little can be done to alter it (except perhaps through some type of physiological intervention). When dealing with maladaptive characteristics such as learning difficulties or aggressive tendencies in children, this assumption can have serious consequences. Think about it: If you had a son who was having difficulty in math, would you want his teacher to be a strong empiricist or a strong nativist? Almost certainly, you would want a teacher who is a strong empiricist and who believes the child's math problems are the result of poor learning experiences, which can be corrected by providing better experiences. Thus, a strong empiricist approach, such as that exemplified by Skinner and other behaviorists, tends to be more optimistic about the possibility of changing behavior for the better. Behaviorists nevertheless have a growing appreciation for the influence of genetic factors on learning and behavior, and in the future we will no doubt see a significant increase in research in this area.

1. Skinner is most similar to (Hull/Watson/Tolman) _____ in arguing that behavior is best viewed from a m_____ perspective.

2. For Skinner, an S-R interpretation can best be applied to behavior that is r_____ and can be _____ conditioned. It cannot be applied to _____ behavior that is under the control of its c_____ and has a more fl_____ quality about it.

3. The Tolmanian rat runs through the maze because it e_____ that doing so will result in food; the Skinnerian rat runs through the maze because, in its p_____ experience, doing so resulted in food.

4. Although he emphasized the role of the environment, Skinner also believed that behavior was fundamentally the result of the interaction of g_____ and the environment. He was in fact quite interested in evidence indicating g_____ limitations on _____ conditioning.

5. Skinner believed that the processes of e_____ and operant conditioning were quite similar in that both involved selecting what was beneficial from what was not beneficial.

6. On a practical level, Skinner believed that genetic explanations for behavior tend to be (optimistic/pessimistic) _____ about the possibility of change.

Behavior Analysis and Applied Behavior Analysis   More so than other behaviorists, Skinner was careful to distinguish between the philosophical aspect of his approach and the experimental science that grew out of that approach. The term *radical behaviorism* refers to the philosophical aspect of Skinner's approach, consisting of the set of assumptions, which we discussed earlier, upon which his behavioral science is based. The science that grew out of radical behaviorism was originally called the ***experimental analysis of behavior,*** but is now more commonly referred to as ***behavior analysis.*** Behavior analysts, following the lead of Skinner, have especially concentrated on researching the various principles of operant conditioning (which are discussed in Chapters 6 through 10).

Like Watson, Skinner was concerned that the principles discovered through research should have practical application. In this regard, he did not disappoint. His work directly led to the establishment of ***applied behavior analysis,*** a technology of behavior in which basic principles of behavior are applied to real-world issues. These applications range from helping people with clinical disorders (such as phobias and schizophrenia), to improving educational practices, to implementing programs that encourage communities to stop polluting and conserve energy. Applied behavior analysis is particularly well established as the treatment of choice for children with developmental disabilities, including autism, and many graduates from behavior analysis programs find work in this field. (See Miltenberger, 1997, for a more extensive list of areas of application.) Applied behavior analysis is also sometimes referred to as *behavior modification* or *behavior therapy*, though the latter term can also refer to more cognitive-behavioral approaches to treatment than would be found in pure applied behavior analysis.

1. Skinner's philosophy of behaviorism (meaning the set of basic assumptions for how best to conduct a science of behavior) is called _____ behaviorism.

2. The science that grew out of that philosophy is called the e_____ a_____ of behavior or, more briefly, _____ _____.

3. The technology that has grown out of that science is known as _____ _____ _____.

QUICK QUIZ M

ADVICE FOR THE LOVELORN

While reading this text you will occasionally encounter advice columns, like this one, in which behavioral concepts are applied to relationship problems. Bear in mind that the advice given is often quite speculative and that real relationship difficulties are too complex to be properly assessed and dealt with through simplistic advice columns. Nevertheless, these columns will, in a fun manner, give you a sense for how behavioral concepts can offer a unique perspective on important aspects of human behavior.

Dear Dr. Dee,

I have very strong feelings for my new girlfriend, but I can't tell if these are feelings of infatuation or love. My friends tell me I am in love, but my parents tell me I am infatuated. How can I tell the difference?

So Confused

Dear So,

The distinction between love and infatuation is a tough one, and many people find it difficult to differentiate between the two. Interestingly, Skinner (1989) suggested that the more subtle an emotional state (and, presumably, the more subtle the differences between emotional states), the more value there is in analyzing that emotion in terms of the circumstances that surround it. In what circumstance, for example, are we most likely to use the term *infatuation*? For starters, are we not more likely to use that term when the level of attachment seems to greatly exceed the total rewards available in the relationship? In particular, isn't it the case that we often apply the word *infatuation* to a relationship that is driven by short-term sexual rewards with few long-term prospects? By contrast, the word *love* is typically applied to a relationship in which a strong level of attachment seems to properly match the available rewards. The relationship seems to have good long-term prospects and is not driven merely by short-term sexual rewards. Thus, for many people, the word *infatuation* implies an "unhealthy" relationship that is doomed to failure, whereas the word *love* implies a "healthy" relationship that has the potential to prosper.

A little thought will likely reveal other differences between infatuation and love. Nevertheless, our brief analysis suggests that if you wish to determine whether you are "in love" or "merely infatuated," you might do well to ponder the rewards offered by that relationship and forget about trying to detect minute differences in feelings.

Behaviorally yours,

Dr. Dee

And Furthermore

The Life of B. F. Skinner

Though quieter and less colorful than Watson, Skinner was nevertheless also the focus of much controversy. As such, it may be worthwhile to briefly describe his life, especially since he is viewed by many as the prototypical behaviorist. Indeed, in a survey of psychology department chairpersons, Skinner was voted the most influential psychologist of the 20th century (Haggbloom et al., 2002).

Burrhus Frederick Skinner was born in Susquehanna, Pennsylvania, in 1904. Raised in a traditional Presbyterian household, Skinner had a relatively normal childhood, though it was not without difficulties. For example, although he was never physically punished as a child (apart from once having his mouth washed out with soap for saying a bad word), he was taught through reprimands and warnings "to fear God, the police, and what people will think" (Skinner, 1967, p. 407). Interestingly, as a behaviorist, he would later conclude that punishment is an ineffective means for managing behavior, often creating more problems than it solves.

One of Skinner's strongest traits, even in childhood, was his love of building and inventing.

> I made slingshots, bows and arrows, blow guns and water pistols from lengths of bamboo, and from a discarded water boiler a steam cannon with which I could shoot plugs of potato and carrot over the houses of our neighbors. . . . I tried again and again to make a glider in which I might fly. (Skinner, 1967, p. 388)

This inventiveness served Skinner well in later years when he was able to build unique devices for studying the behavior of animals, most notably the "Skinner box" (see Chapter 6). Without these inventions, it is conceivable that many of the principles discussed in this text would have remained undiscovered.

Skinner's personality was also characterized by a strange mixture of objectivity and sentimentality (Bjork, 1993). For example, when his younger brother, Ebbie, suddenly died of a cerebral hemorrhage, Skinner observed the death in a surprisingly detached fashion. Nevertheless, he was greatly distressed by the incident and felt pangs of guilt when he later recalled how he had once injured his brother in play. Skinner's objectivity was also apparent in everyday settings. For example, in describing a family friend, Skinner once wrote:

> The doctor and his dog are becoming more than idle amusement. . . . He becomes a fool in the eyes of everyone but me when he attempts to justify the dog's actions. . . . [Pep] comes up to us wagging his tail—"He says 'throw me a stick,'" says the doctor. . . . Lately I've got the habit too. It's quite fun to make up mental processes to fit a dog's every move. (as quoted in Bjork, 1993, p. 63)

As a radical behaviorist, Skinner would later argue that mentalistic terms are often mere inferences derived from observable behavior.

Skinner graduated from a small liberal arts college and, with some encouragement from the famous poet Robert Frost, spent a year trying to establish himself as a writer. Although

(*continued*)

quite disciplined about it, he completed only a few stories and poems and eventually gave up in despair. He sometimes claimed that he had failed as a writer because he had nothing important to say; but he also speculated that his writing was simply too "objective," with too few references to thoughts and feelings, to interest the average reader (Bjork, 1993, p. 56). Years later Skinner would publish a novel called *Walden Two,* but it was an "objective" novel about a utopian community founded on behavioral principles.

Following his failure at becoming a writer, Skinner came to the conclusion that his real interests lay in the study of behavior. Impressed by the writings of John B. Watson, he entered graduate studies at Harvard in 1928. He thrived in that environment. Much of his graduate and postdoctoral training was surprisingly unstructured, and he was often left to his own devices to study whatever he wished. In later years, he would write that he had no sense of ever devising a theory or testing a hypothesis; he simply followed his interests. He discounted the notion of science as a formal system of theory building and hypothesis testing, asserting that real science is much less structured than most scientists describe it to be (Skinner, 1956).

Skinner eventually became a major figure in behaviorism, in a league with the likes of Tolman and Hull. During World War II, he also had an opportunity to apply the principles of conditioning to national defense. While contemplating the widespread destructiveness of bombing attacks, it occurred to him that it might be possible to train pigeons to guide missiles toward specific targets. The basic notion was first to train a pigeon to peck at a moving picture of, say, a ship in order to receive a food reward. The pigeon would then be placed in the nose cone of a missile that was being launched toward a ship. A lens would project the seascape in front of the missile onto a glass screen in front of the pigeon. As the pigeon pecked at the image of the ship, the position of the pecks on the screen would provide feedback to the missile's guidance system. Skinner and his coworkers envisioned squadrons of "kamikaze" pigeons being trained to attack different kinds of targets. After obtaining some funding, they were in fact able to demonstrate that such a device was feasible. Nevertheless, the scientists who viewed the demonstration withdrew their support. The sight of a pigeon tracking a military target across a screen with such accuracy was simply too bizarre, and too amusing, for them to give it serious consideration.

Like Watson before him, Skinner was sometimes the target of false rumors. For example, when Skinner's wife, Eve, did not adjust well to the "joys" of motherhood, Skinner built an "aircrib" (or "baby tender") to ease the burden of raising their youngest daughter, Deborah. The crib was a large, enclosed space with an unbreakable glass window. The baby, wearing only a diaper, lay on a woven plastic sheet (the surface of which felt like linen), while the surrounding air was carefully filtered and maintained at a precise temperature (Figure 1.9). Skinner believed the aircrib to be far superior to the jail-like bars, uncertain temperature fluctuations, and loose bedding of the standard crib. It was also much easier to keep clean. Enthused by his invention and by the way Deborah seemed to thrive, Skinner wrote an article on the device for *Ladies' Home Journal* and set out to market it. Unfortunately, a story arose that Skinner was isolating his daughter in an "operant conditioning chamber" and experimenting on her. According to one version of the story, the daughter eventually went insane and killed herself. The reality is that she had a happy childhood, spent no more time in the aircrib than other children do in a regular crib, and grew up to be quite normal. Nevertheless, the damage was done, and relatively few aircribs were ever sold.[8]

In the early 1970s, Skinner was severely criticized by numerous intellectuals and politicians for his book, *Beyond Freedom and Dignity.* In the book, Skinner (1971) rejected the concept of free will and argued that we must instead "engineer" society to more effectively control human behavior. He had hoped the book would encourage people to devise better programs for eliminating pollution, preventing crime, and so on, and he became quite depressed over the criticism he received. Skinner received a more favorable reaction for his invention of the "teaching machine" and programmed instruction—although in later years, he lamented that this notion too had been largely ignored and never utilized to its full potential. The recent popularity of personal computers, which are ideally suited for programmed instruction, could well change that.

FIGURE 1.9 Skinner's daughter, Deborah, seemed to thrive in the "aircrib" or "baby tender" her father had built for her, so Skinner set out to market it as an improvement over the standard crib with its jail-like bars and poor hygiene. Unfortunately, it led to the completely false rumor that he was conducting conditioning experiments on his daughters, who developed severe psychological disorders as a result.

© Bettmann/corbis

Throughout his later years, Skinner remained intellectually active, carefully engineering his environment to compensate for the effects of aging. He even wrote a book, *Enjoy Old Age,* offering behavioral advice on self-management for the elderly (Skinner & Vaughan, 1983). His final public appearance was on August 10, 1990, when he was presented with a Lifetime Contribution Award by the American Psychological Association. Terminally ill but with little fear of death and as independent as ever, Skinner used his acceptance speech to lambaste the psychological community for its return to mentalistic explanations of behavior. Eight days later he passed away from leukemia at the age of 86. (See Vargas, 1990, for a touching description of Skinner's final days.)

---

[8]Unfortunately, the myth that Skinner had experimented on his daughter still makes the rounds today. A notable example is a recent book by Laura Slater (2004) entitled, *Opening Skinner's Box: Great Psychological Experiments of the Twentieth Century*, in which she repeats the rumors of Deborah's insanity. This prompted an angry response from Skinner's daughter, entitled "I Was Not a Lab Rat," in which she demands that people stop spreading these vicious rumors (Skinner-Buzan, 2004).

SUMMARY

This text introduces you to the basic principles of learning and behavior. More specifically, the text emphasizes principles of classical conditioning—in which reflexive behaviors come to be elicited in new situations—and operant conditioning—in which the probability of a behavior is influenced by its consequences.

Individuals of historical significance in the study of learning include Aristotle, who assumed that knowledge is largely gained from experience (as opposed to being inborn) and believed that learning is based on four laws of association: similarity, contrast, contiguity, and frequency. Descartes proposed that involuntary behaviors, which occur in both humans and animals, are automatically elicited by external stimulation whereas voluntary behaviors, which occur only in humans, are controlled by free will. The British empiricists argued that all knowledge is a function of experience, and they strongly emphasized the laws of association in their study of learning. Structuralists, such as Titchener, assumed that the mind is composed of a finite number of basic elements that can be discovered using the method of introspection. Darwin's theory of evolution established the notion that adaptive characteristics, including the ability to learn, evolve through the process of natural selection. This influenced the functionalists, such as William James, who recommended studying the adaptive processes of the mind. Functionalism eventually led to the establishment of behaviorism, with its emphasis on the study of publicly observable behavior and the environmental events that influence it.

There are several schools of behaviorism. Watson's methodological behaviorism rejects all references to internal events, such as thoughts and feelings, that cannot be directly observed. Hull's neobehaviorism includes references to hypothetical internal events, usually of a physiological nature (such as fatigue or hunger), that are presumed to mediate between the environment and behavior. Tolman's cognitive behaviorism differs from Hull's approach in that the hypothesized intervening variables are of a mentalistic nature, such as expectations and cognitive maps. This approach eventually led to Bandura's social learning theory, which emphasizes the importance of observational learning as well as the reciprocal interaction of internal events, environment, and behavior. By contrast, Skinner's radical behaviorism views internal events as private behaviors subject to the same laws of learning as publicly observable behaviors. Skinner's perspective is molar rather than molecular and does not discount the influence of genetic factors on learning. The science that has grown out of radical behaviorism is called the experimental analysis of behavior, or simply behavior analysis. This science has in turn led to a technology of behaviorism, known as applied behavior analysis, in which basic principles of learning are applied to real-world problems. The chapter ends with a brief biography of Skinner, whom many consider to be the classic behaviorist.

SUGGESTED READINGS

Watson, J. B. (1913). Psychology as the behaviorist views it. *Psychological Review, 20*, 154–177. The article that started it all.

Skinner, B. F. (1953). *Science and human behavior.* New York: Macmillan. A book that many regard as the bible of radical behaviorism.

Skinner, B. F. (1974). *About behaviorism.* New York: Knopf. For the average undergraduate, this introduction to radical behaviorism is probably more accessible than *Science and Human Behavior.*

Barash, D. P. (1982). How it works: Evolution as a process. In *Sociobiology and behavior* (2nd ed.). New York: Elsevier Science. A good introduction to evolution and behavior.

Hergenhahn, B. R. (1988). *An introduction to theories of learning* (6th ed.). Englewood Cliffs, NJ: Prentice-Hall. Contains extensive descriptions of the different approaches to learning and behavior, such as those by Hull and Tolman.

Buckley, K. W. (1989). *Mechanical man: John Broadus Watson and the beginnings of behaviorism.* New York: Guilford Press. A well-written biography of John B. Watson and the various controversies that swirled around him.

Bjork, D. W. (1993). *B. F. Skinner: A life.* New York: Basic Books. A very readable biography of Skinner's life.

STUDY QUESTIONS

Because many students tend to ignore long lists of broad study questions (or learning objectives) that attempt to cover all the material in a chapter, these study questions focus on the most basic information. To determine if you have a grasp of this information, see if you can write out a clear answer to each of these questions. Be aware, however, that obtaining an excellent mark in this course will require more than just a simple reiteration of this basic material.

1. Name and briefly describe the two fundamental forms of learning emphasized in this textbook.
2. Describe the nativist versus empiricist approaches to knowledge.
3. Name and briefly describe the four laws of association.
4. Outline Descartes' dualistic model of human behavior.
5. How did the British empiricists view the acquisition of knowledge and the composition of the conscious mind?
6. Describe the structuralist approach to psychology. Name and define the basic method by which the structuralists gathered data.
7. Describe the functionalist approach to psychology. Where did functionalists stand on the issue of animal experimentation, and what was their reasoning behind this?
8. Describe Darwin's principle of natural selection. What are the three main components of the principle of natural selection?

9. Define the law of parsimony and Morgan's Canon.
10. Describe Watson's methodological behaviorism. How did Watson's position on the nature–nurture debate change over time?
11. Describe Hull's neobehaviorism.
12. Describe Tolman's cognitive behaviorism.
13. Describe Bandura's social learning theory and his concept of reciprocal determinism.
14. Describe Skinner's radical behaviorism. How does his approach to determinism differ from that of Bandura's?
15. In what way was Skinner more similar to Tolman than to Watson and Hull?
16. Why was Skinner cautious about placing too much emphasis on genetic factors in behavior?
17. What is the distinction between radical behaviorism, behavior analysis, and applied behavior analysis?

CONCEPT REVIEW

applied behavior analysis. A technology of behavior in which basic principles of behavior are applied to real-world issues.

behavior. Any activity of an organism that can be observed or somehow measured.

behavior analysis (or experimental analysis of behavior). The behavioral science that grew out of Skinner's philosophy of radical behaviorism.

behaviorism. A natural science approach to psychology that traditionally focuses on the study of environmental influences on observable behavior.

British empiricism. A philosophical school of thought, of which John Locke was a member, maintaining that almost all knowledge is a function of experience.

cognitive behaviorism. A brand of behaviorism that utilizes intervening variables, usually in the form of hypothesized cognitive processes, to help explain behavior. Sometimes called "purposive behaviorism."

cognitive map. The mental representation of one's spatial surroundings.

countercontrol. The deliberate manipulation of environmental events to alter their impact on our behavior.

empiricism. In psychology, the assumption that behavior patterns are mostly learned rather than inherited. Also known as the *nurture* perspective (or, more rarely, as *nurturism*).

evolutionary adaptation. An inherited trait (physical or behavioral) that has been shaped through natural selection.

functionalism. An approach to psychology holding that the mind evolved to help us adapt to the world around us, and that the focus of psychology should be the study of those adaptive processes.

introspection. The attempt to accurately describe one's conscious thoughts, emotions, and sensory experiences.

latent learning. Learning that occurs in the absence of any observable demonstration of learning and only becomes apparent under a different set of conditions.

law of contiguity. A law of association holding that events that occur in close proximity to each other in time or space are readily associated with each other.

law of contrast. A law of association holding that events that are opposite from each other are readily associated.

law of frequency. A law of association holding that the more frequently two items occur together, the more strongly they are associated.

law of parsimony. The assumption that simpler explanations for a phenomenon are generally preferable to more complex explanations.

law of similarity. A law of association holding that events that are similar to each other are readily associated.

learning. A relatively permanent change in behavior that results from some type of experience.

methodological behaviorism. A brand of behaviorism asserting that, for methodological reasons, psychologists should study only those behaviors that can be directly observed.

mind–body dualism. Descartes' philosophical assumption that some human behaviors are bodily reflexes that are automatically elicited by external stimulation, while other behaviors are freely chosen and controlled by the mind.

nativism. The assumption that a person's characteristics are largely inborn. Also known as the *nature* perspective.

natural selection. The evolutionary principle according to which organisms that are better able to adapt to environmental pressures are more likely to survive and reproduce than those that cannot adapt.

neobehaviorism. A brand of behaviorism that utilizes intervening variables, in the form of hypothesized physiological processes, to help explain behavior.

radical behaviorism. A brand of behaviorism that emphasizes the influence of the environment on overt behavior, rejects the use of internal events to explain behavior, and views thoughts and feelings as behaviors that themselves need to be explained.

reciprocal determinism. The assumption that environmental events, observable behavior, and "person variables" (including internal events) reciprocally influence each other.

social learning theory. A brand of behaviorism that strongly emphasizes the importance of observational learning and cognitive variables in explaining human behavior. It has more recently been referred to as "social-cognitive theory."

S-R theory. The theory that learning involves the establishment of a connection between a specific stimulus (S) and a specific response (R).

structuralism. An approach to psychology holding that it is possible to determine the structure of the mind by identifying the basic elements that compose it.

CHAPTER TEST

Chapter tests typically contain fewer hints than quick quizzes do—for example, there is usually only a single blank for an answer, even though the answer may require more than a single word. Unlike the quick quizzes, however, an answer key has been provided at the end. Note too that the question numbers have been scrambled (e.g., the first question on this list is number 9). This allows you to look up the answer to a question immediately without having to worry about inadvertently seeing the answer to the next question. Finally, do not worry if you are initially unable to answer some of the items. Fill-in-the-blank items can be difficult, and this test is designed to be a learning experience more than a form of self-assessment. You may find it difficult to recall some of the information because it is still relatively unfamiliar to you.

9. When Tara saw the lush green lawn, it reminded her of just how dry the lawn had been the previous year. Among the four laws of association, this is best described as an example of the law of _____.

29. Deanna often gets lost when she drives around the city that she lives in. Tolman might say that she has a faulty _____.

17. When Janelle first saw a video of the pop singer Britney Spears, she immediately thought of Paula Abdul because the two performers seemed to have a common style of performance. Among the four laws of association, this is best described as an example of the law of _____.

1. Jordan once became terribly ill while visiting Chicago. As a result, whenever he visits Chicago, he thinks of the illness he suffered at that time. Among the four laws of association, this is best described as an example of the law of _____.

10. After struggling unsuccessfully to completely eliminate his test anxiety, Andres finally accepts that there are some aspects of himself that he can control and some that he cannot. This conclusion is similar to that of the French philosopher _____ and his theory of _____ dualism.

12. In trying to understand her feelings for Juan, Alisha pays close attention to the sensations she feels each time she sees him. This is an example of the method of _____. This was a favorite method of research by psychologists who adhered to the approach known as _____.

27. Hull's theory is a (molar/molecular) _____ type of theory, whereas Tolman's theory is a _____ type.

7. When Anastasia once visited London, it rained *every day for a week*. As a result, whenever she is trapped in a rainstorm, it reminds her of her trip to London. Among the four laws of association, this is best described as an example of the law of _____.

20. The law of _____ holds that simpler explanations are usually preferable explanations.

15. "My cat never gets lost. It's like she has a blueprint in her mind of the exact layout of the entire town." This statement fits best with (name the behaviorist) _____'s brand of behaviorism, known as _____.

11. "Babies know nothing," Kristie pronounced when her sister commented on how intelligent her new baby seemed to be. Kristie obviously believes that the mind of a newborn is a _____ slate (or, in Latin, _____), a notion that was promoted by a group of philosophers known as the _____.

31. Although Roberta just sits there throughout the lecture, she can afterward repeat everything the professor said. This is an example of _____ learning, which illustrates the distinction between learning and _____.

16. Ava tells her friend Trish that she believes that her husband kept yawning during their anniversary dinner because he was subconsciously trying to punish her for having become pregnant. Trish tells Ava to quit being paranoid and that he was probably just tired. Conway Lloyd Morgan would have leaned toward accepting (Ava/Trish) _____'s explanation as more likely correct.

25. Recall the opening vignette to the chapter where, after making love, one behaviorist comments, "That was fine for you, how was it for me?" This joke is most descriptive of which school of behaviorism? _____

23. Shira emphasizes environmental explanations for behavior and believes that thoughts and feelings should be regarded as private behaviors that also need to be explained. As such, she is most likely a _____ behaviorist. To the extent that Shira also conducts research into basic principles of behavior, she can be called a(n) _____. To the extent that she applies those principles to developing better methods for coaching basketball, she can be called a(n) _____.

2. Aristotle was a(n) (nativist/empiricist) _____, whereas Plato was a(n) _____.

32. Learning is a relatively _____ change in behavior that results from some type of _____.

22. When I haven't eaten for several hours, I feel a strong sense of hunger and therefore walk quickly as I head to the cafeteria. This statement fits best with (name the behaviorist) _____'s brand of behaviorism, known as _____.

5. Neal was recently stung by a wasp and is now quite fearful of wasps. This is best seen as an example of _____ conditioning.

30. John's therapist tells him that, although she cares about what he feels, she is more interested in what he did and in the circumstances that affected both his behavior and his feelings. This therapist's approach fits best with _____'s brand of behaviorism, known as _____.

19. Descartes believed that the behavior of (animals/humans/both) _____ is entirely reflexive.

14. Mandy found a five-dollar bill when she took out the trash one day. As a result, she often volunteers now to take out the trash. This is an example of _____ conditioning.

26. A middleman in a business transaction is analogous to what Tolman and Hull referred to as a(n) _____.

33. As originally defined by Watson, behaviorism is a _____ approach to psychology that emphasizes the study of _____ influences on directly _____ behavior.

3. After Jasmine saw her sister talk back to the sassy kid next door, she herself did likewise. This is an example of _____ learning.

18. Ally's therapist tells her that he doesn't care what she thinks and feels; he is concerned only about what she did and about the circumstances that affected her behavior. This therapist's approach fits best with (name the behaviorist) _____'s brand of behaviorism, known as _____.

8. In considering the process of dreaming, a psychologist who adheres to the approach known as _____ would be most concerned with understanding how dreaming facilitates our ability to survive and prosper.

35. Lynne persists in teaching her daughter music despite the insistence of her husband that the child "was born tone deaf." Which of these two has an attitude most similar to that of a behaviorist? _____.

24. Sal claims that the neglect he suffered as a child resulted in low self-esteem, which in turn resulted in his long history of criminal activity. His parole officer tells him that such an explanation is too simplistic, that it ignores the complex manner in which the various facets of life interact with each other, and that Sal needs to acknowledge that his own attitude played a role in creating his difficulties. Among the theorists in this chapter, the one who would most appreciate this statement is _____, because it agrees with his concept of _____ determinism.

4. "Great musicians are born, not made" is an example of the (nativist/empiricist) _____ perspective on behavior, and "practice makes perfect" is an example of the _____ perspective.

28. (Hull/Tolman) _____ viewed behavior from a gestalt perspective, whereas (Hull/Tolman) _____ assumed that behavior consists of a long chain of specific stimulus-response connections. This latter approach is known as a(n) _____ theory of behavior.

13. William James was a (structuralist/functionalist) _____, and Titchener was a _____.

6. The defining characteristic of behaviorism, as originally proposed by Watson, is the emphasis on _____.

21. Removing the television set from the room so you won't be distracted while studying each evening is an example of what Skinner called _____.

34. Skinner's approach to the study of behavior is a (molar/molecular) _____ approach. In this sense, Skinner is quite similar to (Watson/Tolman/Hull) _____.

Visit the book companion Web site at <http://www.academic.cengage.com/psychology/powell> for additional practice questions, answers to the Quick Quizzes, practice review exams, and additional exercises and information.

ANSWERS TO CHAPTER TEST

1. contiguity
2. empiricist; nativist
3. observational
4. nativist (or nature); empiricist (or nurture)
5. classical
6. observable behavior
7. frequency
8. functionalism (or evolutionary)
9. contrast
10. Descartes; mind–body
11. blank; *tabula rasa*; British empiricists
12. introspection; structuralism
13. functionalist; structuralist
14. operant
15. Tolman's; cognitive (or purposive) behaviorism
16. Trish's
17. similarity
18. Watson's; methodological behaviorism
19. animals
20. parsimony
21. countercontrol
22. Hull's; neobehaviorism
23. radical; behavior analyst; applied behavior analyst
24. Bandura; reciprocal
25. methodological behaviorism
26. intervening variable
27. molecular; molar
28. Tolman; Hull; S-R
29. cognitive map
30. Skinner's; radical behaviorism
31. latent; performance
32. permanent; experience
33. natural science; environmental; observable
34. molar; Tolman
35. Lynne

Research Methods

CHAPTER OUTLINE

Based on an actual conversation that took place between a "relationship expert" and a caller on a radio call-in show:

"Hi Dr. Kramer. I need some advice. I'm wondering if I should get married or break off my engagement and finish university first."

"How old are you?"

"Twenty-one."

"Break off your engagement. Statistically, your marriage has a much better chance of surviving if you don't get married until your late 20s."

"Oh, okay."

This chapter introduces you to the basic methods of behavioral research. Once a researcher has developed a hypothesis or has decided on a specific area of interest, such as the effect of reward size on speed of learning, he or she will employ a research method to obtain some behavioral data. Some of the methods for obtaining data include naturalistic observation, case studies, control group designs, and single-subject designs.

The methods used in behavioral research are in many ways similar to those used in other fields of psychology. For example, much behavioral research involves comparisons between "experimental" groups that receive some kind of manipulation (or treatment) and "control" groups that do not receive that manipulation. In some cases, however, the methods are quite distinctive. For example, behavior analysts (as discussed in Chapter 1, these are behaviorists who adhere to Skinner's philosophy of radical behaviorism) have a strong preference for conducting experiments that require only one or, at most, a few subjects. These types of experimental designs, known as *single-subject designs*, have several advantages (as well as disadvantages), which we discuss later in the chapter. Let's begin, however, with an overview of some basic terms and definitions.

Basic Terms and Definitions

Independent and Dependent Variables

All scientific research involves the manipulation and/or measurement of certain variables. A ***variable*** is a characteristic of a person, place, or thing that can change (vary) over time or from one situation to another. Temperature is an example of a variable; temperature varies from day to day, season to season, and place to place. Height and weight are also examples of variables—people come in many different sizes and shapes. Until a person reaches maturity, his or her height will change over a period of time. Weight is even less consistent and can fluctuate endlessly, often in directions we do not particularly like.

Almost anything can be considered a variable. Consider the following singles ad:

Brown-haired, S, M, 25, seeks S, F, aged 20–26, for fun and friendship.

The *S* in this ad stands for "single," which is one category of the variable *marital status*, which can range from single, to common-law married, to married, to divorced, and even to widowed. The *M* stands for "male," which is part of the dichotomous (meaning "two categories") variable *gender* (i.e., male and female). *Age, hair color,* and preference for *fun and friendship* are examples of other variables represented in this ad.

Two types of variables are particularly important in setting up an experiment. The **independent variable** is the aspect of an experiment that systematically varies across the different conditions in the experiment. In other words, the independent variable is what is *manipulated* in an experiment. For example, we may be interested in whether the size of a reward (or "reinforcer") can affect the efficiency of learning. To test this notion, we might conduct a maze learning experiment with rats. Each rat is given 10 trials in which it is placed in a maze and allowed to find its way to the goal box. Depending on the "experimental condition" to which the rat has been randomly assigned, it receives one, two, or three pellets of food each time it reaches the goal box. Thus, the independent variable in this experiment is the number of food pellets the rats in each group receive when they reach the goal box.

The **dependent variable** is the aspect of an experiment that is allowed to vary freely to see if it is affected by changes in the independent variable. In other words, the dependent variable is what is measured in an experiment. In a psychology experiment, this is always some type of behavior. Changes in the dependent variable are *dependent upon* changes in the independent variable (which is a useful phrase to remember to help you distinguish between the dependent and independent variable in an experiment). In the rat experiment, the dependent variable could be the total number of errors (i.e., number of wrong turns) the rat makes while trying to find its way to the goal box. Alternatively, we might simply look at the speed with which the rat reaches the goal box. Either way, a significant difference between groups on this measure will indicate whether the number of food pellets found in the goal box affects the rat's efficiency in learning the maze. In turn, this will provide supportive evidence for our more general notion—which is what we are really interested in—that the size of a reinforcer affects the efficiency of learning.

Functional Relationships

In behavioral research, the dependent variable is almost always some behavior, and the independent variable is some environmental event that is presumed to influence the behavior. The relationship between changes in an independent variable and changes in a dependent variable is known as a **functional relationship**. Thus, behaviorists are typically interested in discovering functional relationships between environmental events and behavior. A functional relationship can also be thought of as a cause-and-effect relationship, with changes in the independent variable being the cause and changes in the dependent variable being the effect.

1. A researcher is interested in studying the effects of viewing television violence on aggression in children. She shows one group of participants an extremely violent movie, another group a moderately violent movie, and a third group a nonviolent movie. In this case, the level of movie violence shown to the children would be considered the _____ variable, and the children's subsequent level of aggressive behavior would be the _____ variable.

2. A dependent variable is considered to be the (cause/effect) _____ in an experiment, whereas the independent variable is considered to be the _____.

3. A _____ relationship is the relationship between a change in an independent variable and an associated change in a dependent variable. Behaviorists are typically concerned with discovering the relationship between changes in e_____ events and changes in b_____.

QUICK QUIZ A

Stimulus and Response

Two terms used repeatedly throughout this text are *stimulus* and *response*. A **stimulus** is any event that can potentially influence behavior, whereas a **response** is a particular instance of a behavior. For example, food is a stimulus that elicits the response of salivation when presented to a hungry dog. Similarly, loud music (a stimulus) might cause your neighbor to bang on the wall (a response), and a high mark on a test (a stimulus) might cause you to grin with delight (a response). The plural for the word *stimulus* is *stimuli*. Thus, a red light is a stimulus, and a red light and a green light are stimuli.

Note that the response of one organism can act as a stimulus that influences the response of another organism. For example, when one rat bites another, that bite is a stimulus that might elicit a retaliatory response from the other rat. In turn, this retaliatory response might then act as a stimulus that induces the first rat to retreat. Similarly, a smile from Shane is a stimulus that encourages Navi to say hello; Navi's hello is in turn a stimulus that encourages Shane to introduce himself. Thus, social interactions generally consist of a chain of alternating responses, with each response acting as a stimulus for the next response from the other person.

Overt and Covert Behavior

It is also important to distinguish between overt and covert behavior. **Overt behavior** is behavior that has the potential for being directly observed by an individual other than the one performing the behavior. In other words, it is behavior that could be publicly observed if others were present. A person's response of saying hello and a rat's response of pressing a lever are both instances of overt behavior. As noted in Chapter 1, behaviorists traditionally have tended to emphasize the study of overt behavior.

Skinner, however, maintained that internal events such as thoughts, feelings, and even sensory experiences (e.g., seeing and hearing) should also be classified as behaviors. Skinner referred to such behaviors as "private behaviors" or "private events," although they are more commonly referred to as covert behaviors. Thus, *covert behavior* is behavior that can be perceived only by the person performing the behavior. In other words, it is behavior that is *subjectively* perceived and is not publicly observable. Dreaming, thinking about your next chess move, visualizing how your date will go on the weekend, and feeling anxiety are all examples of covert behavior. Of course, some covert behaviors have components that could be made publicly observable. A feeling of anxiety, for example, is likely to involve increases in heart rate and muscle tension, both of which could be electronically measured. If such measurements are made, then those particular components of anxiety can be considered overt—which from a traditional behavioral perspective is much preferred over a purely subjective report of anxiety.

Just as the behavior of one person can serve as a stimulus for the behavior of another person, covert and overt behaviors within the same person can act as stimuli for each other. For example, thinking about one's next move in chess (a covert behavior) is a stimulus that influences which chess piece you actually move (an overt behavior), while accidentally moving the wrong chess piece (an overt behavior) is a stimulus that induces you to think unpleasant thoughts about yourself (a covert behavior). As behavior analysts put it, the environment does not stop with the skin: Events both outside the skin and inside the skin can influence our behavior—though behavior analysts maintain that the ultimate cause of the behavior is to be found outside the skin. (For example, what might a behavior analyst consider to be the ultimate cause of a person thinking about a certain chess move and then making that move?)

Appetitive and Aversive Stimuli

Many stimuli, both internal and external, can be classified as appetitive or aversive. An *appetitive stimulus* is an event that an organism will seek out. Food is an appetitive stimulus when we are hungry; water is an appetitive stimulus when we are thirsty. An *aversive stimulus* is an event that an organism will avoid. Electric shock and extreme heat are examples of aversive stimuli. (Note that the word is *aversive* and not *adversive*.)

Appetitive and aversive stimuli might also be defined as those events that people usually describe as pleasant or unpleasant. Such descriptions are often quite accurate, but one has to be careful not to rely on them too much. As the *Calvin and Hobbes* cartoon illustrates, people can vary widely in the types of events they regard as appetitive versus aversive—a point that many parents overlook when they attempt to reinforce or punish a child's behavior. As well, a person may claim that a certain experience is unpleasant, yet work actively

Calvin and Hobbes   by Bill Watterson

to obtain it. For example, someone might describe her pack-a-day smoking habit as "disgusting," yet move heaven and earth to make it to the store in time to buy another pack. Despite what she says, tobacco is clearly an appetitive stimulus for her. The moral of the story is that talk is cheap—or, as behavior analysts sometimes put it, "just verbal behavior." It may or may not accurately reflect the nonverbal behavior it presumably describes.

1. A(n) _____ is any event that can potentially influence behavior; a(n) _____ is a specific instance of behavior.

2. A tone is a s_____, and a tone and a bell are s_____.

3. One person's response can be another person's _____.

4. Julie dislikes Jake, one of the sales personnel who works in her department. Because Julie avoids Jake like the plague, Jake can be considered an _____ stimulus. For example, Julie closes her office door when Jake is nearby, which is an example of a(n) (overt/covert) _____ behavior.

5. Julie also thinks unkind thoughts about Jake and feels anxious when she sees him in the hallway, both of which are examples of _____ behavior.

6. Jake is strongly attracted to Julie and often hangs around her office just to get a glimpse of her. Julie is thus an _____ stimulus for Jake.

7. If we think before we act, then our (covert/overt) _____ behavior serves as a stimulus that influences our (covert/overt) _____ behavior. If we act first and then feel regret later, then our _____ behavior serves as a stimulus that influences our _____ behavior.

Establishing Operations: Deprivation and Satiation

You may have noticed in some of the preceding examples that the appetitiveness or aversiveness of an event depends on a particular state or condition. For example, food is an appetitive stimulus to a hungry rat but might not be an appetitive stimulus to a rat that has just eaten. A procedure that affects the appetitiveness or aversiveness of a stimulus is called an **establishing operation** (Michael, 1982).

Deprivation and satiation are two types of establishing operations. **Deprivation** is the prolonged absence of an event that tends to increase the appetitiveness of that event. If the event is being used as a reinforcer (reward) for some behavior—such as food being used as a reinforcer for lever pressing—then we could also define deprivation as a procedure that increases the reinforcing value of an event. Going without food for a long period of time obviously increases the appetitiveness of food, thereby increasing its ability to serve as a reinforcer for some behavior. Less obviously, deprivation of many other events might also increase their appetitiveness. If you have ever gone without television for a while (as did the first author, when he was a poor, starving graduate student), you may have found it quite interesting when you finally had an opportunity to watch it again. Likewise, lack of social contact for several days (i.e., social deprivation) will usually result in a strong desire for social contact.

In contrast to deprivation, **satiation** refers to the prolonged exposure to (or consumption of) an event, which tends to decrease the appetitiveness of that event. Food is much less effective as a reinforcer for lever pressing if a rat has just eaten a large meal and is thus "satiated" on food. Similarly, if you hear a favorite piece of music too often, you may grow tired of hearing it. In fact, you might even become "sick of it" and avoid it, meaning the song has become aversive.

Although the general rule is that deprivation increases the appetitiveness of an event while satiation decreases its appetitiveness, exceptions can occur. For example, people (and rats, as you will discover in a later chapter) who undertake severe diets sometimes acquire a disorder known as anorexia nervosa. In these cases, severe food deprivation seems to decrease the appetitive value of food rather than increase it, and these individuals begin to eat even less food than the diet allows. People (and rats) who become anorexic also engage in extremely high levels of activity yet seem to find the activity more, not less, reinforcing—that is, they do not seem to "satiate" on the activity. These processes are discussed more fully in Chapter 11.

Contiguity and Contingency

Two terms that are often confused are *contiguity* and *contingency*. Although they sound similar, they actually refer to very different conditions. *Contiguity*, as mentioned in the opening chapter, means "closeness or nearness." Thus, **temporal contiguity** is the extent to which events occur close together in time. Thunder and lightning are temporally contiguous—we hear the thunder and shortly after we see the lightning. Temporal contiguity is an important aspect of learning. A rat will more readily learn to press a lever for food if the food immediately follows the lever press than if it appears several seconds later. Likewise, a child will more readily learn to throw a tantrum for candy if the tantrum is immediately followed by candy.

Spatial contiguity is the extent to which events are situated close to each other in space. This type of contiguity also affects learning (though perhaps not as strongly as temporal contiguity). It is easier for a rat to learn to press a lever for food if the food dispenser is close to the lever as opposed to being several feet away. Likewise, it may take a young child (or a young puppy) somewhat longer to learn that a doorbell, as opposed to a knock, indicates that someone is at the front door. The sound of the knock is spatially contiguous with the door (the sound comes from the door), whereas the sound of the doorbell is not (the sound usually comes from a box located elsewhere in the house).

The term *contingency* has a quite different meaning from contiguity. A *contingency* is a predictive relationship between two events, such that the occurrence of one event predicts the probable occurrence of another. If a rat receives a food pellet whenever it presses a lever, then a contingency exists between lever pressing and food. We then say that the presentation of food is contingent on lever pressing. Likewise, if a child receives a big balloon every time she goes to the dentist, then a contingency exists between visiting the dentist and receiving the balloon. In other words, receiving the balloon is contingent upon visiting the dentist. As you will see later, contingency is an extremely important aspect of learning.

QUICK QUIZ C

1. An e_____ o_____ is a procedure that affects the appetitiveness or aversiveness of a stimulus.

2. Farah has been working out of town and has not seen a movie for over a year. It is likely that the reward value of going to a movie has (increased/decreased) _____ as a function of (satiation/deprivation) _____.

3. The term _____ means "closeness or nearness."

4. Erin says that she once experienced a strong pain in her leg at the precise moment that her son, who was away on a mountain-climbing expedition, broke his leg. Because of the t_____ c_____ between her feeling of pain and her son's injury, Erin now claims that she must have some type of psychic ability.

5. People who live close to each other are more likely to date and fall in love. Thus, s_____ c_____ seems to have a strong effect on the development of romantic relationships.

6. Sasha obtains a high mark on her exams only when she studies diligently. For Sasha, there is a c_____ between studying diligently and doing well on her exams.

7. If a dog receives a dog biscuit only when it begs, then receiving the dog biscuit is c_____ upon the behavior of begging.

Measurement of Behavior

Behavioral Definitions

When we study the effects of certain variables on a behavior, it is important that we properly define the behavior. Such behavioral definitions should be *objective* in the sense that they refer to some observable aspect of the individual's behavior. For example, yelling and striking are observable aspects of aggressive behavior, but feelings of anger are not. Therefore, defining aggression in terms of the physical characteristics of yelling and striking is more precise than defining it as feelings of anger.

Behavioral definitions should also be clearly defined, that is, *unambiguous.* For example, we might define yelling as a loud vocalization that continues for more than 5 seconds and can be heard outside a closed door. Striking might be defined as a rapid arm or leg movement that results in physical contact. From a scientific perspective, an unambiguous definition will ensure that our measurements of the behavior are relatively consistent over time and across settings. Thus, what counts as an aggressive incident today will also count as an aggressive incident tomorrow. Further, if we are investigating various treatments to reduce the number of aggressive incidents (e.g., by rewarding the child for acting nonaggressively), we can be more certain that any observed change in the aggressive behavior is the result of our treatment as opposed to an unconscious shift in our definition of aggression. Finally, an unambiguous behavioral definition will make it easier for other researchers to replicate our results.

Clear definitions of behavior are also beneficial outside the research setting, particularly in tasks such as child-rearing (the ultimate challenge in behavior management). A major problem faced by many children is that parents often shift their standards as to what constitutes appropriate behavior. For example, a parent might constantly tell a child that eating in the living room is wrong, but then allow eating in the living room when visitors arrive or when the family is watching a movie. A clearer definition of what behaviors are appropriate versus inappropriate would be far less confusing to the child and would reduce the probability of the child violating the rules. One highly effective parent we know of uses a "three-warning" rule for situations that require compliance. For example, if one of the children is asked to get ready to go swimming with her aunt, she must comply by the third warning or else suffer a negative consequence (e.g., she will not be allowed to go swimming that day). Because the rule is so well defined and allows the child a certain amount of time "to get mobilized," negative consequences rarely have to be imposed. And even when the child does not comply and does suffer the consequences, she rarely makes a fuss about it because she was well aware of the contingencies from the outset. (This does not mean that the children in this family are rigidly controlled. In fact, one's first impression upon entering the household is that it is quite chaotic, with children running everywhere, laughing and playing. Within clearly defined limits, the children are allowed a great deal of freedom, which they very much appreciate.)

Recording Methods

Depending on how we define a behavior, there are several ways in which we can go about measuring it. Let's look at a few of these methods.

Rate of Response   One of the most popular measures in behavioral research is *rate of response*, which is the frequency with which a response occurs in a certain period of time. Rate measurements are most appropriate when the response is of brief duration, with a well-defined start and finish (i.e., onset and offset). The number of cigarettes smoked per day, the number of words written in a 1-hour writing session, and the number of body stomps in a half-hour broadcast of professional wrestling are all rate measures of behavior.

Certain experimental procedures have been explicitly designed to facilitate measuring behavior in terms of rate. For example, operant conditioning experiments often involve rats pressing levers to earn food. The lever press is a very definable response because once the lever is pressed sufficiently for the microswitch to be activated, a response is electronically recorded. Number of lever presses per session thus provides a precise measure of the rat's food-directed behavior. Rate is also a very *sensitive* measure of behavior and is thus highly favored by some behaviorists (especially radical behaviorists). The rate at which a rat presses a lever for food will vary closely with the number of hours of food deprivation, the type of food being delivered (preferred or non-preferred), and the number of responses required for a food pellet to be obtained.

A *cumulative recorder* is a classic device that measures the total number of responses over time and provides a graphic depiction of the rate of behavior. This instrument consists of a roll of paper that unravels at a slow, constant pace and a movable pen that makes tracks across it (see Figure 2.1). If there are no responses for a period of time, the pen remains stationary while the paper unrolls beneath it. This results in a flat, horizontal line along the paper, with longer lines indicating longer periods of no responding. When a

FIGURE 2.1   Illustration of a cumulative recorder. This device consists of a roll of paper that unravels at a slow, constant pace. If no response is made, the pen remains stationary, resulting in a horizontal line. A high rate of response produces a steep line, and a low rate of response produces a shallow line. The short diagonal slashes indicate the points at which reinforcers were delivered, for example, food pellets delivered to a rat for making a certain number of lever presses. (*Source:* Malone, 1990.)

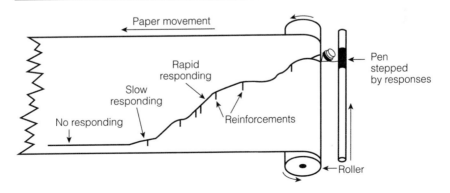

response occurs (e.g., the rat presses the lever), electronic equipment registers the response and produces a slight upward movement of the pen. Thus, a low rate of response produces a line that slopes upward at a shallow angle (because the pen is slowly moving upward while the paper passes beneath it), whereas a high rate of response produces a line that slopes upward at a steep angle. *The important thing to remember is that the steeper the line, the higher the rate of response.* A cumulative record thereby provides an easily read, graphic depiction of changes in the organism's rate of response over time. (Needless to say, these days, response rates are more often recorded by computer software programs. This allows for the generation of various types of descriptive records, including cumulative records, and facilitates various types of complex analyses of the data.)

Intensity   Responding can also be measured in terms of intensity. The *intensity* of a behavior is the force or magnitude of the behavior. For example, in Pavlov's classical conditioning procedure with dogs, a tone was associated with food, such that the tone itself eventually came to elicit salivation.

> **Tone: Food** → *Salivation*
> **Tone** → *Salivation*

The strength of conditioning was typically measured as the amount (magnitude) of saliva produced whenever the tone was sounded by itself. More saliva indicated stronger conditioning. Another intensity measure of behavior is the force with which a rat presses a lever to obtain food. Likewise, it is intensity that we are concerned with when we teach a child to speak softly and to print firmly.

Duration   *Duration* is the length of time that an individual repeatedly or continuously performs a certain behavior. This measure is appropriate when we are concerned with either increasing or decreasing the length of time the behavior occurs. For example, a student may attempt to increase the amount of time he spends studying each week, as well as decrease the amount of time spent watching television.

Speed   Although duration measures are sometimes useful, they are problematic in the sense that they do not indicate certain qualities of the behavior. You may run for an hour, but the speed at which you run (as indicated by the amount of distance you cover during that hour) will be a much more accurate indicator of your fitness level. Thus, *speed* is a measure of how quickly or slowly a behavior occurs, or the rapidity with which one progresses through some type of distance. The length of time it takes for a rat to run through a maze from the start box to the goal box is a measure of speed. (See Figure 2.2 for examples of the different types of mazes that have been used in psychological research.) We are also concerned with speed when we teach a child to eat more quickly (if he tends to dawdle at the dinner table) or more slowly (if he tends to fling food everywhere in a rush to get finished). Studies on

FIGURE 2.2   Three types of mazes used in behavioral research. Although the Hampton Court type of maze was often used by researchers in the early 1900s, it was later largely supplanted by the T-maze and the straight-alley "maze," which, because of their simplicity, proved more useful for investigating basic principles of behavior. (*Source:* Lieberman, 2000.)

(a) Hampton Court maze   (b) T-maze

(c) Straight-alley maze

activity levels in rats often measure both the duration of running (the amount of time the rats spend in a running wheel) as well as the speed of running (the amount of distance covered during that time). (Note, however, that we could also use a rate measure for wheel running, that is, the number of wheel turns per minute.)

Latency   The *latency* of a behavior is the length of time required for the behavior to begin. With respect to classical conditioning of salivation, the strength of conditioning can be measured not in terms of the amount of saliva, but in terms of how soon the dog begins salivating after it hears the tone. Likewise, the amount of time it takes for a student to sit down and begin studying following her evening meal might be a useful measure of the extent to which she finds studying aversive (unpleasant). TV game shows that require contestants to press buzzers when they believe they have the right answer are using a latency measure of the contestants' performance.

Latency, speed, and duration are often confused because they all involve some type of time measurement. To help distinguish between them, consider the behavior of an athlete who specializes in the 100-meter sprint. The amount of time it takes for her to commence running when she hears the starting pistol—which is only a fraction of a second—is a measure of latency, whereas the amount of time it takes for her to complete the race is a measure of speed. The amount of time she trains each day is a measure of duration.

Interval Recording   A particularly efficient way of measuring behavior, often utilized in applied settings, is *interval recording:* the measurement of whether or not a behavior occurs within a series of continuous intervals. For example, if we wish to measure the amount of aggressive behavior in a classroom, we might videotape several hours of class time. We would then have observers view the videotape and record whether or not an aggressive incident occurred within each successive 10-minute interval. The proportion of intervals in which at least one incident occurred would be our measure of aggression. For instance, imagine that we videotape 3 hours (180 minutes) of class time. We then have observers view the videotape and record whether at least one aggressive incident occurred within each successive 10-minute interval. *Note that we are not concerned with how many aggressive incidents occurred in each interval,* only with whether at least one aggressive incident occurred in each interval. The percentage of intervals during which at least one incident occurred is our measure of the behavior. For example, if at least one act of aggression occurred in 12 of the 18 intervals, then $12/18 \times 100 = 66.70\%$.

A major advantage of interval recording is that one does not have to record every single response, which may be difficult if responses occur at a very high rate (e.g., a fistfight that consists of a rapid series of aggressive actions). Interval recording is also useful if it is difficult to determine the point at which the behavior starts and stops. Aggressive incidents are a good example of this in that they sometimes build slowly, and trying to determine the exact moment when the aggression begins may be difficult.

Time-Sample Recording   A variant of interval recording is time-sample recording. In *time-sample recording,* one measures whether or not a behavior occurs within a series of discontinuous intervals (intervals that are spaced apart). For example, to assess the level of aggression in a classroom, we might have an observer unobtrusively enter the classroom for a 10-minute interval at the start of each half-hour and record whether at least one aggressive incident occurred during that interval. The behavior of the students is thus intermittently sampled, and the percentage of these sampled intervals in which an aggressive incident occurred is our measure of aggression. Imagine, for example, that over the course of 6 hours we are able to sample 12 ten-minute intervals. If one or more aggressive incidents occurred in 8 of those intervals, then the level of aggression is calculated as $8/12 \times 100 = 66.7\%$. Although we will not have observed every act of aggression using such a method, and we may even have missed a few whoppers, we will nevertheless have obtained a fairly good assessment of the amount of aggression in that setting. As well, this method of recording is very time efficient for our observer, who can spend most of the day working on other tasks or making observations in other classrooms. *(To reemphasize, remember that for both interval and time-sample recording, we do not measure the number of responses that occur, but rather the number of intervals in which at least one response occurs.)*

Topography Sometimes we are concerned with the behavior's *topography*, which is the physical form of the behavior. For example, rather than record the rate at which a rat presses a lever, we might observe *how* it presses the lever, such as whether it uses its left paw or right paw. Similarly, it is the topography of the behavior that we are concerned with when we teach a child how to dress appropriately, write neatly, and brush his teeth properly. Training a dolphin (or your pet goldfish) to swim through a hoop to obtain a food reward is yet another example in which the topography of the behavior is the focus of concern.

Number of Errors Any behavior in which responses can be categorized as right or wrong can be assessed in terms of the number of errors. For example, the number of wrong turns a rat takes before it finds its way through a maze to the goal box is one measure of how well the rat has learned the maze. Likewise, the number of errors a student makes on an exam is a standard method for determining how well the student knows the material.

1. Behavioral definitions should be o_____ and un_____.

2. The force with which a person can squeeze a device that measures grip strength is a measure of i_____.

3. How quickly a musician plays a musical piece from beginning to end is a measure of _____, whereas the number of hours the musician practices each week is a measure of _____. The amount of time it takes the musician to commence playing following the conductor's cue to begin is a measure of _____.

4. The exact manner in which a person lifts a weight is called the t_____ of the behavior.

5. The time it takes before a response begins is a measure of l_____.

6. The number of fish a person catches in a 1-hour period is a measure of r_____.

7. Recording whether Ashley hiccups during a continuous series of 5-minute time periods is an example of _____ recording, whereas measuring whether a hiccup occurs during a 5-minute period at the start of each hour throughout the day is an example of _____-_____ recording.

8. A device commonly used to measure the ongoing rate of a behavior is a c_____ r_____. On this device, a flat line indicates (no/slow/fast) _____ responding, a steep line indicates _____ responding, and a shallow line indicates _____ responding.

Research Designs

Deciding how to measure a behavior is only part of the problem. We must also determine which method to use to assess the impact of certain variables on that behavior. Several methods are available, and they can be divided into two general types: descriptive methods and experimental methods.

Descriptive Research

Descriptive research involves simply describing the behavior and the situation within which it occurs. Descriptive methods do not involve the manipulation of any variables. Two commonly used descriptive methods are naturalistic observation and case studies.

Naturalistic Observation   *Naturalistic observation* involves the systematic observation and recording of behavior in its natural environment. Note the word *systematic*. We are not talking here about casual observations, which may be strongly biased by the researcher's preconceptions about behavior. Behavioral scientists have as many preconceptions about behavior as the average person does—perhaps even more, because it is their job to study behavior—and are therefore quite susceptible to viewing behavior from a biased perspective. To avoid such biases, researchers attempt to define their variables objectively and unambiguously and make their observations in a consistent and uniform manner.

Jane Goodall's systematic study of chimpanzee behavior in the wild is a classic example of naturalistic observation. Through her detailed observations, we now know that chimpanzees eat meat (they sometimes kill and devour monkeys), use primitive tools (they sometimes dip a twig into a termite hill to capture termites for food), and engage in warfare (chimpanzees from one group have been observed stalking, attacking, and killing members of a neighboring group; see Goodall, 1990).

Naturalistic observation is a commonly used approach in ethology, a branch of zoology that focuses on the study of inherited behavior patterns in animals. Such patterns have presumably evolved to help the animal cope with certain aspects of its natural environment. For this reason, inherited behavior patterns are usually best studied within the natural environment (or at least a close approximation to it), because the behavior may not occur when the animal is removed from that environment. Displays of dominance and submission, for example, may not be evident unless an animal is allowed to freely interact with members of its own species. If such displays do occur in other situations, they may be difficult to identify. For example, a dog's gesture of rolling over on its back and displaying its underbelly can be more clearly seen as a submissive gesture when dogs interact with each other than when they interact with us. One of the authors first realized this when he witnessed the family dog being attacked by a much larger dog. Following a brief skirmish, Trixie rolled over on her back and displayed her stomach, the same behavior she often displayed toward her owners. What had always seemed like a simple request for a tummy scratch also functioned as an inborn gesture of subordination.

Although naturalistic observation is ideal for studying inherited behavior patterns, it also contributes to our understanding of learning. A famous example of this is the "cultural adoption" of food-washing behavior among a troop of macaque monkeys off the coast of Japan. When one monkey acquired the habit of washing sand off a sweet potato by dipping it in lake water (the researchers had left the potatoes on a sandy beach to attract the monkeys to that area), other monkeys in the troop soon imitated this behavior. Interestingly, the oldest monkeys in the troop never adopted this "newfangled way" of cleaning food (Kawamura, 1963).

The naturalistic approach is excellent for gaining rich, detailed information about a behavior and the circumstances in which it typically occurs. A major problem with this approach is that it often leaves us uncertain as to which variables are most important in determining the behavior. For example, if you study childhood aggression by observing children interacting on a playground, you may see many displays of aggressive behavior (e.g., grabbing a toy away from another child, pushing, yelling, etc.). However, it will be difficult to determine *why* these behaviors are occurring. As a naturalistic observer, you cannot intervene or ask the participants any questions for clarification. It will also be difficult to know if an aggressive child has a long history of aggression, is experiencing considerable frustration that day, or has had frequent exposure to violence in the home. In a sense, the natural environment is a vast sea of variables, and sorting out which variables are responsible for which behavior can be a daunting task. Thus, the naturalistic observation approach is often insufficient for gaining a full understanding of a behavior and the variables that influence it.

Case Studies   Another type of descriptive method is the *case study approach*, which involves the intensive examination of one or a few individuals. Case studies can be done in natural settings (as a form of naturalistic observation), or they may involve detailed examination in a more structured setting such as a clinician's office. Case studies are especially prevalent in medical research. Individuals who have suffered certain types of neurological damage often provide us with insight into which areas of the brain control which functions. Similarly, examining the lives of highly gifted individuals, such as Albert Einstein and Judit Polgar (the famous young chess player described in Chapter 1), can sometimes yield important information as to how exceptional skills can be acquired.

The case study approach is frequently employed in some areas of clinical psychology, especially with respect to relatively rare disorders—for example, *fugue states*, in which a person suddenly moves away from home and assumes a different identity—the few case studies available constitute our only source of information. Some clinical case studies have become quite famous. Consider, for example, the case of Anna O., which was reported by Sigmund Freud and his colleague Joseph Breuer (1895/1955). Anna O. is the pseudonym given to a young woman Breuer treated for symptoms of hysteria—a common psychiatric disorder in the latter part of the 19th century. A major characteristic of the disorder was various neurological symptoms, such as limb paralysis, that seemed to have no actual neurological basis, though psychological symptoms, such as "dual" personality and hallucinations, were also common. Breuer and Freud reported that most of Anna O.'s symptoms disappeared when she was encouraged to talk about upsetting events that had occurred to her and that seemed to be related to the onset of her symptoms. This case is generally regarded as the first clear demonstration of the therapeutic effectiveness of *catharsis* (that is, the release of tension that is assumed to automatically result from expressing pent-up thoughts and emotions).

As with naturalistic observations, it is important to ensure that case studies are based on systematic observation and that researcher bias has been reduced to a minimum. Unfortunately, these criteria are sometimes lacking. For example, scholars have recently discovered that the case of Anna O. actually had a far different outcome than that reported by Breuer and Freud. Following her "successful" treatment, Anna O. quickly relapsed and needed to be institutionalized. It was in fact several years before she finally recovered from her hysterical illness, a fact that Breuer and Freud were aware of but never publicly acknowledged. Nevertheless, Breuer and Freud's false report of Anna O.'s recovery helped establish psychoanalysis as the dominant school of psychotherapy in the first half of the 20th century.[1] (For these and other examples of how Freud may have misled people with his reported case studies—which has evolved into quite a controversy—see Esterson, 1993, and Webster, 1995.)

In addition to the problem of researcher bias, case studies are limited in the extent to which the results can be generalized to other people, places, and times. For example, Anna O.'s case history, even if it had been accurate, may not have been at all representative of how most cases of hysteria at that time could best be treated. Because case studies often involve only one person, we have no way of knowing if the case being described is the norm or the exception. The major problem, however, is that, like other descriptive approaches, it is usually difficult to determine which variables are responsible for which behavior. Nevertheless, despite these limitations, the case study method of research, as with the naturalistic observation method, often provides a valuable starting point for further investigations.

---

[1]By contrast, behavioral methods of therapy are usually subjected to rigorous experimentation before being widely adopted by practitioners (although informative case studies are also published). Thus, it is not surprising that in a recent list of "empirically validated therapies"—that is, therapies for which there is good research evidence demonstrating their effectiveness—a large majority of the therapies listed were either behavioral or cognitive-behavioral in orientation (Task Force on Promotion and Dissemination of Psychological Procedures, 1995; see also Wilson, 1997).

1. Two common descriptive methods are n_____ _____ and c_____ _____.

2. Both approaches are susceptible to the problem of researcher b_____ in which the opinions and beliefs of the researcher can unduly influence his or her observations.

3. The major problem with both approaches is that it is often (easy/difficult) _____ to specify which variables influence which behavior.

4. Because the case study approach often involves only one person, the results may be limited in the extent to which they can be g_____ to other people, places, and times.

Experimental Research

Although descriptive research methods such as naturalistic observations and case studies often provide detailed information about behavior, they usually do not allow us to draw firm conclusions about the causes of a behavior. If, for example, we observe that children who read a lot tend to have higher marks in school, is it the case that reading leads to higher marks, or do "bright" children simply like to read? To answer this question, it is necessary to conduct an experiment. In general, in their quest to discover cause-and-effect relationships (that is, functional relationships) between environmental events and behavior, behavioral researchers have a strong preference for the experimental approach to research.

In an experiment, one or more independent variables are systematically varied to determine their effect on a dependent variable (the behavior you suspect will change as a result of changes in the independent variable). Any differences in behavior across the different conditions of the experiment are presumed to be caused by the differences in the independent variable.

Behavioral researchers use two main types of experimental designs: control group designs and single-subject designs. As will be seen, each type of design has its advantages and disadvantages, and the decision to employ one method or the other largely has to do with the nature of the particular issue being investigated.

Control Group Designs   The most common type of experimental design is the *control group design.* In the simplest form of this design, individuals are randomly assigned to either an experimental (or treatment) group or a control group; individuals assigned to the experimental group are exposed to a certain manipulation or treatment, whereas those assigned to the control group are not. Imagine, for example, that 20 rats are randomly assigned to either an experimental group or a control group. Rats in the experimental group are individually placed in an experimental chamber for 30 minutes, during which time they receive a free food pellet every minute. The rats in the control group are treated exactly the same except they receive no food during the 30-minute session. They are simply allowed to snoop around the chamber. The rats in each group receive one session per day for 10 consecutive days. On day 11, a mechanical lever is placed in each chamber, and the rats must learn to press the lever to obtain food. The question of interest is whether the rats that previously received free food will learn to press the lever more readily or less readily than the rats that did not receive free food. Thus, the *independent variable* in this experiment is the presence versus absence of free food during the initial phase of the experiment, and the *dependent variable* is the average amount of time it takes for the rats in each group to learn to press the lever for food. (By the way, research has shown that animals that receive free food subsequently have more difficulty learning how to respond for food [Welker, 1976; Wheatley, Welker, & Miles, 1977]. This suggests that exposure to free reinforcers can sometimes impair an organism's ability to learn how to respond for reinforcers.)

Control group designs are often considerably more complicated than the simple experiment we have described. For example, we might wonder if the damaging effects of free food on ability to learn are dependent on age. Thus, we might rerun this experiment with groups of old rats, middle-aged rats, and young rats. This approach would yield what is known as a *2 × 3 factorial design*, in which there are two independent variables (food and age), the first of which has two levels (free food versus no food) and the second of which has three levels (old age versus middle age versus young age). This experiment would include a total of six groups (old with free food, old with no food, middle-aged with free food, middle-aged with no food, young with free food, and young with no food; see Table 2.1). If free food affects learning ability only in rats of a certain age, then we say that there is an *interaction* between the effects of free food and age. Such interaction effects give us a much finer understanding of the variables in which we are interested, and a lot of research is designed to search for such effects.

A particular type of control group design, often used in certain types of animal research, is a comparative design. A **comparative design** is a type of control group design in which different species constitute one of the independent variables. It is often used to test an evolutionary hypothesis regarding the differences in selective pressures for a particular learning trait between species. Comparative designs can be simple or factorial, and they can involve more than one independent or dependent variable. The main distinction (other than the use of more than one species) between comparative designs and standard control group designs is that in a comparative design you do not have a pure control group that receives no treatment.

For example, if you hypothesize that rats have evolved to deal with small, enclosed environments better than dogs have (or that dogs have evolved to deal with larger, more open environments better than rats have), you could

TABLE 2.1 Six experimental conditions (groups of participants) in a 2 × 3 factorial experiment involving two levels of a "food" variable and three levels of an "age" variable.

	YOUNG (Y)	MIDDLE–AGED (M)	OLD (O)
No food (NF)	NFY	NFM	NFO
Free food (FF)	FFY	FFM	FFO

examine how quickly dogs and rats learn to find a target in a complex maze versus a large open area. This is a 2 × 2 factorial design in which there are two independent variables (species and environment), where each independent variable has two levels (rat versus dog; maze versus open area). (Of course, you would not use exactly the same apparatus for a rat that you would for a dog. Rather, you would attempt to equate the equipment for the particular size and other important traits of each species.) You will note, however, that in no condition does a group receive no treatment. Instead, the control comes in the form of providing each group with the same treatments so that the dependent variable (speed of learning) can be isolated to the independent variables (species or type of environment, or an interaction between the two).

Control group designs are excellent for assessing the general effects of certain variables. Cause-and-effect statements are possible due to the strict control over the environment that allows the experimenter to rule out alternative explanations. Because all subjects receive identical experiences except for the independent variable that is being manipulated, we can be fairly confident that differences between groups in performance are the result of differences in the independent variable. Random assignment of subjects to each condition also ensures that various characteristics of the subjects in each group are likely to be evenly distributed across the experimental and control conditions. Thus, the two groups will be pretty much alike at the onset of the experiment, and any differences found at the end of the experiment can therefore be attributed to our manipulation of the independent variable.

Control group designs, however, are not without their drawbacks. To begin with, this type of design usually requires a large number of subjects (often 10 or more per group). In fact, for statistical reasons, the larger the number of subjects in a group, the more trustworthy the results. But what if you wished to conduct research on the effectiveness of a behavioral treatment for one individual? It would be impractical to conduct an experiment with a large number of subjects just to determine if a certain treatment might be effective for one person. Control group designs are therefore not well suited for investigating the effect of a certain treatment on a particular individual.

A second difficulty with control group designs is that they typically focus on the *average* performance of all subjects in each group. Little attention is given to the performance of individual subjects, even if some subjects differ markedly from the average. For example, going back to our rat study, suppose that 2 out of the 10 rats previously given free food learned to press the lever almost immediately, while the others took much longer. Even if, on average, the rats in this free-food group learned more slowly than the rats in the no-food group, what about the two quick learners? Should we regard them as mere aberrations ("I guess some rats are just brighter than others"), or is it the case that exposure to free food actually facilitates subsequent learning in some individuals? By ignoring individual data, we might never ask such questions. In other words, group data is combined to produce a statistical average, but most individuals within the group deviate from this average; therefore, the averages that are produced may have little relevance to those individuals.

(Question: What implication does this have for the value of the advice given during the radio call-in show in the opening vignette?)

A third limitation of control group designs is that the results are often analyzed and interpreted only at the end of the experiment rather than during the experiment. In some situations, this may be undesirable. If, for example, we are treating a child for self-injurious behavior, we need to be aware throughout whether our treatment is having a positive effect. If the effect is positive, we can maintain the treatment; if the effect is negative, we should immediately halt our treatment and try something different. By contrast, control group designs that measure effects only at the end of the study usually do not provide us with this type of flexibility.

Finally, a weakness *specific* to the comparative type of control group design is that species can differ in more ways than just their learning capacity or style. This limits the type of study that can be conducted, or the species that can be compared. For example, if we were comparing cats and hedgehogs for escape learning, we might find that cats learn to escape relatively quickly when they see a cue related to the onset of shock, whereas hedgehogs tend not to run away from this potentially dangerous situation. Is this because hedgehogs cannot learn? No. It is more likely that hedgehogs employ a different defensive behavior when threatened (rolling into a ball and freezing) than do cats, so the choice of dependent variable (running to escape) in this situation is inappropriate for the species in question.

In conclusion, control group designs are excellent for assessing general relationships between independent and dependent variables. There are drawbacks, however; these designs are inefficient when we are interested in relating the findings to a particular individual, when the focus on average effects results in the neglect of unusual effects displayed by certain individuals, and when there is a need to monitor the individual's progress throughout the study. Alternative designs that do not suffer from these limitations—but have their own limitations—are called single-subject designs.

QUICK QUIZ F

1. In an experiment, a(n) _____ variable is systematically varied (manipulated) to determine its effects on the _____ variable.

2. In the simplest form of a control group design, individuals are r_____ assigned to either an e_____ (or tr_____) group and a _____ group.

3. Control group designs in which behaviors or response to treatments are compared between species are referred to as _____ designs.

4. Briefly stated, three problems with control group designs are

   a._____
   _____

   b._____
   _____

   c._____
   _____

Single-Subject Designs   Unlike control group designs, *single-subject designs* require only one or a few subjects to conduct an entire experiment. There are several types of single-subject designs, four of which are described here.

Simple-Comparison (AB) Design. In a **simple-comparison design,** behavior in a baseline condition is compared to behavior in a treatment condition. Suppose, for example, that Cory wishes to cut down on smoking (as a first step toward quitting) and wonders if he might be able to do so by punishing himself. In a *self-punishment* procedure, people apply an aversive consequence to themselves each time they engage in an unwanted target behavior. Self-punishment of smoking might consist of Cory giving his buddy 25 cents for each cigarette he smokes. (Another way of looking at this is that Cory has implemented a fine or tax on himself to try to reduce the amount he smokes.)

The first step in the program would be for Cory to take a baseline measure of the number of cigarettes he typically smokes each day. The **baseline** is the normal frequency of the behavior that occurs before some intervention. Cory could, for example, keep an index card tucked inside the flap of his cigarette pack and make a check mark on it for each cigarette he smokes.

The baseline period should last several days to provide a good assessment of the typical frequency of Cory's smoking. If it appears that there is a gradual upward or downward trend in the amount smoked during baseline (sometimes the mere act of closely monitoring a behavior can result in some improvement, via a process known as *reactivity*), Cory should continue the baseline period until the behavior stabilizes. Following the baseline, he should then institute the self-punishment procedure for several days. If the treatment is effective, the frequency of smoking during the treatment period should be consistently lower than it was during the baseline period (see Figure 2.3).

FIGURE 2.3   Simple-comparison (AB) design. Hypothetical results using a simple-comparison design to assess the effectiveness of a treatment (self-punishment) on number of cigarettes smoked. The dashed vertical line divides the baseline condition from the treatment condition. Results are consistent with, but do not provide strong evidence for, the notion that the treatment was effective.

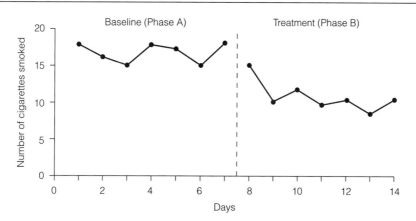

In this type of study, the baseline period is often called the A phase, and the treatment period is called the B phase. Thus, this design is sometimes referred to as an AB design. (Students sometimes think the baseline phase is the B phase because the word *baseline* starts with a *B*. Do not think this way. The *baseline phase is the A phase* because that is the phase we start with, and the treatment phase is the B phase because it follows the A phase. The letters *A* and *B* simply indicate the order in which the conditions occur.)

A major problem with the simple-comparison design is that it does not control for the possibility that some other event occurred at the same time that the treatment was implemented, and it was this other event that caused the change in the behavior. For example, perhaps Cory caught a cold at the same time that he began self-punishment, and it is actually the cold that accounts for the reduction in smoking. The simple-comparison design does not allow us to assess this possibility and thus constitutes a poor experimental design. In other words, it does not clearly demonstrate a functional relationship between the independent variable (self-punishment) and the dependent variable (smoking). At best, it provides only suggestive evidence that the treatment is effective. If you have limited resources and time for investigating a treatment effect, however, and you are simply interested in seeing whether there is some type of improvement, then a simple-comparison design may be sufficient.

Reversal Design. A much better design is the reversal design, which is sometimes also called an ABA or ABAB design (depending on the number of reversals carried out). The **reversal design** is a type of single-subject design that involves repeated alternations between a baseline period and a treatment period. If the behavior systematically changes each time the treatment is instituted and later withdrawn, then a functional relationship has been demonstrated between the treatment and the behavior. In Cory's case, he would begin with the baseline phase, then institute a self-punishment phase, then revert to baseline, and then revert to self-punishment. If the results are something like those depicted in Figure 2.4, with smoking decreasing each time the treatment is implemented and increasing each time the treatment is withdrawn, then we have obtained fairly strong evidence that the treatment is the cause of the improvement. It is extremely unlikely that some other event, such as illness, coincided precisely with each application of the treatment to produce such systematic changes in behavior.

The reversal design has many strengths; and unlike the control group design, it allows an entire experiment to be conducted with a single subject. As such, the reversal design is often ideal for determining the effectiveness of a behavioral intervention for one person. As well, some behaviorists argue that statistical tests are not needed to determine if the changes in behavior are significant (Sidman, 1960). One can often "eyeball" the graph to see if the treatment is working. The underlying logic is that if the results are not clear enough to be judged significant by visual inspection alone, then the treatment should be altered to produce a stronger effect. This forces the investigator to

FIGURE 2.4 Reversal (ABAB) design. Hypothetical results using a reversal design to assess the effectiveness of a treatment (self-punishment) on number of cigarettes smoked. The systematic change in smoking across the alternating conditions provides strong *evidence* that the treatment is the cause of the improvement.

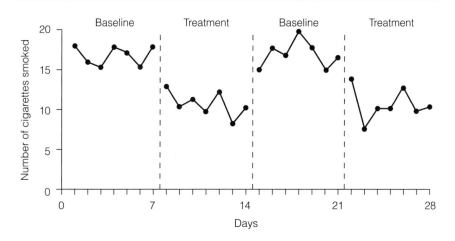

attain precise control over the variables influencing the target behavior and to strive for powerful treatments that produce large effects.

You might be wondering whether results from a reversal design can be generalized to other subjects since we have demonstrated the effect with only one subject. This is an important question because in science we are concerned with finding effects that have generality. With single-subject designs, this problem is typically solved by running the study with more than one subject. Since each subject in the study constitutes an entire experiment, each additional subject constitutes a replication of that experiment. If we find the same pattern of results for all of the subjects submitted to these procedures, the findings are likely to have good generality. For example, if we tried the self-punishment treatment with three additional individuals and they too showed consistent decreases in smoking, then it is quite likely that this treatment will be effective for many individuals (although the nature of the punishing consequence might have to be tailored to each individual; what is punishing for one person might not be punishing for another). In general, results that have been obtained with only four or so individuals often have good generality.

It is also possible to use a reversal design to assess the effectiveness of more than one treatment. For example, imagine that Cory's initial treatment turns out to be relatively ineffective and results in little if any improvement. Rather than withdrawing the treatment and returning to baseline, a better strategy would be to implement a new treatment and see if it produces a stronger effect. In Cory's case, he might decide that the 25-cent fine for each cigarette smoked is insufficiently punishing and that he should instead fine himself a dollar. The implementation of this larger punisher constitutes a new phase of treatment, phase C. If after a week that treatment appears to be successful, Cory can revert

FIGURE 2.5 Two-treatment reversal design. Hypothetical results in which a reversal design was used to assess the effectiveness of two treatment procedures on the number of cigarettes smoked. When the first treatment (B) produced little improvement, a second treatment (C) was immediately implemented. This treatment was then alternated with a baseline period to confirm its effectiveness. This would therefore be called an ABCAC design.

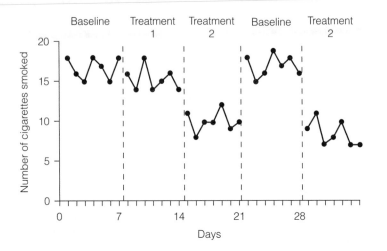

to the baseline for a week and then return to the treatment to confirm its effectiveness. This would then be called an ABCAC design (see Figure 2.5).

Reversal designs have some advantages, but they also have some disadvantages. The main disadvantage is that the behavior must revert to its original baseline frequency when the treatment is withdrawn; otherwise, it will be impossible to determine if the treatment has had an effect. If, for example, the results for Cory's study looked something like those depicted in Figure 2.6, in which smoking does not return to its pretreatment level during the reversal to baseline, we would be in no better situation than if we had run a simple-comparison design. Although the rate of smoking dropped when Cory first instituted the self-punishment procedure, it did not climb back up when the procedure was halted; therefore, we cannot be sure that self-punishment was the actual cause of the initial decrease. Although we may be pleased that Cory is now smoking less than he used to, from a scientific perspective of demonstrating the effectiveness of self-punishment, these results are less than ideal.

We must also bear in mind that some treatments are intended to produce long-lasting effects. For example, a student who is exposed to a new method of teaching math will hopefully experience a permanent increase in his or her math ability. A reversal design would not be appropriate for assessing the effect of such an intervention, because the improvement should remain evident long after the intervention has ended.

A final difficulty with a reversal design is that it may be ethically inappropriate to remove a treatment once some improvement has been obtained. If,

FIGURE 2.6   Reversal (ABAB) design. Hypothetical results in which a reversal design was used to assess the effectiveness of a self-punishment treatment on smoking. In this case, the behavior did not revert to its baseline level when the treatment was withdrawn. Thus, although it is possible that the treatment was the cause of the improvement, these results do not provide strong evidence in this regard.

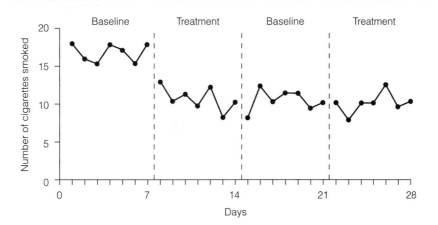

for example, the implementation of a treatment results in the elimination of a person's severe drug addiction, is it reasonable for us to temporarily withdraw the treatment in the hope that the addictive behavior will reappear? Although from a scientific perspective withdrawing the treatment would help confirm its effectiveness, such withdrawal would not be ethical. We must instead look for another method of demonstrating a functional relationship between the implementation of the treatment and the improvement in behavior. One alternative is to use a multiple-baseline design.

1. In a simple-comparison design, behavior in a b_____ condition is compared to behavior in a t_____ condition.

2. A simple-comparison design (does/does not) _____ allow us to determine if there is a f_____ relationship between the independent and dependent variables.

3. A reversal design (also called an _____ design) involves repeated alternations between a _____ period and a _____ period.

4. What type of result do we need to see during the second baseline phase to determine whether our treatment is the cause of the change in the behavior?_____
_____
_____.

5. A reversal design is inappropriate for an experiment in which the treatment produces a (temporary/permanent) _____ change in the behavior.

6. A reversal design is also inappropriate when the act of withdrawing the treatment during the second A phase would lead to e_____ problems.

Multiple-Baseline Design. In a **multiple-baseline design,** a treatment is instituted at successive points in time for two or more persons, settings, or behaviors. As an example of a *multiple-baseline-across-persons* design, imagine that we have three people who wish to try a self-punishment program for smoking. We begin by taking a baseline measurement of smoking for each person. At the end of the first week, we have one person begin the treatment, while the other two carry on with the baseline. At the end of the second week, we have a second person begin the treatment while the third person carries on with the baseline. Finally, at the end of the third week, the third person also begins the treatment. Thus, across the three individuals, the treatment is implemented at different points in time. If the improvement in smoking coincides with the implementation of the treatment for each individual, then a functional relationship between the treatment and the improvement in behavior has been demonstrated (see Figure 2.7).

As an example of a *multiple-baseline-across-settings* design, imagine that the three graphs in Figure 2.7 represent Cory's rate of smoking in three different settings: at work, at home, and at the coffee shop. After a week of baseline, Cory begins self-punishing his smoking, but only at work. After the second week, he begins self-punishing smoking at home while continuing to punish it at work. Finally, after the third week, he also starts punishing his smoking behavior at the coffee shop. If his rate of smoking in each setting drops only at the point when the self-punishment procedure is implemented, then the procedure is highly likely to be the cause of the improvement.

As an example of a *multiple-baseline-across-behaviors* design, imagine that the three graphs in Figure 2.7 represent three of Cory's problem behaviors— for example, smoking, swearing, and nail biting. In this case, we implement the treatment at different times for each behavior. If each behavior shows improvement only when the treatment is implemented, then we have again demonstrated a functional relationship between the treatment and behavior.

The multiple-baseline design is a good alternative to the reversal design in that we do not have to worry about withdrawing the treatment to determine that it is effective. This design is therefore appropriate for situations in which the treatment is likely to produce a permanent change in behavior, or in which it may be unethical to withdraw the treatment once some improvement has been achieved. Nevertheless, this design is limited because we need to have more than one person, setting, or behavior to which the treatment can be applied. It is also possible that the treatment effect might generalize across the different settings or behaviors occurring before the intervention being instituted within those settings or behaviors. For example, as Cory begins to exert more control over his smoking at work, this effect might generalize to his smoking patterns at home and at the coffee shop even before the treatment being applied in those settings. Under such circumstances, it would be difficult to determine whether the treatment was in fact the cause of the improvement.

FIGURE 2.7 Multiple-baseline design. Hypothetical results using a multiple-baseline-across-persons design to assess the effectiveness of a treatment (self-punishment) on number of cigarettes smoked. The three graphs represent the data for three different persons. For each person, the improvement in behavior coincides with the point at which the treatment was implemented. This result shows a functional relationship between the treatment and the improvement in behavior.

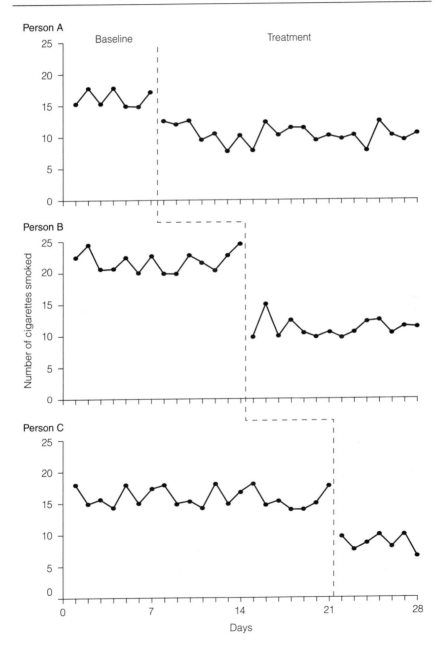

1. With a multiple-baseline design, the treatment is instituted at different points in t_____ for _____ or more p_____, s_____, or b_____.

2. A key advantage of the multiple-baseline design is that we do not have to w_____ the treatment to determine if it is effective.

3. It is therefore a preferable design for situations in which the treatment might result in a (temporary/permanent) _____ change in behavior, or where it might be un_____ to withdraw the treatment.

Changing-Criterion Design. In some circumstances, the treatment is not intended to produce a large, immediate change in behavior but rather a gradual change over time. A useful design for measuring such changes is a **changing-criterion design.** In this type of design, the effect of the treatment is demonstrated by how closely the behavior matches a criterion that is systematically altered.

Imagine, for example, that Cory decides to use self-punishment to gradually reduce his smoking behavior. Following a baseline period, he sets a certain criterion for an allowable number of cigarettes that is only slightly less than the average number of cigarettes he smoked during the baseline. If he successfully meets this criterion for 3 consecutive days, he reduces the allowable limit by two cigarettes. If he meets that criterion for 3 successive days, he reduces the limit by two more cigarettes. He repeats this process until the eventual goal of no smoking has been achieved. The self-punishment procedure consists of tearing up a dollar bill for every cigarette that is smoked over the allowable limit (see Axelrod, Hall, Weiss, & Rohrer, 1974, for a case report of such a procedure).

Hypothetical results for this program are displayed in Figure 2.8. Cory was generally successful in meeting each criterion, with the number of cigarettes smoked per day either matching or falling below the criterion for that day. The three exceptions occurred on days 29, 33, and 34. Because Cory exceeded the criterion on these days, he would have implemented the self-punishment contingency of tearing up a dollar bill.

As noted previously, the changing-criterion design is especially appropriate for situations in which the behavior is intended to change gradually in accord with some changing criterion for performance. Thus, it would be an appropriate design for gradually increasing the amount of time one studies each day or decreasing the amount of time spent playing computer games. It is important, however, that the behavior closely match the criteria; otherwise, it will be difficult to determine if the change in behavior is the result of the treatment or of some other, extraneous factor. The design can, however, be greatly strengthened by including periods in which the criterion suddenly changes in the opposite direction (for example, in the case of Cory, the number of cigarettes allowed would sometimes be raised). If the behavior continues to track the criterion closely even when it changes direction, then we will have obtained strong evidence for the effectiveness of the treatment. In a sense, we

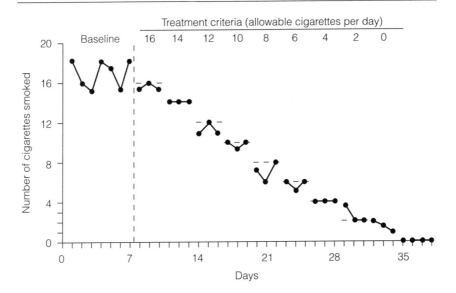

FIGURE 2.8 Changing-criterion design. Hypothetical data illustrating use of a changing-criterion design to assess the effectiveness of self-punishment to gradually reduce smoking. The dashed horizontal lines indicate the changing criterion for maximum allowable number of cigarettes smoked per day.

have created a changing-criterion design that incorporates certain aspects of a reversal design.

The reversal design and multiple-baseline design are the most basic single-subject designs, with the changing-criterion design less often utilized. Other types of single-subject designs have also been devised, each having its advantages and disadvantages (see Barlow & Hersen, 1984; Kazdin, 1994). Most of these have been developed for use in applied settings. In experimental research, the reversal design (or some variation of it) is often employed in studies of operant conditioning. By contrast, the control group design is frequently employed in studies of classical conditioning.

Taken together, the strength of any experimental design is that it enables us to make causal statements about the effects of independent variables on dependent variables. Control over the environment enables the researcher to isolate the effects of the independent variables while controlling for extraneous influences. Despite this advantage, experimental methods also have a major disadvantage. Because of the need to strictly control the environment, experimental settings are sometimes quite artificial, with the result that the findings may have limited applicability to the real world. However, the precise control over the environment that can be obtained with experimental research lends itself to replication, and with each replication across new subjects and new settings, we gain confidence that our findings do have generality.

ADVICE FOR THE LOVELORN

Dear Dr. Dee,

I am suspicious that my boyfriend is having an affair with his old girlfriend. Whenever she is in town, he phones me significantly less often. For example, between May and August, when I know for a fact that she was in town, he phoned me an average of 5.8 times per week, while between September and December, when she was out of town, he phoned an average of 6.4 times per week. I worked it out, and sure enough, this is a statistically significant difference! But when I confronted him with this hard evidence of his unfaithfulness, he denied it and said that I am being paranoid.

Am-I Being Paranoid?

Dear Am-I,

Given the evidence that you have presented, I would have to say yes, you are being paranoid. But worse than that, you are being a poor scientist. For example, you have neglected to consider other factors that might account for the observed difference. Quite apart from his old girlfriend being in town, your boyfriend may be calling less frequently between May and August for several other reasons, such as spending more time in outdoor activities, visiting with relatives, and so on. These other possibilities need to be assessed before you can draw any conclusions about your boyfriend's unfaithfulness.

You also need to recognize that statistically significant differences do not provide hard evidence of anything. What they provide is *supportive* evidence for a certain *possibility*. Thus, even with a highly significant difference between two sets of scores, there is still a slight possibility that the difference is actually due to chance variation. As well, you need to consider that a difference that is *statistically* significant may not be *meaningfully* significant. The difference you have described seems quite small. I bet that if you chart the number of phone calls week by week, as in a simple-comparison design, you will have a hard time spotting much of a difference between the May–August period and the September–December period. And in this particular case, if you cannot see much of a difference by eyeballing the data, then maybe there really isn't much of a difference.

Behaviorally yours,

Dr. Dee

1. In a changing-criterion design, the question of interest is whether the changes in behavior match changes in a c_____ for the behavior that is being systematically al_____.

2. A changing-criterion design is most appropriate for assessing the effect of programs designed to produce a (sudden/gradual) _____ change in behavior.

3. In using this type of design, it is important that the level of behavior closely _____ the changes in the criterion for that behavior.

4. The changing-criterion design can be strengthened by including periods in which the criterion suddenly _____ _____.

Use of Animals in Behavioral Research

Animal research has greatly contributed to our understanding and treatment of serious diseases and illnesses, as well as to our understanding of basic physiological processes. Similarly, many of the basic principles of behavior have been discovered through research with animals, especially rats and pigeons. But if the ultimate goal of such research is to discover principles of behavior that are applicable to humans, why use animals at all? In this section we outline some of the arguments for and against animal research that will help inform your opinion in this highly controversial debate.

Two advantages of using animals in research are the ability to control their genetic makeup and their learning history. Knowledge of an animal's genetic makeup helps us eliminate, or assess, the effects of inherited differences on learning and behavior. Rats, for example, can be bred so that an entire batch of research subjects has virtually identical genes. It is possible to control for genetic differences in humans by studying identical twins, but the number of people we can obtain for such research is necessarily quite limited. Similarly, animals bred for research have had somewhat identical experiences during their upbringing, along with a fairly limited learning history. It is impossible to control for the learning histories of humans who volunteer for psychological research. If we are conducting experiments designed to assess basic principles of learning, then the learning histories of one's subjects could critically influence the outcome of the experiment.

A third advantage to using animals as subjects is that researchers are often able to more strictly control the experimental environment for animals than for humans. This ability is especially important in behavioral research, in which we are attempting to isolate and manipulate certain aspects of the environment to determine their effect on behavior. For example, if we are interested in the effect of food deprivation on activity level in rats (as discussed in Chapter 11), then it is highly advantageous to strictly control the rat's feeding schedule— to a degree that would be impossible in humans. Human subjects participating in ongoing research also have an unfortunate tendency to discuss the research task with their friends when they go home each day, even when they are asked not to do so. These conversations can easily lead to a significant change in the person's behavior during the next experimental session. By contrast, rats and mice tend not to give each other suggestions while lounging about in their home cages following a hard day of lever pressing. Their behavior therefore tends to be more consistent from day to day. In general, because animals are more easily insulated from extraneous influences during the course of the experiment, their behavior is more likely to reflect the true influence of the independent variable.

A fourth reason for using animals in behavioral research is that some research cannot ethically be conducted with humans. This is particularly the case with experimental manipulations that are potentially aversive or harmful. For example, rats have been used to investigate the manner in which classical conditioning might account for unusual instances of drug overdose (this finding is discussed in Chapter 5). Investigations using such an animal model of drug addiction have the potential to save lives but would be impossible to conduct with human subjects. (An *animal model* is a procedure that uses animals to mimic a particular human characteristic or symptom, such as drug addiction or obesity, so it can then be more systematically investigated than would be possible with humans.)

In reaction to these claimed benefits of animal research, critics have offered several counterarguments. One criticism is that because animals are not humans, the findings from animal research necessarily have limited applicability to humans. The physiological processes, genetic tendencies, and learning histories of animals are simply too different for research with animals to be of much relevance to humans. In this text we hope to convince you of the opposite, but the argument should not be dismissed out of hand. Despite the demonstrated benefits of animal research, some research with animals almost certainly does have little applicability to humans. Unfortunately, determining ahead of time which research findings are likely to be applicable to humans is a difficult task. Some of the most applicable findings from animal research, such as basic research on schedules of reinforcement (discussed in Chapter 7), initially would have struck some people as trivial and unimportant. (In fact, some people opposed to behaviorism still regard these findings as trivial and unimportant.)

Perhaps the most fundamental criticism of animal research is that it is morally wrong and that animals have rights similar to humans. Animal rights activists oppose "inhumane" research practices, such as confining animals to cages, subjecting them to electric shock, depriving them of food, and so on. From this perspective, even the reported benefits of animal research for saving lives and improving the human condition are insufficient to justify submitting animals to such morally reprehensible practices.

Beginning in the 1800s, researchers have reacted to such criticism by developing guidelines that weigh the benefits of research against the injurious or aversive nature of the procedures. The first guidelines were formulated in 1876, with the introduction of the British Cruelty to Animals Act. It was in the 1960s, however, that animal care committees and review

And Furthermore

Cruel Starvation or a Healthy Diet: The Ethics of Food Restriction

In many of the animal studies described in this text, food is used as a reward (reinforcer) for performing certain behaviors. As such, the animals are typically food deprived to ensure that they are well motivated to work for food. Pigeons, for example, are typically placed on a diet until their weight is about 80 to 85% of their *free-feeding weight* (which is the amount they weigh when food is constantly available). Some people regard such food restriction procedures as inhumane. But is this really the case?

First, we have to remember that the 80 to 85% level is calculated based on the pigeon's free-feeding weight. Free food is an unnatural state of affairs for a pigeon, which in its natural environment must constantly forage for food. The result is that the weight of a pigeon on free food is well beyond its natural weight. Poling, Nickel, and Alling (1990), for example, found that wild pigeons placed on free food for 42 days experienced an average weight increase of 17%, with some pigeons gaining as much as 30%. (This latter figure is equivalent to a 160-pound individual who, with little to do but eat, balloons up to 208 pounds!) Thus, the weight of a pigeon at 80% of its free-feeding weight may be quite close to what it would be if it were foraging for food in its natural environment.

A second point to bear in mind is that a certain amount of food restriction can be quite healthy. In fact, calorie restriction is the most reliable means known for slowing the aging process. Almost all species tested, ranging from spiders to monkeys, have shown significant increases in both health status and life span when raised on diets that provide 30 to 50% fewer calories than normal (e.g., Weindruch, 1996; Koubova, 2003). (Of course, the animals growing up on these diets are also significantly smaller than normal.) This effect has yet to be confirmed in humans, and sometimes the diet produces negative results when it is suddenly imposed later in life. Nevertheless, enough evidence exists to suggest that a moderate level of calorie restriction—given that one eats adequate amounts of highly nutritious foods—might be a healthy regimen for both people and pigeons.

boards became strongly established. Today, researchers in most professional organizations, including the American Psychological Association, are regulated by ethical standards that provide strict guidelines for the care and use of animals.

It is also worth noting that animal researchers are themselves concerned about the welfare of their animals. Skinner, for example, disliked shocking rats and therefore conducted few studies of punishment (Bjork, 1993). Many researchers also acknowledge that the animal rights movement has served a valuable purpose by ensuring the development of strict standards of ethical conduct. They likewise recognize that the extent to which animal research is justified is a difficult question that individuals must answer for themselves. The important thing, however, is to make it an informed decision. (For a discussion of these issues, see Mukerjee, 1997.)

1. Two advantages to using animals for behavioral research is that one can more strictly control an animal's g_____ makeup and l_____ history.

2. A third advantage to using animals is that the e_____ environment can more easily be controlled for animals than for humans.

3. A fourth advantage to using animals for research is that it would be u_____ to conduct certain types of studies with humans, such as examining the effects of brain lesions on learning ability.

4. Two arguments against the use of animals in research are

a. _____

b. _____

SUMMARY

Behavioral research involves the manipulation and measurement of variables. The independent variable is that aspect of an experiment that is systematically varied across conditions in an experiment and is believed to affect the dependent variable, which is the behavior being measured. Appetitive stimuli are events that are sought out by an organism, whereas aversive stimuli are events that are avoided. Establishing operations are conditions that affect the appetitiveness or aversiveness of an event. Deprivation is one such condition, which tends to increase the appetitiveness of an event, whereas satiation tends to decrease the appetitiveness of an event. A contingency exists if there is a conditional relationship between two events such that the occurrence of one event predicts the likely occurrence of another. This is often the case in experimental research where changes in an independent variable produce changes in a dependent variable.

Behavioral researchers strive to employ objective, unambiguous definitions of behavior. Depending on the research question, there are several ways to measure behavior. Rate of response indicates the frequency with which a response occurs in a certain period of time, and intensity is the force or magnitude of a behavior. Duration is the length of time an ongoing behavior is performed, speed is the time required to perform a complete episode of behavior, and latency is the amount of time it takes for the behavior to commence. Interval recording measures whether a behavior occurs within each of a series of continuous intervals, and time-sample recording measures whether a behavior occurs within a series of discontinuous intervals. Other behavioral measures include topography (the physical form of a behavior) and number of errors.

In addition to selecting a measure of behavior, researchers need to determine the most appropriate method for conducting research. Research methods can be classified as descriptive or experimental. Two descriptive methods are naturalistic observation and the case study approach. Descriptive methods provide rich, detailed information but do not demonstrate causal relationships.

Experimental methods do demonstrate causal relationships and generally take the form of control group or single-subject designs. Control group designs generally involve the random assignment of participants to experimental and nonexperimental (control) conditions. However, control group designs have certain drawbacks, such as requiring large numbers of participants. In contrast, single-subject designs can be used to demonstrate cause-and-effect relationships using only one or a few individuals. Types of single-subject designs include the simple-comparison design, reversal design, multiple-baseline design, and changing-criterion design, each of which has its strengths and weaknesses.

Advantages of using animals as subjects in behavioral research include enhanced control over learning history, genetic background, and experimental environment relative to human participants. Also, animals can be used in studies that cannot ethically be conducted on humans. Disadvantages of using animals are the possibility that findings may have limited application to humans and the notion that animals have the same rights as humans. Ethics committees have been established to weigh the costs and benefits of proposed research involving animals.

SUGGESTED READINGS

Skinner, B. F. (1956). A case history in scientific method. *American Psychologist,* *11*, 221–233. Skinner's interesting and sometimes irreverent view of what the "scientific method" *really* involves, at least from the perspective of his own experience.

Sidman, M. (1960). *Tactics of scientific research: Evaluating experimental data in psychology.* New York: Basic Books. The classic text on single-subject research designs. Although this book is a bit beyond most undergraduates, a quick perusal will give you a sense for the radical behaviorist approach to research.

Kazdin, A. E. (1994). *Behavior modification in applied settings* (5th ed.). Pacific Grove, CA: Brooks/Cole. Contains an extensive discussion of research methods in applied behavior analysis, including additional types of single-subject designs.

Martin, D. W. (2004). *Doing psychology experiments* (6th ed.). Belmont, CA: Wadsworth. A very readable introductory textbook on research methods in psychology.

STUDY QUESTIONS

1. Distinguish between independent and dependent variables. What is a functional relationship?
2. Define stimulus and response. Differentiate between the terms *stimulus* and *stimuli*.

3. Distinguish between overt and covert behavior. Distinguish between appetitive and aversive stimuli.
4. Define establishing operation. Name and describe two types of establishing operations.
5. Distinguish between contiguity and contingency. Name and define two types of contiguity.
6. Define rate of response. Why is rate of response a favored measure of behavior among radical behaviorists?
7. How does one distinguish a high rate of response versus a low rate of response versus a period of no response on a cumulative record?
8. Distinguish between speed, duration, and latency measures of behavior.
9. Distinguish between the intensity and topography of a behavior.
10. Distinguish between interval recording and time-sample recording, and specify how the overall measure of behavior is calculated.
11. Name and describe two types of descriptive research methods. What is the major limitation of these types of research methods?
12. Describe the simplest form of a control group design. How are subjects assigned to the different conditions, and why is this done?
13. What is a comparative design?
14. What are three limitations of control group designs?
15. What are single-subject designs? Describe a simple-comparison design. In what sense is it a "flawed" design?
16. Describe a reversal design. What are the drawbacks to this type of design?
17. Describe a multiple-baseline design. What are two limitations of this type of design?
18. Describe a changing-criterion design. How can it be strengthened? For what types of situations is this design appropriate?
19. List four advantages and two disadvantages of using animals as subjects in behavioral research.

CONCEPT REVIEW

appetitive stimulus. An event that an organism will seek out.

aversive stimulus. An event that an organism will avoid.

baseline. The normal frequency of a behavior before some intervention.

case study approach. A descriptive research approach that involves intensive examination of one or a few individuals.

changing-criterion design. A type of single-subject design in which the effect of the treatment is demonstrated by how closely the behavior matches a criterion that is systematically altered.

comparative design. A type of control group design in which different species constitute one of the independent variables.

contingency. A predictive relationship between two events such that the occurrence of one event predicts the probable occurrence of the other.

control group design. A type of experiment in which, at its simplest, subjects are randomly assigned to either an experimental (or treatment) group or a control group; subjects assigned to the experimental group are exposed to a certain manipulation or treatment, while those assigned to the control group are not.

covert behavior. Behavior that can be *subjectively* perceived only by the person performing the behavior. Thoughts and feelings are covert behaviors.

cumulative recorder. A device that measures total number of responses over time and provides a graphic depiction of the rate of behavior.

dependent variable. That aspect of an experiment that is allowed to freely vary to determine if it is affected by changes in the independent variable.

deprivation. The prolonged absence of an event that tends to increase the appetitiveness of that event.

descriptive research. Research that focuses on describing the behavior and the situation within which it occurs.

duration. The length of time that an individual repeatedly or continuously performs a certain behavior.

establishing operation. A procedure that affects the appetitiveness or aversiveness of a stimulus.

functional relationship. The relationship between changes in an independent variable and changes in a dependent variable; a cause-and-effect relationship.

independent variable. That aspect of an experiment that is made to systematically vary across the different conditions in an experiment.

intensity. The force or magnitude of a behavior.

interval recording. The measurement of whether or not a behavior occurs within a series of continuous intervals. (The number of times that it occurs within each interval is irrelevant.)

latency. The length of time required for a behavior to begin.

multiple-baseline design. A type of single-subject design in which a treatment is instituted at successive points in time for two or more persons, settings, or behaviors.

naturalistic observation. A descriptive research approach that involves the systematic observation and recording of behavior in its natural environment.

overt behavior. Behavior that has the potential for being directly observed by an individual other than the one performing the behavior.

rate of response. The frequency with which a response occurs in a certain period of time.

response. A particular instance of a behavior.

reversal design. A type of single-subject design that involves repeated alternations between a baseline period and a treatment period.

satiation. The prolonged exposure to (or consumption of) an event that tends to decrease the appetitiveness of that event.

simple-comparison design. A type of single-subject design in which behavior in a baseline condition is compared to behavior in a treatment condition.

single-subject design. A research design that requires only one or a few subjects in order to conduct an entire experiment.

spatial contiguity. The extent to which events are situated close to each other in space.

speed. The amount of time required to perform a complete episode of a behavior from start to finish.

stimulus. Any event that can potentially influence behavior. (The plural for stimulus is *stimuli*.)

temporal contiguity. The extent to which events occur close together in time.

time-sample recording. The measurement of whether or not a behavior occurs within a series of discontinuous intervals. (The number of times that it occurs within each interval is irrelevant.)

topography. The physical form of a behavior.

variable. A characteristic of a person, place, or thing that can change (vary) over time or from one situation to another.

CHAPTER TEST

12. Using a(n) _____ recording procedure, we find that during a 10-minute observation, Erik chewed his nails only during the first and second minute, as well as during the fourth, seventh, ninth, and tenth minutes.

27. Being quite addicted to computer games, James decides to implement a program to *gradually* reduce the amount of time that he spends playing these games. A useful design for determining if his program is successful would be a _____ design.

18. The reversal design is also known as a(n) _____ design.

3. Each time it rains, I see an increased number of umbrellas being carried. There appears to be a _____ relationship between the weather and the appearance of umbrellas.

8. You have just eaten a large pizza. It is likely that the reward value of eating a pizza has (increased/decreased) _____ as a function of (which type of establishing operation) _____.

23. The amount of time it takes Robert to read a chapter is a _____ measure of behavior, and the amount of time it took him to begin reading the chapter is a _____ measure of behavior. The total amount of time he spends reading each day is a _____ measure of behavior.

15. In a _____ design, subjects are randomly assigned to a treatment or nontreatment condition.

11. Number of cigarettes smoked each week is a _____ measure of smoking.

19. Animals are often used in behavioral research because this practice allows for greater _____ over learning history, genetic influences, and experimental environment than is possible with humans. As well, animals

are often used when the use of humans would be _____ questionable.

10. The force with which a boxer delivers a blow is a(n) _____ measure of behavior.

26. I wish to test a new drug that I believe will permanently remove the symptoms of a rare neurological disorder. Unfortunately, only three patients who suffer from the disorder have volunteered to take the drug. What would be a useful type of design to demonstrate the effectiveness of this drug? _____.

16. An experiment that utilizes a type of _____ design requires only one or a few subjects.

4. A flash of light is a _____, and two flashes of light are _____. A specific eyeblink that is elicited by a flash of light is a _____.

20. After Trish told Jen that Ryan was the most popular guy in school, Jen became extremely interested in him. Trish's statement about Ryan apparently functioned as an _____ that increased Ryan's value as an _____ stimulus.

7. You have not had a pizza in 4 months. It is likely that the reward value of eating a pizza has (increased/decreased) _____ as a function of (which type of establishing operation) _____.

24. When people feel confident, they tend to stand straight. In this case, we are using a _____ measure of behavior as an index of confidence.

1. Any characteristic of a person, place, or thing that can change can be called a _____.

9. Robbie is afraid of spiders, but Naseem finds them interesting. A spider is a(n) _____ stimulus to Robbie, and a(n) _____ stimulus to Naseem.

6. A knife and spoon are placed side by side in a dinner setting, creating spatial (contiguity/contingency) _____ between the two utensils.

28. Dr. Takeuchi wonders whether the crows that he is studying can solve certain types of problems as well as dogs can. In testing this notion, he would use a type of experimental design known as a _____ design.

13. Using a(n) _____ recording procedure, a school psychologist drops into a classroom for a 20-minute period four times each day and notes whether some type of disruption occurs during the time that he is there.

17. The _____ approach is a descriptive method of research often used by psychiatrists who encounter a very unusual case.

2. In a classical conditioning experiment, one group of dogs first hears a tone and then receives food, while another group of dogs receives food and then hears a tone. Following this, the researcher measures how much the dogs in each group salivate when they simply hear the tone. In this experiment, the order in which tone and food are presented is

the _____ variable, and the amount of salivation to the tone is the _____ variable.

22. On a cumulative recorder, a gradually sloping line indicates a _____ rate of response, and a steep line indicates a _____ rate of response. By contrast, a _____ line indicates no response.

14. Two main approaches to behavioral research are the _____ approach and the _____ approach.

5. Blinking is a(n) _____ behavior, but thinking about blinking is a(n) _____ behavior.

25. Dr. Ross studies the effects of schizoid personality disorder by sitting in the park each day and observing the behavior of street people who are known to be suffering from the disorder. Dr. Ross is using a descriptive research method known as _____.

21. To determine whether drinking coffee in the evening keeps me awake at night, I observe my sleep patterns for a 2-week period in which I drink coffee each evening, followed by a 2-week period in which I do not drink coffee in the evening. I am using a _____ design to conduct this study, which will likely give me (strong/questionable) _____ evidence concerning how coffee affects my sleep patterns.

Visit the book companion Web site at <http://www.academic.cengage.com/psychology/powell> for additional practice questions, answers to the Quick Quizzes, practice review exams, and additional exercises and information.

ANSWERS TO CHAPTER TEST

1. variable
2. independent; dependent
3. functional (or contingent)
4. stimulus; stimuli; response
5. overt; covert
6. contiguity
7. increased; deprivation
8. decreased; satiation
9. aversive; appetitive
10. intensity
11. rate
12. interval
13. time sample
14. descriptive; experimental
15. control group
16. single-subject
17. case study
18. ABA (or ABAB)
19. control; ethically
20. establishing operation; appetitive
21. simple comparison or AB; questionable
22. low (or slow); high (or fast); flat
23. speed; latency; duration
24. topography
25. naturalistic observation
26. multiple-baseline (across persons)
27. changing-criterion
28. comparative

CHAPTER 3

Elicited Behaviors and Classical Conditioning

CHAPTER OUTLINE

At a friend's party, Uma witnessed her boyfriend flagrantly flirting with another woman. She was initially quite angry, but when he later apologized for his actions and was very attentive to her, she experienced unusually strong feelings of attraction toward him. Still, she somehow felt manipulated by the whole affair. After all, her friends had warned her that he had a terrible reputation for playing "mind games."

Elicited Behaviors

The word *elicit* means "to draw out or bring forth." Thus, an elicited behavior is one that is automatically drawn out by a certain stimulus. (Note that the word is *elicit* and not *illicit*, which refers to something illegal, such as an illicit drug.) A sneeze produced by a particle of dust or a startle reaction to the sound of a gunshot are examples of elicited behaviors. They are elicited in the sense that they are automatically drawn out by the stimuli that produce them. In this sense, many such behaviors can also be thought of as involuntary. For example, you do not choose to be startled by a gunshot; your startle reaction is an involuntary response to the gunshot. Similarly, you do not choose to salivate when you bite into a lemon; salivating is an involuntary response to the lemon.

In this chapter, we begin by describing different types of elicited behaviors as well as some simple mechanisms by which they can be modified. This will include a discussion of the opponent-process theory of emotion, an intriguing theory that explains a wide variety of emotional phenomena ranging from symptoms of drug withdrawal to the sense of loss you feel following the breakup of a relationship. The remainder of the chapter will then be devoted to introducing the concept of classical conditioning, the first major type of learning to be discussed in this text.

Reflexes

Reflexes are the most basic form of elicited behavior. A ***reflex*** is a relatively simple, automatic response to a stimulus. (It can also be defined as the *relationship* between such a response and the stimulus that elicits it.) Some reflexes involve only one gland or set of muscles, such as when you salivate in response to a drop of lemon juice or blink in response to a puff of air. Other reflexes are more general in scope, involving the coordinated action of several body parts. For example, the ***startle response***—a defensive reaction to a sudden, unexpected stimulus—involves the automatic tightening of skeletal muscles as well as various hormonal and visceral (internal organ) changes. Similarly, the ***orienting response***—in which we automatically position ourselves to facilitate attending to a stimulus—can involve a relatively major body movement, such as when we automatically turn in response to an unfamiliar noise behind us.

Many reflexes are closely tied to survival. For example, food consumption involves a chain of reflexes including salivation, peristalsis (wave-like actions that push food down the esophagus and through the digestive system), and secretion of digestive juices in the stomach. Conversely, the vomiting reflex serves a protective function by expelling potentially poisonous substances from the digestive system. Other protective reflexes include the *flexion response,* in which we automatically jerk our hand or foot away from a hot or sharp object that we have inadvertently contacted, and the aforementioned startle reaction—designed to ready us for fight or flight if an unexpected stimulus should prove dangerous.

Newborns come "prepackaged" with a host of reflexes that facilitate their survival. For example, if you touch a baby's cheek with your finger, the baby will automatically turn his or her head in that direction. This reflex action is designed to facilitate taking a nipple into the mouth. Once the nipple is in the mouth, the baby's sucking reflex is activated (which in turn elicits a "milk letdown" reflex in the mother). Many of these reflexes disappear within a few years (e.g., the sucking reflex), but others, such as salivating and vomiting, remain with us throughout life.

Many of the simpler reflexes are activated through a reflex arc. A *reflex arc* is a neural structure that underlies many reflexes and consists of a sensory neuron, an interneuron, and a motor neuron. For example, when you quickly jerk your hand away from an open flame, you are exhibiting a flexion response. Upon touching the flame, receptors in the hand stimulate sensory neurons that carry a danger message (in the form of a burst of nerve impulses) toward the spinal cord. Within the spinal cord, interneurons receive this message and immediately pass it on to the motor neurons. These motor neurons then activate the muscles in the arm that pull the hand away from the flame. Simultaneous with this process, pain messages are also sent up the spinal cord to the brain; but by the time they are received and you consciously feel the pain, the hand is already being withdrawn from the flame. Thus, we do not withdraw our hand from the flame because of the pain; we actually begin withdrawing our hand before feeling any pain. Because the flexion response utilizes a simple reflex arc through the spinal cord, we are able to withdraw our hand from the flame much quicker than if the message had to be routed all the way through the brain and then back down to the arm muscles (see Figure 3.1).

1. A simple, involuntary response to a stimulus is called a _____.

2. Reflexes are e_____ in the sense that they are drawn out by stimuli that precede their occurrence.

3. A s_____ reaction is an automatic defensive response to a sudden, unexpected stimulus; the o_____ response consists of movements designed to facilitate attending to a stimulus.

4. Many simple reflexes are activated through a r_____ a_____ that consists of a(n) _____ neuron, a(n) _____ neuron, and a(n) _____ neuron (in that order).

5. Quickly jerking your hand or foot away from contact with an open flame or sharp object is a reflexive action known as a fl_____ response. In such cases, the perception of pain generally (precedes/follows) _____ the response.

FIGURE 3.1 The reflex arc underlying a flexion response. Upon touching the flame, receptors in the finger stimulate sensory neurons that carry the message via nerve impulses toward the spinal cord. Interneurons within the spinal cord receive the message and pass it directly to motor neurons. The motor neurons in turn activate muscles in the arm that pull the finger away from the flame. At the same time this action is occurring, a pain message is sent to the brain. (*Source:* Nairne, 2000.)

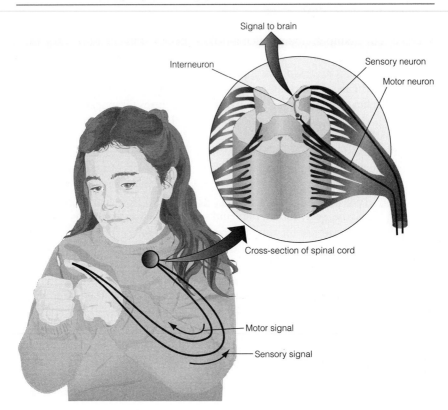

Fixed Action Patterns

Some types of elicited behaviors are more complex than simple reflexes. A *fixed action pattern* is a fixed sequence of responses elicited by a specific stimulus. Fixed action patterns are also sometimes called "modal action patterns" (Domjan, 2003). Examples include web building by spiders, V-shaped formation flying by ducks, and nut burying by some species of squirrels. Dogs and cats display numerous fixed action patterns. Cats compulsively scratch the ground to cover up urine and feces (effective in a litter box but completely ineffective on your carpet) and rub up against the legs of visitors to "mark" them as belonging to their territory. Dogs indicate their desire to play by wagging their tails, stretching out their front legs, and lowering their heads to the ground (see Figure 3.2). In fact, by adopting this posture (and looking completely foolish in front of any visitors), you can effectively ask your dog if

FIGURE 3.2 Fixed action pattern for play. A dog will indicate its desire for play by stretching out its front legs and lowering its head to the ground. (*Source:* Reprinted with the permission of The Free Press, a Division of Simon & Schuster Adult Publishing Group, from THE INTELLIGENCE OF DOGS: Canine Consciousness and Capabilities by Stanley Coren. Copyright © 1994 by Stanley Coren. All rights reserved.

Tail up

Ears up

Mouth open,
tongue exposed

Front end lowered
by bent forepaws

it wishes to play (which of course it will not, given that it now has you looking like an idiot).

For many fixed action patterns, we are able to identify a specific stimulus that sets it in motion. The specific stimulus that elicits a fixed action pattern is called a ***sign stimulus*** or ***releaser***. For example, a male *Betta splendens*, better known as a Siamese fighting fish, immediately takes an aggressive posture at the sight of another male (the releaser), with both fish then spreading out their brilliant red or blue fins and gills. If introduced into the same tank, the two fish will attack each other, sometimes even fighting until death. Similarly, during mating season, a male stickleback fish displays a fixed sequence of aggressive actions when another male enters its territory (Tinbergen, 1951). Interestingly, the sign stimulus for the stickleback's aggressive actions is not the presence of the other male but the sight of its red underbelly. If the red belly is covered up or painted a different color, the intruder will not be attacked. On the other hand, if a pie-shaped or cigar-shaped piece of wood with a red patch on the bottom is introduced into the tank, it will be attacked.

Fixed action patterns tend to be unique to certain species and are therefore sometimes called *species-specific behaviors*. They can also be called instincts, but some researchers dislike this term because it implies that the behavior is more rigid and inflexible than is actually the case. For example, if two rats are subjected to a painful stimulus, such as an electric shock, they will automatically aggress toward each other (Ulrich & Azrin, 1962). In fact, many species will become aggressive in reaction to pain, but in rats it often takes the form of a fixed action pattern in which the two combatants rear up on their hind legs and essentially box by striking out at each other with their front paws. Interestingly, this aggression is more likely to occur in rats that had previously been trained to be aggressive than in those that had not been trained to be aggressive (Baeninger & Ulm, 1969). Thus, the rats' fixed action pattern of aggression is actually somewhat variable and can be significantly modified by experience.

Fixed action patterns are adaptive responses that have evolved to help animals cope with consistent aspects of their environment. The difficulty with such inherited behavior patterns is that a sudden, large-scale change in the environment may render the pattern useless or even harmful. For example, deer have an inborn tendency to run a zigzag pattern when being pursued by a predator. This action, which confuses the predator, greatly increases the deer's chances of survival in the wild; however, this same action greatly reduces its chances of survival when it is being pursued down the highway by an automobile. The inborn tendency to zigzag is a maladaptive way of responding to the modern threat of automobiles. By comparison, an animal that can modify its behavior patterns through learning can better adapt to a changing environment, which is why the ability to learn was an important evolutionary advancement.

1. A _____ _____ _____ is a fixed sequence of responses that occurs in reaction to a specific stimulus.

2. The specific stimulus that elicits a fixed action pattern is called a s_____ stimulus or r_____.

3. Different species of spiders spin different kinds of webs. Web spinning of this sort can thus be considered a sp_____-sp_____ behavior. Such behaviors used to be called i_____, but some researchers dislike this term because it implies that the behavior is more (flexible/inflexible) _____ than is actually the case.

Simple Mechanisms of Learning

Habituation and Sensitization

The repeated presentation of an eliciting stimulus can alter the strength of the elicited behavior. *Habituation* is a decrease in the strength of an elicited behavior following repeated presentations of the eliciting stimulus. For example, we quickly stop attending to low-intensity background noises such as the ticking of a clock or the distant noise of traffic. Similarly, a sudden, unexpected tap on the shoulder may elicit a startle response, while further taps might have no such effect.

By contrast, *sensitization* is an increase in the strength of an elicited behavior following repeated presentations of the eliciting stimulus. For example, soldiers under attack generally do not habituate to the sound of artillery shells exploding nearby. Instead, their startle reaction grows stronger. Needless to say, this greatly contributes to the stress they experience and the inevitable breakdown virtually all soldiers suffer after repeated exposure to battle conditions (though Hollywood would often have you think otherwise).

The effects of habituation and sensitization usually disappear when the stimulus is not presented for a period of time, meaning that the strength of the behavior goes back to its original level. For example, you might habituate to the sound of a neighbor's stereo one evening, only to be once more bothered by it when she first turns it on the next morning. In the few hours since you last heard the music, your habituation to it disappeared and you again responded to the noise like you normally would. But some forms of habituation last for longer periods of time. For example, if you move into an apartment from which you hear the sound of a train each morning, your reaction to the noise will probably be most intense on the first day and then decrease slowly thereafter. Moreover, once you become fully habituated to the noise, you would have to be away from your apartment for several weeks or even months before your reaction to the noise would return to its original level. This type of habituation is known as long-term habituation, as opposed to short-term habituation. Thus, in *long-term habituation*, the response slowly decreases as a result of repeated stimulation and then slowly recovers in the absence of repeated stimulation, whereas in *short-term habituation*, the response quickly decreases and then quickly recovers. In general, long-term habituation tends to occur when presentations of the stimulus are widely spaced (e.g., a train going by your apartment each morning), whereas short-term habituation tends to occur when presentations of the stimulus are narrowly spaced or continuous (e.g., a child next door repeatedly banging on a drum).

Note that sensitization often generalizes to other stimuli. A shell-shocked soldier is likely to jump not only in response to artillery explosions but also to any sudden stimulus. By contrast, habituation is quite stimulus specific, such that any change in the stimulus is likely to result in the reappearance of the habituated response. Thus, many people suddenly become aware of the sound of their car when the motor sounds a bit different or when the car has a slightly different feel to it as they are driving along. Only a slight change is needed to alert the driver that something is potentially wrong (and hopefully, inexpensive to fix). One version of this process is known as the *Coolidge effect*, based on an old joke about former U.S. president Calvin Coolidge. The story has it that he and his wife were once being separately escorted around a chicken farm. When Mrs. Coolidge was informed that the resident rooster was capable of mating several times a day, she replied, "You should tell that to the president." Informed about this, the president asked whether the repeated matings occurred with the same chicken or different chickens. When told that it was different chickens, he replied, "You should tell that to my wife." The Coolidge effect therefore is the enhanced sexual arousal displayed by the males of some species when presented with different sexual partners as opposed to the same sexual partner to whom it has habituated.

Habituated responses can also reappear following the presentation of a seemingly irrelevant novel stimulus, by a phenomenon called ***dishabituation.*** For example, Sherri might quickly habituate to the sound of gunshots at a shooting range. If, however, a handsome stranger approaches and stands nearby, she might again be startled when the next shot is fired. Likewise, couples can sometimes rekindle their romance by traveling to a new and different environment—or even just by treating themselves to a night in a hotel room rather than staying at home.

QUICK QUIZ C

1. An increase in the strength of a behavior following repeated presentations of the eliciting stimulus is called _____.

2. A decrease in the strength of a behavior following repeated presentations of the eliciting stimulus is called _____.

3. Learning to ignore the sound of dripping water is an example of _____; becoming increasingly aware of the sound of a jackhammer on the street below your apartment is an example of _____.

4. The fact that it has been several months since you noticed the sound of the fan in your home computer is an example of l_____-t_____ habituation. Such habituation tends to build up (quickly/slowly) _____ and disappear (quickly/slowly) _____.

5. In general, sensitization is (less/more) _____ stimulus specific than habituation.

6. The presentation of a novel stimulus during a period of habituation can sometimes result in dis_____, in which the habituated response (reappears/disappears) _____.

Why does repeated exposure to certain stimuli sometimes result in habituation and sometimes in sensitization? One factor is the intensity of the eliciting stimulus. A *low-intensity stimulus*, such as the ticking of a clock, typically results in habituation, while a *high-intensity stimulus*, such as exploding artillery shells, typically results in sensitization. A *stimulus of intermediate intensity* often results in an initial period of sensitization followed by habituation. For example, at a shooting range, the first few shots you hear might produce an increasingly strong startle reaction. But you then begin to habituate to the shots, and after awhile you hardly notice them.

Another factor that influences habituation versus sensitization, which can often override the intensity factor, is the adaptive (or evolutionary) significance of the stimulus. For example, which of the following would be easier to habituate to at night: the constant sound of locomotives shuttling railcars back and forth in the rail yard nearby or the sound of a bee buzzing in your bedroom? The buzzing of the bee is a much less intense stimulus than the sound of the trains, and yet many people will find it much easier to habituate to the sound of the trains. Now consider other sensory modalities. Think of smells associated with foods you typically cook in your home. Most people can quickly habituate to the smell of onions and spices, even if quite strong, but will become increasingly bothered by the smell of something rancid, even if relatively weak. Likewise with touch, we habituate easily to firm pressure on our body, such as our body weight pressing down on a chair, so long as it is not painful, whereas we do not habituate to certain other types of pressure, such as tickling or a gentle caress. (See Provine, 2004, for an interesting discussion of the evolutionary and social significance of tickling.)

So what is happening here? Habituation and sensitization are processes that we see across species, even in very simple organisms like worms and snails (e.g., Wicks & Rankin, 1997). From an evolutionary perspective, this suggests that these processes probably have tremendous survival advantages. In a sense, they help us sort information in our environment into two basic categories: currently relevant and currently irrelevant (Eisenstein, Eisenstein, & Smith, 2001). If a stimulus is currently irrelevant, we tend to habituate to it; but if a stimulus is currently relevant—that is, it provides some sort of useful or at least novel information—we tend not to habituate to it. If a stimulus is extremely relevant, perhaps even dangerous, we may even become sensitized to it. It therefore makes sense to become sensitized to the buzzing sound of insects that sting and the smell of something rotten (which could poison us). It also makes sense not to habituate to the caress of a lover, since such touching has, throughout our evolutionary history, been associated with possible reproductive opportunities. This perspective also explains why stimulus intensity can make a difference: low-intensity stimuli are often (though not always) insignificant while high-intensity stimuli are often (though not always) very significant and sometimes potentially dangerous.

Of course, we do not always get it right, and we sometimes become sensitized to things that are really of no danger to us. Wouldn't you love to be able to habituate to the sound of the barking dog next door or the car alarms that go off in the middle of the night? Unfortunately (or fortunately), organisms behave in ways that increase their likelihood of survival and reproduction, which often means erring on the side of caution. The result is that we often become sensitized to stimuli that are not actually dangerous, and we fail to habituate to stimuli that we would really do better to ignore. Add to that individual differences in the tendency to habituate and sensitize (LaRowe, Patrick, Curtin, & Kline, 2006), and sleepless nights due to barking dogs are an unfortunate reality for many of us.

1. One factor that influences whether we habituate or become sensitized to a particular stimulus is the _____ of the eliciting stimulus.

2. In general, repeated presentations of a low-intensity stimulus result in _____, and repeated presentations of a high-intensity stimulus result in _____.

3. A stimulus of intermediate intensity will initially result in a period of _____, which is then followed by _____.

4. From an evolutionary standpoint, if a stimulus is irrelevant or "safe," we tend to _____ to it, whereas if a stimulus is perceived as a signal of danger we will become _____ to it.

5. We often fail to _____ to stimuli (even if they are not actually dangerous) because our nervous system tends to "err on the side of caution" to keep us safe.

QUICK QUIZ D

Opponent-Process Theory of Emotion

Habituation and sensitization represent two opposing tendencies: weaker reactivity to a stimulus versus stronger reactivity. Solomon (1980; see also Solomon & Corbit, 1974) has proposed an intriguing theory of emotion that involves a similar dual mechanism. Known as the opponent-process theory, it is particularly good at explaining the aftereffects of strong emotional responses. Consider, for example, the following anecdote:

> My neighbor's son was struck by lightning as he was returning from a golf course. He was thrown to the ground. His shorts were torn to shreds and he was burned across his thighs. When his companion sat him up, he screamed "I'm dead, I'm dead." His legs were numb and blue and he could not move. By the time he reached the nearest hospital he was *euphoric* [italics added]. (Taussig as quoted in Solomon, 1980, p. 691)

In one sense, the boy's euphoria is logical in that he was lucky to be alive. But in another sense, it is illogical because he was injured and decidedly worse off than before the incident. Should he not have remained at least somewhat distressed about the incident?

Consider, too, the following scenario. Suppose you purchase a lottery ticket during a visit home. Next weekend, your mom phones to tell you the winning numbers—and lo and behold, you discover that you have won $50,000! Wow! You are absolutely elated. Unfortunately, an hour later you receive another call from your mom informing you that she made a mistake on the numbers. It turns out that you *only* won $50. You are now extremely disappointed even though you are still $50 better off than when you climbed out of bed that morning. Within a day, however, your disappointment wears off and you carry on with your impoverished lifestyle as usual.

Now consider an experiment in which a dog is exposed to electric shock (e.g., Katcher et al., 1969). During the shock, the dog's heart rate quickly rises to a peak, decreases slightly, and then stabilizes at a relatively high level. Now guess what happens when the shock is turned off. Does the dog's heart rate return to normal? No, it does not. When the shock is removed, the dog's heart rate plunges to *below* normal and then after a few minutes moves back up to normal (see Figure 3.3). In fact, the pattern of changes in heart rate during and after the shock—an index of the dog's emotional response to shock—is very similar to the emotional pattern displayed in the preceding lottery scenario. In both cases, an event elicits a strong emotional response; but when the event is withdrawn, an opposite response is elicited and then gradually disappears. In fact, this pattern of emotional changes is relatively common.

An explanation for these emotional changes is provided by the opponent-process theory of emotion. The **opponent-process theory** proposes that an emotional event elicits two competing processes: (1) an a-process (or primary process) that is directly elicited by the event, and (2) a b-process (or opponent process) that is elicited by the a-process and serves to counteract the a-process. For example, the presentation of shock directly elicits a tendency for the dog's heart rate to increase, which is the a-process. This increase in

FIGURE 3.3 Heart rate changes accompanying the application and withdrawal of shock. Our emotional responses often follow a similar pattern, with the onset of the emotional event followed by one type of response and the offset of the event followed by an opposite response.

heart rate in turn elicits a compensatory reaction that tries to decrease the heart rate, which is the b-process. The purpose of this compensatory b-process is to counter the sudden increase in heart rate, thereby maintaining a state of internal balance (known as homeostasis). In other words, the b-process tries to prevent the increase in heart rate from becoming too extreme, which could be damaging or even fatal. The actual heart rate elicited by shock is therefore the net result of the tendency for heart rate to increase in the presence of shock (the a-process), minus the compensatory tendency for heart rate to decrease (the b-process; see Figure 3.4). Similarly, in the lottery example, the feeling of elation you experience when you think you have won the lottery is the amount of elation directly elicited by winning the money (the a-process) minus the compensatory reaction to this elation (the b-process), which is trying to keep your elation from becoming too extreme.

1. The opponent-process theory of emotion accounts for why a strong emotional response is often followed by a(n) (similar/opposite) _____ emotional response.

2. The _____-_____ is directly elicited by the emotional event; this in turn elicits the _____-_____, the purpose of which is to maintain a relatively balanced internal state known as h_____.

3. The a-process is also known as the pr_____ process, and the b-process is also known as the o_____ process.

QUICK QUIZ E

FIGURE 3.4 Opponent-process mechanisms that underlie changes in heart rate due to the onset and offset of shock. During the shock, as the b-process acquires strength, it pulls the heart rate down from its initial peak and stabilizes it at a moderately high level. Following shock, when the a-process is no longer active, the b-process pulls the heart rate to below normal, then gradually disappears, allowing the heart rate to return to normal.

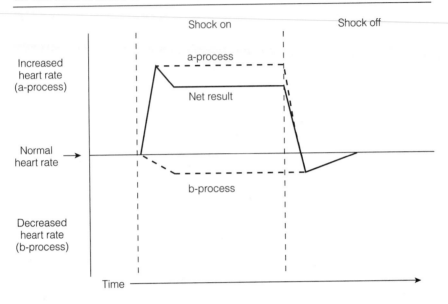

The a- and b-processes have some important characteristics:

1. **The a-process correlates closely with the presence of the emotional event.** As shown in Figure 3.4, the tendency for the heart rate to increase in response to shock is directly tied to the presence of the shock. When the shock is presented, the heart rate immediately increases; when the shock is removed, the heart rate immediately decreases. Similarly, you immediately become elated when you think you have won the lottery, and your elation immediately disappears when you discover that you have not.

2. **The b-process is slow to increase and slow to decrease.** The slow buildup in the b-process accounts for why our emotional response to an event is often strongest at the outset. If you look again at Figure 3.4, you can see that when the shock is first turned on, the dog's heart rate quickly peaks and then declines slightly before stabilizing. The immediate peak happens during the early moments of shock because the b-process is not yet strong enough to counteract the a-process, thereby allowing the a-process free rein to increase the heart rate. After a few moments, though, the b-process becomes strong enough to moderate the a-process, causing a slight decrease in the heart rate before stabilizing. When the shock is removed, the a-process immediately disappears; but the b-process only

FIGURE 3.5 Effects of repeated stimulus presentations on primary and opponent processes. With repeated stimulation, the b-process becomes stronger and takes longer to disappear. The result is that the heart rate rises only slightly above normal during the shock, then drops considerably below normal following the shock and takes a relatively long time to return to normal.

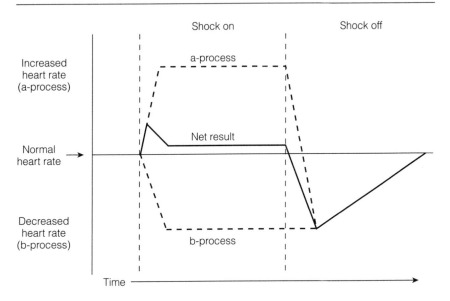

slowly declines. For this reason, when the shock is turned off, the dog's heart rate plunges to well below normal, because all that remains is the b-process that has been trying to pull the heart rate down. (It is as though, in a tug-of-war, the other team suddenly let go of the rope, sending your team flying backward in the direction they were pulling.) Similarly, when you discover that you have not won the lottery, you immediately feel depressed because the counter-reaction to the elation you have been feeling is all that remains. As the b-process gradually weakens, however, your emotional response slowly returns to normal, just as the dog's heart rate slowly returns to normal.

3. **With repeated presentations of the emotional event, the b-process increases in both strength and duration.** This is the most interesting part of the theory. For example, what happens to the dog's heart rate if it is repeatedly shocked? As it turns out, the increase in heart rate during each shock becomes less and less extreme. Additionally, each time the shock is turned off, the dog's heart rate plunges more and more deeply and takes increasingly longer to return to normal (see Figure 3.5). The dog's overt emotional response matches these changes in heart rate. Whereas in the early sessions the dog shows considerable distress in response to the shock, in later sessions it appears more annoyed than distressed. More surprising, though, is the change in the dog's emotional response following the shock. Whereas in the

early sessions the dog appears somewhat relieved when the shock is turned off, in the later sessions it shows signs of extreme pleasure and euphoria, jumping about and greeting the experimenter with enthusiasm.

Similar emotional patterns have been found in humans. For example, S. Epstein (1967) found that military parachutists became less and less terrified with repeated jumps and became more and more elated following each jump. This sense of elation can last several hours among veteran jumpers and probably accounts, at least partially, for the strong attraction some people feel toward parachuting and other high-risk activities.[1]

The opponent-process theory of emotion also has implications for a phenomenon known as revictimization (van der Kolk, 1989). Some people repeatedly become involved in abusive relationships or have great difficulty leaving such relationships. A contributing factor in some cases may be that the person has become hooked on the powerful feelings of pleasure that occur during the "honeymoon period" of forgiveness that often follows an intense period of abuse. This intense pleasure is the compensatory after-reaction (the b-process), which has become greatly strengthened during repeated episodes of abuse. As suggested in the opening vignette to this chapter, a weaker version of this honeymoon effect might even occur in relationships in which one is exposed to a period of emotional distress rather than actual abuse.

It must be remembered that the opponent-process theory, however intriguing, is still a theory; and some of the research fails to support it (e.g., Fanselow, DeCola, & Young, 1993). Furthermore, as you will see in Chapter 5, classical conditioning might often play an important role in the elicitation of opponent processes, especially processes associated with drug use. Nevertheless, opponent-process theory has stimulated a considerable amount of research and has proven extremely useful for enhancing our understanding of emotional responses.

QUICK QUIZ F

1. With repeated presentations of the emotional event, the b-process (increases/decreases) _____ in both s_____ and d_____.

2. The _____-_____ is directly tied to the presence of the emotional event, whereas the ___-_____ is (slow/quick) _____ to increase and (slow/quick) _____ to decrease.

3. Feeling elated while talking on the phone to someone with whom you are in love is an example of the _____-_____. Feeling lovesick after you finally hang up for the night is an example of the _____-_____.

---

[1]Note, however, that emotional changes during skydiving can be a bit more complex than this. Veteran skydivers experience a peak of anxiety just before leaving the plane, followed by a strong sense of elation during the free fall, another peak of anxiety when the chute is being deployed (a high-risk moment), and then a sense of elation after they land. The strong sense of elation that occurs during free fall may be a contributing factor to accidents because veteran jumpers may be tempted to delay deploying the chute until the last possible moment (Delk, 1980).

ADVICE FOR THE LOVELORN

Dear Dr. Dee,

Several months ago I broke up with my boyfriend when he took a job in another city. We were together 5 years, and it had turned into a pretty monotonous relationship by the time it ended. But it sure is taking me a long time to get over it. My friend tells me that I must have some kind of "unresolved dependency issue" for me to be this depressed. She recently broke up with her boyfriend—she went out with him for only a month but claims that she was madly in love—and got over it in a week. Is there something wrong with me, or is my friend just superficial?

Still Depressed

Dear Still,

There may be several reasons why some people take longer than others to recover from a breakup. The opponent-process theory, however, might be particularly applicable in your case. Remember that our primary emotional response to an event typically weakens with repeated exposure, while the emotional after-reaction typically strengthens. Solomon (1980) suggested that these processes are as applicable to love relationships as they are to other emotional events. Couples that have been together for only a short time usually have much stronger feelings of affection for each other than do couples that have been together for a long time. In other words, the emotional response of affection generally decreases over time. When relationships end, however, couples that have been together for a long time experience a much deeper and longer-lasting sense of loss than do couples that have been together for only a short time. According to opponent-process theory, this sense of loss is the compensatory reaction to the relationship, which should be much stronger in those couples that have been together longer. For this reason, it will naturally take more time for you to get over your long-term "monotonous" relationship than for your friend to get over her brief "madly-in-love" relationship.

Behaviorally yours,

Dr. Dee

Classical Conditioning

We have so far discussed those situations in which a certain stimulus (e.g., lemon juice) elicits a particular response (e.g., salivation). We have also noted that repeated presentations of a stimulus can sometimes change the nature of the response, either strengthening it (sensitization), weakening it (habituation), or eliciting a compensatory reaction (the opponent process). But these are relatively simple means of adaptation. Because the world is a complex place filled with a vast array of stimuli, we often need to anticipate whether an event is about to occur and to recognize whether certain events are meaningfully related to other events. For example, when we are first stung by a wasp, it is adaptive for us to associate the pain with the sight and sound of the wasp. It is also adaptive for us to be wary of insects that resemble wasps, because many of them (e.g., honeybees and hornets) also sting. Thus, the ability to relate events to each other allows us to better anticipate the future, thereby greatly facilitating our chances of surviving.

Classical conditioning is a process in which one stimulus that does not elicit a response is associated with a second stimulus that does; as a result, the first stimulus also comes to elicit a response. Classical conditioning is also known as *Pavlovian conditioning*, after Pavlov, who discovered many of the basic principles of classical conditioning. It is also sometimes called *respondent conditioning*, in which case the elicited behaviors are called *respondent behaviors* or simply *respondents*.

Pavlov's Discovery of Classical Conditioning

© Bettman/CORBIS

Ivan P. Pavlov
(1849–1936)

Ivan P. Pavlov (1849–1936), a Russian physiologist, is generally credited with the first systematic investigations into classical conditioning.[2] Beginning in the late 1800s, Pavlov conducted important research on digestive secretions as well as the neural mechanisms that control them. He is, in fact, responsible for much of what we now know about digestion, and he won the Nobel Prize for his discoveries.

As part of this research enterprise, Pavlov also investigated salivation, the initial step in the digestive process. By this time, Pavlov was well aware that salivation could be initiated by psychic factors such as the sight of food (visual perception being regarded as a psychic, meaning psychological, process). He was nevertheless surprised at the amount of control exerted by these factors. He noted, for instance, that different substances affected both the quantity and quality of saliva produced. For example, a moist, edible substance such as meat elicited a small amount of slimy saliva whereas a dry, inedible substance such as sand elicited a large amount of watery saliva (to facilitate spitting it out). These differences existed both when the substances were actually placed in the dogs' mouths and, later, when the dogs were merely shown

[2]At about the same time, an American graduate student by the name of E. B. Twitmyer also conducted experiments on this type of conditioning and even reported his results at the 1904 conference of the American Psychological Association. However, his report generated little interest, and he abandoned the topic, which is fortunate because the term "Twitmyerian conditioning" is a mouthful (see Hothersall, 1984).

Pavlov with his research team. If the assistants seem more tense than the dog, this is not surprising. Pavlov was very demanding of his assistants, but quite concerned about the welfare of his dogs.

these substances. Subsequent research confirmed that these psychic secretions exhibited a great deal of regularity and lawfulness, and Pavlov began to devote more and more resources to their investigation. By 1907, classical conditioning, as it would come to be known, had become the sole focus of his research efforts.

In the decades that followed, Pavlov discovered most of the basic principles of classical conditioning and explored their application in such diverse areas as personality, hypnosis, sleep, and psychopathology. The epitome of the devoted scientist, Pavlov could be a tough taskmaster with students and assistants (once refusing to accept an assistant's excuse that he was late because he had to avoid the revolutionary battles going on in the streets). Yet, in other ways, he was a devoted humanitarian. When the Soviet regime took control—fortunately, the regime continued to support his research endeavors—he was openly critical of its denial of basic rights and religious freedoms. Pavlov also showed great concern for the welfare of his dogs. He invested considerable effort in devising surgical procedures that allowed for the accurate observation of internal mechanisms of digestion while minimizing the animals' discomfort and ensuring a full postoperative recovery.

Basic Procedure and Definitions

To illustrate the process of classical conditioning, we will use one of Pavlov's basic procedures. In this procedure, a dog is trained to salivate to the sound of a metronome.

During these experiments, the dog was restrained in a harness, and a tube was inserted into an incision that had been made in its cheek. Whenever the dog salivated, the saliva would run down the tube into a container where it could be precisely measured (see Figure 3.6). Although the apparatus appears uncomfortable, the dogs in fact habituated to it readily.

FIGURE 3.6 Pavlov's conditioning apparatus. In some of Pavlov's early experiments, a dog was trained to salivate to the sound of a metronome. The dog was restrained in a harness, and a tube was inserted into an incision in its cheek. Whenever the dog salivated, the tube carried the saliva to a container that activated a recording device. (*Source:* Coon, 1998.)

Pavlov's basic procedure worked as follows. Before conditioning, the dogs would automatically salivate in response to the taste of food. Because salivation to food occurs naturally and does not require prior training (conditioning), it is called an *unconditioned response* (UR), and the food is called an *unconditioned stimulus* (US). The sound of a metronome, however, does not elicit salivation and is therefore said to be a *neutral stimulus* (NS) with respect to salivation. During conditioning, the sound of the metronome is presented just before the food, which of course continues to elicit salivation. After conditioning, as a result of having been paired with the food, the metronome itself now elicits salivation. Because salivating to the metronome requires prior training (conditioning), it is called a *conditioned response* (CR), and the sound of the metronome is called a *conditioned stimulus* (CS)[3] (see Figure 3.7).

---

[3]Note that the Russian terms used by Pavlov were originally translated as "conditioned" and "unconditioned." They are, however, more precisely translated as "conditional" and "unconditional." We will continue to use the former terms because they have been in standard use for longer.

FIGURE 3.7   Classical conditioning of salivation. Before conditioning, the dog automatically salivates to the taste of food. During conditioning, the sound of a metronome is presented just before the presentation of food. After conditioning, the metronome itself now elicits salivation. (*Source:* Nairne, 2000.)

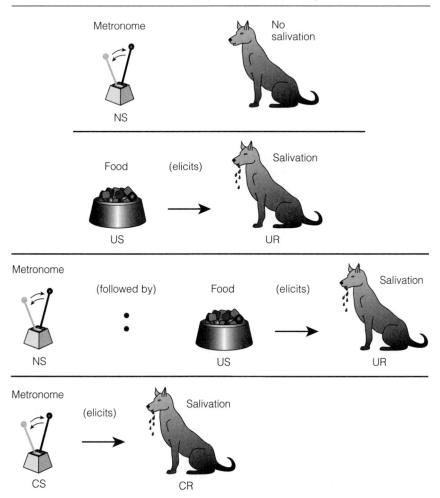

This procedure can be schematically diagrammed as follows.

Before conditioning:
Food → *Salivation*
 US   UR
Metronome → No salivation
  NS   —

During conditioning:
Metronome: Food → *Salivation*
NS (or CS)   US   UR

(During conditioning, the metronome can be labeled either an NS or a CS, because during this phase it begins as an NS and then becomes a CS.)

After conditioning:
Metronome → *Salivation*
    CS   **CR**

Each pairing of the NS and US during conditioning is called a *conditioning trial.*[4] Several conditioning trials are often needed before the NS becomes established as a CS. Measuring the level of conditioning can be done in various ways. The most common procedure is to intersperse the conditioning trials with an occasional *test trial* in which the NS is presented by itself. For example, every once in a while, the metronome can be presented alone to see if it elicits salivation. Alternatively, one can continue to pair the metronome with the food and simply observe whether salivation occurs in the short interval between the start of the metronome and the presentation of food.

As an everyday example of classical conditioning, let us suppose that a child is bitten by a dog and subsequently develops a fear of dogs. This process can be diagrammed as follows (omitting the "before conditioning" phase):

Dog: Bite → *Fear*
  NS   **US**   **UR**
Dog → *Fear*
  CS   **CR**

The bite can be considered an unconditioned stimulus that elicits an unconditioned response of fear (actually more pain than fear, but we will simplify matters a bit). As a result of the bite, the sight of the dog becomes a conditioned stimulus that elicits in the child a conditioned response of fear.

Let us now look more closely at each component of the classical conditioning procedure. The ***unconditioned stimulus (US)*** is a stimulus that naturally elicits a response, and the ***unconditioned response (UR)*** is the response that is naturally elicited by the US. When we say that the response is naturally elicited by the US, we mean that it is an *unlearned* or *innate* reaction to that stimulus. For example, food naturally elicits the response of salivation, and a bite naturally elicits the response of fear (and pain). (Note that the US and UR are sometimes given the abbreviations of UCS and UCR.)

The ***conditioned stimulus (CS)*** is any stimulus that, although initially neutral, comes to elicit a response because it has been associated with an unconditioned stimulus. The metronome is initially neutral with respect to salivation in that it does not naturally elicit salivation.[5] When the

---

[4]It is also sometimes referred to as a *reinforcement trial*, but in this text we will reserve the term *reinforcement* for certain operant conditioning procedures, as discussed in the last half of this text.

[5]Although the metronome is neutral with respect to salivation, it may not be neutral with respect to other types of responses. For example, it is likely a US for an orienting response (turn on the metronome, and the dog will prick up its ears and turn toward it).

Fortunately, Pavlov realized that the value of such experiments lay in their ability to reveal basic principles of behavior, not in their ability to simply make a dog salivate.

"PERHAPS, DR. PAVLOV, HE COULD BE TAUGHT TO SEAL ENVELOPES."

metronome has been associated with food, however, it does elicit salivation. The ***conditioned response (CR)*** is the response, often similar to the UR, that is elicited by the CS. Note that the conditioned response is at most only *similar* to the unconditioned response. It is never identical (a fact that is overlooked in many introductory psychology textbooks). Even when the UR and CR appear identical, as in the case of salivation elicited by the food (US) and by the metronome (CS), there are always some differences. For example, the CR is usually weaker or less intense than the UR. Thus, the dog will salivate less to the metronome than it will to the food. The CR is also sometimes quite different from the UR. For example, as noted earlier, the unconditioned response elicited by a bite is actually somewhat different from the conditioned response elicited by the sight of the dog that bit us. For simplicity, we labeled both responses as fear responses. Nevertheless, the response to the bite is mostly what we would describe as a pain reaction ("Yeow!"), whereas the subsequent response to the dog is one that is more clearly identified as fear (e.g., freezing). The extent to which the CR can differ from the UR is discussed more fully in Chapter 5.

1. Classical conditioning is also known as P_____ conditioning or r_____ conditioning.

2. In the latter case, the behaviors themselves are called _____ behaviors or simply _____.

3. In the metronome example, the metronome is initially a(n) _____ stimulus because it (does/does not) _____ elicit salivation. The food, however, is a(n) _____ stimulus that elicits a(n) _____ response of salivation.

4. During conditioning, the metronome can be labeled as either a(n) _____ stimulus or a(n) _____ stimulus.

5. Following conditioning, the metronome is a(n) _____ stimulus, and the salivation elicited by the metronome is a(n) _____ response.

6. Each pairing of the metronome and the food is called a c_____ tr_____.

7. Write out the term indicated by each of the following abbreviations:

CS: _____

UR: _____

NS: _____

US: _____

8. In the basic classical conditioning procedure, the (CS/US/NS) _____ is paired with the (CS/US/NS) _____, which in turn elicits the (CR/UR) _____. As a result, the first stimulus becomes a (CS/US/NS) _____, which elicits a (CR/UR) _____.

9. Using the appropriate abbreviations, label each component in the following classical conditioning procedure:

Wasp: Painful sting → *Fear*

Wasp → *Fear*

10. Using the format in question 9, diagram a classical conditioning procedure involving the stimuli of "nurse" and "painful injection," and the response of "anxiety." Label each component using the appropriate abbreviations.

11. The CR is (often/always) _____ (similar/identical) _____ to the UR.

12. A CR that appears identical to the UR is almost always (less/more) _____ intense.

13. Define each of the following terms (do not worry if at this point you still have to go back and look at the definitions).

Unconditioned stimulus:

Unconditioned response:

Conditioned stimulus:

Conditioned response:

Appetitive and Aversive Conditioning

Most classical conditioning procedures can be divided into two categories based on whether the US is pleasant or unpleasant. In *appetitive conditioning,* the US is an event that is usually considered pleasant and that an organism seeks out. Examples include food (if the organism is hungry), water (if the organism is thirsty), or addictive drugs (especially if the organism is a drug addict). Sexual stimuli too are regarded as appetitive stimuli, and there is good evidence that sexual responses can be classically conditioned. For example, Rachman and Hodgson (1968) took seven male volunteers and presented them with conditioning trials in which a picture of black, knee-length boots was followed by a picture of a nude woman. After about 30 trials, five of the males became sexually aroused by the sight of the boots. (Do not worry. The researchers later eliminated the conditioning by repeatedly presenting the picture of the boots without the picture of the nude—this process, known as *extinction*, is discussed later.)

In *aversive conditioning,* the US is an event that is usually considered unpleasant and that an organism usually avoids. Examples of aversive USs include an electric shock, a painful bite, and an unpleasant odor. Aversive conditioning often occurs rapidly, especially when the aversive stimulus is quite strong, and sometimes requires only one or two pairings of the NS and the US. This reflects the close relationship between aversive conditioning and survival; to survive, we have evolved in such a way as to quickly learn to dislike those events that cause pain or illness.

Given how easily aversive conditioning can occur, it is not surprising that this type of conditioning probably accounts for many of our fears and anxieties. When the fear is appropriate—as in learning to fear an angry dog that has bitten us—such conditioning is beneficial. When the fear is inappropriate— as when we begin to fear all dogs—such conditioning can be problematic. Therefore, a great deal of effort has gone into the study of fear conditioning, as well as into how such fears can be eliminated. This research has yielded important information on how real-world fears and anxieties can be treated (we discuss this topic more fully in Chapter 5).

When conducting research on fear conditioning in animals, measuring the level of fear can be problematic. Changes in certain physiological responses, such as heart rate, that might indicate fear are difficult to record, especially in small experimental animals such as rats. An ingenious solution to this problem was developed by Estes and Skinner (1941); it is known as the *conditioned suppression* or *conditioned emotional response (CER) paradigm.* In this paradigm, the rat is first trained to engage in some ongoing behavior, such as lever pressing to obtain food (with many lever presses being required to obtain a single pellet). When a steady rate of lever pressing has been established, a fear-conditioning procedure is introduced in which, say, a 30-second tone is presented followed by a 1-second shock. Thus:

30" Tone: 1" Shock → *Fear*
   NS   **US**   **UR**

(In a proper conditioning procedure, each of these conditioning trials is separated by an interval of time, perhaps 30 minutes.) In the initial phase, the rat will become emotionally upset (fearful) whenever it receives a shock and will stop pressing the lever. As conditioning proceeds, however, the tone too will come to elicit fear, and the rat will stop pressing the lever when it hears the tone.

30" Tone → *Fear*
 CS   CR

Thus, the degree to which lever pressing for food is suppressed in the presence of the 30-second tone can be used as an indirect measure of the extent to which the tone elicits fear. Think of the procedure as similar to a gunfighter walking in and out of a saloon. The extent to which the saloon patrons fear the gunfighter can be accurately measured by the extent to which they stop talking to each other when he is in the saloon (you can hear a pin drop!) and resume talking when he leaves the saloon. Similarly, the rat's level of fear can be assessed by the extent to which it stops lever pressing when the tone is sounding and resumes lever pressing when the tone is not sounding.

On a more formal level, conditioned suppression is measured in the form of a *suppression ratio*. A suppression ratio is the number of responses emitted during the CS period divided by the combined number emitted during the CS period and the number emitted during the same length period immediately preceding the CS. Thus,

$$\text{Suppression Ratio} = \frac{\#\text{ of CS responses}}{\#\text{ of CS responses} + \#\text{ of pre-CS responses}}$$

For example, imagine that a rat emits 20 responses during the 30-second pre-CS period followed by 0 responses during a 30-second CS period. In other words, there is total suppression of responding during the CS period. The suppression ratio would be:

$$\frac{0}{0 + 20} = 0$$

Thus, a suppression ratio of 0 indicates total suppression of responding. But what if instead there was only a partial suppression of responding during the CS? For example, what if the rat emitted 10 responses during the CS period? In this case, the suppression ratio would be:

$$\frac{10}{10 + 20} = \frac{10}{30} = .33$$

Now if there was no suppression of responding—that is, the rat emitted the same number of responses during the CS period as during the pre-CS period—the suppression ratio would be:

$$\frac{20}{20 + 20} = \frac{20}{40} = .5$$

Note how the suppression ratio will generally vary between 0 and .5, with a lower ratio indicating greater suppression and more effective conditioning than a higher ratio. A ratio of 0 indicates greater suppression and stronger fear conditioning than a ratio of .33, which in turn indicates greater suppression and stronger fear conditioning than a ratio of .5. Students often find this confusing since the stronger conditioning is indicated by the lower number, which is opposite to the way most ratios work. To keep it straight, simply remember that *a lower ratio indicates less responding, and less responding indicates greater suppression.*

The CER paradigm has proven to be a useful method for investigating fear conditioning in animals and is, in fact, commonly used to study classical conditioning processes. But be especially careful to note that the CR in this type of procedure is the covert response of fear; the CR is *not* the reduction in lever pressing, which serves as the indirect measure of the covert response of fear.

Note that classical conditioning can transform a normally aversive stimulus into an appetitive stimulus. Pavlov found that if a dog received a shock to one of its paws and then received food, the dog would eventually begin to salivate in response to the shock. The dog's overt reactions to the shock, such as tail wagging, further indicated that the shock had lost its aversiveness. Interestingly, if the shock was then applied to a different paw, the dog would not salivate but instead reacted with discomfort. The perception of shock as pleasurable appeared to be quite specific to the body part involved in the conditioning.

As you may already have guessed, this same process might partially account for the development of masochistic tendencies (the tendency to perceive painful stimulation as pleasurable) in humans. The painful stimulation from being whipped, for example, has for some people become associated with feelings of sexual arousal, as a result of which the painful stimulation itself can elicit arousal. Interestingly, as with Pavlov's dogs, people who are masochistic do not perceive all pain as pleasurable; rather, it is only the type of pain that is connected with their erotic experiences (e.g., being whipped) that is perceived as pleasurable. The pain they feel from accidentally stubbing a toe or banging a shin is as aversive for them as it is for anyone else (Rathus, Nevid, & Fichner-Rathus, 2000).

QUICK QUIZ H

1. In _____ conditioning, the US is an event that is usually considered unpleasant and that the organism avoids.

2. In _____ conditioning, the US is an event that is usually considered pleasant and that the organism seeks out.

3. Learning to associate the corner bar with the happy times you experience in that bar is an example of _____ conditioning.

4. Learning to associate your refrigerator with the nauseating smell of spoiled food is an example of _____ conditioning.

5. In a c_____ e_____ response (CER) paradigm, the level of fear elicited by a CS is indicated by the degree to which the rat's rate of lever pressing for food (decreases/increases) _____ in the presence of that stimulus.

6. The CER paradigm is also known as a c_____ s_____ paradigm.

7. The suppression ratio is the number of (pre-CS/CS/post-CS) _____ responses divided by the number of _____ responses plus the number of _____ responses.

8. Total suppression of behavior results in a suppression ratio of (.5/0) _____ whereas no suppression of behavior will result in a suppression ratio of around _____.

And Furthermore

Classical Conditioning and Interpersonal Attraction

Classical conditioning may play an important role in interpersonal attraction. According to the reinforcement-affect model of attraction (Byrne & Clore, 1970; see also Baron & Byrne, 1997), the extent to which we are attracted to someone can be significantly affected by the degree to which the person is associated with events that elicit positive emotions. For this reason, we are generally attracted to people who say and do the kinds of things that make us feel good. Eventually, we feel good just being around such people.

Interestingly, the model also predicts that we can become attracted to a person who is only incidentally associated with positive events. Experiments have revealed that events as innocuous as pleasant background music or a positive news story on the radio can heighten the extent to which a person we are meeting is perceived as attractive. Of course, this means that associating ourselves with pleasant stimuli—pleasant music, attractive clothing, and even a clean car—during an initial date can greatly facilitate the possibility of a second date.

The reinforcement-affect model also suggests that we are less attracted to someone who is associated with aversive events. Obviously, dressing like a slob or drinking to the point of vomiting during a first date is probably not a good idea. Less obviously, inadvertently hearing bad news on the radio or really annoying music may also undermine your prospects for a second date. On the other hand, there may be times when you *want* to be perceived as less attractive. A letter once appeared in a newspaper advice column in which a woman described how she finally managed to dissuade a persistent acquaintance from continually asking her out. She agreed to a date and then ate plenty of garlic beforehand! Her suitor was apparently not a big garlic fan, and she had no further difficulties with him.

Excitatory and Inhibitory Conditioning

In all of the examples so far, and as it is traditionally defined, the NS is associated with the presentation of a US. The metronome is associated with the presentation of food, the dog is associated with a painful bite, and the tone is associated with shock. Conditioning in which the NS is associated with the presentation of a US is known as *excitatory conditioning*. The result of excitatory conditioning is that the CS comes to elicit a certain response, such as salivation or fear.

But what if a stimulus is associated with the absence of the US rather than its presentation? What if, for example, a vicious dog always bites you except when its owner is present? The owner then is a sort of safety signal that indicates the absence of a painful bite. Conditioning in which the NS is associated with the absence or removal of a US is known as *inhibitory conditioning*. The result of inhibitory conditioning is that the CS comes to inhibit the occurrence of a certain response—that is, the response is less likely to occur when that stimulus is present. Thus, although the dog is an excitatory CS for fear, the owner is an inhibitory CS for fear, and your fear of the dog will be suppressed when the owner is present. Similarly, if a rat is consistently shocked when a tone is presented, the tone will become an excitatory stimulus for fear. But if the rat is never shocked when a tone and a light are presented together, the light will become an inhibitory CS for fear because it explicitly signals the absence of shock. In such procedures, the excitatory CS is usually labeled a CS+, and the inhibitory CS is labeled a CS–.

Traditionally, researchers have focused on the study of excitatory conditioning, and most of the basic principles of classical conditioning have been established using excitatory procedures. For this reason, most of the examples in this text are examples of excitatory conditioning. In recent years, however, the study of inhibitory conditioning has begun to attract a good deal of interest (Domjan, 2003).

1. Conditioning associated with the removal of a US is known as _____ conditioning, whereas conditioning associated with the presentation of a US is known as _____ conditioning.

2. Your grandmother always cooks great meals except when your vegetarian sister is present. As a result, you usually salivate a great deal when sitting at your grandmother's table for a meal, but not when your sister is present. Your grandmother's table is an _____ CS for salivation, while your vegetarian sister is an _____ CS for salivation.

3. Most of the basic principles of classical conditioning have been established using procedures that involve _____ conditioning.

4. A conditioned excitatory stimulus (an excitatory CS) is one that is associated with the (presentation/removal) _____ of a US; a conditioned inhibitory stimulus (an inhibitory CS) is one that is associated with the (presentation/removal) _____ of a US.

5. An excitatory CS for fear is one that will (elicit/suppress) _____ a fear response; an inhibitory CS for fear is one that will (elicit/suppress) _____ a fear response.

6. For the residents of Berlin and London during World War II, an air-raid siren would have been a (CS+/CS–) _____ for anxiety, while the all-clear siren would have been a (CS+/CS–) _____ for anxiety.

7. A click is followed by food, while a click and a buzzing noise is never followed by food. In this case, the click will become a (CS+/CS–) _____ and the buzzing noise will become a (CS+/CS–) _____.

Temporal Arrangement of Stimuli

In the classical conditioning examples discussed to this point, the NS was always presented before the US. This temporal arrangement, though, is only one of several ways to arrange the NS and US. In this section, we outline four such arrangements and note the effectiveness of each for producing a conditioned response.

1. **Delayed Conditioning.** In *delayed conditioning,* the onset of the NS precedes the onset of the US, and the two stimuli overlap. For example, if we want a rat to associate a tone with a brief shock, we first present the tone and then, while the tone is still on, present a shock. As shown in Figure 3.8a, the onset of the tone precedes the onset of the shock and the tone is still on when the shock is presented. (Note that it is the point at which the two stimuli are turned on, rather than turned off, that is critical.) A delayed conditioning procedure is often the best arrangement for conditioning, especially if the time between the onset of the NS and the onset of the US (known as the *interstimulus interval* or *ISI*) is relatively short. When conditioning certain autonomic responses (responses controlled by

FIGURE 3.8   Four ways in which presentation of the NS and US can be temporally arranged.

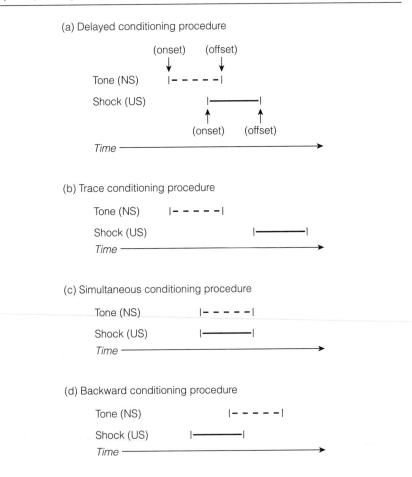

(a) Delayed conditioning procedure

(b) Trace conditioning procedure

(c) Simultaneous conditioning procedure

(d) Backward conditioning procedure

the autonomic nervous system), such as salivation, the optimal ISI is generally in the range of a few seconds. When conditioning skeletal responses (responses controlled by skeletal muscles), such as the eyeblink reflex, the optimal ISI is about a half second. Thus, conditioning generally works best when the onset of the NS more or less immediately precedes the onset of the US; this fact is consistent with the notion that the NS generally serves as a predictor of the US, a notion that is discussed further in Chapter 5. Nevertheless, some forms of classical conditioning do not require a close temporal pairing between the NS and US. One such form, known as taste aversion conditioning, is described in Chapter 11.

2. **Trace Conditioning.** In *trace conditioning,* the onset and offset of the NS precede the onset of the US. In other words, the NS occurs before the US, and the two stimuli do not overlap. For example, a tone is turned on and then off, and this is then followed by the presentation of a shock (see Figure 3.8b). The time between the offset of the NS and the onset of the US (e.g., between the point when the tone was turned *off* and the shock was turned *on*) is called the *trace interval.* Because the tone is no longer present when the shock occurs, you might say that the organism has to "remember" the occurrence of the tone (or, in cognitive parlance, have some "memory trace" of it) to be able to associate the two. Trace conditioning can be almost as effective as delayed conditioning if the trace interval is relatively short (no more than a few seconds). If the trace interval is longer than that, conditioning is unlikely to occur.

3. **Simultaneous Conditioning.** In *simultaneous conditioning,* the onset of the NS and the onset of the US are simultaneous. For example, a tone and a shock are turned on at the same time (see Figure 3.8c). Although simultaneous conditioning involves the closest possible contiguity between the NS and the US, this procedure usually results in poor conditioning. One reason for this is that if the NS occurs at the same time as the US, the NS is no longer a good predictor of the US.

4. **Backward Conditioning.** In *backward conditioning,* the onset of the NS follows the onset of the US. In other words, the US is presented first and the NS is presented later. For example, the rat receives a shock and then hears a tone (see Figure 3.8d). Backward conditioning is traditionally considered the least effective procedure for conditioning. This is especially true for conditioning of an excitatory response like salivation. Nevertheless, under some circumstances, backward excitatory conditioning can be achieved, such as when the NS is a "biologically relevant" stimulus for fear (Keith-Lucas & Guttman, 1975). For example, if instead of using a tone as the NS for shock, we use the sight of a snake, then backward conditioning might occur (see Figure 3.9).

Why does backward conditioning work with the snake but not the tone? Some researchers (e.g., Seligman, 1971) have proposed that many animals have an inherited predisposition to fear certain types of events. From this perspective, rats have an inherited predisposition to fear snakes, because

FIGURE 3.9 A potentially effective backward conditioning procedure in which the NS is a biologically relevant stimulus for a conditioned fear response.

Snake (NS) |– – – – –|

Shock (US) |————|

Time ——————————————→

poisonous snakes have constituted a significant threat to rats throughout their evolutionary history. This predisposition is so strong that even if the snake is presented after the shock, the fear elicited by the shock still becomes associated with the snake. (Needless to say, such predispositions would also facilitate conditioning using a delayed, trace, or simultaneous procedure.)

Backward conditioning can also result in inhibitory conditioning. For example, if a tone sounds just as a shock is being *terminated*, then the tone essentially predicts the removal of shock. The tone in this case may become a safety signal (CS−) that inhibits the occurrence of fear. Similarly, if a child suffers from severe asthma attacks, but feels relief when the doctor gives him an injection, the doctor's presence will become a safety signal that effectively inhibits the child's sense of distress. Whenever this doctor is nearby, the child will feel especially safe and comfortable.

Thus, although delayed conditioning is traditionally thought of as the most effective arrangement, conditioning can occur with other arrangements as well. Although beyond the scope of this text, recent evidence in fact indicates that each type of arrangement can have an impact on behavior (see Domjan, 2003).

QUICK QUIZ J

1. The most successful temporal arrangement for conditioning is delayed conditioning, in which the onset of the NS (precedes/follows) _____ the onset of the US, and the two stimuli (overlap/do not overlap) _____.

2. In delayed conditioning, the time between the onset of the NS and the onset of the US is called the _____ interval (abbreviated _____).

3. In trace conditioning, the (onset/offset) _____ and _____ of the NS precedes the _____ of the US.

4. In trace conditioning, the time between the _____ of the NS and the _____ of the US is called the _____ interval. Trace conditioning can be effective if this interval is relatively (long/short) _____.

5. In simultaneous conditioning, the _____ of the NS occurs at the same time as the _____ of the US. Simultaneous conditioning usually results in (good/poor) _____ conditioning.

6. In backward conditioning, the (US/NS) _____ is presented first and the (US/NS) _____ is presented later. Backward conditioning is generally considered to result in (good/poor) _____ conditioning.

7. Backward conditioning can result in excitatory conditioning of fear when the NS is a b_____ relevant stimulus for fear. Backward conditioning can also result in inhibitory conditioning when the NS signals the (presentation/removal) _____ of the US.

8. Suppose that we attempt to condition a reflex response of sneezing using a flower as the NS and pollen as the US. Name each of the four NS-US arrangements listed.

a._____ conditioning: **Flower** |----|

                                   Pollen |—|

b._____ conditioning: **Flower** |--------|

                                   Pollen |—|

c._____ conditioning: **Flower** |----|

                                   Pollen |———|

d._____ conditioning: **Flower** |----|

                                   Pollen |—|

SUMMARY

In general, elicited behaviors are involuntary reactions to specific stimuli. Examples of elicited behaviors include reflexes and fixed action patterns. Repeated presentations of the same stimulus may decrease the strength of a behavior (known as habituation) or increase the strength of a behavior (known as sensitization) depending on the intensity and evolutionary significance of the eliciting stimulus. A similar dual mechanism is evident in the opponent-process theory of emotion, in which an emotionally arousing event elicits an emotional response (the a-process) that in turn elicits a compensatory response (the b-process).

In classical conditioning, a neutral stimulus is associated with some other stimulus that naturally elicits a response, and as a result the neutral stimulus also comes to elicit a response. In Pavlov's basic procedure, the unconditioned stimulus (US) is the stimulus that naturally elicits a response, and the unconditioned response (UR) is the response that is naturally elicited by the US. The conditioned stimulus (CS) is the stimulus that, although initially a neutral stimulus (NS), comes to elicit a response because it has been associated with the US. The conditioned response (CR) is the response that is elicited by the CS.

In appetitive conditioning, the US is an appetitive stimulus such as food; in aversive conditioning, the US is an aversive stimulus such as a shock. Studies of aversive conditioning are often carried out using a conditioned suppression procedure in which a rat stops lever pressing for food in the presence of a tone that has been paired with a shock. In excitatory conditioning the NS is associated with the presentation of the US, whereas in inhibitory conditioning the NS is associated with the removal of the US.

There can be various temporal arrangements of the NS and US in classical conditioning. In delayed conditioning, the onset of the NS precedes the onset of the US and overlaps with it. In trace conditioning, the onset and offset of the NS precede the onset of the US. In simultaneous conditioning, the NS and US are presented at the same time. Finally, in backward conditioning, the onset of the NS follows the onset of the US. Delayed conditioning and trace conditioning are usually the most effective procedures, with backward conditioning being the least effective. However, backward conditioning can occur under some circumstances, such as when the NS is a biologically relevant stimulus for fear and the US is an aversive stimulus.

SUGGESTED READINGS

Pavlov, I. P. (1927). *Conditioned reflexes* (G. V. Anrep, Trans.). London: Oxford University Press. The best of Pavlov's own books on classical conditioning.

Windholz, G. (1997). Ivan P. Pavlov: An overview of his life and psychological work. *American Psychologist, 52,* 941–946. This commemorative issue of *American Psychologist* on Pavlov's work also contains several other articles on Pavlov's work and on the modern-day status of classical conditioning.

STUDY QUESTIONS

1. What is a reflex?
2. Describe the startle response, orienting response, and flexion response.
3. Describe, or diagram, the sequence of events in a reflex arc.
4. Define fixed action pattern. What is a sign stimulus or releaser?
5. Define habituation and sensitization.
6. What is the effect of high versus low versus moderate stimulus intensity on habituation and sensitization?
7. Distinguish between long-term and short-term habituation.
8. Describe the evolutionary significance of trends in habituation and sensitization.
9. Describe the phenomenon of dishabituation.
10. Define the opponent-process theory of emotion.
11. List three main characteristics of opponent processes.
12. Define classical conditioning.
13. Diagram an example of a classical conditioning procedure using the appropriate abbreviations to label each component.
14. Define the terms *unconditioned stimulus* and *unconditioned response*.
15. Define the terms *conditioned stimulus* and *conditioned response*.
16. Distinguish between appetitive and aversive conditioning.
17. Describe the conditioned suppression (or CER) procedure. Explain how to calculate a suppression ratio.

18. Distinguish between excitatory and inhibitory conditioning.
19. Name and diagram four temporal arrangements of the NS and US. Which two temporal arrangements of the NS and US are traditionally considered to be most effective?

CONCEPT REVIEW

appetitive conditioning. Conditioning procedure in which the US is an event that is usually considered pleasant and that an organism seeks out.

aversive conditioning. Conditioning procedure in which the US is an event that is usually considered unpleasant and that an organism avoids.

backward conditioning. Conditioning procedure in which the onset of the NS follows the onset of the US.

classical conditioning. A process whereby one stimulus that does not elicit a certain response is associated with a second stimulus that does; as a result, the first stimulus also comes to elicit a response.

conditioned response (CR). The response, often similar to the unconditioned response, that is elicited by the conditioned stimulus.

conditioned stimulus (CS). Any stimulus that, although initially neutral, comes to elicit a response because it has been associated with an unconditioned stimulus.

delayed conditioning. Conditioning procedure in which the onset of the NS precedes the onset of the US, and the two stimuli overlap.

dishabituation. The reappearance of a habituated response following the presentation of a seemingly irrelevant novel stimulus.

excitatory conditioning. Conditioning procedure in which the NS is associated with the *presentation* of a US.

fixed action pattern. A fixed sequence of responses elicited by a specific stimulus.

flexion response. The automatic response of jerking one's hand or foot away from a hot or sharp object.

habituation. A decrease in the strength of an elicited behavior following repeated presentations of the eliciting stimulus.

inhibitory conditioning. Conditioning procedure in which the NS is associated with the *absence* or *removal* of a US.

opponent-process theory. A theory proposing that an emotional event elicits two competing processes: (1) an a-process (or primary process) directly elicited by the event, and (2) a b-process (or opponent process) that is elicited by the a-process and serves to counteract the a-process.

orienting response. The automatic positioning of oneself to facilitate attending to a stimulus.

reflex arc. A neural structure that underlies many reflexes and consists of a sensory neuron, an interneuron, and a motor neuron.

reflex. A relatively simple, involuntary response to a stimulus.

sensitization. An increase in the strength of an elicited behavior following repeated presentations of the eliciting stimulus.

sign stimulus (or releaser). A specific stimulus that elicits a fixed action pattern.

simultaneous conditioning. Conditioning procedure in which the onset of the NS and the onset of the US are simultaneous.

startle response. A defensive reaction to a sudden, unexpected stimulus, which involves automatic tightening of skeletal muscles and various hormonal and visceral changes.

trace conditioning. Conditioning procedure in which the onset and offset of the NS precede the onset of the US.

unconditioned response (UR). The response that is naturally elicited by the unconditioned stimulus.

unconditioned stimulus (US). A stimulus that naturally elicits a response.

CHAPTER TEST

4. A sudden loud noise is likely to elicit a(n) _____ reaction, which is a reflexive defensive response to a sudden stimulus.

13. With repeated presentations of the emotional event, the b-process (increases/decreases) _____ in both _____ and _____.

23. Seeing a wasp land on your arm and then watching it as it stings you is an example of a _____conditioning procedure; noticing the wasp at the same moment that you feel the sting is an example of a _____ conditioning procedure.

6. When a subordinate dog submits to a threatening display from a dominant dog, it will often roll over on its back and display its stomach. This sequence of actions is called a _____, and the threatening display from the dominant dog is called the _____ stimulus or _____ for these actions.

14. Classical conditioning is also known as P_____ conditioning or _____ conditioning. In the latter case, the elicited behaviors are referred to as _____.

9. The faint sound of a jackhammer several blocks away will likely result in _____, but the extremely loud sound of a jackhammer right outside your window will likely result in _____. The moderately loud sound of a jackhammer half a block away may result in a period of _____ followed by _____.

26. In general, aversive conditioning occurs (more/less) _____ readily than appetitive conditioning.

2. The most basic type of elicited behavior is the _____, which is a simple, involuntary response to a stimulus.

12. According to the opponent-process theory of emotion, b-processes are (slow/quick) _____ to increase and (slow/quick) _____ to decrease.

18. Imagine an eyeblink conditioning procedure in which the sound of a click is paired with a puff of air to the eye. Each pairing of the click and air puff during conditioning is referred to as a(n) _____.

11. In the opening scenario, Uma witnessed her boyfriend flirting with another woman. First, she experienced intense anger. Later, however, when he apologized for his actions and was very attentive to her, she experienced unusually strong feelings of attraction toward him. An explanation for this pattern of emotional changes is provided by the _____ theory of emotion. In this case, Uma's feelings of anger are an example of the _____ process, and her feelings of affection following his apology are an example of the _____ process.

1. Behaviors that are automatically drawn out by the stimuli that precede them are referred to as _____ behaviors.

20. When you opened the refrigerator last evening, the putrid smell of rotten eggs made you feel extremely nauseous. Today, when you are about to open the refrigerator again, you find yourself experiencing a slight twinge of nausea, even though the refrigerator has been thoroughly cleaned. In classical conditioning terms, the refrigerator has become a(n) _____ stimulus that now elicits a(n) _____ response of nausea. In this case, the nausea produced by the sight of the refrigerator is likely to be (less/more) _____ severe than the nausea produced by the smell of rotten eggs.

5. The reflexive action of pulling your hand away from a hot pot handle is activated through a _____: a neural structure underlying simple reflexes that consists of a (in correct order) _____ _____.

25. Feeling a sting and then seeing the wasp on your arm is an example of a _____ conditioning procedure, which in this case may be (effective/ineffective) _____ because the CS is a _____ for a fear response.

10. You finally habituate to the faint sound of a jackhammer half a block away, such that you cease to notice it. The lights in your house then flicker, at which point you again notice the sound of the jackhammer. This is an example of the process of _____.

15. Imagine an eyeblink conditioning procedure in which the sound of a click is paired with a puff of air to the eye. The puff of air is called the _____ stimulus (abbreviated _____), and the eyeblink that it elicits is called the _____ response (abbreviated _____).

30. In general, long-term habituation is most likely to occur when the stimulus is presented at (narrowly/widely) _____ spaced intervals; in this case, the ability to respond tends to recover (slowly/quickly) _____ when the stimulus is no longer presented.

19. When you opened the refrigerator one evening, the putrid smell of rotten eggs made you feel extremely nauseous. In classical conditioning terms, the putrid smell is a(n) _____ stimulus that elicits a(n) _____ response of nausea.

28. Inadvertently touching a hot object is likely to elicit a(n) _____ response; the sound of a gunshot is likely to elicit a(n) _____ response; the sound of someone talking behind you may elicit a(n) _____ response.

7. Fixed action patterns are sometimes called _____ behaviors because they are often unique to a certain species.

3. The reflexive action of a dog pricking up its ears in response to a sound is an example of a(n) _____ response, which consists of movements designed to facilitate _____.

31. To calculate a suppression ratio, divide the number of responses that occur (during/following/preceding) _____ the CS by the number that occur _____ the CS plus the number that occur _____ the CS.

17. Imagine an eyeblink conditioning procedure in which the sound of a click is paired with a puff of air to the eye. After conditioning, the click becomes a(n) _____ stimulus (abbreviated _____) because it now elicits an eyeblink. The eyeblink elicited by the click is called the _____ response (abbreviated _____).

27. Dana always feels very relaxed when she takes her large dog for a walk, even though the neighborhood is relatively dangerous. This appears to be an example of _____, with the dog functioning as an _____ CS (abbreviated _____).

21. When you opened the refrigerator one evening, the putrid smell of rotten eggs made you feel extremely nauseous. The subsequent response of nausea to the sight of the refrigerator is an example of (aversive/appetitive) _____ conditioning as well as (excitatory/inhibitory) _____ conditioning.

16. Imagine an eyeblink conditioning procedure in which the sound of a click is paired with a puff of air to the eye. Before conditioning, the sound of the click does not elicit an eyeblink; it is therefore considered to be a(n) _____ stimulus.

24. In an experiment involving the conditioning of an eyeblink response to the sound of a click, hearing the click and then a second later feeling the puff of air in your eye is an example of a _____ conditioning procedure. Conversely, feeling the puff of air and then hearing the click is an example of a _____ conditioning procedure. In general, the (former/latter) _____ procedure is likely to produce more effective conditioning.

8. In a restaurant, the parents of a very noisy child hardly notice the commotion. This is an example of _____. However, the customers at neighboring tables are becoming increasingly annoyed by the child. This is an example of _____.

22. Brett is allergic to bee stings. He eats and drinks heartily when he is inside the restaurant, but not when he is seated on the outdoor patio surrounded by flowers. This circumstance is similar to the _____ paradigm, which is also known as the _____ (CER) procedure.

29. In a conditioned suppression ratio, a score of _____ indicates total suppression of the behavior, while a score of around _____ indicates no suppression.

Visit the book companion Web site at <http://www.academic.cengage.com/psychology/powell> for additional practice questions, answers to the Quick Quizzes, practice review exams, and additional exercises and information.

ANSWERS TO CHAPTER TEST

1. elicited
2. reflex
3. orienting; attending to a stimulus
4. startle
5. reflex arc; sensory neuron; interneuron; motor neuron
6. fixed action pattern; sign; releaser
7. species-specific
8. habituation; sensitization
9. habituation; sensitization; sensitization; habituation
10. dishabituation
11. opponent-process; primary (or a-) process; opponent (or b-) process
12. slow; slow
13. increases; strength; duration
14. Pavlovian; respondent; respondents
15. unconditioned stimulus (US); unconditioned response (UR)
16. neutral
17. conditioned; CS; conditioned; CR
18. conditioning trial
19. unconditioned; unconditioned
20. conditioned; conditioned; less
21. aversive; excitatory
22. conditioned suppression; conditioned emotional response
23. delayed; simultaneous
24. trace; backward; former
25. backward; effective; biologically relevant stimulus
26. more
27. inhibitory; inhibitory; CS−
28. flexion; startle; orienting
29. 0; .5
30. widely; slowly
31. during; during; preceding

Classical Conditioning: Basic Phenomena and Various Complexities

Jana enjoys being wildly unpredictable in her relationships, believing that most men find unpredictable women quite exciting. She cancels dates at the last minute, shows up on the guy's doorstep at odd hours of the day or night, and tries as much as possible to be completely spontaneous. Once, she stole a man's bowling trophy and cheese grater, just to see if he would notice. Unfortunately, many of the guys she goes out with seem to be rather stressed out and neurotic, though it usually takes a while before this becomes apparent. She is starting to wonder if there are any good men around these days.

Some Basic Conditioning Phenomena

Acquisition

In classical conditioning, **acquisition** is the process of developing and strengthening a conditioned response through repeated pairings of neutral stimulus (NS) with an unconditioned stimulus (US). In general, acquisition proceeds rapidly during early conditioning trials, then gradually levels off. The maximum amount of conditioning that can take place in a particular situation is known as the *asymptote* of conditioning (see Figure 4.1).

The asymptote of conditioning, as well as the speed of conditioning, is dependent on several factors. In general, *more-intense USs produce stronger and more rapid conditioning than do less-intense USs.* For example, we can obtain stronger conditioning of a salivary response when the US consists of a large amount of food or a highly preferred food than if it consists of a small amount or less preferred food. Likewise, a severe bite from a dog

FIGURE 4.1 A typical acquisition curve in which strength of conditioning increases rapidly during the first few trials and then gradually levels off over subsequent trials.

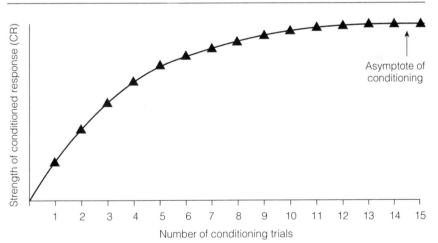

will result in a stronger conditioned fear response than a minor bite will. Similarly, *more-intense NSs result in stronger and more rapid conditioning than do less-intense NSs.* For example, a loud metronome that has been paired with food produces a stronger response of salivation than a faint metronome that has been paired with food. And, not surprisingly, conditioned fear responses to dogs are more readily acquired if the person is bitten by a large dog than by a small dog.

1. The process of strengthening a conditioned response through repeated pairings of an NS with a US is known as _____.

2. In general, conditioning proceeds more (rapidly/slowly) _____ during the early trials of a conditioning procedure.

3. The maximum amount of learning that can take place in a given situation is known as the _____ of learning.

4. In general, a (more/less) _____ intense US produces better conditioning.

5. In general, a (more/less) _____ intense NS produces better conditioning.

Extinction, Spontaneous Recovery, and Disinhibition

Given that a certain stimulus now elicits a conditioned response, is there any way to eliminate the response? In a *process* known as **extinction,** a conditioned response can be weakened or eliminated when the conditioned stimulus (CS) is repeatedly presented in the absence of the US. The term *extinction* also applies to the *procedure* whereby this happens, namely, the repeated presentation of the CS in the absence of the US.

Suppose, for example, that a metronome has been paired with food such that it now elicits a conditioned response of salivation:

> Metronome: Food → *Salivation*
>   NS   US   UR
> Metronome → *Salivation*
>   CS   CR

If we now continue to present the metronome by itself and never again pair it with food (each presentation of the metronome being known as an "extinction trial"), the conditioned response of salivation will eventually die out—that is, the CR of salivation will have been *extinguished.*

> Metronome → No salivation
>   "NS"   —

The process of extinction is the decrease in the strength of the CR, and the procedure of extinction is the means by which this is carried out, namely, the repeated presentation of the metronome without the food.

In a similar manner, if a dog that once bit me never again bites me, my fear response to the dog should eventually extinguish. Unfortunately, some people who were once bitten by a dog continue to fear that dog as well as other dogs, in which case we might say that they have a "phobia" about dogs. But if the person has never again been bitten by the dog, why is his or her fear so persistent? One reason is that people who fear dogs tend to avoid them, and to the extent that they avoid them, their fear response cannot be extinguished. As you will see in later chapters, this tendency to avoid a feared event is a major factor in the development and maintenance of a phobia, and treatment procedures for phobias are often based on preventing this avoidance response from occurring.

Once a CR has been extinguished, one should not assume that the effects of conditioning have been completely eliminated. For this reason, in the above diagram the "NS" following extinction has been placed in quotation marks, since it is no longer a pure neutral stimulus. For one thing, *a response that has been extinguished can be reacquired quite rapidly when the CS (or NS) is again paired with the US.* If we again pair the metronome with food following an extinction procedure, it may take only a few pairings before we achieve a fairly strong level of conditioning. Likewise, if I somehow manage to overcome my phobia of dogs, I might rapidly reacquire that phobia if I again have a frightening experience with dogs.

As further evidence that extinction does not completely eliminate the effects of conditioning, an extinguished response can reappear even in the absence of further pairings between the CS and US. Suppose, for example, that we do extinguish a dog's conditioned salivary response to a metronome by repeatedly presenting the metronome without food. By the end of the extinction session, the metronome no longer elicits salivation. However, if we come back the next morning and sound the metronome, the dog will very likely salivate. In everyday terms, it is almost as if the dog has forgotten that the metronome no longer predicts food. As a result, we are forced to conduct another series of extinction trials, repeatedly sounding the metronome without the food. After several trials, the response is again extinguished. The next day, however, the dog again starts salivating when we present the metronome. At this point, we might be tempted to conclude that we have an awfully dumb dog on our hands. The dog, however, is simply displaying a phenomenon known as spontaneous recovery.

Spontaneous recovery is the reappearance of a conditioned response following a rest period after extinction. Fortunately, spontaneous recovery does not last forever. In general, each time the response recovers it is somewhat weaker and is extinguished more quickly than before (see Figure 4.2). Therefore, after several extinction sessions, we should be able to sound the metronome at the start of the session and find little or no salivation.

The phenomenon of spontaneous recovery is particularly important to remember when attempting to extinguish a conditioned fear response. For example, we might arrange for a dog-phobic child to spend several hours with a dog. At the end of that time, the child's fear of the dog might seem to have been totally eliminated. Nevertheless, we should expect that the fear will at least partially recover the next time the child is confronted with a dog, and that several sessions of extinction may be needed before the fear is completely

FIGURE 4.2   Hypothetical results illustrating a decline in spontaneous recovery across repeated sessions of extinction.

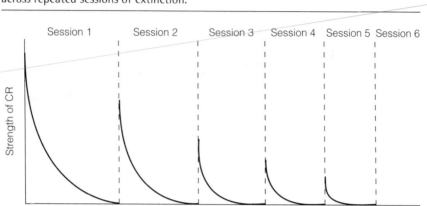

eliminated. Similarly, if you feel terribly anxious with a new date at the start of the evening but more at ease after a couple of hours, do not be disappointed if you again find yourself becoming quite anxious at the start of your next date. It may take several dates with that person before you feel comfortable right from the outset. Likewise, following a breakup, it may take a while before your feelings of attraction to the other person are finally extinguished, and even then they may intermittently reappear for a considerable period of time.

To Pavlov (1927), the phenomenon of spontaneous recovery indicated that extinction is not simply a process of unlearning the conditioning that has taken place. Rather, extinction involves learning something new, namely, to inhibit the occurrence of the CR in the presence of the CS. For example, rather than unlearning the response of salivation to the metronome during extinction, the dog learns to inhibit the response of salivation to the metronome, with the connection between the metronome and salivation still remaining intact on some underlying level. Spontaneous recovery may therefore represent the partial weakening of this inhibition during the rest period between extinction sessions.

Support for the notion that extinction involves a buildup of inhibition is also provided by a phenomenon known as disinhibition. **Disinhibition** is the sudden recovery of a response during an extinction procedure when a novel stimulus is introduced. For example, if we are in the process of extinguishing conditioning to a metronome but then present a novel humming noise in the background, the sound of the metronome may again elicit a considerable amount of salivation.

Metronome: Food → *Salivation*
      NS   US   UR
Metronome → *Salivation*
      CS   CR

Following repeated presentations of the metronome:

> **Metronome** → *Weak salivation* **(Partial extinction)**
> **CS** **CR**

(Presentation of the novel humming noise in background)

> **Novel humming noise { Metronome** → *Salivation*
> **CS** **CR**

Similarly, if your anxiety while giving a speech in class gradually fades, it may suddenly recover when a noisy ceiling fan starts up or someone walks in late. (Note that the phenomenon of disinhibition is similar to dishabituation, discussed in Chapter 3, in which the presentation of a novel stimulus results in the reappearance of a habituated response. To distinguish these concepts, it will help to remember that dis*habituation* involves the reappearance of a *habituated* response, and dis*inhibition* involves the recovery of a response that has become partially *inhibited* due to extinction.)[1]

1. In the *process* of extinction, a conditioned response grows weaker because _____.

2. The *procedure* of extinction involves _____

3. Once a CR has been extinguished, reacquisition of that response tends to occur (more/less) _____ rapidly than the original conditioning.

4. The sudden recovery of an extinguished response following some delay after extinction is known as s_____ r_____.

5. With repeated sessions of extinction, each time a response recovers, it is usually somewhat (weaker/stronger) _____ and extinguishes more (slowly/quickly) _____.

6. Pavlov believed that this phenomenon indicates that extinction involves the (inhibition/unlearning) _____ of a conditioned response.

7. The sudden recovery of a response during an extinction procedure when a novel stimulus is introduced is called _____.

QUICK QUIZ B

Stimulus Generalization and Discrimination

Classical conditioning would not be very useful if it only enabled us to learn about relationships between particular stimuli. For example, if we are bitten by a spider, it would not be very helpful for us to fear only that particular spider (which, in

---

[1] Another reason that extinction of real-world fears can be difficult is that we might not identify all of the CSs that are helping to elicit the fear response. For example, in the case of a dog phobia, CSs other than the dog—such as the sound of growling or worried looks on the faces of others—may also be involved. Presenting only the stimulus of a aggressive dog over and over again will not necessarily weaken the association between those additional CSs and the US.

any case, we probably obliterated the moment it bit us). From an evolutionary perspective, it would be far more adaptive to learn to fear other spiders as well, particularly those spiders that look similar to the one that bit us. Fortunately, this is precisely what happens, through a process known as stimulus generalization.

In classical conditioning, *stimulus generalization* is the tendency for a CR to occur in the presence of a stimulus that is similar to the CS. In general, the more similar the stimulus is to the original CS, the stronger the response. For example, if a dog is conditioned to salivate to a tone that has a pitch of 2,000 Hz, it will salivate to similar tones as well. But it will salivate more strongly to a 1,900-Hz tone or a 2,100-Hz tone than it will to a 1,000-Hz tone or a 3,000-Hz tone. In other words, tones that are most similar to the original CS will elicit the strongest response. Similarly, after being bitten by a dog, a child will probably fear not only that particular dog but other dogs as well. And the child is particularly likely to fear dogs that closely resemble the dog that bit him.

The process of generalization is most readily apparent when the stimuli involved are physically similar and vary along a continuum. Tones of varying pitch or loudness and lights of varying color or brightness are examples of such stimuli. However, generalization can also occur across nonphysical dimensions, particularly in humans who use language. *Semantic generalization* is the generalization of a conditioned response to verbal stimuli that are similar in *meaning* to the CS. For example, if humans are exposed to a conditioning procedure in which the sight of the word *car* is paired with shock, that word eventually becomes a CS that elicits a fear response. When participants are shown other words, generalization of the fear response is more likely to occur to those words that are similar in meaning to *car*, such as *automobile* or *truck*, than to words that look similar, such as *bar* or *tar*. Thus, the meaning of the word is the critical factor in semantic generalization. For this reason, words that have similar meaning for an individual—for example, *Jennifer Lopez* and *J-Lo*—are likely to generate the same conditioned emotional response.

The opposite of stimulus generalization is *stimulus discrimination,* the tendency for a response to be elicited more by one stimulus than another. For example, if the dog salivates in the presence of the 2,000-Hz tone but not in the presence of a 1,900-Hz tone, then we say that it is able to *discriminate*, or has *formed a discrimination*, between the two stimuli. Such discriminations can be deliberately trained through a procedure known as *discrimination training*. If we repeatedly present the dog with one type of trial in which a 2,000-Hz tone is always followed by food and another type of trial in which a 1,900-Hz tone is never followed by food, the dog will soon learn to salivate in the presence of the 2,000-Hz tone and not in the presence of the 1,900-Hz tone.

Conditioning Phase (with the two types of trials presented several times in *random order*)

    2,000-Hz tone: Food → *Salivation*
        NS   US   UR
    1,900-Hz tone: No food
        NS   —

Test Phase

2,000-Hz tone → *Salivation*
    CS+   CR
1,900-Hz tone → No salivation
    CS–   —

As a result of training, the 2,000-Hz tone has become an excitatory CS (or CS+) because it predicts the presentation of food, and the 1,900-Hz tone has become an inhibitory CS (or CS–) because it predicts the absence of food. The discrimination training has, in effect, countered the tendency for generalization to occur. (Note that the two types of trials were presented in random order during the conditioning phase. If they were instead presented in alternating order, the dog might associate the presentation of food with every second tone rather than with the tone that has a pitch of 2,000 Hz.)

As you may have already guessed, discrimination training is a useful means for determining the sensory capacities of animals. For example, by presenting an animal with a CS+ tone and a CS– tone that are successively more and more similar, we can determine the animal's ability to discriminate between tones of different pitch. If it salivates to a CS+ of 2,000 Hz and does not salivate to a CS– of 1,950 Hz, then it has shown us that it can distinguish between the two. But if it salivates to both a CS+ of 2,000 Hz and a CS– of 1,950 Hz, then it cannot distinguish between the two.

Generalization and discrimination play an important role in many aspects of human behavior. Phobias, for example, involve not only the classical conditioning of a fear response but also an overgeneralization of that fear response to inappropriate stimuli. For example, a woman who has been through an abusive relationship may develop feelings of anxiety and apprehensiveness toward all men. Eventually, however, through repeated interactions with men, this tendency will decrease and she will begin to adaptively discriminate between men who are potentially abusive and those who are not. Unfortunately, such discriminations are not always easily made, and further bad experiences could greatly strengthen her fear. Moreover, if the woman begins to avoid all men, then the tendency to overgeneralize may remain, thereby significantly impairing her social life. As noted earlier, if we avoid that which we are afraid of, it is difficult for us to overcome our fears.

1. Stimulus generalization is the tendency for a (CR/UR) _____ to occur in the presence of stimuli that are similar to the original (CS/US) _____. In general, the more (similar/different) _____ the stimulus, the stronger the response.

2. The generalization of a conditioned response to stimuli that are similar in meaning to a verbal CS is called s_____ generalization.

3. The opposite of stimulus generalization is stimulus _____. This can be defined as _____
_____
_____.

4. Feeling "icky" around all objects that look like a snake is an example of stimulus _____, whereas feeling icky only around snakes is an example of stimulus _____.

5. Suppose Cary disliked his physics instructor and, as a result, came to dislike all science instructors. This example illustrates the process of over-_____.

Discrimination Training and Experimental Neurosis

Overgeneralization is not the only way that processes of discrimination versus generalization influence the development of psychological disorders. For example, Pavlov (1927, 1928) reported an interesting discovery made by a colleague, Shenger-Krestovnikova, that arose during a discrimination training procedure. In this experiment, an image of a circle signaled the presentation of food and an ellipse signaled no food (see Figure 4.3). In keeping with normal processes of discrimination, the dog dutifully learned to salivate when it saw the circle (a CS+) and not to salivate when it saw the ellipse (a CS−). Following this, the ellipse was gradually made more circular, making it more difficult for the dog to determine when food was about to appear. When the ellipse was almost completely circular, the dog was able to make only a weak discrimination, salivating slightly more in the presence of the circle than in the presence of the ellipse. Interestingly, continued training with these stimuli did not result in any improvement. In fact, after several weeks, the discrimination was lost. More interestingly, however, the hitherto well-behaved dog became extremely agitated during each session—squealing, wriggling about, and biting at the equipment. It acted as though it was suffering a nervous breakdown.

Pavlov called this phenomenon ***experimental neurosis,*** an experimentally produced disorder in which animals exposed to unpredictable events develop neurotic-like symptoms. Pavlov hypothesized that human neuroses might develop in a similar manner. Situations of extreme uncertainty can be stressful, and prolonged exposure to such uncertainty might result in the development of neurotic symptoms. Thus, in the opening vignette to this chapter,

FIGURE 4.3 Discrimination training procedure used by Shenger-Krestovnikova in which the picture of a circle functioned as the CS+ and the picture of the ellipse functioned as the CS−.

it is not surprising that Jana's boyfriends often display increasing symptoms of neuroticism as the relationship progresses. A little uncertainty in one's romantic relationships can be exciting, but extreme uncertainty might eventually become aversive.

In carrying out their studies of experimental neurosis, Pavlov and his assistants also discovered that different dogs displayed different symptoms. Some dogs displayed symptoms of anxiety when exposed to the procedure, while others became catatonic (rigid) and acted almost hypnotized. Additionally, some dogs displayed few if any symptoms and did not have a nervous breakdown. Pavlov speculated that such differences reflected underlying differences in temperament. This was an extension of one of Pavlov's earlier observations that some dogs condition more easily than others. Shy, withdrawn dogs seem to make the best subjects, conditioning easily, whereas active, outgoing dogs are more difficult to condition (which is quite the opposite of what Pavlov had originally expected).

Based on results such as these, Pavlov formulated a theory of personality in which inherited differences in temperament interact with classical conditioning to produce certain patterns of behavior. This work served to initiate the study of the biological basis of personality (Gray, 1999). For example, Eysenck (1957) later utilized certain aspects of Pavlov's work in formulating his own theory of personality. A major aspect of Eysenck's theory is the distinction between introversion and extroversion. In very general terms, introverts are individuals who are highly reactive to external stimulation (hence, cannot tolerate large amounts of stimulation and tend to withdraw from such stimulation), condition easily, and develop anxiety-type symptoms in reaction to stress. By contrast, extroverts are less reactive to external stimulation (hence, can tolerate, and will even seek out, large amounts of stimulation), condition less easily, and develop physical-type symptoms in reaction to stress. Eysenck's theory also proposes that psychopaths, individuals who engage in antisocial behavior, are extreme extroverts who condition very poorly. As a result, they experience little or no conditioned anxiety when harming or taking advantage of others, such anxiety being the underlying basis of a conscience.

Both Pavlov's and Eysenck's theories of personality are considerably more complicated than presented here, involving additional dimensions of personality and finer distinctions between different types of conditioning, especially excitatory and inhibitory conditioning. Thus, extroverts do not always condition more poorly than introverts, and additional factors are presumed to influence the development of neurotic symptoms (Clark, Watson, & Mineka, 1994; Eysenck, 1967; Monte, 1999). Nevertheless, processes of classical conditioning interacting with inherited differences in temperament could well be major factors in determining one's personality.

The experimental neurosis paradigm indicates that prolonged exposure to unpredictable events can sometimes have serious effects on our well-being. We will explore this topic in more detail in Chapter 9.

1. In Shenger-Krestovnikova's experiment the animal suffered a nervous breakdown when exposed to a CS+ and a CS– that were made progressively (more/less) _____ similar.

2. Pavlov referred to this nervous breakdown as e_____ n_____, an experimentally produced disorder in which animals exposed to unp_____ events develop n_____-like symptoms.

3. Pavlov and his assistants noted that the dogs displayed two general patterns of symptoms. Some dogs became _____while other dogs became _____. In addition, (all/not all) _____ dogs developed symptoms.

4. Pavlov believed that these differences between dogs reflected (learned/inherited) _____ differences in t_____.

5. In Eysenck's theory, introverts are (more/less) _____ reactive to external stimulation than extroverts are and therefore (can/cannot) _____ tolerate large doses of stimulation.

6. Introverts also condition (more/less) _____ easily than extroverts.

7. Introverts seem to develop a_____-type symptoms in reaction to stress, whereas extroverts develop p_____-type symptoms.

8. Psychopaths are extreme (introverts/extroverts) _____ who condition (very easily/very poorly) _____. They therefore feel little or no conditioned _____ when harming or manipulating others.

Two Extensions to Classical Conditioning

The normal classical conditioning procedure involves associating a single neutral stimulus with a US. But stimuli rarely exist in isolation. For example, a neighborhood bully does not exist as an isolated element in a child's world. The bully is associated with a variety of other stimuli, such as the house he lives in, the route he takes to school, and the kids he hangs around with. If a child is assaulted by the bully and learns to fear him, will he also fear the various objects, places, and people with which the bully is associated? In more technical terms, can classical conditioning of a CS also result in the development of a conditioned response to various stimuli that have been, or will be, associated with the CS? The processes of higher-order conditioning and sensory preconditioning indicate that it can.

Higher-Order Conditioning

Suppose you are stung by a wasp while out for a run one day and, as a result, develop a terrible fear of wasps. Imagine, too, that following the development of this fear, you notice a lot of wasps hanging around the trash bin outside your apartment building. Could the trash bin also come to elicit a certain amount of fear, or at least a feeling of edginess or discomfort? In a process known as ***higher-order conditioning,*** a stimulus that is associated with a CS can also become a CS. Thus, the trash bin could very well come to elicit a fear response through its association with the wasps. This process can be diagrammed as follows:

(**Step 1:** Basic conditioning of a fear response to wasps. As part of a higher-order conditioning procedure, this first step is called *first-order conditioning,* and the original NS and CS are respectively labeled NS_1 and CS_1.)

> **Wasp: Sting** → *Fear*
> NS_1 US   UR
> **Wasp** → *Fear*
> CS_1 CR

(**Step 2:** Higher-order conditioning of the trash bin through its association with wasps. This second step is sometimes also called *second-order conditioning,* and the new NS and CS are labeled NS_2 and CS_2.)

> **Trash bin: Wasp** → *Fear*
> NS_2 CS_1 CR
> **Trash bin** → *Fear*
> CS_2 CR

Note that the CS_2 generally elicits a weaker response than the CS_1 (which, as noted in Chapter 3, generally elicits a weaker response than the US). Thus, the fear response produced by the trash bin is likely to be much weaker than the fear response produced by the wasps. This is not surprising given that the trash bin is only *indirectly* associated with the unconditioned stimulus (i.e., the wasp sting) upon which the fear response is actually based.

An experimental example of higher-order conditioning might involve pairing a metronome with food so that the metronome becomes a CS_1 for salivation, and then pairing a light with the metronome so that the light becomes a CS_2 for salivation (see Figure 4.4). In diagram form:

(**Step 1:** First-order conditioning)

> **Metronome: Food** → *Salivation*
> NS_1 US   UR
> **Metronome** → *Salivation*
> CS_1 CR

(**Step 2:** Second-order, or higher-order, conditioning)

> **Light: Metronome** → *Salivation*
> NS_2 CS_1 CR
> **Light** → *Salivation*
> CS_2 CR

The light now elicits salivation although it has never been directly paired with food. (For consistency, we will continue to use Pavlov's salivary conditioning procedure as the basic experimental example throughout much of this chapter.

FIGURE 4.4 In this example of higher-order conditioning, a metronome is paired with food and becomes a CS_1 for salivation, following which a light paired with the metronome becomes a CS_2 for salivation. (*Source:* Nairne, 2000.)

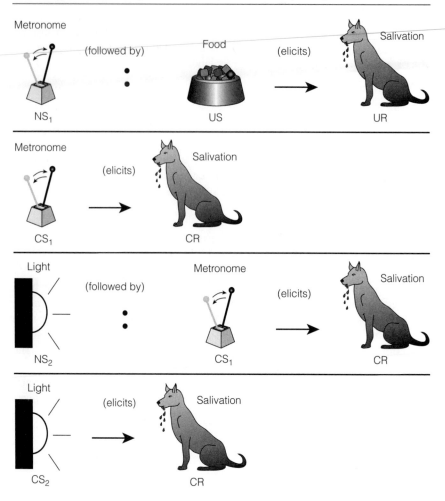

In reality, however, modern researchers use other procedures to study classical conditioning, such as the conditioned emotional response [CER] procedure discussed in Chapter 3.)

We could also attempt *third-order conditioning* by pairing yet another stimulus, such as the sound of a tone, with the light. However, third-order conditioning is difficult to obtain, and when it is obtained, the conditioned response to a third-order conditioned stimulus (the CS_3) is likely to be very weak.

Higher-order conditioning is commonly used in advertising. Advertisements often pair a company name or product with objects, events, or people (usually attractive people) that have been conditioned to elicit positive emotional responses. For example, the advertisement in Figure 4.5

FIGURE 4.5   An example of higher-order conditioning in advertising. The adver-tiser assumes that the positive emotional response elicited by the sight of the attrac-tive model will be associated with the clothes, increasing the probability that some readers of the ad will purchase the clothes.

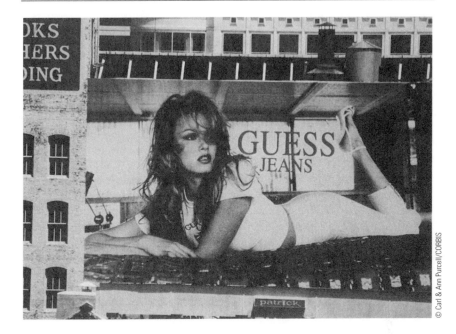

© Carl & Ann Purcell/CORBIS

presents an attractive woman in conjunction with a certain product. The assumption is that the sight of the woman elicits a positive emotional response, partly conditioned through various cultural experiences, that will be associated with the product and thereby increase the probability that readers of the ad will wish to purchase that product. (Of course, readers who are concerned about sexism in advertising would likely find the advertisement offensive, in which case they might be less likely to purchase that product.)

1. In _____-_____ conditioning, an already established CS is used to condition a new CS.

2. In general, the CS_2 elicits a (weaker/stronger) _____ response than the CS_1.

3. In higher-order conditioning, conditioning of the CS_1 is often called _____ -order conditioning, while conditioning of the CS_2 is called _____-order conditioning.

4. In a higher-order conditioning procedure in which a car is associated with an attrac-tive model, the attractive model is the (CS_1/CS_2) _____ and the car is the (CS_1/CS_2) _____.

QUICK QUIZ E

And Furthermore

When Celebrities Misbehave

As mentioned, advertisers are aware that we are more likely to buy products that are associated with celebrities . . . but will any celebrity do? Some companies will shy away from a celebrity who has been convicted of a crime or implicated in some sort of scandal. For example, when basketball star Kobe Bryant was accused of sexual assault in 2003 (a case that was eventually dismissed), he lost his endorsement deal with McDonald's. When Mary-Kate Olsen checked into a treatment facility in 2004 because of an eating disorder, "Got Milk?" ads featuring the Olsen twins were no longer used by the California Milk Processor Board (CMPB). Companies like McDonald's and CMPB are particularly sensitive to indiscretions by their celebrity endorsers, because their corporate image is aimed at being "wholesome" and "family oriented."

© Image courtesy of The Advertising Archives

Do all advertisers react this way to celebrity scandal? Not necessarily. When photos were published in 2005 by the *Daily Mirror* (a British tabloid) that showed model Kate Moss allegedly using cocaine, she immediately lost some lucrative endorsements with fashion companies, including H & M and Burberry, as well as several modeling contracts. Interestingly, this short-term loss was not sustained; according to Forbes.com (a leading business and finance news site), not only did Burberry resign Moss to an endorsement deal, but other high-end clients were quick to sign her to new contracts. Why would companies want their products associated with a drug-using model?

The fashion industry thrives on what is "edgy," and many designers and retailers want their products to be associated with things that are dark and dangerous, as well as sexy. While some companies (like H & M, which has made statements about its antidrug stance in the wake of the Moss cocaine scandal) try to maintain a clean image, others are comfortable being associated with the darker side of life. Thus, if consumers associate a product with the dangerous and less-than-pure image of Kate Moss, then they are making exactly the association the retailer was hoping for. (And they can put on that eyeliner, and feel a little bit dangerous, without having to resort to cocaine use of their own!)

Sensory Preconditioning

We have seen that an event that is *subsequently* associated with wasps, such as trash bins, can become a CS for fear. What about an event that was *previously* associated with wasps, such as a toolshed that once had a wasps' nest hanging in it? Will walking near the shed now also elicit feelings of anxiety?

In **sensory preconditioning**, when one stimulus is conditioned as a CS, another stimulus it was previously associated with can also become a CS. If you previously associated the toolshed with wasps and then acquired a fear of wasps as a result of being stung, you might also feel anxious when walking near the toolshed. This process can be diagrammed as follows:

(**Step 1:** Preconditioning phase in which the toolshed is associated with wasps)

> **Toolshed: Wasps**
> NS_2 NS_1

(**Step 2:** Conditioning of wasps as a CS_1)

> **Wasp: Sting** → *Fear*
> NS_1 **US**   **UR**
> **Wasp** → *Fear*
> CS_1 **CR**

(**Step 3:** Presentation of the toolshed)

> **Toolshed** → *Fear*
> CS_2 **CR**

The toolshed now elicits a fear response, although it was never directly associated with a wasp sting.

An experimental example of sensory preconditioning involves first presenting a dog with several pairings of two neutral stimuli such as a light and a metronome. The metronome is then paired with food to become a CS for salivation. As a result of this conditioning, the light, which has never been directly paired with the food but has been associated with the metronome, also comes to elicit salivation (see Figure 4.6). This process can be diagrammed as follows:

(**Step 1:** Preconditioning phase, in which the light is repeatedly associated with the metronome)

> **Light: Metronome** (10 presentations of light followed by metronome)
> NS_2 NS_1

(**Step 2:** Conditioning of the metronome as a CS_1)

> **Metronome: Food** → *Salivation*
> NS_1 **US**   **UR**
> **Metronome** → *Salivation*
> CS_1 **CR**

(**Step 3:** Presentation of the light)

> **Light** → *Salivation*
> CS_2 **CR**

FIGURE 4.6 In this example of sensory preconditioning, a dog is presented with several pairings of a light and a metronome. The metronome is then paired with food and becomes a conditioned stimulus for salivation. As a result, the light that was previously paired with the metronome also becomes a conditioned stimulus for salivation. (*Source:* Nairne, 2000.)

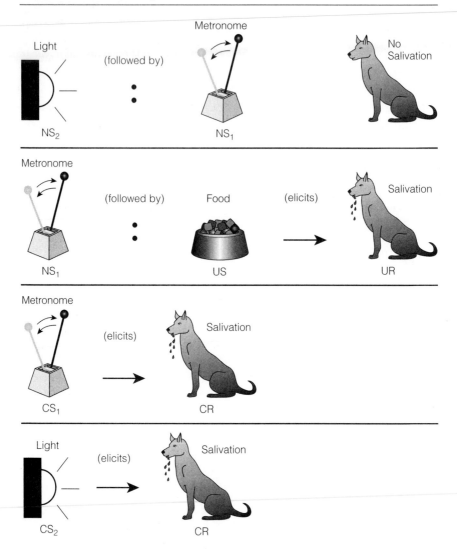

As with higher-order conditioning, the response elicited by the light (CS_2) is generally weaker than the response elicited by the metronome (CS_1). Likewise, the fear response elicited by the toolshed (CS_2) is likely to be weaker than the fear response elicited by the wasps (CS_1).

Although it was once believed necessary to pair the neutral stimuli hundreds of times in the preconditioning phase (e.g., Brogden, 1939), it is now known that this type of conditioning works best if the stimuli are paired relatively few times (R. F. Thompson, 1972). This prevents the animal from becoming overly familiar with the stimuli prior to conditioning. (As you will see in a later section on *latent inhibition*, neutral stimuli that are familiar are more difficult to condition as CSs than are unfamiliar stimuli.) Another unusual finding with sensory preconditioning is that the procedure is sometimes more effective when the two stimuli in the preconditioning phase are presented simultaneously as opposed to sequentially (Rescorla, 1980). This result is unusual because it contradicts what we find with NS-US pairings, in which simultaneous presentation of the two stimuli is relatively ineffective.

Sensory preconditioning is significant because it demonstrates that stimuli can become associated with each other in the absence of any identifiable response (other than an orienting response). In this sense, sensory preconditioning can be viewed as a form of *latent learning*, which was first discussed in Chapter 1. Just as Tolman's rats learned to find their way around a maze even when it seemed as if

Is this scenario more likely an example of higher-order conditioning or of sensory preconditioning? (You will find the answer when you complete the end-of-chapter test.)

"HE'S BEEN AT IT TOO LONG. NOW, WHEN THE BELL RINGS, DR. PAVLOV SALIVATES."

there were no significant consequences for doing so (i.e., food had not yet been introduced into the goal box), animals will associate stimuli with each other even when those stimuli seem to have little significance for them.

Suppose you suddenly developed a strong fear of dogs after being severely bitten. As a result, you are now anxious about in-line skating because, on several occasions in the past, you witnessed people walking their dogs on the in-line skating paths.

1. This example illustrates the phenomenon of _____ _____.

2. The in-line skating paths will probably elicit a (stronger/weaker) _____ fear response than will the sight of the dogs.

3. Sensory preconditioning often works best when the two neutral stimuli are paired (relatively few /hundreds of) _____ times in the preconditioning phase.

4. Unlike NS-US pairings in normal conditioning, NS-NS pairings in sensory preconditioning can produce stronger conditioning when the two stimuli are presented (sequentially/simultaneously) _____.

Three Examples of Specificity in Classical Conditioning

In the preceding section, we examined two ways in which the classical conditioning process can be extended to conditioning of additional CSs. In this section, we discuss three procedures—overshadowing, blocking, and latent inhibition—in which conditioning occurs to specific stimuli only, despite close pairing of other stimuli with the US. Two of these procedures (overshadowing and blocking) involve the presentation of what is known as a compound stimulus. A *compound stimulus* consists of the simultaneous presentation of two or more individual stimuli (e.g., the sound of a metronome is presented at the same time as a light).

Overshadowing

If you were stung by a wasp during a walk in the woods, would it make sense to develop a conditioned fear response to every stimulus associated with that event (e.g., the trees surrounding you, the butterfly fluttering by, and the cloud formation in the sky)? No, it would not. Rather, it would make more sense to develop a fear of those stimuli that were most salient (that really stood out) at the time of being stung, such as the sight of the wasp.

In *overshadowing,* the most salient member of a compound stimulus is more readily conditioned as a CS and thereby interferes with conditioning of the least salient member. In the wasp example, you are likely to develop a conditioned fear response to the most distinctive stimuli associated with that event, such as the sight of the wasp and perhaps the buzzing sound it makes.

An experimental example of overshadowing might involve first pairing a compound stimulus, such as a bright light and a faint-sounding metronome, with food. After several pairings, the compound stimulus becomes a CS that elicits salivation. However, when each member of the compound is tested separately, the bright light elicits salivation while the faint metronome elicits no salivation (or very little salivation). In diagram form:

(**Step 1:** Conditioning of a compound stimulus as a CS. Note that the compound stimulus consists of the simultaneous presentation of the two bracketed stimuli.)

> **[Bright light + Faint metronome]: Food** → *Salivation*
> NS   US   UR
> **[Bright light + Faint metronome]** → *Salivation*
>   CS   CR

(**Step 2:** Presentation of each member of the compound separately)

> **Bright light** → *Salivation*
>   CS   CR
> **Faint metronome** → **No salivation**
>   NS   —

Due to the presence of the bright light during the conditioning trials, no conditioning occurred to the faint metronome. This is not because the faint metronome is unnoticeable. If it had been paired with the food by itself, it could easily have become an effective CS. Only in the presence of a more salient stimulus does the less salient stimulus come to elicit little or no response (see Figure 4.7).

Head managers make use of the overshadowing effect when they assign an assistant to announce an unpopular decision. Although the employees might recognize that the head manager is mostly responsible, the assistant is the most salient stimulus and will, as a result, bear the brunt of the blame. It is thus the assistant who is likely to become most disliked by the employees. On the other hand, head managers often make a point of personally announcing popular decisions, thereby attracting most of the positive associations to themselves even if they have been only minimally involved in those decisions. Similarly, the positive feelings generated by the music of a rock band will be most strongly associated with the most salient member of that band (e.g., the lead singer)—a fact that often leads to problems when other band members conclude that they are not receiving their fair share of the accolades.

Blocking

The phenomenon of overshadowing demonstrates that, in some circumstances, mere contiguity between a neutral stimulus and a US is insufficient for conditioning to occur. An even clearer demonstration of this fact is provided by a phenomenon known as blocking. In ***blocking,*** the presence of an established CS interferes with conditioning of a new CS. Blocking is similar to overshadowing, except that the compound consists of a neutral stimulus and a CS rather than two neutral stimuli that differ in salience. For example, suppose that a light is first conditioned as a CS for salivation. If the light is then combined with a

FIGURE 4.7 In this example of overshadowing, a bright light and a faint-sounding metronome are simultaneously presented as a compound stimulus and paired with food. After several pairings, the compound stimulus becomes a CS that elicits salivation. However, when each member of the compound is tested separately, the bright light elicits salivation but the faint-sounding metronome does not. (*Source:* Nairne, 2000.)

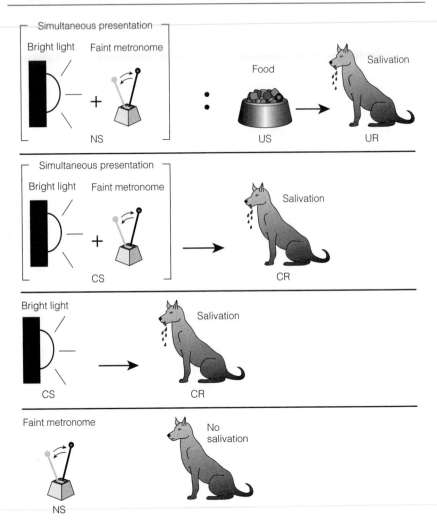

metronome to form a compound, and this compound is then paired with food, little or no conditioning occurs to the metronome. In diagram form:

(Step 1: Conditioning of the light as a CS)

> **Light: Food → *Salivation***
>   **NS**   **US**   **UR**
> **Light → *Salivation***
>   **CS**   **CR**

(**Step 2:** Several pairings of a compound stimulus with the US)

[Light + Metronome]: Food → *Salivation*
      CS + NS   **US**   **UR**

(**Step 3:** Presentation of each member of the compound separately. The question at this point is whether conditioning occurred to the metronome.)

Light → *Salivation*
  CS   **CR**
Metronome → No salivation
    NS   **—**

In step 2, the presence of the light blocked conditioning to the metronome. An everyday (but overly simplistic) way of thinking about what is happening here is that the light already predicts the food, so the dog pays attention only to the light. As a result, the metronome does not become an effective CS despite being paired with the food (see Figure 4.8).

For a real-life example of the blocking effect, imagine that you have to make an unpopular announcement to your employees. The phenomenon of blocking suggests that you would do well to make it a joint announcement with another manager who is already disliked by the employees (one who is already an aversive CS). The employees might then attribute most or all of the bad news to the unpopular manager, and you will be left relatively unscathed.

The phenomenon of blocking garnered a lot of attention when it was first demonstrated (Kamin, 1969). It clearly indicates that mere contiguity between an NS and a US is insufficient to produce conditioning. Rather, it seems that a more crucial factor in conditioning is the extent to which the NS comes to act as a signal or predictor of the US. In more cognitive terms (Tolman would have loved blocking), the act of conditioning can be said to produce an "expectation" that a particular event is about to occur. When the light is conditioned as a CS, the dog comes to expect that food will follow the light. Later, when the metronome is presented at the same time as the light, the metronome provides no additional information about when food will occur; hence, no conditioning occurs to it. We will again encounter this notion of expectations when we discuss the Rescorla-Wagner theory of conditioning in Chapter 5.[2]

---

[2]A different way of thinking about this (again, popular with researchers who have a preference for cognitive interpretations of such matters) is that *increases in conditioning* can occur only to the extent that a US is *unexpected* or *surprising*. Once a US is fully expected, such as when a light by itself reliably predicts the occurrence of food, no further conditioning can occur. In more general terms, we learn the most about something when we are placed in a position of uncertainty and must then strive to reduce that uncertainty. Once the uncertainty has been eliminated, learning ceases to occur. Thus, in blocking, no conditioning (no new learning) occurs to the neutral stimulus, because the presence of the CS that it has been combined with ensures that the animal is not surprised when the US soon follows.

FIGURE 4.8 In this example of blocking, a light is first conditioned as a CS for salivation. When the light is then combined with a metronome to form a compound stimulus, and this compound stimulus is paired with food, the metronome does not become a conditioned stimulus. The presence of the already established CS blocks conditioning to the metronome. (*Source:* Nairne, 2000.)

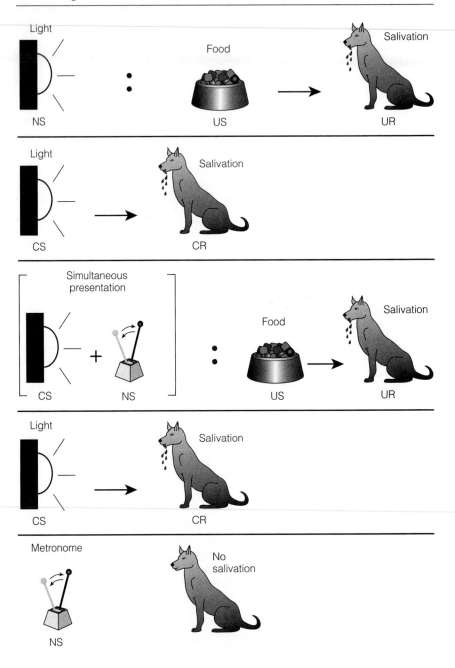

Latent Inhibition

Do we condition more readily to stimuli that are familiar or unfamiliar? You might think that familiar stimuli are more readily conditioned: If we already know something about a topic, it seems easier to learn more about it. In fact, in what is known as *latent inhibition,* a familiar stimulus is more difficult to condition as a CS than is an unfamiliar (novel) stimulus.[3] Or, stated the other way around, *an unfamiliar stimulus is more readily conditioned than a familiar stimulus.* For example, if, on many occasions, a dog has heard the sound of a metronome prior to conditioning, then a standard number of conditioning trials might result in little or no conditioning to the metronome.

(**Step 1:** Stimulus preexposure phase in which a neutral stimulus is repeatedly presented)

> **Metronome** (40 presentations)
>   **NS**

(**Step 2:** Conditioning trials in which the preexposed neutral stimulus is now paired with a US)

> **Metronome: Food** → *Salivation* (10 trials)
>   **NS**   **US**   **UR**

(**Step 3:** Test trial to determine if conditioning has occurred to the metronome)

> **Metronome** → **No salivation**
>   **NS**   —

If the dog had not been preexposed to the metronome and it had been a novel stimulus when first paired with food, then the 10 conditioning trials would have resulted in significant conditioning to the metronome. Because of the preexposure, however, no conditioning occurred (see Figure 4.9). It will take many more pairings of metronome and food before the metronome will reliably elicit salivation.

Latent inhibition prevents the development of conditioned associations to redundant stimuli in the environment. Such stimuli are likely to be relatively inconsequential with respect to the conditioning event. For example, if a rabbit in a grassy field is attacked by a coyote and then escapes, it will be much more adaptive for the rabbit to associate the attack with the novel scent of the coyote than with the familiar scent of grass. The scent of the coyote is a good predictor of a possible attack, and a conditioned fear response to that scent will help the rabbit avoid such attacks in the future. A conditioned fear response to grass, however, will be completely maladaptive because the rabbit is surrounded by grass day in and day out and often feeds on it. It is the novel stimuli preceding the presentation of a US that are most likely to be meaningfully related to it.

---

[3]Latent inhibition is also known as the *CS preexposure effect.* A related phenomenon, known as the *US preexposure effect,* holds that conditioning is slower with familiar, as opposed to unfamiliar, USs.

FIGURE 4.9 In latent inhibition, familiar stimuli are more difficult to condition as CSs than novel stimuli. If a dog has, on many occasions, heard the sound of a metronome prior to conditioning being implemented, then it will be difficult to obtain conditioning to the metronome using a standard number of conditioning trials. (*Source:* Nairne, 2000.)

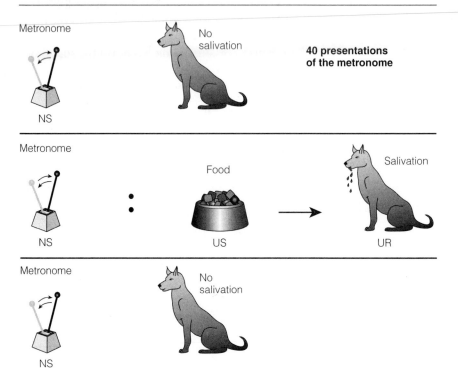

Problems concerning latent inhibition are evident in people who have schizophrenia (Lubow & Gewirtz, 1995). These individuals often have great difficulty attending to relevant stimuli in their environment and are instead distracted by irrelevant stimuli, such as various background noises or people passing nearby. Experiments have revealed that people with schizophrenia display less latent inhibition than is normal—that is, they condition more easily to familiar stimuli—indicating that the disorder partly involves an inability to screen out redundant stimuli. Experiments have also revealed that drugs used to treat schizophrenia tend to increase levels of latent inhibition, thereby normalizing the person's attentional processes.

1. A compound stimulus consists of the (simultaneous/successive) _____ presentation of two or more separate stimuli.

2. In _____, the most salient member of a compound stimulus is more readily conditioned as a CS and thereby interferes with conditioning of the less salient member.

3. In _____, the presence of an established CS interferes with conditioning of another stimulus.

4. In _____, a familiar stimulus is more difficult to condition as a CS than is an unfamiliar stimulus.

5. In a(n) _____ procedure, the compound stimulus consists of a neutral stimulus and a CS, whereas in a(n) _____ procedure, the compound stimulus consists of two neutral stimuli.

6. Latent inhibition (prevents/promotes) _____ the development of conditioned associations to redundant stimuli.

7. Because Jez has a history of getting into trouble, he often catches most of the blame when something goes wrong, even when others are also responsible for what happened. This is most similar to the phenomenon of _____.

ADVICE FOR THE LOVELORN

Dear Dr. Dee,

My friend has started dating someone who is quite aggressive toward her. I am worried for her safety, yet she says she's known him for years and he is not that frightening. To the rest of us, it is obvious that the guy is dangerous. Is she blinded by love?

Deeply Concerned

Dear Deeply,

On the one hand, your friend is more familiar with this person than you are, so it may be that her judgment is indeed more accurate. On the other hand, her increased familiarity with him might also mean that it will take longer for her to become fearful of him. This is in keeping with the process of latent inhibition, in which we condition less readily to familiar stimuli than to unfamiliar stimuli. This is yet another factor that might contribute to people remaining in an abusive relationship even though the people around them clearly recognize the danger signals. So it may be that she is blinded by latent inhibition, not love.

Behaviorally yours,

Dr. Dee

Additional Phenomena

In this section, we briefly cover some additional ways in which the process of classical conditioning can be affected by modifications in the typical conditioning procedure.

Temporal Conditioning

In all of the preceding examples, the CS is a distinctive, external stimulus of some sort, such as a light, a metronome, or a dog. But this need not always be the case. *Temporal conditioning* is a form of classical conditioning in which the CS is the passage of time. For example, if a dog is given a bite of food every 10 minutes, it will eventually salivate more strongly toward the end of each 10-minute interval than at the start of the interval. The end of the 10-minute interval is the effective CS for salivation. Similarly, residents of a city who experience a bombing attack each night at 2:00 A.M. for several nights in a row will likely start feeling anxious as 2:00 A.M. approaches, even in the absence of any clock indicating the time. The various cues that we use to estimate time, some of which are internal, are sufficient to elicit the feelings of anxiety.

Occasion Setting

As we have learned, classical conditioning involves establishment of an association between two events, such as between the sound of a metronome and the taste of food or between the sight of a wasp and the feel of its sting. To date, however, we have largely ignored the fact that these two events do not exist in isolation but instead occur within a certain context. This context often comes to serve as an overall predictor of the relationship between these two events. Imagine, for example, that a metronome is followed by food, but only when a light is on. When the light is off, the metronome is not followed by food. The conditioning procedure would look something like this:

(**Step 1:** Presentation of light-metronome and metronome-alone trials in random order)

    Light on { Metronome: Food → *Salivation*
        NS   **US**   **UR**
    Light off { Metronome: No food
        NS   **—**

Not surprisingly, in this circumstance, we are likely to find that the metronome elicits salivation only when the light is on and not when it is off.

(**Step 2:** Test trials)

    Light on { Metronome → *Salivation*
             CS   **CR**
    Light off { Metronome → No salivation
             NS   **—**

The light in this instance is referred to as an *occasion setter* because it predicts the occasions on which the metronome is followed by food. Its presence therefore comes to control the extent to which the metronome serves as a CS for salivation. Thus, **occasion setting** is a procedure in which a stimulus (i.e., an occasion setter) signals that a CS is likely to be followed by the US with which it is associated. The presence of this stimulus then facilitates the occurrence of the CR in response to the CS.

An occasion setter can be associated not only with the presentation of a US but also with a change in the intensity of the US. Imagine, for example, that an abused child receives his worst beatings from his parents whenever they are drinking alcohol. Thus:

> **Alcohol absent { Parents: Mild abuse → *Mild anxiety***
> **Alcohol present { Parents: Severe abuse → *Strong anxiety***

Although the child typically feels a mild amount of anxiety around his parents, the sight or smell of alcohol in the presence of his parents greatly increases his anxiety. Thus:

> **Alcohol absent { Parents → *Mild anxiety***
> **Alcohol present { Parents → *Strong anxiety***

The conditioned response of anxiety to the parents is intensified by the presence of alcohol. The alcohol is therefore an occasion setter that heightens the child's anxiety in the presence of the parents.

Because the real world consists of a complex mixture of stimuli, occasion setting is an important factor in many instances of classical conditioning. Women are typically more anxious about being harassed while walking by a construction worker at a construction site than while walking by a construction worker in an office complex. And hikers are more anxious around bears with cubs than they are around bears without cubs. The additional stimuli present in these circumstances (construction site and bear cubs) indicate a higher probability of certain events (harassment and bear attack).

1. In temporal conditioning, the (NS/US) _____ is presented at regular intervals, with the result that the end of each interval becomes a (CS/US) _____ that elicits a (CR/UR) _____.

2. In classical conditioning, o_____ s_____ is a procedure in which a stimulus signals that a CS is likely to be followed by the _____. This stimulus is called a(n) _____ _____, and serves to (facilitate/retard) _____ the occurrence of the (UR/CR) _____.

3. Kessler became very accustomed to having a snack at about 4 o'clock each afternoon. As a result, he now finds that he automatically starts thinking about food at about 4 o'clock each afternoon, even before he notices the time. These automatic thoughts of food seem to represent an example of _____ conditioning.

4. Brandon notices that the doctor gives him an injection only when a nurse is present in the examining room. As a result, he feels more anxious about the medical exam when the nurse is present than when the nurse is absent. In this case, the nurse functions as an o_____ s_____ for his conditioned feelings of anxiety.

QUICK QUIZ H

External Inhibition

Remember how the presentation of a novel stimulus during an extinction procedure can result in a sudden recovery of the conditioned response? According to Pavlov, the presentation of the novel stimulus at the same time as the CS seems to disrupt the buildup of inhibition that was occurring during extinction; therefore, this process is known as *disinhibition*. The process of external inhibition is the mirror opposite of disinhibition. In *external inhibition*, the presentation of a novel stimulus at the same time as the conditioned stimulus produces a decrease in the strength of the conditioned response. In other words, the presence of the novel stimulus inhibits the occurrence of the CR.

Suppose, for example, that the sound of the metronome has been strongly associated with food so that it reliably elicits salivation:

> Metronome: Food → *Salivation*
> NS   US   UR
> Metronome → *Salivation*
> CS   CR

If we now present a light at the same time as the metronome, then the metronome will elicit considerably less salivation.

> Light { Metronome → *Little salivation*
>   CS   **Weak CR**

A simple way of thinking about this is that the dog has been distracted by the light and therefore reacts less strongly to the metronome.

In a similar fashion, if you happen to be feeling anxious because some wasps are buzzing around your table at an outdoor cafe, you may find that the occurrence of an unusual event, such as the sound of a violinist who begins entertaining the patrons, will somewhat alleviate the anxiety. In fact, this process works well enough that people in anxiety-arousing situations sometimes deliberately create a distracting stimulus. For example, on a recent television talk show, a popular morning show host described how he used to sometimes jab himself with a darning needle just before the start of his segments to alleviate some of the anxiety he was experiencing!

US Revaluation

At the beginning of this chapter, we mentioned how more-intense stimuli produce stronger conditioning than do less-intense stimuli. For example, a strong shock will produce stronger fear conditioning than a weak shock does. But what would happen if we conducted our conditioning trials with one level of shock and then presented a different level of shock by itself on a subsequent nonconditioning trial? In other words, would changing the intensity or value of the US after the conditioning of a CS also change the strength of response to the CS?

Imagine, for example, that the sound of a metronome is followed by a small amount of food, with the result that the metronome comes to elicit a small amount of saliva.

Metronome: Small amount of food → *Weak salivation*
      NS   US   UR

Metronome → *Weak salivation*
      CS   CR

Once this conditioning has been established, we now present the dog with a large amount of food, which elicits a large amount of saliva.

Large amount of food → *Strong salivation*
      US   UR

What type of response will now be elicited by the metronome? As it turns out, the dog is likely to react to the metronome as though it predicts a large amount of food rather than a small amount of food.

Metronome → *Strong salivation*
      CS   CR

Note that the metronome was never directly paired with the large amount of food; the intervening experience with the large amount by itself produced the stronger level of conditioned salivation.

Therefore, **US revaluation** involves the postconditioning presentation of the US at a different level of intensity, thereby altering the strength of response to the previously conditioned CS. It is called US *revaluation* because the *value* or magnitude of the US is being changed. Depending on whether the value is increased or decreased, this procedure can also be called *US inflation* or *US deflation*. The preceding scenario is an example of US inflation. As an example of US deflation, imagine that you salivate profusely when you enter Joe's restaurant because you love their turkey gumbo. You then get a new roommate, who as it turns out, is a turkey gumbo fanatic and prepares turkey gumbo meals for you five times a week. Needless to say, so much turkey gumbo can become monotonous (an instance of long-term habituation), and you finally reach a point where you have little interest in turkey gumbo. As a result, when you next enter Joe's restaurant, you salivate very little. The value of turkey gumbo has been markedly reduced in your eyes, which in turn affects your response to the restaurant that has been associated with it.

In everyday terms, it seems like what is happening in US revaluation is that the animal has learned to expect the US whenever it sees the CS. The intensity of its response is thus dependent on the animal's most recent experience with the US. On a more theoretical level, as with blocking, US revaluation suggests that conditioning generally involves the creation of an association between the CS and the US (i.e., a stimulus-stimulus, or S-S, association) as opposed to an association between the NS and the UR (i.e., a stimulus-response, or S-R, association). These theoretical issues are more fully discussed in Chapter 5. (You will also see that US revaluation might play a role in the development of some human phobias.)

1. In e_____ i_____ the presentation of a (novel/familiar) _____ stimulus at the same time as the conditioned stimulus produces a(n) (increase/decrease) _____ in the strength of the conditioned response.

2. The (US/CS) _____ r_____ procedure involves the (pre/post) _____ conditioning presentation of the (CS/US) _____ at a different level of intensity.

3. Shahid usually salivates when he enters Joe's restaurant because he loves their turkey gumbo. One time, however, when the waiters were all dressed like clowns and bagpipes were playing in the background, he salivated much less. This appears to be an instance of _____ _____.

4. Nikki feels all excited when she sees her father arrive home each evening because he always brings her some licorice. One day her mother bought her a lot of licorice earlier in the day, and Nikki had no desire for licorice when evening came around. As a result, she was not as excited when her father came home that evening. In this example, her father is a (CS/US) _____ through his association with licorice. Being satiated with licorice therefore reduced the value of the (CS/US) _____ that typically followed her father's arrival home. As a result, her (CR/UR) _____ of excitement on seeing her father was greatly reduced. This process is known as _____ _____ .

Pseudoconditioning

We hope you are now pretty familiar with the basic classical conditioning procedure and some of the phenomena associated with it. Be aware, however, that determining whether classical conditioning has occurred is not always as straightforward as it might seem. A phenomenon known as *pseudoconditioning* poses a particular problem. In **pseudoconditioning**, an elicited response that appears to be a CR is actually the result of sensitization rather than conditioning. Suppose, for example, that we try to condition a leg withdrawal reflex (leg flexion) in a dog by presenting a light flash followed by a slight shock to its foot.

Light flash: Shock → *Leg flexion*

After a few pairings of the light with the shock, we now find that the flexion response occurs immediately when the light is flashed.

Light flash → *Leg flexion*

On the surface, it seems that the light flash has become a CS and that we have successfully conditioned a flexion response. But have we? What if instead of flashing a light, we sound a beep and find that, lo and behold, it too elicits a response?

Beep → *Leg flexion*

What is going on here?

Remember the process of sensitization in which the repeated presentation of an eliciting stimulus can sometimes increase the strength of the elicited response? Well, sensitization can result in the response being elicited by other stimuli as well. For example, soldiers with war trauma exhibit an enhanced startle response, not just to the sound of exploding artillery shells but to certain other stimuli as well, including doors slamming, cars backfiring, or even an unexpected tap on the shoulder. Similarly, if a dog has been shocked in the paw a couple of times, it would not be at all surprising if any sudden stimulus in that setting could make the dog quickly jerk its leg up. Therefore, although we thought we had established a CR—which is the result of a CS having been associated with a US—in reality we have simply produced a hypersensitive dog that automatically reacts to almost any sudden stimulus.

Pseudoconditioning is a potential problem whenever the US is some type of emotionally arousing stimulus. Fortunately, there are ways of determining the extent to which a response is the result of pseudoconditioning rather than real conditioning. One alternative is to employ a control condition in which the NS and US are presented separately. For example, while subjects in the experimental group receive several pairings of the light flash and the shock, subjects in the control group receive light flashes and shocks that are well separated in time.

Experimental group | *Control group*
Light flash: Shock → *Leg flexion* | **Light flash // Shock → *Leg flexion***

(The symbol / / for the control group means that the light flash and the shock are *not* paired together and are instead presented far apart from each other.) When the animals in each group are then exposed to the light flash presented on its own, we find the following:

Experimental group | *Control group*
Light flash → *Strong leg flexion* | **Light flash → *Weak leg flexion***

The level of responding shown by the control group is presumed to reflect the amount of sensitization (pseudoconditioning) due to the use of an upsetting stimulus such as a shock. However, because the response shown by the experimental group is stronger than that shown by the control group, conditioning is assumed to have occurred, with the difference between the two groups indicating the strength of conditioning. Classical conditioning experiments typically utilize one or more control groups like this to assess how much actual conditioning has taken place versus how much the subject's responses are the result of nonconditioning factors such as sensitization.

1. When an elicited response that appears to be a CR is actually the result of sensitiza-tion, we say that _____ has taken place.

2. The above phenomenon is a potential problem whenever the US produces a strong em_____ response.

3. An appropriate control procedure to test for this phenomenon involves pre-senting a control group of subjects with the NS and US (close together/quite separate) _____. Whatever responding is later elicited by the NS in this group is assumed to be the result of s_____ rather than real conditioning.

Warning _____

In this chapter, you have been exposed to a considerable number of condition-ing procedures, some of which are quite similar (such as overshadowing and blocking). Be sure to *overlearn* these procedures, as students often confuse them, especially under the stress of examination conditions.

SUMMARY

Strengthening a conditioned response by pairing a CS (or NS) with a US is known as acquisition. In general, early conditioning trials produce more rapid acquisition than do later trials. Weakening a conditioned response by repeat-edly presenting the CS by itself is known as extinction. Spontaneous recovery is the reappearance of a previously extinguished response after a rest period, and disinhibition is the sudden recovery of an extinguished response follow-ing introduction of a novel stimulus.

In stimulus generalization, we learn to respond similarly to stimuli that resemble an original stimulus. One version of stimulus generalization, known as semantic generalization, involves generalization of a response to verbal stimuli that are similar in meaning to the original stimulus. In stimulus discrimination, we respond to one stimulus more than another, a process that is established through discrimination training. Pavlov dis-covered that dogs that were exposed to a difficult discrimination problem often suffered from nervous breakdowns, a phenomenon that he called experimental neurosis.

In higher-order conditioning, a previously conditioned stimulus (CS_1) is used to condition a new stimulus (CS_2). The CS_2 elicits a weaker response than the CS_1 does because there is only an indirect association between the CS_2 and the US. In sensory preconditioning, when one stimulus is conditioned as a CS, another stimulus with which it was previously associ-ated also becomes a CS.

Certain situations can also interfere with the process of conditioning. For example, overshadowing occurs when the most salient member of a compound stimulus is more readily conditioned as a CS and thereby interferes with the conditioning of a less salient member. Blocking occurs when the presence of an established CS during conditioning interferes with conditioning of a new CS. Familiar stimuli are also more difficult to condition than unfamiliar stimuli, a phenomenon known as latent inhibition.

In temporal conditioning, the effective CS is the passage of time between USs that are presented at regular intervals. With occasion setting, an additional stimulus (an occasion setter) indicates whether a CS will be followed by a US; the CS therefore elicits a CR only in the presence of the occasion setter. External inhibition occurs when the presentation of a novel stimulus at the same time as the CS reduces the strength of the CR. US revaluation involves exposure to a stronger or weaker US following conditioning, which then alters the strength of response to the previously conditioned CS. Pseudoconditioning is a false form of conditioning in which the response is actually the result of sensitization rather than classical conditioning.

SUGGESTED READINGS

Eysenck, H. J. (1967). *The biological basis of personality*. Springfield, IL: Charles C Thomas. Indicates the extent to which Pavlov's work influenced Eysenck's theory of personality and, hence, many other theories of personality.

Lieberman, D. A. (2000). *Learning: Behavior and cognition* (3rd ed.). Belmont, CA: Wadsworth. For students who may find it helpful to read alternative descriptions of these various classical conditioning phenomena.

STUDY QUESTIONS

1. Define acquisition. Draw a graph of a typical acquisition curve, and indicate the asymptote of conditioning.
2. Define the processes of extinction and spontaneous recovery.
3. Define disinhibition. How does it differ from dishabituation?
4. Describe stimulus generalization and semantic generalization.
5. What is stimulus discrimination? Outline an example of a discrimination training procedure.
6. Define experimental neurosis, and describe Shenger-Krestovnikova's procedure for producing it.
7. Define higher-order conditioning, and diagram an example.

8. Define sensory preconditioning, and diagram an example.
9. Define overshadowing, and diagram an example.
10. Define blocking, and diagram an example.
11. Define latent inhibition, and diagram an example.
12. What is temporal conditioning? Describe an example.
13. Define occasion setting, and diagram an example.
14. Define external inhibition. Diagram an example.
15. Define US revaluation, and diagram an example.
16. How does pseudoconditioning differ from classical conditioning? How can one experimentally determine whether a response is the result of classical conditioning or pseudoconditioning?

CONCEPT REVIEW

acquisition. The process of developing and strengthening a conditioned response through repeated pairings of an NS (or CS) with a US.

blocking. The phenomenon whereby the presence of an established CS interferes with conditioning of a new CS.

compound stimulus. A complex stimulus that consists of the simultaneous presentation of two or more individual stimuli.

disinhibition. The sudden recovery of a response during an extinction procedure when a novel stimulus is introduced.

experimental neurosis. An experimentally produced disorder in which animals exposed to unpredictable events develop neurotic-like symptoms.

external inhibition. A decrease in the strength of the conditioned response due to the presentation of a novel stimulus at the same time as the conditioned stimulus.

extinction. The process whereby a conditioned response can be weakened or eliminated when the CS is repeatedly presented in the absence of the US; also, the procedure whereby this happens, namely, the repeated presentation of the CS in the absence of the US.

higher-order conditioning. The process whereby a stimulus that is associated with a CS also becomes a CS.

latent inhibition. The phenomenon whereby a familiar stimulus is more difficult to condition as a CS than is an unfamiliar (novel) stimulus.

occasion setting. A procedure in which a stimulus (known as an *occasion setter*) signals that a CS is likely to be followed by the US with which it is associated.

overshadowing. The phenomenon whereby the most salient member of a compound stimulus is more readily conditioned as a CS and thereby interferes with conditioning of the least salient member.

pseudoconditioning. A situation in which an elicited response that appears to be a CR is actually the result of sensitization rather than conditioning.

semantic generalization. The generalization of a conditioned response to verbal stimuli that are similar in meaning to the CS.

sensory preconditioning. In this phenomenon, when one stimulus is conditioned as a CS, another stimulus it was previously associated with can also become a CS.

spontaneous recovery. The reappearance of a conditioned response following a rest period after extinction.

stimulus discrimination. The tendency for a response to be elicited more by one stimulus than another.

stimulus generalization. The tendency for a CR to occur in the presence of a stimulus that is similar to the CS.

temporal conditioning. A form of classical conditioning in which the CS is the passage of time.

US revaluation. A process that involves the postconditioning presentation of the US at a different level of intensity, thereby altering the strength of response to the previously conditioned CS.

CHAPTER TEST

12. In higher-order conditioning, the CS_2 generally elicits a (stronger/weaker) _____ response than does the CS_1.

5. The fact that you learned to fear wasps and hornets, as well as bees, after being stung by a bee is an example of the process of _____.

8. During an eyeblink conditioning procedure, you blinked not only in response to the sound of the click but also when someone tapped you on the shoulder. Your response to the tap on the shoulder may be indicative of _____ conditioning, which means that the elicited response is likely the result of _____ rather than classical conditioning.

18. While playing tennis one day, you suffer a minor ankle sprain. Two weeks later you severely twist your ankle while stepping off a curb. The next time you play tennis, you find yourself surprisingly worried about spraining your ankle. This is an example of _____.

23. According to Eysenck, psychopaths tend to be extreme (extroverts/introverts) _____ who condition (easily/poorly) _____.

20. Midori feels anxious whenever the manager walks into the store accompanied by the owner because the manager always finds fault with the employees when the owner is there. This is best seen as an example of _____ with the owner functioning as the _____.

14. Two examples of specificity in conditioning, known as _____ and _____, involve pairing a compound stimulus with a US.

2. Following an experience in which you were stung by a bee and subsequently developed a fear of bees, you are hired for a 1-day job in which your task is to catch bees for a biologist. During the day, you never once

get stung by a bee. As a result, your fear of bees will likely (decrease/increase) _____, a process known as _____.

10. The researcher feels that you have done such a fine job catching bees that she hires you for another day. At the start of the next day, you will likely find that your fear of bees has (completely disappeared/partially returned) _____, a phenomenon known as _____.

22. By the end of the second day, your fear of bees has mostly disappeared. However, you then hear thunder in the distance and become a bit worried about whether you should immediately head back to the lab. You decide first to catch one more bee, but find that your fear of bees is now somewhat stronger. The sudden recovery of your fear response is an example of a process known as _____.

15. Marty once played in an all-star game alongside Bobby Orr (a famous and talented hockey player). Marty scored two goals and an assist, as did Orr. Orr was later voted the game's most valuable player, while Marty's name was barely mentioned. This situation seems analogous to the _____ effect in classical conditioning.

25. Remember the cartoon of Pavlov learning to salivate to the bell after watching the dogs being conditioned? Of the two types of extensions to classical conditioning, this is most similar to _____. This situation might have arisen during conditioning if the dogs were being fed bites of juicy steak, the *sight* of which for most humans is probably a (CS_1/CS_2) _____ for salivation. The bell would then become a (CS_1/CS_2) _____ through its association with the sight of the steak.

19. Jared's parents always start arguing at about midnight each night. As a result, he wakes up feeling anxious each night just before midnight. This seems to be an example of _____ conditioning.

3. Consider the following example:

    (Step 1)
    John: Rude behavior → *Anger*
    John → *Anger*

    (Step 2)
    Amir: John → *Anger*
    Amir → *Anger*

    This is an example of _____ conditioning.

11. In higher-order conditioning, conditioning of the CS_1 is sometimes called _____ conditioning, and conditioning of the CS_2 is called _____ conditioning.

6. The *procedure* of extinction involves the _____ _____.

24. The gradual strengthening of a classically conditioned fear response by repeated pairings of a tone with a shock is an example of the process of _____. During this process, early pairings of tone and shock are likely to produce (larger/smaller) _____ increments in conditioning compared to later pairings.

1. The maximum amount of conditioning that can take place in a particular situation is known as the _____ of conditioning.

9. Consider the following example:

   (Step 1: Repeated experiences in restaurant)
   Restaurant: Yoshi

   (Step 2: Not in restaurant)
   Yoshi: Argument → *Tension*
   Yoshi → *Tension*

   (Step 3)
   Restaurant → *Tension*

   This process is best seen as an example of _____.

4. Based partially on Pavlov's work on experimental neurosis, Eysenck concluded that (introverts/extroverts) _____ tend to be highly reactive to external stimulation, condition easily, and develop anxiety-type symptoms in reaction to stress. By contrast, _____ are less reactive, condition less easily, and develop physical-type symptoms in reaction to stress.

17. You once played in an all-star game alongside Antonio, an unknown basketball player just like you. Antonio, however, is a very tall and noticeable player on the court. Although you both played equally well, almost all the credit for the win went to _____, which seems analogous to the _____ effect in classical conditioning.

13. If the scent of ammonia and the ticking of a clock are combined to form a compound stimulus, then the two stimuli are being presented (simultaneously/successively) _____.

26. Alan finds that he can lessen his hunger pangs while waiting for dinner by watching an exciting television show. This is most similar to the concept of _____.

21. Rasheed had never experienced a more difficult multiple-choice test. Virtually every alternative for every question looked equally correct. By the end of the exam, he felt extremely anxious. Rasheed's experience is somewhat analogous to a phenomenon discovered by Pavlov's associates, which they called _____.

16. A student has great difficulty focusing on the relevant material being discussed in class and is easily distracted. This student might also display (stronger/weaker) _____ evidence of _____ inhibition compared to the average student.

7. A person who fears dogs also feels anxious when he hears the word *canine*. This is an example of _____.

Visit the book companion Web site at <http://www.academic.cengage.com/psychology/powell> for additional practice questions, answers to the Quick Quizzes, practice review exams, and additional exercises and information.

ANSWERS TO CHAPTER TEST

1. asymptote
2. decrease; extinction
3. higher-order conditioning
4. introverts; extroverts
5. stimulus generalization
6. repeated presentations of the CS without the US
7. semantic generalization
8. pseudo; sensitization
9. sensory preconditioning
10. partially returned; spontaneous recovery
11. first-order; second-order
12. weaker
13. simultaneously
14. blocking; overshadowing
15. blocking (with Orr being analogous to an established CS)
16. weaker; latent
17. Antonio; overshadowing
18. US revaluation
19. temporal
20. occasion setting; occasion setter
21. experimental neurosis
22. disinhibition
23. extroverts; poorly
24. acquisition; larger
25. higher-order conditioning; CS_1; CS_2
26. external inhibition

CHAPTER 5

Classical Conditioning: Underlying Processes and Practical Applications

CHAPTER OUTLINE

Estella thought Juan looked a bit tipsy as he left the picnic to drive home. She wondered if she should tell him that the supposedly nonalcoholic punch he had been drinking was actually spiked with vodka. On the other hand, he had only had a single glass. He surely couldn't be drunk.

Underlying Processes in Classical Conditioning

By now, you probably realize that classical conditioning is not as simple a process as it first seems. It is a complex phenomenon that is only slowly yielding its secrets to researchers. The following sections discuss major theoretical notions concerning the underlying processes of classical conditioning. As you will learn, some of these theories have resulted in findings with great practical importance.

S-S Versus S-R Learning

There are two basic ways to conceptualize the type of learning that occurs in classical conditioning. One way, which conforms to the general S-R approach promoted by Watson and Hull, is to view classical conditioning as a process of directly attaching a reflex response to a new stimulus. According to this *S-R (stimulus-response) model* of conditioning, the neutral stimulus (NS) becomes directly associated with the unconditioned response (UR) and therefore comes to elicit the same response as the UR. For example, when bitten by a dog, a child directly associates the dog with the pain and fear that were elicited by the bite and therefore experiences fear when he or she next encounters the dog. Similarly, if I can somehow cause you to salivate in the presence of a tone (such as by presenting food immediately after the tone), then the response of salivation will become connected to the tone, and you will subsequently salivate whenever you hear the tone. In each case, the purpose of the unconditioned stimulus (US) is simply to elicit the UR so that it occurs in close proximity to the NS, thereby allowing a connection to be created between the NS and the UR (see Figure 5.1).

Another way of conceptualizing classical conditioning is the *S-S (stimulus-stimulus) model* of conditioning, in which the NS becomes directly associated with the US and, because of this association, comes to elicit a response that is

FIGURE 5.1 According to the S-R model of conditioning, the NS is directly associated with the UR.

Pavlov was a physiologist who believed that classical conditioning was an effective, though indirect, way of studying neurological processes in the brain. Thus, he often made inferences about the kinds of neurological processes that are activated during conditioning. He claimed that presentation of a US, such as food, activated an area of the cerebral cortex (the outermost layer of the brain) that was responsible for sensing the occurrence of that event. Activation of this "food center" in the brain in turn activated another part of the cortex (the "salivation center") that produced the unconditioned response of salivation.

Food → *Activates food center in cortex* → *Activates salivation center in cortex* → **Salivation**

Pavlov also believed that the presentation of a neutral stimulus, such as a light, activated another area of the cortex responsible for detecting that type of stimulus. According to Pavlov, when the light is presented just before the food during conditioning, a connection is formed between the area of the cortex activated by the light and the area activated by the food. As a result, activation of the light center of the cortex also activates the food center of the cortex, resulting in salivation. In other words, Pavlov believed that the presentation of the light set in motion the following sequence of events:

Light → *Activates light center in cortex* → *Activates food center in cortex* → *Activates salivation center in cortex* → **Salivation**

Pavlov's notions about the kinds of neurological processes underlying classical conditioning are now considered to be incorrect. These processes are known to be considerably more complex than he presumed. Nevertheless, this does not negate all aspects of Pavlov's theory. For example, consider the notion that the conditioned stimulus (CS) is somehow a direct substitute for the US. In at least some cases, it seems as though animals do react to the CS as if it were the US. The dog salivates to the tone just as it does to food. More importantly, the dog may even approach the light and start to lick it, as though pairing the light with the food resulted in the light being perceived as edible (Pavlov, 1941). This sort of phenomenon, now known as *sign tracking*, is discussed more fully in Chapter 11.

Pavlov's theory can be classified as a type of S-S theory because it involves the formation of a neurological association between an NS and a US. Nevertheless, on a behavioral level, it is similar to an S-R theory insofar as it predicts that the conditioned response (CR) will be the same, or at least highly similar, to the UR. Although this is often the case, the major problem with this theory is that it sometimes is not the case. In fact, sometimes the CR and the UR differ substantially. For example, a rat that receives a foot shock (the US) will probably jump (the UR). However, if it sees a light (CS) that has been paired with a foot shock, it will freeze (the CR). Why would the rat jump in one instance and freeze in the other? An examination of the rat's

FIGURE 5.2   According to the S-S model of conditioning, the NS is directly associated with the US.

Tone: Food ⟶ *Salivate*
NS   US   UR

related to the US. Thus, a child who is bitten by a dog associates the dog with the bite, and because of that association the child comes to fear the dog. Likewise, pairing a tone with food results in the tone being associated with food, as a result of which the tone comes to elicit salivation. An everyday mentalistic way of thinking about it is that the tone makes the dog think of the food, and because it is thinking of food, it now salivates (see Figure 5.2). Although the S-R and S-S models might seem mutually exclusive (i.e., it seems as though both cannot be correct) and have often been pitted against each other by theorists, many researchers now believe that both types of processes may be involved in conditioning. Many basic conditioning procedures do seem to cause an association to develop between the NS and the US (an S-S association)—as shown, for example, by the phenomena of blocking and US revaluation that were discussed in the last chapter. Other instances of conditioning, however, seem to involve the establishment of an S-R association (see Domjan, 2003, for further details). Nevertheless, modern theories of conditioning have generally emphasized the establishment of S-S associations. In particular, they have attempted to specify how the NS and US become associated during the conditioning process—a problem that Pavlov himself grappled with.

1. In the _____-_____ model of classical conditioning, conditioning is viewed as a process of directly attaching a reflex response to a new stimulus.

2. In the _____-_____ model of classical conditioning, conditioning involves establishing a direct connection between an NS and a US.

3. Tyrell was once bitten by Rover, the neighbor's dog, and as a result he developed a strong fear of the dog. However, when he heard that Rover had to have all his teeth removed, Tyrell's fear of the dog completely disappeared. This suggests that Tyrell's fear response was based on an _____-_____ association. (Think: Was Tyrell's fear based on associating Rover with the response of fear or with the possibility of being bitten?) According to Chapter 4, this is also an example of (US revaluation/blocking) _____.

Stimulus–Substitution Versus Preparatory–Response Theory

An early S-S theory of conditioning was introduced by Pavlov (1927). According to Pavlov's ***stimulus-substitution theory,*** the CS acts as a substitute for the US. For example, pairing a tone with food results in the tone becoming a substitute for the food, eliciting salivation just as the food does.

natural response to danger gives us a clue. If a rat is attacked by a snake, jumping straight up (and rats can really jump!) may cause the snake to miss. On the other hand, if a rat detects a snake in the vicinity, tensing its muscles and freezing will minimize the possibility of being detected or, if the rat is attacked, will enable it to jump quickly. This suggests that the purpose of the CR, rather than merely being a version of the UR, is to ready the organism for the occurrence of the US.

Thus, according to ***preparatory-response theory,*** the purpose of the CR is to prepare the organism for the presentation of the US (Kimble, 1961, 1967). The dog salivates to the tone to get ready for food, and the rat freezes in response to the light to get ready for the shock. Note that in one case, the preparatory response is highly similar to the UR, whereas in the other case it is quite different. Thus, unlike stimulus-substitution theory, preparatory-response theory allows for situations in which the CR and the UR are different. In some cases, conditioning can even result in a CR that appears to be the opposite of the original UR. We examine this possibility in the next section, in which we discuss a version of preparatory-response theory known as the compensatory-response model.

QUICK QUIZ B

1. According to _____-_____ theory, the CS acts as a substitute for the US.

2. According to _____-_____ theory, the purpose of the CR is to prepare the organism for the occurrence of the US.

3. According to _____-_____ theory, the CR and UR should always be the same or at least highly similar. As it turns out, this is (true/false) _____.

Compensatory-Response Model

An interesting example of preparatory-response theory involves cases in which conditioning eventually results in a CR that appears to be the opposite of the original UR. This type of conditioning often occurs with drug reactions, so we will illustrate it using the example of heroin. Imagine that a heroin addict always injects heroin in the presence of certain environmental cues, such as a particular room and/or with certain friends. Heroin has several effects on the body, but we will focus on just one of them for now, which is a decrease in blood pressure. Shooting up with heroin involves the following sequence of events:

> **Heroin-related cues: Heroin → *Decreased blood pressure***
>   **NS**   **US**   **UR**

If this was a normal conditioning procedure, one might expect that the heroin-related cues will eventually become a CS that will itself elicit a decrease in blood pressure. But in reality, quite the opposite occurs. With repeated drug use, the presence of the heroin-related cues elicit not a decrease in blood pressure, but an *increase* in blood pressure!

Heroin-related cues → *Increased blood pressure*
         CS   **CR**

How can this be? Remember the opponent-process theory of emotion that we learned about in Chapter 3. Recall how certain stimuli can elicit both a primary response (the a-process) and a compensatory response (the b-process). According to the ***compensatory-response model,*** a CS that has been repeatedly associated with the primary response (a-process) to a US will eventually come to elicit a compensatory response (b-process).

To help clarify this, let us examine the heroin example in more detail. Repeatedly injecting heroin does not simply elicit a response, but instead sets in motion a chain of events. The heroin directly elicits an immediate decrease in blood pressure (the a-process) that in turn elicits a compensatory increase in blood pressure (the b-process).

Heroin → *Decreased blood pressure* → *Increased blood pressure*
              (a-process)   *(b-process)*

In terms of stimuli and responses, the heroin is a US that naturally elicits a decrease in blood pressure, and the decrease in blood pressure is itself a US that naturally elicits an increase in blood pressure. Therefore, the decrease in blood pressure is both an unconditioned response (UR) to heroin and an unconditioned stimulus (US) that elicits a compensatory increase in blood pressure.

Heroin → *Decreased blood pressure* → *Increased blood pressure*
  US   UR / US   UR

Notice that there are two USs in this sequence that the heroin-related cues in the environment could potentially become associated with: the heroin, or the decrease in blood pressure that results from the heroin.

What happens in compensatory conditioning is that the heroin-related cues, such as being in a certain room, become associated not with the heroin but with the primary response to heroin—that is, with the decrease in blood pressure. As a result, these cues eventually come to elicit the compensatory reaction to that response. So the actual conditioning that takes place with heroin is as follows:

Heroin-related cues: Decreased blood pressure → *Increased blood pressure*
         NS   **US**   **UR**
Heroin-related cues → *Increased blood pressure*
         CS   **CR**

Why would this type of compensatory conditioning occur? Remember how, in the opponent-process theory, the compensatory reactions to a US serve to maintain a state of homeostasis (internal balance). If these compensatory reactions start occurring before the US is presented, they will be even more effective in minimizing the disturbance produced by the US. For example, if the compensatory reaction to the heroin (an increase in blood pressure) can be elicited just before the injection of heroin, then the immediate physical reaction to the heroin (the decrease in blood pressure) will be effectively moderated. In this sense, a conditioned compensatory response allows the body to prepare itself *ahead of time* for the onslaught of the drug. Conditioned compensatory responses therefore constitute an extreme form of preparatory response to certain environmental events.

1. According to the _____-_____ model of drug conditioning, a CS that has been associated with (a drug/primary response to a drug) _____ will eventually come to elicit a c_____ reaction. Another way of looking at it is that the CS has become associated with the (a-process/b-process) _____ and therefore eventually comes to elicit the (a-process/b-process) _____.

2. Diagram the *actual* events involved in the conditioning of an increase in blood pressure in response to a hypodermic needle that has been consistently associated with heroin administration (*hint*: the US in this conditioning is not heroin):

Needle: _____ → _____
    NS   US   UR

Needle → _____
    CS   CR

3. Shock naturally elicits an increase in heart rate. In this case, shock is a (NS/CS/US) _____ and the increase in heart rate is a (CR/UR) _____.

4. Following from question 3, an increase in heart rate naturally elicits a compensatory decrease in heart rate. For this sequence of events, the increase in heart rate is a (NS/CS/US) _____ and the decrease in heart rate is (CR/UR) _____.

5. Following from question 4, a tone that is repeatedly paired with shock will eventually come to elicit a compensatory decrease in heart rate. Diagram the actual events involved in this type of conditioning (paying particular attention to what the actual US consists of).

Tone: _____ → _____
    NS   US   UR

Tone → _____
    CS   CR

QUICK QUIZ C

The compensatory-response model obviously has important implications for *drug addiction*. Drug addictions are partly motivated by a tendency to avoid the symptoms of drug withdrawal, which are essentially the compensatory responses to the effect of the drug. For example, heroin produces a decrease in blood pressure as well as a combination of other effects, which the drug user experiences as pleasant feelings of relaxation and euphoria. This relaxing effect of heroin in turn elicits compensatory reactions that, on their own, are experienced as unpleasant feelings of tension. Repeated heroin use therefore results in the following process of conditioning:

Heroin-related cues: Relaxing effect of heroin → *Tension & agitation*
      NS   **US**   **UR**
Heroin-related cues → *Tension & agitation*
      CS   **CR**

Thus, a heroin addict will, after repeated heroin use, begin to experience unpleasant symptoms of tension and agitation simply by being in the presence of cues associated with heroin use. These symptoms are what the drug addict interprets as symptoms of withdrawal.

The presence of drug-related cues is therefore one of the strongest reasons why people continue to battle cravings long after they have stopped using a drug. Think of an individual who always uses heroin in a particular environment, goes into a rehab program, and then returns home to her usual environment. When she returns to the environment in which she had previously used heroin, she will very likely become agitated, which she will interpret as withdrawal symptoms and a craving for heroin. And to escape from these symptoms, she will be sorely tempted to once more take heroin.

To the extent that withdrawal symptoms are elicited by CSs associated with drug use, then removing those CSs should weaken the withdrawal symptoms and make it easier to remain abstinent. This possibility is supported by anecdotal evidence. Many American soldiers became heroin users during their tour of duty in Vietnam, leading to fears that they would remain addicted when they returned home. These fears, however, did not materialize (Robins, 1974). One explanation for this is that the drastic change in environment when the soldiers returned home removed many of the cues associated with heroin use, thereby alleviating the symptoms of withdrawal and making it easier for them to remain heroin free.

Unfortunately, for many people trying to kick a habit, whether it is alcohol, cigarettes, or heroin, it is often not possible to completely avoid all cues associated with the drug. For this reason, modern treatments for drug addiction often include procedures designed to extinguish the power of drug-related cues. For example, someone attempting to quit smoking may be required to remain in the presence of cigarettes for a long period of time without smoking. Repeated presentations of the CS (the sight of the cigarettes) in the absence of the US (nicotine ingestion) should result in weaker and weaker CRs (cravings for a smoke). Of course, this process can initially be very difficult—and in the case of severe alcoholism, even dangerous due to the severity of withdrawal symptoms. It therefore requires careful management, but once accomplished can significantly reduce the possibility of a relapse. (See also Sokolowska, Siegel, & Kim,

2002, for a discussion of how some CSs can be internal, such as feelings of stress that lead to smoking, and how the effect of these internal cues may also need to be extinguished.)

The compensatory-response model also has implications for *drug tolerance* (Siegel, 1983, 2005). For example, if you have a habit of always drinking in a particular setting, then the various cues in that setting—people greeting you as you walk in the front door of the bar; the stool you always sit on—become CSs for the effect of alcohol. The presence of these CSs will initiate physiological reactions that compensate for the alcohol you are about to consume. As a result, in the presence of these CSs, you should have greater tolerance for alcohol than you would in their absence.

Research has confirmed this association. In a study by McCusker and Brown (1990), participants consumed alcohol in either an "alcohol expected" environment (i.e., alcohol was consumed in a simulated lounge during the evening with pub noises playing in the background) or an "alcohol unexpected" environment (i.e., alcohol was consumed during the day in an office environment). Those who consumed alcohol in the expected environment performed significantly better on various measures of cognitive and motor functioning compared to those who consumed alcohol in the unexpected environment. They also showed smaller increases in pulse rate. This suggests that the alcohol-related cues in the expected condition (evening, lounge setting) elicited compensatory reactions that partially compensated for the effects of the alcohol (see also Bennett & Samson, 1991).

On the other side of the coin, if you consume alcohol in an environment where you typically do not drink (e.g., a business luncheon), the alcohol could have a much stronger effect on you than if you consumed it in an environment where you typically do drink (e.g., a bar). This means that your ability to drive safely could be significantly more impaired following a lunchtime martini than after an evening drink at a bar. Worse yet, even if you do consume the drink at a bar, consider what happens when you leave that setting. Your compensatory reactions might be reduced significantly because you have now removed yourself from the alcohol-related cues that elicit those reactions. As a result, you may become more intoxicated during the drive home from the bar than you were in the bar (Linnoila, Stapleton, Lister, Guthrie, & Eckhardt, 1986). This means that the amount of alcohol you consume is not, by itself, a reliable gauge for determining how intoxicated you are. (Thus, going back to the opening vignette for this chapter, why should Estella be especially concerned about Juan's ability to drive?)[1]

It should be noted that there are exceptions to the typical compensatory reactions to a CS. Stimuli associated with drug use sometimes elicit druglike

---

[1]The type of alcohol consumed can also have an effect. People become significantly more intoxicated following consumption of an unusual drink (such as a strange liqueur) rather than a familiar drink (such as beer). The familiar drink can be seen as a CS for alcohol that elicits compensatory reactions to the alcohol (Remington, Roberts, & Glautier, 1997).

And Furthermore

Conditioned Compensatory Responses and Drug Overdose

The compensatory-response model has also been used to explain incidents of *drug overdose*. Many "overdose" fatalities do not, in fact, involve an unusually large amount of the drug. For example, heroin addicts often die after injecting a dosage that has been well tolerated on previous occasions. A critical factor appears to be the setting within which the drug is administered. As we have seen, if a heroin addict typically administers the drug in the presence of certain cues, those cues become CSs that elicit compensatory reactions to the drug. An addict's tolerance to heroin therefore is much greater in the presence of those cues than in their absence.

Anecdotal evidence supports this possibility. Siegel (1984) interviewed 10 survivors of heroin overdose, 7 of whom reported that the overdose had been preceded by an unusual change in the setting or drug administration procedure. For example, one woman reported that she overdosed after hitting a vein on the first try at injecting the drug, whereas she usually required several tries. Further evidence comes from studies with rats that had become addicted to heroin. When the cues usually associated with heroin were absent, the rats' ability to tolerate a large dose was markedly reduced to the point that many of the rats died. Thus, heroin-tolerant rats who were administered a very strong dose of heroin in a novel setting were more likely to die than those who received the dose in the setting previously associated with the drug (Siegel, Hinson, Krank, & McCully, 1982).

Siegel (1989) describes two cases that clearly illustrate the dangers of drug overdose resulting from conditioning effects.

The respondent (E. C.) was a heavy user of heroin for three years. She usually self-administered her first, daily dose of heroin in the bathroom of her apartment, where she lived with her mother. Typically, E. C.

reactions rather than drug-compensatory reactions. In other words, the stimuli become associated with the primary response to the drug rather than the compensatory response. For example, in one study, rats became more sensitive to cocaine when it was administered in the usual cocaine administration environment than in a different one (Hinson & Poulos, 1981). The CSs for cocaine administration apparently elicited reactions that mimicked the drug, thereby strengthening its effect. There is also evidence that stimuli associated with drug use sometimes elicit both drug compensatory responses in one system of the body and druglike responses in another. For example, a CS for caffeine, such as a cup of decaffeinated coffee that has many of the cues associated with coffee but without the caffeine, produces a caffeine-like increase in alertness and a caffeine-compensatory decrease in salivation in moderate caffeine users (Rozen, Reff, Mark, & Schull, 1984; see also Eikelboom & Stewart, 1982; Lang, Ross, & Glover, 1967). Thus, the circumstances in which conditioning results in druglike reactions versus drug-compensatory reactions are complex and not entirely understood (Siegel, 1989). (See also "Conditioned Compensatory Responses and Drug Overdose" in the And Furthermore box.)

would awake earlier than her mother, turn on the water in the bathroom (pretending to take a shower), and self-inject without arousing suspicion. However, on the occasion of the overdose, her mother was already awake when E. C. started her injection ritual, and knocked loudly on the bathroom door telling E. C. to hurry. When E. C. then injected the heroin, she immediately found that she could not breathe. She was unable to call her mother for help (her mother eventually broke down the bathroom door and rushed E. C. to the hospital, where she was successfully treated for heroin overdose). (pp. 155–156)

Siegel goes on to explain that the mother knocking on the bathroom door was an unusual cue that may have disrupted the environmental CSs that would normally have elicited compensatory reactions to the heroin. In other words, the knocking was a novel stimulus that resulted in *external inhibition* of the compensatory CRs that would normally have occurred in that setting.

The second example described by Siegel involves administration of a drug to a patient to alleviate the pain of pancreatic cancer.

The patient's [17-year-old] son, N. E., regularly administered the [morphine] in accordance with the procedures and dosage level specified by the patient's physician. . . . The patient's condition was such that he stayed in his bedroom which was dimly lit and contained much hospital-type apparatus necessary for his care. The morphine had always been injected in this environment. For some reason, on the day that the overdose occurred, the patient dragged himself out of the bedroom to the living room. The living room was brightly lit and different in many ways from the bedroom/sickroom. The patient, discovered in the living room by N. E., appeared to be in considerable pain. Inasmuch as it was time for his father's scheduled morphine injection, N. E. injected the drug while his father was in the living room. N. E. noticed that his father's reaction to this injection was atypical; his pupils became unusually small, and his breathing shallow. . . . The father died some hours later. (pp. 156–157)

Two years later, N. E. took a class in which conditioning effects on drug tolerance were discussed, at which point he realized the implications of these effects for his own experience.

1. According to the compensatory-response model of drug addiction, symptoms of withdrawal are likely to be (stronger/weaker) _____ in the presence of drug-related cues. This is because the drug-related cues tend to elicit (primary/compensatory) _____ responses to the drug that are experienced as cravings.

2. In keeping with the compensatory-response model, modern treatments for drug addiction often recommend (exposure to/removal of) _____ drug-related cues to allow (conditioning/extinction) _____ of the cravings to take place.

3. We tend to have (higher/lower) _____ tolerance for a drug in the presence of cues associated with taking the drug.

4. Suppose an addict always injects heroin in her bedroom at home, but one time stays overnight at a friend's house and decides to take an injection there. The addict will likely experience a(n) (increased/decreased) _____ reaction to the drug at her friend's house.

5. A person who drinks a glass of wine in a fine restaurant is likely to be (more/less) _____ affected by the alcohol than if she drank the same amount of wine in a courtroom.

Rescorla–Wagner Theory

One of the most influential theories of classical conditioning was proposed by Rescorla and Wagner (1972). Their theory attempted to explain the effect of each conditioning trial on the strength, or what might be called the "associative value," of the CS in its relationship to the US. The *Rescorla-Wagner theory* proposes that a given US can support only so much conditioning, and this amount of conditioning must be distributed among the various CSs available. Another way of saying this is that there is only so much associative value to be distributed among the various cues associated with the US.

One assumption of this theory is that *stronger USs support more conditioning than do weaker USs*. For example, the use of a highly preferred food as the US produces a stronger conditioned response of salivation than does a less preferred food. Imagine, for example, that a tone paired with a highly preferred food (say, steak) elicits a maximum of 10 drops of saliva, while a tone paired with a much less preferred food (say, dog food) elicits only 5 drops of saliva. If we regard each drop of saliva as a unit of associative value, then we could say that the highly preferred food supports a maximum associative value of 10 units, while the less preferred food supports a maximum associative value of 5 units.

We can use the following format to diagram the changes in the associative value (we will assume the highly preferred food is the US):

Tone (V = 0): **Food** (*Max* = 10) → *Salivation*
Tone (V = 10) → *Salivation*

The letter V will stand for the associative value of the CS (which at the start of conditioning is 0). The term *Max* will stand for the maximum associative value that can be supported by the US once conditioning is complete. In our example, imagine V as the number of drops of saliva the tone elicits—0 drops of saliva to begin with and 10 drops once the tone is fully associated with the food—and *Max* as the maximum number of drops of saliva that the tone can potentially elicit if it is fully associated with the food. (If this is starting to look a bit mathematical to you, you are correct. In fact, the model can be expressed in the form of an equation. For our purposes, however, the equation is unnecessary.)[2]

Now suppose that a compound stimulus consisting of a tone and a light are repeatedly paired with the food, to the point that the compound stimulus obtains the maximum associative value.

[Tone + Light] (V = 0): **Food** (*Max = 10*) → *Salivation*
[Tone + Light] (V = 10) → *Salivation*

This associative value, however, must somehow be distributed between the two component members of the compound. For example, if the tone is a bit

---

[2]The equation for the Rescorla-Wagner model is $\Delta V = k(\lambda - V)$, where V is the associative value of the CS, λ ("lambda") represents the maximum associative value that the CS can hold (i.e., the asymptote of learning), and k is a constant that represents the salience of the CS and US (with greater salience supporting more conditioning). For additional information on the use of this equation, see the additional information for this chapter that is posted at the textbook Web site.

more salient than the light, then the tone might have picked up 6 units of associative value while the light picked up only 4 units. In other words, when tested separately, the tone elicits 6 drops of saliva while the light elicits 4.

Tone $(V = 6) \rightarrow$ *Salivation*
Light $(V = 4) \rightarrow$ *Salivation*

If the tone was even more salient than the light—for example, it was a very loud tone and a very faint light—then *overshadowing* might occur, with the tone picking up 9 units of associative value and the light only 1 unit:

[Loud tone + Faint light] $(V = 0)$: **Food** $(Max = 10) \rightarrow$ *Salivation*
Loud tone $(V = 9) \rightarrow$ *Salivation*
Faint light $(V = 1) \rightarrow$ *Salivation*

The loud tone now elicits 9 drops of saliva (a strong CR) while the faint light elicits only 1 drop of saliva (a weak CR). Thus, the Rescorla-Wagner explanation for the overshadowing effect is that there is only so much associative value available (if you will, only so much spit available) for conditioning, and if the more salient stimulus in the compound picks up most of the associative value, then there is little associative value left over for the less salient stimulus.

As can be seen, the Rescorla-Wagner theory readily explains conditioning situations involving compound stimuli. Take, for example, a *blocking* procedure. One stimulus is first conditioned to its maximum associative value:

Tone $(V = 0)$: **Food** $(Max = 10) \rightarrow$ *Salivation*
Tone $(V = 10) \rightarrow$ *Salivation*

This stimulus is then combined with another stimulus for further conditioning trials:

[Tone + Light] $(V = 10 + 0 = 10)$: **Food** $(Max = 10) \rightarrow$ *Salivation*

But note that the food supports a maximum associative value of only 10 units, and the tone has already acquired that much value. The light can therefore acquire no associative value because all of the associative value has already been assigned to the tone. Thus, when the two stimuli are later tested for conditioning, the following occurs:

Tone $(V = 10) \rightarrow$ *Salivation*
Light $(V = 0) \rightarrow$ **No salivation**

So far we have described the Rescorla-Wagner theory in relation to changes in associative value. The theory has also been interpreted in more cognitive terms. To say that a CS has high associative value is similar to saying that it is a strong predictor of the US, or that the subject strongly "expects" the US whenever it encounters the CS. Thus, in the previous example, to say that the tone has high associative value means that it is a good predictor of food and that the dog "expects" food whenever it hears the tone. In the case of blocking, however, the tone is such a good predictor of food that the light with which it is later paired becomes redundant, and the presence of the light does not affect the subject's expectations about food. As a result, no conditioning occurs to the light. In general, then, conditioning can be viewed as a matter of building the subject's expectations that one event will follow another.

The Rescorla-Wagner theory also leads to some counterintuitive predictions. Consider what happens if you first condition two CSs to their maximum associative value and then combine them into a compound stimulus for further conditioning. For example, suppose we condition a tone to its maximum associative value, as follows:

> **Tone** $(V = 0)$: **Food** *(Max = 10)* → *Salivation*
> **Tone** $(V = 10)$ → *Salivation*

and then do the same for the light:

> **Light** $(V = 0)$: **Food** *(Max = 10)* → *Salivation*
> **Light** $(V = 10)$ → *Salivation*

We now combine the tone and the light into a compound stimulus and conduct further conditioning trials:

> **[Tone + Light]** $(V = 10 + 10 = 20)$: **Food** *(Max = 10)* → *Salivation*

Note that the tone and the light together have 20 units of associative value (10 for the tone and 10 for the light). However, the maximum associative value that can be supported by the food at any one moment is only 10 units. This means that the associative value of the compound stimulus must decrease to match the maximum value that can be supported by the US. Thus, according to the Rescorla-Wagner theory, after several pairings of the compound stimulus with food, the total associative value of the compound stimulus will be reduced to 10:

> **[Tone + Light]** $(V = 10)$ → *Salivation*

This in turn means that when each member in the compound is tested separately, its value also will have decreased. For example:

> **Tone** $(V = 5)$ → *Salivation*
> **Light** $(V = 5)$ → *Salivation*

Thus, even though the tone and light were subjected to further pairings with the food, the associative value of each decreased (i.e., each stimulus elicited less salivation than it originally did when it had been conditioned individually).

The effect we have just described is known as the *overexpectation effect,* the decrease in the conditioned response that occurs when two separately conditioned CSs are combined into a compound stimulus for further pairings with the US. It is as though presenting the two CSs together leads to an "overexpectation" about what will follow. When this expectation is not fulfilled, the subject's expectations are modified downward. As a result, each CS in the compound loses some of its associative value.

ADVICE FOR THE LOVELORN

Dear Dr. Dee,

My friend says that if you are deeply and madly in love with someone, then you will necessarily be much less interested in anyone else. I think my friend is wrong. There is no reason why someone can't be deeply in love with more than one person at a time. So who is right?

The Wanderer

Dear Wanderer,

I honestly do not know who is right. But your friend's hypothesis seems somewhat consistent with the Rescorla-Wagner theory. If feelings of love are to some extent classically conditioned emotional responses, then the more love you feel for one person (meaning that he or she is a distinctive CS that has strong associative value), the less love you should feel for alternative partners who are simultaneously available (because there is little associative value left over for those other CSs). In other words, there is only so much love (so much associative value) to go around, and strong romantic feelings for one person will likely result in weak romantic feelings for others. In keeping with this, you can occasionally encounter people who report being so "in love" with someone—at least in the early stages of a relationship—that they are attracted to no one else. (I remember a male movie star some years ago commenting upon this, remarking that he had never thought it possible that he could so completely lose interest in all other women.) It is the case, however, that some people are strongly attracted to many different partners, though perhaps what is attracting them in such cases is some quality that those partners have in common, such as a high degree of physical attractiveness. But would we then define such attraction as love?

Behaviorally yours,

Dr. Dee

Although the Rescorla-Wagner model has been a source of inspiration for researchers, not all of its predictions have been confirmed. As a result, revisions to the model have been proposed along with alternative models. Some behaviorists have also criticized the common practice of interpreting the Rescorla-Wagner model in cognitive terms by arguing that the concept of associative value, which can be objectively measured by the strength of the CR, makes inferences about mentalistic processes, such as expectations, unnecessary (e.g., Pierce & Epling, 1995). Despite these debates, however, few models have been as productive in furthering our understanding of the underlying processes of classical conditioning.

1. The Rescorla-Wagner theory proposes that a given _____ can support only so much conditioning, and this amount of conditioning must be distributed among the various _____ available.

2. In general, stronger USs support (more/less) _____ conditioning than weaker USs.

3. According to the Rescorla-Wagner theory, overshadowing occurs because the more salient CS picks up (most/little) _____ of the associative value available in that setting.

4. According to the Rescorla-Wagner theory, blocking occurs because the (CS/NS) _____ in the compound has already picked up all of the available associative value.

5. Suppose a compound stimulus has an associative value of 25 following conditioning. According to the Rescorla-Wagner theory, if one CS has acquired 15 units of associative value, the other CS must have acquired _____ units of associative value.

6. Suppose a tone and a light are each conditioned with food to a maximum associative value of 8 units. If the tone and light are combined into a compound stimulus for further conditioning trials, the associative value of each stimulus must necessarily (decrease/increase) _____. This is known as the o_____ effect.

Practical Applications of Classical Conditioning

Understanding Phobias

A particularly salient way that classical conditioning affects our lives is through its involvement in the development of fears and anxieties. As already noted, a conditioned fear response can be elicited by a previously neutral stimulus that has been associated with an aversive stimulus. In most cases, this sort of fear conditioning is a highly adaptive process because it motivates the individual to avoid a dangerous situation. A person who is bitten by a dog and learns to fear dogs is less likely to be bitten in the future simply because he or she will tend to avoid dogs.

This process, however, occasionally becomes exaggerated, with the result that we become very fearful of events that are not at all dangerous or only minimally dangerous. Such extreme, irrational fear reactions are known as phobias. In many cases, these phobias seem to represent a process of *over-generalization*, in which a conditioned fear response to one event has become overgeneralized to other harmless events. Thus, although it may be rational to fear a mean-looking dog that once bit you, it is irrational to fear a friendly-looking dog that has never bitten you.

Watson and Rayner's "Little Albert"   The importance of classical conditioning and overgeneralization in the development of phobias was first noted by John B. Watson and his student (and wife-to-be) Rosalie Rayner. In 1920, Watson and Rayner published a now-famous article in which they described their attempt to condition a fear response in an 11-month-old infant named Albert. Albert was a very healthy, well-developed child, whose mother worked as a wet nurse in the hospital where the tests were conducted. Albert was described as "stolid and unemotional," almost never cried, and had never been seen to display rage or fear. In fact, he seemed to display an unusual level of emotional stability.

The researchers began the experiment by testing Albert's reactions to a variety of objects. These included a white rat, a rabbit, a dog, some cotton wool, and even a burning newspaper. None of the objects elicited any fear, and in fact Albert often attempted to handle them. He was, however, startled when the experimenters made a loud noise by banging a steel bar with a hammer. The experimenters thus concluded that the loud noise was an unconditioned stimulus that elicited a fear response (or, more specifically, a startle reaction), whereas the other objects, such as the rat, were neutral stimuli with respect to fear:

Loud noise → *Fear (as indicated by startle reaction)*
   US   **UR**
Rat → **No fear**
NS   —

In the next part of the experiment, Watson and Rayner (1920) paired the loud noise (US) with the white rat (NS). The rat was presented to Albert, and just as his hand touched it, the steel bar was struck with the hammer. In this first conditioning trial, Albert "jumped violently and fell forward, burying his face in the mattress. He did not cry, however" (p. 4). He reacted similarly when the trial was repeated, except that this time he began to whimper. The conditioning session was ended at that point.

The next session was held a week later. At the start of the session, the rat was handed to Albert to test his reaction to it. He tentatively reached for the rat, but he quickly withdrew his hand after touching it. Since, by comparison, he showed no fear of some toy blocks that were handed to him, it seemed that a slight amount of fear conditioning to the rat had occurred during the previous week's session. Albert was then subjected to further pairings of the rat with the noise, during which he became more and more fearful. Finally, at one point, when the rat was presented without the noise, Albert "began to crawl so rapidly that he was caught with difficulty before reaching the edge of the table" (Watson & Rayner, 1920, p. 5). Albert's strong avoidance reaction suggested that the rat had indeed become a conditioned fear stimulus as a result of its association with the noise. This process can be diagrammed as follows:

Rat: Loud noise → *Fear*
  NS   US   UR
Rat → *Fear* (as indicated by crying and crawling away from the rat)
  CS   CR

In subsequent sessions (during which Albert occasionally received further pairings of the rat with the noise to "freshen" the conditioning), Albert showed not only a fear of the rat but also of objects that were in some way similar to the rat, such as a rabbit, a fur coat, a dog, and even a Santa Claus mask. In other words, Albert's fear response had generalized to objects that were similar to the original CS. His conditioned fear to the rat, and his generalized fear of similar objects, persisted even following a 30-day break, although the intensity of his reactions was somewhat diminished. At that point, Albert's mother moved away, taking Albert with her, so further tests could not be conducted. Watson and Rayner were therefore unable to carry out their stated plan of using behavioral procedures to eliminate Albert's newly acquired fear response.

Watson and Rayner with Little Albert. (The white rat is beside Albert's left arm.)

Courtesy of Prof. Benjamin Harris, University of New Hampshire

Although the Little Albert experiment is often depicted as a convincing demonstration of phobic conditioning in a young infant, it is actually quite limited in this regard. For example, it took several pairings of the loud noise with the rat before the rat reliably elicited a strong fear reaction; additionally, although Albert's fear reaction remained evident following a 30-day rest period, it had also started to diminish by that time. By contrast, real-life phobias usually require only one pairing of the US with the CS to become established, and they often grow stronger over time. Watson and Rayner (1920) also noted that Albert displayed no fear so long as he was able to suck his thumb, and the experimenters had to repeatedly remove his thumb from his mouth during the sessions to enable a fear reaction to be elicited. This suggests that Albert's fear response was relatively weak since it was easily countered by the pleasure derived from thumb sucking.

Thus, although Watson and Rayner (1920) speculated about the possibility of Albert growing up to be a neurotic individual with a strange fear of furry objects, it is quite likely that he did not develop a true phobia and soon got over any aversion to furry objects. In fact, more recent evidence suggests that additional factors are often involved in the development of a true phobia. Some of these factors are discussed in the next section.[3]

1. A phobia is an extreme, irrational fear reaction to a particular event. From a classical conditioning perspective, it seems to represent a process of over-_____.

2. In the Little Albert experiment, the rat was originally a(n) _____ stimulus, while the loud noise was a(n) _____ stimulus.

3. Albert's startle response to the noise was a(n) _____ response, while his crying in response to the rat was a(n) _____ response.

4. One difference between Albert's fear conditioning and conditioning of real-life phobias is that the latter often require (only one/more than one) _____ conditioning trial.

5. Unlike real-life phobias, Albert's fear of the rat seemed to grow (stronger/weaker) _____ following a 30-day break.

6. Albert's fear response was (present/absent) _____ whenever he was sucking his thumb, which suggests that the fear conditioning was actually relatively (strong/weak) _____.

QUICK QUIZ F

---

[3]It has been noted that the Little Albert study can also be interpreted as an example of operant conditioning (e.g., Goodwin, 2005). More specifically, because the loud noise occurred when the baby reached for the rat—meaning that the noise followed the reaching response and served to punish that response—the process can be described as an example of *positive punishment* (which is discussed in Chapter 6).

And Furthermore

The Ethics of the Little Albert Experiment

By today's standards, the Little Albert study is highly unethical, and many people are astounded that such an experiment could ever have taken place. The lack of established ethical guidelines for psychological research at that time no doubt played a role. But it is also interesting to note that the Little Albert study hardly raised an eyebrow at the time it was published. In fact, Watson received far more criticism for his research with rats (from animal rights activists) than he ever did for his research with Albert (Buckley, 1989). This might seem strange to us, living as we do in an era when people are quite sensitive to issues of child abuse and maltreatment. But in Watson's era, such issues, though not ignored, were certainly given less attention. Nevertheless, Watson and Rayner were not completely oblivious to the possible harm their procedures might create. For example, they deliberately chose Albert as a subject because of his strong emotional stability, which to them implied that they could do him "relatively little harm by carrying out such experiments . . ." (Watson & Rayner, 1920, p. 3). They also "comforted themselves" with the notion that the experiences Albert would receive during the experiment were probably not much different from what he would naturally encounter when he left "the sheltered environment of the nursery for the rough and tumble of the home" (p. 3). Unfortunately, Watson and Rayner's cautious concerns seemed to disappear later in the article when they joked about the possibility of Albert's fear response remaining with him when he grew into adulthood:

> The Freudians twenty years from now, unless their hypotheses change, when they come to analyze Albert's fear of a seal skin coat . . . will probably tease from him the recital of a dream which upon their analysis will show that Albert at three years of age attempted to play with the pubic hair of the mother and was scolded violently for it. (Watson & Rayner, 1920, p. 14)

One can only hope that this statement was more an example of Watson's bravado and an attempt to convince others of the superiority of his behavioral approach than any belief that he and Rayner had induced a permanent phobia in Albert. In any event, the Little Albert experiment certainly illustrates the need for stringent ethical standards regarding the use of humans (especially children) in experimental research.

Additional Factors in Phobic Conditioning   Not all phobias are acquired through a direct process of classical conditioning. Indeed, many people with phobias are unable to recall any particular conditioning event before the development of their symptoms (Marks, 1969). Additionally, most people exposed to extremely frightening events do not develop phobias. For example, the vast majority of people exposed to air raids during the World War II endured them rather well, developing only short-term fear reactions that quickly disappeared (Rachman, 1977). Researchers have therefore suggested several additional variables that, singly or in combination, may be involved in the development of phobic symptoms. These include observational learning, temperament, preparedness, history of control, incubation, US revaluation, and selective sensitization.

Observational Learning. Many phobias are acquired through observation of fearful reactions in others. For example, in World War II a major predictor of whether children developed a fear of air raids was whether their mothers displayed such fears. As well, airmen who became phobic of combat often developed their symptoms after witnessing fear reactions in a crew mate (Rachman, 1977).

This tendency to acquire conditioned fear reactions through observation may be inherited (Mineka, 1987). If so, a display of fear by another person may be conceptualized as an unconditioned stimulus that elicits an unconditioned fear response in oneself:

Display of fear by others → *Fear* (in oneself)
        US   UR

A neutral stimulus that is associated with this display might then become a conditioned stimulus for fear:

Snake: Display of fear by others → *Fear*
 NS   US   UR
Snake → *Fear*
 CS   CR

The result is that a person who has had no direct confrontation with snakes may indirectly acquire a conditioned fear of snakes. (The other way in which observational learning of a fear response can occur is through higher-order conditioning. This process is discussed in the section on observational learning in Chapter 12.)

Temperament. **Temperament,** an individual's base level of emotionality and reactivity to stimulation, is to a large extent genetically determined. Temperament seems to affect how easily a conditioned response can be acquired. As noted in Chapter 4, Pavlov found that dogs that were shy and withdrawn conditioned more readily than dogs that were active and outgoing. Similarly, individuals with certain temperaments may be more genetically susceptible than others to the development of conditioned fears (Clark, Watson, & Mineka, 1994).

Even Watson, who made a career out of downplaying the role of genetic influences in human behavior, acknowledged the possible influence of temperament. Watson and Rayner (1920) deliberately chose Albert as a subject under the assumption that his emotional stability would grant him a good deal of immunity against the harmful effects of their procedures. They also noted that "had he been emotionally unstable probably both the directly conditioned response [to the rat] and those transferred [to similar stimuli] would have persisted throughout the month unchanged in form" (p. 12), when in fact his fears had somewhat diminished following the 30-day break. Thus, they believed that Albert did not have the sort of temperament that would facilitate acquiring a phobia.

Preparedness. The concept of **preparedness** refers to a genetically based predisposition to learn certain kinds of associations more easily than others (Seligman, 1971). Thus, we may have an inherited predisposition to develop fears to certain types of objects or events. This notion was initially proposed by Valentine (1930), who attempted to replicate Watson and Rayner's experiment with his 1-year-old daughter by blowing a loud whistle whenever she touched certain objects. When the object she touched was a pair of opera glasses, she displayed no fear, even to the sound of the whistle. When the object was a caterpillar, however, some fear was elicited. By contrast, Valentine observed a 2-year-old who became fearful of dogs "at slight provocation." He concluded that people may have an innate tendency to fear certain kinds of events (such as insects and certain other animals) and that Watson had been able to successfully condition Albert to fear rats because of this tendency.

More recent evidence for the role of preparedness in fear conditioning includes a study by Cook and Mineka (1989). They exposed laboratory-raised rhesus monkeys to videotapes edited to show another monkey reacting either fearfully or nonfearfully to either a fear-relevant stimulus (toy snake or toy crocodile) or a fear-irrelevant stimulus (flowers or toy rabbit). Only those monkeys who observed the model reacting fearfully to the fear-relevant stimulus acquired a conditioned fear reaction to that stimulus. Similarly, Soares and Öhman (1993) found that human subjects displayed physiological signs of anxiety in reaction to certain subliminal stimuli—pictures presented so briefly that subjects were consciously unaware of the content—that had been paired with uncomfortable levels of electric shock. This reaction occurred when the pictures were of fear-relevant stimuli (snakes and spiders) as opposed to fear-irrelevant stimuli (flowers and mushrooms). This result supports the notion that humans, too, may be predisposed to learn certain types of fears more readily than others. (The concept of preparedness is more fully discussed in Chapter 11.)

Students often confuse the concepts of temperament and preparedness. In people, temperament refers to differences between people in how emotionally reactive they are, which in turn affects how easily they can develop a phobia. Preparedness (as it relates to phobias) refers to differences between phobias in how easily they can be acquired. Thus, temperament refers to how extensively a particular person can acquire a phobia, while preparedness affects how easily a particular type of phobia can be acquired. For example, the fact that Jason more easily develops a phobia than does Samantha reflects the role of temperament; the fact that, for both of them, a phobia of snakes is more easily acquired than a phobia of toasters reflects the role of preparedness.

1. From a conditioning perspective, viewing a display of fear in others can be conceptualized as a(n) _____ stimulus that elicits a(n) _____ response of fear in oneself. The event the other person is reacting to might then become a(n) _____ stimulus that elicits a(n) _____ response of fear in oneself.

2. The term _____ refers to an individual's genetically determined level of emotionality and reactivity to stimulation. It (does/does not) _____ seem to affect the extent to which responses can be classically conditioned.

3. The concept of p_____ holds that we are genetically programmed to acquire certain kinds of fears, such as fear of snakes and spiders, more readily than other kinds.

4. Travis rolled his pickup truck, yet he had no qualms about driving home afterwards; Cam was in a minor fender bender last week and remained petrified of driving for several days afterward. These different outcomes may reflect inherited differences in t_____ between the two individuals.

5. The fact that many people are more petrified of encountering snakes than they are of being run over by cars, even though the latter is a far more relevant danger in the world in which they live, reflects differences in _____ for acquiring certain kinds of fears.

History of Control. Another factor that may influence susceptibility to fear conditioning is a history of being able to control important events in one's environment. For example, in one study, young monkeys who had a history of controlling the delivery of food, water, and treats (such as by pulling a chain) were considerably less fearful of a mechanical toy monster than were monkeys who had simply been given these items regardless of their behavior (Mineka, Gunnar, & Champoux, 1986). Living in an environment where they had some degree of control over important events seemed to effectively immunize them against the traumatic effects of encountering a strange and frightening object. Presumably, these monkeys would also have been less susceptible to classical conditioning of fear responses, although this prediction was not directly tested. The harmful effects of prolonged exposure to uncontrollable events, and the beneficial effects of prior exposure to controllable events, are further examined in Chapter 9 under the topic of learned helplessness.

Incubation. When a phobia develops through a direct process of classical conditioning, an important question must be asked: Why does the conditioned fear not extinguish with subsequent exposures to the CS? To some extent, extinction does not occur, because the person tends to avoid the feared stimulus (the CS) so that repeated exposure to the CS in the absence of the US does not take place. Additionally, however, because of this tendency to move away from the feared stimulus, any exposures that do occur are likely to be very brief. According to Eysenck (1968), such brief exposures may result in a phenomenon known as "incubation." *Incubation* refers to the strengthening of a conditioned fear response as a result of brief exposures to the aversive CS.[4] For example, a child who is bitten by a dog and then runs away each time he encounters a dog may find that his fear of dogs grows worse even though he is never again bitten. As a result, what may have

---

[4]The term *incubation* has also been used to refer simply to the increased strength of a fear response that one may experience following a rest period after fear conditioning, with no reference to brief exposures to the CS (e.g., Corsini, 2002).

started off as a moderate fear of dogs may evolve over time into a severe fear. In fact, this process might even result in a conditioned fear that is actually stronger than the unconditioned fear that was originally elicited when the child was bitten. Thus, the CR would be stronger than the UR, which contradicts the general rule that a CR is weaker than the UR. It also contradicts the general rule that the presentation of the CS without the US will result in extinction. Note, too, that covert exposures to the feared stimulus—as in worrying about it—might also result in incubation (Wells & Papageorgiou, 1995). Incubation is, of course, the reason for the old adage that if you fall off a horse you should immediately get back on. If you wait, you might later become too fearful to get back on. Note, however, that some researchers believe that the process of incubation has yet to be convincingly demonstrated (Levis & Brewer, 2001).

US Revaluation. As noted in Chapter 4, exposure to a US of a different intensity (i.e., a different *value*) than that used during conditioning can alter the strength of the response to a previously conditioned CS. This process could play a major role in human phobias (Davey, 1992). Consider, for example, a skateboarder who experiences a minor injury as a result of a fall:

Skateboarding: Minor injury → *Slight anxiety*
Skateboarding → *Slight anxiety*

Because the injury was relatively minor, skateboarding elicits only a slight amount of conditioned anxiety, most of which will likely extinguish as the skateboarder continues the activity. But imagine that this person later is in a car accident and suffers a severe injury:

Severe injury → *Strong anxiety*

What might happen is that he might now display a strong degree of anxiety to skateboarding:

Skateboarding → *Strong anxiety*

It is as though the skateboarder finally realizes just how painful an injury can be. And given that skateboarding is associated with being injured, it now elicits strong feelings of anxiety.

The preceding example involves direct exposure to a US of different intensity; however, the process of US revaluation can also occur through observational learning. A student of one of the authors reported that she developed a phobia about snowboarding after first spraining her leg in a minor snowboarding accident—which resulted in only minor anxiety about snowboarding—and then witnessing someone else suffer a severe snowboarding accident. In this circumstance, observational learning resulted in US inflation, which then led to the phobia.

US inflation can also occur through verbally transmitted information. Consider the following case described by Davey, de Jong, and Tallis (1993):

> M. F. (male, aged 29 yr) worked as a bank employee. On one occasion the bank was robbed, and during the robbery M. F. was threatened with a gun. He had not been particularly anxious at the time and returned to work the next day without complaining of any residual fear symptoms. However, 10 days after the robbery

he was interviewed by the police, and during this interview he was told that he was very lucky to be alive because the bank robber was considered to be a dangerous man who had already killed several people. From this point on M. F. did not return to work and developed severe PTSD symptoms. (p. 496)

This latter example suggests that we have to be particularly careful about the sort of information we convey to people who have suffered potentially traumatic events because that information itself might induce a traumatic reaction. Indeed, research has shown that individuals who have been exposed to a traumatic event and are then given psychological debriefings—a structured form of posttrauma counseling designed to prevent the development of posttraumatic stress disorder (PTSD)—are sometimes *more* likely to develop symptoms of PTSD than those who did not receive such debriefings (e.g., Mayou & Ehlers, 2000; Sijbrandij, Olff, Reitsma, Carlier, & Gersons, 2006). It seems that the debriefing itself sometimes heightens the effect of the trauma, possibly by giving victims the impression that the trauma was more severe than they would otherwise have thought. Because psychological debriefings are now widely employed by various agencies, research is urgently needed to determine the extent to which such debriefings are helpful versus harmful.

Selective Sensitization. Yet another process that could influence the development of a phobia is **selective sensitization,** which is an increase in one's reactivity to a potentially fearful stimulus following exposure to an unrelated stressful event. For example, people with *agoraphobia* (fear of being alone in a public place) often report that the initial onset of the disorder occurred during a period in which they were emotionally upset or suffered from some type of physical illness (Rachman, 1977). Similarly, an individual going through a stressful divorce might find that her previously minor anxiety about driving in heavy traffic suddenly develops into severe anxiety. The stressful circumstance surrounding the divorce affects her reactions not only to the divorce but to other potentially aversive events as well. Therefore, during turbulent times in one's life, minor fears and anxieties may become exacerbated into major fears and anxieties (Barlow, 1988).

1. We will probably be (more/less) _____ susceptible to acquiring a conditioned fear response if we grow up in a world in which we experience little or no control over the available rewards.

2. Brief exposures to a feared CS in the absence of the US may result in a phenomenon known as _____ in which the conditioned fear response grows (stronger/weaker) _____. This runs counter to the general principle that presentation of the CS without the US usually results in e_____.

3. According to the concept of _____ revaluation, phobic behavior might sometimes develop when the person encounters a (more/less) _____ intense version of the (CS/US) _____ than was used in the original conditioning. This process can also occur through o_____ l_____ or through v_____ transmitted information.

QUICK QUIZ H

4. The process of s_____ s_____ refers to an increase in one's reactivity to a potentially fearful stimulus following exposure to a stressful event, even though the stressful event is (related/unrelated) _____ to the feared stimulus.

Treating Phobias

Perhaps more than any other disorder, phobias are highly susceptible to treatments based on behavioral principles of conditioning. In this section, we discuss the two basic types of treatment: systematic desensitization and flooding.

Systematic Desensitization   Recall how Watson and Rayner had intended to use behavioral procedures to eliminate Albert's fears but were unable to do so because his mother suddenly moved away. A few years later, Mary Cover Jones (1924) did carry out such a treatment (under Watson's supervision) with Peter, a 2-year-old boy who had an extreme fear of rabbits. Jones's treatment strategy consisted of first feeding Peter cookies while presenting a rabbit at a considerable distance. It was assumed that the positive emotional response elicited by the cookies would overcome the mild anxiety elicited by the distant rabbit. Over successive sessions, the rabbit was gradually brought closer to Peter as he continued to eat cookies. Within a few months, Peter was holding the rabbit in his lap while munching on cookies. As a result of this gradual conditioning procedure, Peter's fear of the rabbit was eliminated.

Although Jones's treatment procedure, carried out in 1924, had effectively eliminated a phobia, it languished in obscurity until Joseph Wolpe (1958) essentially rediscovered it 30 years later. As a graduate student, Wolpe conducted research on fear conditioning in cats exposed to electric shocks. The cats displayed a strong fear of both the experimental chamber in which they had been shocked and the room containing the chamber. A major indication of this fear was the cats' refusal to eat while in the room (an example of conditioned suppression). Wolpe then devised a treatment plan to eliminate the fear. He began by feeding the cats in a room that was quite dissimilar from the original "shock" room. Then, over a period of days, the cats were fed in rooms that were made progressively similar to the shock room. Eventually they were able to eat in the original room and even in the experimental cage in which they had been shocked. This procedure effectively eliminated the conditioned fear response in all 12 cats that Wolpe studied.

Wolpe (1958) interpreted the cats' improvements to be the result of ***counterconditioning,*** in which a CS that elicits one type of response is associated with an event that elicits an incompatible response. In Wolpe's study, the experimental room originally elicited a fear response because of its association with shock. Later, it elicited a positive emotional reaction after it had become associated with food. Wolpe proposed that the underlying process in counterconditioning is ***reciprocal inhibition,*** in which certain responses are incompatible with each other, and the occurrence of one response necessarily inhibits the other. Thus, the positive emotional response elicited by food inhibited the cats' anxiety because the two responses countered each other.

As a result of his success, Wolpe (1958) began to ponder ways of applying this treatment procedure to human phobias. Although both he and Jones had successfully used food to counter feelings of anxiety, Wolpe felt that this approach would be impractical for most treatment situations involving humans. He toyed with other types of responses that might counter anxiety, such as anger and assertiveness (i.e., the client was taught to act angry or assertive in situations that were normally associated with fear), but then he finally hit upon the use of deep muscle relaxation. Deep muscle relaxation is largely incompatible with the experience of anxiety (Jacobson, 1938), making it ideal from Wolpe's perspective as a tool for counterconditioning.

Wolpe (1958) also realized that real-life exposure to a phobic stimulus was impractical in some treatment scenarios. For example, it would be extremely difficult to expose a person with a fear of thunderstorms to a succession of storms that are made progressively frightening. To solve this dilemma, Wolpe decided to have the patient simply visualize the feared stimulus. A series of visualized scenarios could then be constructed that would represent varying intensities of the feared event. For example, the person could imagine a storm some distance away that had only a mild amount of thunder and lightning, then a storm that was somewhat closer with a bit more thunder and lightning, and so on. One drawback to this procedure is that the counterconditioning occurs only to the visualized event, and it will then have to generalize to the real event. Nevertheless, if the visualization is fairly vivid, the amount of generalization to the real world should be considerable.

Thus, three basic aspects of Wolpe's (1958) treatment procedure, which is generally known as *systematic desensitization*, are as follows:

1. **Training in relaxation.** An abbreviated version of Jacobson's (1938) deep muscle relaxation procedure is commonly employed for inducing relaxation, but other methods such as meditation or hypnosis have also been used.
2. **Creation of a hierarchy of imaginary scenes that elicit progressively intense levels of fear.** Experience has shown that about 10 to 15 scenes are sufficient, starting with a scene that elicits only a minor degree of fear (e.g., for a dog-phobic individual, it might be visualizing a friendly poodle tied to a tree at a distance of several yards) and finishing with a scene that elicits a tremendous amount of anxiety (e.g., visualizing standing beside a large dog that is barking).
3. **Pairing of each item in the hierarchy with relaxation.** Starting with the least fearful scene in the hierarchy, the person is asked to visualize the scene for about 10 to 30 seconds and then engage in a short period of relaxation. This process is repeated until the first scene no longer elicits anxiety, at which point the process is carried out using the next scene. By the time the top item in the hierarchy is reached, most of the person's conditioned fear will have been eliminated, resulting in only a residual amount of fear

to what was once an intensely fearful scene. The fear response to this final scene is also eliminated, at which point it is quite likely that the person will now feel significantly less anxious when confronted with the phobic stimulus in real life.

Thus, *systematic desensitization* is a behavioral treatment for phobias that involves pairing relaxation with a succession of stimuli that elicit increasing levels of fear. Although Wolpe (1958) emphasized, mostly for convenience, the use of imaginary stimuli (the procedure then being referred to as *imaginal desensitization*), the treatment can also be carried out with real phobic stimuli. This version of desensitization is sometimes referred to as *in vivo desensitization*. Mary Cover Jones's (1925) treatment of Peter's rabbit phobia is an example of *in vivo* desensitization. As with imaginal desensitization, *in vivo* desensitization usually makes use of relaxation to counter the person's fear response. For example, a dog-phobic client might move gradually closer to a real dog, pausing after each step and relaxing for several seconds. Additionally, the process might first be carried out with a very small dog and then gradually progress to a very large dog. *In vivo* desensitization has an obvious advantage in that one does not have to worry about whether the treatment effect will generalize to a real-life stimulus because one is already working with a real-life stimulus. As previously noted, however, it is often difficult or impossible to arrange such systematic real-life exposures. Additionally, in severely phobic clients, the real stimulus might elicit a tremendous amount of anxiety. In such cases, it might be wiser to first use imaginal desensitization to eliminate much of the fear, and then switch to *in vivo* desensitization to complete the process. More detailed information on systematic desensitization can be found in behavior modification texts such as Miltenberger (1997) and Spiegler and Guevremont (1998).

Considerable research has been carried out on systematic desensitization. The procedure has proven to be highly effective in certain circumstances. For example, systematic desensitization tends to be quite effective with patients who have relatively few phobias that are quite specific in nature (e.g., a fear of dogs and spiders). By contrast, people who suffer from social phobias tend to experience a general fear of many different social situations and do not respond as well to this form of treatment. Additionally, when using imaginal desensitization, the client must be able to clearly visualize the feared event and experience anxiety while doing so. Unfortunately, some individuals are unable to visualize clearly, or they feel no anxiety even with clear visualization. In these cases, *in vivo* desensitization is the better alternative.

Wolpe (1958) assumed that systematic desensitization is a counterconditioning procedure that works through the process of reciprocal inhibition. Not everyone agrees. Some researchers (e.g., Eysenck, 1976) have claimed that systematic desensitization is really just a simple matter of extinction, in which a CS is repeatedly presented in the absence of the US. From this perspective, systematic desensitization for a dog-phobic individual works because it involves repeated presentations of dogs (or images of dogs) in the absence of anything bad happening. Evidence for the extinction explanation comes from the fact that relaxation is not always needed for the treatment to be effective; gradual exposure to the feared stimulus is by itself often sufficient. On the other hand, in support of the counterconditioning explanation, severe phobias respond better to treatment when relaxation is included (Wolpe, 1995). The exact mechanism by which systematic desensitization produces its effects is, however, still unknown, and it could well be that *both* extinction and counterconditioning are involved.

1. Associating a stimulus that already elicits one type of response with an event that elicits an incompatible response is called c_____. Wolpe believed that the underlying process is r_____ i_____ in which certain types of responses are (compatible/incompatible) _____ with each other, and the occurrence of one type of response necessarily i_____ the other.

2. Mary Cover Jones used the stimulus of _____ to counter Peter's feelings of anxiety, while Wolpe, in his s_____ d_____ procedure, used _____.

3. The three basic components of Wolpe's procedure are:

a. _____

b. _____

c. _____

4. A version of Wolpe's procedure that uses real-life rather than imaginary stimuli is called _____ _____ _____. A major advantage of this procedure is that one does not have to worry about whether the treatment effect will g_____ to the real world.

5. Wolpe's procedure is very effective with people who have (few/many) _____ phobias that are highly (general/specific) _____. Thus, this procedure (does/does not) _____ work well with people who have a social phobia.

6. One bit of evidence against the counterconditioning explanation for this type of treatment is that relaxation (is/is not) _____ always necessary for the treatment to be effective. On the other hand, in keeping with the counterconditioning explanation, relaxation does seem to facilitate treatment when the phobia is (nonspecific/severe) _____.

Flooding   Consider a rat that continues to avoid a goal box in which it was once shocked, even though no further shocks will ever be delivered. One way to eliminate this phobic behavior is to place the rat in the goal box and insert a barrier that prevents it from leaving. Forced to remain in the box, the rat will initially show considerable distress, but this distress will disappear as time passes and no shock is delivered. By simply preventing the avoidance response from occurring, we can eliminate the rat's irrational fear.

The treatment procedure that makes use of this response-prevention principle is *flooding therapy:* a behavioral treatment that involves prolonged exposure to a feared stimulus, thereby providing maximal opportunity for the conditioned fear response to be extinguished (Spiegler & Guevremont, 1998). This method can be contrasted with systematic desensitization, in which exposure to the feared stimulus not only occurs gradually but also involves pairing the feared event with a response that will counteract the fear (such as relaxation). Flooding is more clearly based on the principle of extinction as opposed to counterconditioning.

As with systematic desensitization, there are two basic types of flooding procedures. In *imaginal flooding,* the client is asked to visualize, as clearly as possible, a scenario involving the feared event. For example, an individual who is spider phobic might imagine waking up at night to find a large, hairy spider on the pillow beside her. A person with a fear of heights might imagine having to climb down a fire escape from a 10th-floor apartment. The greater the level of fear induced by the visualized scenario, the better.

The client first visualizes the scenario in the therapist's office and then practices visualizing it at home. Although the level of fear during visualization may initially increase, it should eventually begin to decrease and finally will be extinguished. Once the fear response to one scenario has been extinguished, the fear response to other scenarios (e.g., having to remove a spider from the kitchen sink) can be similarly extinguished. After extinction has occurred in several scenarios, the client will likely experience considerably less fear when encountering the feared event in the real world.

In vivo flooding is an alternative to imaginal flooding. *In vivo* flooding consists of prolonged exposure to the actual feared event. Consider, for example, a woman who is extremely fearful of balloons (perhaps because someone once burst a balloon in her face when she was a young child). An *in vivo* flooding procedure might involve filling a room with balloons and then having the woman enter the room, close the door, and remain inside for an hour or more. After a few sessions of this, her fear of balloons might well be eliminated.

Of course, flooding is something that people have been intuitively aware of for centuries. The famous German poet and philosopher Goethe described how, as a young man, he had cured himself of a fear of heights by climbing the tower of the local cathedral and standing on the ledge. He repeated this procedure until his fear was greatly alleviated (Lewes, 1965). As with *in vivo* desensitization, *in vivo* flooding is advantageous because it does not require the treatment effect to generalize from an imagined encounter to a real encounter. It is also not dependent on a person's visualization ability. Unfortunately, *in vivo* flooding can be highly aversive. It is also not a realistic alternative with some types of feared events, such as house fires, which are impossible to replicate in the therapy setting. (See also "Was Sigmund Freud a Behavior Analyst?" in the And Furthermore box.)

One concern with any type of flooding therapy is that the stress involved may result in medical complications. As well, clients who have a history of other

And Furthermore

Was Sigmund Freud a Behavior Analyst?

Students sometimes wonder how, if conditioning principles are so effective in treating certain disorders, other therapeutic systems that use decidedly different methods for treating such disorders could have become so well established. One possibility is that these other systems might sometimes make use of behavioral principles but have neglected to advertise the fact. For example, few people are aware that Sigmund Freud, the founder of psychoanalysis, very much appreciated the therapeutic value of direct exposure to one's fears. This is apparent in the following description of Freud and his followers on a holiday outing in 1921 (Grosskurth, 1991). During an excursion in the mountains, they climbed a tower to a platform that was surrounded by an iron railing at hip level.

> Freud suggested that they all lean forward against the railing with their hands behind their backs, their feet well back, and imagine that there was nothing there to prevent them from falling. This was an exercise Freud had devised for overcoming the fear of heights, from which he had suffered as a young man. Jones [one of Freud's most devoted followers] teased him that it didn't seem very psychoanalytic. (p. 21)

Despite Jones's opinion, Freud (1919/1955) was so impressed with the effectiveness of direct exposure to one's fears that he explicitly recommended it as an adjunct to standard psychoanalysis:

> One can hardly master a phobia if one waits till the patient lets the analysis influence him to give it up. He will never in that case bring into the analysis the material indispensable for a convincing resolution of the phobia. One must proceed differently. Take the example of agoraphobia; there are two classes of it, one mild, the other severe. Patients belonging to the first class suffer from anxiety when they go into the streets by themselves, but they have not yet given up going out alone on that account; the others protect themselves from the anxiety by altogether ceasing to go about alone. With these last, one suc-ceeds only when one can induce them by the influence of the analysis to behave like phobic patients of the first class—that is to go into the street and to struggle with the anxiety while they make the attempt. One starts, therefore, by moderating the phobia so far; and it is only when that has been achieved at the physician's demand that the associations and memories [of childhood trauma and unconscious conflicts] come into the patient's mind which enable the phobia to be resolved. (pp. 165–166)

Of course, one can only wonder how Freud could have determined that the final resolution of the phobia was due to the retrieval of childhood memories rather than the cumulative effects of further exposure. (See also Thyer, 1999, for an example of how Carl Jung, another psycho-dynamic therapist, used an exposure-based procedure to treat a case of railroad phobia.)

psychiatric disorders may experience an exacerbation of their fears as a result of this type of treatment. One must be particularly cautious about using flooding to treat clients suffering from posttraumatic stress disorder (a severe stress reac-tion produced by a traumatic event such as an accident or wartime experience).

It is also important that the duration of each exposure, whether *in vivo* or imaginal, be sufficiently long (at least 30 to 45 minutes), otherwise the fear may not be extinguished or, worse yet, may grow more intense. In this sense, flooding is a riskier procedure than systematic desensitization (Spiegler & Guevremont, 1998).

Hybrid Approaches to the Treatment of Phobias   Systematic desensitization and flooding are the most basic behavioral approaches to the treatment of phobic behavior. Several variations of these approaches have been devised, which often combine aspects of each along with additional processes such as observational learning. Such approaches are generally known as *exposure-based treatments* or *exposure therapies* and are now considered the treatment of choice for phobic disorders (Spiegler & Guevremont, 1998).

For example, Öst (1989) described a method for rapidly eliminating specific phobias, such as a specific fear of injections or spiders, in a single session. The major component of the treatment package was an *in vivo exposure* procedure in which clients were encouraged to approach the feared object as closely as possible, remain there until the anxiety faded away, and then approach the object even more closely. This process continued until the client had approached the object closely and her reported level of fear toward the object had been reduced by 50% or more. Note that this exposure procedure is similar to systematic desensitization in that it is somewhat gradual, and similar to flooding in that the client is encouraged to endure a fairly intense level of anxiety each step of the way.

Öst's (1989) treatment package included several additional components. For example, throughout the procedure, most clients were accompanied by a person (the therapist) who acted as a model to demonstrate to the client how to interact with the feared object (such as how to use a jar to capture a spider). The therapist also helped the client physically contact the feared object—for example, by first touching the object while the client touched the model's hand, then touching the object while the client also touched the object, and then gradually removing his hand while the patient continued touching the object. The therapeutic use of modeling in this manner is called *participant modeling*, *contact desensitization*, or *guided participation*, and it has been shown to greatly facilitate fear reduction (Bandura, 1975; Bandura, Blanchard, & Ritter, 1969).

Öst (1989) reported that out of 20 female patients who had been treated with this method (interestingly, men rarely volunteer for such treatment), 19 showed considerable improvement following an average session length of only 2.1 hours. As well, 18 of the clients remained either much improved or completely recovered at long-term follow-up (follow-up information was gathered an average of 4 years after treatment). Needless to say, these results are quite encouraging, especially because most of the clients had suffered from their phobia for several years before treatment. (Question: Although the results are encouraging, what is a major weakness of this study in terms of its methodology [which the author himself readily acknowledged]?)

1. In flooding therapy, the avoidance response is (blocked/facilitated) _____, thereby providing maximal opportunity for the conditioned fear to _____.

2. Two types of flooding therapy are _____ flooding in which one visualizes the feared stimulus, and _____ flooding in which one encounters a real example of the feared stimulus.

3. For flooding therapy to be effective, the exposure period must be of relatively (long/short) _____ duration.

4. Modern-day therapies for phobias are often given the general name of e_____-b_____ treatments.

5. Öst's single-session procedure combines the gradualness of s_____ d_____ with the prolonged exposure time of f_____. This procedure also makes use of p_____ m_____, in which the therapist demonstrates how to interact with the feared object.

Aversion Therapy for Eliminating Problem Behaviors

Some behavior problems stem from events being overly enticing rather than overly aversive. For example, nicotine and alcohol can be highly pleasurable, with the result that many people become addicted to these substances. Similarly, pedophiles have inappropriate feelings of sexual attraction to young children. Obviously, one way to counter these problem behaviors is to directly reduce the attractiveness of the relevant stimuli.

Aversion therapy reduces the attractiveness of a desired event by associating it with an aversive stimulus (Spiegler & Guevremont, 1998). An ancient version of this treatment was suggested by the Roman writer Pliny the Elder, who recommended treating overindulgence in wine by secretly slipping the putrid body of a large spider into the bottom of the wine drinker's glass. The intention was that the feelings of revulsion elicited by a mouthful of spider would become associated with the wine, thereby significantly reducing the person's desire for wine (Franks, 1963). More recent versions of this therapy are somewhat less primitive. For example, the taste of alcohol has sometimes been paired with painful electric shocks. An alternative version—which is more similar to Pliny's treatment in that it makes use of stimuli associated with ingestion—involves pairing the taste of alcohol with nausea. In this case, the client is first given an *emetic*, which is a drug that produces nausea. As the nausea develops, the client takes a mouthful of alcohol. This procedure is repeated several times; as well, the type of alcohol is varied across trials to ensure generalization. Research has shown that such nausea-based treatments are more effective than shock-based treatments, presumably because we have a biological tendency to quickly associate nausea with substances that we ingest (Baker & Cannon, 1979; Masters, Burish, Hollon, & Rimm, 1987). This tendency, known as taste aversion conditioning, is discussed more fully in Chapter 11.

Aversion therapy has also been used with smoking, with similar results. Early attempts to pair smoking and electric shock were relatively ineffective, possibly because physical pain is not a biologically relevant response to smoking. A more effective procedure has been to pair smoking with nicotine-induced nausea. This procedure, known as "rapid smoking," involves having the client smoke continuously, inhaling every 6 to 10 seconds (Danaher, 1977). Within a few minutes, extreme feelings of nausea are elicited and the person will be unable to continue. One session is usually sufficient to produce at least temporary abstinence. This is especially the case with smokers who do not yet have a strong physical addiction to smoking and who smoke more for the pleasure of smoking—which the aversive conditioning counteracts—than for the avoidance of withdrawal symptoms (Zelman, Brandon, Jorenby, & Baker, 1992). Long-term abstinence is much less certain but can be facilitated through the use of additional treatment procedures (such as *relapse prevention training*, in which the person learns to identify and cope with situations in which there is a high risk of resuming the problematic behavior [Marlatt & Gordon, 1985]). Rapid smoking is, however, very stressful, usually resulting in extreme increases in heart rate. Thus, this type of treatment must be employed cautiously, particularly if the client has a history of medical difficulties (Lichtenstein & Glasgow, 1977). (In other words, do not try this at home!)

Aversion therapy has also been used to treat sex offenders (Hall, Shondrick, & Hirschman, 1993). In the case of pedophiles, photographic images of unclothed children may be paired with drug-induced nausea or a powerfully unpleasant scent such as ammonia. As part of a comprehensive treatment package, such procedures help reduce the risk that the individual will reoffend following release from prison.[5]

Aversion therapy is sometimes carried out with the use of imaginal stimuli rather than real stimuli. This version of the treatment is usually called *covert sensitization*. For example, a person addicted to smoking might imagine experiencing extreme illness and vomiting each time she tries to smoke. Alternatively, she might visualize being forced to smoke cigarettes that have been smeared with feces. As with imaginal desensitization, the effectiveness of this procedure is dependent on the client's ability to visualize images clearly and to experience strong feelings of revulsion in response to these images. The treatment effect also has to generalize from the visualized event to the real event, which, as in imaginal versus *in vivo* desensitization and flooding, is likely to result in some loss of effectiveness. Thus, covert sensitization may be somewhat less effective than aversion therapy, which utilizes exposure to the actual stimulus.

---

[5]Although aversion therapy for pedophiles does reduce the likelihood that they will reoffend, such treatments should be understood within the context of the generally pessimistic outcomes for sex offenders. On average, these treatments have not been demonstrated to be a "cure" for most offenders (Kirsch & Becker, 2006).

1. In _____ therapy, one attempts to reduce the attractiveness of an event by associating that event with an unpleasant stimulus.

2. A standard treatment for alcoholism is to associate the taste of alcohol with feelings of n_____ that have been induced by consumption of an e_____.

3. A highly effective procedure for reducing cigarette consumption, at least temporarily, is r_____ s_____.

4. In general, aversion therapy is (more/less) _____ effective when the unpleasant response that is elicited is biologically relevant to the problematic behavior.

5. Aversion therapy is sometimes carried out using _____ stimuli rather than real stimuli. This type of treatment procedure is known as _____ sensitization.

Medical Applications of Classical Conditioning

There is a growing body of evidence indicating that processes of classical conditioning have significant medical implications. For example, Russell et al. (1984) were able to condition guinea pigs to become allergic to certain odors by pairing those odors with an allergy-inducing protein. People who have allergies may suffer from a similar process, in which their allergic reaction is elicited not only by the substance that originally caused the allergy but also by stimuli associated with that substance. Thus, for a person who is allergic to pollen, even the mere sight of flowers might elicit an allergic reaction.

> **Flowers: Pollen** → *Allergic reaction*
>   NS   US   UR
> **Flowers** → *Allergic reaction*
>   CS   CR

Other studies have shown that various aspects of the immune system can be classically conditioned. For example, Ader and Cohen (1975) exposed rats to an immunosuppressive drug paired with saccharin-flavored water. These rats were then given an injection of foreign cells, followed by a drink of either saccharin-flavored water or plain water. The rats that drank the saccharin-flavored water produced fewer antibodies in reaction to the foreign cells than did the rats that drank the plain water. The flavored water had apparently become a CS for immunosuppression.

In a real-world extension of this study, Bovbjerg et al. (1990) found that women who received chemotherapy in a hospital setting displayed evidence of immunosuppression when they later returned to the hospital. The hospital environment had become associated with the immunosuppressive effect of the chemotherapy and was now a CS for a conditioned immunosuppressive response, thus:

> **Hospital: Chemotherapy** → *Immunosuppression*
>   NS   US   UR
> **Hospital** → *Immunosuppression*
>   CS   CR

Other studies have shown that classical conditioning can be used to *strengthen* immune system functioning. For example, one team of researchers gave human subjects a taste of sherbet followed by shots of adrenaline (Buske-Kirschbaum, Kirschbaum, Stierle, Jabaij, & Hellhammer, 1994). Adrenaline tends to increase the activity of natural killer cells, which are an important component of the body's immune system. After pairing the sweet sherbet with the adrenaline, the sweet sherbet itself elicited an increase in natural killer cell activity. Hence:

Sweet sherbet: Adrenaline → *Increased natural killer cell activity*
　　NS　　　　　US　　　　　　　　　　　UR
Sweet sherbet → *Increased natural killer cell activity*
　　CS　　　　　　　　　CR

(See also Solvason, Ghanta, & Hiramoto, 1988.)

The medical implications of such findings are enormous. Obviously, many patients would benefit considerably from enhanced immune functioning during the course of their illness. Other patients, however—namely those who suffer from autoimmune diseases, such as arthritis, in which the immune system seems to be overactive—would benefit from a procedure that could reliably weaken their immune system. (See Exton et al., 2000, for a review of research into this issue; also Ader, 2003.)

As the preceding discussion suggests, classical conditioning has important implications for our understanding of the placebo effect (Siegel, 2002). In drug research, a placebo is an inert substance that appears to be a drug but in reality has no pharmacological value. In double-blind control studies, placebos are given to a control group to assess the effects of "expectancy" upon the patient's symptoms, such effects being known as placebo effects. Only when the drug effect is stronger than the placebo effect is the drug considered effective.

In classical conditioning terms, the placebo effect can be seen as the result of pairing the appearance of the drug (originally an NS) with the active ingredients of the drug (the US). Thus, conditioning a placebo effect for aspirin, in which the active ingredient is acetylsalicylic acid, would involve the following:

White pill: Acetylsalicylic acid→ **Headache removal**
　　NS　　　　　US　　　　　　　　　UR
White pill → **Headache removal**
　　CS　　　　　　CR

The possibility that this type of process underlies the placebo effect is supported by the fact that such effects are much more likely to occur following a period of treatment with the active drug (e.g., Kantor, Sunshine, Laska, Meisner, & Hopper, 1966). Also supportive of a conditioning interpretation is the finding that repeated administration of a placebo by itself tends to reduce its effectiveness, which suggests that a process of extinction is taking place (Lasagna, Mosteller, von Felsinger, & Beecher, 1954).

If conditioning processes do underlie placebo effects, research into this process might allow us to better control such effects. Placebos could then be used, for example, to reduce the frequency with which a patient has to take the

And Furthermore

Classical Conditioning, Gulf War Syndrome, and Multiple Chemical Sensitivity

Processes of classical conditioning may be implicated in the controversial disorder known as Gulf War syndrome. Many veterans returning home from that war in 1991 began suffering from a wide array of symptoms—nausea, headaches, sleep problems, and rashes—which they attributed to their experiences in the war. The precise cause of these symptoms has been difficult to determine. Based on a conditioning model, Ferguson and Cassaday (1999) have proposed that the cluster of symptoms displayed by these veterans is virtually identical to that induced by interleukin-1, a small protein produced by the immune system during periods of stress or illness that causes inflammatory reactions in the body. They suggested that the chronic stresses and chemical agents the veterans were exposed to during the war produced an increase in interleukin-1 production and its resultant symptoms. These symptoms then became associated with the sights, sounds, and smells of the war zone. At home, these symptoms were again elicited when the veterans encountered stimuli that were similar to those encountered in the war zone.

One veteran reported that he experienced a headache any time he smelled petroleum, which had been a particularly prevalent smell in the war zone at that time. According to the Ferguson and Cassaday (1999) model, this veteran had presumably been exposed to toxic levels of petroleum fumes, which elicited an increase in interleukin-1 and its perceived symptoms, such as a headache. Through the process of conditioning, the smell of petroleum became a conditioned stimulus that by itself elicited interleukin-1 symptoms:

Petroleum smell: Toxic petroleum fumes → *Interleukin-1 symptoms*
      NS   US   UR
Petroleum smell → *Interleukin-1 symptoms*
      CS   CR

If this conditioning explanation of Gulf War syndrome is accurate, it suggests two possible treatment strategies: (1) administration of drugs to block the effect of interleukin-1 and (2) delivery of cognitive-behavioral treatments designed to eliminate the conditioned associations.

Similar conditioning processes may account for a type of environmental illness known as multiple chemical sensitivity or MCS (Bolla-Wilson, Wilson, & Bleecker, 1988). People with MCS develop symptoms in response to low levels of common odorous substances. As with the Gulf War veteran, MCS patients sometimes report that the onset of their illness was preceded by exposure to toxic levels of an odorous substance. From a conditioning perspective, it may be that the toxic substance served as a US that elicited a variety of symptoms. The odor of that substance then became a CS, with the symptoms (the CRs) generalizing to a variety of odors. Consistent with this interpretation, MCS patients do not report developing their symptoms following exposure to toxic levels of a substance that has no odor.

Both Gulf War syndrome and MCS have been controversial diagnoses, with some physicians maintaining that these illnesses are "merely psychological." A classical conditioning interpretation, however, allows us to interpret these illnesses as psychological in the sense of being conditioned but quite real in the sense of involving true physiological reactions over which the patient has little or no control.

real drug, thereby possibly reducing some of the side effects associated with that drug. Additionally, we may be able to devise ways in which the placebo effect can be combined with the effect of the real drug to produce an enhanced form of treatment (see Siegel, 2002).

1. When Christopher entered his friend's house, he noticed a dog dish beside the door. He soon began experiencing symptoms of asthma and assumed that the house was filled with dog dander (particles of fur or skin), to which he is allergic. Only later did he discover that his friend's children had placed the dish by the door in anticipation of soon owning a dog. In fact, no dog had yet been in the house. Assuming that Christopher's reaction is an example of higher-order conditioning, diagram the conditioning process that resulted in Christopher's allergic reaction. Label each component using the appropriate abbreviations.

2. Diagram the classical conditioning process in Ader and Cohen's (1975) study of immunosuppression. Label each component using the appropriate abbreviations.

3. Supporting the possibility that placebo effects are classically conditioned responses, such effects are more likely to occur (following/preceding) _____ a period of treatment with the real drug. As well, repeated presentations of the placebo by itself tends to (reduce/increase) _____ its effectiveness, which suggests that e_____ may be taking place.

SUMMARY

According to the S-S approach to classical conditioning, conditioning involves the formation of an association between the NS and the US. In contrast, the S-R approach claims that conditioning involves the formation of an association between the NS and a reflex response. Pavlov's stimulus-substitution theory was an early S-S approach in which the CS is presumed to act as a substitute for the US. The fact that the CR is sometimes different from the UR does not support this theory; rather, it seems like the CR response often serves to prepare the organism for the onset of the US (the preparatory-response theory of conditioning). In one version of preparatory-response theory, known as the compensatory-response model, the CS is viewed as eliciting opponent processes that counteract the effect of the US. This approach has significant application to understanding addiction. The Rescorla-Wagner theory accounts for certain conditioning phenomena (e.g., blocking) by proposing that a given US can support only so much conditioning, which must be distributed among the various CSs available.

The principles of classical conditioning are useful in understanding and treating phobias. This was first demonstrated by Watson and Rayner (1920), who conditioned an 11-month-old infant named Albert to fear a rat by associating presentations of the rat with a loud noise. True phobic conditioning, however, may involve several additional factors, including observational learning, temperament, preparedness, history of control, incubation, US revaluation, and selective sensitization.

One treatment procedure for phobias is systematic desensitization. This is a counterconditioning procedure in which a CS that elicits one type of response is associated with another stimulus that elicits a different response. Counterconditioning works through the process of reciprocal inhibition, in which one type of response can inhibit the occurrence of another incompatible response. The three components of systematic desensitization are (1) training in deep muscle relaxation, (2) creation of a hierarchy of imaginary scenes that elicit progressively intense levels of fear, and (3) pairing each item in the hierarchy with relaxation. In one variant of this procedure, known as *in vivo* desensitization, the imaginary scenes are replaced by a hierarchy of real-life encounters with the feared stimulus. An alternative treatment procedure for phobias is flooding, which involves prolonged exposure to a feared stimulus, thus allowing the conditioned fear response to be extinguished. More recent exposure-based treatments for phobias often combine characteristics of both systematic desensitization and flooding as well as observational learning.

Aversion therapy attempts to reduce the attractiveness of a desired event by associating it with an aversive stimulus. Examples include associating nausea with alcohol ingestion or cigarette smoking and, in pedophiles, associating the smell of ammonia with the sight of young children. In a technique known as covert sensitization, aversion therapy is carried out with the use of imaginal stimuli rather than real stimuli.

Classical conditioning has been shown to have medical implications. For example, neutral stimuli that have been associated with an allergy-inducing substance can become CSs that elicit a conditioned allergic response. Research has also revealed that stimuli that have been paired with a drug that alters immune system functioning can become CSs that likewise alter immune system functioning. Related studies provide evidence that classical conditioning is involved in the creation of the placebo effect, with the placebo being a CS that elicits a druglike response due to previous pairing with the actual drug.

SUGGESTED READINGS

Pavlov, I. P. (1941). *Conditioned reflexes and psychiatry*. (W. H. Gantt, Trans.). New York: International Publishers. Pavlov's attempt to apply the principles of conditioning to understanding various forms of human neuroses.

Wolpe, J. (1958). *Psychotherapy by reciprocal inhibition*. Stanford, CA: Stanford University Press. Wolpe's original book describing his development of systematic desensitization.

Spiegler, M. D., & Guevremont, D. C. (1998). *Contemporary behavior therapy* (3rd ed.). Pacific Grove, CA: Brooks/Cole. An excellent introductory text on behavior therapy describing many different treatment procedures, including some procedures not mentioned in this chapter.

STUDY QUESTIONS

1. Distinguish between S-R and S-S models of conditioning.
2. Describe stimulus-substitution theory. What is the major weakness of this theory?
3. Describe the preparatory-response theory of conditioning.
4. Describe the compensatory-response model of conditioning. How does the compensatory-response model account for drug overdoses that occur when an addict seems to have injected only a normal amount of the drug?
5. Describe the Rescorla-Wagner theory. Describe how the Rescorla-Wagner theory accounts for overshadowing and blocking.
6. Describe the overexpectation effect and how the Rescorla-Wagner theory accounts for it.
7. Briefly describe the Watson and Rayner experiment with Little Albert and the results obtained.
8. Describe how observational learning can affect the acquisition of a phobia. Assuming that the look of fear in others can act as a US, diagram an example of such a process.
9. Describe how temperament and preparedness can affect the acquisition of a phobia.
10. Describe how selective sensitization and incubation can affect the acquisition of a phobia.
11. Describe how history of control and US revaluation can affect the acquisition of a phobia.
12. What is counterconditioning? Name and define the underlying process.
13. Define systematic desensitization and outline its three components.
14. Define flooding. Be sure to mention the underlying process by which it is believed to operate. Also, what is the distinction between imaginal and *in vivo* versions of flooding (and desensitization)?
15. Define aversion therapy. What is covert sensitization?

16. Diagram an example of a classical conditioning procedure that results in an alteration (strengthening or weakening) of immune system functioning. Diagram an example of a classical conditioning process involved in the creation of a placebo effect.

CONCEPT REVIEW

aversion therapy. A form of behavior therapy that attempts to reduce the attractiveness of a desired event by associating it with an aversive stimulus.

compensatory-response model. A model of conditioning in which a CS that has been repeatedly associated with the primary response (a-process) to a US will eventually come to elicit a compensatory response (b-process).

counterconditioning. The procedure whereby a CS that elicits one type of response is associated with an event that elicits an incompatible response.

flooding therapy. A behavioral treatment for phobias that involves prolonged exposure to a feared stimulus, thereby providing maximal opportunity for the conditioned fear response to be extinguished.

incubation. The strengthening of a conditioned fear response as a result of brief exposures to the aversive CS.

overexpectation effect. The decrease in the conditioned response that occurs when two separately conditioned CSs are combined into a compound stimulus for further pairings with the US.

preparatory-response theory. A theory of classical conditioning that proposes that the purpose of the CR is to prepare the organism for the presentation of the US.

preparedness. An evolved predisposition to learn certain kinds of associations more easily than others.

reciprocal inhibition. The process whereby certain responses are incompatible with each other, and the occurrence of one response necessarily inhibits the other.

Rescorla-Wagner theory. A theory of classical conditioning that proposes that a given US can support only so much conditioning and that this amount of conditioning must be distributed among the various CSs available.

selective sensitization. An increase in one's reactivity to a potentially fearful stimulus following exposure to an unrelated stressful event.

S-R (stimulus-response) model. As applied to classical conditioning, this model assumes that the NS becomes directly associated with the UR and therefore comes to elicit the same response as the UR.

S-S (stimulus-stimulus) model. A model of classical conditioning that assumes that the NS becomes directly associated with the US, and therefore comes to elicit a response that is related to that US.

stimulus-substitution theory. A theory of classical conditioning that proposes that the CS acts as a substitute for the US.

systematic desensitization. A behavioral treatment for phobias that involves pairing relaxation with a succession of stimuli that elicit increasing levels of fear.

temperament. An individual's base level of emotionality and reactivity to stimulation that, to a large extent, is genetically determined.

CHAPTER TEST

8. The three steps in systematic desensitization are (1) training in _____, (2) creation of a _____ of feared stimuli, and (3) pairing _____ with each item in the _____.

21. In the Little Albert study, the loud noise was the (CS/US) _____, while the white rat was the (CS/US) _____. Little Albert's fear of other furry objects illustrates the process of stimulus _____.

3. Lothar's job has recently become quite stressful. Interestingly, he is also developing a fear of driving through rush hour traffic. This is best described as an example of _____.

13. The _____ approach proposes that classical conditioning involves establishing a direct connection between an NS and a US.

25. Tara's slight fear of spiders turns into a major phobia when she witnesses a friend become hospitalized after being bitten by a spider. This is an example of _____.

7. The procedure of pairing the frightening sight of a hornet with an appetitive stimulus such as candy is an example of _____. This type of procedure is effective due to the process of _____.

20. When Uncle Bob and Aunt Shirley were separated, they each gave Little Lucas great Christmas presents, with the result that he developed strong positive feelings for both of them. They then resolved their difficulties and moved back together. They now give Little Lucas one great present from the two of them. The Rescorla-Wagner theory predicts that Little Lucas's positive feelings for each will become (stronger/weaker/unaffected) _____. This is known as the _____ effect.

9. Desensitization and flooding procedures that utilize thoughts about the feared stimulus are known as _____ procedures, whereas procedures that involve exposure to the real stimulus are known as _____ procedures.

2. While playing with a spider, Suyen was frightened by the sound of a firecracker. As a result, she acquired a lasting fear of spiders, but not of firecrackers. This is an illustration of the concept of _____.

17. According to the Rescorla-Wagner theory, overshadowing occurs because the _____ stimulus picks up most of the associative value.

26. Many fatalities seemingly due to drug overdose appear to actually be the result of taking the drug in the presence of cues (associated/ not associated) _____ with drug use thereby resulting in

a (weaker/stronger) _____ compensatory response and a (higher/lower) _____ level of drug tolerance.

14. Whenever I see Attila, the neighbor's dog, I am reminded that he once bit me, which makes me quite nervous. This sequence of events fits best with an (S-R/S-S) _____ approach to classical conditioning.

10. In _____ therapy, one attempts to (decrease/increase) _____ the attractiveness of a *desired* event by pairing it with an (appetitive/aversive) _____ stimulus. An imagery-based form of this therapy is called _____.

6. Traditional advice has it that if you fall off a horse you should immediately get back on and keep riding until your fear has disappeared. This approach is similar to the therapeutic technique known as _____. Furthermore, getting back on immediately allows no opportunity for brief exposures to the feared stimulus that could result in _____ of the conditioned fear response.

24. Evidence for the role of conditioning in placebo effects includes the fact that such effects are more likely (following/preceding) _____ a period of treatment with (a fake/the real) _____ drug. Also, repeated administration of a placebo reduces its effectiveness, which suggests that a process of _____ is taking place.

12. The _____ approach to learning, views classical conditioning as a process of directly attaching a reflex response to a new stimulus.

18. According to the Rescorla-Wagner theory, _____ occurs because the (CS/NS/US) _____ in the compound has already picked up most of the available associative value.

4. Bo was never afraid of bees until he saw his best friend, Emmet, react with a look of horror to the sight of a bee. Bo now becomes quite anxious each time he sees a bee. This is best described as an example of _____ learning.

15. A cat salivates to the sound of your alarm clock in anticipation of a breakfast feeding. It also freezes at the sight of another cat in anticipation of an attack. These examples best illustrate the _____ theory of conditioning.

23. Tika's slight fear of snakes turns into a major phobia when she suffers a serious illness. This is an example of the process of _____.

1. The ease with which an individual can acquire a conditioned fear response may be influenced by that person's base level of emotionality and reactivity to stimulation, which is known as t_____. This may, to a large extent, be (genetically/environmentally) _____ determined.

11. Fionn experiences an allergic reaction whenever people even talk about dogs. In the terminology of classical conditioning, the talk about dogs appears to be a (use the abbreviation) _____ while the allergic reaction is a _____.

19. According to the _____ effect, if two fully conditioned stimuli are combined into a compound stimulus that is then subjected to further pairings with the US, the associative value of each member of the compound will (increase/decrease) _____.

5. Gina's parents are extremely concerned about her well-being, and as a result they do almost everything for her. By contrast, Sara's parents make sure that she does a lot of things on her own. Between the two of them, _____ may be less susceptible to the development of a phobia, insofar as a history of being able to _____ important events in one's environment may (reduce/increase) _____ one's suscep-tibility to acquiring a phobia.

16. Research on classical conditioning processes in drug addiction suggests that the withdrawal symptoms evoked by the sight of a desired drug are actually _____ reactions to the drug that have come to be elic-ited by environmental cues associated with that (drug/primary response to the drug) _____.

22. Tran's slight fear of rats turns into a major phobia when he is told by his parents that rats are much more dangerous than he previously suspected. This is an example of _____.

Visit the book companion Web site at <http://www.academic.cengage. com/psychology/powell> for additional practice questions, answers to the Quick Quizzes, practice review exams, and additional exercises and information.

ANSWERS TO CHAPTER TEST

1. temperament; genetically
2. preparedness
3. selective sensitization
4. observational
5. Sara; control; reduce
6. flooding; incubation
7. counterconditioning; reciprocal inhibition
8. relaxation; hierarchy; relaxation; hierarchy
9. imaginal; *in vivo*
10. aversion; decrease; aversive; covert sensitization
11. CS; CR
12. S-R
13. S-S

14. S-S
15. preparatory-response
16. compensatory (or opponent or b-process); primary response to the drug
17. more salient
18. blocking; CS
19. overexpectation; decrease
20. weaker; overexpectation
21. US; CS; generalization
22. US revaluation
23. selective sensitization
24. following; the real; extinction
25. US revaluation
26. not associated; weaker; lower

CHAPTER 6

Operant Conditioning: Introduction

CHAPTER OUTLINE

"Hurry up," Joe growled as Sally carefully searched the selection of videos.

"Oh, don't be so grumpy," she said sweetly, hooking her arm into his.

"Just pick one, damn it!"

She quickly picked out a video, then gave him a hug as they walked to the checkout counter. (Based on a real incident observed in a video store.)

In the last few chapters, we focused on elicited behavior and the type of learning known as classical conditioning. Elicited behavior is controlled by the stimuli that precede it. Recall how in Pavlov's classic experiment food elicited salivation and how, after a tone had been paired with food, it too elicited salivation:

Tone: Food → *Salivation*
Tone → *Salivation*

Note how the target response in this type of learning always occurs at the end of the sequence. The preceding stimulus, by itself, is sufficient to elicit the response. In this sense, the process is very reflexive: Present the stimulus and the response automatically follows.

But is everything we do this reflexive? Does the sight of this text, for example, automatically elicit the response of reading? Obviously it does not (though students who tend to procrastinate might sometimes wish that it did). Rather, if you had to explain why you are reading this text, you are likely to say you are reading it in order to achieve something—such as an understanding of the subject matter or a high grade in a course. Reading the text is oriented toward some goal, a consequence, and this consequence is the reason for the behavior. Indeed, most behaviors that concern us each day are motivated by some consequence. For example, we go to a restaurant for a meal, we turn on a radio to hear music, and we ask someone out on a date hoping he or she will accept. When we fail to achieve the desired outcome, we are unlikely to continue the behavior. How long would you persist in asking someone out on a date if that person never accepted?

Behaviors that are influenced by their consequences are called *operant behaviors*, and the effects of those consequences upon behavior are called *operant conditioning*. They are called operant conditioning because the response *operates on the environment* to produce a consequence. This type of learning is also called *instrumental conditioning* because the response is *instrumental* in producing the consequence.

1. Operant behaviors are influenced by their _____.

2. Elicited behavior is a function of what (precedes/follows) _____ it; operant behavior is a function of what (precedes/follows) _____ it.

3. Another name for operant conditioning is _____ conditioning.

Historical Background

Although people have used operant conditioning for thousands of years (e.g., in raising children, training animals, etc.), this kind of learning was not subjected to scientific analysis until the late 1800s when Edwin L. Thorndike investigated the learning ability of animals.

Thorndike's Law of Effect

The first experimental studies of operant conditioning were undertaken by Edwin L. Thorndike in the 1890s. As a graduate student, Thorndike was interested in animal intelligence. Many people at that time were speculating that animals were capable of higher forms of reasoning. Particularly impressive were stories about lost dogs and cats finding their way home over long distances. As Thorndike (1898) noted, however, "Dogs get lost hundreds of times and no one ever notices it or sends an account of it to a scientific magazine, but let one find his way from Brooklyn to Yonkers and the fact immediately becomes a circulating anecdote" (p. 4). Thorndike (1911)

Edwin L. Thorndike
(1874–1949)

also said that such depictions did not provide ". . . a psychology of animals, but rather a *eulogy* of animals. They have all been about animal *intelligence*, never about animal *stupidity*" (p. 22).

Thorndike was not suggesting that animals could not be intelligent, but rather that we should not accept anecdotes as fact, nor should we assume that animals behaving in a particular way are doing so for intelligent reasons. It was not only the lay public that caused Thorndike to argue for caution in interpreting animal behavior. Some of his contemporary researchers were also guilty of noncritical analysis of animal intelligence. In particular, George John Romanes was known for interpreting the mental processes of animals as analogous to human thought processes, and he did so freely in his book, *Mental Evolution in Man* (Romanes, 1989). Thorndike, and others, were skeptical of this and rejected Romanes' anecdotal approach to the study of animal behavior. Thorndike's skepticism was driven by a belief that the intellectual ability of animals could be properly assessed only through *systematic investigation.*

Of the many experiments Thorndike (1898) conducted with animals, the most famous one involved cats. In a typical experiment, a hungry cat was enclosed in a puzzle box, and a dish of food was placed outside. To reach the food, the cat had to learn how to escape from the box, such as by stepping on a treadle that opened a gate. The first time the cat was placed in the puzzle box, several minutes passed before it accidentally stepped on the treadle and opened the gate. Over repeated trials, it learned to escape the box more quickly. There

A convincing example of animal intelligence.

was, however, no sudden improvement in performance as would be expected if the cat had experienced a "flash of insight" about how to solve the problem. Rather, it seemed as though the response that worked (stepping on the treadle) was gradually strengthened, while responses that did not work (e.g., clawing at the gate, chewing on the cage) were gradually weakened (see Figure 6.1).

FIGURE 6.1 Thorndike's puzzle box. In a typical experiment, a hungry cat was enclosed in a puzzle box and a dish of food was placed outside the box. To reach the food, the cat had to learn how to escape from the box by stepping on a treadle that opened the gate. The graph illustrates the general decrease across trials in the amount of time it took the cat to escape. (*Source:* Nairne, 2000.)

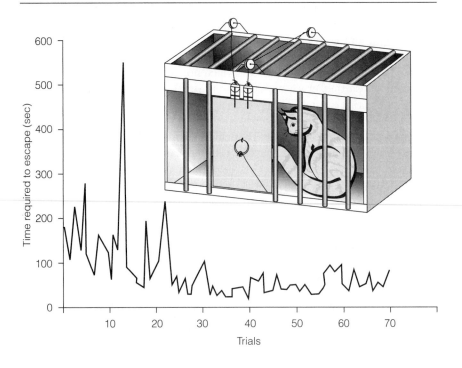

Thorndike suspected that a similar process governed all learning, and on this basis he formulated his famous law of effect.[1]

The *law of effect* states that behaviors leading to a satisfying state of affairs are strengthened or "stamped in," while behaviors leading to an unsatisfying or annoying state of affairs are weakened or "stamped out." In other words, the *consequences* of a behavior determine whether that behavior will be repeated. Thorndike's law of effect is a hallmark in the history of psychology. However, it was another young scientist by the name of Burrhus Frederick Skinner who fully realized the implications of this principle for understanding and changing behavior.

Skinner's Selection by Consequences

Skinner came upon the study of operant conditioning by a somewhat different route. As a graduate student in the late 1920s, he was well aware of Thorndike's law of effect. However, like many psychologists of the time, he believed that behavior could best be analyzed as though it were a reflex. He also realized, like Pavlov, that a scientific analysis of behavior required finding a procedure that yielded regular patterns of behavior. Without such regularity, which could be achieved only in a well-controlled environment, it would be difficult to discover the underlying principles of behavior.

In this context, Skinner set out to devise his own procedure for the study of behavior, eventually producing one of the best-known apparatuses in experimental psychology: the operant conditioning chamber, or "Skinner box." In a standard Skinner box for rats, the rat is able to earn food pellets by pressing a response lever or bar (see Figure 6.2).

Skinner's procedure is known as the "free operant" procedure because the rat freely responds with a particular behavior (like pressing a lever) for food, and it may do so at any rate. The experimenter controls the contingencies within the operant chamber, but the animal is not forced to respond at a particular time. This contrasts with other procedures for studying animal learning, such as maze learning, in which the experimenter must initiate each trial by placing the rat in the start box.[2] Skinner demonstrated that the rate of behavior in an operant chamber was controlled by the conditions that he established in his experiments. Later, Skinner invented a variant of the operant chamber for pigeons, in which the pigeon pecks an illuminated

---

[1]Although Thorndike's research led to a general tendency to reject anecdotal approaches to animal learning and behavior, some researchers believe that he may have overstated the case that animals do not experience sudden increases in learning. They claim that evidence is available for such "insight" learning, depending on the task and the species examined (see Wasserman & Zentall, 2006, for a comprehensive review).

[2]Although the terms *operant conditioning* and *instrumental conditioning* are often used interchangeably, the term *instrumental conditioning* is sometimes reserved for procedures that involve distinct learning trials, such as maze learning experiments, as opposed to Skinner's free operant procedure.

FIGURE 6.2 Operant conditioning chamber for rats. When the rat presses the lever (or bar), a food pellet drops into the food tray. Aversive stimuli can be presented by delivering an electric shock through the floor grids. (*Source:* Lieberman, 2000.)

plastic disc called a response key (named after the telegraph key) to earn a few seconds of access to food (see Figure 6.3). Many of the principles of operant conditioning, particularly those concerning schedules of reinforcement (discussed in Chapter 7), were discovered with the use of this key-pecking procedure.

FIGURE 6.3 Operant conditioning chamber for pigeons. When the pigeon pecks the response key (a translucent plastic disc that can be illuminated with different-colored lights), grain is presented in the food cup for a period of a few seconds. (*Source:* Domjan, 2000.)

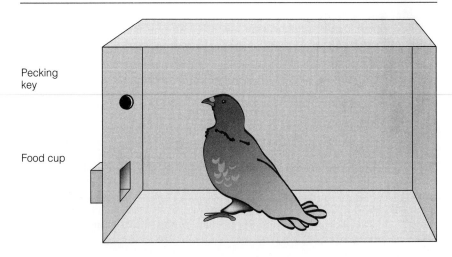

With the evolution of the Skinner box, Skinner's beliefs about the nature of behavior also changed. He abandoned the notion that all behavior could be analyzed in terms of reflexes and, along with other learning theorists, came to believe that behaviors can be conveniently divided into two categories. One category consists of involuntary, reflexive-type behaviors, which as Pavlov had demonstrated can often be classically conditioned to occur in new situations. Skinner referred to such behavior as *respondent behavior*. The other category, which Skinner called *operant behavior*, consists of behaviors that seem more voluntary in nature and are controlled by their consequences rather than by the stimuli that precede them. It was this type of behavior that Thorndike had studied in his puzzle box experiments and upon which he had based his law of effect. It was this type of behavior that most interested Skinner as well. He spent the rest of his life investigating the basic principles of operant conditioning and applying those principles to important aspects of human behavior (see Bjork, 1993; Skinner, 1938, 1967).

1. Thorndike's cats learned to solve the puzzle box problem (gradually/suddenly) _____.

2. Based on his research with cats, Thorndike formulated his famous _____ of _____, which states that behaviors that lead to a(n) _____ state of affairs are strengthened, while behaviors that lead to a(n) _____ state of affairs are weakened.

3. According to Thorndike, behaviors that worked were st_____ i__, while behaviors that did not work were st_____ o___.

4. The Skinner box evolved out of Skinner's quest for a procedure that would, among other things, yield (regular/irregular) _____ patterns of behavior.

5. In the original version of the Skinner box, rats earn food by p_____ a _____; in a later version, pigeons earn a few seconds of access to food by p_____ at an illuminated plastic disc known as a _____ _____.

6. Skinner's procedures are also known as fr_____ o_____ procedures in that the animal controls the rate at which it earns food.

7. Skinner originally thought all behavior could be explained in terms of _____, but he eventually decided that this type of behavior could be distinguished from another, seemingly more voluntary type of behavior known as _____ behavior.

Operant Conditioning

Operant conditioning is a type of learning in which the future probability of a behavior is affected by its consequences. Note that this is essentially a restatement of Thorndike's law of effect. Skinner, however, was dissatisfied with Thorndike's mentalistic description of consequences as being either satisfying or annoying. Satisfaction and annoyance are internal states inferred from the animal's behavior. Skinner avoided any speculation about what the animal (or person) might be thinking or feeling and simply emphasized the effect of the consequence on the future *probability* of the behavior. The animal might be thinking, or feeling, but those behaviors are not explicitly measured or analyzed.

Note that Skinner's principle of operant conditioning bears a striking resemblance to Darwin's principle of natural selection (which forms the basis of the theory of evolution). According to the principle of natural selection, members of a species that inherit certain adaptive characteristics are more likely to survive and propagate, thereby passing that characteristic on to offspring. Thus, over many generations, the frequency of those adaptive characteristics within the population will increase and become well established. Similarly, according to the principle of operant conditioning, behaviors that lead to favorable outcomes are more likely to be repeated than those that do not lead to favorable outcomes. Thus, operant conditioning is sort of a mini-evolution of an organism's behaviors, in which behaviors that are adaptive (lead to favorable outcomes) become more frequent while behaviors that are nonadaptive (do not lead to favorable outcomes) become less frequent.

The operant conditioning process can be conceptualized as involving three components: (1) a response that produces a certain consequence (e.g., lever pressing produces a food pellet), (2) the consequence that serves to either increase or decrease the probability of the response that preceded it (e.g., the consequence of a food pellet increases the rat's tendency to again press the lever), and (3) a discriminative stimulus that precedes the response and signals that a certain consequence is now available (e.g., a tone signals that a lever press will now produce food). These components are examined in more detail in the next section.

Operant Behavior

An *operant behavior* is a class of emitted responses that result in certain consequences; these consequences, in turn, affect the future probability or strength of those responses. Operant responses are sometimes simply called *operants*. Suppose, for example, that a rat presses a lever and receives a food pellet, with a result that it is more likely to press the lever in the future.

Lever press → **Food pellet**
The effect: The future probability of lever pressing increases.

Or Jonathan might tell a joke and receive a frown from the person he tells it to. He is now less likely to tell that person a joke in the future.

Tell a joke → **Person frowns**
The effect: The future probability of telling a joke decreases.

In each case, the behavior in question (the lever pressing or the joke telling) is an operant response (or an "operant") because its occurrence results in the delivery of a certain consequence, *and* that consequence affects the future probability of the response.

In contrast to classically conditioned behaviors, which are said to be *elicited by stimuli* (e.g., food elicits salivation), operant behaviors are technically said to be *emitted by the organism* (e.g., the rat emits lever presses or the person emits the behavior of telling jokes). This wording is used to indicate that operant behavior appears to have a more voluntary, flexible quality to it compared to elicited behavior, which is generally more reflexive and automatic. (Does this mean that operant behavior is entirely the organism's "choice?" Not necessarily. In fact, as we have pointed out, the behavior comes to be controlled by the contingencies of reinforcement and punishment that follow the behavior, and it can be argued that the sense of voluntariness accompanying such behavior is merely an illusion.)

Note, too, that operant behavior is usually defined as a *class of responses*, with all of the responses in that class capable of producing the consequence. For example, there are many ways a rat can press a lever for food: hard or soft, quick or slow, right paw or left paw. All of these responses are effective in depressing the lever and producing food, and therefore they all belong to the same class of responses known as "lever presses." Similarly, Jonathan could tell many different jokes, and he could even tell the same joke in many different ways, all of which might result in a laugh. Defining operants in terms of classes has proven fruitful because it is easier to predict the occurrence of a class of responses than it is to predict the *exact* response that will be emitted at a particular point in time. For example, it is easier to predict that a hungry rat will press a lever to obtain food than it is to predict exactly how it will press the lever on any particular occasion.

1. Skinner's definition of operant conditioning differs from Thorndike's law of effect in that it views consequences in terms of their effect upon the strength of behavior rather than whether they are s_____ing or a_____ing.

2. Operant conditioning is similar to the principle of natural selection in that an individual's behaviors that are (adaptive/nonadaptive) _____ tend to increase in frequency, while behaviors that are _____ tend to decrease in frequency.

3. The process of operant conditioning involves the following three components: (1) a r_____ that produces a certain _____, (2) a c_____ that serves to either increase or decrease the likelihood of the _____ preceded it, and (3) a d_____ stimulus that precedes the _____ and signals that a certain _____ is now available.

4. Classically conditioned behaviors are said to be e_____ by the stimulus, while operant behaviors are said to be e_____ by the organism.

5. Operant responses are also simply called _____.

6. Operant behavior is usually defined as a(n) _____ of responses rather than a specific response.

Operant Consequences: Reinforcers and Punishers

The second component of an operant conditioning procedure is the consequence that either increases (strengthens) or decreases (weakens) the frequency of a behavior. Consequences that strengthen a behavior are called reinforcers, and consequences that weaken a behavior are called punishers. More specifically, an event is a ***reinforcer*** if (1) it follows a behavior, and (2) the future probability of that behavior *increases*. Conversely, an event is a ***punisher*** if (1) it follows a behavior, and (2) the future probability of that behavior *decreases*.

Diagrams of operant conditioning procedures generally use the following symbols. Reinforcers are usually given the symbol S^R (which stands for *reinforcing stimulus*), and punishers are given the symbol S^P (which stands for *punishing stimulus*). The operant response is given the symbol R. Using these abbreviations, a diagram of a procedure in which a lever press is reinforced by the delivery of a food pellet looks like this:

> *Lever press* → **Food pellet**
> $\quad$ **R** $\qquad\qquad$ **S^R**

The food pellet is a reinforcer because it follows the lever press *and* increases the future probability of lever pressing. A diagram of Jonathan's failed attempt at humor, in which a frown punished his behavior of telling jokes, looks like this:

> *Tell a joke* → **Person frowns**
> $\quad$ **R** $\qquad\qquad$ **S^P**

The frown is a punisher because it follows the joke *and* the future probability of joke telling decreases.

Note that, from an operant conditioning perspective, we do *not* say that the person or animal has been reinforced or punished; rather, it is the behavior that has been reinforced or punished. Only the behavior increases or decreases in frequency. (There is actually a lesson in this. If you want a child to stop doing something, should you tell her that her behavior displeases you or that she displeases you? Similarly, when your roommate does something that bothers you, will it be more constructive to tell him that his behavior disturbs you or that he disturbs you? Is it easier for people to change their behavior or to change who they are?)

It is also important to differentiate the terms *reinforcer* and *punisher* from *reinforcement* and *punishment*. *Reinforcer* and *punisher* both refer to the specific *consequences* used to strengthen or weaken a behavior. In the previous examples, the food pellet is a reinforcer for lever pressing, and the frown is a punisher for joke telling. In contrast, the terms *reinforcement* and *punishment* usually refer to the *process* or *procedure* by which a certain consequence changes the strength of a behavior. Thus, the use of food to increase the strength of lever pressing is an example of reinforcement, while the food itself is a reinforcer. Similarly, the process of frowning to encourage Jonathan to stop telling jokes is an example of punishment, while the frown itself is a punisher. In summary, the terms *reinforcer* and *punisher* refer to the actual consequences of the behavior; the terms *reinforcement* and *punishment* refer to the process or procedure of strengthening or weakening a behavior by instituting those consequences.

Note, too, that reinforcers and punishers are defined entirely by their effect on behavior. For example, a laugh is a reinforcer for the behavior of joke telling only to the extent that joke telling then increases. If, for some reason, joke telling decreased as a result of the laugh (maybe the person telling the joke delights in disgusting his listeners and does not want them to find his joke funny), the laugh would by definition be a punisher. It is important to remember this, because events that on the surface seem like reinforcers or punishers do not always function in that manner. We encountered this notion in Chapter 2 in our discussion of the distinction between appetitive and aversive events (and particularly in the cartoon depiction of Calvin ravenously eating what he believes to be a bowl of maggot soup). In similar fashion, a teacher might yell at her students for being disruptive, and as a result the students become *more* (not less) disruptive. Although the teacher is clearly trying to punish the disruptive behavior, the yelling is actually having the opposite effect. By definition, therefore, the yelling is a reinforcer because it is causing the disruptive behavior to increase in frequency (perhaps because disruptive students find that other students admire them if they upset the teacher).

Thus, the safest bet is to define consequences as reinforcers and punishers in relation to their effect on behavior and not in relation to how pleasant or unpleasant they seem. It is for this reason that many behaviorists prefer the term *reinforcer* rather than *reward*, the latter term being too strongly associated with events that are seemingly pleasant (e.g., affection, food, money). For example, the teacher's yelling is hardly what anyone would call a reward, but technically speaking it is a reinforcer for the students' disruptive behavior. Not all behaviorists are this strict in their terminology, however, and they sometimes use the terms *reward* and *reinforcer* interchangeably (e.g., Bandura, 1997; Herrnstein, 1997).[3] Moreover, because students often find it helpful to think of consequences in terms of whether they are pleasant or unpleasant, we will sometimes make use of such terms in our discussion of consequences. In other words, to help you gain an initial grasp of this material, we will sometimes be rather informal in the terminology we use. (Note, however, that such informality may not be acceptable in an examination on this material.)

Finally, you should be aware that punishment is not the only means of weakening a behavior. A response that has been strengthened through reinforcement can also be weakened by the withdrawal of reinforcement. *The weakening of a behavior through the withdrawal of reinforcement for that behavior*

---

[3]Furthermore, some behaviorists use the term *reward* to refer to the effect of the consequence on the animal as opposed to the behavior (Rachlin, 1991). For example, a dog biscuit can be both a reinforcer for the dog's *behavior* of begging and a reward to the *dog* for having carried out such a behavior. Thus, reinforcers strengthen behavior, while rewards make us happy.

is known as extinction. For example, a child who has learned to whine for candy in the supermarket will eventually cease whining when behaving that way no longer results in candy. Likewise, a roommate who tells gross jokes because of the outraged reaction he gets from his religiously inclined roommates will eventually stop telling such jokes if the roommates stop reacting that way. Extinction is usually a much gentler process than punishment; one drawback to it, however, is that it is typically a much slower process. Extinction and the various issues associated with it are more fully discussed in Chapter 8.

QUICK QUIZ D

1. Simply put, reinforcers are those consequences that s_____ a behavior, while punishers are those consequences that w_____ a behavior.

2. More specifically, a reinforcer is a consequence that (precedes/follows) _____ a behavior and (increases/decreases) _____ the probability of that behavior. A punisher is a consequence that (precedes/follows) _____ a behavior and (increases/decreases) _____ the probability of that behavior.

3. The terms *reinforcement* and *punishment* refer to the pr_____ or pr_____ whereby a behavior is strengthened or weakened by its consequences.

4. Strengthening a roommate's tendency toward cleanliness by thanking her when she cleans the bathroom is an example of _____, while the thanks itself is a _____.

5. Eliminating a dog's tendency to jump up on visitors by scolding her when she does so is an example of _____, while the scolding itself is a _____.

6. Reinforcers and punishers are defined entirely by their _____ on behavior. For this reason, the term *reinforcer* is often preferred to the term _____ because the latter is too closely associated with events that are commonly regarded as pleasant or desirable.

7. When Moe stuck his finger in a light socket, he received an electric shock. As a result, he now sticks his finger in the light socket as often as possible. By definition, the electric shock was a _____ because the behavior it followed has (increased/decreased) _____ in frequency.

8. Each time Edna talked out in class, her teacher immediately came over and gave her a hug. As a result, Edna no longer talks out in class. By definition, the hug is a(n) _____ because the behavior it follows has (increased/decreased) _____ in frequency.

9. When labeling an operant conditioning procedure, punishing consequences (punishers) are given the symbol _____ (which stands for _____ _____), while reinforcing consequences (reinforcers) are given the symbol _____ (which stands for _____ _____). The operant response is given the symbol _____.

10. When we give a dog a treat for fetching a toy, we are attempting to reinforce (the behavior of fetching the toy/the dog that fetched the toy) _____.

11. When we chastise a child for being rude, we are attempting to punish (the child who was rude/the child's rude behavior) _____.

12. Weakening a behavior through the w_____ of reinforcement for that behavior is known as extinction.

13. Clayton stopped plugging in the toaster after he received an electric shock while doing so. This is an example of (punishment/extinction) _____.

14. Manzar stopped using the toaster after it no longer made good toast. This is an example of (punishment/extinction) _____.

Operant Antecedents: Discriminative Stimuli

The operant response and its consequence are the most essential components of the operant conditioning procedure. In most circumstances, however, a third component can also be identified. When a behavior is consistently reinforced or punished in the presence of certain stimuli, those stimuli will begin to influence the occurrence of the behavior. For example, if lever pressing produces food only when a tone is sounding, the rat soon learns to press the lever only when it hears the tone. This situation can be diagrammed as follows:

Tone: *Lever Press* → **Food pellet**
S^D　　　R　　　　S^R

This sequence can be read as follows: In the presence of the tone, if the rat presses the lever, it will receive food. The tone is called a discriminative stimulus. Discriminative stimuli are traditionally given the symbol S^D (pronounced "es-dee"). A *discriminative stimulus* (S^D) is a stimulus in the presence of which responses are reinforced and in the absence of which they are not reinforced. In other words, a discriminative stimulus is a signal that indicates that a response will be followed by a reinforcer.

Another example: If Susan always laughs at Jonathan's jokes, then he is more likely to tell her a joke. Susan is an S^D for Jonathan's behavior of telling jokes. This can be diagrammed as follows:

Susan: *Tell her a joke* → **She laughs**
S^D　　　R　　　　S^R

Discriminative stimuli are said to "set the occasion for" the behavior, meaning that the behavior is more likely to occur in the presence of those stimuli. Discriminative stimuli do not elicit behavior in the manner of a CS or US in classical conditioning. For example, the tone does not automatically elicit a lever press; it merely increases the probability that a lever press will occur. Whether or not lever pressing occurs is still a function of its consequence (food), and the S^D simply indicates that this consequence is now available. Similarly, the presence of Susan does not automatically elicit the behavior of joke telling in Jonathan; rather, he is simply more likely to tell a joke in her presence. Therefore, rather than saying that the S^D elicits the behavior, we say that the person or animal emits the behavior in the presence of the S^D. (Remember, it is only in classical conditioning that we say that the stimulus *elicits* the behavior. In operant conditioning, we say that the organism *emits* the behavior.)

The discriminative stimulus, the operant behavior, and the reinforcer or punisher constitute what is known as the **three-term contingency**. The three-term contingency can also be viewed as consisting of an *antecedent event* (an antecedent event is a *preceding* event), a *behavior*, and a *consequence* (which can be remembered by the initials *ABC*).

Antecedent	Behavior	Consequence
Susan:	*Tell her a joke* →	She laughs
S^D	R	S^R
Tone:	*Lever press* →	Food pellet
S^D	R	S^R

Another way of thinking about this sequence is that you notice something (Susan), do something (tell a joke), and get something (Susan laughs). Similarly, you notice that it is 7:00 P.M., you turn on the TV, and you get to see your favorite sitcom. Or maybe your dog notices that you have popcorn, begs persistently, and gets some of the popcorn. Many students find this sequence easy to remember: Notice something, do something, get something. (As you will see later, however, the consequence in some cases involves losing or avoiding something rather than getting something.)

So far, we have dealt only with stimuli that are associated with reinforcement. Stimuli can also be associated with punishment. A stimulus that signals that a response will be punished is called a **discriminative stimulus for punishment**. For example, if a water bottle signals that meowing will result in being sprayed with water (rather than being fed), a cat will quickly learn to stop meowing whenever it sees the water bottle.

Water bottle:	*Meow* →	Get sprayed
S^D	R	S^P

Similarly, a motorist who receives a fine for speeding in the presence of a police car will soon learn to stop speeding in the presence of police cars.

Police car:	*Speed* →	Receive fine
S^D	R	S^P

For the speeding motorist, the presence of a police car is a discriminative stimulus for punishment.

A discriminative stimulus may also signal the occurrence of extinction; that is, the stimulus signals the nonavailability of a previously available reinforcer. If, for example, lever pressing is typically followed by the presentation of food, but only when a tone is sounding and not when a buzzer is sounding, then:

Tone:	*Lever press* →	Food pellet
S^D	R	S^R
Buzzer:	Lever press →	No food
S^Δ	R	—

The buzzer in this case is a *discriminative stimulus for extinction,* which is a stimulus that signals the absence of reinforcement. A discriminative stimulus for extinction is typically given the symbol S^Δ (pronounced "es-delta"). As noted earlier, the process of extinction is more fully discussed in Chapter 8.[4]

Finally, you should be aware that processes of operant and classical conditioning overlap such that a particular stimulus can simultaneously act as both a discriminative stimulus and a conditioned stimulus. For example, consider a tone that serves as an S^D for the operant behavior of lever pressing:

> **Tone:** *Lever press* → **Food**
> $\ \ S^D \qquad\ \ R \qquad\quad S^R$

The tone is closely associated with food; and food, of course, elicits salivation. This means that during the course of our operant conditioning procedure the tone will also become a conditioned stimulus (CS) that elicits salivation as a conditioned response (CR). Thus, if we ignore the lever pressing and concentrate just on the salivation, then what is happening is this:

> **Tone: Food** → *Salivation*
> $\ \ NS\quad$US$\qquad$UR
> **Tone** → *Salivation*
> $\ \ CS\qquad$CR

Whether the tone should be considered an S^D or a CS depends on the response to which one is referring. It is an S^D with respect to the operant response of lever pressing and a CS with respect to the classically conditioned response of salivation. (See Table 6.1 for a summary of the differences between classical and operant conditioning.)

---

1. The operant conditioning procedure usually consists of three components: (1) a d_____ s_____, (2) an o_____ response, and (3) a c_____.

2. A discriminative stimulus is usually indicated by the symbol _____.

3. A discriminative stimulus is said to "_____ for the behavior," meaning that its presence makes the response (more/less) _____ likely to occur.

4. A discriminative stimuli (does/does not) _____ elicit behavior in the same manner as a CS.

5. Using the appropriate symbols, label each component in the following three-term contingency (assume that the behavior will be strengthened):

Phone rings: *Answer phone* → Conversation with friend

_____   _____   _____

---

[4]Note that the symbols for discriminative stimuli are not entirely standardized. Some textbooks use S+ (positive discriminative stimulus) to denote the discriminative stimulus for reinforcement, and S– (negative discriminative stimulus) to denote the discriminative stimulus for extinction or punishment. In *Sniffy, the Virtual Rat,* for example, the symbols S+ and S– are used as opposed to S^D and S^Δ.

TABLE 6.1 Differences between operant and classical conditioning. Note that these are *traditional* differences. As you will see in Chapter 11, the distinction between classical and operant conditioning is sometimes less clear than what is depicted here.

CLASSICAL CONDITIONING	OPERANT CONDITIONING
Behavior is generally seen as involuntary and inflexible.	Behavior is generally seen as voluntary and flexible.
Behavior is said to be "elicited by the stimulus."	Behavior is said to be "emitted by the organism."
This type of conditioning typically involves innate patterns of behavior (URs).	This type of conditioning often does not involve innate patterns of behavior.
Behavior is a function of what comes before it; that is, the preceding stimulus is critical and the consequences are largely irrelevant.	Behavior is a function of what comes after it; that is, the consequences are critical and the preceding stimulus merely "sets the occasion for the behavior."
Conditioning involves a stimulus-stimulus-response (S-S-R) sequence.	Conditioning involves a stimulus-response-stimulus (S-R-S) sequence.

In general, to determine if operant or classical conditioning is involved, the most important question to ask is whether the behavior is a function of what precedes it (classical conditioning) or what might follow it (operant conditioning).

6. The three-term contingency can also be thought of as an ABC sequence, where A stands for _____ event, B stands for _____, and C stands for _____.

7. Another way of thinking about the three-term contingency is that you _____ something, _____ something, and _____ something.

8. A stimulus in the presence of which a response is punished is called a _____ _____ for _____.

9. A bell that signals the start of a round and therefore serves as an S^D for the operant response of beginning to box may also serve as a(n) (S^D/CS) _____ for a fear response. This is an example of how the two processes of _____ conditioning and _____ conditioning often overlap.

Four Types of Contingencies

We have seen that there are two main types of consequences in operant conditioning: reinforcers and punishers. If the response is followed by a reinforcer, then we say that a *contingency of reinforcement* exists (meaning that the delivery of the reinforcer is contingent upon the response); if the response is followed by a punisher, then a *contingency of punishment* exists. However, contingencies of reinforcement and punishment can be further divided into two subtypes: positive and negative. This results in four basic types of contingencies (response–consequence relationships): positive reinforcement, negative reinforcement, positive punishment, and negative punishment. Because these are sometimes confusing to students, we describe them in some detail here.

As you learned previously, reinforcement is a procedure that strengthens a behavior, and punishment is a procedure that weakens a behavior. That part is pretty straightforward, but this next part can be tricky. When combined with the words *reinforcement* or *punishment*, the word *positive* means only that the behavior is followed by the *presentation* or addition of something (think of a + [positive] sign, which means "add"). Thus, the word *positive*, when combined with the terms *reinforcement* or *punishment*, does *not* mean good or pleasant; it means only that the response has resulted in something being added or presented. The event that is presented could either be pleasant (receiving a compliment) or unpleasant (getting yelled at).

Similarly, the word *negative*, when combined with the words *reinforcement* or *punishment*, means only that the behavior is followed by the *removal* of something; that is, something is subtracted from the situation (think of a – [negative] sign, which means "subtract"). The word *negative*, therefore, in this context, does *not* mean bad or unpleasant; it means only that the response results in the removal of something. The something that is removed could be an event that is pleasant (your dessert is taken away) or an event that is unpleasant (the person stops yelling at you).

To summarize, in the case of positive reinforcement and positive punishment, the word *positive* means only that the behavior has resulted in something being presented or added. In negative reinforcement and negative punishment, the word *negative* means only that the behavior has resulted in something being removed or subtracted. The word *reinforcement*, of course, means that the behavior will increase in strength, and the word *punishment* means that the behavior will decrease in strength.

Thus, to determine which type of contingency is involved in any particular instance, ask yourself the following two questions: (1) *Does the consequence consist of something being presented or withdrawn?* If the consequence consists of something being presented, then it is a *positive* contingency; if the consequence consists of something being withdrawn, then it is a *negative* contingency. (2) *Does the consequence serve to strengthen or weaken the behavior?* If it strengthens the behavior, then we are dealing with a process of *reinforcement*; if it weakens the behavior, then we are dealing with a process of *punishment*. Apply these two questions to any examples that you encounter, and you will generally have no problem with sorting out these four types of contingencies in the following sections.

1. The word *positive*, when combined with the words *reinforcement* or *punishment*, means only that the behavior is followed by the _____ of something. The word *negative*, when combined with the words *reinforcement* or *punishment*, means only that the behavior is followed by the _____ of something.

2. The word *positive*, when combined with the words *reinforcement* or *punishment*, (does/does not) _____ mean that the consequence is good or pleasant. Similarly, the term *negative*, when combined with the words *reinforcement* or *punishment*, (does/does not) _____ mean that the consequence is bad or unpleasant.

3. Within the context of reinforcement and punishment, positive refers to the (addition/subtraction) _____ of something, and negative refers to the (addition/subtraction) _____ of something.

4. Reinforcement is related to a(n) (increase/decrease) _____ in behavior, whereas punishment is related to a(n) (increase/decrease) _____ in behavior.

Positive Reinforcement

Positive reinforcement consists of the *presentation* of a stimulus (one that is usually considered pleasant or rewarding) following a response, which then leads to an increase in the future strength of that response. Loosely speaking, the behavior results in the delivery of something the recipient likes, so the person or animal is more likely to behave that way in the future. Some of the earlier illustrations have been examples of positive reinforcement. The standard rat procedure in which lever pressing produces food is an example of positive reinforcement because the consequence of food leads to an increase in lever pressing. It is reinforcement because the behavior increases in frequency, and it is positive reinforcement because the consequence involves the presentation of something—namely, food (which we would call a positive reinforcer). Here are some additional examples of positive reinforcement:

$$\underset{\text{R}}{\text{Turn on TV}} \rightarrow \underset{\text{S}^{\text{R}}}{\text{See the show}}$$

$$\underset{\text{R}}{\text{Smile at person}} \rightarrow \underset{\text{S}^{\text{R}}}{\text{The person smiles at you}}$$

$$\underset{\text{R}}{\text{Order coffee}} \rightarrow \underset{\text{S}^{\text{R}}}{\text{Receive coffee}}$$

$$\underset{\text{R}}{\text{Study diligently for quiz}} \rightarrow \underset{\text{S}^{\text{R}}}{\text{Obtain an excellent mark}}$$

$$\underset{\text{R}}{\text{Compliment partner}} \rightarrow \underset{\text{S}^{\text{R}}}{\text{Receive a kiss}}$$

Negative Reinforcement

Negative reinforcement is the *removal* of a stimulus (one that is usually considered unpleasant or aversive) following a response, which then leads to an increase in the future strength of that response. Loosely speaking, the behavior results in the prevention or removal of something the person or animal hates, so the subject is more likely to behave that way in the future. For example, if by pressing a lever a rat terminates an electric shock that it is receiving, it will become more likely to press the lever the next time it receives an electric shock. This is an example of reinforcement because the behavior increases in strength; it is negative reinforcement because the consequence consists of taking something away. Here are some additional examples:

> *Open umbrella* → **Escape rain**
>   **R**   **S^R**
>
> *Claim illness* → **Avoid writing an exam**
>   **R**   **S^R**
>
> *Take aspirin* → **Eliminate headache**
>   **R**   **S^R**
>
> *Turn on the heater* → **Escape the cold**
>   **R**   **S^R**

The last example is interesting because it illustrates how it is sometimes a matter of interpretation as to whether something is an example of negative reinforcement or positive reinforcement. Does the person turn on the heater to escape the cold (negative reinforcement) or to obtain warmth (positive reinforcement)? Either interpretation would be correct.

Negative reinforcement involves two types of behavior: escape and avoidance. *Escape behavior* results in the termination (stopping) of an aversive stimulus. In the example of the person getting rained on, by opening the umbrella the person stops this from happening. Likewise, taking aspirin removes a headache, and turning on the heater allows one to escape the cold. Avoidance is similar to escape except that *avoidance behavior* occurs before the aversive stimulus is presented and therefore prevents its delivery. For example, if the umbrella were opened before stepping out into the rain, the person would avoid getting rained on. And by pretending to be ill, a student avoids having to write an exam. Escape and avoidance are discussed in more detail in Chapter 9.

1. When you reached toward the dog, he nipped at your hand. You quickly pulled your hand back. As a result, he now nips at your hand whenever you reach toward him. The consequence for *the dog's behavior of nipping* consisted of the (presentation/removal) _____ of a stimulus (namely, your hand), and his behavior of nipping subsequently (increased/decreased) _____ in frequency; therefore, this is an example of _____ reinforcement.

2. When the dog sat at your feet and whined during breakfast one morning, you fed him. As a result, he sat at your feet and whined during breakfast the next morning. The consequence for the dog's whining consisted of the (presentation/removal) _____ of a stimulus, and his behavior of whining subsequently (increased/decreased) _____ in frequency; therefore, this is an example of _____ reinforcement.

QUICK QUIZ G

3. Karen cries while saying to her boyfriend, "John, I don't feel as though you love me." John gives Karen a big hug saying, "That's not true, dear, I love you very much." If John's hug is a reinforcer, Karen is (more/less) _____ likely to cry the next time she feels insecure about her relationship. More specifically, this is an example of _____ reinforcement of Karen's crying behavior.

4. With respect to escape and avoidance, an _____ response is one that *terminates* an aversive stimulus, while an _____ response is one that *prevents* an aversive stimulus from occurring. Escape and avoidance responses are two classes of behavior that are maintained by (positive/negative) _____ reinforcement.

5. Turning down the heat because you are too hot is an example of an (escape/ avoidance) _____ response; turning it down before you become too hot is an example of an (escape/avoidance) _____ response.

Positive Punishment

Positive punishment consists of the *presentation* of a stimulus (one that is usually considered unpleasant or aversive) following a response, which then leads to a *decrease* in the future strength of that response. Loosely speaking, the behavior results in the delivery of something the person or animal hates, so the subject is less likely to behave that way in the future. For example, if a rat received a shock when it pressed a lever, it would stop pressing the lever. This is an example of punishment because the behavior decreases in strength, and it is positive punishment because the consequence involves the presentation of something (i.e., shock). Consider some further examples of positive punishment:

> *Talk back to the boss* → **Get reprimanded**
> $\quad$ **R** $\qquad\qquad\qquad$ **S^P**
> *Swat at the wasp* → **Get stung**
> $\quad\quad$ **R** $\qquad\qquad$ **S^P**
> *Meow constantly* → **Get sprayed with water**
> $\quad\quad$ **R** $\qquad\qquad\qquad$ **S^P**

In each case, the behavior is followed by the presentation of an aversive stimulus, with the result that there is a decrease in the future probability of the behavior.

People frequently confuse positive punishment with negative reinforcement. One reason for this is the fact that many behaviorists, including Skinner, use the term *negative reinforcer* to refer to an aversive (unpleasant) stimulus and the term *positive reinforcer* to refer to an appetitive (pleasant) stimulus. Unfortunately, people with less knowledge of the field have then assumed that the presentation of a negative reinforcer is an instance of negative reinforcement, which it is not. Within the framework presented here, it is instead an instance of positive punishment.

Negative Punishment

Negative punishment consists of the *removal* of a stimulus (one that is usually considered pleasant or rewarding) following a response, which then leads to a *decrease* in the future strength of that response. Loosely speaking, the behavior results in the removal of something the person or animal likes, so the subject is less likely to behave that way in the future. Here are some examples of negative punishment:

Stay out past curfew → **Lose car privileges**
      R S^P

Argue with boss → **Lose job**
     R S^P

Play with food → **Lose dessert**
     R S^P

Tease sister → **Sent to room (loss of social contact)**
      R S^P

In each case, it is punishment because the behavior decreases in strength, and it is negative punishment because the consequence consists of the removal of something. The last example is known as "time-out" and is employed by many parents as a replacement for spanking. Removal of social contact is usually one consequence of such a procedure; more generally, however, the child loses the opportunity to receive any type of positive reinforcer during the time-out interval. Children find such situations to be quite unpleasant, with the result that even very brief time-outs can be quite effective.

Consider another example of negative punishment: Jonathan's girlfriend, who is quite jealous, completely ignored him (withdrew her attention from him) when she observed him having a conversation with another woman at a party. As a result, he stopped talking to the other women at the party.

Jonathan talks to other women → **His girlfriend ignores him**
              R S^P

Jonathan's behavior of talking to other women at parties has been negatively punished. It is punishment in that the frequency with which he talked to other women at the party declined, and it is negative punishment because the consequence that produced that decline was the withdrawal of his girlfriend's attention.

Question: In this scenario, Jonathan's behavior has been negatively punished. But what contingencies are operating on the girlfriend's behavior? When she ignored him, he stopped talking to other women at the party. Given that this occurred, she might ignore him at future parties if she again sees him talking to other women. If so, her behavior has been negatively reinforced by the fact that it was effective in getting him to stop doing something that she disliked. If we diagram this interaction from the perspective of each person, we get the following:

For Jonathan:
I talk to other women → **My girlfriend ignores me**
        R S^P

For his girlfriend:

I ignore Jonathan → **He stops talking to other women**
      R S^R

As you can see, a reduction in one person's behavior as a result of punishment can negatively reinforce the behavior of the person who implemented the punishment. This is the reason we are so often enticed to use punishment: Punishment is often successful in immediately getting a person to stop behaving in ways that we dislike. That success then reinforces our tendency to use punishment in the future, which of course can create major problems in the long run. We discuss the uses and abuses of punishment more fully in Chapter 9.

Some students mistakenly equate behaviorism with the use of punishment. It is important to recognize that behaviorists actually emphasize the use of positive reinforcement. Indeed, Skinner (1953) believed that many societal problems can be traced to the overuse of punishment as well as negative reinforcement. For example, teachers too often control their students by attempting to punish maladaptive behavior rather than by reinforcing adaptive behavior. Moreover, the educational system in general is designed in such a way that students too often study to avoid failure (a negative reinforcer) rather than to obtain knowledge (a positive reinforcer). As a result, schooling is often more onerous and less effective than it could be.

Similarly, in interpersonal relationships, people too often attempt to change each other's behavior through the use of aversive consequences, such as complaining, when positive reinforcement for appropriate behavior might work just as well or better. Marsha, for example, says that Roger forgets to call whenever he is going to be late, even though she often complains about it. Perhaps a more effective approach would be for her to express her appreciation when he does call.

Furthermore, although many people believe that the key to a great relationship is open communication, research has shown that a much more important element is the ratio of positive (pleasant) interactions to negative (aversive) interactions. In fact, one of the best predictors of a successful marriage is when the positives outweigh the negatives by a ratio of about five to one (Gottman, 1994). Even volatile relationships, in which there seems to be an enormous amount of bickering, can thrive if the number of positive exchanges, such as teasing, hugging, and praising, greatly outweigh the number of negative exchanges.

To help strengthen your understanding of the four types of contingencies— positive reinforcement, negative reinforcement, positive punishment, and negative punishment—and deal with examples that are potentially confusing, see also "Four Types of Contingencies: Tricky Examples" in the And Furthermore box.[5]

---

[5]Note that the labels for the two types of punishment are not standardized. For example, positive and negative punishment are sometimes called *Type 1* and *Type 2 punishment* (e.g., Chance, 1994) or *punishment by contingent application* and *punishment by contingent withdrawal* (e.g., L. Miller, 1997).

And Furthermore

Four Types of Contingencies: Tricky Examples

After learning about the four types of contingencies, students are sometimes dismayed when they encounter examples that suddenly confuse them. When this happens, the contingency typically has been worded in an unusual way. For example, suppose that a mother tells her son that *if he does not clean his room, then he will not get dessert.* What type of contingency is the mother specifying? To begin with, it sounds like a negative contingency because the consequence seems to involve the threatened loss of something—namely, the dessert. It also sounds like reinforcement because the goal is to increase the probability of a certain behavior—cleaning the room. We might therefore conclude that this is an example of negative reinforcement. But does this make sense? In everyday terms, negative reinforcement involves strengthening a behavior by removing something that the person dislikes, while here we are talking about removing something that the person likes. So what type of contingency is this?

To clarify situations like this, it helps to reword the example in terms of the *occurrence* of a behavior rather than its *nonoccurrence* because in reality it is only the occurrence of a behavior that is reinforced or punished. By doing so, and depending on the behavior we focus on, this example can be interpreted as fitting either of two types of contingencies. On one hand, if we focus on the behavior of cleaning the room, it can be viewed as an example of positive reinforcement: *if the son cleans his room, he can have dessert.* On the other hand, if we focus on the behavior of "doing something other than cleaning the room" (or something other than following his mother's instructions), it can be viewed as an example of negative punishment: *if the son does something other than clean his room, he will not get dessert.* Thus, all behaviors other than room cleaning, such as watching television, will result in the loss of dessert. In fact, to the extent that the mother made her request in a threatening manner, she probably intended something like the latter. But note how she could just as easily have worded her request in the form of positive reinforcement—"If you clean your room, you can have some dessert"—and how much more pleasant that sounds. Unfortunately, many parents too often choose the unpleasant version, especially when they are frustrated or angry, which in turn helps to create a decidedly unpleasant atmosphere in the household.

---

1. When Sasha was teasing the dog, it bit her. As a result, she no longer teases the dog. The consequence for *Sasha's behavior* of teasing the dog was the (presentation/removal) _____ of a stimulus, and the teasing behavior subsequently (increased/decreased) _____ in frequency; therefore, this is an example of _____ _____.

2. Whenever Sasha pulled the dog's tail, the dog left and went into another room. As a result, Sasha now pulls the dog's tail less often when it is around. The consequence for pulling the dog's tail was the (presentation/removal) _____ of a stimulus, and the behavior of pulling the dog's tail subsequently (increased/decreased) _____ in frequency; therefore, this is an example of _____ _____.

QUICK QUIZ H

3. When Alex burped in public during his date with Stephanie, she got angry with him. Alex now burps quite often when he is out on a date with Stephanie. The consequence for burping was the _____ of a stimulus, and the behavior of belching subsequently _____ in frequency; therefore, this is an example of _____ _____.

4. When Alex held the car door open for Stephanie, she made a big fuss over what a gentleman he was becoming. Alex no longer holds the car door open for her. The consequence for holding open the door was the _____ of a stimulus, and the behavior of holding open the door subsequently _____ in frequency; therefore, this is an example of _____ _____.

5. When Tenzing shared his toys with his brother, his mother stopped criticizing him. Tenzing now shares his toys with his brother quite often. The consequence for sharing the toys was the _____ of a stimulus, and the behavior of sharing the toys subsequently _____ in frequency; therefore, this is an example of _____ _____.

Positive Reinforcement: Further Distinctions

Because behaviorists so strongly emphasize positive reinforcement, let us have a closer look at this type of contingency. More specifically, we will examine various categories of positive reinforcement.

Immediate Versus Delayed Reinforcement

A reinforcer can be presented either immediately after a behavior occurs or following some delay. In general, *the more immediate the reinforcer, the stronger its effect on the behavior.* Suppose, for example, that you wish to reinforce a child's quiet playing by giving him a treat. The treat should ideally be given while the quiet period is still in progress. If, instead, you deliver the treat several minutes later, while he is engaged in some other behavior (e.g., banging a stick on his toy box), you might inadvertently reinforce that behavior rather than the one you wish to reinforce.

The weak effect of delayed reinforcers on behavior accounts for some major difficulties in life. Do you find it tough to stick to a diet or an exercise regime? This is because the benefits of exercise and proper eating are delayed and therefore weak, whereas the enjoyable effects of alternate activities, such as watching television and drinking a soda, are immediate and therefore powerful. Similarly, have you ever promised yourself that you would study all weekend, only to find that you completely wasted your time reading novels, watching television, and going out with friends? The immediate reinforcement associated with these recreational activities effectively outweighed the delayed reinforcement associated with studying. Of course, what we are talking about here is the issue of self-control, a topic that is more fully discussed in Chapter 10.

The importance of immediate reinforcement is so profound that some behaviorists (e.g., Malott, 1989; Malott & Suarez, 2004) argue that a delayed reinforcer does not, on its own, actually function as a "reinforcer." They point to experimental evidence indicating that delaying a reinforcer by even a few seconds can often severely influence its effectiveness (e.g., Grice, 1948; Keesey, 1964; see also J. Williams, 1973). This finding suggests that delayed reinforcers, to the extent that they are effective, may function by a different mechanism from immediate reinforcement, especially in humans. Thus, receiving a good mark on that essay you wrote last week does not reinforce the behavior of essay writing in the same way that immediately receiving a food pellet reinforces a rat's tendency to press a lever (or immediately seeing your mother's smile reinforces your tendency to give her another compliment). Rather, in the case of humans, behaviors that appear to be strengthened by long-delayed reinforcers are often under the control of rules or instructions that we have received from others or generated for ourselves. These rules or instructions describe to us the delayed consequences that can result from a behavior (e.g., "Gee, if I work on that essay tonight, I am likely to get a good mark on it next week"), thereby bridging the gap between the behavior and the consequence.

In this text, for simplicity, we will ignore some of the complexities associated with the issue of rules and delayed reinforcement, though we will briefly discuss rule-governed behavior in Chapter 12. For the present purposes, it is sufficient to note that delayed reinforcement is usually much less potent, and perhaps even qualitatively different, than immediate reinforcement. This also makes clear the crucial importance of immediate reinforcement when dealing with young children (and animals) who have little or no language capacity, since the use of rules is essentially dependent on language.

1. In general, the more _____ the reinforcer, the stronger its effect on behavior.

2. It is sometimes difficult for students to study in that the reinforcers for studying are _____ and therefore w_____, whereas the reinforcers for alternative activities are _____ and therefore s_____.

3. It has been suggested that delayed reinforcers (do/do not) _____ function in the same manner as immediate reinforcers. Rather, the effectiveness of delayed reinforcers in humans is largely dependent on the use of i_____ or r_____ to bridge the gap between the behavior and the delay.

QUICK QUIZ I

Primary and Secondary Reinforcers

A *primary reinforcer* (also called an *unconditioned reinforcer*) is an event that is innately reinforcing. Loosely speaking, primary reinforcers are those things we are born to like rather than learn to like and that therefore naturally reinforce our behavior. Examples of primary reinforcers are food, water, proper temperature (neither too hot nor too cold), and sexual contact.

Many primary reinforcers are associated with basic physiological needs, and their effectiveness is closely tied to a state of deprivation. For example, food is a highly effective reinforcer when we are food deprived and hungry but not when we are satiated. Some primary reinforcers, however, do not seem to be associated with a physiological state of deprivation. An animal (or person) cooped up in a boring environment will likely find access to a more stimulating environment highly reinforcing and will perform a response such as lever pressing (or driving to the mall) to gain such access. In cases such as this, the deprivation seems more psychological than physiological.

A *secondary reinforcer* (also called a *conditioned reinforcer*) is an event that is reinforcing because it has been associated with some other reinforcer. Loosely speaking, secondary reinforcers are those events that we have learned to like because they have become associated with other things that we like. Much of our behavior is directed toward obtaining secondary reinforcers, such as good marks, fine clothes, and a nice car. Because of our experiences with these events, they can function as effective reinforcers for our current behavior. Thus, if good marks in school are consistently associated with praise, then the good marks themselves can serve as reinforcers for behaviors such as studying. And just seeing a professor who once provided you with lots of praise and encouraged you to make the most of your life may be an effective reinforcer for the behavior of visiting her after you graduate.

Conditioned stimuli that have been associated with appetitive unconditioned stimuli (USs) can also function as secondary reinforcers. For example, the sound of a metronome that has been paired with food to produce a classically conditioned response of salivation:

$$\text{Metronome: Food} \rightarrow \textit{Salivation}$$
$$\text{NS} \qquad \text{US} \qquad \text{UR}$$
$$\text{Metronome} \rightarrow \textit{Salivation}$$
$$\text{CS} \qquad \text{CR}$$

Can then be used as a secondary reinforcer for an operant response such as lever pressing:

$$\textit{Lever press} \rightarrow \text{Metronome}$$
$$\text{R} \qquad \text{S}^{\text{R}}$$

Because the metronome has been closely associated with food, it can now serve as a reinforcer for the operant response of lever pressing. The animal essentially seeks out the metronome because of its pleasant associations. Similarly, we may seek out music that has been closely associated with a romantic episode in our life because of its pleasant associations.

Discriminative stimuli associated with positive reinforcers can likewise function as secondary reinforcers. A tone that has served as an S^D signaling the availability of food for lever pressing:

$$\text{Tone: } \textit{Lever press} \rightarrow \text{Food}$$
$$\text{S}^{\text{D}} \qquad \text{R} \qquad \text{S}^{\text{R}}$$

can then function as a secondary reinforcer for some other behavior, such as running in a wheel:

Run in wheel → Tone
    R S^R

An important type of secondary reinforcer is known as a generalized reinforcer. A ***generalized reinforcer*** (also known as a ***generalized secondary reinforcer***) is a type of secondary reinforcer that has been associated with several other reinforcers. For example, money is a powerful generalized reinforcer for humans because it is associated with an almost unlimited array of other reinforcers including food, clothing, furnishings, entertainment, and even dates (insofar as money will likely increase our attractiveness to others). In fact, money can become such a powerful reinforcer that some people would rather just have the money than the things it can buy. Social attention, too, is a highly effective generalized reinforcer, especially for young children (though some aspects of it, such as touching, are probably also primary reinforcers). Attention from caretakers is usually associated with a host of good things such as food and play and comfort, with the result that attention by itself can become a powerful reinforcer. It is so powerful that some children will even misbehave to get someone to pay attention to them.

Generalized reinforcers are often used in behavior modification programs. In a "token economy," tokens are used in institutional settings—such as mental institutions, prisons, or classrooms for problem children—to increase the frequency of certain desirable behaviors, such as completing an assigned task, dressing appropriately, or behaving sociably. Attendants deliver the tokens immediately following the occurrence of the behavior. These tokens can later be exchanged for "backup reinforcers" such as treats, trips into the community, or television viewing time. In essence, just as the opportunity to earn money—and what it can buy—motivates many of us to behave appropriately, so too does the opportunity to earn tokens—and what they can be exchanged for—motivates the residents of that setting to behave appropriately. (See Miltenberger, 1997, for an in-depth discussion of token economies.)

Note that an event can function as both a primary reinforcer and a secondary reinforcer. A Thanksgiving dinner, for example, can be both a primary reinforcer, in the sense of providing food, and a secondary reinforcer due to its association with a beloved grandmother who prepared many similar dinners in your childhood.

Finally, just as stimuli that are associated with reinforcement can become secondary reinforcers, so also can the *behaviors* that are associated with reinforcement. For example, children who are consistently praised for helping others might eventually find the behavior of helping others to be reinforcing in and of itself. They will then help others, not to receive praise but because they "like to help." We might then describe such children as having an altruistic nature. By a similar mechanism, even hard work can sometimes become a secondary reinforcer (see "Learned Industriousness" in the And Furthermore box).

And Furthermore

Learned Industriousness

Some people seem to enjoy hard work while others do not. Why is this? According to *learned industriousness theory*, if working hard (displaying high effort) on a task has been consistently associated with reinforcement, then working hard might itself become a secondary reinforcer (Eisenberger, 1992). This can result in a generalized tendency to work hard. Experiments with both humans and animals have confirmed this possibility. For example, rats that have received reinforcers for emitting forceful lever presses will then run faster down an alleyway to obtain food (Eisenberger, Carlson, Guile, & Shapiro, 1979). Similarly, students who have received reinforcers for solving complex math problems will later write essays of higher quality (Eisenberger, Masterson, & McDermitt, 1982). Experiments have also confirmed the opposite: Rats and humans that have received reinforcers for displaying low effort on a task will show a generalized tendency to be lazy (see Eisenberger, 1992). (Something to think about if you have a strong tendency to take the easy way out.)

QUICK QUIZ J

1. Events that are innately reinforcing are called _____ reinforcers. They are sometimes also called un_____ reinforcers.

2. Events that become reinforcers through their association with other reinforcers are called _____ reinforcers. They are sometimes also called _____ reinforcers.

3. Honey is for most people an example of a _____ reinforcer, while a coupon that is used to purchase the honey is an example of a _____ reinforcer.

4. A (CS/US) _____ that has been associated with an appetitive (CS/US) _____ can serve as a secondary reinforcer for an operant response. As well, a stimulus that serves as a(n) _____ for an operant response can also serve as a secondary reinforcer for some other response.

5. A generalized reinforcer (or generalized secondary reinforcer) is a secondary reinforcer that has been associated with _____.

6. Two generalized secondary reinforcers that have strong effects on human behavior are _____.

7. Behavior modification programs in institutional settings often utilize generalized reinforcers in the form of t_____. This type of arrangement is known as a t_____ e_____.

Intrinsic and Extrinsic Reinforcement

In the preceding discussion, we noted that operant behavior itself can sometimes be reinforcing. Such a behavior is said to be intrinsically reinforcing or motivating. Thus, **intrinsic reinforcement** is reinforcement provided by the mere act of performing the behavior. We rollerblade because it is invigorating, we party with friends because we like their company, and we work hard at something partly because hard work has, through experience, become enjoyable (though you are probably still not convinced about that one). Animals, too, sometimes engage in activities for their own sake. In some of the earliest research on intrinsic motivation, it was found that with no additional incentive, monkeys repeatedly solved mechanical puzzles (Harlow, Harlow, & Meyer, 1950).

Unfortunately, many activities are not intrinsically reinforcing and instead require additional incentives to ensure their performance. ***Extrinsic reinforcement*** is the reinforcement provided by some consequence that is external to the behavior (i.e., an "extrinsic reinforcer"). For example, perhaps you are reading this text solely because of an upcoming exam. Passing the exam is the extrinsic consequence that is motivating your behavior. Other examples of extrinsically motivated behaviors are driving to get somewhere, working for money, and dating an attractive individual merely to enhance your prestige.

Unfortunately, the distinction between intrinsic and extrinsic reinforcers is not always clear. For example, is candy an intrinsic or extrinsic reinforcer? In one sense, candy seems like an intrinsic reinforcer because eating it is an enjoyable activity; yet the candy exists external to the behavior that is being reinforced. In such cases, it often helps to focus on the behavior that is being strengthened. Imagine, for example, that we offer candy to a child to strengthen the behavior of being quiet in the supermarket. The candy is clearly an extrinsic reinforcer for the behavior of *being quiet,* but with respect to the behavior of *eating candy,* the candy is the critical component in an intrinsically reinforcing activity. In any case, do not fret too much if you encounter an example that seems confusing. The most important thing is to be able to distinguish situations in which the motivation is clearly intrinsic (taking a bath for the pleasure of it) from those in which the motivation is clearly extrinsic (taking a bath because you have been paid to do so).

Question: What happens if you are given an extrinsic reinforcer for an activity that is already intrinsically reinforcing? What if, for example, you love rollerblading and are fortunate enough to be hired one weekend to blade around an amusement park while displaying a new line of sportswear? Will the experience of receiving payment for rollerblading increase, decrease, or have no effect on your subsequent enjoyment of the activity?

Although you might think that it would increase your enjoyment of rollerblading (since the activity is not only enjoyable but also associated with money), many researchers claim that experiences like this can *decrease* intrinsic interest. For example, Lepper, Green, and Nisbett (1973) found that children who enjoyed drawing with Magic Markers became less interested following a session in which they had been promised, and then received, a "good player" award for drawing with the markers. In contrast, children who did not receive an award or who received the award unexpectedly after playing with the markers did not show a loss of interest. Similar results have been reported by other investigators (e.g., Deci & Ryan, 1985). However, some researchers have

And Furthermore

Positive Reinforcement of Artistic Appreciation

B. F. Skinner (1983) once described how two students used positive reinforcement to instill in their new roommate an appreciation of modern art. These students had several items of modern art in their apartment, but the roommate had shown little interest in them and was instead proceeding to "change the character" of the space. As a counterploy, the students first decided to pay attention to the roommate only when they saw him looking at one of the works of art. Next, they threw a party and arranged for an attractive young woman to engage him in a discussion about the art. They also arranged for him to receive announcements from local art galleries about upcoming art shows. After about a month, the roommate himself suggested attending a local art museum. Interestingly, while there, he just "happened" to find a five-dollar bill lying at his feet while he was looking at a painting. According to Skinner, "It was not long before [the two students] came again in great excitement—to show me his first painting" (p. 48).

found that extrinsic rewards have no effect on intrinsic interest (e.g., Amabile, Hennessey, & Grossman, 1986) or actually produce an *increase* in intrinsic interest (e.g., Harackiewicz, Manderlink, & Sansone, 1984). Unfortunately, despite these mixed findings, it is the damaging effects of extrinsic rewards on intrinsic motivation that are often presented to the public (e.g., Kohn, 1993). But is this a fair assessment of the evidence? Are the harmful effects of reinforcement the rule or the exception?

Cameron and Pierce (1994) attempted to answer this question by conducting a meta-analysis of 96 well-controlled experiments that examined the effects of extrinsic rewards on intrinsic motivation. (A meta-analysis is a statistical procedure that combines the results of several separate studies, thereby producing a more reliable overall assessment of the variable being studied.) The meta-analysis by Cameron and Pierce indicates that extrinsic rewards usually have little or no effect on intrinsic motivation. External rewards can occasionally undermine intrinsic motivation, but only when *the reward is expected* (i.e., the person has been instructed beforehand that she will receive a reward), *the reward is tangible* (e.g., it consists of money rather than praise), and *the reward is given for simply performing the activity* (and not for how well it is performed). It also turns out that verbal rewards, such as praise, often produce an increase in intrinsic motivation, as do tangible rewards given for high-quality performance (see Deci & Ryan, 1985). Cameron and Pierce (1994) conclude that extrinsic rewards can be safely applied in most circumstances and that the limited circumstances in which they decrease intrinsic motivation are easily avoided. Bandura (1997) likewise has argued that the dangers of extrinsic rewards on intrinsic motivation have been greatly overstated. (See Cameron, 2001; Cameron, Banko, & Pierce, 2001; Cameron & Pierce, 2002;

and Deci, Koestner, & Ryan, 2001a, 2001b, for further contributions to this debate.)[6] (See also "Positive Reinforcement of Artistic Appreciation" in the And Furthermore box.)

1. An _____ motivated activity is one in which the activity is itself reinforcing; an _____ motivated activity is one in which the reinforcer for the activity consists of some type of additional consequence that is not inherent to the activity.

2. Running to lose weight is an example of an _____ motivated activity; running because it "feels good" is an example of an _____ motivated activity.

3. In their meta-analysis of relevant research, Cameron and Pierce (1994) found that extrinsic rewards decrease intrinsic motivation only when they are (expected/unexpected) _____, (tangible/verbal) _____, and given for (performing well/merely engaging in the behavior) _____ _____.

4. They also found that extrinsic rewards generally increased intrinsic motivation when the rewards were (tangible/verbal) _____, and that tangible rewards increased intrinsic motivation when they were delivered contingent upon (high/low) _____ quality performance.

Natural and Contrived Reinforcers

The distinction between intrinsic and extrinsic reinforcers is closely related to the distinction between natural and contrived reinforcers. *Natural reinforcers* are reinforcers that are naturally provided for a certain behavior; that is, they are a typical consequence of the behavior within that setting. Money is a natural consequence of selling merchandise; gold medals are a natural consequence of hard training and a great performance. *Contrived reinforcers* are reinforcers that have been deliberately arranged to modify a behavior; they are not a typical consequence of the behavior in that setting. For example, although television is the natural reinforcer for the behavior of turning on the set, it is a contrived reinforcer for the behavior

---

[6]It is also the case that some consequences that appear to function as positive reinforcers might in reality be more aversive. For example, many years ago, a player for the Pittsburgh Pirates told me (Russ Powell) that he hated baseball because there were so many young players trying to replace him. It seemed like the consequence that motivated his playing was no longer the love of baseball, nor even the desire to obtain a good salary; rather, it was the threatened *loss* of a good salary if he didn't play well. According to Skinner (1987), human behavior is too often controlled by these types of negative consequences—working to avoid the loss of a paycheck and studying to avoid failure (especially prevalent in students who procrastinate until they are in serious danger of failing). It is therefore not surprising that these activities often seem less than intrinsically interesting.

of, say, accomplishing a certain amount of studying. In the latter case, we have created a contrived contingency in an attempt to modify the person's study behavior.

Note that *intrinsic reinforcers are always natural reinforcers, while extrinsic reinforcers can be either natural or contrived*. For example, an actor's "feeling of satisfaction" is an intrinsic, natural reinforcer for a good performance. By contrast, compliments by customers are extrinsic, natural reinforcers for a chef's behavior of creating a wonderful meal; and candy is an extrinsic, contrived reinforcer for a child's behavior of sitting quietly in a doctor's office. In other words, some extrinsic reinforcers are part of the typical contingencies in our environment, while others have been artificially imposed to modify a particular behavior. Needless to say, concerns about the effects of extrinsic reinforcement on intrinsic motivation have focused mostly on situations in which extrinsic reinforcers have been artificially manipulated, or contrived.

Although contrived reinforcers are often seen as a hallmark of behaviorism, behaviorists strive to utilize natural reinforcers whenever possible (Sulzer-Azaroff & Mayer, 1991). When contrived reinforcers are used, the ultimate intention is to let the "natural contingencies" eventually take over if at all possible. For example, although we might initially use tokens to motivate a patient with schizophrenia to socialize with others, our hope is that the behavior will soon become "trapped" by the natural consequences of socializing (e.g., smiles and pleasant comments from others) such that the tokens can eventually be withdrawn. Similarly, although we might initially use praise to increase the frequency with which a child reads, the natural (and intrinsic) reinforcers associated with reading will hopefully take over so that the child will begin reading even in the absence of praise.

Note, too, that natural contingencies tend to produce more efficient behavior patterns than do contrived contingencies (Skinner, 1987). Although a coach might use praise to reinforce correct throwing actions by a young quarterback, the most important factor in producing correct throws will be the natural consequence of where the ball goes.

To distinguish between intrinsic versus extrinsic reinforcers and natural versus contrived reinforcers, just remember that the former is concerned with the extent to which the behavior itself is reinforcing while the latter is concerned with the extent to which a reinforcer has been artificially imposed so as to manipulate a behavior. Note, too, that the extent to which a reinforcer has been artificially imposed is not always clear; hence, it is always possible to find examples in which it is ambiguous as to whether the reinforcer is contrived or natural. Are grades in school a natural reinforcer or a contrived reinforcer? It depends on whether one's grades are a typical aspect of the learning environment, at least within the school system, or a contrived aspect. In any event, as with intrinsic versus extrinsic motivation, the important thing is to be able to distinguish those situations in which the reinforcers are clearly contrived—as often occurs in a behavior modification program—from those in which the reinforcers are more natural.

1. A(n) _____ reinforcer is a reinforcer that typically occurs for that behavior in that setting; a(n) _____ reinforcer is one that typically does not occur for that behavior in that setting.

2. You flip the switch and the light comes on. The light coming on is an example of a(n) (contrived/natural) _____ reinforcer; in general, it is also an example of an (intrinsic/extrinsic) _____ reinforcer.

3. You thank your roommate for helping out with the housework in an attempt to motivate her to help out more often. To the extent that this works, the thank-you is an example of a(n) (contrived/natural) _____ reinforcer; it is also an example of an (intrinsic/extrinsic) _____ reinforcer.

4. In applied behavior analysis, although one might initially use (contrived/natural) _____ consequences to first develop a behavior, the hope is that, if possible, the behavior will become tr_____ by the n_____ c_____ associated with that behavior.

5. In most cases, the most important consequence in developing highly effective forms of behavior will be the (contrived/natural) _____ consequences of that behavior.

6. (Intrinsic/Extrinsic) _____ reinforcers are always natural reinforcers, while _____ reinforcers can be either natural or contrived.

Shaping

Positive reinforcement is clearly a great way to strengthen a behavior, but what if the behavior that we wish to reinforce never occurs? For example, what if you want to reinforce a rat's behavior of pressing a lever but are unable to do so because the rat never presses the lever? What can you do? The solution is to use a procedure called shaping.

Shaping is the gradual creation of new operant behavior through reinforcement of successive approximations to that behavior. With our rat, we could begin by delivering food whenever it stands near the lever. As a result, it begins standing near the lever more often. We then deliver food only when it is facing the lever, at which point it starts engaging in that behavior more often. In a similar manner, step-by-step, we reinforce touching the lever, then placing a paw on the lever, and then pressing down on the lever. When the rat finally presses down on the lever with enough force, it closes the microswitch that activates the food magazine. The rat has now earned a reinforcer on its own. After a few more experiences like this, the rat begins to reliably press the lever whenever it is hungry. By reinforcing successive approximations to the target behavior, we have managed to teach the rat an entirely new behavior.

Another example of shaping: How do you teach a dog to catch a Frisbee? Many people simply throw the Frisbee at the dog, at which point the dog probably wonders what on earth has gotten into its owner as the Frisbee sails over its head. Or possibly the dog runs after the Frisbee, picks it up after it falls on the ground, and then makes the owner chase after him to get the Frisbee back. Karen Pryor (1999), a professional animal trainer, recommends the following procedure. First, reinforce the dog's behavior of taking the Frisbee from your hand and immediately returning it. Next, raise the criterion by holding the Frisbee in the air to make the dog jump for it. When this is well established, toss the Frisbee slightly so the dog jumps and catches it in midair. Then toss it a couple of feet so he has to run after it to catch it. Now gradually throw it further and further so the dog has to run farther and farther to get it. Remember to provide lots of praise each time the dog catches the Frisbee and returns it.

Shaping is obviously a fundamental procedure for teaching animals to perform tricks. During such training, the trainers often use a sound, such as a click from a handheld clicker, to reinforce the behavior. The sound has been repeatedly paired with food so that it has become a secondary reinforcer. The benefit of using a sound as a reinforcer is that it can be presented immediately upon the occurrence of the behavior, even if the animal is some distance away. Also, if food were presented each time the correct behavior occurred, the animal would quickly satiate, at which point the food would become ineffective as a reinforcer. By using a secondary reinforcer such as a click, with food delivered only intermittently, satiation will take longer to occur, thereby allowing for longer training sessions.

Most of our behaviors have, to some extent, been learned or modified through shaping. For example, when children first learn to eat with a knife and fork, parents might praise even very poor attempts. Over time, though, they expect better and better performance before offering praise. In a similar manner, with children we gradually shape the behavior of dressing appropriately, speaking politely, and writing legibly. And shaping is not confined merely to childhood. All of us are in the position of receiving constant feedback about our performance—be it ironing clothes, cooking a meal, or slamdunking a basketball—thus allowing us to continually modify our behaviors and improve our skills. In such circumstances, it is usually the natural consequences of the behavior—the extent to which we are successful or unsuccessful—that provide the necessary reinforcement for gradual modifications of the behavior.

For further information on shaping as applied to both animals and humans, you might wish to obtain a copy of Karen Pryor's (1999) highly readable book, *Don't Shoot the Dog*. Pryor also has a Web site on "clicker training" (shaping through the use of clicks as secondary reinforcers) that can be accessed via the Internet (just search for "clicker training"). Clicker training has become increasingly popular with dog owners and is being used to shape behavior in everything from birds to horses and even llamas and elephants. Interestingly, Pryor observes that many animals greatly enjoy the "game" of clicker training. (See also "Training Ishmael" in the And Furthermore box.)

An excellent demonstration of the power of shaping.

ADVICE FOR THE LOVELORN

Dear Dr. Dee,

My boyfriend has a terrible tendency to boss me around. I have tried to counter this tendency by being especially nice to him, but the problem seems to be getting worse. He also refuses to discuss it or see a counselor. He says I am too sensitive and that I am making a mountain out of a molehill. What should I do?

Just About Hadenough

Dear Just,

You should first recognize that some people have a long history of reinforcement for being dominant or aggressive, and that it can sometimes be difficult to alter such tendencies. In fact, you might eventually have to bail out of this relationship, particularly because he refuses to discuss what seems to be an obvious problem.

Nevertheless, you might also wish to consider the possibility that you are inadvertently reinforcing his aggressiveness. Remember how, in the opening vignette to this chapter, the young woman reacted to her partner's angry demands by a show of affection. While this might reduce his anger in the short run, it might also reinforce his tendency to be aggressive. After all, not only was his anger effective in getting her to hurry up, it also resulted in a hug. The next time he wants her to hurry up or desires affection, what better way than to get angry?

As a first step, you might wish to take careful note of the situations in which your boyfriend becomes bossy. If it appears that you might be reinforcing his bossiness by being particularly nice to him when he acts that way, you could try offering him little or no attention when he behaves like that and lots of attention when he behaves more appropriately. Can this work? In her book *Don't Shoot the Dog*, Karen Pryor (1999) relates the following story about a woman who implemented just such a program:

> A young woman married a man who turned out to be very bossy and demanding. Worse yet, his father, who lived with them, was equally given to ordering his daughter-in-law about. It was the girl's mother who told me this story. On her first visit she was horrified at what her daughter was going through. "Don't worry, Mother," the daughter said. "Wait and see." The daughter formed the practice of responding minimally to commands and harsh remarks, while reinforcing with approval and affection any tendency by either man to be pleasant and thoughtful. In a year, she had turned them into decent human beings. Now they greet her with smiles when she comes home and leap up—both of them—to help with the groceries. (p. 30)

By reinforcing successive approximations toward decent behavior and not reinforcing bossy behavior (yet still responding minimally to their requests), this woman was apparently able to shape more appropriate behavior in her husband and father-in-law. Remember, though, such problems are often difficult to manage and may require professional help.

Behaviorally yours,

Dr. Dee

And Furthermore

Training Ishmael

Although the principles of reinforcement and shaping are easy enough to learn, apply-ing those principles can be another matter. In this case, there is no substitute for the experience of shaping behavior in a live animal. Dogs are ideal subjects for this, with cats and birds also being quite suitable. However, many people live in apartments where such pets are not allowed. Fortunately, apartment dwellers are often allowed to keep fish, and some fish are in fact surprisingly trainable. Goldfish, for example, have been trained to swim through hoops, push ping pong balls around, and (according to one report from an acquaintance who swore she saw it on television) pull a string to ring a tiny bell for food.

To illustrate the process of using reinforcement to train a fish, let us consider some training that I (Russ Powell) conducted with Ishmael, a 2-inch long, dark blue, male *Betta splendens* (Siamese fighting fish). Ishmael lives by himself in a 1-gallon acrylic tank with gravel and a few plants. It might seem to you that a 1-gallon tank is awfully small, but bettas have evolved to survive in small pools of water in their native Thailand. Isolation from other fish is also a natural state of affairs for a betta because the sight of another male, or something similar to it, often elicits the fixed action pattern of aggression that we discussed in Chapter 3. As it turns out, this natural proclivity for small living quarters and relative isolation is an advantage when it comes to training bettas, because this setup mimics some of the features of an operant conditioning chamber.

The interesting thing about training a male betta is that two types of reinforcers are available. One, of course, is food, and this generally works as well with bettas as it does with other animals (though bettas are sometimes fussy eaters). Unfortunately, being such small fish, they can be given only a few bites of food per day, which means that each training session must be kept quite short to prevent overfeeding. The other type of reinforcer is the presentation of a mirror that allows them to see a mirror image of themselves. This mirror image is often perceived as another male, which then elicits the fixed action pattern of aggression. Interestingly, the opportunity to aggress like this can serve as a positive reinforcer that can be used to strengthen some other behavior (Melvin, 1985; T. Thompson, 1963). Note that this is an excellent example of how positive reinforcers are not necessarily the kinds of events that one would classify as pleasant. If bettas had human-like feelings, one could only assume from their behavior that they hate the sight of another male; nevertheless, they will learn to perform a response in order to see that male.

As an informal demonstration of the effectiveness of mirror presentation as a reinforcer with Ishmael, mirror presentations were made contingent upon the behavior of turning a half-circle, first in a clockwise and then in a counterclockwise direction. A clockwise turn was defined as a clockwise movement from, at minimum, a left-facing position (from the

(continued)

observer's perspective) to a right-facing position in the tank. A counterclockwise turn was defined as a counterclockwise movement from, at minimum, a right-facing position to a left-facing position. Each training session lasted 10 minutes, which was measured with a kitchen timer.

During an initial baseline period, Ishmael's clockwise and counterclockwise circling habits were recorded throughout the session with 10 mirror presentations presented noncontingently (independent of any behavior) at random points in time. (*Question: Why include mirror presentations in the baseline period?*) During this period, Ishmael showed a slight preference for turning in a counterclockwise direction (see Figure 6.4). A clockwise turn was selected for initial training beginning in session 5. Rather than simply waiting for a clockwise turn and then presenting the mirror, past experience with another betta suggested that the turning behavior could be established more rapidly by using a shaping procedure. Thus, mirror presentations were initially made contingent upon successive approximations to the required behavior (i.e., slight turns in the correct direction were initially reinforced, and progressively complete turns were subsequently reinforced). Shaping proceeded rapidly, with Ishmael quickly establishing a pattern of clockwise turns. For the remainder of session 5 and for the following three sessions, he exhibited a clear preference for such turns.

Beginning in session 9, the contingency was reversed with counterclockwise turns reinforced and clockwise turns extinguished. Possibly due to the short length of each training session, counterclockwise turns did not become well established until session 13 (even with shaping), which was maintained for the following three sessions. A reversal was then attempted in which clockwise turns were again reinforced and counterclockwise turns were extinguished (hence, overall, this was an ABCB design).

FIGURE 6.4 Number of clockwise and counterclockwise turns made by Ishmael across different phases of the demonstration.

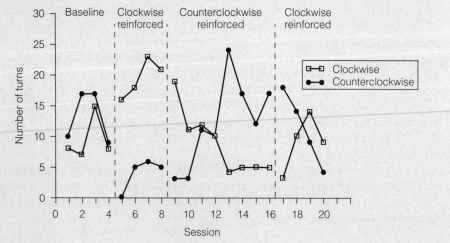

This time, three sessions were required before Ishmael developed a preference for turning in the newly reinforced direction. In session 20, however, the number of turns in either direction—as well as, it seemed, his general activity level—dropped sharply, especially toward the end of the session. During the first 5 minutes of the next session, he mostly sat at the bottom of the tank reacting minimally to the mirror. No circling behavior occurred. It appeared as though long-term habituation had set in such that the mirror was no longer sufficiently reinforcing to motivate the target behavior, and the session was therefore terminated. Ishmael showed a similar lack of interest in the mirror over the following 2 days as well.

Despite this less-than-ideal conclusion, the results generally confirmed that mirror presentation was an effective reinforcer for Ishmael's circling behavior. Most impressive was the initial learning of a clockwise turn, which occurred very rapidly. With food as a reinforcer, Ishmael also learned to bump, but not push, a ping pong ball—it was easy to get him to hover near the ball, but difficult to get him to contact it—to swim through a wire hoop for food—which was relatively easy to accomplish—and to nip at the bent end of a plastic-coated paper clip, which was extremely easy to accomplish. (As for Ishmael, he easily trained his owner [me] to give him extra food by staring longingly at me and acting very excited when I came home each evening.) Further information on betta training can be found in the *Chapter 6: Additional Information* section of the book companion Web site (the URL is at the end of the chapter).

Now for the answer to the question about including mirror presentations in the baseline period: Intermittent presentation of the mirror by itself generates a lot of excitement and movement. Hence, noncontingent presentation of the mirror during the baseline period controls for the increase in circling that will likely occur simply due to the increased movement caused by mirror presentation alone.

1. Shaping is the creation of _____ operant behavior through the reinforcement of s_____ a_____ to that behavior.

2. In clicker training with dogs, the click is a s_____ reinforcer that has been established by first pairing it with f_____.

3. The advantages of using the click as a reinforcer is that it can be delivered i_____. It can also prevent the animal from becoming s_____.

QUICK QUIZ M

SUMMARY

In contrast to elicited behaviors that are automatically evoked by the stimuli that precede them, operant behaviors are controlled by their consequences. Thus, in operant (or instrumental) conditioning, the future probability of a response is affected by its consequence. Reinforcers are consequences that increase the probability of (or strengthen) a response, whereas punishers decrease the probability of (or weaken) a response. In positive reinforcement and positive punishment, the consequence involves the presentation of a stimulus, whereas in negative reinforcement and negative punishment, the consequence involves the removal of a stimulus.

When a behavior has been consistently reinforced or punished in the presence of certain stimuli, those stimuli will begin to influence the occurrence of the behavior. A discriminative stimulus is a stimulus in the presence of which a response has been reinforced and in the absence of which it has not been reinforced.

Immediate reinforcers have a much stronger effect on behavior than do delayed reinforcers. Primary reinforcers are events that are innately reinforcing; secondary reinforcers are events that become reinforcing because they have been associated with other reinforcers. A generalized secondary reinforcer is a secondary reinforcer that has been associated with many other reinforcers. Intrinsic reinforcement occurs when performing a behavior is inherently reinforcing; extrinsic reinforcement occurs when the effective reinforcer is some consequence that is external to the behavior. Extrinsic reinforcement can undermine intrinsic interest in a task when the reinforcer is expected, tangible, or is made contingent on mere performance of the task. Extrinsic reinforcement can strengthen intrinsic interest when the reinforcer consists of verbal praise or is made contingent on high-quality performance.

Shaping is the creation of novel behavior through the reinforcement of gradual approximations to that behavior. Effective shaping is often carried out with the use of a secondary reinforcer, such as the sound of a whistle or a click that can be delivered immediately following the occurrence of the appropriate behavior.

SUGGESTED READINGS

Thorndike, E. L. (1898). Animal intelligence: An experimental study of the associative processes in animals. *Psychological Review Monograph Supplement, 2*, 1–109. A classic work in the field.

Kohn, A. (1993). *Punished by rewards.* Boston: Houghton Mifflin. One of the harshest criticisms of the use of rewards to motivate people.

Pryor, K. (1975). *Lads before the wind: Adventures in porpoise training.* New York: Harper & Row. An engaging account of Pryor's experiences in becoming a dolphin trainer.

Pryor, K. (1999). *Don't shoot the dog: The new art of teaching and training* (Rev. ed.). New York: Bantam Books. Pryor's most popular book on the art of shaping behavior as applied to everything from dogs to horses to humans.

Cameron, J., & Pierce, W. D. (2002). *Rewards and intrinsic motivation: Resolving the controversy.* New York: Greenwood Publishing. An ardent defense of the use of rewards to motivate people.

STUDY QUESTIONS

1. State Thorndike's law of effect. What is operant conditioning (as defined by Skinner), and how does this definition differ from Thorndike's law of effect?
2. Explain why operant behaviors are said to be emitted and why they are defined as a "class" of responses.
3. Define the terms *reinforcer* and *punisher.*
4. What is the difference between the terms *reinforcement* and *reinforcer?*
5. What is a discriminative stimulus? Define the three-term contingency and diagram an example.
6. Define positive reinforcement and diagram an example. Define negative reinforcement and diagram an example. (For each example, include the appropriate symbols.)
7. Define positive punishment and diagram an example. Define negative punishment and diagram an example. (For each example, include the appropriate symbols.)
8. What are the similarities and differences between negative reinforcement and positive punishment?
9. How does immediacy affect the strength of a reinforcer? How does this often lead to difficulties for students in their academic studies?
10. Distinguish between primary and secondary reinforcers, and give an example of each.
11. What is a generalized reinforcer? What are two examples of such reinforcers?
12. Define intrinsic and extrinsic reinforcement, and provide an example of each.
13. Under what three conditions does extrinsic reinforcement undermine intrinsic interest? Under what two conditions does extrinsic reinforcement enhance intrinsic interest?
14. Define natural and contrived reinforcers, and provide an example of each.
15. Define shaping. What are two advantages of using a secondary reinforcer, such as a sound, as an aid to shaping?

CONCEPT REVIEW

avoidance behavior. Behavior that occurs before the aversive stimulus is presented and therefore prevents its delivery.

contrived reinforcers. Reinforcers that have been deliberately arranged to modify a behavior; they are not a typical consequence of the behavior in that setting.

discriminative stimulus (S^D). A stimulus in the presence of which responses are reinforced and in the absence of which they are not reinforced.

discriminative stimulus for extinction (S$^\Delta$). A stimulus that signals the absence of reinforcement.

discriminative stimulus for punishment. A stimulus that signals that a response will be punished.

escape behavior. A behavior that results in the termination of an aversive stimulus.

extrinsic reinforcement. The reinforcement provided by a consequence that is external to the behavior, that is, an extrinsic reinforcer.

generalized (or generalized secondary) reinforcer. A type of secondary reinforcer that has been associated with several other reinforcers.

intrinsic reinforcement. Reinforcement provided by the mere act of performing the behavior; the performance of the behavior is inherently reinforcing.

law of effect. As stated by Thorndike, the proposition that behaviors that lead to a satisfying state of affairs are strengthened or "stamped in," while behaviors that lead to an unsatisfying or annoying state of affairs are weakened or "stamped out."

natural reinforcers. Reinforcers that are naturally provided for a certain behavior; that is, they are a typical consequence of the behavior within that setting.

negative punishment. The removal of a stimulus (one that is usually considered pleasant or rewarding) following a response, which then leads to a decrease in the future strength of that response.

negative reinforcement. The removal of a stimulus (one that is usually considered unpleasant or aversive) following a response, which then leads to an increase in the future strength of that response.

operant behavior. A class of emitted responses that result in certain consequences; these consequences, in turn, affect the future probability or strength of those responses.

operant conditioning. A type of learning in which the future probability of a behavior is affected by its consequences.

positive punishment. The presentation of a stimulus (one that is usually considered unpleasant or aversive) following a response, which then leads to a decrease in the future strength of that response.

positive reinforcement. The presentation of a stimulus (one that is usually considered pleasant or rewarding) following a response, which then leads to an increase in the future strength of that response.

primary reinforcer (or unconditioned reinforcer). An event that is innately reinforcing.

punisher. An event that (1) follows a behavior and (2) decreases the future probability of that behavior.

reinforcer. An event that (1) follows a behavior and (2) increases the future probability of that behavior.

secondary reinforcer (or conditioned reinforcer). An event that is reinforcing because it has been associated with some other reinforcer.

shaping. The gradual creation of new operant behavior through reinforcement of successive approximations to that behavior.

three-term contingency. The relationship between a discriminative stimulus, an operant behavior, and a reinforcer or punisher.

CHAPTER TEST

31. Shaping is (A) the reinforcement of a new operant behavior, (B) the gradual reinforcement of a new operant behavior, (C) the reinforcement of
successive approximations to a new operant behavior, (D) the creation of
new operant behavior through successive approximations to reinforcement, (E) none of the preceding. ____

20. A positive reinforcer is a stimulus, (A) the presentation of which
increases the strength of a response, (B) the presentation of which
follows a response and increases the strength of that response, (C) the
presentation of which decreases the strength of a response, (D) the
presentation of which follows a response and decreases the strength of
that response. _____

2. Elicited behaviors are controlled by the events that (precede/
follow) _____ their occurrence, while operant behaviors are controlled by the events that (precede/follow) _____
their occurrence.

14. An easy way to remember the three-term contingency is that you _____
something, _____ something, and _____ something.

25. Behaviors that are performed for their own sake are said to be _____
motivated; behaviors that are performed to achieve some additional
incentive are said to be _____ motivated.

11. Reinforcers and punishers are defined entirely by their _____
on behavior.

8. An event is a punisher if it _____ a behavior and the future
probability of that behavior _____.

23. Money and praise are common examples of _____ reinforcers.

12. If the rat does not press the lever, then it does not receive a shock.
As a result, the rat is more likely not to press the lever. This is an
example of (A) negative reinforcement, (B) negative punishment,
(C) positive reinforcement, (D) positive punishment. _____
(*Think carefully about this.*)

28. At the zoo one day, you notice that a zookeeper is leading a rhinoceros
into a pen by repeatedly whistling at it as the animal moves. It is probably
the case that the whistle has been paired with _____ and is
now functioning as a _____.

1. Compared to most elicited behaviors, operant behaviors seem (more/
less) _____ automatic and reflexive.

15. The three-term contingency can be thought of as an ABC sequence in which A stands for _____, B stands for _____, and C stands for _____.

27. The gradual development of new operant behavior through reinforcement of _____ to that behavior is called _____.

6. Operant responses are sometimes simply called _____.

21. Each time a student studies at home, she is praised by her parents. As a result, she no longer studies at home. This is an example of what type of contingency? _____

17. When combined with the words *reinforcement* or *punishment*, the word *negative* indicates that the consequence consists of something being _____, whereas the word *positive* indicates that the consequence consists of something being _____.

10. The terms *reinforcer* or *punisher* refer to the specific _____ that follows a behavior, whereas the terms *reinforcement* or *punishment* refer to the _____ or_____ whereby the probability of a behavior is altered by its consequences.

24. Harpreet very much enjoys hard work and often volunteers for projects that are quite demanding. According to _____ theory, it is likely the case that, for Harpreet, the act of expending a lot of effort has often been _____.

3. According to Thorndike's _____, behaviors that lead to a _____ state of affairs are strengthened, whereas behaviors that lead to an _____ state of affairs are weakened.

30. A generalized secondary reinforcer is one that has become a reinforcer because it has been associated with (A) a primary reinforcer, (B) a secondary reinforcer, (C) several secondary reinforcers, (D) several primary reinforcers, or (E) several reinforcers (either primary or secondary). _____

19. When Beth tried to pull the tail of her dog, he bared his teeth and growled threateningly. Beth quickly pulled her hand back. The dog growled even more threateningly the next time Beth reached for his tail, and she again pulled her hand away. Eventually Beth gave up, and no longer tries to pull the dog's tail. The dog's behavior of baring his teeth and growling served to (positively/negatively) _____ (punish/reinforce) _____ Beth's behavior of trying to pull his tail. Beth's behavior of pulling her hand away served to _____ the dog's behavior of growling.

32. Achieving a record number of strikeouts in a game would be a(n) (natural/contrived) _____ reinforcer for pitching well; receiving a bonus for throwing that many strikeouts would be a(n) _____ reinforcer.

5. Operant behaviors are usually defined as a _____ of responses, all of which are capable of producing a certain _____.

16. A stimulus that signals that a response will be punished is called a _____ for punishment.

22. Events that are innately reinforcing are called _____ reinforcers; events that become reinforcers through experience are called _____ reinforcers.

9. A reinforcer is usually given the symbol _____, while a punisher is usually given the symbol _____. The operant response is given the symbol _____, while a discriminative stimulus is given the symbol _____.

26. Steven has fond memories of his mother reading fairy tales to him when he was a child, and as a result he now enjoys reading fairy tales as an adult. For Steven, the act of reading fairy tales is functioning as what type of reinforcer? (A) primary, (B) secondary, (C) intrinsic, (D) extrinsic, (E) both (B) and (C). _____

4. Classically conditioned behaviors are said to be _____ by stimuli; operant behaviors are said to be _____ by the organism.

18. Referring to this chapter's opening vignette, among the four types of contingencies described in this chapter, Sally's actions toward Joe probably best illustrate the process of _____. In other words, Joe's abusive behavior will likely (increase/decrease) _____ in the future as a result of Sally's actions.

7. An event is a reinforcer if it _____ a behavior and the future probability of that behavior _____.

29. Major advantages of using the sound of a click for shaping are that the click can be delivered _____ and the animal is unlikely to _____ upon it.

13. A discriminative stimulus is a stimulus that signals that a _____ is available. It is said to "_____" for the behavior.

Visit the book companion Web site at <http://www.academic.cengage.com/psychology/powell> for additional practice questions, answers to the Quick Quizzes, practice review exams, and additional exercises and information.

ANSWERS TO CHAPTER TEST

1. less
2. precede; follow
3. law of effect; satisfying; unsatisfying (or annoying)
4. elicited; emitted
5. class; consequence
6. operants
7. follows; increases
8. follows; decreases
9. S^R; S^P; R; S^D

10. consequence (event); process; procedure
11. effect
12. D (because *"lever press"* → shock" is the effective contingency)
13. reinforcer; set the occasion
14. notice; do; get
15. antecedent; behavior; consequence
16. discriminative stimulus

17. removed (or subtracted); presented (or added)
18. positive reinforcement; increase
19. positively; punish; negatively reinforce
20. B
21. positive punishment
22. primary; secondary (or conditional)
23. generalized (or generalized secondary)
24. learned industriousness; positively reinforced
25. intrinsically; extrinsically
26. E
27. successive (or gradual) approximations; shaping
28. food; secondary reinforcer
29. immediately; satiate
30. E
31. C
32. natural; contrived

Schedules and Theories of Reinforcement

"I don't understand why Alvin is so distant," Mandy commented. "He was great when we first started going out. Now it's like pulling teeth to get him to pay attention to me."

"So why do you put up with it?" her sister asked.

"I guess I'm in love with him. Why else would I be so persistent?"

Schedules of Reinforcement

In this section, we discuss schedules of reinforcement. A *schedule of reinforcement* is the response requirement that must be met to obtain reinforcement. In other words, a schedule indicates what exactly has to be done for the reinforcer to be delivered. For example, does each lever press by the rat result in a food pellet, or are several lever presses required? Did your mom give you a cookie each time you asked for one, or only some of the time? And just how persistent does Mandy have to be before Alvin will pay attention to her? As you will discover in this section, different response requirements can have dramatically different effects on behavior. Many of these effects (known as *schedule effects*) were first observed in experiments with pigeons (Ferster & Skinner, 1957), but they also help to explain some puzzling aspects of human behavior that are often attributed to internal traits or desires.

Continuous Versus Intermittent Schedules

A *continuous reinforcement schedule* is one in which each specified response is reinforced. For example, each time a rat presses the lever, it obtains a food pellet; each time the dog rolls over on command, it gets a treat; and each time Karen turns the ignition in her car, the motor starts. Continuous reinforcement (abbreviated CRF) is very useful when a behavior is first being shaped or strengthened. For example, when using a shaping procedure to train a rat to press a lever, reinforcement should be delivered for each approximation to the target behavior. Similarly, if we wish to encourage a child to always brush her teeth before bed, we would do well to initially praise her each time she does so.

An *intermittent (or partial) reinforcement schedule* is one in which only some responses are reinforced. For example, perhaps only some of the rat's lever presses result in a food pellet, and perhaps only occasionally did your mother give you a cookie when you asked for one. Intermittent reinforcement obviously characterizes much of everyday life. Not all concerts we attend are enjoyable, not every person we invite out on a date accepts, and not every date that we go out on leads to an enjoyable evening. And although we might initially praise a child each time she properly completes her homework, we might soon praise her only occasionally in the belief that such behavior should persist in the absence of praise.

There are four basic (or simple) types of intermittent schedules: fixed ratio, variable ratio, fixed interval, and variable interval. We will describe each one along with the characteristic response pattern produced by each. Note that this characteristic response pattern is the stable pattern that emerges once the organism has had considerable exposure to the schedule. Such stable patterns are known as *steady-state behaviors*, in contrast to the more variable patterns of behavior that are evident when an organism is first exposed to a schedule.

1. A s_____ of reinforcement is the r_____ requirement that must be met to obtain reinforcement.

2. On a c_____ reinforcement schedule (abbreviated _____), each response is reinforced, whereas on an i_____ reinforcement schedule, only some responses are reinforced. The latter is also called a p_____ reinforcement schedule.

3. Each time you flick the light switch, the light comes on. The behavior of flicking the light switch is on a(n) _____ schedule of reinforcement.

4. When the weather is very cold, you are sometimes unable to start your car. The behavior of starting your car in very cold weather is on a(n) _____ schedule of reinforcement.

5. S_____ e_____ are the different effects on behavior produced by different response requirements. These are the stable patterns of behavior that emerge once the organism has had sufficient exposure to the schedule. Such stable patterns are known as st_____-st_____ behaviors.

Four Basic Intermittent Schedules

Fixed Ratio Schedules   On a *fixed ratio (FR) schedule,* reinforcement is contingent upon a fixed, predictable number of responses. For example, on a fixed ratio 5 schedule (abbreviated FR 5), a rat has to press the lever 5 times to obtain a food pellet. On an FR 50 schedule, it has to press the lever 50 times to obtain a food pellet. Similarly, earning a dollar for every 10 carburetors assembled on an assembly line is an example of an FR 10 schedule, while earning a dollar for each carburetor assembled is an example of an FR 1 schedule. Note that an FR 1 schedule is the same as a CRF (continuous reinforcement) schedule in which each response is reinforced (thus, such a schedule can be correctly labeled as either an FR 1 or a CRF).

FR schedules generally produce a high rate of response along with a short pause following the attainment of each reinforcer (see Figure 7.1). This short pause is known as a *postreinforcement pause.* For example, a rat on an FR 25 schedule will rapidly emit 25 lever presses, munch down the food pellet it receives, and then snoop around the chamber for a few seconds before rapidly emitting another 25 lever presses. In other words, it will take a short break following each reinforcer, just as you might take a short break after reading each chapter in a textbook or completing a particular assignment. Note, too, that each pause is followed by a quick return

FIGURE 7.1 Response patterns for FR, variable ratio (VR), fixed interval (FI), and variable interval (VI) schedules. This figure shows the characteristic pattern of responding on the four basic schedules. Notice the high response rate on the fixed and variable ratio schedules, moderate response rate on the variable interval schedule, and scalloped response pattern on the fixed interval schedule. Also, both the fixed ratio and fixed interval schedules are accompanied by postreinforcement pauses. (*Source:* Modified from Nairne, 2000.)

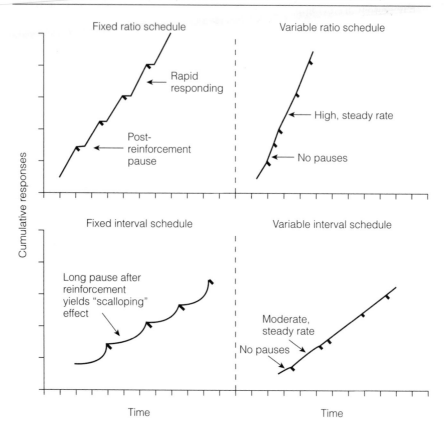

to a high rate of response. Thus, the typical FR pattern is described as a "break-and-run" pattern—a short break followed by a steady run of responses.

Similarly, students sometimes find that when they finally sit down to start work on the next chapter or assignment, they quickly become involved in it. Perhaps this is why just starting a task is often the most important step in overcoming procrastination; once you start, the work often flows naturally. For this reason, it is sometimes helpful to use certain tricks to get started, such as beginning with a short, easy task before progressing to a more difficult task. Alternatively, you might promise yourself that you will work for only 5 or 10 minutes and then quit for the evening if you really do not feel like carrying on. What often happens is that once the promised time period has passed, it is actually quite easy to carry on.

In general, higher ratio requirements produce longer postreinforcement pauses. This means that you will probably take a longer break after completing a long assignment than after completing a short one. Similarly, a rat will show longer pauses on an FR 100 schedule than on an FR 30 schedule. With very low ratios, such as FR 1 (CRF) or FR 2, there may be little or no pausing other than the time it takes for the rat to munch down the food pellet. In such cases, the next reinforcer is so close—only a few lever presses away—that the rat is tempted to immediately go back to work. (If only the reinforcers for studying were so immediate!)

Schedules in which the reinforcer is easily obtained are said to be very *dense* or *rich*, while schedules in which the reinforcer is difficult to obtain are said to be very *lean*. Thus, an FR 5 schedule is considered a very dense schedule of reinforcement compared to an FR 100. During a 1-hour session, a rat can earn many more food pellets on an FR 5 schedule than it can on an FR 100. Similarly, an assembly line worker who earns a dollar for each carburetor assembled (a CRF schedule) can earn considerably more during an 8-hour shift than can a worker who earns a dollar for every 10 carburetors assembled (an FR 10 schedule).

In general, "stretching the ratio"—moving from a low ratio requirement (a dense schedule) to a high ratio requirement (a lean schedule)—should be done gradually. For example, once lever pressing is well established on a CRF schedule, the requirement can be gradually increased to FR 2, FR 5, FR 10, and so on. If the requirement is increased too quickly—for example, CRF to FR 2 and then a sudden jump to FR 20—the rat's behavior may become erratic and even die out altogether. Likewise, if you try to raise the requirement too high—say, to FR 2000—there may be a similar breakdown in the rat's behavior. Such breakdowns in behavior are technically known as **ratio strain,** a disruption in responding due to an overly demanding response requirement.

Ratio strain is what most people would refer to as burnout, and it can be a big problem for students faced with a heavy workload. Some students, especially those who have a history of getting by with minimal work, may find it increasingly difficult to study under such circumstances and may even choose to drop out of college. If they had instead experienced a gradual increase in workload over a period of several months or years, they might have been able to put forth the needed effort to succeed.

1. On a(n) _____ _____ schedule, reinforcement is contingent upon a fixed number of responses.

2. A schedule in which 15 responses are required for each reinforcer is abbreviated _____.

3. A mother finds that she always has to make the same request three times before her child complies. The mother's behavior of making requests is on an _____ schedule of reinforcement.

4. An FR 1 schedule of reinforcement can also be called a _____ schedule.

5. A fixed ratio schedule tends to produce a (high/low) _____ rate of response, along with a p_____ p_____.

6. An FR 200 schedule of reinforcement will result in a (longer/shorter) _____ pause than an FR 50 schedule.

7. The typical FR pattern is sometimes called a b_____-and-r_____ pattern, with a _____ pause that is followed immediately by a (high/low) _____ rate of response.

8. An FR 12 schedule of reinforcement is (denser/leaner) _____ than an FR 100 schedule.

9. A very dense schedule of reinforcement can also be referred to as a very r_____ schedule.

10. Over a period of a few months, Aaron changed from complying with each of his mother's requests to complying with every other request, then with every third request, and so on. The mother's behavior of making requests has been subjected to a procedure known as "s_____ the r_____."

11. Graduate students often have to complete an enormous amount of work in the initial year of their program. For some students, the workload involved is far beyond anything they have previously encountered. As a result, their study behavior may become increasingly (erratic/stereotyped) _____ throughout the year, a process known as r_____ s_____.

Variable Ratio Schedules On a *variable ratio (VR) schedule,* reinforcement is contingent upon a varying, unpredictable number of responses. For example, on a variable ratio 5 (VR 5) schedule, a rat has to emit an *average* of 5 lever presses for each food pellet, with the number of lever responses on any particular trial varying between, say, 1 and 10. Thus, the number of required lever presses might be 3 for the first pellet, 6 for the second pellet, 1 for the third pellet, 7 for the fourth pellet, and so on, with the overall average being 5 lever presses for each reinforcer. Similarly, on a VR 50 schedule, the number of required lever presses may vary between 1 and 100, with the average being 50.

VR schedules generally produce a high and steady rate of response with little or no postreinforcement pause (see Figure 7.1). The lack of a postreinforcement pause is understandable if you consider that each response on a VR schedule has the potential of resulting in a reinforcer. For example, on a VR 50 schedule in which the response requirement for each reinforcer varies between 1 and 100, it is possible that the very next lever press will produce another food pellet, even if the rat has just obtained a food pellet.

The real world is filled with examples of VR schedules. Some predatory behaviors, such as that shown by cheetahs, are on VR schedules in that only some attempts at chasing down prey are successful. In humans, only some acts of politeness receive an acknowledgment, only some residents who are called upon by canvassers will make a contribution, and only some CDs that we buy are enjoyable. Many sports activities, such as shooting baskets in basketball and shots on goal in hockey, are also reinforced largely on a VR schedule. A colleague just stopped by and joked that his golf drive is probably on a VR 200 schedule. In other words, he figures that an average of about one in every 200 drives is a good one. I (Russ Powell) replied that my own drives are probably on a much leaner schedule with the result that ratio strain has set in, which is fancy behaviorist talk for "I so rarely hit the ball straight that I have just about given up playing."

Variable ratio schedules help to account for the persistence with which some people display certain maladaptive behaviors. Gambling is a prime example in this regard: The unpredictable nature of these activities results in a very high rate of behavior. In fact, the behavior of a gambler playing a slot machine is the classic example of human behavior controlled by a VR schedule. Certain forms of aberrant social behavior may also be accounted for by VR schedules. For example, why do some men persist in using cute, flippant remarks to introduce themselves to women when the vast majority of women view such remarks negatively? One reason is that a small minority of women actually respond favorably, thereby intermittently reinforcing the use of such remarks. For example, Kleinke, Meeker, and Staneske (1986) found that although 84% of women surveyed rated the opening line "I'm easy. Are you?" as poor to terrible, 14% rated it as either very good or excellent!

Variable ratio schedules of reinforcement may also facilitate the development of an abusive relationship. At the start of a relationship, the individuals involved typically provide each other with an enormous amount of positive reinforcement (a very dense schedule). This strengthens the relationship and increases each partner's attraction to the other. As the relationship progresses, such reinforcement naturally becomes somewhat more intermittent. In some situations, however, this process becomes malignant, with one person (let us call this person the victimizer) providing reinforcement on an extremely intermittent basis, and the other person (the victim) working incredibly hard to obtain that reinforcement. Because the process evolves gradually (a process of slowly "stretching the ratio"), the victim may have little awareness of what is happening until the abusive pattern is well established. What would motivate such an unbalanced process? One source of motivation is that the less often the victimizer reinforces the victim, the more attention (reinforcement) he or she receives from the victim. In other words, the victim works so hard to get the partner's attention that he or she actually reinforces the very process of being largely ignored by that partner. Of course, it does not necessarily have to be a one-way process, and there may be relationships in which the partners alternate the role of victim and victimizer. The result may be a volatile relationship that both partners find exciting but that is constantly on the verge of collapse due to frequent periods in which each partner experiences "ratio strain."

1. On a variable ratio schedule, reinforcement is contingent upon a _____ un_____ _____ of responses.

2. A variable ratio schedule typically produces a (high/low) _____ rate of behavior (with/without) _____ a postreinforcement pause.

3. An average of 1 in 10 people approached by a panhandler actually gives him money. His behavior of panhandling is on a _____ schedule of reinforcement.

4. As with an FR schedule, an extremely lean VR schedule can result in r_____ s_____.

Fixed Interval Schedules On a *fixed interval (FI) schedule,* reinforcement is contingent upon the first response after a fixed, predictable period of time. For a rat on a fixed interval 30-second (FI 30-sec) schedule, the first lever press *after* a 30-second interval has elapsed results in a food pellet. Following that, another 30 seconds must elapse before a lever press will again produce a food pellet. Any lever pressing that occurs during the interval, before the 30-second period has elapsed, is ineffective. Similarly, trying to phone a friend who is due to arrive home in exactly 30 minutes will be effective only after the 30 minutes have elapsed, with any phone calls before that being ineffective.

FI schedules often produce a "scalloped" (upwardly curved) pattern of responding, consisting of a postreinforcement pause followed by a gradually increasing rate of response as the interval draws to a close (see Figure 7.1). For example, a rat on an FI 30-sec schedule will likely emit no lever presses at the start of the 30-second interval. This will be followed by a few tentative lever presses perhaps midway through the interval, with a gradually increasing rate of response thereafter. By the time the interval draws to a close and the reinforcer is imminent, the rat will be emitting a high rate of response, with the result that the reinforcer will be attained as soon as it becomes available.

Would the behavior of trying to phone someone who is due to arrive home in 30 minutes also follow a scalloped pattern (assuming they do not have a cell phone)? If we have a watch available, it probably would not. We would simply look at our watch to determine when the 30 minutes have elapsed and then make our phone call. The indicated time would be a discriminative stimulus (S^D) for when the reinforcer is available (i.e., the person is home), and we would wait until the appropriate time before phoning. But what about the behavior of looking at your watch during the 30 minutes (the reinforcer for which would be noticing that the interval has elapsed)? You are unlikely to spend much time looking at your watch at the start of the interval. As time progresses, however, you will begin looking at it more and more frequently. In other words, your behavior will follow the typical scalloped pattern of responding.

The distribution of study sessions throughout the term can also show characteristics of an FI scallop. At the start of a course, many students engage in little or no studying. This is followed by a gradual increase in studying as the first exam approaches. The completion of the exam is again followed by little or no studying until the next exam approaches. Unfortunately, these postreinforcement pauses are often too long, with the result that many students obtain much poorer marks than they would have if they had studied at a steadier pace throughout. (Note, however, that studying for exams is not a pure example of an FI schedule because a certain amount of work must be accomplished during the interval to obtain the reinforcer of a good mark. On a pure FI schedule, any responding that happens during the interval is essentially irrelevant.)

1. On a fixed interval schedule, reinforcement is contingent upon the _____ response following a _____, pr_____ period of _____.

2. If I have just missed the bus when I get to the bus stop, I know that I have to wait 15 minutes for the next one to come along. Given that it is absolutely freezing out, I snuggle into my parka as best I can and grimly wait out the interval. Every once in a while, though, I emerge from my cocoon to take a quick glance down the street to see if the bus is coming. My behavior of looking for the bus is on a(n) _____ (use the abbreviation) schedule of reinforcement.

3. In the example in question 2, I will probably engage in (few/frequent) _____ glances at the start of the interval, followed by a gradually (increasing/decreasing) _____ rate of glancing as time passes.

4. Responding on an FI schedule is often characterized by a sc_____ pattern of responding consisting of a p_____ p_____ followed by a gradually (increasing/decreasing) _____ rate of behavior as the interval draws to a close.

5. On a pure FI schedule, any response that occurs (during/following) _____ the interval is irrelevant.

Variable Interval Schedules   On a *variable interval (VI) schedule,* reinforcement is contingent upon the first response after a varying, unpredictable period of time. For a rat on a variable interval 30-second (VI 30-sec) schedule, the first lever press after an *average* interval of 30 seconds will result in a food pellet, with the actual interval on any particular trial varying between, say, 1 and 60 seconds. Thus, the number of seconds that must pass before a lever press will produce a food pellet could be 8 seconds for the first food pellet, 55 seconds for the second pellet, 24 seconds for the third, and so on, the average of which is 30 seconds. Similarly, if each day you are waiting for a bus and have no idea when it will arrive, then looking down the street for the bus will be reinforced after a varying, unpredictable period of time—for example, 2 minutes the first day, 12 minutes the next day, 9 minutes the third day, and so on, with an average interval of, say, 10 minutes (VI 10-min).

VI schedules usually produce a moderate, steady rate of response with little or no postreinforcement pause (see Figure 7.1). By responding at a relatively steady rate throughout the interval, the rat on a VI 30-sec schedule will attain the reinforcer almost as soon as it becomes available. Similarly, if you need to contact a friend about some emergency and know that she always arrives home sometime between 6:00 P.M. and 6:30 P.M., a good strategy would be to phone every few minutes throughout that time period. By doing so, you will almost certainly contact her within a few minutes of her arrival.

Because VI schedules produce predictable response rates, as well as predictable rates of reinforcement, they are often used to investigate other aspects of operant conditioning, such as those involving matters of choice between alternative sources of reinforcement. You will encounter examples of this when we discuss choice behavior in Chapter 10.

1. On a variable interval schedule, reinforcement is contingent upon the _____ response following a _____, un_____ period of _____.

2. You find that by frequently switching stations on your radio, you are able to hear your favorite song an average of once every 20 minutes. Your behavior of switching stations is thus being reinforced on a _____ schedule.

3. In general, variable interval schedules produce a (low/moderate/high) _____, (steady/fluctuating) _____ rate of response with little or no _____.

Comparing the Four Basic Schedules   The four basic schedules produce quite different patterns of behavior, which vary in both the rate of response and in the presence or absence of a postreinforcement pause. These characteristics are summarized in Table 7.1.

As can be seen, ratio schedules (FR and VR) produce higher rates of response than do interval schedules (FI and VI). This makes sense because the reinforcer in such schedules is entirely "response contingent"; that is, it depends entirely on the number of responses emitted. For this reason, a rat on a VR 100 schedule can double the number of food pellets earned in a 1-hour session by doubling its rate of lever pressing. Similarly, a door-to-door salesman can double the number of sales he makes during a day by doubling the number of customers he calls on (assuming that he continues to give an adequate sales pitch to each customer). Compare this to an interval schedule

TABLE 7.1   Characteristic response rates and postreinforcement pauses for each of the four basic intermittent schedules. These are only general characteristics; they are not found under all circumstances. For example, an FR schedule with a very low response requirement, such as FR 2, is unlikely to produce a postreinforcement pause. By contrast, an FR schedule with a very high response requirement, such as FR 2000, may result in a ratio strain and a complete cessation of responding.

	FR	VR	FI	VI
Response rate	High	High	Increasing	Moderate
Postreinforcement pause	Yes	No	Yes	No

in which reinforcement is mostly time contingent. For example, on an FI 1-minute schedule, no more than 50 reinforcers can be earned in a 50-minute session. Under such circumstances, responding at a high rate throughout each interval does not pay off and is essentially a waste of energy. Instead, it makes more sense to respond in a way that will maximize the possibility of attaining the reinforcer soon after it becomes available. On an FI schedule, this means responding at a gradually increasing rate as the interval draws to a close; on a VI schedule, this means responding at a moderate, steady pace throughout the interval.

It can also be seen that fixed schedules (FR and FI) tend to produce postreinforcement pauses, whereas variable schedules (VR and VI) do not. On a variable schedule, there is always the possibility of a relatively immediate reinforcer, even if one has just attained a reinforcer, which tempts one to immediately resume responding. By comparison, on a fixed schedule, attaining one reinforcer means that the next reinforcer is necessarily some distance away. On an FR schedule, this results in a short postreinforcement pause before grinding out another set of responses; on an FI schedule, the postreinforcement pause is followed by a gradually increasing rate of response as the interval draws to a close and the reinforcer becomes imminent.

1. In general, (ratio/interval) _____ schedules tend to produce a high rate of response. This is because the reinforcer in such schedules is entirely r_____ contingent, meaning that the rapidity with which responses are emitted (does/does not) _____ greatly affect how soon the reinforcer is obtained.

2. On _____ schedules, the reinforcer is largely time contingent, meaning that the rapidity with which responses are emitted has (little/considerable) _____ effect on how quickly the reinforcer is obtained.

3. In general, (variable/fixed) _____ schedules produce little or no postreinforcement pausing because such schedules provide the possibility of relatively i_____ reinforcement, even if one has just obtained a reinforcer.

4. In general, _____ schedules produce postreinforcement pauses because obtaining one reinforcer means that the next reinforcer is necessarily quite (distant/close) _____.

QUICK QUIZ F

Other Simple Schedules of Reinforcement

Duration Schedules   On a duration schedule, reinforcement is contingent on performing a behavior continuously throughout a period of time. On a *fixed duration (FD) schedule,* the behavior must be performed continuously for a fixed, predictable period of time. For example, the rat must run in the wheel for 60 seconds to earn one pellet of food (an FD 60-sec schedule). Likewise, Julie may decide that her son can watch television each evening only after he completes 2 hours of studying (an FD 2-hr schedule).

On a ***variable duration (VD) schedule,*** the behavior must be performed continuously for a varying, unpredictable period of time. For example, the rat must run in the wheel for an average of 60 seconds to earn one pellet of food, with the required time varying between 1 second and 120 seconds on any particular trial (a VD 60-sec schedule). And Julie may decide to reinforce her son's studying with cookies and other treats at varying points in time that happen to average out to about one treat every 30 minutes (a VD 30-min schedule). (*Question: How do FD and VD schedules differ from FI and VI schedules?*)

Although duration schedules are sometimes useful in modifying certain human behaviors, such as studying, they are in some ways rather imprecise compared to the four basic schedules discussed earlier. With FR schedules, for example, one knows precisely what was done to achieve the reinforcer, namely, a certain number of responses. On an FD schedule, however, what constitutes "continuous performance of behavior" during the interval could vary widely. With respect to wheel running, for example, a "lazy" rat could dawdle along at barely a walk, while an "energetic" rat might rotate the wheel at a tremendous pace. Both would receive the reinforcer. Similarly, Julie's son might read only a few pages during his 2-hour study session or charge through several chapters; in either case, he would receive the reinforcer of being allowed to watch television. Remember too, from Chapter 6, how reinforcing the mere performance of an activity with no regard to level of performance can undermine a person's intrinsic interest in that activity. This danger obviously applies to duration schedules. One therefore needs to be cautious in their use.

Response-Rate Schedules   As we have seen, different types of intermittent schedules produce different rates of response (i.e., they have different *schedule effects*). These different rates are essentially by-products of the schedule. However, in a ***response-rate schedule,*** reinforcement is directly contingent upon the organism's rate of response. Let's examine three types of response-rate schedules.

Which of these workers is on a ratio schedule of reinforcement?

In ***differential reinforcement of high rates (DRH),*** reinforcement is contingent upon emitting *at least* a certain number of responses in a certain period of time—or, more generally, reinforcement is provided for responding at a fast rate. The term *differential reinforcement* means simply that one type of response is reinforced while another is not. In a DRH schedule, reinforcement is provided for a high rate of response and not for a low rate. For example, a rat might receive a food pellet only if it emits at least 30 lever presses within a period of a minute. Similarly, a worker on an assembly line may be told that she can keep her job only if she assembles a minimum of 20 carburetors per hour. By requiring so many responses in a short period of time, DRH schedules ensure a high rate of responding. Athletic events such as running and swimming are prime examples of DRH schedules in that winning is directly contingent on a rapid series of responses.

In ***differential reinforcement of low rates (DRL),*** a minimum amount of time must pass between each response before the reinforcer will be delivered— or, more generally, reinforcement is provided for responding at a slow rate. For example, a rat might receive a food pellet only if it waits at least 10 seconds between lever presses. So how is this different from an FI 10-sec schedule? Remember that on an FI schedule, responses that occur during the interval have no effect; on a DRL schedule, however, responses that occur during the interval do have an effect—an adverse effect in that they *prevent* reinforcement from occurring. In other words, responding during the interval must *not* occur in order for a response following the interval to produce a reinforcer.

Human examples of DRL schedules consist of situations in which a person is required to perform some action slowly. For example, a parent might praise a child for brushing her teeth slowly or completing her homework slowly, given that going too fast generally results in sloppy performance. Once the quality of performance improves, reinforcement can then be made contingent on responding at a normal speed.

In ***differential reinforcement of paced responding (DRP),*** reinforcement is contingent upon emitting a series of responses at a set rate—or, more generally, reinforcement is provided for responding neither too fast nor too slow. For example, a rat might receive a food pellet if it emits 10 consecutive responses, with each response separated by an interval of no less than 1.5 and no more than 2.5 seconds. Similarly, musical activities, such as playing in a band or dancing to music, require that the relevant actions be performed at a specific pace. People who are very good at this are said to have a good sense of timing or rhythm. Further examples of DRP schedules can be found in noncompetitive swimming or running. People often perform these activities at a pace that is fast enough to ensure benefits to health and a feeling of well-being, yet not so fast as to result in exhaustion and possible injury. In fact, even competitive swimmers and runners, especially those who compete over long distances, will often set a specific pace throughout much of the race. Doing so ensures that they have sufficient energy at the end for a last-minute sprint (DRH) to the finish line, thereby maximizing their chances of clocking a good time.

1. On a (VD/VI) _____ schedule, reinforcement is contingent upon responding continuously for a varying period of time; on an (FI/FD) _____ schedule, reinforcement is contingent upon the first response after a fixed period of time.

2. As Tessa sits quietly, her mother occasionally gives her a hug as a reward. This is an example of a _____ _____ schedule.

3. In practicing the slow-motion form of exercise known as tai chi, Yang noticed that the more slowly he moved, the more thoroughly his muscles relaxed. This is an example of d_____ reinforcement of _____ _____ behavior (abbreviated _____).

4. On a video game, the faster you destroy all the targets, the more bonus points you obtain. This is an example of _____ reinforcement of _____ _____ behavior (abbreviated _____).

5. Frank discovers that his golf shots are much more accurate when he swings the club with a nice, even rhythm that is neither too fast nor too slow. This is an example of _____ reinforcement of_____ behavior (abbreviated _____).

Noncontingent Schedules   On a *noncontingent schedule of reinforcement,* the reinforcer is delivered *independently* of any response. In other words, a response is not required for the reinforcer to be obtained. Such schedules are also called *response-independent schedules.* There are two types of noncontingent schedules: fixed time and variable time.

On a *fixed time (FT) schedule,* the reinforcer is delivered following a fixed, predictable period of time, regardless of the organism's behavior. For example, on a fixed time 30-second (FT 30-sec) schedule, a pigeon receives access to food every 30 seconds regardless of its behavior. Likewise, many people receive Christmas gifts each year, independently of whether they have been naughty or nice—an FT 1-year schedule. FT schedules therefore involve the delivery of a "free" reinforcer following a predictable period of time.

On a *variable time (VT) schedule,* the reinforcer is delivered following a varying, unpredictable period of time, regardless of the organism's behavior. For example, on a variable time 30-second (VT 30-sec) schedule, a pigeon receives access to food after an average interval of 30 seconds, with the actual interval on any particular trial ranging from, say, 1 second to 60 seconds. Similarly, you may coincidentally run into an old high school chum about every 3 months on average (a VT 3-month schedule). VT schedules therefore involve the delivery of a free reinforcer following an unpredictable period of time. (*Question: How do FT and VT schedules differ from FI and VI schedules?*)

1. On a non_____ schedule of reinforcement, a response is not required to obtain a reinforcer. Such a schedule is also called a response i_____ schedule of reinforcement.

2. Every morning at 7:00 A.M. a robin perches outside Marilyn's bedroom window and begins singing. Given that Marilyn very much enjoys the robin's song, this is an example of a _____ _____ 24-hour schedule of reinforcement (abbreviated _____).

3. For farmers, rainfall is an example of a noncontingent reinforcer that is typically delivered on a _____ _____ schedule (abbreviated _____).

Noncontingent reinforcement may account for some forms of superstitious behavior. In the first investigation of this possibility, Skinner (1948b) presented pigeons with food every 15 seconds (FT 15-sec) regardless of their behavior. Although you might think that such free reinforcers would have little effect on the pigeons' behavior (other than encouraging them to stay close to the feeder), quite the opposite occurred. Six of the eight pigeons began to display ritualistic patterns of behavior. For example, one bird began turning counterclockwise circles, while another repeatedly thrust its head into an upper corner of the chamber. Two other pigeons displayed a swaying pendulum motion of the head and body. Skinner believed these behaviors evolved because they had been accidentally reinforced by the coincidental presentation of food. For example, if a pigeon just happened to turn a counterclockwise circle before food delivery, that behavior would be accidentally reinforced and increase in frequency. This would increase the likelihood of the same behavior occurring the next time food was delivered, which would further strengthen it. The eventual result would be a well-established pattern of turning circles, as though turning circles somehow caused the food to appear.

Some researchers have argued that Skinner's evidence for superstitious behavior in the pigeon may not be as clear-cut as he believed. They claim that at least some of the ritualistic behaviors he observed may have consisted of innate tendencies, almost like fidgeting behaviors, that are often elicited during a period of waiting (Staddon & Simmelhag, 1971). These tendencies, which are discussed in Chapter 11, are known as *adjunctive behaviors.* Nevertheless, other experiments have replicated the effect of noncontingent reinforcement on the development of superstitious behavior. Ono (1987), for example, placed students in a booth that contained three levers and a counter. The students were told that "if you do something, you may get points on the counter" (p. 263). They were also told to get as many points as possible. In reality, the points were delivered on either an FT or VT schedule, so the students' behavior actually had no effect on point delivery. Nevertheless, most students developed at least temporary patterns of superstitious lever pulling; that is, they pulled the lever as though it were effective in producing points. Interestingly, one student started with lever pulling but then coincidentally received a point after simply touching the counter. This led to a superstitious pattern of climbing on the counter and touching different parts of the apparatus, apparently in the belief that this action produced the points. She then jumped off the apparatus at just the time that she received another point, which led to a superstitious pattern of repeatedly jumping in the air and touching the ceiling! After several minutes of this, she finally quit, apparently as a result of fatigue.

Professional athletes and gamblers are particularly prone to the development of superstitions, some of which may evolve in the manner that Skinner suggests. Under constant threat of losing their position to an eager newcomer, professional athletes are constantly on the lookout for anything that might enhance their performance. As a result, unusual events that precede a fine performance, such as humming a certain tune or wearing an unusual article of clothing, may be quickly identified and then deliberately reproduced in the hopes of reproducing that performance. Gamblers display even stronger tendencies toward the development of superstitions, probably because the activity in which they are engaged is even more uncertain in its outcome. Bingo players, for example, commonly carry lucky pendants, stuffed animals, or pieces of jewelry to each game, and they are often adamant (almost pathologically so) about obtaining cards that contain certain patterns or are drawn from the top or bottom of the stack. Many of these rituals probably evolved because they were at one time associated with a big win.

Herrnstein (1966) noted that superstitious behaviors can sometimes develop as by-products of contingent reinforcement for some other behavior. For example, a businessman might believe it is important to impress customers with a firm handshake—when in fact it is merely the handshake, and not the firmness of the handshake, that is the critical factor. (Unfortunately, such a superstition could have serious consequences if the businessman then attempts to branch out into the Asian market, where a firm handshake is often regarded as a sign of disrespect.) Similarly, some managers might come to believe that "pushing the panic button" is an effective way to deal with crises, simply because it is usually followed by a successful outcome. What they fail to realize is that a low-key approach might have been equally if not more effective—and certainly a lot less stressful.

Question: Although Skinner's (1948b) original demonstration of superstitious behavior involved the use of a fixed time schedule, you might wish to consider whether superstitious behavior in humans is more likely to develop under a fixed or variable time schedule. To answer this, think about the types of situations in which you are particularly likely to find superstitious behavior in humans. Is it in situations that involve predictable events or unpredictable events? Obviously, it is unpredictable events, such as games of chance, performance in sports, fishing ("Jana's lucky lure"), and so forth. In this sense, at least from a human perspective, superstitious behavior can be seen as an attempt to make an unpredictable situation more predictable.

1. When noncontingent reinforcement happens to follow a particular behavior, that behavior may (increase/decrease) _____ in strength. Such behavior is referred to as s_____ behavior.

2. Herrnstein (1966) noted that superstitious behaviors can sometimes develop as a by-product of c_____ reinforcement for some other behavior.

3. As shown by the kinds of situations in which superstitious behaviors develop in humans, such behaviors seem most likely to develop on a(n) (VT/FT) _____ schedule of reinforcement.

What happens if a noncontingent schedule of reinforcement is superimposed on a regular, contingent schedule of reinforcement? What if, for example, a pigeon responding on a VI schedule of food reinforcement also receives extra reinforcers for free? Will the pigeon's rate of response on the VI schedule increase or decrease? In fact, the pigeon's rate of response on the response-dependent schedule will decrease (Rachlin & Baum, 1972). Just as people on welfare sometimes become less inclined to look for work, the pigeon that receives free reinforcers will work less vigorously for the contingent reinforcers. Suggestive evidence of this effect can also be found among professional athletes. One study, conducted several years ago, found that major league pitchers who had signed long-term contracts showed a significant decline in number of innings pitched relative to pitchers who only signed a 1-year contract (O'Brien, Figlerski, Howard, & Caggiano, 1981) (see Figure 7.2). Insofar as a long-term contract virtually guarantees a hefty salary regardless of performance, these results suggest that athletic performance may suffer when the money earned is no longer contingent on performance. (*Question: Can you think of alternative explanations for this finding?*)

At this point, you might be thinking that noncontingent reinforcement is all bad, given that it leads to superstitious behavior in some situations and to poor performance in others. In fact, noncontingent reinforcement is sometimes quite beneficial. More specifically, it can be an effective means of reducing the frequency of maladaptive behaviors. For example, children who act out often do so to obtain attention. If, however, they are given a sufficient amount of attention on a noncontingent basis, they will no longer have to act out to obtain it. Noncontingent reinforcement has even been shown to reduce the frequency of self-injurious behavior. Such behavior, which can consist of head-banging or biting chunks of flesh out of one's arm, is sometimes displayed by people who suffer from retardation or autism; it can be notoriously difficult to treat. In many cases, the behavior appears to be maintained by the attention it elicits from caretakers. Research has shown, however, that if the caretakers provide the individual with plenty of attention on a noncontingent basis, then the frequency of their self-injurious behavior may be greatly reduced (e.g., Hagopian, Fisher, & Legacy, 1994). In a sense, such individuals no longer have to injure themselves to receive attention because they are now receiving lots of attention for free.

FIGURE 7.2 Average number of innings pitched by major league pitchers in the years before and after signing long-term contracts. (*Source:* Coon, 1998. Data from O'Brien et al., 1981.)

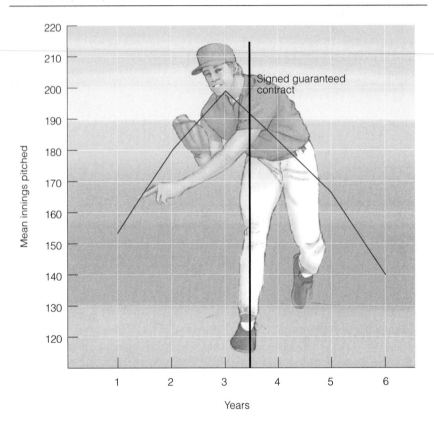

Interestingly, the beneficial effects of noncontingent reinforcement can be seen as providing empirical support for the value of what Carl Rogers (1959), the famous humanistic psychologist, called "unconditional positive regard." Unconditional positive regard refers to the love, respect, and acceptance that one receives from significant others, regardless of one's behavior. Rogers assumed that such regard is a necessary precondition for the development of a healthy personality. From a behavioral perspective, unconditional positive regard can be viewed as a form of noncontingent social reinforcement, which can indeed have beneficial effects. In fact, it seems likely that proper child rearing requires healthy doses of both noncontingent reinforcement, which gives the child a secure base from which to explore the world and take risks, and contingent reinforcement, which helps to shape the child's behavior in appropriate ways, maximize skill development, and prevent the development of passivity. Thus, Abraham Maslow (1971), another famous humanistic psychologist, argued that child rearing should be neither too restrictive nor too lenient, which in behavioral terms can be taken to imply that the social reinforcement children receive should be neither excessively contingent nor excessively noncontingent.

1. During the time that a rat is responding for food on a VR 100 schedule, we begin delivering additional food on a VT 60-second schedule. As a result, the rate of response on the VR schedule is likely to (increase/decrease/remain unchanged) _____.

2. In many mixed martial arts matches, each fighter typically receives a guaranteed purse, regardless of the outcome. In the Ultimate Fighter series, the winner of the final match is awarded a major contract in the UFC while the loser receives nothing. As a result, Karo is not surprised when he notices fighters in the latter event (more/less) _____ often fighting to the point of complete exhaustion, since the monetary reinforcer tied to the match is (contingent/not contingent) _____ upon winning the match.

3. A child who is often hugged during the course of the day, regardless of what he is doing, is in humanistic terms receiving unconditional positive regard. In behavioral terms, he is receiving a form of non_____ social reinforcement. As a result, this child may be (more/less) _____ likely to act out in order to receive attention.

Complex Schedules of Reinforcement

All of the schedules previously described are relatively simple in that there is only one basic requirement. On the other hand, a **complex schedule** consists of a combination of two or more simple schedules. There are a wide variety of such schedules, three of which are described here. Two other types of complex schedules—multiple schedules and concurrent schedules—are discussed in later chapters.

Conjunctive Schedules A *conjunctive schedule* is a type of complex schedule in which the requirements of two or more simple schedules must be met before a reinforcer is delivered. For example, on a conjunctive FI 2-minute FR 100 schedule, reinforcement is contingent upon completing 100 lever presses *and* completing at least one lever press following a 2-minute interval.

Many of the contingencies that we encounter in everyday life are examples of conjunctive schedules. The wages you earn on a job are contingent upon working a certain number of hours each week *and* doing a sufficient amount of work so that you will not be fired. Likewise, Jon's fiancée might have chosen to marry him because he is kind *and* humorous *and* interesting *and* drives a Porsche. With any one of these components missing, he would not have received the reinforcer of being engaged to her.

Adjusting Schedules In an *adjusting schedule,* the response requirement changes as a function of the organism's performance while responding for the previous reinforcer. For example, on an FR 100 schedule, if the rat completes all 100 responses within a 5-minute interval, we may then increase the requirement to 110 responses (FR 110). In other words, because it has performed so well, we expect even better performance in the future.

In a similar fashion, when Seema displayed excellent ability in mastering her violin lessons, she and her parents decided to increase the amount she had to learn each week. And when Lily's high school students performed poorly on their exams, she gradually decreased the amount of material they had to learn each week. (It is, of course, in this manner that standards in school become gradually lowered, often to the detriment of the students.)

Note that the process of shaping also involves an adjusting schedule insofar as the criterion for reinforcement is raised depending on the animal's performance. As soon as the rat has learned to stand near the lever to get food, one raises the criterion to touching the lever, placing a paw on the lever, and so forth. The requirement for reinforcement changes as soon as the rat has successfully met the previous requirement.

1. A complex schedule is one that consists of _____.

2. In a(n) _____ schedule, the response requirement changes as a function of the organism's performance while responding for the previous reinforcer, while in a(n) _____ schedule, the requirements of two or more simple schedules must be met before the reinforcer is delivered.

3. To the extent that a gymnast is trying to improve his performance, he is likely on a(n) _____ schedule of reinforcement; to the extent that his performance is judged according to both the form and quickness of his moves, he is on a(n) _____ schedule.

Chained Schedules A *chained schedule* consists of a sequence of two or more simple schedules, each of which has its own S^D and the last of which results in a terminal reinforcer. In other words, the person or animal must work through a series of component schedules to obtain the sought-after reinforcer. A chained schedule differs from a conjunctive schedule in that the two component schedules must be completed in a particular order, which is not required in a conjunctive schedule.

As an example of a chained schedule, a pigeon in a standard operant conditioning chamber is presented with a VR 20 schedule on a green key, followed by an FI 10-sec schedule on a red key, which then leads to the terminal reinforcer of food. Thus, an average of 20 responses on the green key will result in a change in key color to red, following which the first response on the red key after a 10-second interval will be reinforced by food. The food is the terminal reinforcer that supports the entire chain. This chain can be diagrammed as follows:

$$\begin{array}{ccc} \text{VR 20} & & \text{FI 10-sec} \\ \text{Green key: } \textit{Peck} \rightarrow & \text{Red key: } \textit{Peck} \rightarrow & \text{Food} \\ S^D \qquad\quad R & S^R/S^D \qquad\quad R & S^R \end{array}$$

Note that the presentation of the red key is both a secondary reinforcer for completing the preceding VR 20 schedule and an S^D for responding on the subsequent FI 10-sec schedule. Note, too, that this is an example of a *two-link chain*, with the VR 20 schedule constituting the first, or initial, link and the FI 10-sec schedule constituting the second, or terminal, link. By adding yet another schedule to the start of the chain, we can create a three-link chain, for example:

$$\begin{array}{ccccccc}
\textbf{VI 30-sec} & & \textbf{VR 20} & & \textbf{FI 10-sec} & & \\
\textbf{White key: } \textit{Peck} \rightarrow & \textbf{Green key: } \textit{Peck} \rightarrow & \textbf{Red key: } \textit{Peck} \rightarrow & \textbf{Food} \\
S^D \quad R & S^R/S^D \quad R & S^R/S^D \quad R & S^R
\end{array}$$

In this case, both the green and red keys function as secondary reinforcers that help maintain behavior throughout the chain.

1. A chained schedule consists of a sequence of two or more simple schedules, each of which has its own _____ and the last of which results in a t_____ r_____.

2. Within a chain, completion of each of the early links ends in a(n) s_____ reinforcer, which also functions as the _____ for the next link of the chain.

QUICK QUIZ L

Once pigeons learn which schedule is associated with which key, they generally show the appropriate response patterns for those schedules. In the preceding example, this would be a moderate, steady rate of response on the white key, a high rate of response on the green key, and a scalloped pattern of responding on the red key. Nevertheless, responding tends to be somewhat weaker in the earlier links of a chain than in the later links. This can be seen most clearly when each link consists of the same schedule. For example, Kelleher and Fry (1962) presented pigeons with a three-link chained schedule with each link consisting of an FI 60-sec schedule:

$$\begin{array}{ccccccc}
\textbf{FI 60-sec} & & \textbf{FI 60-sec} & & \textbf{FI 60-sec} & & \\
\textbf{White key: } \textit{Peck} \rightarrow & \textbf{Green key: } \textit{Peck} \rightarrow & \textbf{Red key: } \textit{Peck} \rightarrow & \textbf{Food} \\
S^D \quad R & S^R/S^D \quad R & S^R/S^D \quad R & S^R
\end{array}$$

The pigeons displayed very long pauses and a slow rate of response on the white key compared to the other two keys. The greatest amount of responding occurred on the red key.

Why would the earlier links of the chain be associated with weaker responding? One way of looking at it is that in the later links, the terminal reinforcer is more immediate and hence more influential; while in the early links, the terminal reinforcer is more distant and hence less influential (remember that delayed reinforcement is less effective than immediate reinforcement). Another way of looking at it is that the secondary reinforcers supporting behavior in the early links are less directly associated with food and are therefore relatively weak (e.g., the green key is associated with food only indirectly through its association with the red key). From this perspective, a chained schedule can be seen as the operant equivalent of higher-order classical conditioning—in which, for example, a tone (CS_1) associated with food (US) elicits less salivation than the food does, and a light (CS_2) associated with the tone elicits less salivation than the tone does. Similarly, in the example of the chained schedule, the red key associated with the food is a less powerful reinforcer than the food, and the green key associated with the red key is a less powerful reinforcer than the red key. (If you find that you can no longer remember the concept of higher-order classical conditioning, you should go back and review it.)

The difference in response strength between the early and later links in a chain is representative of a more general behavioral principle known as the goal gradient effect. The **goal gradient effect** is an increase in the strength and/or efficiency of responding as one draws near to the goal. For example, rats running through a maze to obtain food tend to run faster and make fewer wrong turns as they near the goal box (Hull, 1932). Similarly, a student writing an essay is likely to take shorter breaks and work more intensely as she nears the end. Dolphin trainers are well aware of the goal gradient effect. Dolphins who are trained to perform long chains of behaviors have a tendency to drift toward "sloppy" performance during the early parts of the chain, and trainers have to be vigilant to ensure that the dolphin's behavior is not reinforced when this occurs (Pryor, 1975). (Perhaps the most profound example of a goal gradient, however, is that shown by people who desperately need to urinate and become speed demons as they near the washroom.)

An efficient way to establish responding on a chained schedule is to train the final link first and the initial link last, a process known as *backward chaining*. Using the pigeon example, the pigeon would first be trained to respond on the red key to obtain food. This will establish the red key as a secondary reinforcer through its association with food. As a result, the presentation of the red key can then be used to reinforce responding on the green key. Once this is established, the presentation of the green key can be used to reinforce responding on the white key.

In these examples, each link in the chain required the same type of behavior; namely, key pecking. It is also possible to create behavior chains in which each link consists of a different behavior.[1] For example, a rat might have to climb over a barrier and then run through a tunnel to obtain food. This can be diagrammed as follows:

Barrier: *Climb over barrier* → Tunnel: *Run through tunnel* → Food
S^D R S^R/S^D R S^R

Note that the sight of the tunnel is both a secondary reinforcer for climbing over the barrier and a discriminative stimulus for then running through the tunnel.

---

[1]Behavior chains that require the same type of response in each link are called *homogeneous chains*; behavior chains that require a different type of response in each link are called *heterogeneous chains*.

As with the previous examples, backward chaining would be the best way to train this sequence of behaviors. Thus, the rat would first be trained to run through the tunnel for food. Once this is established, it would be taught to climb over the barrier to get to the tunnel, with the sight of the tunnel acting as a secondary reinforcer for this action. In this manner, very long chains of behavior can be established. In one reported example, a rat was trained to go up a ladder, cross a platform, climb a rope, cross a bridge, get into a little elevator box, release the pulley holding the box, lower the box "paw over paw" to the floor, and then press a button to obtain the food (Pryor, 1975). Of course, each of these behaviors also had to be shaped (through reinforcement of successive approximations to the target behavior). Shaping and chaining are thus the basic means by which circus and marine animals are trained to perform some remarkable feats (see Figure 7.3).

Most human endeavors involve response chains, some of which are very long. The act of reading this chapter, for example, consists of reading section after section, until the terminal reinforcer of completing the entire chapter has been attained. Completing each section serves as both a secondary reinforcer for having read that section as well as an S^D for reading the next section. Reading the chapter is in turn part of a much larger chain of behaviors that include attending lectures, taking notes, and studying—the terminal reinforcer for which is passing the course. Fortunately, backward chaining is not required for the development of such chains, because language enables us to describe to one another the required sequence of behaviors (as in a course syllabus). In other words, for humans, response chains are often established through instructions.

Unfortunately, in the case of very long chains, such as completing a course, the terminal reinforcer is often extremely distant, with the result that behavior is easily disrupted during the early part of the chain (remember the goal gradient principle). It is much easier to be a diligent student the night before the midterm than during the first week of the semester. Can anything be done to

FIGURE 7.3 Through shaping and chaining, animals can be taught to display some remarkable behaviors.

© Newscom

© Hulton Archive/ Getty Images

alleviate this problem? One possibility is to make the completion of each link in the chain more salient (i.e., more noticeable), thereby enhancing its value as a secondary reinforcer. Novelists, for example, need to write hundreds, or even thousands, of pages before the terminal reinforcer of a completed book is attained. To keep themselves on track, some novelists keep detailed records of their progress, such as charting the number of words written each day as well as the exact dates on which chapters were started and completed (Wallace & Pear, 1977). These records outline their achievements, thereby providing a much-needed source of secondary reinforcement throughout the process. Similarly, students sometimes keep detailed records of the number of hours studied or pages read. They might also compile a "to do" list of assignments and then cross off each item as it is completed. Crossing off an item provides a clear record that the task has been accomplished and also functions as a secondary reinforcer that helps motivate us (Lakein, 1973).

1. Responding tends to be weaker in the (earlier/later) _____ links of a chain. This is an example of the g_____ g _____ effect in which the strength and/or efficiency of responding (increases/decreases) _____ as the organism approaches the goal.

2. An efficient way to train a complex chain, especially in animals, is through b_____ chaining, in which the (first/last) _____ link of the chain is trained first. However, this type of procedure usually is not required with verbally proficient humans, with whom behavior chains can be quickly established through the use of i_____.

3. One suggestion for enhancing our behavior in the early part of a long response chain is to make the completion of each link more s_____, thereby enhancing its value as a s_____ reinforcer.

Theories of Reinforcement

In this section, we briefly discuss some major theories of reinforcement. We begin with Clark Hull's early drive reduction view of reinforcement. This is followed by a brief description of a highly influential approach known as the Premack principle. This principle is of immense practical importance, and it has helped revolutionize the manner in which the process of reinforcement is now conceptualized. In fact, the two other theoretical approaches that we discuss—the response deprivation hypothesis and the bliss point approach—can be viewed as direct outgrowths of the Premack principle.

Drive Reduction Theory

An early approach to understanding reinforcement, and one that was strongly championed by Hull (1943), is *drive reduction theory*. According to this theory, an event is reinforcing to the extent that it is associated with a reduction in some type of physiological drive. Thus, food deprivation produces a "hunger drive," which then propels the animal to seek out food. When food is obtained, the hunger drive is reduced. At the same time, the behavior that preceded this drive reduction, and led to the food, is automatically strengthened. In very simple terms (in actuality, the theory is more complex than this), if a hungry rat in a maze turns left just before it finds food in the goal box, the act of turning left in the maze will be automatically strengthened by the subsequent reduction in hunger.

We touched upon this theory in Chapter 6 when we noted that primary reinforcers are often those events that seem to reduce a physiological need. From this perspective, secondary reinforcers are events that have become reinforcers because they have been associated with a primary reinforcer and, hence, with some type of drive reduction. Thus, a person enjoys collecting cookbooks because cooking is associated with eating food, which in turn has been associated with a reduction in hunger. According to Hull, all reinforcers are associated, either directly or indirectly, with some type of drive reduction.

In Chapter 6 we also noted that a major problem with this physiological view of reinforcement is that some reinforcers do not seem to be associated with any type of drive reduction. A rat will press a lever to obtain access to a running wheel, a chimpanzee will press a button so that it can obtain a peek into another room, and teenagers will spend considerable amounts of money to be exposed to earsplitting, and potentially damaging, levels of rock music. It is difficult to see how such events are associated with a reduction in some type of physiological need. Instead, it seems as though the motivation for such behavior exists more in the reinforcing stimulus than in some type of internal state.

Motivation that is derived from some property of the reinforcer, as opposed to an internal drive state, is referred to as *incentive motivation.* Playing a video game for the fun of it, attending a concert because you enjoy the music, and working to earn enough money to buy a Porsche are examples of behaviors that are motivated by incentives. Even events that seem to be clearly associated with drive reduction can be strongly affected by incentive factors. For example, going to a restaurant for a meal might be largely driven by hunger; however, the fact that you prefer a restaurant that serves hot, spicy food is an example of incentive motivation. The spiciness of the food plays no role in the reduction of hunger; it is simply a form of sensory stimulation that you find highly reinforcing.

In conclusion, most theorists no longer believe that drive reduction theory can offer a comprehensive account of reinforcement, and this approach has now been largely abandoned. Some recent approaches have instead emphasized observable behavior patterns as opposed to hypothetical internal processes in their explanation of the reinforcement process. A major step in this direction was the Premack principle.

1. According to drive reduction theory, an event is reinforcing if it is associated with a reduction in some type of p_____ drive.

2. According to this theory, a s_____ reinforcer is one that has been associated with a p_____ reinforcer.

3. A major problem with drive reduction theory is that _____
_____.

4. The motivation that is derived from some property of the reinforcer is called
_____ motivation.

5. Research has shown that hungry rats will perform more effectively in a T-maze
when the reinforcer for a correct response (right turn versus left turn) consists of several small pellets as opposed to one large pellet (Capaldi, Miller, &
Alptekin, 1989). Chickens will also run faster down a runway to obtain a popcorn kernel presented in four pieces than in one whole piece (Wolfe & Kaplon,
1941). The fact that several small bites of food is a more effective reinforcer
than one large bite is consistent with the notion of (drive reduction/incentive
motivation) _____.

The Premack Principle

Remember how we earlier noted that Skinner defined reinforcers (and punishers) by their effect on behavior? This unfortunately presents us with a
problem. In the real world, it would be nice to know ahead of time whether
a certain event can function as a reinforcer. One way to do this, of course,
would be to take something the person or animal seems to like and use
that as a reinforcer. But it is not always easy to determine what a person
or animal likes. Moreover, events that we might believe should be liked
might not actually function as reinforcers. To a 5-year-old boy, a kiss from
his mother is great if he needs comforting, but not when he is trying to
show off to his friends. Fortunately, the Premack principle provides a more
objective way to determine whether something can be used as a reinforcer
(Premack, 1965).

The Premack principle is based on the notion that reinforcers can often
be viewed as behaviors rather than stimuli. For example, rather than saying
that lever pressing was reinforced by *food* (a stimulus), we could say that
lever pressing was reinforced by the act of *eating food* (a behavior). Similarly,
rather than saying that playing appropriately was reinforced by *television*, we
could instead say that it was reinforced by *watching television*. When we view
reinforcers in this manner—as behaviors rather than stimuli—then the
process of reinforcement can be conceptualized as a sequence of two behaviors:
(1) the behavior that is being reinforced, followed by (2) the behavior that is
the reinforcer. Moreover, according to Premack, by comparing the frequency
of various behaviors, we can determine whether one can be used as a reinforcer for the other.

More specifically, the **Premack principle** states that a high-probability
behavior can be used to reinforce a low-probability behavior. For example,
when a rat is hungry, eating food has a higher likelihood of occurrence
than running in a wheel. This means that eating food (the high-probability
behavior [HPB]) can be used to reinforce the target behavior of running in

a wheel (the low-probability behavior [LPB]). In other words, the rat will run in the wheel to obtain access to the food:

> **Target behavior**   **Consequence**
> *Running in a wheel* (LPB) → **Eating food** (HPB)
>   R   S^R

On the other hand, if the rat is not hungry, then eating food is less likely to occur than running in a wheel. In this case, running in a wheel can be used as a reinforcer for the target behavior of eating food. In other words, the rat will eat to obtain access to the wheel.

> **Target behavior**   **Consequence**
> *Eating food* (LPB) → **Running in a wheel** (HPB)
>   R   S^R

By focusing on the relative probabilities of behaviors, the Premack principle allows us to quickly identify potential reinforcers in the real world. If Kaily spends only a few minutes each morning doing chores, but at least an hour reading comic books, then the opportunity to read comic books (a higher-probability behavior) can be used to reinforce doing chores (a lower-probability behavior).

> *Do chores* → **Read comic books**
>   R   S^R

In fact, if you want an easy way to remember the Premack principle, just think of Grandma's rule: First you work (a low-probability behavior), then you play (a high-probability behavior).

The Premack principle has proven to be very useful in applied settings. For example, a person with autism who spends many hours each day rocking back and forth might be very unresponsive to consequences that are normally reinforcing for others, such as receiving praise. The Premack principle, however, suggests that the opportunity to rock back and forth can be used as an effective reinforcer for another behavior that we might wish to strengthen, such as interacting with others. Thus, the Premack principle is a handy principle to keep in mind when confronted by a situation in which normal reinforcers seem to have little effect.

1. The Premack principle holds that reinforcers can often be viewed as _____ rather than stimuli. For example, rather than saying that the rat's lever pressing was reinforced with food, we could say that it was reinforced with _____ food.

2. The Premack principle states that a _____ _____ behavior can be used as a reinforcer for a _____ _____ behavior.

3. According to the Premack principle, if you crack your knuckles 3 times per hour and burp 20 times per hour, then the opportunity to _____ can probably be used as a reinforcer for _____.

4. If you drink five soda pops each day and only one glass of orange juice, then the opportunity to drink _____ can likely be used as a reinforcer for drinking _____.

5. If *Chew bubble gum* → Play video games is a diagram of a reinforcement procedure based on the Premack principle, then chewing bubble gum must be a (lower/higher) _____ probability behavior than playing video games.

6. What is Grandma's rule, and how does it relate to the Premack principle?

Response Deprivation Hypothesis

The Premack principle requires us to know the relative probabilities of two behaviors before we can judge whether one will be an effective reinforcer for the other. But what if we have information on only one behavior? Is there any way that we can tell whether that behavior can function as a reinforcer before actually trying it out?

The *response deprivation hypothesis* states that a behavior can serve as a reinforcer when (1) access to the behavior is restricted and (2) its frequency thereby falls below its preferred level of occurrence (Timberlake & Allison, 1974). The preferred level of an activity is its baseline level of occurrence when the animal can freely engage in that activity. For example, imagine that a rat typically runs for 1 hour a day whenever it has free access to a running wheel. This 1 hour per day is the rat's preferred level of running. If the rat is then allowed free access to the wheel for only 15 minutes per day, it will be unable to reach this preferred level and will be in a state of deprivation with regard to running. According to the response deprivation hypothesis, the rat will now be willing to work (e.g., press a lever) to obtain additional time on the wheel.

> *Lever press* → **Running in a wheel**
>   **R**   **S^R**

The response deprivation approach also provides a general explanation for why contingencies of reinforcement are effective. Contingencies of reinforcement are effective to the extent that they create a condition in which the organism is confronted with the possibility of a certain response falling below its baseline level. Take Kaily, who enjoys reading comic books each day. If we establish a contingency in which she has to do her chores before reading comic books, her baseline level of free comic book reading will drop to zero. She will therefore be willing to do chores to gain back her comic book time.

> *Do chores* → **Read comic books**
>   **R**   **S^R**

You will notice that the diagram given here is the same as that given for the Premack principle. In this case, however, reading comic books is a reinforcer because the contingency pushes free comic book reading to below its preferred rate of occurrence. The relative probabilities of the two behaviors are irrelevant, meaning that it does not matter if the probability of reading comic books is higher or lower than the probability of doing chores. The only thing that matters is whether comic book reading is now in danger of falling below its preferred level. Thus, the response deprivation hypothesis is applicable to a wider range of conditions than the Premack principle. (Question 4 in the Quick Quiz will help clarify this.)

To help distinguish between the Premack principle and the response deprivation hypothesis, ask yourself whether the main point seems to be the frequency of one behavior relative to another (in which case the Premack principle is applicable) or the frequency of one behavior relative to its baseline (in which case the response deprivation hypothesis is applicable).

1. According to the response deprivation hypothesis, a response can serve as a reinforcer if free access to the response is (provided/restricted) _____ and its frequency then falls (above/below) _____ its baseline level of occurrence.

2. If a child normally watches 4 hours of television per night, we can make television watching a reinforcer if we restrict free access to the television to (more/less) _____ than 4 hours per night.

3. The response deprivation hypothesis differs from the Premack principle in that we need only know the baseline frequency of the (reinforced/reinforcing) _____ behavior.

4. Kaily typically watches television for 4 hours per day and reads comic books for 1 hour per day. You then set up a contingency whereby Kaily must watch 4.5 hours of television each day in order to have access to her comic books. According to the Premack principle, this will likely be an (effective/ineffective) _____ contingency. According to the response deprivation hypothesis, this could be an (effective/ineffective) _____ contingency.

QUICK QUIZ P

Behavioral Bliss Point Approach

The response deprivation hypothesis assumes there is an optimal level of behavior that an organism strives to maintain. This same assumption can be made for the manner in which an organism distributes its behavior between two or more activities. According to the **behavioral bliss point approach,** an organism with free access to alternative activities will distribute its behavior in such a way as to maximize overall reinforcement (Allison, 1983). For example, a rat that can freely choose between running in a wheel and exploring a maze might spend 1 hour per day running in the wheel and 2 hours exploring the maze. This distribution of behavior represents the optimal reinforcement available from those two activities—that is, the behavioral bliss point—for that particular rat.

Note that this optimal distribution of behavior is based on the notion that each activity is freely available. When activities are not freely available—as when the two activities are intertwined in a contingency of reinforcement—then the optimal distribution may become unattainable. Imagine, for example, that a contingency is created in which the rat now has to run in the wheel for 60 seconds to obtain 30 seconds of access to the maze:

Wheel running **(60 seconds)** → **Maze exploration (30 seconds)**
R $\quad\quad\quad\quad\quad\quad\quad\quad\quad\quad$ **S^R**

It will now be impossible for the rat to reach its behavioral bliss point for these two activities. When they are freely available, the rat prefers twice as much maze exploration (2 hours) as wheel running (1 hour). But our contingency forces the rat to engage in twice as much wheel running as maze exploration. To obtain the preferred 2 hours of maze exploration, the rat would have to engage in 4 hours of running, which is far beyond its preferred level for that activity. Thus, it will be impossible for the rat to attain its behavioral bliss point for those activities.

A reasonable assumption as to what will happen in such circumstances is that the rat will compromise by distributing its activities in such a way as to draw as near as possible to its behavioral bliss point. For instance, it might choose to run a total of 2 hours per day to obtain 1 hour of maze exploration. This is not as enjoyable as the preferred distribution of 1 hour of running and 2 hours of maze exploration; but, given the contingencies, it will have to do. Likewise, most of us are forced to spend several more hours working and several fewer hours enjoying the finer things in life than we would if we were independently wealthy and could freely do whatever we want. The behavioral bliss point for our varied activities is essentially unattainable. Instead, faced with certain contingencies that must be met in order to survive, we distribute our activities in such a way as to draw as near to the bliss point as possible.

The behavioral bliss point approach assumes that organisms attempt to distribute their behavior so as to maximize overall reinforcement. This, of course, is a very rational way to behave. In Chapter 10, you will encounter an alternative theory, known as melioration theory, which maintains that organisms, including people, are not that rational and that various processes often entice the organism away from maximization. Note, too, that none of the theories discussed in this chapter take account of an animal's innate tendencies toward certain patterns of behavior, which may affect how easily certain behaviors can be trained. In Chapter 11, you will encounter a theory that does take account of such tendencies.

1. According to the behavioral _____ _____ approach, an organism that (is forced to/can freely) _____ engage in alternative activities will distribute its behavior in such a way as to (optimize/balance) _____ the available reinforcement.

2. Contingencies of reinforcement often (disrupt/enhance) _____ the distribution of behavior such that it is (easy/impossible) _____ to obtain the optimal amount of reinforcement.

3. Given this state of affairs, how is the organism likely to distribute its activities?

ADVICE FOR THE LOVELORN

Dear Dr. Dee,

I recently began dating a classmate. We get along really well at school, so it seemed like we would be a perfect match. Unfortunately, once we started dating, our relationship seemed to lose a lot of its energy, and our lives seemed a lot less satisfying. Someone suggested that we must each have an unconscious fear of commitment. What do you think?

Less Than Blissful

Dear Less,

I suppose it is possible that you have an unconscious fear of commitment—if there is such a thing as an unconscious fear of commitment. On the other hand, it may be that the amount of time you spend interacting with one another at school is actually the optimal amount of time, given the various reinforcers available in your relationship. Spending additional time together (which also means spending less time on alternative activities) has, for each of you, resulted in a distribution of behavior that is further removed from your behavioral bliss point. Obviously, a good relationship should move you toward your bliss point, not away from it. Try being just friends-at-school again, and see if that restores some of the satisfaction in your relationship.

Behaviorally yours,

Dr. Dee

SUMMARY

A schedule of reinforcement is the response requirement that must be met to obtain a reinforcer. Different types of schedules produce different patterns of responding, which are known as schedule effects.

In a continuous schedule of reinforcement, each response is reinforced. In an intermittent schedule of reinforcement, only some responses are reinforced. There are four basic intermittent schedules. On a fixed ratio schedule, a fixed number of responses is required for reinforcement, while on a variable ratio schedule, a varying number of responses is required. Both schedules produce a high rate of response, with the fixed ratio schedule also producing a postreinforcement pause. On a fixed interval schedule, the first response after a fixed period of time is reinforced, while on a variable interval schedule, the first response after a varying period of time is reinforced. The former produces a scalloped pattern of responding, whereas the latter produces a moderate, steady pattern of responding.

On a fixed duration schedule, reinforcement is contingent upon responding continuously for a fixed, predictable period of time; on a variable duration schedule, reinforcement is contingent upon responding continuously for a varying, unpredictable period of time. Response-rate schedules specifically reinforce the rate of response. For example, on a DRH schedule, reinforcement is contingent on a high rate of response, whereas on a DRL schedule, it is contingent on a low rate of response. On a DRP schedule, reinforcement is contingent on a particular rate of response—neither too fast nor too slow. By contrast, on a noncontingent schedule of reinforcement, the reinforcer is delivered following a certain period of time regardless of the organism's behavior. The time period can either be fixed (a fixed time schedule) or varied (a variable time schedule). Noncontingent schedules sometimes result in the development of superstitious behavior.

A complex schedule consists of two or more simple schedules. In a conjunctive schedule, the requirements of two or more simple schedules must be met before a reinforcer is delivered; in an adjusting schedule, the response requirement changes as a function of the organism's performance during responding for the previous reinforcer. On a chained schedule, reinforcement is contingent upon meeting the requirements of two or more successive schedules, each with its own discriminative stimulus. Responding tends to become stronger and/or more efficient toward the end of the chain, which is an instance of the goal gradient effect. Behavior chains are often best established by training the last link first and the first link last.

According to drive reduction theory, an event is reinforcing if it is associated with a reduction in some type of internal physiological drive. However, some behaviors seem motivated more by the external consequence (known as incentive motivation) than by an internal drive state. The Premack principle assumes that high-probability behaviors can be used as reinforcers for low-probability behaviors. The response deprivation hypothesis states that a behavior can be used as a reinforcer if access to the behavior is restricted so that its frequency falls below its baseline rate of occurrence. The behavioral bliss point approach assumes that organisms distribute their behavior in such a manner as to maximize their overall reinforcement.

SUGGESTED READINGS

Ferster, C. B., & Skinner, B. F. (1957). *Schedules of reinforcement.* New York: Appleton-Century-Crofts. The seminal book on schedule effects. Not a book for light reading, but glancing through it will give you a sense of the history of behavior analysis and what real schedule effects look like.

Herrnstein, R. J. (1966). Superstition: A corollary of the principle of operant conditioning. In W. K. Honig (Ed.), *Operant behavior: Areas of research and application.* New York: Appleton-Century-Crofts. A discussion of the behavioral approach to superstitious behavior. The discussion of human superstitions at the end of the article would be of most interest to undergraduates.

Timberlake, W., & Farmer-Dougan, V. A. (1991). Reinforcement in applied settings: Figuring out ahead of time what will work. *Psychological Bulletin*, *110*, 379–391. Reviews the Premack principle and the response deprivation approach to reinforcement and its usefulness in applied settings.

STUDY QUESTIONS

1. What is a schedule of reinforcement?
2. Distinguish between continuous and intermittent schedules of reinforcement.
3. Define fixed ratio schedule. Describe the typical pattern of responding produced by this schedule.
4. Define variable ratio schedule. Describe the typical pattern of responding produced by this schedule.
5. Define fixed interval schedule. Describe the typical pattern of responding produced by this schedule.
6. Define variable interval schedule. Describe the typical pattern of responding produced by this schedule.
7. Name and define two types of duration schedules.
8. What are three types of response-rate schedules?
9. Name and define the two types of noncontingent schedules.
10. What is a conjunctive schedule? What is an adjusting schedule?
11. What is a chained schedule? Diagram and label an example of a chained schedule.
12. What type of reinforcer serves to maintain behavior throughout the early links in a chain? What is the best way to establish responding on a chained schedule in animals?
13. Define the goal gradient effect and give an example.
14. Describe the drive reduction theory of reinforcement. What is a major difficulty with this theory? What is incentive motivation?
15. Outline the Premack principle. Give an example of the Premack principle from your own life.
16. Outline the response deprivation hypothesis. Give an example of the response deprivation hypothesis from your own life.
17. Describe the behavioral bliss point approach to reinforcement.

CONCEPT REVIEW

adjusting schedule. A schedule in which the response requirement changes as a function of the organism's performance while responding for the previous reinforcer.

behavioral bliss point approach. The theory that an organism with free access to alternative activities will distribute its behavior in such a way as to maximize overall reinforcement.

chained schedule. A schedule consisting of a sequence of two or more simple schedules, each with its own S^D and the last of which results in a terminal reinforcer.

complex schedule. A schedule consisting of a combination of two or more simple schedules.

conjunctive schedule. A type of complex schedule in which the requirements of two or more simple schedules must be met before a reinforcer is delivered.

continuous reinforcement schedule. A schedule in which each specified response is reinforced.

differential reinforcement of high rates (DRH). A schedule in which reinforcement is contingent upon emitting at least a certain number of responses in a certain period of time—or, more generally, reinforcement is provided for responding at a fast rate.

differential reinforcement of low rates (DRL). A schedule in which a minimum amount of time must pass between each response before the reinforcer will be delivered—or, more generally, reinforcement is provided for responding at a slow rate.

differential reinforcement of paced responding (DRP). A schedule in which reinforcement is contingent upon emitting a series of responses at a set rate—or, more generally, reinforcement is provided for responding neither too fast nor too slow.

drive reduction theory. According to this theory, an event is reinforcing to the extent that it is associated with a reduction in some type of physiological drive.

fixed duration (FD) schedule. A schedule in which reinforcement is contingent upon continuous performance of a behavior for a fixed, predictable period of time.

fixed interval (FI) schedule. A schedule in which reinforcement is contingent upon the first response after a fixed, predictable period of time.

fixed ratio (FR) schedule. A schedule in which reinforcement is contingent upon a fixed, predictable number of responses.

fixed time (FT) schedule. A schedule in which the reinforcer is delivered following a fixed, predictable period of time, regardless of the organism's behavior.

goal gradient effect. An increase in the strength and/or efficiency of responding as one draws near to the goal.

incentive motivation. Motivation derived from some property of the reinforcer, as opposed to an internal drive state.

intermittent (or partial) reinforcement schedule. A schedule in which only some responses are reinforced.

noncontingent schedule of reinforcement. A schedule in which the reinforcer is delivered independently of any response.

Premack principle. The notion that a high-probability behavior can be used to reinforce a low-probability behavior.

ratio strain. A disruption in responding due to an overly demanding response requirement.

response deprivation hypothesis. The notion that a behavior can serve as a reinforcer when (1) access to the behavior is restricted and (2) its frequency thereby falls below its preferred level of occurrence.

response-rate schedule. A schedule in which reinforcement is directly contingent upon the organism's rate of response.

schedule of reinforcement. The response requirement that must be met to obtain reinforcement.

variable duration (VD) schedule. A schedule in which reinforcement is contingent upon continuous performance of a behavior for a varying, unpredictable period of time.

variable interval (VI) schedule. A schedule in which reinforcement is contingent upon the first response after a varying, unpredictable period of time.

variable ratio (VR) schedule. A schedule in which reinforcement is contingent upon a varying, unpredictable number of responses.

variable time (VT) schedule. A schedule in which the reinforcer is delivered following a varying, unpredictable period of time, regardless of the organism's behavior.

CHAPTER TEST

21. On a _____ schedule, reinforcement is contingent upon the first response *during* a varying period of time. (A) fixed interval, (B) variable time, (C) fixed time, (D) variable interval, (E) none of the preceding.

6. On a _____ schedule (abbreviated _____), reinforcement is contingent upon a fixed, predictable number of responses. This produces a _____ rate of response often accompanied by a _____ _____.

17. On a (use the abbreviation) _____ schedule, a minimum amount of time must pass between each response before the reinforcer will be delivered. On a _____ schedule, reinforcement is contingent upon emitting at least a certain number of responses in a certain period of time. On a _____ schedule, reinforcement is contingent on emitting a series of responses at a specific rate.

10. If Jason is extremely persistent in asking Neem out for a date, she will occasionally accept his invitation. Of the four basic schedules, Jason's behavior of asking Neem for a date is most likely on a _____ _____ schedule of reinforcement.

36. Russ is so impressed with how quickly his betta learned to swim in a circle that he keeps doubling the number of circles it has to perform in order to receive a reinforcer. This is an example of an _____ schedule of reinforcement (one that is particularly likely to suffer from r_____ s_____).

8. On a _____ schedule, a response *must not occur* until 20 seconds have elapsed since the last reinforcer. (A) VI 20-sec, (B) VT 20-sec, (C) FT 20-sec, (D) FI 20-sec, (E) none of the preceding.

28. Postreinforcement pauses are most likely to occur on which two types of simple intermittent schedules? _____ _____.

16. On _____ schedules, reinforcement is contingent upon the rate of response.

31. Shawna often goes for a walk through the woods, but she rarely does yardwork. According to the _____, walking through the woods could be used as a _____ for yardwork.

5. On a _____ schedule (abbreviated _____), reinforcement is contingent upon the first response after a fixed period of time. This produces a _____ pattern of responding.

13. A _____ schedule generally produces a high rate of response with a short pause following the attainment of each reinforcer. In general, the higher the requirement, the (longer/shorter) _____ the pause.

29. On a _____ schedule, a response cannot be reinforced until 20 seconds have elapsed since the last reinforcer. (A) VI 20-sec, (B) VT 20-sec, (C) FT 20-sec, (D) FI 20-sec, (E) none of the preceding.

37. Ahmed's daily routine consists of swimming without rest for 30 minutes, following which he takes a break. This most closely resembles a(n) _____ schedule of reinforcement.

3. If a dog receives a treat each time it begs for one, its begging is being maintained on a(n) _____ schedule of reinforcement. If it only sometimes receives a treat when it begs for one, its begging is being maintained on a(n) _____ schedule of reinforcement.

27. Dersu often carried a lucky charm with him when he went out hunting. This is because the appearance of game was often on a (use the abbreviation) _____ schedule of reinforcement.

32. Gina often goes for a walk through the woods, and even more often she does yardwork. According to the _____, walking through the woods could still be used as a reinforcer for yardwork given that one restricts the frequency of walking to _____ its_____ level.

26. On a fixed interval schedule, reinforcement is contingent upon the first response _____ a fixed period of time. (A) during, (B) before, (C) after, (D) none of the preceding.

9. Neem accepts Jason's invitation for a date only when she has "nothing better to do." Of the four basic intermittent schedules, Jason's behavior of asking Neem for a date is best described as being on a _____ schedule of reinforcement.

38. When Deanna screams continuously, her mother occasionally pays attention to her. This is most likely an example of a(n) _____ schedule of reinforcement.

30. Drinking a soda to quench your thirst is an example of _____ reduction; drinking a soda because you love its tangy sweetness is an example of _____ motivation.

4. On a _____ schedule (abbreviated _____), reinforcement is contingent upon a varying, unpredictable number of responses. This produces a _____ rate of response.

24. A pigeon pecks a green key on a VI 60-sec schedule, which results in the insertion of a foot-treadle into the chamber. The pigeon then steps on the treadle 10 times, following which it receives food. To train this chain of behaviors, one should start with _____.

11. Neem accepts Jason's invitation for a date only when he has just been paid his monthly salary. Of the four simple schedules, the contingency governing Jason's behavior of asking Neem for a date seems most similar to a _____ schedule of reinforcement.

35. "If I'm not a success in every aspect of my life, my family will reject me." This is a severe example of a _____ schedule of reinforcement.

25. Dagoni works for longer and longer periods of time and takes fewer and fewer breaks as his project nears completion. This is an example of the _____ effect.

18. On a _____ schedule of reinforcement, the reinforcer is delivered independently of any response.

7. On a _____ schedule (abbreviated _____), reinforcement is contingent upon the first response after a varying interval of time. This produces a _____ rate of response.

15. Gambling is often maintained by a _____ schedule of reinforcement.

20. On a _____ schedule (abbreviated _____), the reinforcer is delivered following a varying period of time. It differs from a VI schedule in that a response (is/is not) _____ required to obtain the reinforcer.

33. Anna ideally likes to exercise for 1 hour each morning, followed by a 30-minute sauna, in turn followed by a half hour of drinking coffee and reading the newspaper. Unfortunately, due to other commitments, she actually spends 45 minutes exercising, followed by a 15-minute sauna, and a half hour drinking coffee and reading the paper. According to the _____ approach, Anna's ideal schedule provides the _____ amount of overall reinforcement that can be obtained from those activities. Her actual distribution of behavior represents her attempt to draw as near to the _____ point as possible for these activities.

1. A _____ is the response requirement that must be met to obtain reinforcement.

22. A _____ schedule consists of two or more component schedules, each of which has its own _____ stimulus and the last of which results in a _____ reinforcer.

34. The abbreviation DRL refers to _____ reinforcement of _____ rate behavior.

14. As noted in the opening scenario to this chapter, Mandy found that she had to work harder and harder to entice Alvin to pay attention to her. It is quite likely that her behavior was on a _____ schedule of reinforcement. As a result, she began experiencing periods of time where she simply gave up and stopped trying. Eventually, she stopped seeing him altogether. When her sister asked why, Mandy, having just read this chapter, replied, "_____ _____."

2. Different response requirements have different effects on behavior. These effects are known as _____.

23. A pigeon pecks a green key on a VR 9 schedule, then a red key on an FI 20-sec, following which it receives food. The reinforcer for pecking the green key is the presentation of the _____, which is a _____ reinforcer.

12. Eddy finds that he has to thump his television set twice before the picture will clear up. His behavior of thumping the television set is on a (be specific and use the abbreviation) _____ schedule of reinforcement.

19. On a _____ schedule (abbreviated _____), the reinforcer is delivered following a fixed interval of time, regardless of the organism's behavior.

Visit the book companion Web site at <http://www.academic.cengage.com/psychology/powell> for additional practice questions, answers to the Quick Quizzes, practice review exams, and additional exercises and information.

ANSWERS TO CHAPTER TEST

1. schedule of reinforcement (reinforcement schedule)
2. schedule effects
3. continuous; intermittent
4. variable ratio; VR; high, steady
5. fixed interval; FI; scalloped
6. fixed ratio; FR; high; postreinforcement pause
7. variable interval; VI; moderate, steady
8. E
9. variable interval
10. variable ratio
11. fixed interval
12. FR 2
13. fixed ratio; longer
14. variable ratio; ratio strain
15. variable ratio
16. response rate
17. DRL; DRH; DRP
18. noncontingent
19. fixed time; FT

20. variable time; VT; is not
21. E
22. chained; discriminative; terminal
23. red key; secondary
24. treadle press
25. goal gradient
26. C
27. VT
28. fixed interval and fixed ratio
29. D
30. drive; incentive
31. Premack principle; reinforcer
32. response deprivation hypothesis; below; baseline
33. behavioral bliss point; optimal (maximum); bliss
34. differential; low
35. conjunctive
36. adjusting; ratio strain
37. FD
38. VD

Extinction and Stimulus Control

Poppea gained access to Nero, and established her ascendancy. First she used flirta-tious wiles, pretending to be unable to resist her passion for Nero's looks. Then, as the emperor fell in love with her, she became haughty, and if he kept her for more than two nights she insisted that she was married and could not give up her marriage.

TACITUS, *The Annals of Imperial Rome*

Extinction

In the past few chapters, we have concentrated on strengthening oper-ant behavior through the process of reinforcement. However, as previously noted, a behavior that has been strengthened through reinforcement can also be weakened through extinction. ***Extinction*** is the nonreinforcement of a pre-viously reinforced response, the result of which is a decrease in the strength of that response. As with classical conditioning, the term *extinction* refers to both a procedure and a process. The *procedure* of extinction is the nonrein-forcement of a previously reinforced response; the *process* of extinction is the resultant decrease in response strength.

Take, for example, a situation in which a rat has learned to press a lever for food:

$$\textbf{\textit{Lever press}} \rightarrow \textbf{Food}$$
$$\textbf{R} \qquad \textbf{S}^{\textbf{R}}$$

If lever pressing is no longer followed by food:

$$\textbf{\textit{Lever press}} \rightarrow \textbf{No food}$$
$$\textbf{R} \qquad \text{—}$$

then the frequency of lever pressing will decline. The act of withholding food delivery following a lever press is the procedure of extinction, and the resul-tant decline in responding is the process of extinction. If lever pressing ceases entirely, the response is said to have been *extinguished*; if it has not yet ceased entirely, then the response has been only *partially extinguished*.

Similarly, consider a child who has learned to whine to obtain candy:

$$\textbf{\textit{Whining}} \rightarrow \textbf{Candy}$$
$$\textbf{R} \qquad \textbf{S}^{\textbf{R}}$$

If whining no longer produces candy:

$$\textbf{\textit{Whining}} \rightarrow \textbf{No candy}$$
$$\textbf{R} \qquad \text{—}$$

the frequency of whining will decline. The procedure of extinction is the nondelivery of candy following the behavior, and the process of extinction is the resultant decline in the behavior. If the whining is completely eliminated, then it has been extinguished. If whining still occurs, but at a lower frequency, then it has been partially extinguished.

An important, but often neglected, aspect of applying an extinction procedure is to ensure that the consequence being withheld is in fact the reinforcer that is maintaining the behavior. You might believe that the consequence of candy is reinforcing a child's tendency to whine, when in fact it is the accompanying attention from the parent. If this is the case, and the parent continues to provide attention for whining (for example, by arguing with the child each time he or she whines), then withholding the candy might have little or no effect on the behavior. Of course, another possibility is that the whining is being maintained by both the candy and attention, in which case withholding the candy might only partially extinguish the behavior. Thus, determining the effective reinforcer that is maintaining a behavior is a critical first step in extinguishing a behavior.

1. Extinction is the _____ of a previously _____ response, the result of which is a(n) _____ in the strength of that response.

2. Whenever Jana's friend Karla phoned late in the evening, she would invariably begin complaining about her coworkers. In the beginning, Jana listened attentively and provided emotional support. Unfortunately, Karla started phoning more and more often, with each call lasting longer and longer. Jana began to wonder if she was reinforcing Karla's behavior of phoning and complaining, so she decided to screen her late-evening calls and not answer any such calls from Karla. Eventually, Karla stopped phoning at that time, and they resumed a normal friendship that excluded lengthy complaints over the phone. Jana used the (procedure/process) _____ of extinction when she stopped answering Karla's late-evening calls, while the _____ of extinction is the eventual cessation of such calls.

3. In carrying out an extinction procedure, an important first step is to ensure that the consequence being withdrawn is in fact the _____.

Side Effects of Extinction

When an extinction procedure is implemented, it is often accompanied by certain side effects. It is important to be aware of these side effects because they can mislead one into believing that an extinction procedure is not having an effect when in fact it is.

1. **Extinction Burst.** The implementation of an extinction procedure does not always result in an immediate decrease in responding. Instead, one often finds an *extinction burst*, a temporary increase in the frequency and intensity of responding when extinction is first implemented. Suppose, for example, that we reinforce every fourth lever press by a rat (an FR 4 schedule of reinforcement). When extinction is implemented, the rat will initially react by pressing the lever both more rapidly and more forcefully. The rat's behavior is analogous to our behavior when we plug money into

298 CHAPTER 8 Extinction and Stimulus Control

a candy machine, press the button, and receive nothing in return. We do not just give up and walk away. Instead, we press the button several times in a row, often with increasing amounts of force. Our behavior toward the machine shows the same increase in frequency and intensity that characterizes an extinction burst.

2. **Increase in Variability.** An extinction procedure can also result in an increase in the variability of a behavior (Antonitis, 1951). For example, a rat whose lever pressing no longer produces food might vary the manner in which it presses the lever. If the rat typically pressed the lever with its right paw, it might now try pressing it with its left paw. As well, if the rat usually pressed the lever in the center, it might now press it more to one side or the other. Similarly, when confronted by a candy machine that has just stolen our money, we will likely vary the manner in which we push the button, such as holding it down for a second before releasing it. And we will almost certainly try pressing other buttons on the machine to see if we can at least obtain a different selection.[1]

3. **Emotional Behavior.** Extinction is often accompanied by emotional behavior (Zeiler, 1971). The hungry pigeon that suddenly finds that key pecking no longer produces food soon becomes agitated (as evidenced, for example, by quick jerky movements and wing flapping). Likewise, people often become upset when confronted by a candy machine that does not deliver the goods. Such emotional responses are what we typically refer to as *frustration.*

4. **Aggression.** One type of emotional behavior that is particularly common during an extinction procedure is aggression. In fact, extinction procedures have been used to study aggressive behavior in animals. For example, research has shown that a pigeon whose key pecking is placed on extinction will reliably attack another pigeon (or model of a pigeon) that happens to be nearby (Azrin, Hutchinson, & Hake, 1966). Extinction-induced aggression (also called frustration-induced aggression) is also common in humans. People often become angry with those who block them from obtaining an important goal. For that matter, even uncooperative vending machines are sometimes attacked.

5. **Resurgence.** A rather unusual side effect of extinction is **resurgence,** the reappearance during extinction of other behaviors that had once been effective in obtaining reinforcement (Epstein, 1985). Hull (1934), for example, trained rats to first run a 20-foot pattern through a maze to obtain food, then a 40-foot pattern. When all running was then placed on extinction, the rats initially persisted with the 40-foot pattern, then returned to the 20-foot pattern before quitting. It was as though they were attempting to make the food reappear by repeating a pattern that

---

[1]Although we have treated them separately in this text, the increase in response variability during extinction is sometimes regarded as one aspect of an extinction burst. In other words, an extinction burst can be defined as an increase in the rate, intensity, and variability of responding following the implementation of an extinction procedure.

had earlier been effective. Resurgence resembles the psychoanalytic concept of *regression*, which is the reappearance of immature behavior in reaction to frustration or conflict. Thus, a husband faced with a wife who largely ignores him might begin spending increasing amounts of time at his parents' house. Faced with the lack of reinforcement in his marriage, he returns to a setting that once provided a rich source of reinforcement.

6. **Depression.** Extinction can also lead to depressive-like symptoms. For example, Klinger, Barta, and Kemble (1974) had rats run down an alleyway for food and then immediately followed this with an assessment of the rats' activity level in an open field test. Thus, each session consisted of two phases: (1) running down an alleyway for food, followed by (2) placement in an open area that the rats could freely explore. When extinction was implemented on the alleyway task, activity in the open field test first increased to above normal, then decreased to below normal, followed by a return to normal (see Figure 8.1).

FIGURE 8.1   Changes in rats' activity level in an open field test as a function of extinction on a preceding straight-alley maze task. (*Source:* Adapted from "Cyclic activity changes during extinction in rats: A potential model of depression," by E. Klinger, S. G. Barta, & E. D. Kemble, 1974, *Animal Learning and Behavior,* 2, pp. 313–316. Copyright © 1974 by the Psychonomic Society. Adapted with permission.)

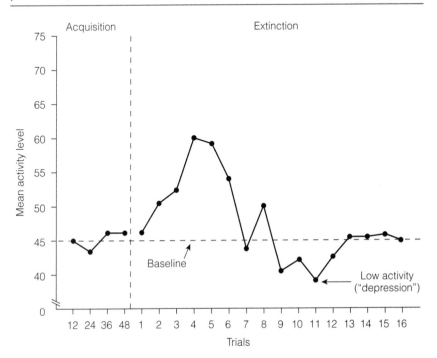

Klinger et al. (1974) noted that low activity is a common symptom of depression; moreover, depression is often associated with loss of reinforcement (Lewinsohn, 1974). For example, if someone dies, the people for whom that individual was a major source of reinforcement are essentially experiencing extinction, and they will likely become depressed for a period of time. And one symptom of such depression is a low level of activity. The fact that a similar process occurs in rats suggests that a temporary period of depression (accompanied by a decrease in activity) following the loss of a major reinforcer should be regarded as a normal aspect of disengagement from that reinforcer (Klinger, 1975).

These various side effects of extinction can obviously be an impediment to successfully implementing an extinction procedure. Note, too, how these side effects can be inadvertently strengthened if one suddenly gives in and provides the subject with the sought-after reinforcer. Imagine, for example, Bobbie has learned that by begging at the supermarket he can usually entice his mother into buying him some candy. One day, however, Bobbie's mother decides to withhold the candy, with the result that he becomes very loud and persistent (an extinction burst) as well as emotionally upset and aggressive. If Bobbie's mother now gives in and buys him some candy, what type of behavior has she reinforced? Obviously not the behavior of being polite and well mannered in the supermarket. In this way, parents sometimes inadvertently shape their children into throwing severe temper tantrums, a tendency that could have serious consequences if maintained later in life. After all, what the media calls "road rage"—or "air rage" when passengers become belligerent on airline flights—might, in many cases, be simply an adult version of a temper tantrum, a behavior pattern that was inadvertently established in childhood. (See also discussion of *partial reinforcement effect* later in this chapter.)

QUICK QUIZ B

1. Krissy asked her father to buy her a toy, as he usually did, when they were out shopping. Unfortunately, Krissy's father had spent all of his money on building supplies and told her that he had nothing left for a toy. The first thing that might happen is that Krissy will (increase/decrease) _____ the frequency with which she asks for a toy and ask for a toy with a (louder/softer) _____ voice. This process is known as an e_____ b_____.

2. Krissy is also likely to ask for the toy in many different ways because extinction often results in an increase in the v_____ of a behavior.

3. Krissy might also begin showing a lot of e_____ behavior, including a_____.

4. When her father still refuses to buy her a toy, Krissy suddenly asks her dad to pick her up and carry her, something she has not asked for since she was much smaller. This could be an example of r_____, or what psychoanalysts call r_____.

5. On the trip home, Krissy, who never did get a toy, sat silently and stared out the window. This is not surprising, because extinction is sometimes followed by a temporary period of d_____.

ADVICE FOR THE LOVELORN

Dear Dr. Dee,

*Why is it that I act so weird whenever I break up with a guy? One day I am intent on rees-
tablishing the relationship, the next day I am so angry I don't ever want to see him again.
Then I usually get all depressed and lie around in bed for days on end.*

What a Rollercoaster

Dear What,

Sounds like extinction to me. The loss of a relationship is the loss of a major reinforcer in
your life. You therefore go through many of the side effects that accompany extinction.
You experience an extinction burst ("intent on reestablishing the relationship"), become
angry ("don't ever want to see the guy again"), and eventually get depressed.

Solution: Extinction effects are a normal part of life, so don't expect that you shouldn't feel
something. But you might be able to moderate your feelings a bit so they are not quite so
painful. In particular, stay active as much as possible and seek out alternative sources of
reinforcement. And try to avoid lying in bed for days on end, as this will only further reduce
the reinforcement in your life. In fact, lying in bed for days on end will make just about
anyone depressed, regardless of his or her relationship status!

Behaviorally yours,

Dr. Dee

Resistance to Extinction

Resistance to extinction is the extent to which responding persists after an
extinction procedure has been implemented. A response that is very persistent
is said to have high resistance to extinction, while a response that disappears
quickly is said to have low resistance to extinction (see Figure 8.2). For example, a dog that continues to beg for food at the dinner table for 20 minutes
after everyone has stopped feeding, it is displaying much higher resistance to
extinction than does a dog that stops begging after 5 minutes.

Resistance to extinction can be affected by a number of factors, including
the following:

Schedule of Reinforcement. The schedule of reinforcement is the
most important factor influencing resistance to extinction. According to the

FIGURE 8.2 Two hypothetical extinction curves. Following an initial period of reinforcement at the start of the session, the extinction procedure is implemented. This results in a brief extinction burst, followed by a decline in responding. The decline is more gradual in the top example than in the bottom example and hence illustrates greater resistance to extinction.

partial reinforcement effect, behavior that has been maintained on an intermittent (partial) schedule of reinforcement will extinguish more slowly than behavior that has been maintained on a continuous schedule. Thus, lever pressing that has been reinforced on an FR 10 schedule will take longer to extinguish than lever pressing that has been reinforced on a CRF (FR 1) schedule. Similarly, lever pressing that has been reinforced on an FR 100 schedule will take longer to extinguish than lever pressing that has been reinforced on an FR 10 schedule. Resistance to extinction is particularly strong when behavior has been maintained on a variable ratio schedule (G. S. Reynolds, 1975); thus, a VR 20 schedule will produce greater resistance to extinction than an FR 20 schedule.

One way of thinking about the partial reinforcement effect is that the less frequent the reinforcer, the longer it takes the animal to "discover" that reinforcement is no longer available (Mowrer & Jones, 1945). It obviously takes much longer for an animal to discover that reinforcement is no longer available when it has been receiving reinforcement on, say, a VR 100 schedule than on a CRF schedule. A less mentalistic interpretation is that there is a much greater contrast between a CRF schedule and extinction than between a VR 100 schedule and extinction. On a VR 100 schedule, the animal has learned to emit many responses in the absence of reinforcement; hence, it is more persistent in its responding when an extinction procedure is implemented (E. J. Capaldi, 1966).

The partial reinforcement effect helps account for certain types of annoying or maladaptive behaviors that are difficult to eliminate. Dogs that beg for food are often extremely persistent. Paradoxically, this is sometimes the result of previously unsuccessful attempts at extinction. Imagine, for example, that all family members agree to stop feeding the dog at the dinner table. If one person nevertheless slips the dog a morsel when it is making a particularly big fuss, the begging will become both more intense and more persistent. This means that the next attempt at extinction will be even more difficult. Of course, the partial reinforcement effect also suggests a possible solution to this problem. If behavior that has been continuously reinforced is less resistant to extinction, then it might help to first spend several days reinforcing each instance of begging. Then, when extinction is implemented, the dog's tendency to beg might extinguish more rapidly (Lerman & Iwata, 1996).

History of Reinforcement.   In general, the more reinforcers an individual has received for a behavior, the greater the resistance to extinction. Lever pressing will extinguish more rapidly if a rat has previously earned only 10 reinforcers for lever pressing than if it has earned 100 reinforcers. Likewise, a child who has only recently picked up the habit of whining for candy should stop relatively quickly when the behavior is placed on extinction, as opposed to a child who has been at it for several weeks. From a practical perspective, this means it is much easier to extinguish an unwanted behavior, such as whining for candy, when it first becomes evident (hence the saying, "nip it in the bud"). There is, however, a limit in the extent to which further reinforcers will produce increased resistance to extinction. Furomoto (1971), for example, found that resistance to extinction for key pecking in pigeons reached its maximum after about 1,000 reinforcers.

Magnitude of the Reinforcer.   The magnitude of the reinforcer can also affect resistance to extinction. For example, large-magnitude reinforcers sometimes result in greater resistance to extinction than small-magnitude reinforcers. Thus, lever pressing might take longer to extinguish following a training period in which each reinforcer consisted of a large pellet of food than if the reinforcer were a small pellet of food. Lever pressing might also take longer to extinguish if the reinforcer was a highly preferred food item than if it were a less-preferred food item. From a practical perspective, this means that a dog's behavior of begging at the dinner table might extinguish more easily if you first spend several days feeding it small bites of less-preferred morsels (Lerman & Iwata, 1996). Unfortunately, one problem with this strategy is that the effect of reinforcer magnitude on resistance to extinction is not entirely consistent. In fact, researchers sometimes find that smaller reinforcers result in greater resistance to extinction (e.g., Ellis, 1962).

Degree of Deprivation. Not surprisingly, the degree to which an organism is deprived of a reinforcer also affects resistance to extinction. In general, the greater the level of deprivation, the greater the resistance to extinction (Perin, 1942). A rat that is only slightly hungry will cease lever pressing more quickly than a rat that is very hungry. This suggests yet another strategy for extinguishing a dog's tendency to beg at the table: Feed the dog before the meal.

Previous Experience With Extinction. When sessions of extinction are alternated with sessions of reinforcement, the greater the number of prior exposures to extinction, the quicker the behavior will extinguish during subsequent exposures (Bullock & Smith, 1953). For example, if a rat experiences several sessions of extinction randomly interspersed with several sessions of reinforcement, it will eventually learn to stop lever pressing soon after the start of an extinction session. The rat has learned that if it has not received reinforcement soon after the start of a session, then it is likely that no reinforcement will be forthcoming for the remainder of the session. Similarly, a child might learn that if he does not receive candy within the first 10 minutes of whining during a trip to the supermarket, he might as well give up for the day.

Distinctive Signal for Extinction. Extinction is greatly facilitated when there is a distinctive stimulus that signals the onset of extinction. As briefly noted in Chapter 6, such a stimulus is called a *discriminative stimulus for extinction*; it is more fully discussed later in this chapter.

QUICK QUIZ C

1. R_____ to _____ is the extent to which responding persists after an extinction procedure is implemented.

2. According to the p_____ r_____ effect, responses that have been maintained on an intermittent schedule will show (more/less) _____ resistance to extinction than responses that have been reinforced on a continuous schedule.

3. Among the four basic intermittent schedules, the (use the abbreviation) _____ schedule is particularly likely to produce strong resistance to extinction.

4. In general, a behavior that has been reinforced many times is likely to be (much easier/more difficult) _____ to extinguish.

5. Resistance to extinction is generally greater when the behavior that is being extinguished has been reinforced with a (high/low) _____-magnitude reinforcer, though the opposite effect has also been found.

6. In general, there is a(n) (direct/inverse) _____ relationship between resistance to extinction and the organism's level of deprivation for the reinforcer.

7. Previous experience with extinction, as well as a distinctive signal for extinction, tends to produce a(n) (increase/decrease) _____ in resistance to extinction.

Spontaneous Recovery

Although extinction is a reliable process for weakening a behavior, it would be a mistake to assume that once a response has been extinguished, it has been permanently eliminated. As with extinction of a classically conditioned response, extinction of an operant response is likely to be followed by spontaneous recovery (Skinner, 1938). As you will recall, *spontaneous recovery* is the reappearance of an extinguished response following a rest period after extinction. Suppose, for example, that we extinguish a rat's behavior of lever pressing. The next day, when we place the rat back in the experimental chamber, it will probably commence lever pressing again. It is almost as though it has forgotten that lever pressing no longer produces food. Nevertheless, the behavior will likely be weaker than it was at the start of the extinction phase the day before, and will extinguish more quickly given that we continue to withhold reinforcement. Similarly, on the third day, we might again find some recovery of lever pressing, but it will be even weaker than the day before and will extinguish even more quickly. This process might repeat itself several times, with each recovery being weaker and more readily extinguished than the previous one. Following several extinction sessions, we will eventually reach the point at which spontaneous recovery does not occur (apart from a few tentative lever presses every once in a while), and the behavior will have essentially been eliminated (see Figure 8.3). Likewise, a child's tendency to throw tantrums in the supermarket to obtain candy might require several visits to the supermarket during which a tantrum does not produce candy before the behavior is fully eliminated. In short, when applying an extinction procedure, you have to be persistent.

Skinner (1950) proposed that spontaneous recovery is a function of discriminative stimuli (S^Ds) associated with the start of the session. For an experimental rat, the experience of being taken from the home cage, weighed, and placed in an operant chamber is itself a signal for the availability of food. ("Oh, goody,

FIGURE 8.3 Graph of hypothetical data illustrating spontaneous recovery across repeated sessions of extinction.

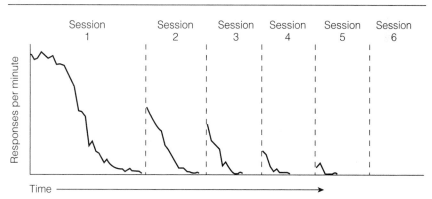

I'm being weighed. That means I'll soon be able to earn some food by lever pressing.") Only after repeated exposure to these events without receiving food does the rat at last fail to show the learned behavior. Similarly, for the child who has learned to throw tantrums in the supermarket to receive candy, entering the supermarket is itself an S^D for the availability of candy. The child will require repeated exposure to the sequence of entering the supermarket, throwing a tantrum, and not receiving candy before this cue becomes ineffective.

1. S_____ _____ is the reappearance of an extinguished response at a later point in time.

2. In general, each time this occurs, the behavior is (weaker/stronger) _____ than before and extinguishes (more/less) _____ readily.

3. Skinner believed that this phenomenon is a function of _____ that are uniquely associated with the start of the session.

Differential Reinforcement of Other Behavior

The process of extinction can be greatly facilitated by both extinguishing the target behavior *and* reinforcing the occurrence of a replacement behavior. This procedure is known as ***differential reinforcement of other behavior (DRO),*** which is the reinforcement of any behavior other than the target behavior that is being extinguished. One variant of this procedure, known as *differential reinforcement of incompatible behavior (DRI)*, involves reinforcing a behavior that is specifically incompatible with the target behavior. Paying attention to a child only if he is doing something other than fighting with his little sister is a DRO procedure; paying attention to him only when he is interacting in a friendly manner with his little sister is a DRI procedure.

DRO and DRI procedures tend to be more effective than simple extinction procedures because the target behavior is weakened both by the lack of reinforcement for that behavior and by the reinforcement of alternative behaviors that come to replace it. Hence, it is easier to extinguish a child's habit of whining for candy at a supermarket if you not only withdraw the reinforcement for whining but also explicitly reinforce well-mannered behaviors. Unlike a straight extinction procedure, in a DRO or DRI procedure the child is not being deprived of reinforcement within that setting; this approach will thereby reduce or eliminate possible side effects normally resulting from extinction. Note that the reinforcement for well-mannered behavior can include the very candy for which the child has been whining. He can therefore still obtain candy, but only if he exhibits a proper pattern of behavior. (The candy, of course, can then be gradually phased out—or replaced by a healthier treat—as the appropriate behavior becomes firmly established.)

A particularly useful type of differential reinforcement procedure is called *functional communication training* (or *differential reinforcement of functional communication*). Many unwanted behaviors occur because the child is attempting to attain an important reinforcer, such as attention, but is doing

And Furthermore

Extinction of Bedtime Tantrums in Young Children

A common difficulty faced by many parents is training children to go to bed at night without fussing or throwing a tantrum. The problem often arises because parents pay attention to a child who is throwing a tantrum and getting out of bed, thereby inadvertently reinforcing the very behavior that is annoying them. Of course, the obvious solution to this problem is for the parents to place the child's tantrums on extinction by leaving the child alone in his or her room until he or she finally falls asleep. Research has in fact shown this to be a highly effective procedure. Rickert and Johnson (1988), for example, randomly assigned children to either a systematic ignoring condition (extinction), scheduled awakenings throughout the night (to comfort the child), or a control condition in which parents carried on as normal. In the systematic ignoring condition, the parents were told to initially check on their child's safety when the child made a fuss and then ignore all further cries. Results revealed that children who underwent the extinction procedure experienced considerably greater improvement in their sleep patterns than the children in the other two conditions.

Thus, extinction seems to be an effective treatment for this type of problem. Unfortunately, it suffers from a major drawback. Many parents find it impossible to totally ignore their children's persistent heartfelt pleas during the night, especially during the initial stages of treatment when such pleas are likely to be magnified in both intensity and duration (the typical extinction burst). As a result, "graduated extinction procedures" have been devised that are more acceptable to parents and less upsetting to the child. Adams and Rickert (1989), for example, instructed parents to wait for a predetermined period of time, based on what they felt was an acceptable duration, before responding to the child's calls. The parents were also instructed to comfort the child for only 15 seconds or less. Combined with a consistent bedtime routine, this less-stringent procedure was quite effective in helping many parents, and children, finally to get a good night's sleep (see Mindell, 1999, for a review).

so inappropriately. If the child is instead taught to communicate his or her need for the reinforcer in a socially appropriate manner ("Gee Mom, I'm really bored. Can you help me find something interesting to do?"), then the frequency of inappropriate behaviors (such as misbehaving to get mom's attention) is likely to decrease. So in *functional communication training*, the behavior of clearly and appropriately communicating one's desires is differentially reinforced (e.g., Durand, 1990).

Differential reinforcement procedures can reduce many of the unwanted side effects of extinction, such as frustration and aggression. As a general rule, therefore, whenever one attempts to extinguish an unwanted behavior, one should also provide plenty of reinforcement for more appropriate behavior (Miltenberger, 1997).

1. The procedure of reinforcing all behaviors except the particular target behavior that you wish to extinguish is known as d_____ r_____ of o_____ behavior (abbreviated _____).

2. The procedure of reinforcing only those behaviors that are specifically incompatible with the target behavior that you wish to extinguish is known as _____ _____ of _____ behavior (abbreviated _____).

3. Giving a dog a treat whenever it does something other than jump up on visitors as they enter the house is an example of a (use the abbreviation) _____ procedure. Giving a dog a treat for sitting quietly when visitors enter the house is an example of a _____ procedure.

4. DRO and DRI procedures are useful in that they tend to reduce many of the side effects associated with an _____ procedure.

Stimulus Control

As previously noted, when a behavior has been consistently reinforced in the presence of a certain stimulus, that stimulus will begin to affect the probability of the behavior. This stimulus, known as a discriminative stimulus (S^D), does not automatically elicit the behavior in the manner of a CS eliciting a reflex; it merely signals the availability of reinforcement, thereby increasing the probability that the behavior will occur. Such behavior is then said to be under *stimulus control,* meaning that the presence of a discriminative stimulus reliably affects the probability of the behavior.

For example, if a 2,000-Hz tone signals that lever pressing will lead to food:

$$\textbf{2,000-Hz Tone: } \textit{Lever press} \rightarrow \textbf{Food}$$
$$S^D \qquad\qquad R \qquad\qquad S^R$$

and the rat thus learns to press the lever only in the presence of the tone, the behavior of lever pressing is said to be under stimulus control. Similarly, the sound of a ringing telephone has strong stimulus control over whether people will pick it up and say hello. People never answer phones that are not ringing and almost always answer phones that are ringing. Here are some other examples of stimulus control (with the S^D italicized):

- At *red lights*, we stop; at *green lights*, we proceed.
- If *someone smiles at us*, we smile at them.
- In an *elevator*, we stand facing the front rather than the back.
- When we hear an *ambulance siren behind us*, we pull our car over to the side of the road and slow down or stop.
- When the *professor begins lecturing*, students cease talking among themselves (hint, hint).[2]

_____

[2]Some of these examples also represent a special type of stimulus control known as an *instructional control* ("Do not drive through red lights, or you will get a ticket!"). The concept of instructional control is discussed in the section on rule-governed behavior in Chapter 12.

In this section, we will look more closely at discriminative stimuli and their effects on behavior. Note that some of the principles discussed, such as stimulus generalization, represent operant versions of principles discussed in earlier chapters on classical conditioning.

Stimulus Generalization and Discrimination

In our discussion of classical conditioning, we noted that stimuli that are similar to a CS can also elicit a CR, by a process known as stimulus generalization. A similar process occurs in operant conditioning. In operant conditioning, *stimulus generalization* is the tendency for an operant response to be emitted in the presence of a stimulus that is similar to an S^D. In general, the more similar the stimulus, the stronger the response. Take, for example, a rat that has learned to lever press for food whenever it hears a 2,000-Hz tone. If we then present the rat with a series of tones that vary in pitch, we will find that it also presses the lever in the presence of these other tones, particularly in the presence of a tone that is similar to the original S^D. Thus, the rat will display a higher rate of lever pressing in the presence of an 1,800- or 2,200-Hz tone, both of which are more similar to the original S^D, than in the presence of a 1,200- or 2,800-Hz tone, which are less similar.

This tendency to generalize across different stimuli can be depicted in a *generalization gradient,* which is a graphic description of the strength of responding in the presence of stimuli that are similar to the S^D and that vary along a continuum. As shown in Figure 8.4, gradients can vary in their degree of steepness. A relatively steep gradient indicates that rate of responding drops sharply as the stimuli become increasingly different from the S^D, while a relatively flat gradient indicates that responding drops gradually as the stimuli become increasingly different from the S^D. In other words, a flat gradient indicates more generalization, while a steep gradient indicates less generalization.[3]

As in classical conditioning, the opposite of stimulus generalization in operant conditioning is *stimulus discrimination,* the tendency for an operant response to be emitted more in the presence of one stimulus than another. More generalization means less discrimination, and less generalization means more discrimination. Thus, a steep gradient indicates weak generalization and strong discrimination, whereas a flat gradient indicates strong generalization and weak discrimination.

---

[3]Generalization gradients are also used to indicate the extent of stimulus generalization in classical conditioning. Imagine, for example, that the 2,000-Hz tone in Figure 8.4 is a CS that has been associated with food and now elicits a conditioned salivary response. A steep generalization gradient would indicate weak generalization of the CR across tones, while a flat gradient would indicate strong generalization of the CR across tones.

FIGURE 8.4 Two hypothetical generalization gradients depicting rate of lever pressing in the presence of tones that vary in pitch between 1,200 and 2,800 Hz ("Hertz" is the number of sound waves per second generated by a sound source). In both examples, tones that are more similar to the original S^D (a 2,000-Hz tone) are associated with stronger responding. However, generalization is much greater in the bottom gradient, which is relatively flat, than in the top gradient, which is relatively steep.

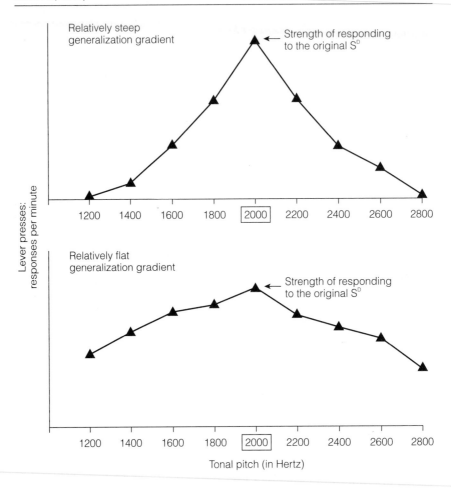

Tonal pitch (in Hertz)

1. A behavior is said to be under s_timulus_____ c_ontrol_____ when it is highly likely to occur in the presence of a certain stimulus.

2. In operant conditioning, the term s_timulus_____ g_enereliation_____ refers to the tendency for a response to be emitted in the presence of stimuli that are similar to the original ___S^D_____. The opposite process, called s_timulus_____ d_iscrimination__, refers to the tendency for the response to be emitted more in the presence of one stimulus than another.

3. In general, stimuli that are (more/less) __more__ similar produce stronger generalization.

4. A _generalization_ _gradient_ _____ indicates the strength of responding to stimuli that vary along a continuum.

5. In a graph that depicts a _generalization_ _gradient_ _____, a relatively flat line indicates more _generalization_ and less _discrimination_. A relatively steep line indicates more _discrimination_ and less _generalization_.

6. When Jonathan looked at his watch and noticed that it was 12:30 P.M., he decided that it was time for lunch. Jonathan's eating behavior appears to be under strong _stimulus_ _control_.

7. Jonathan always goes for lunch around 12:30, with the range being somewhere between 12:25 and 12:35 P.M. The generalization gradient for this behavior across various points in time would therefore be much (steeper/flatter) _steeper_ than if the range was between 12:00 and 1:00. This indicates a pattern of strong (discrimination/generalization) _discrimination_ and weak _generalization_ for Jonathan's lunch-going behavior across different points in time.

Discrimination training, as applied to operant conditioning, involves reinforcement of responding in the presence of one stimulus (the S^D) and not another stimulus. The latter is called a **discriminative stimulus for extinction,** which is a stimulus that signals the absence of reinforcement. A discriminative stimulus for extinction is typically given the symbol S$^\Delta$ (pronounced "es-delta"; remember that one can also use the symbol S+ in place of S^D and S− in place of S$^\Delta$). For example, if we wish to train a rat to discriminate between a 2,000-Hz tone and a 1,200-Hz tone, we would present the two tones in random order. Whenever the 2,000-Hz tone sounds, a lever press produces food; whenever the 1200-Hz tone sounds, a lever press does *not* produce food.

> **2,000-Hz Tone:** *Lever press* → **Food**
> S^D R S^R
> **1,200-Hz Tone:** *Lever press* → **No food**
> S$^\Delta$ R −

After repeated exposure to these contingencies, the rat will soon learn to press the lever in the presence of the 2,000-Hz tone and not in the presence of the 1,200-Hz tone. We can then say that the rat's behavior of lever pressing is under strong stimulus control.

In similar fashion, if the manager where you work complies with your requests for a day off only when he appears to be in a good mood and does not comply when he appears to be in a bad mood, you learn to make requests only when he is in a good mood. The manager's appearance exerts strong stimulus control over the probability of your making a request. In this sense, one characteristic of people who have good social skills is that they can make fine discriminations between social cues—such as facial expression and body posture—which enables them to maximize the amount of social reinforcement (and minimize the amount of social punishment) obtained during their exchanges with others. Likewise, college roommates are more likely to live in harmony to the extent that they learn to discriminate each other's social cues and modify their actions appropriately.

1. In a discrimination training procedure, responses that occur in the presence of the (use the symbols) S^D, $S+$ are reinforced, while those that occur in the presence of the S^{Δ}, $S-$ are not reinforced. This latter stimulus is called a d_iscriminative_ stimulus_ for e_xtinction_.

2. An "Open for Business" sign is an _____ for entering the store and making a purchase, while a "Closed for Business" sign is an _____ for entering the store and making a purchase.

The Peak Shift Effect

An unusual effect often produced by discrimination training is the peak shift effect. According to the *peak shift effect,* the peak of a generalization gradient following discrimination training will shift from the S^D to a stimulus that is further removed from the S^{Δ} (Hanson, 1959). This constitutes an exception to the general principle that the strongest response in a generalization gradient occurs in the presence of the original S^D.

Suppose, for example, that we first train a rat to press a lever in the presence of a 2,000-Hz tone. We then conduct a test for generalization across a range of tones varying in pitch between 1,200 and 2,800 Hz, and we find a generalization gradient like that shown in the top panel of Figure 8.5. We then submit the rat to a discrimination training procedure in which we reinforce lever pressing in the presence of a 2,000-Hz tone (S^D) and not in the presence of a 1,200-Hz tone (S^{Δ}). When this has been successfully accomplished (the rat responds only in the presence of the 2,000-Hz tone and not in the presence of the 1,200-Hz tone), we again test for generalization across a range of tones. What we are likely to find with this rat is a generalization gradient something like that depicted in the bottom panel of Figure 8.5. Look carefully at this gradient. How does it differ from the gradient in the top portion of the figure, which represents generalization in the absence of discrimination training?

One obvious difference is that, with discrimination training, the gradient drops off more sharply on the side toward the S^{Δ}, which simply means that this rat strongly discriminates between the S^{Δ} and the S^D. But what is the other difference between the two graphs? Before discrimination training (the top panel), the strongest response occurs to the S^D (the 2,000-Hz tone). Following discrimination training (the bottom panel), the strongest response shifts away from the S^D to a stimulus that lies in a direction opposite to the S^{Δ} (in this case, it shifts to a 2,200-Hz tone). This shift in the peak of the generalization gradient is the peak shift effect.

FIGURE 8.5 Illustration of a peak shift effect following discrimination training. Prior to discrimination training (top panel), the gradient is relatively flat. Following discrimination training (bottom panel), in which a 1,200-Hz tone has been established as an S^Δ, the strongest response occurs not in the presence of the S^D (the 2,000-Hz tone), but in the presence of a stimulus further removed from the S^Δ. The gradient in the bottom panel therefore illustrates the peak shift effect.

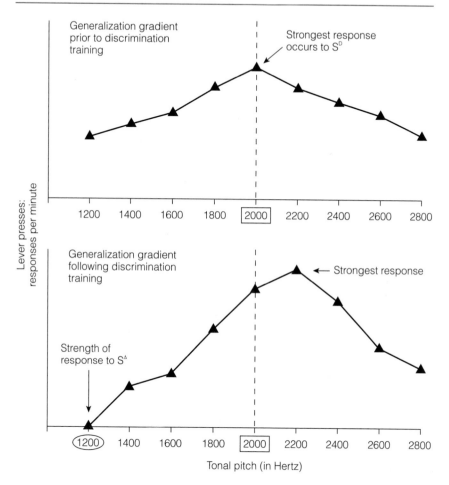

Perhaps a fanciful example will help clarify the peak shift effect. Suppose that Mr. Shallow identifies women entirely on the basis of how extraverted versus introverted they are. Jackie, with whom he had a very boring relationship, was an introvert (an S^Δ), while Dana, with whom he had a wonderfully exciting relationship, was an extravert (an S^D). He then moves to a new city and begins touring the singles bars seeking a new mate. According to the peak shift effect, he will likely seek out a woman who is even more extraverted than Dana.

One explanation for the peak shift effect is that during discrimination training, subjects respond in terms of the relative, rather than the absolute values, of stimuli (Kohler, 1918/1939). Thus, according to this interpretation, the rat does not learn merely that a 2,000-Hz tone indicates food and a 1,200-Hz tone indicates no food; rather, it learns that a higher-pitched tone indicates food and a lower-pitched tone indicates no food. Given a choice, the rat therefore emits the strongest response in the presence of a tone that has an even higher pitch than the original S^D. Likewise, Mr. Shallow chooses a woman who is even more extraverted than Dana because greater extraversion is associated with a better relationship.

Another explanation for the peak shift effect is that, despite discrimination training, the S^D is still somewhat similar to the S^Δ and has acquired some of its inhibitory properties (Spence, 1937). From this perspective, the 2,000-Hz tone (the S^D) is somewhat similar to the 1,200-Hz tone (the S^Δ), making the 2,000-Hz tone slightly less attractive than it would have been if the S^Δ had never been trained. Thus, a tone that has a slightly higher pitch than 2,000 Hz, and is thereby less similar to the 1,200-Hz tone, will result in the highest rate of responding. Likewise, Mr. Shallow seeks a woman who is very extraverted because he is attempting to find a woman who is even more dissimilar from Jackie, with whom he had such a poor relationship.[4]

1. In the peak shift effect, the peak of a generalization gradient, following discrimination training _____, shifts away from the _discriminative stimulus_ to a stimulus that is further removed from the S^Δ _____.

2. If an orange key light is trained as an S^D in a key pecking task with pigeons, and the pigeons are then exposed to other key colors ranging from yellow on one end of the continuum to red on the other (with orange in the middle), then the peak of the generalization gradient will likely be to a (yellowish-orange/orange/orange-reddish) _orange-reddish_ key light.

3. If a pigeon undergoes discrimination training in which a yellow key light is explicitly established as an S^Δ and an orange key light is explicitly established as the S^D, the strongest response in the generalization gradient will likely be to a (yellowish-orange/orange/orange-reddish) _orange-reddish_ key light. This effect is known as the _peak_ _shift_ effect.

Multiple Schedules and Behavioral Contrast

Stimulus control is often studied using a type of complex schedule known as a multiple schedule. A **multiple schedule** consists of two or more independent schedules presented in sequence, each resulting in reinforcement and each having a distinctive S^D. For example, a pigeon might first be presented with a red key that signals an FI 30-sec schedule, completion of which

---

[4]The peak shift effect is also found in classical conditioning following discrimination training between a CS+ and a CS−. For example, if the CS+ was a 2,000-Hz tone and the CS− was a 1,200-Hz tone, what would the peak shift effect consist of?

results in food. The key light then changes to green, which signals a VI 30-sec schedule, completion of which also results in food. These two schedules can be presented in either random or alternating order, or for set periods of time (such as 2 minutes on the red FI 30-sec schedule followed by 2 minutes on the green VI 30-sec schedule followed by another 2 minutes on the red FI 30-sec schedule, etc.). The following schematic shows the two schedules presented in alternating order:

$$\begin{array}{ccccccc} \textbf{FI 30-sec} & & & & \textbf{VI 30-sec} & & \\ \textbf{Red key: } \textit{Key peck} \rightarrow \textbf{Food/Green key: } \textit{Key peck} \rightarrow \textbf{Food/Red key: etc.} \\ S^D & R & S^R & S^D & R & S^R & S^D \end{array}$$

Note that a multiple schedule differs from a chained schedule in that a chained schedule requires that all of the component schedules be completed before the sought-after reinforcer is delivered. For example, on a *chain* FI 30-sec VI 30-sec schedule, both the FI and VI components must be completed to obtain food. On a *multiple* FI 30-sec VI 30-sec schedule, however, completion of each component schedule results in food.

On a multiple schedule, stimulus control is demonstrated when the subject responds differently in the presence of the S^Ds associated with the different schedules. For example, with sufficient experience on a multiple FI 30-sec VI 30-sec schedule, a pigeon will likely show a scalloped pattern of responding on the red key signaling the FI component, and a moderate, steady pattern of responding on the green key signaling the VI component. The pigeon's response pattern on each key color will be the appropriate pattern for the schedule of reinforcement that is in effect on that key.

1. On a ___multiple___ schedule, two or more schedules are presented (sequentially/simultaneously) _sequentially_, with each resulting in a r_esponse_ and having its own distinctive _discriminative stimulus; s^D_

2. This type of schedule differs from a chained schedule in that a _reinforcement_ is provided after each component schedule is completed.

3. On a multiple FR 50 VR 50 schedule, we are likely to find a high rate of response on the (FR/VR/both) _both_ component(s) along with a p_ost_ _reinforcement_ pause on the (FR/VR/both) _FR_ component(s).

QUICK QUIZ I

An interesting phenomenon that can be investigated using multiple schedules is behavioral contrast. *Behavioral contrast* occurs when a change in the *rate of reinforcement* on one component of a multiple schedule produces an opposite change in the *rate of response* on another component (G. S. Reynolds, 1961). In other words, as the rate of reinforcement on one component changes in one direction, the rate of response on the other component changes in the other direction.

There are two basic contrast effects: positive and negative. In a *negative contrast effect*, an increase in the rate of *reinforcement* on one component produces a decrease in the rate of *response* on the other component. Suppose, for example, that a pigeon first receives several sessions of exposure to a multiple VI 60-sec VI 60-sec schedule:

VI 60-sec   **VI 60-sec**
Red key: *Key peck* → **Food/Green key:** *Key peck* → **Food/etc.**

Because both schedules are the same, the pigeon responds equally on both the red key and the green key. Following this, the VI 60-sec component on the red key is changed to VI 30-sec, which provides a higher rate of reinforcement (on average, two reinforcers per minute as opposed to one reinforcer per minute):

VI 30-sec   **VI 60-sec**
Red key: *Key peck* → **Food/Green key:** *Key peck* → **Food/etc.**

With more reinforcement now available on the red key, the pigeon will decrease its rate of response on the green key, which is associated with the unchanged VI 60-sec component. Simply put, because the first component in the sequence is now more attractive, the second component seems relatively less attractive. The situation is analogous to a woman whose husband has suddenly become much more affectionate and caring at home; as a result, she spends less time flirting with other men at work. The men at work seem relatively less attractive compared to her Romeo at home.

In *positive behavioral contrast,* a decrease in rate of *reinforcement* on one component results in an increase in rate of *response* on the other component. If, for example, on a multiple VI 60-sec VI 60-sec schedule:

VI 60-sec   **VI 60-sec**
Red key: *Key peck* → **Food/Green key:** *Key peck* → **Food/etc.**

the first VI 60-sec component is suddenly changed to VI 120-sec:

VI 120-sec   **VI 60-sec**
Red key: *Key peck* → **Food/Green key:** *Key peck* → **Food/etc.**

the pigeon will increase its rate of response on the unchanged VI 60-sec component. As one component becomes less attractive (changing from VI 60-sec to VI 120-sec), the unchanged component becomes relatively more attractive. The situation is analogous to the woman whose husband has become less caring and affectionate at home; as a result, she spends more time flirting with other men at work. The men at work seem relatively more attractive compared to the dud she has at home.

Positive contrast effects are also evident when the change in one component of the multiple schedule involves not a decrease in the amount of reinforcement but implementation of a punisher, such as a mild electric shock. As the one alternative suddenly becomes punishing, the remaining alternative, which is still reinforcing, is viewed as even more attractive (Brethower & Reynolds, 1962). This might explain what happens in some volatile relationships in which couples report strong overall feelings of affection for each other (Gottman, 1994). The intermittent periods of aversiveness seem to heighten the couple's appreciation of each other during periods of affection. Such relationships can therefore thrive, *given* that the positive aspects of the relationship significantly outweigh the negative aspects.[5]

> ### Warning
>
> Remember that with positive and negative contrast, we are concerned with how changing the rate of *reinforcement* on the first component of a multiple schedule affects the rate of *responding* on the second component. The rate of responding will, of course, also change on the first component because the schedule of reinforcement on that component has changed; but that is not surprising. What is surprising is the change in response rate on the second component, even though the schedule of reinforcement in that component has remained the same. Thus, it is the *change in response rate* on the second component that is the focus of concern in behavioral contrast.

QUICK QUIZ J

1. In _negative_ behavioral contrast, an increase in reinforcement on one alternative results in a(n) (increase/decrease) _decrease_ in (responding/reinforcement) _responding_ on the other alternative.

2. In _positive_ behavioral contrast, a decrease in reinforcement on one alternative results in a(n) _increase_ in _responding_ on the other alternative.

3. A pigeon that experiences a shift from a multiple FR 10 VI 60-sec schedule to a multiple FR 100 VI 60-sec schedule will likely (increase/decrease) _increase_ its rate of response on the VI 60-sec component.

4. When Levin (a lonely bachelor in Tolstoy's novel *Anna Karenina*) proposed to the beautiful young Kitty, she rejected him. Levin was devastated and decided to devote the rest of his life to his work. Kitty, in turn, was subsequently rejected by the handsome young military officer, Vronsky, whom she had mistakenly assumed was intent on marrying her. Kitty was devastated and deeply regretted having turned down Levin, whom she now perceived to be a fine man. A year later, they encountered each other at a social gathering. Relative to individuals who have not experienced such hardships in establishing a relationship, we would expect their affection for each other to be much (deeper/shallower) _deeper_ than normal. This can be seen as an example of (positive/negative) _positive_ behavioral contrast.

---

[5]Similar contrast effects occur when there is a shift in the magnitude of a reinforcer (Crespi, 1942). For example, rats that experience a sudden switch from receiving a small amount of food for running down an alleyway to receiving a large amount of food for running down the same alleyway will run faster for the large amount (a positive contrast effect) than if they had always received the large amount. And those that are shifted from a large amount to a small amount will run slower (a negative contrast effect).

An additional type of contrast effect is ***anticipatory contrast,*** in which the rate of response varies inversely with an upcoming ("anticipated") change in the rate of reinforcement (B. A. Williams, 1981). For example, Pliskoff (1963) found that pigeons increased their rate of responding for reinforcement when they were presented with a stimulus signaling that extinction was imminent. In other words, faced with the impending loss of reinforcement, the pigeons responded all the more vigorously for reinforcement while it was still available.

Anticipatory contrast seems analogous to what many of us have experienced—that things we are about to lose often seem to increase in value. For example, Lindsay views her relationship with Bryce as rather dull and uninteresting until she learns that Bryce might be romantically interested in another woman. Faced with the possibility that she might lose him, she now becomes intensely interested in him. Unfortunately, some people may use anticipatory contrast as a deliberate tactic to strengthen a partner's feelings of attachment. Read again the anecdote at the beginning of this chapter about Poppea's relationship with the Roman emperor Nero. In behavioral terms, Poppea first established herself as an effective reinforcer for Nero; then, to further increase her value, intermittently threatened to withdraw herself from Nero's company. In anticipation of possibly losing her, Nero became even more attached.

The occurrence of these contrast effects indicates that behaviors should not be viewed in isolation. Consequences for behavior in one setting can greatly affect the strength of behavior in another setting. Consider, for example, a young girl who is increasingly neglected at home, perhaps because her parents are going through a divorce. She might try to compensate for this circumstance by seeking more attention at school (a positive contrast effect), perhaps to the point of misbehaving. Although the parents might blame the school for her misbehavior, she is in fact reacting to the lack of reinforcement at home. Thus, to borrow a concept from humanistic psychology, behavior needs to be viewed in a holistic manner, with the recognition that behavior in one setting can be influenced by contingencies operating in other settings.

QUICK QUIZ K

1. An increase in the rate of responding for an available reinforcer when faced with the possibility of losing it in the near future is known as _anticipatory_ contrast.

2. If Jackie hears her mother say that it is getting close to her bedtime, she is likely to become (more/less) ___more___ involved in the computer game she is playing.

3. Vronsky (another character in Tolstoy's *Anna Karenina*) falls deeply in love with Anna, who is the wife of another man. For several months, they carry on a passionate affair. When Anna, however, finally leaves her husband to be with him, Vronsky finds that he soon becomes bored with their relationship. The fact that his feelings for Anna were much stronger when their relationship was more precarious is in keeping with the principle of _ant_ contrast.

And Furthermore

St. Neots' Margin

The anticipatory contrast effect described by Pliskoff (1963) reflects the pigeon's reaction to a potential difficulty—namely, the impending loss of a reinforcer. According to British writer Colin Wilson (1972), such difficulties may provide our lives with a sense of meaning when more pleasant stimuli have failed. Wilson's description of how he discovered this concept provides an interesting illustration.

> In 1954, I was hitch-hiking to Peterborough on a hot Saturday afternoon. I felt listless, bored and resentful: I didn't want to go to Peterborough—it was a kind of business trip—and I didn't particularly long to be back in London either. There was hardly any traffic on the road, but eventually I got a lift. Within ten minutes, there was an odd noise in the engine of the lorry. The driver said: 'I'm afraid something's gone wrong—I'll have to drop you off at the next garage.' I was too listless to care. I walked on, and eventually a second lorry stopped for me. Then occurred the absurd coincidence. After ten minutes or so, there was a knocking noise from *his* gearbox. When he said: 'It sounds as if something's gone wrong,' I thought: 'Oh *no!*' and then caught myself thinking it, and thought: 'That's the first definite reaction I've experienced today.' We drove on slowly—he was anxious to get to Peterborough, *and by this time, so was I.* He found that if he dropped speed to just under twenty miles an hour, the knocking noise stopped; as soon as he exceeded it, it started again. We both listened intently for any resumption of the trouble. Finally, as we were passing through a town called St. Neots, he said: 'Well, I think if we stay at this speed, we should make it.' And I felt a surge of delight. Then I thought: 'This is absurd. My situation hasn't *improved* since I got into the lorry—in fact, it has got worse, since he is now crawling along. All that has happened is that an inconvenience has been threatened and then the threat withdrawn. And suddenly, my boredom and indifference have vanished.' I formulated then the notion that there is a borderland or threshold of the mind that can be stimulated by pain or inconvenience, but not pleasure. (p. 27)

Wilson labeled the concept *St. Neots' margin* after the town they were driving through at the time. He proposes that such difficulties create "meaning" by forcing us to concentrate, and that the absence of such concentration makes life dull and uninteresting. But we can also view these difficulties as a type of contrast effect in which we are in danger of losing a reinforcer. As a result, we respond more vigorously for the reinforcer and value it more highly.

Contrast effects may therefore provide our lives with a sense of meaning that might otherwise be missing. Wilson describes, for example, how the writer Sartre claimed that he never felt so free as during the war when, as a member of the French Resistance, he was in constant danger of being arrested. In danger of losing his freedom, he truly appreciated his freedom. Consider too Balderston's (1924) play, *A Morality Play for the Leisured Class*, which recounts the story of a man who dies and finds himself in the afterlife. When a shining presence tells him that he can have any pleasure he desires by merely wishing it, he is overjoyed and fully indulges himself. He soon discovers, however, that things quickly lose their value when they are so easily attained. Facing an eternity of profound boredom (in which contrast effects are completely absent), he finally exclaims that he would rather be in hell—at which point the presence asks: "And wherever do you think you *are*, sir?"

Fading and Errorless Discrimination Learning

While discrimination training is an effective way for establishing stimulus control, it has its limitations. For example, during the process of learning to discriminate an S^D from an S^Δ, the subject will initially make several "mistakes" by responding in the presence of the S^Δ. Because such responses do not result in reinforcement, the subject is likely to become frustrated and display a great deal of emotional behavior. It would be helpful, therefore, if there were a method of discrimination training that minimized these effects.

Errorless discrimination training is a procedure that minimizes the number of errors (i.e., nonreinforced responses to the S^Δ) and reduces many of the adverse effects associated with discrimination training. It involves two aspects: (1) The S^Δ is introduced early in training, soon after the animal has learned to respond appropriately to the S^D, and (2) the S^Δ is presented in weak form to begin with and then gradually strengthened. This process of gradually altering the intensity of a stimulus is known as *fading*. (For example, one can *fade in* music by presenting it faintly to begin with and gradually turning up the volume, or *fade out* music by presenting it loudly to begin with and gradually turning down the volume.)

Terrace (1963a) used errorless discrimination training to establish a red–green discrimination in pigeons. The pigeons were first trained to peck a red key on a VI 60-sec schedule of reinforcement. As soon as this behavior was established, occasional 5-second periods of extinction were presented in which the key light was switched off. Since pigeons tend not to peck a dark key, the dark key was easily established as an effective S^Δ for not responding. The VI period and the extinction period were then gradually lengthened until they each lasted 3 minutes. Following this, the dark key was illuminated with a faint greenish hue that was slowly intensified. As the green key color was faded in (as an S^Δ) and gradually replaced the dark key, the pigeons emitted almost no responses toward it; that is, they made almost no errors. By comparison, pigeons that were exposed to standard discrimination training, in which the dark key was suddenly replaced by a brightly lit green key, made numerous responses on it before finally discriminating it from the red S^D. The pigeons exposed to the errorless procedure also showed few of the adverse side effects of discrimination training, such as emotional behavior.

Errorless procedures can also be used to transfer control from one type of stimulus to another. For example, Terrace (1963b) first trained pigeons to discriminate between a red key as the S^D and a green key as the S^Δ. He then gradually faded in a vertical line (the new S^D) on the red key and a horizontal line (the new S^Δ) on the green key, while at the same time fading out the colors. Eventually, the pigeons were pecking a colorless key that had a vertical line and not pecking a colorless key that had a horizontal line. With virtually no errors, stimulus control for pecking had been transferred from key color (red versus green) to line orientation (vertical versus horizontal).

Errorless discrimination training may have practical applications. For example, Haupt, Van Kirk, and Terraciano (1975) used an errorless procedure to enhance the learning of basic arithmetic skills. In their study, a 9-year-old girl who had a history of difficulties in basic arithmetic was given a series of addition problems using a standard drill procedure and a series of subtraction problems using an errorless procedure. The standard drill procedure for the addition problems consisted of presenting the problems on flash cards in which the answers were initially covered. If the child did not know the answer, the answer was uncovered and shown to her. The errorless procedure for the subtraction problems was similar except that the answer on each flash card was initially left exposed to view and then, over successive presentations, gradually blocked out by adding successive sheets of cellophane. The correct answer was thus initially available as a prompt for the correct answer and then gradually faded out. During a subsequent test, the girl made significantly fewer errors on the subtraction problems, for which the errorless procedure had been used, than on the addition problems, for which the standard drill procedure had been used.

Although errorless discrimination training might seem like the perfect answer to many unresolved problems in education, it has some serious drawbacks. Discriminations that have been established through errorless training are more difficult to modify at a later time. For example, Marsh and Johnson (1968) taught pigeons to discriminate between two key colors in which one color was the S^D and the other the S^Δ. Pigeons that had been taught to discriminate using an errorless procedure experienced extreme difficulty learning a new discrimination in which the meaning of the key colors was reversed (i.e., the color that had previously been the S^Δ now became the S^D, and vice versa). In contrast, pigeons that had learned the original discrimination in the normal error-filled way handled the reversal quite handily. Thus, although normal discrimination training has more adverse side effects compared to errorless discrimination training, it also results in greater flexibility when what is learned has to be modified later. For this reason, errorless procedures may be most useful in rote learning of basic facts, such as arithmetic and spelling, in which the substance of what is learned is unlikely to change. With material that requires greater flexibility, however, such as that typically found in most college-level courses, errorless learning might be a significant impediment (Pierce & Epling, 1999).[6]

1. In errorless_____ discrimination training, the S^Δ must be presented (early/later) _early___ in the training procedure, and at very (weak/strong) _weak____ intensity to begin with.

2. This type of discrimination training is likely to produce (more/less) _less____ emotional behavior compared to the standard form of discrimination training.

3. This type of discrimination training is also likely to produce behavior patterns that are (easy/difficult) _difficult___ to modify at a later point in time.

4. Gradually altering the intensity of a stimulus is called _fading___.

QUICK QUIZ L

---

[6]This accords with the more general finding, briefly mentioned in Chapter 1, that experiencing a certain amount of difficulty during the learning process can enhance long-term retention and understanding (Schmidt & Bjork, 1992).

Stimulus Control Procedures for the Study of Memory

There has been an enormous interest in recent decades in studying the cognitive underpinnings of behavior. Although much of this work has been carried out by cognitive psychologists with human subjects, some behaviorists have also participated by studying cognitive processes in animals. As noted in the introductory chapter, this field of study is known as *animal cognition,* or *comparative cognition,* and it can be seen as an outgrowth of Tolman's (1948) early work on cognitive maps.

Memory processes in animals have been a particularly important area of study in animal cognition, and one that might seem to present a rather unique challenge. With humans, we closely identify memory with various kinds of verbal behavior. For example, your professor will likely assess your memory for the material you are now studying by giving you a quiz or an exam at some future time when you will be required to verbally respond (in writing) to various verbal stimuli (questions). Animals, however, do not have such verbal ability, so how then can we study their memory?

In answering this question, we need to consider that the act of remembering is, to a large extent, a matter of stimulus control. For example, on a multiple-choice test, each question presents a series of statements (verbal stimuli), but only one of them corresponds to material that you studied earlier. To the extent that the material is well remembered, you will be able to clearly discriminate the correct statement from the other alternatives. If the material is not well remembered—an all too common occurrence, unfortunately—you could very well end up selecting a wrong alternative.

In studying animal memory a similar procedure is used; that is, at one time the animal is shown a certain stimulus and is then required to identify that stimulus at a later time in order to receive a reinforcer. A procedure often used for this these types of studies is called delayed matching-to-sample. In *delayed matching-to-sample,* the animal is first shown a sample stimulus and then, following some delay, is required to select that stimulus out of a group of alternative stimuli. To the extent that the animal is able to select the correct stimulus, it can be said to remember it.

An example of a matching-to-sample task for pigeons is shown in Figure 8.6. The chamber contains three response keys. In the basic procedure, the two side keys are initially dark while a sample stimulus, such as a triangle, is shown on the center key. When the pigeon pecks this sample stimulus (note that a response is required at this point to ensure that the pigeon has noticed the stimulus), a delay period is entered in which all three keys are dark. Following the delay period, a test period is entered in which the center key is dark and the two side keys are illuminated, one with a triangle and the other with a square. Pecking the triangle (which "matches the sample") is immediately reinforced with food, while pecking the square simply instigates a time-out period followed by the presentation of another trial. Thus, to earn food, the pigeon must select the correct alternative by remembering which stimulus it was shown before the delay.

FIGURE 8.6 The series of events in a delayed matching-to-sample task. The pigeon is first required to peck at the sample stimulus, which initiates a delay interval in which all keys are dark. Following the delay, a test phase occurs in which pecking at the stimulus that matches the sample results in food. The position of the correct stimulus randomly alternates across trials between the right and left keys; the sample stimulus randomly alternates between a square and a triangle.

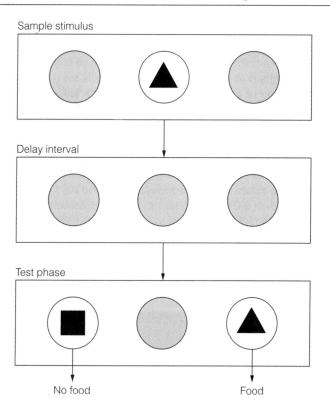

Sample stimulus

Delay interval

Test phase

No food   Food

Using this procedure, one can test memory processes in pigeons by systematically altering various aspects of the procedure, such as the similarity of the stimuli during the test phase, the length of time the sample stimulus is presented, the length of the delay period, and the extent to which the delay period includes the presentation of other stimuli that could potentially interfere with the pigeon's memory for the sample stimulus. A particularly interesting capacity that has been investigated in this way is called *directed forgetting*. Directed forgetting occurs when you have been told to forget something—such as when your math professor makes a mistake in a calculation and tells you to forget what he just wrote on the board (assuming that you understood what he was writing in the first place)—and as a result, you do indeed have poorer memory for that material than you would have had without the instruction to forget. Figure 8.7 shows an example of a directed

FIGURE 8.7 A delayed matching-to-sample procedure for investigating directed forgetting. During a *remember trial*, the O (the "remember" stimulus) during the delay interval indicates that a test trial will be occurring as usual. During a *forget trial*, the X (the "forget" stimulus) during the delay interval indicates that a test phase will not occur and that the sample stimulus can be forgotten. Forget trials, however, occasionally end with a test phase.

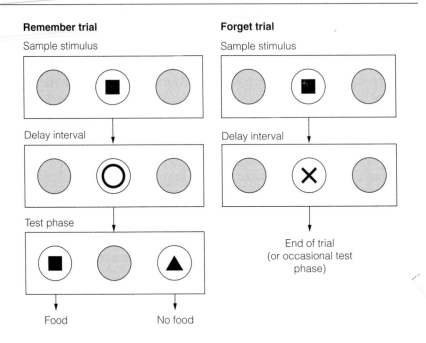

forgetting procedure for pigeons. The sample stimulus is presented as usual. During the delay period, however, the pigeon is shown either an O on the center key, which indicates that it must remember the sample stimulus, or an X, which indicates that it can forget the sample stimulus because the trial will be starting over again. In essence, the O tells the pigeon that everything is okay and that the test phase will be occurring as normal, whereas the X tells the pigeon something like, "Whoops, made a mistake; we'll be starting over again, so you may as well forget what you've just been shown."

The question, therefore, is whether pigeons are actually less likely to remember the sample stimulus when they have been shown the X (the forget cue) as opposed to the O (the remember cue). The way to test this is to occasionally fool the pigeon by presenting the X and then proceeding to the test phase anyway (sort of like an evil professor who later on tests you on lecture material that he explicitly said would not be on the exam). When this is done, it turns out that pigeons do in fact perform worse in the test phase following the forget cue than they do following the remember cue. In other words, when the pigeons are "told" that they need not remember a particular stimulus, they do in fact display poorer memory for that stimulus in the future (e.g., Maki & Hegvik, 1980; see also Kaiser, Sherburne, & Zentall, 1997).

Directed forgetting in pigeons is just one of the phenomena that have been investigated using a delayed matching-to-sample procedure. Other procedures for studying memory in animals have also been devised, some of which more closely resemble the animals' natural environment. This is important because some animals have evolved a staggering capacity for remembering certain kinds of events that can only be demonstrated in an environment that closely resembles their natural environment. The Clark's nutcracker, for example, stores seeds in many thousands of caches scattered over several kilometers and has to retrieve a large number of these caches to survive the winter. Studies conducted within relatively naturalistic enclosures have shown that the birds do indeed seem to remember where they hide these seeds, as opposed to just stumbling across them by accident, and appear to use various landmarks (e.g., rocks and shrubs) to locate them (e.g., Gibson & Kamil, 2001; Vander Wall, 1982). Now if only we could evolve a capacity that good for remembering where we put our car keys.[7]

---

1. Memory is often a matter of _stimulus_ _control_ in which one is first exposed to a stimulus and is then required to respond to that stimulus at a later time.

2. A useful procedure for studying memory is a _delayed_ _matching_ to _sample_ task. In it, the animal is first shown a s_ample_ stimulus and then, following some _delay_, is required to select that stimulus out of a group of alternative stimuli.

3. In a directed forgetting task, the pigeon is shown a cue during the _remember_ period, which signals whether the _sample_ stimulus needs to be _remembered_ or can be f_orgotten_.

4. On such tasks, pigeons are (less/more) _____ likely to select the correct stimulus following exposure to the forget cue.

Stimulus Control: Additional Applications

There are many ways in which stimulus control can be used to manage behavior. Perhaps the most impressive use of stimulus control is by animal trainers, especially those who train animals for public performance. Dolphin trainers, for example, use a mere whistle or gesture to set off a dazzling array of leaps and twirls. Indeed, the control is so precise that the dolphins often seem like robots, an impression that probably contributes to the growing opposition to such shows. Not only has the animal been removed from its natural

---

[7]Although for simplicity we have made the assumption that such tasks as delayed matching-to-sample constitute a means for investigating cognitive processes in animals, some behavior analysts (not surprisingly) have argued that many of these results can be interpreted in noncognitive terms (e.g., Epling & Pierce, 1999).

environment, it now appears to be a slave to the trainer's every whim. (Karen Pryor, 1999, however, contends that the reality is quite different, with such training—especially training through positive reinforcement—being much more a two-way process of communication than brute force control.)

A particularly useful form of stimulus control for animal management is *targeting*. Targeting involves using the process of shaping to train an animal to approach and touch a particular object, as in training a dog to touch the end of a stick with its nose. Targeting is a key aspect of teaching dolphins to make their impressive leaps. The dolphin first receives reinforcement for touching a target stick with its nose, following which the stick is raised higher and higher, enticing the dolphin to leap higher and higher to touch it. Targeting is commonly used to manage animals in zoos. By simply moving the target stick, zookeepers can lead the animals from one cage to another or position them precisely for medical examinations. Animals can also be taught to target a point of light from a laser beam, which then allows the handler to send the animal to a spot some distance away. This can be a useful procedure for directing search-and-rescue dogs in disaster areas that are difficult for the handler to traverse (Pryor, 1999).

Stimulus control can also be used to eliminate certain types of problem behaviors. Pryor (1999), for example, describes how she once experienced considerable difficulty in training a dolphin to wear suction cups over its eyes (as part of an intended demonstration of the dolphin's ability to swim solely by sonar). Although the cups did not hurt, the dolphin refused to wear them and would cleverly sink to the bottom of the pool for several minutes whenever it saw Pryor approaching with the cups. Initially stumped, Pryor finally hit on the idea of reinforcing the behavior of sinking by giving the dolphin a fish whenever it did so (which, she reports, seemed to greatly surprise the dolphin). Soon, the dolphin was sinking at high frequency to earn fish, at which point Pryor began to reinforce the behavior only after a cue had been presented. In short order, the dolphin was sinking only on cue, meaning that the behavior was now under strong stimulus control. Pryor found that she was then able to reintroduce the suction cups and place them on the dolphin without difficulty. In the absence of the cue for sinking, the dolphin no longer had a tendency to sink to avoid the cups. In similar fashion, a dog that has been trained to bark on cue may be less likely to bark at other times. In short, by putting a behavior "on cue," the behavior is less likely to occur in the absence of the cue.

Stimulus control is obviously an important aspect of human behavior, though we sometimes overlook it as a simple means for facilitating certain aspects of our own behavior. Consider Stephanie, who promises herself that she will take vitamins each evening but so often forgets to do so that she eventually gives up. All she really needs to do is create a salient cue for taking vitamins, such as placing the vitamin bottle beside the alarm clock that she sets each evening. Likewise, the person who remembers to take his umbrella in the morning is the person who sets it beside the door the night before when he hears that it will likely rain next day.

Stimulus control is also useful for creating an effective study environment. Too often students attempt to study in settings that contain strong cues for nonstudy behaviors, such as interacting with others or watching television. Most students do far better to study in a setting where such cues are kept to a minimum. For example, Heffernan and Richards (1981) found that students who isolated themselves from interpersonal distractions reported a major improvement in their study habits. More recently, Plant, Ericsson, Hill, and Asberg (2005) found that students who reported studying in quiet, solitary environments had higher grade point averages (GPAs). Although the study was only correlational, the results are consistent with the possibility that students who study in such environments engage in higher-quality studying, which Plant et al. relate to the importance of high-quality, deliberate practice in the development of expert performance (see "Deliberate Practice and Expert Performance" in the And Furthermore box in Chapter 1). A particularly interesting result was that students who studied alone also tended to study fewer hours, which further supports the notion that they were engaging in high-quality studying such that they did not need to study long hours to do well.[8]

Likewise, Skinner (1987) recommends establishing a particular setting, such as a certain desk, that is used only for studying. Over time, the desk will become so strongly associated with the act of studying that just sitting at the desk will facilitate one's ability to study. Of course, this kind of stimulus control cannot be established overnight. Sitting at a desk for 3 hours at a time trying to study but daydreaming instead will only associate the desk with the act of daydreaming. Better to begin with short, high-quality study periods and then gradually progress to longer study periods (although, as the Calvin and Hobbes cartoon suggests, not too gradually).

An example of a procedure to improve study habits was reported by Fox (1962). The program began by first examining each student's schedule and finding a 1-hour period each day that was always available for studying. The students were instructed to spend at least part of that hour studying their most difficult subject matter. They were also told to conduct that studying only in a particular setting (such as a certain room in the library), to have only their study materials with

Calvin and Hobbes   by Bill Watterson

---

[8]This is not to say that studying with others is necessarily ineffective. High-quality group studying can be of significant benefit; the problem is that most students studying with others do not engage in high-quality studying.

them when they were in that setting, and not to be in that setting on other occasions. Most important, if they became bored or started to daydream, they were to complete just a bit more studying (such as reading one page) and then leave the setting. Finally, any studying done outside the special 1-hour period had to be done elsewhere. Initially, none of the students could study throughout the 1-hour period, but over time they gradually built up the ability to do so. A similar procedure was then carried out for each of their other courses. Soon the students were studying each of their courses for 1 hour per day, with a good level of concentration. The students were also given instruction in other academic skills, such as how to read a textbook and take lecture notes. Consequently, all of the students experienced considerable improvement in their grades.

Stimulus control procedures are also the treatment of choice for sleep-onset insomnia, in which people have difficulty falling asleep. For example, Bootzin, Epstein, and Wood (1991) recommend the following procedure:

1. Go to bed only when you are sleepy.
2. Use the bed only for sleeping (or sex). Do not lie in bed to read, study, or watch television.
3. If you cannot fall asleep within 10 to 20 minutes, get out of bed and go to another room. Go back to bed only when you feel sleepy.
4. Repeat the above rule as often as necessary. This rule should also be applied if you are unable to fall asleep after a middle-of-the-night awakening.
5. Use your alarm to get up at the same time each morning, regardless of how you slept the night before.
6. Do not take naps during the day.

The obvious goal of the program is to make lying in bed a strong cue for sleeping. Research has shown this to be an effective program, with many people reporting considerable improvement in their sleep habits both immediately following the program and at long-term follow-up (Lichstein & Riedel, 1994).

QUICK QUIZ N

1. Training a rhinoceros to touch the end of a stick with its nose is an example of a useful behavior management technique called ~~targeting~~.

2. Jaclyn's cat has a terrible habit of jumping up on the kitchen counter whenever Jaclyn is preparing food. How might Jaclyn use a stimulus control procedure to eliminate this behavior? _____.

3. Briefly put, six rules for overcoming sleep-onset insomnia through the use of stimulus control are (chances are that you will have to check back to fill these out):

(1) _go to bed only when sleepy._

(2) _use on bed only for sleeping (or sex)._

(3) _if sleep doesn't come in 10 to 20 mins, go to another room_

(4) _repeat rules even if you can't fall asleep in the middle of the night_

(5) _use alarm to get up at the same time each morning_

(6) _do not take naps_

And Furthermore

Edwin Guthrie: Stimulus Control for the Practical Person

Edwin Guthrie (1886–1959) was a famous learning theorist who strongly emphasized the role of stimulus control because, from his perspective, all learning is a function of one basic principle: If a behavior occurs in the presence of certain stimuli, that behavior becomes automatically attached to those stimuli (Guthrie, 1952). Repeat those stimuli, and the person or animal must necessarily repeat the behavior. In other words, Guthrie's theory is an extreme version of an S-R theory.

Guthrie's theory makes a startlingly blunt prediction about behavior. Whatever you did the last time you were in a certain setting is exactly what you will do the next time you are in that setting. Suppose, for example, that the last time you walked down a certain hallway, you entered the first doorway to the right. Guthrie's theory predicts that the next time you walk down that hallway, you will again enter the first doorway to the right, *given that all the stimuli are the same as when you last walked down that hallway.* Of course, this last part is the catch. The stimuli that precede a behavior—and this can include both internal and external stimuli—are never exactly the same from one occasion to the next. Instead, they are only more or less similar, with the result that a behavior is only more or less likely to be repeated. Note also that the consequences of the behavior—for example, perhaps you entered the first doorway to the right because it leads to the cafeteria where you bought coffee—do not enter into the equation. Guthrie viewed consequences as having only an indirect effect on behavior, though his explanation for how this works is too complex to delve into here.

Guthrie himself did little research, and the research that was done provided only equivocal support for his theory. As a result, it receives relatively little attention from modern-day researchers. Nonetheless, Guthrie's approach still has its adherents and is still considered a major theory of learning (Hergenhahn, 1988). Perhaps one reason for its enduring attraction is the simplicity of the theory (scientists often find a parsimonious explanation quite attractive, possibly because they so often have to deal with complexities). Another reason is the engaging practicality of the theory. Guthrie by nature was a pragmatic individual and often used homey, practical examples for illustration.

One of Guthrie's most cited examples is that of a young girl who each day threw her coat on the floor when she arrived home and was each day scolded by her mother (Guthrie, 1952). On the surface, we might speculate that the girl repeated the behavior because it was reinforced by the attention she received from her mother. From Guthrie's perspective, however, the mother's reaction had little effect on the behavior. Rather, the stimuli that the girl encountered when she entered the house had become so strongly connected to the response of throwing the coat on the floor that this response automatically occurred each time she entered. To solve the problem, the mother began to insist that the child pick up her coat, go back

(continued)

outside, and then practice the behavior of entering the house and hanging up the coat. The stimuli present when the girl entered the house then became associated with the act of hanging up the coat rather than throwing it on the floor, and the new behavior supplanted the old. Thus, from Guthrie's perspective, problem behaviors in a certain setting can often be rectified by deliberately practicing appropriate behaviors in that setting.

Another example is that of a student who was having difficulty studying because she was continually distracted by the sound of a neighbor's radio (Guthrie, 1952). Instead of trying to force herself to study, the student read mystery stories. The stories were so interesting that she was able to read them without being distracted by the sound of the radio. Within a week, the behavior of concentrating while reading had become so firmly established in that setting that she was then able to switch back to her study materials and concentrate well despite the radio.

This last example implies that students who have difficulty concentrating might sometimes do well to study something interesting before they study something boring. Starting with interesting material might establish a strong level of concentration that will then carry over to the less interesting material. This, of course, seems to contradict Grandma's rule—or the Premack principle, if you will—which contends that you should work before you play (applied to studying, this suggests that you should start with less interesting material and finish off with more interesting material). Guthrie, by contrast, seems to suggest that it might sometimes be useful to play before you work.

SUMMARY

Extinction is the nonreinforcement of a previously reinforced response, the result of which is a decrease in the strength of that response. Implementation of an extinction procedure is often followed by an extinction burst, which is a temporary increase in the rate and intensity of a behavior. Extinction is also followed by an increase in the variability of behavior and in emotional behavior, especially aggression. Extinction can also be accompanied by resurgence—the sudden appearance of a different behavior that had previously been reinforced—and depression.

Resistance to extinction is the extent to which responding persists during extinction. According to the partial reinforcement effect, an intermittent schedule of reinforcement, especially a VR schedule, produces greater resistance to extinction than a continuous schedule. Resistance also varies directly with the number of times the behavior has been reinforced, the magnitude of the reinforcers that have been used, and the extent to which the animal has been deprived of the reinforcer. Previous experience with extinction tends to lower resistance to extinction, as does the presence of a discriminative stimulus for extinction (known as an S^Δ).

Spontaneous recovery is the reappearance of an extinguished response following a rest period after extinction. With repeated sessions of extinction, however, the amount of recovery gradually diminishes. The process of extinction can be facilitated through differential reinforcement of other behaviors (especially incompatible behaviors).

A behavior is said to be under stimulus control when the presence of an S^D reliably affects the likelihood of a behavior. The tendency to respond to stimuli similar to the S^D is called stimulus generalization; the tendency not to respond to such stimuli is stimulus discrimination. A graph that indicates the degree of generalization to similar stimuli is a generalization gradient. A flat gradient indicates strong generalization; a steep gradient indicates weak generalization. The peak shift effect is the tendency, following discrimination training, for the peak of a generalization gradient to shift to one side of the S^D, to a point that is further removed from the S^Δ.

A multiple schedule consists of two or more schedules presented in sequence, each resulting in reinforcement and each having a distinctive S^D. Multiple schedules are used to study contrast effects. In a negative contrast effect, an increase in reinforcement on one component of a multiple schedule produces a decrease in responding on the other component. In a positive contrast effect, a decrease in the reinforcement on one component produces an increase in responding on the other component. In anticipatory contrast, the rate of response varies inversely with an upcoming ("anticipated") change in the rate of reinforcement.

Errorless discrimination training is a procedure that minimizes the number of errors and reduces many of the side effects associated with discrimination training. It involves presenting the S^Δ early in training, beginning in weak form and then gradually strengthening it (known as a fading procedure). A drawback to errorless discrimination training is that behavior acquired in this fashion is later more difficult to modify.

In a delayed matching-to-sample procedure, the animal is first shown a sample stimulus and then required to select that stimulus out of a set of alternatives following a delay period. This procedure is used to study memory processes in animals, such as directed forgetting in pigeons.

Stimulus control procedures have been applied to a number of behavior problems, ranging from managing animals in zoos to facilitating the act of studying to treating insomnia.

SUGGESTED READINGS

Guthrie, E. R. (1952). *The psychology of learning* (Rev. ed.). New York: Harper & Row. (Original work published in 1935). Guthrie's very readable book outlines his provocatively simple theory of learning, backed up by plenty of down-home practical examples.

Lerman, D. C., & Iwata, B. A. (1996). Developing a technology for the use of operant extinction in clinical settings: An examination of basic and applied research. *Journal of Applied Behavior Analysis, 29,* 345–382. A nice overview of the use of extinction in applied settings.

Mindell, J. A. (1999). Empirically supported treatments in pediatric psychology: Bedtime refusal and night wakings in young children. *Journal of Pediatric Psychology, 24,* 465–481. Sleepless parents, or those who do not wish to become sleepless parents, will likely appreciate this overview of various methods for getting children to stay in bed at night.

STUDY QUESTIONS

1. Define extinction as it applies to operant conditioning. Be sure to distinguish between the process of extinction and the procedure of extinction.
2. What is an extinction burst? What is resurgence?
3. What are four side effects of extinction, other than extinction burst and resurgence?
4. What is resistance to extinction? Be sure to distinguish between low resistance and high resistance to extinction.
5. Define the partial reinforcement effect. Of the four basic intermittent schedules, which produces the strongest resistance to extinction?
6. How is resistance to extinction affected by history of reinforcement, magnitude of reinforcement, degree of deprivation, and previous experience with extinction?
7. What is spontaneous recovery, and how is it affected by successive sessions of extinction?
8. Define a DRO procedure. How does it differ from a DRI procedure? To eliminate a behavior, why is a DRO procedure more effective than a straight extinction procedure?
9. Define stimulus control. What would be an example of stimulus control of behavior at a hockey game and at a church service?
10. Define stimulus generalization and stimulus discrimination *as they occur in operant conditioning.*
11. What is an S^{Δ}? Diagram an example of a discrimination training procedure (be sure to include the appropriate abbreviations for each component).
12. What is a generalization gradient? How does the shape of the gradient reflect the degree of generalization?
13. Define the peak shift effect. Illustrate your answer with a graph of a generalization gradient.
14. Define a multiple schedule. Diagram an experimental example involving the response of lever pressing for food on an FR 20 and VI 30-sec schedule,

and the stimuli of tone and light. Be sure to include the appropriate label for each component (S^D, etc.).

15. Define positive and negative contrast effects, and give an example of each.
16. Define anticipatory contrast and give an example.
17. Describe errorless discrimination training and the two basic aspects of this procedure. What is a major drawback of such training?
18. Using a diagram, describe the delayed matching-to-sample procedure for studying memory in pigeons.
19. How might a bird owner use stimulus control to eliminate a parrot's tendency to squawk for long periods of time? How might a novelist use stimulus control to facilitate the act of writing?

CONCEPT REVIEW

anticipatory contrast. The process whereby the rate of response varies inversely with an upcoming ("anticipated") change in the rate of reinforcement.

behavioral contrast. A change in the rate of *reinforcement* on one component of a multiple schedule produces an opposite change in the rate of *response* on another component.

delayed matching-to-sample. An experimental procedure in which the animal is first shown a sample stimulus and then, following some delay, is required to select that stimulus out of a group of alternative stimuli.

differential reinforcement of other behavior (DRO). Reinforcement of any behavior other than a target behavior that is being extinguished. One variant of this is called differential reinforcement of incompatible behavior (DRI), in which the behavior that is being reinforced is specifically incompatible with the behavior being extinguished.

discrimination training. As applied to operant conditioning, the differential reinforcement of responding in the presence of one stimulus (the S^D) and not another.

discriminative stimulus for extinction (S^Δ). A stimulus that signals the absence of reinforcement.

errorless discrimination training. A discrimination training procedure that minimizes the number of errors (i.e., nonreinforced responses to the S^Δ) and reduces many of the adverse effects associated with discrimination training.

extinction. The nonreinforcement of a previously reinforced response, the result of which is a decrease in the strength of that response.

extinction burst. A temporary increase in the frequency and intensity of responding when extinction is first implemented.

fading. The process of gradually altering the intensity of a stimulus.

generalization gradient. A graphic description of the strength of responding in the presence of stimuli that are similar to the S^D and vary along a
continuum.

multiple schedule. A complex schedule consisting of two or more independent schedules presented in sequence, each resulting in reinforcement and
each having a distinctive S^D.

negative contrast effect. The process whereby an increase in the rate of
reinforcement on one component of a multiple schedule produces a decrease
in the rate of *response* on the other component.

partial reinforcement effect. The process whereby behavior that has been
maintained on an intermittent (partial) schedule of reinforcement extinguishes more slowly than behavior that has been maintained on a continuous schedule.

peak shift effect. Following discrimination training, the peak of a generalization gradient will shift from the S^D to a stimulus that is further removed
from the S^Δ.

positive behavioral contrast. The process whereby a decrease in rate of reinforcement on one component of a multiple schedule produces an increase
in the rate of response on the other component.

resistance to extinction. The extent to which responding persists after an
extinction procedure has been implemented.

resurgence. The reappearance during extinction of other behaviors that had
once been effective in obtaining reinforcement.

spontaneous recovery. The reappearance of an extinguished response following a rest period after extinction.

stimulus control. A situation in which the presence of a discriminative stimulus reliably affects the probability of a behavior.

stimulus discrimination. In operant conditioning, the tendency for an
operant response to be emitted more in the presence of one stimulus than
another.

stimulus generalization. In operant conditioning, the tendency for an operant response to be emitted in the presence of a stimulus that is similar to
an S^D.

CHAPTER TEST

16. When Asha's parents won the lottery and bought her lots of neat play-
things, she became (less/more) _____less_____ interested in school.
This is an example of a __negative__ contrast effect.

4. When Erin was babysitting Lucie, it took hours before Lucie would stop
pestering her for a treat (Erin had been instructed not to give her any
treats). The next time Erin babysits Lucie, Lucie will (probably/probably
not) _____ resume asking for a treat. This can be considered
an example of an extinction effect known as _____. This may
be occurring in this case because the entry of a babysitter into the house

is, for Lucie, a _____ stimulus indicating that a treat will soon become available.

10. Lucie is ecstatic when Tamsen is her babysitter, and completely indifferent when Natasha is her babysitter. This is because Tamsen tends to give her treats, but Natasha does not. Thus, Tamsen is an (give the abbreviation) S^D, S^+ _____ for the availability of treats, while Natasha is an S^Δ, S^- _____.

27. More persistent is to less persistent as (high/low) ___high___ resistance to extinction is to ___low___ resistance to extinction.

15. When Trish's friend Laura spread some nasty rumors about her, Trish stopped talking to her. Laura did not understand the reason for Trish's silence and initially (increased/decreased) ___increased___ the frequency with which she attempted to talk to Laura. From the perspective of this being an extinction process, Laura's behavior can be seen as an example of a(n) ___extinction burst___.

9. Right after Gina was stung by a hornet, she was as likely to run away from houseflies as from hornets, which is an example of stimulus ___generalization___ One year later, we find that Gina runs away from hornets but not houseflies, which is an example of stimulus ___discrimination___.

19. Lana finds that the children in her class are extremely unruly. To solve this problem, she announces that whenever she is holding up a flag, the children can run around and do whatever they want. Then, periodically throughout the day, she holds up the flag for a few minutes and lets the children run around like crazy. She also finds that when the flag is not being held up, the children are now relatively (quiet/noisy) ___quiet___, insofar as the behavior of running around is now under ___stimulus control___.

5. When Erin was babysitting Lucie, it took hours before Lucie would stop pestering her for a treat. Erin could likely have speeded up this process through the use of a (give the abbreviation) ___DRO (or DRI)___ procedure.

11. When Mehgan lived in Vancouver, she dated Mike, who was quite uneducated, and David, who was moderately educated. She had a boring time with Mike and a great time with David. She then moved to Dallas and set her sights on meeting someone new. According to the ___peak shift___ effect, we would expect her to be most interested in meeting someone (as educated as/more educated than) ___more educated___ David.

21. In behavioral ___contrast___, a change in the rate of ___reinforcement___ on one component of a multiple schedule is followed by a(n) (similar/opposite) ___opposite___ change in the rate of ___response___ on the other component.

7. On a generalization gradient, the strongest response typically occurs to the ___SD S^D___.

13. The nonreinforcement of a previously reinforced response defines the ___procedure___ of extinction, while the resultant decrease

in the strength of that response defines the ___process___ of extinction.

3. A dog whose begging for food has been reinforced 200 times is likely to show greater ___resistance___ to extinction than a dog whose begging has been reinforced only 10 times.

29. A useful procedure for studying memory is a delayed ___matching___ to ___sample___ task, in which the animal is shown a ___sample___ stimulus and then is later required to select that stimulus out of a group of alternative stimuli.

17. Yan lives in a very crowded city, so he teaches his little boy to stay in close contact with his right hand whenever they are walking in a crowd. This is similar to a behavior management technique known as ___targeting___ that is used to guide animals.

6. When the commander yells "Charge!" all of his troops climb out of the trench and start running toward the enemy. The behavior of these troops is obviously under strong ___stimulus___ control.

25. While teaching his daughter the letters of the alphabet, Vern would say each letter as he showed it to her and then encourage her to repeat what he said. He then began to say the letters more and more softly, with the result that she eventually said them on her own without any prompt from him. This can be seen as an example of ___errorless___ discrimination learning. One problem with this type of method is that the learning that results from this procedure tends to be (inflexible/ too flexible) ___inflexible___.

22. When Trish's friend Laura spread some nasty rumors about her, Trish stopped talking to her. Laura tried very hard to get Trish to talk to her. She also became emotionally (upset/distant) ___upset___, which included becoming quite ___angry___ with Trish.

2. When visiting a foreign resort last summer, you frequently encountered a group of children in the street who were trying to sell souvenirs. Although you always rejected their sales pitches, they were incredibly persistent. Chances are that this persistence results because their behavior of selling merchandise is on a(n) ___VR ; intermittent___ schedule of reinforcement. Another factor would be that the children seemed quite poor; hence, they were relatively ___deprived___ of the sought-after reinforcer.

8. A ___generalization___ gradient indicates the strength of responding in the presence of stimuli that are similar to the ___S^P___ and that vary along a ___continuum___.

23. When Tamara first moved to the city, she went out each evening and had a great time. One evening at a nightclub, however, she had a frightening experience that really turned her off the club scene. Interestingly, she subsequently became (more/less) ___more___ interested in other activities, including her job. This may be an example of a(n) ___positive___ contrast effect.

14. The first step in carrying out an extinction procedure is to identify the _reinforcer_ that is maintaining the behavior.

18. When Trish's friend Laura spread some nasty rumors about her, Trish stopped talking to her. Laura tried very hard to get Trish to talk to her but quickly gave up. Laura's behavior of trying to interact with Trish seems to have (low/high) _low_ resistance to extinction.

24. Ahmed found school only slightly interesting. Unfortunately, his lack of studying led to some very poor marks one semester, with the result that he faced the real threat of being forced to withdraw for a year. Throughout the rest of the semester, Ahmed was probably (more/ less) _more_ interested in his schoolwork. This can be seen as an example of _anticipatory_ contrast.

12. A multiple schedule consists of two or more independent schedules presented (simultaneously/sequentially) _sequentially_, each resulting in a _reinforcement_ and each having a distinctive _S^D_.

28. In a _directed_ forgetting task, the pigeon is shown a cue during the _delay_ period, which signals whether the sample stimulus needs to be remembered or can be forgotten.

1. When Trish's friend Laura spread some nasty rumors about her, Trish stopped talking to her. Laura tried hard to get Trish to talk to her. She even asked Trish if she would like to go to the local video arcade, which had been a favorite activity of theirs when they first became friends. This may be an example of an extinction effect known as _resurgence_.

20. When Trish's friend Laura spread some nasty rumors about her, Trish stopped talking to her. Laura tried many different ways to get Trish to talk to her: phoning her, e-mailing, writing letters, and sending messages through mutual friends. The many ways in which Laura attempted to interact with Trish are indicative of an effect that often accompanies extinction, which is an increase in the _variability_ of a behavior.

26. When Trish's best friend Laura spread some nasty rumors about her, Trish stopped talking to her. Laura tried very hard to get Trish to talk to her. When Trish refused, Laura eventually became _depressed_, one symptom of which was a relatively (low/high) _low_ level of activity.

Visit the book companion Web site at <http://www.academic.cengage.com/ psychology/powell> for additional practice questions, answers to the Quick Quizzes, practice review exams, and additional exercises and information.

ANSWERS TO CHAPTER TEST

1. resurgence
2. intermittent (VR); deprived
3. resistance
4. probably; spontaneous recovery; discriminative

5. DRO (or DRI)
6. stimulus
7. S^D
8. generalization gradient; S^D; continuum

9. generalization; discrimination
10. S^D (or S+); S^Δ (or S−)
11. peak shift; more educated than
12. sequentially; reinforcer; S^D
13. procedure; process
14. reinforcer
15. increased; extinction burst
16. less; negative
17. targeting
18. low
19. quiet; stimulus control
20. variability
21. contrast; reinforcement; opposite; response
22. upset; angry
23. more; positive
24. more; anticipatory
25. errorless; inflexible
26. depressed; low
27. high; low
28. directed; delay
29. matching; sample; sample

CHAPTER 9

Escape, Avoidance, and Punishment

CHAPTER OUTLINE

James informed Misha, his new girlfriend, that he was once married to a woman who had been diagnosed with depression. He explained that she had stopped working, moped around the house all day, and would often break down and start crying. Despite his best efforts to be supportive, they finally got a divorce. Misha felt a lot of sympathy for James, who was obviously a very caring fellow. After several months, though, she noticed that she herself was becoming depressed. Although James was often quite affectionate, he would also become angry with her or, worse yet, grow coldly silent for no apparent reason. He also had a tendency to contradict her whenever she offered her opinion on some matter, and he took special pains to point out her mistakes (because, he said, he loved her so much that he wanted to be honest with her). Misha then learned that James' former wife had made a remarkable recovery soon after their divorce.

This chapter explores the effects of aversive consequences on behavior. We begin by examining the role of negative reinforcement in the development of escape and avoidance behaviors. As you will see, this process plays a critical role in the development and maintenance of phobic and obsessive-compulsive disorders in humans. We follow this with a discussion of punishment, in which the presentation or withdrawal of consequences serves to suppress a behavior. We discuss some of the undesirable side effects of punishment as well as some ways punishment can be effective. The chapter concludes with a discussion of the harmful effects of noncontingent punishment, in which the punishing stimulus is delivered independently of the individual's behavior.

Escape and Avoidance

As you will recall from Chapter 6, negative reinforcement consists of the removal of an aversive stimulus following a response, which then leads to an increase in the strength of that response. For example, if we wave our hands at a bothersome wasp and the wasp flies away, we will likely repeat that action with the next wasp that annoys us. Negative reinforcement is associated with two types of behavior: (1) *escape behavior*, in which performance of the behavior terminates the aversive stimulus, and (2) *avoidance behavior*, in which performance of the behavior prevents the aversive stimulus from occurring. Thus, we escape from the rain when we run indoors after it has started; we avoid the rain when we head indoors before it has started.

Typically, one first learns to escape from an aversive stimulus and then to avoid it. This process can be demonstrated using a *shuttle avoidance procedure*, in which an animal has to shuttle back and forth in a box to avoid an aversive stimulus. In one version of this procedure, a rat is placed in a chamber divided by a low barrier. A stimulus of some sort, such as a light, is presented for, say,

FIGURE 9.1 Escape and avoidance in a shuttle avoidance task. As shown in the top panel, the animal first learns to escape from the shock by climbing over the barrier whenever a shock occurs. Later, as it learns that the light predicts the occurrence of shock, it climbs over the barrier whenever the light appears, thereby avoiding the shock (as shown in the bottom panel). (*Source:* Nairne, 2000.)

10 seconds, followed by a mild electric shock. The rat can escape the shock by climbing over the barrier to the other side of the compartment, as it will quickly learn to do whenever it feels a shock (see top panel of Figure 9.1). Technically speaking, at this early point in the process, the presence of shock is a discriminative stimulus that sets the occasion for the escape behavior of crossing the barrier. Crossing the barrier is then negatively reinforced by the removal of shock:

> **Shock:** *Cross barrier* → **Removal of shock**
> S^D .... **R** .... S^R

Now, remember that the shock is preceded by the presentation of a light, which is essentially a warning signal that a shock is about to occur. As the rat learns to associate the light with the shock, it will begin crossing the barrier whenever the light is presented and before the shock begins (see bottom panel of Figure 9.1). The light is now the effective discriminative stimulus for the avoidance response of crossing the barrier.

> **Light:** *Cross barrier* → **Avoidance of shock**
> S^D .... **R** .... S^R

In similar fashion, we might first learn to escape from an upsetting conversation with a racist acquaintance by inventing an excuse for leaving. After a few experiences, however, we might begin actively avoiding that individual before any encounter. By doing so, we avoid having to endure any exposure to that person's racist views.

1. Behavior that terminates an aversive stimulus is called ___escape___ behavior, whereas behavior that prevents an aversive stimulus from occurring is called ___avoidance___ behavior.

2. Typically, one first learns to ___escape___ from an aversive stimulus, and then to ___avoid___ it.

3. Julio initially takes vitamin C whenever he has a cold, in the hope that it will shorten the duration of his symptoms. Feeling that this is effective, he begins taking it daily in the hope that it will keep him from contracting a cold. Julio initially took the vitamin C to (avoid/escape) ___escape___ the symptoms of a cold; he later took it to ___avoid___ the symptoms of a cold.

4. In the shuttle avoidance procedure described previously, the rat first learns to ___escape___ from the shock, with the ___shock___ acting as the S^D for the behavior. The rat later learns to ___avoid___ the shock, with the ___light___ acting as the S^D for the behavior.

Two-Process Theory of Avoidance

Researchers have generally shown more interest in studying avoidance behavior than escape behavior. This is because, from a theoretical perspective, escape behavior is relatively easy to understand. For example, when escaping from shock by climbing over a barrier, the rat moves from a clearly aversive situation to a nonaversive situation. But the motivation underlying avoidance behavior is less apparent. When climbing over a barrier to avoid shock, the rat seems to be moving from one nonaversive situation (no shock) to another nonaversive situation (no shock). How can a lack of change function as a reinforcer?

An early attempt to explain avoidance behavior was the *two-process theory of avoidance* (also known as the *two-factor theory of avoidance*) proposed by Mowrer (1947, 1960). According to this theory, two processes are involved in learning an avoidance response. The first process is classical conditioning of a fear response to a CS. For example, in the shuttle avoidance procedure described previously, the light that precedes the shock becomes a CS that elicits a conditioned fear reaction:

Light: Shock → *Fear*
  NS   US   UR
Light → *Fear*
  CS   CR

Once this conditioned fear has been established, it then forms the basis of an operant conditioning procedure. If the CS generates a conditioned fear response, then moving away from the CS should result in a reduction of fear. This reduction of fear should in turn serve as a negative reinforcer for the response that produced it. In our experimental example, presentation of the light elicits a conditioned fear response, while climbing over the barrier produces a reduction in fear that serves as a negative reinforcer for climbing over the barrier.

Light: *Climb over barrier* → **Reduction in fear**
S^D **R** S^R

Thus, Mowrer's *two-process theory of avoidance* proposes that avoidance behavior is the result of two distinct processes: (1) classical conditioning, in which a fear response comes to be elicited by a CS, and (2) operant conditioning, in which moving away from the CS is negatively reinforced by a reduction in fear.

1. It is relatively easy to understand the process underlying (escape/avoidance) _escape_ conditioning because the organism moves from an _aversive_ situation to a non _aversive_ situation. By contrast, it is more difficult to understand _avoidance_ conditioning because the organism moves from a(n) _nonaversive_ situation to another _nonaversive_ situation.

2. According to Mowrer, avoidance is the result of two distinct processes: (1) _classical_ conditioning of a _fear_ response, and (2) _operant_ conditioning in which an avoidance response is n _egatively reinforced_ by a reduction in _fear._.

Mowrer's two-process theory generated an enormous amount of research, with the result that researchers soon discovered several apparent difficulties with it. One problem was that avoidance responses are often extremely persistent. R. L. Solomon, Kamin, and Wynn (1953), for example, found that dogs would continue to jump a barrier to avoid shock for hundreds of trials even though the shock apparatus had been disconnected and avoidance was no longer necessary. One dog, for example, made more than 600 avoidance responses before the experimenters finally gave up and put a stop to the session.

On the surface, it seems as though two-process theory cannot account for such persistence. If the animal repeatedly encounters the CS in the absence of the US, then fear of the CS should eventually extinguish—meaning that the animal should eventually stop jumping over the barrier. But it seemed as though the behavior would not extinguish. Why not?

A possible answer to this question is provided by a modification of two-process theory known as the *anxiety conservation hypothesis* (R. L. Solomon & Wynne, 1954). According to this approach, avoidance responses usually occur so quickly that there is insufficient exposure to the CS for the conditioned fear to fully extinguish—that is, a good deal of the conditioned fear is conserved because exposures to the CS are too brief for extinction to take place.[1]

---

[1]It is also possible, according to Eysenck's (1968) theory of incubation (discussed in Chapter 5), that such brief exposures might sometimes strengthen a conditioned fear response, which would further counteract the process of extinction.

For this reason, avoidance responses can be extremely persistent. In addition, supporters of two-process theory have pointed out that avoidance responses are not as persistent as sometimes claimed (Levis, 1989). If one continues to expose the animal to the aversive CS, extinction will often eventually occur given that there are no further pairings of the CS with the US. Thus, the fact that avoidance responses are extremely persistent might not be as damaging a criticism of two-process theory as was first assumed.

Researchers, however, also discovered a second, more serious difficulty with two-process theory. They found that, after repeated avoidance trials, animals appeared to show no evidence of fear but continued to make the avoidance response anyway (R. L. Solomon & Wynn, 1953). In other words, once the animals had become adept at making the avoidance response, they seemed to become almost nonchalant and relaxed while carrying it out. This constituted a major problem for two-process theory: If the animals were no longer afraid of the CS, how could avoidance of the CS have been negatively reinforced by a reduction in fear?

This was a pretty damaging criticism, and for a while it looked as though two-process theory was pretty much on the ropes. Levis (1989), however, has argued that although animals in avoidance experiments may become significantly *less* fearful with experience, there is no evidence that they become completely nonfearful. In fact, evidence suggests that if an animal completely loses its fear of the aversive CS, then, just as two-process theory predicts, the avoidance response ceases to occur. But as long as some fear remains, the avoidance response continues, suggesting that fear reduction is still functioning as a negative reinforcer for the behavior (Levis & Boyd, 1979).

Various other theories have been proposed to account for avoidance behavior. According to *one-process theory*, for example, the act of avoidance is negatively reinforced simply by the lower rate of aversive stimulation it is associated with (Herrnstein, 1969; Herrnstein & Hineline, 1966). Thus, the rat in a shuttle avoidance task persistently climbs over the barrier when the light comes on because this action results in a decreased rate of shock, and not because it results in decreased feelings of fear. The attractive aspect of this theory is that it does away with any reference to an internal state of fear, the existence of which has to be inferred. The overall reduction in aversive stimulation that accompanies avoidance is regarded as a sufficient explanation for the behavior. By contrast, Bolles' (1970) *species-specific defense reaction theory* contends that many avoidance behaviors are actually elicited behaviors rather than operant behaviors. (This theory is described in Chapter 11.) Evidence exists both for and against each of these theories. (See Domjan, 2003, for an overview of these and other theories of avoidance.)

The debate over the processes underlying avoidance behavior will likely continue for some time, and it could well be that several processes are involved. At the very least, avoidance behavior is turning out to be more complicated than researchers originally suspected. Fortunately, the knowledge gained from all this theorizing and research is proving to have a practical application, particularly in the analysis and treatment of anxiety disorders, a topic to which we turn next.

1. One apparent problem with two-process theory is that, even after hundreds of trials, the avoidance response does not seem to e_x_t_i_n_g_u_i_s_h_____.

2. However, according to the a_n_x_i_e_t_y_____ c_o_n_s_e_r_v_a_t_i_o_n_____ hypothesis, avoidance responses usually occur so (quickly/slowly) _q_u_i_c_k_l_y_____ that exposures to the (CS/US) ___C_S_____ are too (long/brief) _b_r_i_e_f____ for _e_x_t_i_n_c_t_i_o_n____ to take place.

3. A second problem with Mowrer's theory is that after sufficient experience with avoiding the aversive CS, the animals no longer show any ___f_e_a_r_____, yet continue to make the avoidance response. Levis, however, contends that such animals are nevertheless still (slightly/strongly) _s_l_i_g_h_t_l_y____ fearful, otherwise the avoidance response would extinguish.

4. According to the one-process theory of avoidance, the avoidance response is negatively reinforced by a reduction in overall rate of av_e_r_s_i_v_e_____ st_i_m_u_l_a_t_i_o_n_, as opposed to a reduction in ___f_e_a_r____.

5. According to species-specific defense reaction theory, avoidance responses are often (learned/innate) __I_n_n_a_t_e_____ reactions to aversive stimulation that are automatically (emitted/elicited) ___e_l_i_c_i_t_e_d_____ in dangerous situations.

Avoidance Conditioning and Phobias

In Chapter 5, we noted that the basis of many phobias is the development of a classically conditioned fear response, which then fails to extinguish because the individual avoids the feared stimulus. At that time, we focused on the classical conditioning aspect of a phobia. Let us now examine the role of avoidance learning in phobic development.

As noted, avoidance learning appears to be a fundamental process in the development and maintenance of phobic behavior. This is no doubt one reason for the intense interest researchers have shown in studying avoidance. Indeed, demonstrations of avoidance learning in laboratory rats have often been regarded as applicable to phobic conditioning in humans. But is avoidance conditioning in the laboratory a true analogue of human phobic conditioning? Does a rat avoid shock in a shuttle avoidance procedure in the same manner that a person avoids dogs after being bitten? In fact, some have argued that there are considerable differences between avoidance conditioning in an experimental setting and human phobic conditioning.

Mineka (1985), for example, has claimed that there are two limitations in applying models of experimental avoidance to human phobias. The first limitation concerns the nature of what is being avoided. *In experimental avoidance conditioning, the animal avoids the aversive US.* For example, in the shuttle avoidance procedure discussed earlier, the rat avoids the shock (US) by climbing over the barrier whenever it sees the light (CS). *In human phobias, however, people avoid the CS.* A person who has been attacked by a dog and now has a severe phobia of dogs not only avoids being attacked by a dog but also avoids the possibility of even encountering a dog. A person who has a fear of elevators because he was once trapped in an elevator does not simply

And Furthermore

Repression: Avoidance of Distressing Thoughts?

Repression is one of the most contentious concepts in present-day psychology. Simply defined (and ignoring some of the complexities), repression refers to the removal of anxiety-provoking thoughts from conscious awareness. Beginning in the 1980s, many therapists became intensely interested in this concept. In particular, they discovered that many clients were able to uncover seemingly forgotten memories of childhood abuse when encouraged to do so, and these memories seemed to be related to their symptoms (J. L. Herman, 1992). A controversy arose, however, when some memory researchers warned that such "recovered memories" might often be false memories of traumatic incidents that never occurred (e.g., Loftus, 1993).

Can the principles of conditioning offer us any insight into this controversy? As it turns out, repression can be viewed as a type of avoidance response. More specifically, the process of repression might be a covert form of avoidance conditioning in which the event being avoided is not an external event, such as a phobic object, but an internal thought. The memory of a childhood trauma is therefore an aversive stimulus that generates anxiety, which in turn motivates one to escape from the anxiety by thinking of something else. With practice, one eventually learns to think of something else before the memory even arises, thereby avoiding the memory (e.g., Levis, 1995; see also Skinner, 1953). To the extent that the memory is consistently avoided, never entering consciousness, then it meets the definition of being repressed. Indeed, Levis (1988) utilized this notion to devise a procedure for "reactivating" memories of traumatic events that had apparently been forgotten.

The process of repression is, therefore, consistent with some basic principles of conditioning. Principles of conditioning, however, also suggest that it may be possible to create false memories of abuse. If covert behavior is governed by many of the same principles as overt behavior, then it is conceivable that a therapist might inadvertently shape the production of novel thought patterns that depict a history of abuse and then reinforce the behavior of labeling such thoughts as memories. Consistent with this notion of shaping, some therapists admit that the process of uncovering repressed memories is often gradual,

avoid being trapped in an elevator; he avoids elevators altogether, planning his day well ahead of time so that riding an elevator will not become an issue.

A second limitation of experimental avoidance is that the avoidance behavior seems to condition less readily than does avoidance behavior in a phobia. Experimental avoidance typically requires at least a few pairings of the CS and the US (e.g., light and shock) before avoidance has been reliably established. As well, *experimental avoidance response is usually less than 100% certain,* with the animal occasionally reencountering the aversive US. For example, in a shuttle avoidance task, the rat will occasionally be tardy in climbing over the barrier, with the result that it sometimes receives a shock.

with the memories first appearing as fragmented images that are then strengthened and clarified by repeatedly thinking about them. As well, some therapists warn clients to discuss their recovered memories only with other survivors of abuse, who will reinforce the clients' behavior of believing that these memories are real. The overall result is that clients may become increasingly proficient at generating mental images of childhood trauma that they believe to be genuine memories (Pendergrast, 1995). Furthermore, even when it is claimed that memory recovery has occurred without any "suggestive influence" by the therapist (e.g., Levis & Brewer, 2001), it is possible that other factors, such as exposure to media stories about recovered memories, have played a role.[2]

Of course, the possibility that reinforcement and shaping may be involved in generating recovered memories does not prove that recovered memories are mostly false. It could be that by first uncovering and confirming a fragmented memory of abuse, a sort of desensitization occurs that then allows a more complete memory to emerge (Levis, 1995). On the other side of the coin, however, the fact that the process of repression is explainable in terms of avoidance conditioning does not constitute strong evidence that repression actually occurs and that recovered memories are often real. Thus, if our behavioristic analysis of recovered memories offers any insight into this controversy, it is simply that there are no easy answers. One would therefore do well to approach this issue with caution.

Finally, in an interesting aside to the controversy over recovered memories, L. S. Newman and Baumeister (1996) have proposed a cognitive-behavioral explanation for why some individuals become strongly committed to apparently false memories of UFO abductions. They point out that abduction memories share many of the characteristics of masochistic experiences (in which erotic pleasure is derived from pain and humiliation). In particular, stories of UFO abductions, like masochistic experiences, typically involve feelings of complete helplessness and the loss of one's normal identity. Newman and Baumeister also note that abduction accounts, like masochistic tendencies, are more common among individuals who are relatively successful, yet stressed out by their responsibilities. The act of "remembering" an alien abduction might therefore be a form of masochism that allows the "abductee" to temporarily escape from a stressful lifestyle, thereby negatively reinforcing the production of such memories.

By contrast, human phobias often require only a single, brief conditioning trial to produce an avoidance response that is strong and persistent. For example, a very strong and persistent dog phobia may develop following a single dog attack.

---

[2] Such a claim may also reflect a tendency to underestimate the subtle ways in which a therapist can influence a client. It is said that one lesson learned by the "animal magnetists" in the early days of research into what is now called hypnosis was the extent to which the patient can detect and respond to very subtle cues emitted by the hypnotist. The cues were so subtle that people often missed them, resulting in speculation that hypnotism sometimes created a telepathic link between the patient and the hypnotist (Ellenberger, 1970).

1. According to Mineka, one limitation in applying experimental models of avoidance to human phobias is that the animals are usually avoiding the aversive (CS/US) _____US_____ whereas human phobics are avoiding the aversive _____CS_____.

2. According to Mineka, a second limitation of applying experimental models of avoidance to phobias is that avoidance behavior in an experiment conditions (more/less) _____less_____ readily than does avoidance behavior in a phobia.

3. Experimental avoidance usually requires (one/a few) _____a few_____ conditioning trial(s), while phobic conditioning usually requires _____one_____ conditioning trial(s). Also, (experimental/phobic) _____experimental_____ conditioning is less than 100% certain.

In response to Mineka's (1985) concerns about the applicability of experimental avoidance conditioning to human phobias, Stampfl (1987) proposed that an adequate experimental analogue of a human phobia would require (1) the reliable establishment of a fear response with only a single, brief pairing of the CS and US, (2) subsequent avoidance of the CS as well as the US, and (3) the occurrence of successful avoidance on 100% of trials. Stampfl acknowledged that when using these criteria the typical avoidance-conditioning procedure is an inadequate analogue of human phobic conditioning. He then devised an experimental procedure that produced avoidance conditioning that met all three criteria.

Stampfl's (1987) procedure focuses on the fact that human phobics typically make the avoidance response early in the chain of events leading up to the feared stimulus. For example, a person with an elevator phobia will plan his day well ahead of time so that he will not be faced with any pressure to take an elevator. He may, for example, arrange an appointment with a dentist whose office is on the main floor of an office building. This type of planning is important because not doing so could result in a direct encounter with a phobic stimulus, which in turn could greatly increase the cost involved in avoiding it (such as by having to climb the stairs to get to a dentist's office on the 23rd floor). Thus, *the phobic individual learns to make the avoidance response early on in the chain of events so as to minimize the effort of avoiding.*

The opportunity to make an early avoidance response is typically absent from most avoidance-conditioning procedures. Stampfl, however, designed an apparatus that provided just such an opportunity. As depicted in Figure 9.2, the apparatus consisted of an alleyway that was 5 feet in length and contained a dark compartment at one end. Each rat was first allowed to explore the alleyway at its leisure, during which time it came to strongly prefer the black compartment (rats generally prefer the dark). The rat was then given a foot shock while in the black compartment, at which point it fled to the far end of the alleyway. Three minutes later, a conveyor belt was turned on that began to slowly carry the rat toward the dark compartment. During this first trial, most rats waited until they reached the black sidewall area of the apparatus before running back to the far end. When they did run back to the far end, they broke a photobeam

FIGURE 9.2 Illustration of a 5-foot automated alleyway similar to the one used by Stampfl (1987).

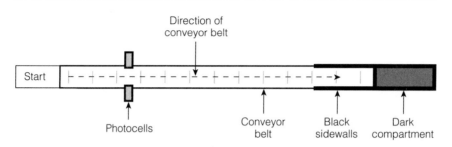

that stopped the conveyor belt for a 3-minute period. The conveyor belt then started up again, and the procedure was repeated. This initial session lasted 2 hours. During the second session, the response requirement for stopping the conveyor belt was increased from FR 1 to FR 10 (that is, the rat had to run back and cross the photobeam 10 times before the conveyor belt would stop).

Stampfl (1987) found that the rats soon learned to run back to the safe area immediately after the conveyor belt started up. In other words, rather than waiting until they reached the black sidewalls before running back, they began running back after traveling only a short distance. In this manner, they were able to minimize the effort involved in breaking the photobeam and stopping the belt. Moreover, under these circumstances, the rats completely avoided entering the black compartment on more than 1,000 consecutive trials, thereby consistently avoiding the aversive CS that was associated with shock. Furthermore, this persistent avoidance response resulted from only a single brief exposure to shock.

In summary, Stampfl's results confirm that a critical factor in the maintenance of phobic behavior is that the avoidance response occurs early in the sequence of events leading up to the phobic stimulus, thereby minimizing the effort involved in making the response. Such early responding greatly reduces the extent to which the avoidance response can be extinguished because the individual experiences little or no exposure to the aversive CS. In terms of the anxiety conservation hypothesis discussed earlier, exposure to the aversive stimulus is so minimal that the avoidance response is extremely resistant to extinction. It is therefore not surprising that phobic behaviors are often extremely persistent.

1. A critical aspect of Stampfl's experimental analogue of phobic conditioning is that the avoidance response can occur (early/late) _early_ in the sequence of events leading up to the feared CS, thereby (maximizing/minimizing) _minimizing_ the amount of effort involved in making the response.

2. This results in (little/considerable) _little_ exposure to the feared CS, thereby greatly (increasing/reducing) _reducing_ the likelihood that the fear response will e_xtinguish_.

QUICK QUIZ E

"I THINK I WAS BETTER OFF WHEN I WAS OBSESSIVE-COMPULSIVE."

Avoidance Conditioning and Obsessive-Compulsive Disorder

Phobia is one type of disorder in which avoidance conditioning plays a critical role. Another is *obsessive-compulsive disorder (OCD)*, a disorder characterized by persistent thoughts, impulses, or images (called obsessions), and repetitive, stereotyped actions (called compulsions) that are carried out in response to the obsessions. For example, a person might have an obsessive worry about contacting germs; this leads to a compulsive tendency to take a shower and clean the house many times each day. Or a person might have an obsessive worry about whether she locked her apartment door when she left that morning, which leads to a compulsive pattern of returning to the apartment several times a day to check it. Note that the person recognizes that the compulsive behavior is clearly excessive but nevertheless feels compelled to perform the action. (Interestingly, cleaning and checking are the two most common forms of compulsive behavior.)

OCD was once considered a particularly difficult disorder to treat. This changed when clinicians began analyzing OCD in terms of avoidance conditioning, especially Mowrer's two-process theory of avoidance conditioning (Rachman & Hodgson, 1980). The applicability of this theory to OCD lies in the fact that obsessions and compulsions have opposite effects on anxiety. In general, obsessions are associated with an increase in anxiety, whereas compulsions are associated with a decrease in anxiety. For example, a person who has a contamination fear and is a compulsive cleaner usually experiences an increase in anxiety after exposure to situations in which "contamination" might have occurred, such as when taking out the garbage. Garbage elicits such a strong anxiety response that any part of the body that has been exposed to garbage also elicits an anxiety response. Taking a shower, however, results in the removal of this anxiety. From the perspective of two-process theory, the feeling of anxiety is a classically conditioned response elicited by contact with the garbage, while showering is an operant response that is negatively reinforced by a reduction in anxiety.

The role of avoidance in OCD is virtually the same as in phobic behavior, except that OCD typically involves an active avoidance response while phobic behavior typically involves a passive avoidance response. More specifically, a person with OCD will generally *do* something to reduce anxiety (such as showering), whereas a person with a phobia will generally *not do* something to reduce anxiety (such as not going near a dog). Nevertheless, individuals with OCD might also utilize passive avoidance responses (e.g., by avoiding garbage whenever possible) such that some of their behavior patterns can also be characterized as phobic.

Two-process theory helped clarify our understanding of OCD and led to the development of the first effective treatment for the disorder. If a compulsive behavior pattern (such as excessive washing) is maintained by avoidance of an anxiety-arousing event (such as contact with germs), then preventing the avoidance response from occurring should result in the eventual extinction of anxiety. This treatment method is known as ***exposure and response prevention (ERP),*** a method of treating OCD that involves prolonged exposure to the anxiety-arousing event while not engaging in the compulsive behavior pattern that reduces the anxiety (e.g., Steketee & Foa, 1985).

As with recent versions of exposure-based treatments for phobic behavior, ERP combines the graduated exposure of systematic desensitization with the prolonged exposure of flooding therapy. For example, a compulsive cleaner might be required to first touch objects associated with slight anxiety (such as door handles and hand rails), then objects associated with moderate anxiety (such as garbage cans and dogs), and finally objects associated with intense anxiety (such as dead birds and dog excrement). These graduated exposures are first carried out imaginally—given that the person has good imagery ability—and then *in vivo*—given that live exposure to the anxiety-arousing event is practical. The exposures are also relatively long, often 90 minutes or more, to ensure sufficient time for the anxiety to begin to extinguish. In addition to scheduled treatment sessions, the client is told to practice exposures at home. The client is also told not to perform any compulsive behavior patterns; for example, a compulsive washer might be instructed to avoid all nonessential showers except for one 10-minute shower every 5 days! Once the obsessive-compulsive pattern has been successfully eliminated, normal patterns of behavior are then reestablished (Steketee & Foa, 1985).

Mowrer's two-process theory has therefore proven quite useful in enhancing our understanding and treatment of OCD. Nevertheless, two-process theory does not provide an entirely adequate explanation for OCD (Steketee & Foa, 1985). For example, people with OCD are usually unable to recall any particular conditioning event that could account for the obsessional anxiety response. People who have a contamination fear, for example, typically do not recall, say, falling into a cesspool before the onset of the fear. On the other hand, onset of OCD does often coincide with a period of stress. One possibility, therefore, is that stress sensitizes certain individuals in such a way that normal concerns, such as those about cleanliness and safety, become greatly exaggerated. Thus, just as the process of selective sensitization might lead to the development of a phobia (as discussed in Chapter 5), so too it might lead to the development of OCD. Furthermore, just as genetic factors may predispose some people to develop a phobia (also discussed in Chapter 5), so too some people might have a genetic predisposition toward developing OCD (Billet, Richter, & Kennedy, 1998).

On a more cognitive level, people with OCD often hold the irrational belief that they should be in complete control of their thoughts—failing to realize that intrusive thoughts are not uncommon and that most people simply ignore them. In other words, they fail to realize that some thoughts are essentially respondents (reflexes) that are automatically elicited by certain stimuli, and that it is futile to try to control such thoughts (as though they were operants). People with OCD also have a tendency to feel personally responsible for events that are highly improbable. They therefore carry out various safety actions, such as rechecking doors and stoves, that other people would not bother with (Salkovskis, 1998). Given the involvement of cognitive factors in OCD, attempts have been made to combine ERP with cognitive therapy on the assumption that directly modifying these false belief systems might enhance treatment. However, the specific efficacy of these cognitive interventions has not yet been firmly established, and ERP by itself remains the treatment of choice for OCD (Foa, Franklin, & Kozak, 1998; Tolin & Steketee, 2007).

QUICK QUIZ F

1. Janice continually worries that her alarm clock might not be set, and that she will wake up late for class. She therefore checks the alarm clock about 20 times each night before finally falling asleep. The persistent thoughts about the alarm clock not being set are classified as a(n) (compulsion/obsession) _obsession_ while the frequent checking of the clock is classified as a(n) _compulsion_.

2. In general, (compulsions/obsessions) _obsessions_ are associated with an increase in anxiety, whereas _compulsions_ are associated with a decrease in anxiety.

3. From the perspective of two-process theory, this decrease in anxiety likely functions as a n_egative_ r_einforcer_ for the compulsive behavior.

4. Exposure and response prevention (ERP) therapy for OCD involves prolonged exposure to anxiety-arousing events while (engaging/not engaging) _not engaging_ in the (obsessive/compulsive) _compulsive_ behavior that serves to reduce the anxiety.

5. ERP is similar to systematic desensitization in that exposure to the anxiety-provoking event is usually (gradual/sudden) _gradual_. It is similar to flooding therapy in that exposure to the anxiety-provoking event is (brief/prolonged) _prolonged_.

6. People with OCD are usually (able/unable) _unable_ to recall a particular conditioning event that was the cause of the obsessional anxiety response. The

disorder often arises, however, during times of s~~tress~~ _____. This suggests that a process of s~~elective~~ s~~ensitization~~ may exacerbate normal concerns about cleanliness and safety.

7. People with OCD fail to realize that intrusive thoughts are (common/uncommon) __common__ and that such thoughts are often (controllable/uncontrollable) __uncontrollable__. They also (take/fail to take) __take__ responsibility for highly (probable/improbable) __improbable__ events.

8. Combined with ERP, cognitive interventions for OCD have been found to provide (much/little) __little__ additional benefit.

Punishment

Escape and avoidance conditioning involves the strengthening of a behavior through the removal of an aversive stimulus. By contrast, punishment involves the weakening of a behavior through the application of an aversive stimulus or the removal of an appetitive stimulus. In this section, we discuss various types of punishment, as well as issues to be concerned with in the application of punishment. We also briefly describe various theories of punishment.

Types of Punishment

Let us begin by reviewing the basic distinction between positive and negative punishment. *Positive punishment consists of the presentation of a certain event following a response, which then leads to a decrease in the future strength of that response.* In simple everyday terms, the behavior results in the delivery of something the person or animal hates, so the subject is less likely to behave that way in the future. Receiving a spanking for swearing and being reprimanded for talking back to the boss are both examples of positive punishment (given that these consequences result in a subsequent decrease in the frequency of these behaviors).

By contrast, *negative punishment consists of the removal of a certain event following a response, which then leads to a decrease in the future strength of that response.* In everyday terminology, the behavior results in the removal of something the person or animal likes, so the subject is less likely to continue that behavior in the future. A loss of employment for being obnoxious and a loss of dessert for complaining at the dinner table are both examples of negative punishment (again, given that the consequence results in a subsequent decrease in such behavior). Note that the events being removed are the types of pleasant events that can also serve as positive reinforcers; thus, negative punishment can also be defined as the loss of a positive reinforcer (a pleasant event) following a response.

There are two basic types of negative punishment: time-out and response cost. *Time-out* involves the loss of access to positive reinforcers for a brief period of time following the occurrence of a problem behavior. Time-out has become popular with modern-day parents, who frequently attempt to punish a child's misbehavior by sending her to the bedroom or by making her sit in a corner for several minutes. Unfortunately, time-out procedures are often poorly applied, with the result that they have little effect on the problem behavior. For example, time-out is likely to be ineffective if the time-out setting is actually more reinforcing than the setting from which the child was removed. In fact, sending a child to his room for acting out at the dinner table might reinforce rather than punish the behavior of acting out if the child dislikes sitting at the dinner table. Another problem is that parents often use time-outs that are too long. The purpose of time-out is not to get the child "out of your hair" for a period of time but to facilitate the development of more appropriate behaviors. Those appropriate behaviors need to be reinforced, which cannot be done if the child is sitting in his room for hours on end. Time-out periods should therefore be quite brief, especially for young children. In fact, a time-out period as short as a minute may be all that is required to effectively suppress the unwanted behavior, especially if one immediately sets out to reinforce more appropriate behaviors as soon as the child is returned to the normal setting (Miltenberger, 1997).

The other type of negative punishment is *response cost,* which is the removal of a specific reinforcer following the occurrence of a problem behavior. Receiving a fine (which leads to loss of money) for speeding or taking a child's toys away for playing too roughly are examples of response cost. One advantage of response cost is that one can easily adjust the severity of the punishment to suit the behavior being punished. Slight aggression with a younger sibling could result in the loss of dessert, while more severe aggression could result in the loss of dessert and the opportunity to watch television that evening. A drawback to response cost, however, is that you must clearly identify a reinforcer that, if removed, will have an impact on behavior. It therefore requires a more careful analysis of the situation than a time-out procedure does. (See Miltenberger, 1997, for a more complete discussion of time-out and response cost procedures.)

Note that negative punishment is quite different from extinction, even though both involve the removal of reinforcers and both result in a decrease in the strength of a behavior. In the case of extinction, a behavior that used to produce a reinforcer no longer does, and the person therefore stops performing the behavior. If Jason used to receive cookies as a result of whining, but he no longer receives cookies by whining, then he will eventually stop whining. In the case of negative punishment, however, performing the behavior results in the loss of a reinforcer that the person would otherwise possess. Imagine, for example, that Jason has already received some cookies but then starts whining for a soda pop. If, each time he whines, one of his cookies is taken away, then he is likely to stop whining. Thus, to distinguish between extinction and negative punishment, ask yourself whether the behavior grows weaker because *performing the behavior no longer leads to something* (in which case, the process is extinction), or because *performing the behavior leads to the removal of something that you would otherwise possess* (in which case the process is negative punishment).

1. When the cat sat at your feet and meowed annoyingly during breakfast one morning, you sprayed it with water. As a result, the cat did not come near the table or meow the next time you sat down for a meal. The consequence for the cat's begging consisted of the (presentation/removal) _presentation_ of a stimulus, and the cat's behavior subsequently (decreased/increased) _decreased_ in frequency. Therefore, this is an example of _positive_ _punishment_.

2. Negative punishment involves the (presentation/removal) _removal_ of a stimulus following a response that subsequently results in a (increase/decrease) _decrease_ in the likelihood of that response occurring again.

3. When Bobbi threw a temper tantrum, her mother turned off the television program that Bobbi was watching. Bobbi's mother is attempting to apply a (response cost/time-out) _response-cost_ procedure.

4. When Bobbi threw a temper tantrum, Bobbi's mother made her sit in the corner for a minute. Bobbi's mother is attempting to apply a (response cost/time-out) _time-out_ procedure.

5. A(n) (advantage/disadvantage) _disadvantage_ of a time-out procedure is that one (does/does not) _does_ have to clearly identify a specific reinforcer before implementing the procedure. An (advantage/disadvantage) _advantage_ of a response cost procedure is that one (can/cannot) _can_ easily modify the severity of the punishment to suit the behavior.

6. When Val began whining, her mother immediately stopped playing with her and left the room. Val quickly stopped whining. This is an example of (extinction/negative punishment) _negative punishment_

7. Val's mother used to play with Val whenever she whined but then stopped doing so. As a result, Val's whining soon ceased. This is an example of (extinction/negative punishment) _extinction_.

8. If the frequency of a behavior decreases because performing the behavior no longer leads to something, the process involved is (extinction/negative punishment) _extinction_. If the frequency of a behavior decreases because performing the behavior leads to the removal of something, the process involved is _negative punishment_

Punishment can also be differentiated in other ways. For example, just as one can distinguish between intrinsic and extrinsic reinforcement, one can distinguish between intrinsic and extrinsic punishment. *Intrinsic punishment* is punishment that is an inherent aspect of the behavior being punished. In other words, the activity itself is punishing, such that the person performing the behavior is now less likely to repeat it. Watching an upsetting television show is intrinsically punishing if you stop watching such shows in the future because of their upsetting nature. *Extrinsic punishment* is punishment that is not an inherent aspect of the behavior being punished, but simply follows the behavior. In other words, the activity is followed by a separate event that serves to punish the activity. Being chastised after lighting up a cigarette ("Are you still indulging in that filthy habit?") is extrinsically punishing if it subsequently reduces how frequently you smoke.

One can also distinguish between primary and secondary punishers. A *primary (or unconditioned) punisher* is an event that is innately punishing. Loosely speaking, these are events that we are born to dislike. Electric shock, intense heat, and loud noise are examples of primary punishers. A *secondary (or conditioned) punisher* is an event that has become punishing because it has in the past been associated with some other punisher. For example, if shock is an effective punisher, then a tone that has been paired with shock in a classical conditioning procedure:

Tone: Shock → *Fear*
  NS   **US**   **UR**
Tone → *Fear*
  CS   **CR**

will become a conditioned aversive stimulus that can then be used as a secondary punisher. For example, presentation of the tone could now be used to punish wheel running:

Running in a wheel → **Tone**
     R S^P

Human behavior is often under the control of secondary punishers. A traffic ticket might effectively punish our tendency to speed, and an icy stare from our partner might effectively punish our tendency to drink too much at a party. Both the fine and the stare are punishing because they have been associated with other types of aversive events: loss of money in the one case and heated arguments in the other.

A special type of secondary punisher is a *generalized (or generalized secondary) punisher,* which is an event that has become punishing because it has in the past been associated with many other punishers. The icy stare is probably best categorized as a generalized punisher because disapproving looks have no doubt been associated with numerous unpleasant events such as reprimands as a child, marital arguments as an adult, and disciplinary action during one's stint in the army.

QUICK QUIZ H

1. Exercising to the point of exhaustion is for many people likely to be an (extrinsically/intrinsically) _intrisically_ punishing event.

2. The bad taste of rotting food will likely, for most people, function as a (primary/secondary) _primary_ punisher, while a restaurant that has served such food will function as a _secondary_ punisher.

3. Looking at an old photo album reminds you of your loneliness as a child, the loss of a favorite pet, and a childhood friend who died. As a result, you stop looking at it. The old photo album can be classified as a g_eneralized_ punisher. Looking at it is also (intrinsically/extrinsically) _extrinsically_ punishing.

Problems with the Use of Punishment

Although many people are of the opinion that behaviorists promote the use of punishment, behaviorists in fact have a general bias against it. This bias results from several problems that are associated with punishment (e.g., Newsom, Favell, & Rincover, 1983; Van Houten, 1983):

1. **Punishment of an inappropriate behavior does not directly strengthen the occurrence of appropriate behavior.** *It may even result in a general suppression of behavior.* A child who has been punished for playing aggressively will not necessarily begin playing more cooperatively, which is really the intended goal. She might instead simply stop playing with other children, which is not at all desirable.

2. **The person delivering the punishment could become an S^D for punishment, with the result that the unwanted behavior is suppressed only when that person is present.** The child, for example, might come to view the father as a discriminative stimulus for punishment and therefore continue to misbehave when the father is absent. The child has thus learned not to get caught for misbehaving rather than not to misbehave.

3. **Punishment might simply teach the individual to avoid the person who delivered the punishment.** A child who is severely punished by his father might begin minimizing the time spent with his father. This would obviously be less than ideal, especially if the father has much to offer the child.

4. **Punishment is likely to elicit a strong emotional response.** This is especially the case with the use of positive punishment, such as spanking or yelling, which is likely to result in crying or other displays of distress. These strong emotional responses are not only unpleasant but will also interfere with any subsequent attempt to teach the child more appropriate behavior. A child who is crying uncontrollably is not in an ideal state for learning anything new, such as how to play appropriately.

5. **Punishment can sometimes elicit an aggressive reaction.** Earlier in this text, we mentioned how a painful stimulus, such as electric shock, can elicit attack behavior in rats. Humans can also react with anger when subjected to aversive stimulation. This anger can be directed toward the individual responsible for the aversive event or, if there are inhibitions about doing so, can be directed toward a substitute target. Thus, a child who is severely punished for being noisy might not aggress toward the parent who spanked her but will instead aggress toward her younger sibling.

6. **The use of punishment, through the process of modeling, could teach the person that punishment is an acceptable means of controlling behavior.** The child whose behavior is being punished might come to believe that punishment is an appropriate method for controlling others. For this reason, children who are abused will sometimes (but not always) begin to abuse others. (The effect of modeling on aggression will be more fully discussed in Chapter 12.)

7. **Because punishment often has an immediate effect in stopping an unwanted behavior, the use of punishment is often strongly reinforced.** If hitting one's children has the immediate effect of getting them to stop making noise (an immediate negative reinforcer), then the behavior of hitting them has been strongly reinforced. The use of punishment can therefore be quite seductive, enticing the parent to use it more and more frequently, possibly to the point of being clearly abusive.

1. Punishment, especially (positive/negative) __positive__ punishment, can often elicit a strong e__motional__ reaction. This reaction might include __aggression__ that, if not directed toward the punisher, might be directed toward a substitute target.

2. Punishment of an inappropriate behavior (will/will not) __will not__ directly strengthen the occurrence of an appropriate behavior. It might even result in a general s__uppression__ of behavior.

3. The use of punishment could, through the process of m__odeling__, teach the recipient that punishment is an acceptable means for modifying a person's behavior.

4. Yelling at your dog for chewing your slippers might teach the dog to avoid __you__ rather than the slippers.

5. Yelling at your dog for chewing your slippers might also teach your dog not to chew the slippers only when __you are present__.

6. If punishment has an i__mmediate__ effect in getting someone to stop annoying us, this result can then act as a strong n__egative__ r__einforcement__ for using punishment in the future.

Benefits and the Effective Use of Punishment

For the reasons outlined previously, most behaviorists tend to avoid or minimize the use of punishment. Nevertheless, there may be some circumstances in which punishment is judged appropriate, such as in quickly suppressing a potentially dangerous behavior in a young child (for example, stopping the child from jabbing at another child's face with a sharpened pencil). This is especially the case given that alternative interventions, such as extinction and reinforcement of other behaviors, often take considerable time to have an effect. In addition to quickly suppressing a particular behavior pattern, punishment can have some beneficial side effects (e.g., Newsom et al., 1983; Van Houten, 1983):

1. **Punishment can sometimes lead to an increase in social behavior.** For example, a young child who has been punished by a time-out period for playing aggressively with his sister may become more affectionate toward his sister when the time-out period has ended. Thus, although punishment does not directly teach more appropriate behaviors, such behaviors can sometimes arise as a side effect. Why would such increases in social

And Furthermore

Punishment and Procrastination

Do you procrastinate? If so, you are definitely not alone. In one survey, 83% of college students admitted to procrastinating on academic tasks, with 50% admitting to procrastinating at least half the time (L. J. Solomon & Rothblum, 1984). What you may not be aware of is that procrastination is also a problem for many professors. It is a particular problem for new faculty members who are under intense pressure to publish in order to obtain tenure but who, at the same time, are often given relatively heavy teaching loads. The result is that new faculty often spend too much time preparing for teaching and too little time writing articles, thereby running the risk of not obtaining tenure at the end of their probationary period.

Robert Boice (e.g., 1989, 1996) has conducted detailed analyses of the work habits of new faculty members, distinguishing those who are productive from those who are not. A major finding was that productive faculty tended to engage in regular, short writing sessions spread throughout the week, whereas nonproductive faculty tended to engage in occasional "binge" episodes of writing spread far apart—that is, they generally procrastinated in their writing, but when they did write, they wrote intensely for long periods of time. Although these procrastinators generally believed that long, intense writing sessions are necessary to be productive, and that they merely needed to increase the frequency of such sessions, Boice concluded that binge writing was itself part of the problem. However invigorated one might feel during an intense session of writing—and procrastinators often reported this—this pattern of work is so effortful that one soon starts to avoid it. In essence, *binge writing sessions are sufficiently aversive that they punish the act of writing.*

The temporary effect that Skinner (1938) found when he attempted to punish a rat's behavior led him to conclude that punishment is an ineffective means for producing a lasting change in behavior. Skinner's experiment, however, utilized a relatively weak form of punishment: a device that slapped the rat on the paw when it attempted to press a lever. Subsequent research revealed that more intense forms of punishment, such as strong electric shocks, are capable of suppressing behavior for much longer periods of time (Azrin & Holz, 1966).

Avoidance Theory of Punishment The *avoidance theory of punishment* holds that punishment actually involves a type of avoidance conditioning in which the avoidance response consists of any behavior other than the behavior being punished (e.g., Dinsmoor, 1954). In other words, just as the behavior of jumping over a barrier is strengthened by shock avoidance in a shuttle avoidance situation, so too is the behavior of doing "anything

behavior occur? One possibility is that they represent innately determined appeasement gestures that are evoked by the punishment; in other words, when we are punished, we may have an inherited tendency to become more sociable in an effort to restore our relationships with others.

2. **Paradoxically, punishment sometimes results in an improvement in mood, such as less crying**. This is the opposite of what one would usually expect, which is that punishment would lead to more emotional behavior, not less. In some cases, however, it may be that the child was crying because he or she was in some way agitated; in such cases, the punishment might distract the child and disrupt the agitation.

3. **Punishment can increase attention to the environment,** as shown by increased eye contact and interest in ongoing activities. In other words, punishment, such as in the form of a shout, might motivate children to become more vigilant to what is happening around them. This can be especially valuable with children who tend to ignore the world around them, such as children who suffer from autism.

In summary, under some circumstances, the application of punishment may be justified and beneficial. If punishment is used, however, the following requirements should be met to maximize the possibility that it will be effective.

1. **As much as possible, punishment should be immediate rather than delayed.** Unfortunately, in the real world, delayed punishment is often the rule rather than the exception. A child's misbehavior is frequently discovered only several minutes or hours after its occurrence, and the delivery of a reprimand following such a long delay may have little effect. This is particularly the case with very young children and animals who, because they are unable to understand explanations, are unlikely to associate the punishment with the unwanted behavior. For example, yelling at a dog for making a mess on the carpet several hours after the incident has occurred will probably only upset the animal and do little to prevent future mishaps.

2. **At least at the outset, punishment should consistently follow each occurrence of the unwanted behavior.** Punishment tends to be less effective in suppressing a behavior when only some instances of the unwanted behavior are punished. In other words, unlike intermittent reinforcement, which has a strong effect on behavior, intermittent punishment tends to have a relatively weak effect on behavior. Nevertheless, once the behavior has been effectively suppressed, then intermittent punishment may be sufficient to maintain the suppression (Clark, Rowbury, Baer, & Baer, 1973).[3]

---

[3]One reason that intermittent punishment may be ineffective is that, particularly for intrinsically rewarding behaviors, it might produce a situation equivalent to intermittent reinforcement. In other words, to the extent that a behavior is reinforced on any nonpunished trial, then the behavior is being intermittently reinforced. And since intermittently reinforced behaviors tend to be quite persistent, this might counter the effects of the punishment being delivered on other trials. Needless to say, even when using continuous punishment, one should attempt to eliminate, so far as possible, any reinforcers for the unwanted behavior.

3. **Punishment should be intense enough from the outset to suppress the target behavior** (though—and this is the tricky part—not so intense as to be unnecessarily abusive). If one begins with a very mild punisher that is ineffective, and then gradually increases the intensity, it might require a very intense punisher to eventually suppress the unwanted behavior. For example, N. E. Miller (1960) presented rats with a very mild shock whenever they entered an alleyway, and then gradually increased the intensity of the shock until it effectively punished the rats' behavior. He found that these rats ceased responding only with very high levels of shock, far beyond what would normally have been required to suppress such a behavior. Likewise, a father who initially uses a very mild reprimand to try to get his daughter to stop teasing the dog, and then gradually increases the severity of the reprimand, might eventually have to deliver a very severe reprimand or worse before she will comply. But if the father had started with a moderately severe reprimand, the daughter might immediately complied, thereby saving the two of them (as well as the dog) a lot of grief. By starting with such a mild intervention and then gradually increasing its severity, the father essentially allowed the daughter to adapt to the punishing stimulus.

4. **Negative punishment is generally preferable to positive punishment.** Negative punishment procedures, such as time-out and response cost, are generally less likely to produce many of the harmful side effects associated with punishment as opposed to positive punishment procedures such as spanking and yelling. Negative punishment can, nevertheless, become abusive, such as when children are forced to endure extremely long time-out periods or are exposed to severe response cost procedures, such as removal of sufficient food.

5. **With individuals who have language capacity, punishment is more effective when accompanied by an explanation.** A possible reason for this is that an explanation will help clarify the exact behavior that is being punished, thereby making it easier for the child to avoid punishment in the future. This accords with the more general recommendation that children should be given frequent feedback about their behavior, both good and bad, because this will greatly facilitate the children's attempts to learn appropriate behavior (Craig, Kermis, & Digdon, 1998).

6. **Punishment of inappropriate behavior should be combined with positive reinforcement for appropriate behavior.** This is perhaps the most important rule. As with extinction, punishment of unwanted behavior will be more effective if it is combined with differential reinforcement for other behavior, especially behavior that is incompatible with the target behavior. As the appropriate behavior is strengthened, it will come to supplant the inappropriate behavior. Thus, to simply apply a time-out period to a child for playing inappropriately might have little effect if the child has not been adequately reinforced for playing appropriately. Time-out periods should, therefore, be followed by abundant reinforcement for appropriate behavior. In fact, differential positive reinforcement

for appropriate behavior (which might include *functional communication training* as discussed in Chapter 8) should always be considered the primary tool for eliminating unwanted behaviors. For a complete discussion of issues involved in the punishment of human behavior, see Axelrod and Apsche (1983).

1. Beneficial side effects of punishment include increases in s͟o͟c͟i͟a͟l͟ behavior, improvements in m͟o͟o͟d͟, and increased att͟e͟n͟t͟i͟o͟n͟ to the environment.

2. With verbally proficient humans, punishment tends to be more effective when it is accompanied by an e͟x͟p͟l͟a͟n͟a͟t͟i͟o͟n͟.

3. In general, when implementing a punishment procedure, one should begin with a punisher of sufficient i͟n͟t͟e͟n͟s͟i͟t͟y͟ to s͟u͟p͟p͟r͟e͟s͟s͟ the behavior.

4. Unlike reinforcement, punishment tends to have a stronger impact on behavior if delivered (consistently/intermittently) c͟o͟n͟s͟i͟s͟t͟e͟n͟l͟y͟.

5. In general, when attempting to punish a maladaptive behavior, one should also attempt to r͟e͟i͟n͟f͟o͟r͟c͟e͟ more adaptive behavior.

6. If punishment is to be used, it should be im͟m͟e͟d͟i͟a͟t͟e͟, since d͟e͟l͟a͟y͟e͟d͟ punishment tends to be relatively ineffective.

7. In general, n͟e͟g͟a͟t͟i͟v͟e͟ punishment is preferable to p͟o͟s͟i͟t͟i͟v͟e͟ punishment because the former is likely to have fewer side effects.

Theories of Punishment

Although a good deal of research has gone into investigating the effectiveness of punishment, less attention has been paid to developing and testing various theories of punishment. We will nevertheless briefly consider three theoretical approaches to punishment.

Conditioned Suppression Theory This theory is based on early work by Skinner (1938). He found that although punishment can quickly suppress a behavior, the behavior often quickly recovers to prepunishment levels when the punishment is withdrawn. What Skinner (1953) assumed was happening was that punishment generates an emotional response that tends to suppress any ongoing appetitive behavior. Crudely put, when the rat is shocked for pressing a lever that produces food, it becomes so upset that it loses interest in the food and therefore does not press the lever to obtain it. If, however, the shock is withdrawn, the rat resumes lever pressing as soon as it calms down enough for its interest in food to be revived. By analogy, if Tyler no longer teases his sister after being scolded for doing so, it is simply because he is too upset to pay much attention to his sister. Thus, the ***conditioned suppression theory of punishment*** assumes that punishment does not weaken a behavior but instead produces an emotional response that interferes with the occurrence of the behavior.

Based on these results, Boice has devised workshops for faculty members to help them overcome their tendency to procrastinate. A major component of these workshops is to learn to write in brief daily sessions, perhaps only 30 minutes per day at first, with the act of stopping on time considered as important as starting on time. The goal is to break the tendency to engage in binge writing sessions, and to begin to experience writing as less effortful and more enjoyable. Combined with other tactics, such as establishing a balanced lifestyle, arranging a comfortable writing environment, and seeking out mentors for feedback, these workshops have proven to be very effective in helping many faculty members become more productive.

Although Boice's advice is directed toward faculty, it also has obvious implications for students. Do you procrastinate in your studying because studying in your view is associated with long hours of hard work? If so, you may wish to consider the benefits of shorter, more consistent study sessions. For example, suppose that you do most of your studying during, say, 5 weeks out of a 15-week term. During the other 10 weeks, when there are no exams or pressing assignments, you typically do little or no studying—although you do spend a lot of time feeling guilty about it. What if, during those 10 weeks, you consistently studied one extra hour per day, 5 days per week (perhaps even combining it with the stimulus control training described in Chapter 8)? Although 1 hour per day might seem minor, consider that it adds up to 50 extra hours of studying by the end of the semester! That is a whopping amount of studying that could have a significant impact on your grades (especially if it is high-quality studying), and it would very likely make the end of the semester less stressful for you. Something to think about.

The tendency to procrastinate represents a lack of self-control, an issue that we focus on in Chapter 10. The lesson for now, however, is that some of our self-control problems might arise from trying to do too much, thereby punishing the very behavior pattern that we are trying to nurture. In such cases, brief daily sessions may be the solution.

---

other than lever pressing" reinforced by shock avoidance in a punishment-of-lever-pressing situation. Thus, in carrying out the following punishment procedure:

$$\textit{Lever press} \rightarrow \textbf{Shock}$$
$$\textbf{R} \qquad\quad \textbf{S}^{\textbf{P}}$$

one is actually carrying out the following avoidance conditioning procedure:

$$\textit{Any behavior other than lever pressing} \rightarrow \textbf{No shock}$$
$$\textbf{R} \qquad\qquad\qquad\qquad \textbf{S}^{\textbf{R}}$$

in which any behavior other than lever pressing is negatively reinforced by the absence of shock (e.g., Dinsmoor, 1954). Similarly, according to this theory, Tyler no longer teases his sister after being scolded for doing so because any behavior he carries out other than teasing his sister is negatively reinforced by the absence of a scolding. If correct, this means that punishment procedures are actually a form of negative reinforcement.

As with conditioned suppression theory, the avoidance theory of punishment assumes that punishment does not directly weaken a behavior. It simply replaces the punished behavior with an avoidance response of some sort. A disadvantage of this theory, however, is that it carries with it all of the theoretical difficulties associated with avoidance conditioning, some of which we discussed earlier in this chapter.

The Premack Approach to Punishment As you will recall from Chapter 5, the Premack principle holds that a high-probability behavior (HPB) can be used to reinforce a low-probability behavior (LPB). As it turns out, the opposite can be applied to punishment. According to the *Premack principle of punishment,* an LPB can be used to punish HPB (Premack, 1971a).

Take, for example, a rat that is both hungry and tuckered out from exercising. The rat in this condition is much more likely to eat food (an HPB) than to run in a wheel (an LPB). In terms of the Premack principle of reinforcement, this means that the behavior of eating can be used as a reinforcer for the behavior of running in a wheel:

$$\textit{Running in a wheel (LPB)} \rightarrow \textbf{Eating food (HPB)}$$
$$\textbf{R} \qquad\qquad\qquad\qquad \textbf{S}^{\textbf{R}}$$

According to the Premack principle of punishment, however, one can also use running in a wheel to punish the response of eating:

$$\textit{Eating food (HPB)} \rightarrow \textbf{Running in a wheel (LPB)}$$
$$\textbf{R} \qquad\qquad\qquad\qquad \textbf{S}^{\textbf{P}}$$

If eating food is followed by the consequence of being forced to run in a motorized wheel, the rat will be less likely to eat than if this consequence did not exist. To bring this point home, imagine how much easier it would be for a person who hates exercising to stick to a diet if she were forced to run a mile each time she ate something not on the diet.

Note that this approach implicitly assumes that punishment is the opposite of reinforcement: If reinforcement strengthens behavior, then punishment weakens behavior. In this sense, it differs from the previous two theories in that it views punishment as the mirror opposite of reinforcement. (See Domjan, 2003, for an extended discussion concerning theories of punishment.)

QUICK QUIZ K

1. According to the conditioned suppression theory of punishment, the application of punishment does not directly w__eaken__ a behavior; instead, it produces an em__otional__ reaction that tends to interfere with ongoing behavior.

2. This theory was based on evidence that punishment tends to produce only a (temporary/permanent) __temporary__ effect. This effect, however, probably results from using relatively (strong/weak) __weak__ forms of punishment.

3. According to the a__voidance__ theory of punishment, a rat stops lever pressing when lever pressing is followed by shock because the occurrence of any

behavior other than lever pressing is n<u>egatively</u> r<u>einforced</u> by the nonoccurrence of shock.

4. According to the punishment version of the Premack principle, the occurrence of a <u>low</u> <u>probability</u> behavior can be used to punish the occurrence of a <u>high</u> <u>probability</u> behavior. This means that if Sally rarely washes dishes and often bites her nails, then the behavior of <u>biting nails</u> can be used to punish the occurrence of <u>washing dishes</u>.

Effects of Noncontingent Punishment

In the typical escape/avoidance procedure, the aversive stimulus is controllable in the sense that the animal is able to make a response that significantly reduces its effect. Likewise, in a punishment procedure, the animal has some semblance of control because it does not make the response, then it will not be punished. In both cases, some type of contingency exists. But what if such a contingency were absent? What if the aversive event was essentially uncontrollable (and even unpredictable), such that whatever you do, you are unable to influence your exposure to that event? In the same manner that noncontingent reinforcement has some unique effects on behavior (as discussed in Chapter 7), so too does noncontingent punishment. Let us therefore spend the remainder of this chapter examining some of these effects.

Learned Helplessness

Consider the following experiment by Seligman and Maier (1967). The experiment began with an initial phase in which dogs were suspended in a harness and exposed to one of three conditions. In an *inescapable-shock condition*, the dogs received a series of shocks but were unable to do anything about them. In an *escapable-shock condition*, the dogs received shocks but were able to terminate each shock by pressing a panel with their snout. Each dog in this condition was also *yoked to* (paired up with) a dog in the first condition, such that when it turned off the shock for itself, it also turned off the shock for its partner dog in the other condition. Thus, the only difference between these two dogs was that the dog in the escapable-shock condition had control over the shocks while the dog in the inescapable-shock condition did not. Finally, some dogs were in a *no-shock control condition:* These dogs were never shocked and simply waited out the session suspended in the harness.

In the next phase of the experiment, all of the dogs were exposed to a shuttle avoidance procedure in which the task was to learn to avoid shock by jumping over a barrier, each shock being preceded by a 10-second period of darkness. The dogs exposed to the no-shock control condition in the initial phase of the experiment soon learned to avoid the shock by jumping over the barrier during the period of darkness that preceded the shock. The dogs exposed to the escapable-shock condition also learned the avoidance task quickly. The dogs from the inescapable-shock condition, however, behaved quite differently. When shocked, many of them initially ran around in great distress but then lay on the floor and whimpered. They made no effort to escape the shock. Even stranger, the few dogs that did by chance jump over the barrier, successfully escaping the shock, seemed unable to learn from this experience and failed to repeat it on the next trial. In summary, the prior exposure to inescapable shock seemed to impair the dogs' ability to learn to escape shock when escape later became possible. This phenomenon is known as *learned helplessness,* a decrement in learning ability that results from repeated exposure to uncontrollable aversive events.

Seligman and Maier (1967) theorized that the dogs became helpless because they had learned during exposure to inescapable shock that any attempt to escape was useless—in other words, that there was a *lack of contingency* between making a response and achieving a certain outcome. As a result, when confronted with shock in a new situation, they simply gave up. Other researchers, however, have proposed alternative explanations. For example, one theory suggests that animals exposed to inescapable aversive stimulation are distressed, and because of this distress they have difficulty attending to the relationship between behavior and its outcomes. Evidence for this theory includes the fact that if animals are given a very salient feedback stimulus whenever they make a successful escape response, such as by sounding a loud bell, the learned helplessness effect may disappear and the animals may once more learn such tasks effectively (Maier, Jackson, & Tomie, 1987).

Learned helplessness may account for certain difficulties experienced by humans. For example, Dweck and Reppucci (1973) found that children who attempted to answer unsolvable problems later had considerable difficulty answering solvable problems. This suggests that children who have difficulty passing math exams in school, possibly because of poor teaching, might grow up to become "math-anxious" individuals who quickly give up when confronted by any sort of math problem. Learned helplessness has also been related to certain forms of depression (Seligman, 1975). People who suffer a series of uncontrollable aversive events—loss of a job, physical illness, divorce, and so on—may become extremely passive and despondent. Like animals exposed to inescapable shock, they show little interest in improving their lot in life. (See also the opening vignette to this chapter.)

Fortunately, researchers have discovered a way to eliminate learned helplessness. The helpless animal will eventually recover its ability to escape on its own if it is repeatedly forced to escape the aversive stimulus—for example, if it is repeatedly dragged from the shock side of the chamber to the no-shock side (Seligman & Maier, 1967; Seligman, Rosellini, & Kozak, 1975). In similar fashion, behavioral treatments for depression often involve encouraging the patient to accomplish a graded series of tasks, starting with relatively minor tasks, such as writing a letter, and progressing to more difficult tasks, such as seeking a new job (Seligman, 1975).

Research has also suggested a means for preventing the development of learned helplessness. Experiments have revealed that prior exposure to escapable shock often immunizes an animal against becoming helpless when it is later exposed to inescapable shock (Seligman et al., 1975); the animal will persist in trying to escape the shock rather than give up. This suggests that a history of successfully overcoming minor adversities might immunize a person against depression when the person is later confronted by more serious difficulties. As a tree is strengthened by exposure to winds strong enough to bend but not break its limbs, so too individuals seem to be strengthened by exposure to manageable amounts of misfortune.

1. The original experiments on learned _helplessness_ revealed that dogs that had first been exposed to inescapable shock had (no difficulty/difficulty) _difficulty_ learning an escape response when later exposed to (escapable/inescapable) _escapable_ shock.

2. It seemed as though these dogs had learned that there (is/is not) _is not_ a contingency between their behavior and the offset of shock.

3. This effect can be overcome by (forcing/enticing) _forcing_ the dogs to make an escape response. As well, dogs that have had previous exposure to escapable shock are (more/less) _less_ susceptible to becoming helpless when later exposed to inescapable shock.

4. Learned helplessness may account for various difficulties in humans, including the clinical disorder known as d_epression_.

QUICK QUIZ L

Masserman's Experimental Neurosis

As you may recall, experimental neurosis is an *experimentally produced disorder in which animals exposed to unpredictable events develop neurotic-like symptoms.* We first encountered this phenomenon in our discussion of Pavlov's work on discrimination training in dogs (see Chapter 4). He and his colleagues discovered that dogs that had difficulty discriminating which cues predicted the delivery of food seemed to experience a nervous breakdown. Pavlov hypothesized that human neuroses might likewise develop as a result of exposure to unpredictable events.

A variation on Pavlov's procedure, involving the use of aversive rather than appetitive stimuli, was developed by Masserman (1943). He found that cats that experienced unpredictable electric shocks or blasts of air while eating often developed a pattern of neurotic-like symptoms. For example, normally quiet cats became restless and agitated, and normally active cats became withdrawn and passive—sometimes even to the point of becoming rigidly immobile (a symptom known as catalepsy). The cats also developed phobic responses to cues associated with feeding (since feeding had become associated with shock), as well as unusual "counterphobic" responses (for example, a cat might run to the goal box, stick its head inside the box, and then simply stare at the experimenter but not eat). It generally took only two or three presentations of the aversive stimulus to elicit these symptoms, which might then last several months.

More recent work (but with rats, not cats) has shown that many of these symptoms are similar to those found in posttraumatic stress disorder (PTSD)

ADVICE FOR THE LOVELORN

Dear Dr. Dee,

I am in a relationship that is starting to depress me, though most of what is happening is quite subtle. For example, when I am really excited about something, my partner will usually act quite disinterested. Similarly, when I suggest doing something that I believe will be fun, she usually turns it down and suggests something else. She also gets snippy with me (or worse yet, gives me the silent treatment) at the most unexpected moments.

I have tried talking to her about it, but she says that I am overreacting and then points to how affectionate she usually is (which is true).

So Am I Overreacting?

Dear So,

Sounds like you are in a relationship where much of your behavior is being subtly punished, some of it on a noncontingent basis. Thus, you are starting to perceive that whatever you do makes little difference. So it is not surprising that you are becoming depressed. You need to calmly point out to your partner the damaging effects of what she is doing, and the extent to which it is making you depressed.

First, however, you might wish to examine your own behavior to see if you are doing something to reinforce this pattern of behavior in your partner. Relationship problems are usually a two-way street, with neither party solely responsible for the difficulty. For example, perhaps you acquiesce to your partner's wishes so often that you are essentially reinforcing her for behaving this way. If that is the case, you may need to become a bit more assertive about your wishes. In fact, it could well be that she would be much happier if you were more assertive and your relationship with each other was more balanced.

Behaviorally yours,

Dr. Dee

---

in humans (e.g., Foa, Zinbarg, & Rothbaum, 1992). PTSD is a disorder that results from exposure to unpredictable life-threatening events, such as tornadoes, physical and sexual assaults, and battlefield experiences. Symptoms include sleep difficulties, exaggerated startle response, and intrusive recollections about the trauma. As well, victims often demonstrate fear and avoidance of trauma-associated stimuli (phobias), as well as a general numbing of responsiveness (for example, a restricted range of emotions). Although the subjective symptoms of PTSD, such as intrusive recollections, are impossible to replicate in animals (we have no idea what animals are actually thinking), many of the overt symptoms, such as phobic behavior, agitation, and passivity, are similar to those shown by animals subjected to noncontingent, unpredictable aversive stimulation.

Experimental neurosis is therefore proving to be a useful means for investigating the development of traumatic symptoms. For instance, as a general rule, traumatic symptoms are more easily induced in animals when the aversive stimulus is delivered in an environment that the animal has long associated with safety or some type of appetitive event. For example, unpredictable shocks delivered in a setting in which the animal typically eats food are especially likely to induce neurotic symptoms (Masserman, 1943). This suggests that symptoms of PTSD are more likely to arise when a person is, for example, unexpectedly attacked in the safety of his or her own home as opposed to a strange or dangerous area of town. The person who is attacked at home generalizes the experience and perceives the world at large as a dangerous, unpredictable place, with the result that he or she thereafter remains constantly vigilant (Foa et al., 1992).

You may be wondering how Masserman's experimental neurosis procedure differs from learned helplessness. The basic difference is that the typical learned helplessness procedure involves repeated exposure to aversive events that are predictable but uncontrollable. It is equivalent to being beaten up every day at 8:00 A.M. At first you try to escape from the beating, but eventually you give up any hope of escape. Masserman's experimental neurosis, on the other hand, involves infrequent but unpredictable exposure to aversive events. It is analogous to being unexpectedly dragged off every once in a while and beaten. The result is constant hypervigilance and an array of psychological and behavioral symptoms. But note that unpredictability also implies uncontrollability, so there is considerable overlap between the symptoms produced by learned helplessness and those produced by Masserman's experimental neurosis procedure (Foa et al., 1992).

1. Experimental neurosis occurs when animals exposed to unp_redictable_____ events develop neurotic-like symptoms.

2. Masserman (1943) found that normally quiet cats exposed to unpredictable shocks or blasts of air became (restless and agitated/withdrawn and passive)_restless____, whereas normally active cats became (restless and agitated/withdrawn and passive) _withdrawn__.

3. When food was paired with unpredictable shock, the cats also developed p_hobic_____ and counter_phobic_____ responses to the food.

4. Evidence suggests that neurotic symptoms are more likely to develop when the traumatic event occurs in an environment that the animal (or person) generally regards as (safe/dangerous) _safe_____.

5. Learned helplessness can be viewed as resulting from repeated exposure to aversive events that are p_redictable____ but un_controllable__; experimental neurosis can be viewed as resulting from exposure to events that are u_npredictable___.

And Furthermore

Dissociative Identity Disorder: A Behavioral Perspective

Some clinicians believe that the most severe disorder produced by exposure to traumatic events is dissociative identity disorder (DID; formerly called multiple personality disorder). The essential characteristic of this disorder is two or more personality states (or alter personalities) that repeatedly take control of behavior. Patients also suffer from extensive amnesia, with some personalities often unaware of the existence of other personalities. In the classic case of Eve White, for example (portrayed in the 1957 movie *The Three Faces of Eve*), the original personality of Eve White was reportedly unaware of an alter personality named Eve Black. Eve Black, however, was fully aware of Eve White and enjoyed making life difficult for her (Thigpen & Cleckley, 1957). This type of amnesia bears some similarity to repression, and in fact many clinicians prefer to conceptualize hidden memories of abuse as dissociated memories rather than repressed memories. Unfortunately, as with the concept of repression, the concept of DID is extremely controversial.

Behaviorists have traditionally viewed multiple personalities as distinct patterns of behavior (both overt and covert) that have arisen in response to distinctly different contingencies of reinforcement (Skinner, 1953). This reasoning has been carried a step further in the *posttraumatic model* of DID, which holds that DID usually results from childhood trauma (e.g., Ross, 1997). According to this model, an abused child can more easily cope with everyday life by usually forgetting about the abusive incidents and by pretending that the abuse is happening to someone else. In behavioral terms, this self-deception can be conceptualized as a type of covert avoidance response—"Nothing bad is happening to me"—that is negatively reinforced by a reduction in anxiety. As a result, the child learns to compartmentalize the distressing experience into a separate personality pattern that has its own dispositions and memories (Kohlenberg & Tsai, 1991; Phelps, 2000). This style of coping may become so habitual that it eventually results in the formation of dozens, or even hundreds, of separate personality states.

Others, however, have argued that DID is usually not the result of trauma but instead the result of suggestive influence (Lilienfeld et al., 1999; Spanos, 1996). According to this *sociocognitive model* (which can also be conceptualized as a cognitive-behavioral model), the patient's displays of alter personalities have been inadvertently shaped through processes of social reinforcement and observational learning. Supportive evidence for this model includes the following:

- The first clear observations of alter personalities are often obtained following exposure to a therapist who communicates to the patient that displays of alter personalities will be considered appropriate (and hence socially reinforced)—such as by asking the patient "if there is another thought process, part of the mind, part, person or force" within or who wishes to communicate with the therapist (e.g., Braun, 1980, p. 213).
- The number of alter personalities displayed by patients usually increases as therapy progresses, as does the patients' ability to quickly switch from one alter to another (Ross, 1997). This suggests that a process of shaping may be involved.

- The number of DID cases rose sharply following dramatic presentations of the disorder to the public during the 1970s and 1980s, such as the case of Sybil, which became a best-selling book (Schreiber, 1973) and a popular movie. This suggests that observational learning may have played a role in the increased prevalence of the disorder.
- Many (though not all) of the patients' memories of childhood trauma are memories that were recovered during therapy (Kluft, 1998). As noted in our previous discussion of repression, such recovered memories might sometimes be false.

Direct evidence for the role of behavioral processes in DID was reported by Kohlenberg (1973). He found that by manipulating the amount of reinforcement a patient received for displaying one of three alter personalities, he was able to change the amount of time that a particular personality was displayed. He then devised a successful treatment program that included reinforcing displays of the personality that acted normally and ignoring displays of other personalities.

Supporters of the posttraumatic model (e.g., Gleaves, 1996; Ross, 1997; Ross & Norton, 1989) and the sociocognitive model (e.g., Lilienfeld et al., 1999; Powell & Gee, 1999; Spanos, 1994, 1996) have each presented a series of arguments and counterarguments in support of their positions. The result has been some movement toward a middle ground. Ross (1997), for example, now acknowledges that at least some cases of DID have been artificially induced in therapy, while Lilienfeld et al. (1999) have acknowledged that a tendency toward developing DID-type symptoms might sometimes be the result of trauma. Likewise, Phelps (2000) has presented a behavioral account of DID, arguing that, although alter personalities could conceivably arise from a history of childhood trauma, therapists might also inadvertently strengthen displays of alter personalities through processes of social reinforcement.

SUMMARY

Negative reinforcement plays an important role in the development of escape and avoidance behaviors. A typical procedure for studying escape and avoidance is a shuttle avoidance task. In it, the rat first learns to escape shock by climbing over a barrier whenever it feels a shock; it then learns to avoid shock by climbing over the barrier in the presence of a cue that predicts shock delivery.

According to Mowrer's two-process theory, avoidance behavior results from (1) classical conditioning, in which a fear response comes to be elicited by a CS, and (2) operant conditioning, in which moving away from the CS is negatively reinforced by a reduction in fear. One criticism of this theory is that the avoidance response is extremely persistent, even when the aversive US is no longer presented. According to the anxiety conservation hypothesis, however, avoidance occurs so quickly that there is insufficient exposure to the CS for extinction of the fear response to take place. A second criticism of two-process theory is that once the animals become accustomed to making the avoidance response, they no longer seem fearful of the CS—hence, it seems that reduction in fear cannot serve as a negative reinforcer for avoidance. One answer to this criticism is that, although the animals may be significantly less fearful, they may still be slightly fearful.

Mineka pointed out that experimental avoidance conditioning in animals differs in several ways from phobic conditioning in humans. More specifically, the animals avoid the aversive US whereas phobic humans avoid the CS, and phobic conditioning in humans often requires only a single trial to produce extremely persistent avoidance. Stampfl, however, showed that phobic-like avoidance could be achieved in rats by providing them with the opportunity to make the avoidance response early in the chain of events leading up to the CS, thereby minimizing the amount of effort involved.

Avoidance conditioning plays a role in obsessive-compulsive disorders. Obsessions produce an increase in anxiety that is then reduced by carrying out the compulsive behavior pattern. Treatment procedures have been developed involving prolonged exposure to the anxiety-arousing event without engaging in the compulsive behavior pattern, thereby allowing the anxiety to be extinguished.

Positive punishment involves the presentation of an aversive stimulus, whereas negative punishment involves the removal of an appetitive stimulus. Two common forms of negative punishment are time-out, which involves the removal of access to all reinforcers, and response cost, which involves the removal of a specific reinforcer. Intrinsic punishment is punishment that is an inherent aspect of the behavior being punished, whereas extrinsic punishment is punishment that is not an inherent aspect of the behavior being punished. A primary punisher is one that is naturally punishing, and a secondary punisher is an event that is punishing because it has been associated with some other punisher. A generalized punisher has been associated with many other punishers.

There are several problems with the use of punishment, including a general suppression of behavior, avoidance of the person carrying out the punishment, elicitation of strong emotional responses, and an increase in aggressive behavior. Nevertheless, beneficial side effects can also occur, such as improvements in social behavior, mood, and attention to the environment. Punishment is more effective if delivered immediately, consistently, and at sufficient intensity to suppress the behavior. It also helps if punishment is accompanied by an explanation and if it is combined with positive reinforcement for appropriate behavior.

According to the conditioned suppression theory of punishment, punishment suppresses a behavior because it produces an emotional response that interferes with the behavior. According to the avoidance theory of punishment, punishment is a type of avoidance conditioning in which the avoidance response consists of doing anything other than the behavior that is being punished. The Premack principle, as applied to punishment, holds that low-probability behaviors can be used as punishers for high-probability behaviors.

Learned helplessness is a decrement in learning ability following exposure to inescapable aversive stimulation. Learned helplessness can be overcome by repeatedly forcing the animal to make the avoidance response. It can be prevented by providing an animal with prior exposure to escapable aversive stimulation. In Masserman's experimental neurosis procedure, animals are exposed to unpredictable aversive stimulation. This produces symptoms that are similar to those experienced by people who have developed posttraumatic stress disorder.

SUGGESTED READINGS

Newsom, C., Favell, J., & Rincover, A. (1983). The side effects of punishment. In S. Axelrod & J. Apsche (Eds.), *The effects of punishment on human behavior*. New York: Academic Press. A nice overview of the harmful, as well as beneficial, side effects of punishment.

Sidman, M. (1989). *Coercion and its fallout*. Boston: Authors Cooperative. A strong indictment by a major behaviorist of the use of punishment to control human behavior.

Spanos, N. P. (1996). *Multiple identities & false memories: A sociocognitive perspective*. Washington, DC: American Psychological Association.

Lilienfeld, S. O., Kirsch, I., Sarbin, T. R., Lynn, S. J., Chaves, J. F., Ganaway, G. K., & Powell, R. A. (1999). Dissociative identity disorder and the sociocognitive model: Recalling the lessons of the past. *Psychological Bulletin*, *125*, 507–523. This article and Spanos's book together constitute the most comprehensive presentation of the sociocognitive (or cognitive-behavioral) perspective on multiple personality disorder.

STUDY QUESTIONS

1. Distinguish between escape and avoidance behavior.
2. Describe the evolution of avoidance behavior in a shuttle avoidance procedure.
3. Describe Mowrer's two-process theory of avoidance behavior.
4. Outline two criticisms of two-process theory.
5. What is the anxiety conservation hypothesis? Outline Levis's answer to the problem of the "nonchalant" rat.
6. In what ways is experimental avoidance conditioning different from human phobic conditioning?
7. According to Stampfl, what is a critical factor in the development and maintenance of phobic behavior?
8. How can two-process theory account for obsessive-compulsive disorder?
9. Distinguish between time-out and response cost procedures.
10. What is the distinction between extrinsic punishment and intrinsic punishment?
11. What is the distinction between a primary punisher and a secondary punisher? What is a generalized punisher?
12. Briefly outline the various problems listed concerning the use of punishment.
13. What is the major advantage of punishment over extinction? What are three beneficial side effects of punishment?
14. Outline the six characteristics of effective punishment.

15. Describe the conditioned suppression theory of punishment.
16. Describe the avoidance theory of punishment.
17. Describe the Premack approach to punishment.
18. Describe the basic procedure that was first used to demonstrate learned helplessness in dogs and the outcome that was observed.
19. How can learned helplessness in dogs be eliminated? How can dogs be immunized against the development of learned helplessness?
20. Describe Masserman's procedure for inducing experimental neurosis, and list some of the symptoms he observed.

CONCEPT REVIEW

avoidance theory of punishment. Punishment involving a type of avoidance conditioning in which the avoidance response consists of any behavior other than the behavior being punished.

conditioned suppression theory of punishment. The assumption that punishment does not weaken a behavior, but instead produces an emotional response that interferes with the occurrence of the behavior.

exposure and response prevention (ERP). A method of treating obsessive-compulsive behavior that involves prolonged exposure to anxiety-arousing events while not engaging in the compulsive behavior pattern that reduces the anxiety.

extrinsic punishment. Punishment that is not an inherent aspect of the behavior being punished but that simply follows the behavior.

generalized (or generalized secondary) punisher. An event that has become punishing because it has in the past been associated with many other punishers.

intrinsic punishment. Punishment that is an inherent aspect of the behavior being punished.

learned helplessness. A decrement in learning ability that results from repeated exposure to uncontrollable aversive events.

Premack principle of punishment. A low-probability behavior (LPB) can be used to punish a high-probability behavior (HPB).

primary (or unconditioned) punisher. Any event that is innately punishing.

response cost. A form of negative punishment involving the removal of a specific reinforcer following the occurrence of a behavior.

secondary (or conditioned) punisher. An event that has become punishing because it has in the past been associated with some other punisher.

time-out. A form of negative punishment involving the loss of access to positive reinforcers for a brief period of time following the occurrence of a problem behavior.

two-process theory of avoidance. The theory that avoidance behavior is the result of two distinct processes: (1) classical conditioning, in which a fear response comes to be elicited by a CS, and (2) operant conditioning, in which moving away from the CS is negatively reinforced by a reduction in fear.

CHAPTER TEST

11. According to Mowrer, the two processes that underlie avoidance behavior are (1) c_lassical_ conditioning, in which a _fear_ response comes to be elicited by a CS, and (2) _operant_ conditioning, in which moving away from the CS is _negatively_ reinforced by a reduction in _fear_.

3. According to the _avoidance_ theory of punishment, if a rat is shocked for pressing a lever, then any behavior other than _lever pressing_ will be _negatively_ reinforced by the nonoccurrence of shock.

27. If a father punishes his son for being aggressive with his playmates, the son may learn not to be aggressive only when the father is _present_.

8. Otto woke up one night to find an intruder standing over him in his bedroom. When the intruder saw that Otto was awake, he stabbed him and fled. Boyd was walking through a strange part of town one night when he too was stabbed. In keeping with certain research findings on experimental _neurosis_, the person most likely to suffer symptoms of PTSD is _Otto_.

14. One criticism of Mowrer's two-process theory is that animals continue to make the avoidance response even though they no longer seem to be _afraid_ of the CS. One reply to this criticism is that although the animals may become significantly less _fearful_ of the CS, they do not in fact become completely _non-fearful_.

20. A person who checks her apartment door dozens of times each night to make sure that it is locked probably experiences a(n) _increase_ in anxiety when she thinks about whether the door is locked and a(n) _decrease_ in anxiety when she checks it. This then acts as a _negative_ reinforcer for the behavior of checking.

15. According to the _one-process_ theory of avoidance, I avoid bees simply because I am then less likely to be stung and not because I feel a reduction in fear.

9. Obert did not want to go to school one morning and so pretended that he was ill. Sure enough, his mother fell for the trick and let him stay home that day. Thereafter, Obert often pretended that he was ill so that he did not have to go to school. Obert's tendency to pretend that he was ill was strengthened through the process of _negative reinforcement_.

28. One problem with spanking a child for spilling food is that the spanking will likely elicit a strong _emotional_ response that will temporarily prevent the child from eating appropriately. The child may also become _aggressive_ as a result of the spanking, which might later be directed to his little brother or sister. He might also learn that an effective means of controlling others is through the use of _punishment_.

2. Skinner concluded that punishment generates a conditioned _emotional_ reaction that then suppresses any appetitive behavior, and that the appetitive behavior (will/will not) _will_ quickly recover once the punishment is withdrawn. Later research showed that this may be because Skinner had

used a relatively (strong/weak) ___weak___ form of punishment in his research.

19. Mowrer's two-process theory seems highly applicable to obsessive-compulsive disorder in that the occurrence of an obsessive thought is associated with a(n) ___increase___ anxiety, while performance of a compulsive behavior is associated with a(n) ___decrease___ in anxiety.

13. One criticism of Mowrer's two-process theory is that an avoidance response often does not seem to ___extinguish___, even after hundreds of trials. According to the ___anxiety conservation___ hypothesis, however, this is because exposures to the aversive ___CS___ are too brief for ___extinction___ to take place.

4. According to the Premack principle, if Rick smokes a lot and rarely vacuums, then ___smoking___ can serve as an effective punisher for ___vacuuming___.

22. Losing your wallet by being careless is an example of a (negative/positive) ___negative___ punisher, while getting a shock by being careless is an example of a ___positive___ punisher (assuming in each case that the behavior ___decreased___ in frequency).

12. According to Mowrer, I go out of my way to avoid bees because behaving this way has been (positively/negatively) ___negatively___ (reinforced/punished) ___reinforced___ by a ___reduction___ in fear.

29. One problem with spanking a child for being noisy while playing is that this will likely have an ___immediate___ effect in suppressing the behavior, which then serves as a strong reinforcer for the use of spanking on future occasions.

25. If you spank a dog for making a mess on the carpet, the dog might learn to avoid ___you___ than avoid making a mess on the carpet.

10. The theoretical difficulty with avoidance behavior, as opposed to escape behavior, is that the individual is moving from one (aversive/nonaversive) ___nonaversive___ situation to another, and it is difficult to see how a lack of change serves as a reinforcer.

31. The beneficial side effects of punishment can include increases in s___ocial___ behavior, improvements in m___ood___, and increased a___ttention___ to the environment.

21. One difference between OCD and a phobia is that a phobia usually requires a(n) (passive/active) ___passive___ avoidance response, while OCD usually requires a(n) ___active___ avoidance response.

7. Pietro is having great difficulty sleeping, is easily startled, and has developed various phobias. Pietro's symptoms are similar to those shown by Masserman's cats that were exposed to ___unpredictable___ aversive stimulation. This set of symptoms in experimental animals is known as experimental ___neurosis___; in humans, it is known as ___posttraumatic___ stress disorder.

16. According to Mineka, there are limitations in the extent to which experimental demonstrations of avoidance are analogous to human phobias. For example, in an experimental demonstration of avoidance that involves a tone and an aversive air blast, the rat avoids the ___air blast___, which is a (CS/US) ___US___. By comparison, the bee-phobic person who was once stung avoids ___bees___, which is a (CS/US) ___CS___.

1. For children who are old enough to understand language, punishment should always be combined with an _explanation_.

23. Making a child sit in a corner for being too noisy is an example of a _time-out_ procedure, while turning off the television set when the child is too noisy is an example of a _response-cost_ procedure.

5. When Renee was in elementary school, she was cruelly teased by a class-mate each recess. The teachers ignored her pleas for help, as did her other classmates. Seligman would predict that, as time passes, Renee is likely to (decrease/increase) _decrease_ efforts to stop the teasing. In other words, she will begin to suffer from learned _helplessness_. She may also become clinically _depressed_.

17. According to Mineka, there are limitations in the extent to which experimental demonstrations of avoidance are analogous to human phobias. For example, in an experimental demonstration of avoidance that involves a tone and an aversive air blast, the rat will likely require (one/more than one) _more than one_ conditioning trial. By comparison, a bee phobia may be acquired after _one_ conditioning trial(s). As well, the rat's avoidance behavior is likely to be (more/less) _less_ consistent than the bee phobic's avoidance behavior.

26. One problem with spanking a child for being noisy while playing is that he might not only stop being noisy but also stop _playing_.

30. A parent who wishes to punish her little girl for playing too roughly with the cat would do well to impose the punishing consequence _immediately_ after the occurrence of the unwanted behavior and, at least initially, on a(n) (consistent/unpredictable) _consistent_ basis. The parent should also _positively reinforce_ the behavior of playing appropriately with the cat.

6. According to learned helplessness research, Clint is (more/less) _less_ likely to become depressed following a bitter divorce if his own parents divorced when he was a child and he later recovered from the experience.

24. Hugh got injured at work while goofing around, and as a result he became less likely to goof around. Eduardo got reprimanded by the boss for goofing around, and he also became less likely to goof around. Getting injured is a (primary/secondary) _primary_ punisher for the behavior of goofing around, while getting reprimanded is a _secondary_ punisher.

18. Stampfl demonstrated that a critical factor in phobic conditioning is the possibility of making an (early/late) _early_ avoidance response, thereby minimizing the amount of _effort_ involved in avoiding the feared event.

Visit the book companion Web site at <http://www.academic.cengage.com/psychology/powell> for additional practice questions, answers to the Quick Quizzes, practice review exams, and additional exercises and information.

ANSWERS TO CHAPTER TEST

1. explanation
2. emotional; will; weak
3. avoidance; lever pressing; negatively
4. vacuuming; smoking
5. decrease; helplessness; depressed
6. less
7. unpredictable; neurosis; posttraumatic
8. neurosis; Otto
9. negative reinforcement
10. nonaversive
11. classical; fear; operant; negatively; fear
12. negatively; reinforced; reduction
13. extinguish; anxiety conservation; CS; extinction
14. afraid; fearful; nonfearful
15. one-process
16. air blast; US; bees; CS
17. more than one; one; less
18. early; effort
19. increase; decrease
20. increase; decrease; negative
21. passive; active
22. negative; positive; decreases
23. time-out; response cost
24. primary; secondary
25. you
26. playing
27. present (or nearby)
28. emotional; aggressive; punishment.
29. immediate
30. immediately; consistent; positively reinforce
31. social; mood; attention

CHAPTER 10

Choice, Matching, and Self-Control

Mark was becoming quite frustrated by Jan's insistence that they were spending too much time together. He told her that if two people truly love each other, they should want to spend as much time together as possible. Jan countered that she did love him but that spending too much time together was making their relationship dull and boring. For her, life was more fulfilling when she interacted with a variety of people each day.

Operant conditioning in the real world is rarely a matter of being offered only one source of reinforcement. Instead, individuals typically choose between alternative sources of reinforcement. In this chapter, we examine some of the principles by which such choices are made—especially the principle of matching, which stipulates that the amount of behavior directed toward an alternative is proportional to the amount of reinforcement we receive from that alternative. We also examine the types of choices involved when people attempt to exert "self-control" over their behavior.

Choice and Matching

Concurrent Schedules

In operant conditioning experiments, investigations of choice behavior often make use of a type of complex schedule known as a concurrent schedule. A *concurrent schedule of reinforcement* consists of the simultaneous presentation of two or more independent schedules, each leading to a reinforcer. The organism is thus allowed a choice between responding on one schedule versus the other.

For example, a pigeon may be given a choice between responding on a red key that is associated with a VR 20 schedule of reinforcement and a green key that is associated with a VR 50 schedule of reinforcement (see Figure 10.1). We can diagram this situation as follows:

Which alternative would you choose? If you think of this situation as analogous to choosing between two slot machines, one of which pays off after an average of 20 quarters are plugged in and the other of which pays off after an average of 50 quarters are plugged in, the choice becomes easy. You would

FIGURE 10.1 Illustration of a two-key operant procedure in which two schedules of reinforcement are simultaneously available, in this case, a VR 20 schedule on the red key and a VR 50 schedule on the green key. The two schedules thus form the two components of a *concurrent VR 20 VR 50* schedule of reinforcement. (*Source:* Domjan, 2003.)

pick the better-paying machine, that is, the one that requires an average of only 20 quarters to produce a win (if you can fight off everyone else who wants that machine). Similarly, the pigeon will come to develop an exclusive preference for the VR 20 alternative (Herrnstein & Loveland, 1975).

Choice between concurrent VR schedules is easy because an exclusive preference for the richer alternative clearly provides the better payoff. But what about concurrent VI schedules? What if, for example, a pigeon is presented with a concurrent VI 30-sec VI 60-sec schedule?

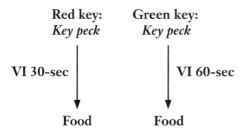

Remember that on VI schedules, reinforcers become available at unpredictable points in time (and any responses before that point will not result in reinforcement). Given this unpredictability, will the bird just randomly distribute its responses between the two alternatives, hoping to catch the reinforcers on each alternative as they become available (just as in trying to phone two friends at home, you might repeatedly dial each number in random order hoping to catch each person soon after he or she arrives home)? Herrnstein (1961) carried out just such an experiment using various schedule values and found that the pigeon's behavior under such circumstances is actually quite systematic. It is so systematic, in fact, that it led to the formulation of what is known as the matching law.

1. Many behaviors are reinforced on a c_____ schedule in which two or more in_____ schedules of reinforcement are s_____ available.

2. If a VR 25 and VR 75 schedule of reinforcement are simultaneously available, your best strategy would be to choose the _____ schedule (100/50/25) _____% of the time.

The Matching Law

The *matching law* holds that the proportion of responses emitted on a particular schedule matches the proportion of reinforcers obtained on that schedule (note that it is *proportion* of responses and reinforcers and not *number* of responses and reinforcers). Thus, a pigeon will emit approximately twice as many responses on the VI 30-sec schedule as on the VI 60-sec schedule because the rate of reinforcement on the former will be twice as great as on the latter (an average of two reinforcers per minute on the VI 30-sec schedule versus one reinforcer per minute on the VI 60-sec schedule). Similarly, a pigeon will emit three times as many responses on a VI 10-sec schedule as it will on a VI 30-sec schedule because the VI 10-sec schedule provides three times the rate of reinforcement (an average of six reinforcers per minute on the VI 10-sec schedule versus two per minute on the VI 30-sec schedule). *The matching law therefore predicts a consistent relationship between the proportion of reinforcers obtained on a certain alternative and the proportion of responses emitted on that alternative.* If a pigeon earns 10% of its reinforcers on a particular alternative, then it will emit 10% of its responses on that alternative; if it earns 60% of its reinforcers on an alternative, then it will emit 60% of its responses on it.

The matching law can also be expressed in the form of an equation:

$$\frac{R_A}{R_A + R_B} = \frac{S^R_A}{S^R_A + S^R_B}$$

where R is the number of responses emitted, S^R is the number of reinforcers earned, and the subscripts A and B refer to the two schedules of reinforcement. Thus, R_A is the number of responses emitted on schedule A, R_B is the number of responses emitted on schedule B, S^R_A is the number of reinforcers earned on schedule A, and S^R_B is the number of reinforcers earned on schedule B. Therefore, the term to the left of the equal sign:

$$\frac{R_A}{R_A + R_B}$$

indicates the proportion of responses emitted on schedule A. It is the number of responses emitted on schedule A divided by the total number emitted on both schedules. The term to the right of the equal sign:

$$\frac{S^R_A}{S^R_A + S^R_B}$$

indicates the proportion of reinforcers earned on schedule A. It is the number of reinforcers earned on schedule A divided by the total number earned on both schedules.

To illustrate how the equation works, let us look at some hypothetical data from an experiment involving a choice between a VI 30-sec and a VI 60-sec schedule. If the pigeon picks up most or all of the reinforcers available on each alternative in a 1-hour session, it should obtain about twice as many reinforcers on the VI 30-sec schedule as on the VI 60-sec. Imagine that this is essentially what happens: Our hypothetical pigeon obtains 119 reinforcers on the VI 30-sec schedule and 58 reinforcers (about half as many) on the VI 60-sec schedule. Plugging these values into the right-hand term of the equation, we get

$$\frac{S^R_{VI\,30\text{-s}}}{S^R_{VI\,30\text{-s}} + S^R_{VI\,60\text{-s}}} = \frac{119}{119 + 58} = \frac{119}{117} = .67$$

which means that the proportion of reinforcers obtained from the VI 30-sec schedule is .67. In other words, 67% (about 2/3) of the reinforcers acquired during the session are obtained from the VI 30-sec schedule, and 33% (about 1/3) are obtained from the VI 60-sec schedule (meaning that twice as many reinforcers are obtained from the VI 30-sec schedule). As for responses, imagine that our hypothetical pigeon emits 2,800 responses on the VI 30-sec schedule and 1,450 responses on the VI 60-sec schedule. Plugging these values into the left-hand term of the equation, we get

$$\frac{R_{VI\,30\text{-s}}}{R_{VI\,30\text{-s}} + R_{VI\,60\text{-s}}} = \frac{2,800}{2,800 + 1,450} = \frac{2,800}{4,250} = .66$$

Thus, the proportion of responses emitted on the VI 30-sec schedule is .66. In other words, 66% of the responses are emitted on the VI 30-sec schedule (and 34% are emitted on the VI 60-sec schedule). In keeping with the matching law, this figure closely matches the proportion of reinforcement obtained on that schedule (.67). In other words, the proportion of responses emitted on the VI 30-sec schedule approximately matches the proportion of reinforcers earned on that schedule. (For results from Herrnstein's [1961] original matching experiment in which pigeons chose between several different combinations of schedules, see Figure 10.2).

FIGURE 10.2   Experimental results depicting the proportion of responses emitted by two pigeons on key A. Different combinations of schedules were offered on key A versus key B across the different conditions of the experiment, with the schedule values ranging from VI 90-sec to VI 540-sec to extinction (no reinforcers available). As the schedule combinations changed and the proportion of reinforcers earned on key A increased from approximately .1 to 1.0, the proportion of responses emitted on key A increased in similar fashion. (*Source:* Adapted from "Relative and absolute strength of response as a function of frequency of reinforcement," by R. J. Herrnstein, 1961, *Journal of Experimental Analysis of Behavior, 4,* pp. 267–272. Copyright © 1961 by the Society for the Experimental Analysis of Behavior, Inc. Reprinted with permission.)

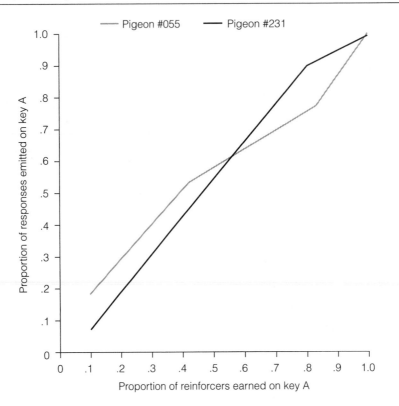

Matching appears to be a basic principle of choice behavior, applicable to a variety of situations and species. For example, Houston (1986) investigated the extent to which the pied wagtail, an insectivorous bird in Britain, distributed its foraging behavior between two separate patches of food: (1) a stretch of territory along the banks of the Thames River, which the territorial owner defended from other wagtails (and only some birds owned territories), and (2) an open meadow that any wagtail could visit and feed upon as part of the flock. Those birds that owned territories tended to walk circular routes within their territories, feeding off insects that were regularly washed up by the river. If, however, food along the river was scarce, the owner could fly over to the meadow and feed with the flock.

(In a sense, finding nothing to eat at home, the bird had the option of eating out at the local restaurant.) Houston found that the proportion of time a bird spent in one food patch versus the other (its own territory versus the public meadow) approximately matched the proportion of food it obtained in that patch.

Matching is also applicable to human social behavior. For example, in a group situation, we must choose between directing our conversation to one person or another, each of whom provides a different rate of reinforcement (in the form of comments or acknowledgments). In one investigation, Conger and Killeen (1974) asked student volunteers to participate with three other students in a discussion session on drug abuse. Each volunteer was unaware that the other members of the group were actually confederates of the experimenter. During the discussion session, while the volunteer was talking, the two confederates sat on either side and intermittently expressed approval in response to whatever the volunteer happened to be saying at that time. The experimenters systematically varied the frequency of verbal approvals delivered by each of the confederates. They found that the relative amount of time the volunteer looked at each confederate matched the relative frequency of verbal approval delivered by that confederate. If one confederate delivered twice as many approvals as the other confederate, then that confederate was looked at twice as often. In general, these results suggest that the principle of matching may underlie various aspects of human social interaction.

QUICK QUIZ B

1. According to the matching law, the (number/proportion) _____ of _____ on an alternative matches the (number/proportion) _____ of _____ obtained on that alternative.

2. On a concurrent VI 60-sec VI 120-sec schedule, the pigeon should emit about (half/twice) _____ as many responses on the VI 60-sec alternative as opposed to the VI 120-sec alternative.

3. If a pigeon emits 1,100 responses on key A and 3,100 responses on key B, then the proportion of responses on key A is _____. If the pigeon also earned 32 reinforcers on key A and 85 reinforcers on key B, then the proportion of reinforcers earned on key A is _____. This pigeon (did/did not) _____ approximately match pr_____ of r_____ to pr_____ of _____.

Deviations from Matching

Although matching provides a good description of behavior in many choice situations, a variety of exceptions have been noted. In general, there are three types of exceptions, or deviations, from matching (Baum, 1974, 1979). The first deviation, which is quite common, is called undermatching. In **undermatching,** the proportion of responses on the richer schedule versus the poorer schedule is less different than would be predicted by matching (to remember this, think of *under*matching as *less* different). For example, the matching law predicts that the proportion of responses should be .67 on the

And Furthermore

Basketball and the Matching Law

In an interesting application of the matching law to sports activities, Vollmer and Bourret (2000) examined the allocation of 2- versus 3-point shots made by male and female basketball players at a major university. The question of interest was whether the players would match the proportion of shots taken from the 3-point range to the proportion of reinforcers (baskets) they obtained from that range. The researchers found that such matching did indeed occur (particularly when the matching equation was altered somewhat to account for the greater value of 3-point shots). In other words, if a certain player obtained about 35% of his or her points from the 3-point range, then about 35% of his or her shots tended to occur from that range. The authors speculated that this ability to match the proportion of shots attempted from a certain range to the proportion of points obtained from that range may be a distinguishing characteristic of player excellence. One author, for example, described how he casually observed a local street game in which 3-point shots were frequently attempted even though they were almost never successful. In other words, these less-skillful players did not display the same tendency to match that the university players had displayed (this was a top-ranked university, by the way). The matching law may, therefore, prove useful in evaluating the skill level of basketball players.

You may have noticed that this type of matching suggests that basketball shots are reinforced on a VI schedule, which contradicts the typical notion that shot-making in such activities is reinforced on a VR schedule (with rate of reinforcement largely dependent on the number of shots attempted). The authors of this study, however, suggest that basketball shots may in fact be reinforced on a combination (conjunctive) VR–VI schedule, with reinforcement dependent both on the number of shots attempted (the VR component) and on defensive lapses by the opposition that occur at unpredictable points in time (the VI component). (See also Reed, Critchfield, & Martens, 2006, for an application of the matching law to play selection in National Football League games during the 2004 season.)

richer VI 30-sec schedule and .33 on the poorer VI 60-sec schedule. If we instead find proportions of .60 and .40, respectively, then undermatching has occurred. There is less of a difference in responding between the richer and poorer schedules than would be predicted by matching.

Undermatching can occur when there is little cost for switching from one schedule to another. For example, in our previous description of a hypothetical matching experiment, we actually left out an important aspect of the procedure. Whenever the pigeon switches from one key to another, the act of doing so initiates a slight delay of, say, 2 seconds during which no response will be effective in producing a reinforcer, even if a reinforcer happens to be available at that time. It is as though, when the pigeon switches from one key to another, the first peck on the new key is simply a statement of intent that says, "I now want to try this key," following which there is a 2-second delay before any peck can actually earn a reinforcer. This delay feature is called a *changeover delay* or *COD*.

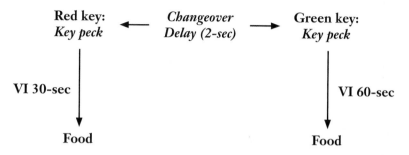

Without a COD, a pigeon will simply alternate pecks back and forth on each key, catching each reinforcer as soon as it becomes available. Only when a slight cost for switching is added to the situation does the pigeon spend more time on the richer alternative.

The COD can be thought of as the experimental equivalent of a foraging situation in which the animal has to travel a certain distance between food patches. If two food patches are extremely close together (say, each patch is separated by only a narrow stream), then undermatching is likely to occur. The animal will simply move back and forth from one side to another, looking for prey, even if one side is generally a much richer area in which to hunt. If, however, the two patches are more widely separated (say, the stream is some-what broad), then the animal is more likely to match the amount of time it spends on one side of the stream to the number of prey that it obtains on that side. It will spend proportionately more time on the rich side of the stream, and less time on the poor side of the stream.

A second deviation from matching is called overmatching. In **overmatching,** the proportion of responses on the richer schedule versus the poorer schedule is more different than would be predicted by matching (to remember this, think of *over*matching as *more* different). For example, the matching law predicts that the proportion of responses should be .67 on the richer VI 30-sec schedule and .33 on the poorer VI 60-sec schedule. If we instead find proportions of .80 and .20, respectively, then overmatching has occurred. There is more of a difference in responding between the richer and poorer schedules than would be predicted by matching.

Overmatching can occur when the cost of moving from one alternative to another is very high. For example, Baum (1974) found that overmatching occurred when a pigeon had to walk around a partition and climb across a wooden hurdle to switch from one response key to another. The pigeon switched less often and spent more time on the richer alternative than the matching law would predict. Similarly, a predator that has to cross a mountain ridge to move from one food patch to another might make the trip only infrequently and spend considerably more time in the richer food patch than predicted by matching.

1. When the difference in the proportion of responding on richer versus poorer alternatives is greater than would be predicted by matching, we say that _____ has occurred.

2. When the difference in the proportion of responding on richer versus poorer alternatives is less than would be predicted by matching, we say that _____ has occurred.

3. In experimental studies of matching, the act of switching from one alternative to another results in a c_____ d_____: a short period of time that must pass before any response can produce a reinforcer.

4. This experimental procedure seems analogous to foraging situations in which an animal has to t_____ a certain d_____ from one food patch to another.

5. In general, food patches that are separated by a very great distance will produce _____ matching, while food patches that are separated by a very short distance will produce _____ matching.

The final deviation from matching is called bias. **_Bias from matching_** occurs when one alternative attracts a higher proportion of responses than would be predicted by matching, regardless of whether that alternative contains the richer or poorer schedule of reinforcement. For example, suppose that our two schedules are VI 30-sec and VI 60-sec, and that we alternate which schedule is associated with the red key versus the green key. The matching law predicts that the proportion of responses on the red key should be .67 when the richer VI 30-sec schedule is presented on it, and .33 when the poorer VI 60-sec schedule is presented on it. But if the proportions instead turned out to be .77 when the VI 30-sec schedule is presented on it and .43 when the VI 60-sec schedule is presented on it, then bias has occurred (see Table 10.1).

TABLE 10.1 Hypothetical results indicating bias from matching. More responses are emitted on the red key, both when it is the richer alternative (VI 30-sec) and when it is the poorer alternative (VI 60-sec), than would be predicted by matching. (Of course, this also means that fewer responses are emitted on the green key than would be predicted by matching.)

CONDITION A (RICHER SCHEDULE ON RED KEY)	PREDICTED	OBTAINED
Red Key: VI 30-sec	.67	.77
Green Key: VI 60-sec	.33	.23
CONDITION B (POORER SCHEDULE ON RED KEY)		
Red Key: VI 60-sec	.33	.43
Green Key: VI 30-sec	.67	.57

The pigeon is emitting 10% more responses on the red key than predicted by matching, both when it is the richer alternative and when it is the poorer alternative. (Of course, this also means that the pigeon is emitting 10% fewer responses on the green key.) In a sense, the pigeon seems to like red and therefore expends extra effort on the red key over and above the amount of responding dictated by the schedule of reinforcement. Similarly, in a conversation with a group of individuals, Erin might spend additional time directing her conversation toward Jason, whom she finds very attractive. For example, on one day, he provides 72% of the reinforcers during a conversation, but she nevertheless looks at him 84% of the time; on another day, he provides only 23% of the reinforcers, but she nevertheless looks at him 36% of the time. In each case, she looks at him more than would be predicted by matching. His attractiveness is an additional factor, over and above the amount of conversational reinforcement he offers, that influences how much she looks at him.

Bias can be a precise way to measure preference. For example, on a concurrent VI 60-sec VI 60-sec schedule, the pigeon should respond equally on the two alternatives. But what if each alternative leads to a different reinforcer, perhaps wheat on one side and buckwheat on the other? Under these circumstances, the extent to which the pigeon biases its responding toward the schedule leading to wheat indicates the extent of the pigeon's preference for wheat. In fact, Miller (1976) carried out just such an experiment and found that pigeons preferred wheat over buckwheat by a ratio of about 1.4 to 1.0. If we think of key pecks as equivalent to how much money pigeons would be willing to spend for one alternative versus the other, then the pigeons were willing to spend $1.40 on a bag of wheat compared to only $1.00 for a bag of buckwheat. Bias in matching can, therefore, be used to indicate degree of preference for different reinforcers.

In summary, undermatching occurs when the difference in responding between the richer and poorer schedules is less than predicted by matching. Overmatching occurs when the difference in responding between the richer and poorer schedules is more than predicted by matching, and bias occurs when one response alternative receives more responses than predicted by matching regardless of whether it contains the richer or poorer schedule. Each of these deviations has been incorporated into more complex versions of the matching law (Baum, 1974).

As with the phenomenon of behavioral contrast (discussed in Chapter 8), the matching law reminds us that operant behavior should often be viewed in context. The amount of behavior directed toward an alternative is a function of the amount of reinforcement available on that alternative as well as the amount of reinforcement available on other alternatives. This notion has important implications for everyday behavior. For example, although a child might spend little time reading, this does not mean that reading is not a reinforcing activity for that child. If other highly reinforcing activities, such as computer games and television, happen to be simultaneously available, reading may be losing out simply because it provides less reinforcement (especially immediate reinforcement) than those other activities.

Thus, a simple but effective way to motivate the child to read might be to limit the amount of time those other activities are available. In the absence of such alternatives, the child might naturally gravitate toward reading as a source of reinforcement.

1. When greater responding is shown for a particular alternative than would be predicted by matching, irrespective of the amount of reinforcement obtained from that alternative, we say that the organism has a b_____ for that alternative.

2. Food patches that differ in the type of prey found within them may produce the type of deviation from matching known as _____.

3. When a bear obtains 70% of its food from a nearby stream, it spends 80% of its time at the stream; when it obtains 30% of its food from the stream, it spends 25% of its time at the stream. When a cougar obtains 20% of its food in a particular canyon, it spends 35% of its time in that canyon; when it obtains 65% of its food from that canyon, it spends 80% of its time in the canyon. Which animal shows systematic evidence of bias? _____.

Matching and Melioration

The matching law describes how behavior is distributed across various alternatives in a choice situation. It does not, however, explain why this pattern of distribution occurs. You might think that it occurs simply because it somehow maximizes one's overall level of reinforcement, a proposition known as *maximization (or optimization) theory* (e.g., Rachlin, 1978). An alternative explanation, however, is called melioration theory (to *meliorate* means "to make better"). According to **melioration theory,** the distribution of behavior in a choice situation shifts toward those alternatives that have higher value regardless of the long-term effect on the overall amount of reinforcement (Herrnstein, 1990). For example, suppose that when a pigeon is *first* confronted with a concurrent VI 30-sec VI 60-sec schedule, it emits an *equal* number of responses on both alternatives. The responses emitted on the VI 30-sec schedule will result in twice as many reinforcers as those emitted on the VI 60-sec schedule. Thus, in terms of benefits (reinforcers obtained) versus costs (responses made), the VI 30-sec schedule will have a much higher value than the VI 60-sec schedule, because the bird will have obtained twice as many reinforcers on the VI 30-sec schedule for the same amount of work. This will make the VI 30-sec schedule a very attractive alternative to the pigeon, with the result that the pigeon will be tempted in subsequent sessions to shift more and more of its behavior in that direction. This shifting, however, will cease at the point of matching, because that is the point at which the two alternatives have about equal value. The pigeon will still be earning twice as many reinforcers on the VI 30-sec schedule, but in doing so it will be expending twice as many responses on that alternative. Thus, the cost of each alternative (in responses made) will now match the benefits obtained from that alternative (in reinforcers earned). Melioration in this situation is thus a sort of leveling-out process, in which behavior shifts until the two alternatives have about equal value in costs versus benefits.

At this point, you might be thinking that melioration is rather trivial. Why would an animal or person not shift behavior toward the richer alternative? The problem is that this tendency to move toward the richer alternative can sometimes result in a substantial reduction in the total amount of reinforcement obtained. There are three ways in which this can occur.

First, an alternative may not require as much responding as one is distributing toward it to obtain all of the available reinforcers. Consider, for example, a pigeon that is presented with a concurrent VR 100 VI 30-sec schedule (note that the first alternative is a VR schedule). On the VR 100 alternative, 100 responses on average will result in a reinforcer, while on the VI 30-sec alternative, the first response after an average interval of 30 seconds will result in a reinforcer. What is the pigeon's best strategy in this situation?

The best strategy is for the pigeon to spend most of its time on the VR schedule, in which the number of reinforcers obtained is directly tied to the number of responses made, and then briefly switch to the VI alternative about every 30 seconds or so to pick up any reinforcer that might have become available on that alternative. This strategy will maximize the amount of reinforcement obtained. In reality, pigeons tend to match the amount of time spent on the VI schedule to the number of reinforcers earned on that schedule, thereby spending more time on the VI schedule and less time on the VR schedule than they should (Herrnstein & Heyman, 1979). Thus, if a pigeon happens to obtain 60% of its reinforcers from the VI 30-sec schedule, it will spend 60% of its time responding on the VI 30-sec schedule and only 40% of its time responding on the VR 100 schedule—a distribution of behavior that greatly reduces the overall amount of reinforcement obtained during the session. Hence, the pigeon's tendency to match (meliorate) has the effect of producing an overall level of reinforcement that is suboptimal.

In similar fashion, Henry, a salesman with a large manufacturing company, might spend too much time courting clients who are relatively easy sells (in reality, he only needs to call on such clients once a month to make a sale), and too little time courting retailers who are relatively difficult sells (who need to be intensively courted before a sale can be made). If Henry shifted some of his time away from the easy clients and toward the difficult clients, he might experience almost no loss of business from the former and a substantial gain in business from the latter. Unfortunately, because the rich schedule of reinforcement provided by the easy clients is very attractive to him, he continues to spend too much time with his easy clients and too little time with his difficult clients.

As another example, consider the manner in which many students distribute study time between the courses they are taking. Students often spend the most time studying for their most enjoyable course and the least time studying for their least enjoyable course. Yet the least enjoyable course is probably the one on which students should spend the most time studying. The result is that they spend the least time studying those courses that require the most work.

1. According to _____ theory, the distribution of behavior in a choice situation shifts toward that alternative that has a (lower/higher) _____ value. This shifting will cease at the point where the two outcomes are (approximately equal/maximally different) _____ in costs versus benefits.

2. A rat faced with a concurrent VR 60 VI 80-sec schedule will spend more time on the _____ schedule than necessary to pick up all of the available reinforcers on that schedule. This result is consistent with _____ theory but contradicts what is known as max_____ (or op_____) theory.

3. Shona spends a lot of time cleaning her apartment, which she quite enjoys, and little time studying, which she does not enjoy. Chances are that this distribution of behavior, which results from the tendency to _____, (will/will not) _____ maximize the amount of reinforcement in her life.

A second problem with melioration is that overindulgence in a highly reinforcing alternative can often result in long-term habituation to that alternative, thus reducing its value as a reinforcer. Suppose, for example, that you suddenly become so rich that you can eat as much as you want of whatever you want. Before becoming rich, you rarely ate lobster, which you absolutely loved. Now, with your newfound wealth, you begin eating lobster almost every day. The problem is that if you eat lobster this frequently, you will likely become habituated to it, such that, although still enjoyable, it is no longer the heavenly treat that it once was. For this reason, many people fondly remember those times in their lives when they had limited resources and had to struggle a bit to get by. The overall amount of reinforcement they experienced at that time, when highly valued items such as lobster could be experienced in only small quantities and truly enjoyed, actually may have been much greater than it is now.[1]

This same process can be a contributing factor to the development of substance abuse. If drinking in a bar is a highly enjoyable activity, you might begin shifting more and more of your behavior in that direction. Eventually, you will be spending so much time in the bar that the overall amount of reinforcement in your life is substantially reduced—both because drinking is no longer as enjoyable as when you drank less frequently, and because you are now in the bar so much that you are missing out on reinforcers from other nonalcohol-related activities. You may in fact be fully aware that your alcohol-oriented life is not very satisfying (in fact, such awareness is a defining characteristic of an addiction) yet find it very difficult to break free and reject the pleasure of heading to the bar for another evening of positive reinforcement.

Many of the previous examples can also be seen as instances of a *third, more general problem, which is that melioration is often the result of behavior being too strongly governed by immediate consequences as opposed to delayed consequences.* The immediate reinforcement available from studying more enjoyable courses tempts one away

---

[1]See also the article entitled, "What Is Wrong With Daily Life in the Western World?" in Skinner (1987). Skinner does not use the term *melioration*, but many of the examples he provides can be interpreted as examples of this process.

ADVICE FOR THE LOVELORN

Dear Dr. Dee,

My boyfriend spends almost all his time with me, which I find depressing. I try to tell him that I need some breathing space, but he seems to think that if I truly loved him, I would want to be with him always. What is your opinion on this?

Smothered

Dear Smothered,

Sounds as if your love relationship may have fallen prey to the damaging effects of melioration. Although some people believe that being in love with someone means wanting to be with that person always, the reality is that too much togetherness can result in a severe case of habituation. Add to this the possibility that the two individuals involved are also spending much less time interacting with other people, and it could well be that the overall amount of reinforcement in their lives is actually less than it was before they met. This suggests that some relationships might improve if the couple spent a bit less time together and worked a bit harder at maintaining other sources of social reinforcement (given that this does not become a cheap excuse for having an affair!). So, behaviorally speaking, I agree with you.

Behaviorally yours,

Dr. Dee

from working on less enjoyable courses and maximizing one's overall grade point average at the end of the term (a delayed reinforcer). And the immediate reinforcement available from going to the bar each evening tempts one away from moderating one's drinking and eventually establishing a more healthy and satisfying lifestyle (a delayed reinforcer). The difficulties that arise from the strong preference for immediate reinforcers over delayed reinforcers are described more fully in the following section.

1. One problem with melioration is that this tendency may result in (over/under) _____ indulgence of a favored reinforcer with the result that we may experience long-term h_____ to it. This means that our enjoyment of life may be greatest when we (do/do not) _____ have all that we want of highly valued items.

2. Another problem is that melioration can result in too much time being spent on those alternatives that provide relatively i_____ reinforcement and not enough time on those that provide d_____ reinforcement.

QUICK QUIZ F

Self-Control

In our discussion of melioration, we noted that people often engage in suboptimal patterns of behavior. Moreover, although people realize that these patterns are suboptimal, they seem unable to change them. They decide to quit smoking but do not persist more than a day; they are determined to go for a run each morning but cannot get out of bed to do so; they resolve to study each evening but spend most evenings either watching television or socializing. In short, they know what to do, but they do not do it. To use the common vernacular, they lack self-control.

Why people have such difficulty controlling their own behavior has long been a matter of conjecture. Plato maintained that people engage in actions that are not in their best interest because of a lack of education, and that once they realize that it is to their benefit to behave appropriately, they will do so. Aristotle disagreed, however, noting that individuals often behave in ways that they clearly recognize as counterproductive. Many people, at least in this culture, would probably agree with Aristotle. They would probably also contend that self-control seems to require a certain mental faculty called willpower. A person who behaves wisely and resists temptations is said to have a lot of willpower, whereas a person who behaves poorly and yields to temptations is said to have little willpower. But is the concept of willpower, as used in this manner, really an explanation? Or is it one of those false explanations based on circular reasoning?

"Sam quit smoking. He must have a lot of willpower."
"How do you know he has a lot of willpower?"
"Well, he quit smoking, didn't he?"

The term *willpower*, used in this way, merely describes what Sam did—that he was able to quit smoking. It does not explain why he was able to quit smoking. For this reason, telling someone that they need to use more willpower to quit smoking is usually a pointless exercise. They would love to use more willpower—if only someone would tell them what it is and where to get it.

In the remainder of this chapter, we discuss some behavioral approaches to self-control. These approaches generally reject the traditional concept of willpower and instead focus on the relationship between behavior and its outcomes. We begin with Skinner's rudimentary analysis of self-control.

Skinner on Self-Control

Skinner (1953) viewed self-control, or "self-management," not as an issue of willpower but as an issue involving conflicting outcomes. For example, drinking alcohol can lead to both positive outcomes (e.g., increased confidence and feelings of relaxation) and negative outcomes (e.g., a hangover along with that idiotic tattoo you found on your arm the next morning). Skinner also proposed that managing this conflict involves two types of responses: a *controlling response* that serves to alter the frequency of a *controlled response*.

Suppose, for example, that to control the amount of money you spend, you leave most of your money at home when heading out one evening. The act of leaving money at home is the controlling response, while the amount you subsequently spend is the controlled response. By emitting the one response, you affect the other.

Skinner (1953) listed several types of controlling responses, some of which are described here.

Physical Restraint With this type of controlling response, you physically manipulate the environment to prevent the occurrence of some problem behavior. Leaving money at home so that you will spend less during an evening out is one example; loaning your television set to a friend for the rest of the semester so that you will be more likely to study than watch television is another.

Depriving and Satiating Another tactic for controlling your behavior is to deprive or satiate yourself, thereby altering the extent to which a certain event can act as a reinforcer. For example, you might make the most of an invitation to an expensive dinner by skipping lunch, thereby ensuring that you will be very hungry at dinnertime. Conversely, if you are attempting to diet, you might do well to shop for groceries immediately *after* a meal. If you are satiated, as opposed to hungry, during your shopping trip, you will be less tempted to purchase fattening items such as ice cream and potato chips.

Doing Something Else To prevent yourself from engaging in certain behaviors, it is sometimes helpful to perform an alternate behavior. Thus, people who are trying to quit smoking often find it helpful to chew gum, and people who are trying to diet often find it helpful to sip sugar-free sodas.

Self-Reinforcement and Self-Punishment A self-control tactic that might seem obvious from a behavioral standpoint is to simply reinforce your own behavior. Although Skinner suggested that this might work, he also noted a certain difficulty with it. In the typical operant conditioning paradigm, the reinforcer is delivered only when the appropriate response is emitted. The rat must press the lever to receive food, the child must clean his room to receive a cookie, and the student must study and perform well on an exam to receive a high mark. In the case of self-reinforcement, however, this contingency is much weaker. You might promise yourself that you will have a pizza after completing 3 hours of studying, but what is to stop you from *not* studying and having the pizza anyway? To use Martin and Pear's (1999) terminology, what is to stop you from "short-circuiting" the contingency and immediately consuming the reward without performing the intended behavior?

A similar problem exists with the use of self-punishment. You might promise yourself that you will do 20 push-ups following each cigarette smoked, but what is to stop you from smoking a cigarette anyway and not bothering with the push-ups? Note too that if you do perform the push-ups, it might punish not only the act of smoking but also the act of carrying through on your promise to punish yourself. As a result, you will be less likely to do the push-ups the next time you have a smoke. In fact, research has shown that people who attempt to use self-punishment often fail to deliver the consequences to themselves (Worthington, 1979).

Thus, some behaviorists believe that self-reinforcement and self-punishment do not function in the same manner as normal reinforcement and punishment (Catania, 1975). Rachlin (1974), for example, has proposed that self-reinforcement might simply make the completion of an intended behavior more *salient*, thereby enhancing its value as a secondary reinforcer. For example, eating a pizza after 3 hours of studying might simply be the equivalent of setting off fireworks and sounding the trumpets for a job well done. There is also some evidence that self-delivered consequences are more effective when the person perceives that other people are aware of the contingency, suggesting that the social consequences for attaining or not attaining the intended goal are often an important aspect of so-called *self*-reinforcement or *self*-punishment procedures (Hayes et al., 1985).

Despite these concerns, Bandura (1976) and others maintain that self-delivered consequences can function in much the same manner as externally delivered consequences, given that the individual has been properly socialized to adhere to self-set standards and to feel guilty for violating such standards. It is also the case that many people do make use of self-reinforcement and self-punishment procedures in trying to control their behavior. Heffernan and Richards (1981), for example, found that 75% of students who had successfully improved their study habits reported using self-reinforcement. Conversely, Gary Player, the senior golfer, is a staunch believer in the value of self-punishment for maintaining a disciplined lifestyle—such as by forcing himself to do an extra 200 sit-ups (over and above the normal 800!) after a game in which he has let himself become irritable (Kossoff, 1999). Self-delivered contingencies are, therefore, a recommended component of many self-management programs (D. L. Watson & Tharp, 2002).

1. Behavioral approaches largely (accept/reject) _____ the concept of willpower as an explanation for self-control.

2. Skinner analyzed self-control from the perspective of a _____ response that alters the frequency of a subsequent response that is known as the _____ response.

3. Suppose you post a reminder on your refrigerator about a long-distance phone call you should make this weekend. Posting the reminder is the _____ response, while making the call on the weekend is the _____ response.

4. Folding your arms to keep from chewing your nails is an example of the use of p_____ r_____ to control your behavior.

5. A problem with the use of self-reinforcement is that we may be tempted to consume the _____ without engaging in the behavior. This problem is known as s_____-_____ the contingency.

6. This can also be a problem in the use of s_____-p_____, in which case we may engage in the behavior and not p_____ ourselves.

7. Some people believe that self-reinforcement is really a way of making the completion of a behavior (more/less) _____ salient, thereby enhancing its value as a s_____ reinforcer.

8. There is also some evidence that self-reinforcement is more effective when others (know/do not know) _____ about the contingency that we have arranged for ourselves.

9. Bandura believes that self-reinforcement and self-punishment can work for people who are likely to feel g_____ if they violate standards that they have set for themselves.

Self-Control as a Temporal Issue

Skinner recognized that self-control issues involve choice between conflicting consequences, but others have emphasized that a frequent, critical aspect of this conflict is that one is choosing between alternatives that differ in the extent to which the consequences are immediate versus delayed (e.g., Rachlin, 1974). As noted earlier, immediate consequences are generally more powerful than delayed consequences, a fact that can readily lead to suboptimal choices. Take, for example, a student who can either go out for the evening and have a good time (which is a relatively immediate or "smaller sooner reward") or study in the hopes of achieving an excellent grade (which is a relatively delayed or "larger later reward"). In a straight choice between having a fun evening and an excellent grade, she would clearly choose the excellent grade. But the fun evening is immediately available and hence powerful, and she will be sorely tempted to indulge herself in an evening's entertainment. Similarly, a pigeon who must choose between pecking a green key that leads to an immediate 2 seconds of access to grain (a smaller sooner reward) or pecking a red key that leads to a 10-second delay followed by 6 seconds of access to grain (a larger later reward) will strongly prefer the small, immediate reward. Thus, *from a*

And Furthermore

B. F. Skinner: The Master of Self-Control

It is ironic that B. F. Skinner, the staunch determinist, was in fact very much an expert in the art of self-control. Of course, from his perspective, he was merely exerting "countercontrol" over the environmental variables that determined his behavior. Although he maintained that the ultimate cause of our behavior lies in the environment, he admitted that "to a considerable extent an individual does appear to shape his own destiny" (Skinner, 1953, p. 228). As it turns out, Skinner proved to be his own best example in this regard.

In behavioral terms, Skinner engineered his environment to be as effective and reinforcing as possible, particularly with respect to his academic work. In Chapter 8, for example, we mentioned how he recommended creating an environment devoted specifically to writing, thereby establishing strong stimulus control over that activity. In addition to this, Skinner (1987) wrote so regularly, at the same time each day, that it seemed to generate a kind of circadian rhythm. Evidence of this occurred when, upon traveling to a different time zone, he would experience the urge to engage in "verbal behavior" at his regular writing time back home! Moreover, in true behaviorist fashion (what is good for the pigeon is good for the behaviorist), Skinner carefully monitored the amount of time he wrote each day and plotted it on a cumulative record. He recognized that the most important factor in being productive was consistency.

> Suppose you are at your desk two hours a day and produce on average 50 words an hour. That is not much, but it is about 35,000 words a year, and a book every two or three years. I have found this to be reinforcing enough. (Skinner, 1987, p. 138; see also Boice, 1996)

Although many people equate self-control with living a rigid and disciplined lifestyle, it was quite the opposite in Skinner's case. After he had once overworked himself to the point where he began to experience symptoms of angina, he resolved to lead a more relaxed and stress-free existence. He restricted his writing activities to a few hours each morning and devoted the rest of the day to less taxing activities, including watching football on television, listening to music, and reading mystery novels (R. Epstein, 1997). For Skinner, relaxation was not only enjoyable but also a critical factor in being an effective academic. In a paper entitled, *How to Discover What You Have to Say: A Talk to Students,* he described it thus:

> Imagine that you are to play a piano tomorrow night with a symphony orchestra. What will you do between now and then? You will get to bed early for a good night's rest. Tomorrow morning you may practice a little but not too much. During the day, you will eat lightly, take a nap, and in other ways try to put yourself in the best possible condition for your performance in the evening. Thinking effectively about a complex set of circumstances is more demanding than playing a piano, yet how often do you prepare yourself to do so in a similar way? (Skinner 1987, p. 133)

In a sense, Skinner very much lived his behaviorism. Just as Freud spent a few minutes each day analyzing his dreams, Skinner spent a few minutes each day analyzing the variables that controlled his behavior (R. Epstein, 1997). To all appearances, it was a successful endeavor. As former student Robert Epstein put it, "Fred was the most creative, most productive, and happiest person I have ever known. I cannot prove that his exceptional self-management skills were the cause, but I have no doubt whatsoever that they were" (p. 564).

temporal perspective, lack of self-control arises from the fact that our behavior is more heavily influenced by immediate consequences than by delayed consequences.

Self-control can also involve choice between a smaller sooner punisher and a larger later punisher—only in this instance it is selection of the smaller sooner alternative that is most beneficial. In deciding whether to go to the dentist, for example, we choose between enduring a small amount of discomfort in the near future (from minor dental treatment) and risking a large amount of discomfort in the distant future (from an infected tooth). Unfortunately, the prospect of experiencing discomfort in the near future (from a visit to the dentist) might exert such strong control over our behavior that we avoid going to the dentist, with the result that we suffer much greater discomfort later on. Likewise, a rat given a choice between accepting a small shock immediately or receiving a strong shock following a 10-second delay might choose the latter over the former, with the result that it experiences considerably more shock than it had to.

Of course, in many self-control situations, the full set of controlling consequences is a bit more complicated than a simple choice between two rewards or two punishers. Choosing not to smoke, for example, leads to both a smaller sooner punisher in the form of withdrawal symptoms and a larger later reward in the form of improved health; whereas continuing to smoke leads to a smaller sooner reward in the form of a nicotine high and a larger later punisher in the form of deteriorating health. Note, too, that later consequences are usually less certain than sooner consequences. There is no guarantee that you will become sick and die an early death if you continue to smoke (though you would be foolish to chance it), nor is there any guarantee that you will become radiantly healthy if you quit smoking (you might, after all, catch some disease that is not related to smoking). You can, however, be pretty certain that your next cigarette will be enjoyable, and that if you quit smoking you will soon experience withdrawal symptoms. Thus, delayed consequences often present a sort of double whammy: Their value is weakened because they are delayed and because they are less certain. Given this combination of factors, it is easy to understand how delayed consequences sometimes have such weak effects on behavior (see Table 10.2).

Self-control issues in the real world therefore often involve a rather complex set of contingencies (e.g., Brigham, 1978). To investigate this issue, however, researchers have typically focused on relatively simple choices, most commonly a choice between a smaller sooner reward and a larger later reward.

TABLE 10.2 Full set of immediate and delayed consequences for the alternatives of quitting smoking versus continuing to smoke.

	IMMEDIATE CONSEQUENCE (CERTAIN)	DELAYED CONSEQUENCE (UNCERTAIN)
Quitting smoking	Withdrawal symptoms	Improvement in health
Continuing to smoke	Nicotine high	Deterioration in health

The task of choosing between such alternatives is known as a *delay of gratification* task because the person or animal must forgo the smaller sooner reward (i.e., the subject has to "delay gratification") to obtain the larger later reward. Thus, in such tasks, ***self-control*** consists of choosing a larger later reward over a smaller sooner reward; the opposite of self-control, known as ***impulsiveness***, consists of choosing a smaller sooner reward over a larger later reward.

1. From a temporal perspective, self-control problems arise from the extent to which we are (more/less) _____ heavily influenced by delayed consequences.

2. Self-control is shown by choice of a (smaller sooner/larger later) _____ reward over a _____ reward. It can also be shown by choice of a (smaller sooner/larger later) _____ punisher over a _____ punisher.

3. With respect to choice between rewards, the opposite of self-control is called i_____, which is demonstrated by choice of a (smaller sooner/larger later) _____ reward over a _____ reward.

4. An additional problem in self-control situations is that the delayed consequences tend to be (more/less) _____ certain than the immediate consequences.

5. Outline the full set of consequences involved in choosing between studying and not studying:

	Immediate	*Delayed*
Studying		
Not studying		

Mischel's Delay of Gratification Paradigm

Some of the earliest systematic research using a delay-of-gratification procedure was carried out by the social learning theorist, Walter Mischel (e.g., 1966, 1974). In a typical experiment, a child was led into a room that contained two items (such as pretzels and marshmallows), one of which was clearly preferred. The child was told that he or she could attain the preferred item by simply waiting for the experimenter to return. If the child wished, however, the experimenter could be summoned by sounding a signal, at which point the child received only the smaller, nonpreferred item. The question of interest was to see what sorts of strategies some children used to wait out the delay period and obtain the larger reward.

Researchers who conducted such studies quickly noted that the extent to which children avoided attending to a reward had a significant effect on their resistance to temptation. For example, one strategy employed by many children was to simply avert their eyes from the promised rewards or cover their eyes with their hands. Many children also adopted Skinner's tactic of "doing something else," such as talking or singing to themselves or inventing games. Children were also better able to wait out the delay period when the rewards were not present as opposed to when they were present.

Thus, resistance to temptation was greatly enhanced by not attending to the tempting reward.

Later research revealed that the manner in which children thought about the rewards also made a difference. Children who were instructed to focus on the abstract properties of the rewards, such as viewing pretzels as tiny logs or marshmallows as clouds, did better than children who focused on the rewards as concrete objects (i.e., seeing pretzels for what they are). Note that all of these strategies are quite different from what one might suppose should happen from a "positive thinking" perspective, which usually recommends keeping one's attention firmly fixed on the desired outcome. In these studies, children who focused on the desired outcome, and conceptualized it as a desired outcome, generally became impulsive and were unable to wait long enough to receive the larger later reward. (See Mischel, 1966, 1974, for comprehensive reviews of this research.)

An interesting aspect of this research is the follow-up evaluations conducted on children who participated in some of the earliest studies (Shoda, Mischel, & Peake, 1990). These children were, on average, 4 years old in the original studies and 17 years old at follow-up. The children who, in the original study, had devised tactics that enabled them to wait for the preferred reward were, many years later, more "cognitively and socially competent"—meaning that they could cope well with frustrations, were academically proficient, and got along well with their peers. This suggests that one's ability to devise appropriate tactics to delay gratification is a basic skill that can enhance many areas of one's life.

1. Children who are (most/least) _____ successful at a delay of gratification task generally keep their attention firmly fixed on the desired treat.

2. While waiting for dessert, Housam imagines that the Jell-O looks like wobbly chunks of glass. By contrast, Ruby views the Jell-O as, well, Jell-O. Between the two of them, _____ is less likely to get into trouble by eating the Jell-O before being told that it is okay to do so. This is because delay of gratification can be enhanced by thinking about the desired reward in ab_____ rather than c_____ terms.

QUICK QUIZ I

The Ainslie–Rachlin Model of Self-Control

While the Mischel studies focused on some of the processes involved in resisting an immediately available temptation, the Ainslie–Rachlin model of self-control focuses on the fact that preference between smaller sooner and larger later rewards can shift over time (Ainslie, 1975; Rachlin, 1974). For example, have you ever promised yourself in the morning that you would study all afternoon, only to find yourself spending the afternoon socializing with friends? In the morning, you clearly preferred studying over socializing that afternoon; but when the afternoon actually arrived, you preferred socializing over studying. In other words, you experienced a reversal of preference as time passed and the smaller sooner reward (socializing) became imminent. The Ainslie–Rachlin model provides an explanation for this reversal of preference and suggests ways to minimize its occurrence and facilitate attainment of the larger later reward.

The Ainslie–Rachlin model is based on the assumption that the value of a reward is a "hyperbolic" function of its delay. In simple terms, what this means is that the delay curve for a reward—which describes the relationship between reward value and time delay—is upwardly scalloped (similar to an FI scallop) with decreasing delays producing larger and larger increments in value. In other words, the value of a reward increases more and more sharply as delay decreases and attainment of the reward becomes imminent (see Figure 10.3).

For example, think about a young child who has been promised a birthday party. When the party is still 3 weeks away, it is likely to be worth very little to him. Three weeks is a long time for a young child, and if you ask him if he would rather have the birthday party in 3 weeks or a chocolate bar right now, he just might prefer the chocolate bar. In other words, a birthday party at 3 weeks' delay is worth less than one chocolate bar available immediately. A week later, with the birthday party still 2 weeks away, you might find that

FIGURE 10.3 Graph indicating relationship between reward value and delay. Moving from left to right along the horizontal axis represents passage of time, with reward delivery drawing ever nearer. As delay decreases (reward draws near), reward value increases slowly at first and then more and more sharply as the reward becomes imminent.

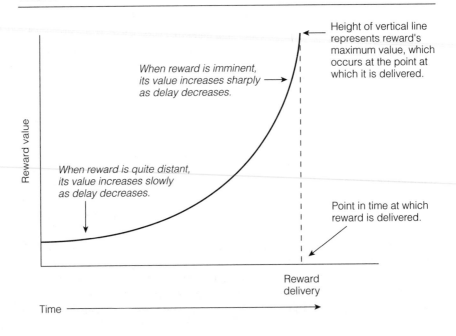

little has changed and that he would still be willing to trade the birthday party for the chocolate bar. The value of the birthday party at 2 weeks' delay has increased very little, if at all, compared to its value the previous week. When the party is 1 week away, however, you might find that the value of the party has increased significantly and that you would now have to offer him two or three chocolate bars before he would agree to cancel the party. And by the time another week has passed and the day of the birthday party has arrived, he may be so excited that he would reject a year's worth of chocolate bars in order to have that party. The value of the party increased sharply as it became imminent.

Much of the experimental evidence for such upwardly scalloped delay functions is derived from research with rats and pigeons, for whom delays of even a few seconds have significant effects on preference. A hungry pigeon, for example, might show weak preference for a reinforcer that is delayed by 15 seconds, slightly stronger preference for one that is delayed by 10 seconds, moderately stronger preference for one that is delayed by 5 seconds, and very strong preference for one that is available immediately (0 second delay). The value of the reward increased only slightly between 15 and 10 seconds, moderately between 10 and 5 seconds, and greatly between 5 and 0 seconds. The delay curve for this pigeon would therefore be relatively flat between 15 and 10 seconds, moderately sloped between 10 and 5 seconds, and steeply sloped between 5 and 0 seconds, which is similar to the delay curve shown in Figure 10.3.

QUICK QUIZ J

1. The Ainslie–Rachlin model is based on the finding that as a reward becomes imminent, its value increases more and more (slowly/sharply) _____, yielding a "delay curve" (or delay function) that is upwardly sc_____.

2. I offer to give people a thousand dollars. People are told that they will receive the thousand dollars in either 3 months, 2 months, 1 month, or immediately. Between which of the following conditions are we likely to find the largest difference in level of excitement about receiving the money: 3 months versus 2 months, 2 months versus 1 month, or 1 month versus immediately? _____.
Between which conditions would we find the second largest difference in level of excitement? _____.

The manner in which delay functions account for preference reversal is shown in Figure 10.4. At an early point in time, when both rewards are still distant, the larger later reward (LLR) is clearly preferred. As time passes, however, and the smaller sooner reward (SSR) becomes imminent, its value increases sharply and comes to outweigh the value of the LLR. Thus, the student who, when she wakes up in the morning, decides that she will definitely study that evening is at the far left end of the distribution, where the delay curve for the LLR (receiving a high mark) is still higher than that of the SSR (going out for an evening of socializing). As evening approaches, however, and the possibility of going out (the SSR) becomes imminent, the delay curve

FIGURE 10.4 Graph indicating relative values of a smaller sooner reward (SSR) and a larger later reward (LLR) as time passes. At an early point in time, before the SSR becomes imminent, its value is less than the value of the LLR. As time passes, however, and the SSR becomes imminent, its value increases sharply and comes to outweigh the value of the LLR.

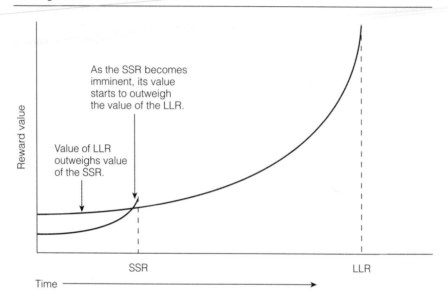

for the latter rises sharply, with the result that the student will be strongly tempted to socialize that evening. By doing so, however, she risks losing the LLR of an excellent grade.

Such preference reversals have been demonstrated experimentally with pigeons. Green, Fisher, Perlow, and Sherman (1981) presented pigeons with a choice between two schedules of reinforcement. In one condition, a peck on the red key resulted in 2-sec access to grain following a 20-sec delay (the SSR), while a peck on the green key resulted in 6-sec access to grain following a 24-sec delay (the LLR). In this circumstance the pigeons strongly preferred the LLR; they selected it on more than 80% of the trials. In another condition, a peck on the red key resulted in 2-sec access to grain following a 2-sec delay, while a peck on the green key resulted in 6-sec access to grain following a 6-sec delay. This latter condition is equivalent to the first condition because the LLR occurs 4 seconds later than the SSR; but it is different in that both alternatives are now much closer. Under this circumstance the pigeons strongly preferred the SSR, which was almost immediately available. Thus, just as the Ainslie–Rachlin model predicts, when the SSR reward was imminent, its value outweighed the value of the LLR. When both the SSR and the LLR were further away, the pigeons strongly preferred the LLR. As the delay values changed, the pigeons displayed a reversal of preference between the two alternatives.

Human subjects making hypothetical choices have also demonstrated preference reversals. In one study by Ainslie and Haendel (1983), most participants said that they would prefer to receive a $100 certified check that can be immediately cashed to a $200 certified check that can be cashed in 2 years. However, when the delays for both alternatives were increased by 6 years—a $100 check that can be cashed in 6 years versus a $200 check that can be cashed in 8 years—subjects preferred the $200 alternative. Thus, with both alternatives quite distant, the LLR was preferred; at much shorter delays, the SSR alternative was preferred. (See Critchfield & Kollins, 2001, for a summary of research findings using this procedure.)

1. If confronted by a choice between one food pellet available in 10 seconds and two food pellets available in 15 seconds, a rat would likely choose the (former/latter) _____. But if 9 seconds are allowed to pass before the rat can make a choice, then it will likely choose the (former/latter) _____.

2. In the above example, as the (smaller sooner/larger later) _____ reward becomes imminent, its value comes to outweigh the value of the (smaller sooner/larger later) _____ reward.

QUICK QUIZ K

Given that this type of preference reversal occurs, the question arises as to whether anything can be done about it. Two alternatives suggest themselves: changing the shape of the delay function for the LLR and making a commitment response.

Changing the Shape of the Delay Function for the Larger Later Reward The basic reason preference reversal occurs is because the LLR has low value at long delays; that is, its delay curve is deeply scalloped. If the delay curve were less deeply scalloped—meaning that the value of the LLR did not decline so drastically as a function of delay—then it would stand a better chance of outweighing any temptations that crop up along the way. This type of situation is illustrated in Figure 10.5.

Herrnstein (1981) suggested several variables that can affect the shape of a delay function. For example, *there appear to be innate differences in impulsivity between species.* Delays of only a few seconds can make a huge difference for rats and pigeons; such delays make little or no difference for humans, whose behavior is often directed toward consequences that will be delivered several hours, days, or even years in the future. (As noted earlier, humans' ability to use language to represent distant events may play a critical role in this behavior.) Thus, delay functions for humans are generally less deeply scalloped than they are for other animals.

There may also be differences between individuals, with some individuals more impulsive than others. People with antisocial personality disorder, which seems to have a strong genetic basis, are generally very impulsive (Kaplan, Sadock,

FIGURE 10.5 Graph indicating relative values of a smaller sooner reward (SSR) and a larger later reward (LLR) in which the delay function for the LLR is less deeply scalloped (somewhat flatter). Under such conditions, the value of the LLR will remain higher than the value of the SSR even as the SSR becomes imminent.

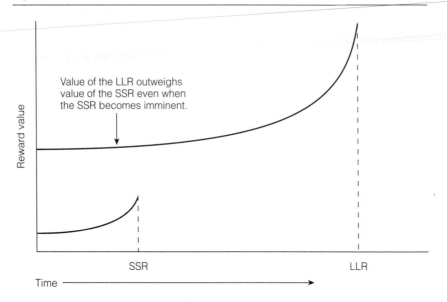

& Grebb, 1994). Such individuals presumably have deeply scalloped delay functions. Less extreme differences no doubt exist among normal individuals in the population. Some people may have an inborn temperament that predisposes them toward displaying the necessary patience to achieve long-term outcomes, whereas others have a temperament that predisposes them toward being rather impulsive.

Within individuals, age can make a difference. In general, *people become less impulsive as they grow older.* Although young children find it difficult to resist having a cookie before dinner, most adults are quite capable of doing so (well, at least more often than when they were kids). In fact, an increased ability to resist temptation and pursue long-term goals is considered a hallmark of maturity.

Related to age, another variable that affects impulsiveness is repeated experience with responding for delayed rewards. As children grow older, caretakers require them to display more and more patience—such as by forcing them to wait until after dinner to have a dessert—thereby gradually shaping their ability to delay gratification. Interestingly, in a scene from Skinner's (1948a) novel *Walden II,* which depicts a utopian community designed around behavioral principles, children are described as waiting in front of their meals for a short time before eating. With successive meals, the waiting period was gradually lengthened. Although such a procedure might sound frightfully authoritarian, it is probably not much different from what most parents carry out less formally as they expect their children to gradually display more and more patience as they grow older. Interestingly, the efficacy of Skinner's approach has been demonstrated experimentally. Research has shown that both pigeons (Mazur & Logue, 1978) and children (Newman & Kanfer, 1976) demonstrate an increased ability to resist the temptation of a smaller sooner reward after being exposed to large rewards that are systematically delayed for longer and longer periods of time.

The availability of other sources of reinforcement may be yet another factor that influences impulsiveness. Many people find that they are more impulsive during periods characterized by a lack of overall reinforcement. Thus, Kimberly experiences a strong urge to resume smoking after she loses her job, and Mike begins drinking heavily after his girlfriend leaves him. Under depressing or stressful circumstances, long-term goals seem to lose their relevance, and immediate temptations become quite powerful. This evidence suggests that, to maximize the possibility of resisting temptations, it helps if one's environment contains a plentiful supply of reinforcement. A student attempting to study for long periods of time in a dingy, cramped corner of the basement will likely find it extremely difficult to persist. Far better, as Skinner (1987) noted, is to arrange a study environment that is both pleasant and comfortable. Good lighting, a comfortable chair, and a well-organized desk (to eliminate the frustration of being unable to find things)—perhaps accompanied by some pleasant music in the background and a cup of coffee to sip on—will enable the act of studying to compete more effectively with such temptations as watching television or playing a computer game. Self-reinforcement procedures may also play a role here in that they ensure that the person intermittently engages in some pleasant activities while attempting to complete a difficult task, for example, by playing computer games for 15 minutes following every 2 hours of studying (the trick, of course, being to keep the game playing to only 15 minutes).

Finally, as noted in our discussion of behavior chains (Chapter 7), *we can more easily maintain responding for a distant goal by setting up an explicit series of subgoals.* The successful completion of each subgoal provides a salient form of secondary reinforcement that helps maintain progress toward a larger later reward. Additionally, because the secondary reinforcement from the completion of a subgoal is relatively immediate, it can compete more effectively with any temptations that crop up along the way. Note, however, that the subgoals should be relatively precise. Completing a vaguely worded goal such as "work on my term paper tonight" is likely to be considerably less reinforcing than completing the more explicit goal of "finish a comprehensive outline of my term paper tonight." The latter is a clearer indicator of progress and will therefore serve as a stronger reinforcer.

1. One strategy for increasing self-control is to make the delay function (or delay curve) for the larger later reward (more/less) _____ deeply scalloped.

2. The delay functions for a pigeon will likely be (more/less) _____ deeply scalloped than those for a human.

3. The delay functions for a 6-year-old child will likely be (more/less) _____ deeply scalloped than those for a 15-year-old.

4. Exposure to gradually increasing delays seems to make the delay function (more/less) _____ deeply scalloped.

5. A person is likely to be (more/less) _____ impulsive in a pleasant environment as opposed to an unpleasant environment.

6. From the perspective of the Ainslie–Rachlin model, the setting up and attainment of a subgoal related to a delayed reward serves to (raise/lower) _____ the delay function for that reward, making it (more/less) _____ deeply scalloped.

Making a Commitment Response   Flattening out the delay gradient for the larger later reward (making it less deeply scalloped) is perhaps the ideal answer to problems of self-control. It seems unlikely, however, that this tactic will always be successful. For a person who smokes, the immediate reinforcement to be derived from having a cigarette (both positive reinforcement in the form of a nicotine high and negative reinforcement in the form of eliminating or avoiding withdrawal symptoms) is likely to be a powerful temptation. In such circumstances, the exercise of self-control might be facilitated through the use of a "commitment response" (Rachlin, 1974, 1991). A *commitment response* is an action carried out at an early point in time that serves either to eliminate or greatly reduce the value of an upcoming temptation.[2]

As an example of a commitment response, consider a student who, in the morning, decides that she definitely needs to study that evening. At this early point in time, the value of studying to ensure a good mark outweighs the value of alternate activities, such as going out with friends or watching television. Through experience, however, the student has learned that these early-morning preferences mean little when evening rolls around and more immediate reinforcement from other activities becomes available. To ensure that she studies tonight, she knows that she has to somehow eliminate ahead of time the various temptations that will arise. Thus, that morning, she gives her younger brother $20 and instructs him to keep it if she fails to study that evening. By making this monetary commitment, she has essentially locked herself into studying. As illustrated in Figure 10.6, the aversive consequence that would result from not studying (her obnoxious brother having a good time at her expense) has so reduced the value of any alternate activity that it no longer

---

[2]The commitment response is sometimes instead called a *precommitment response* (e.g., Logue, 1995).

FIGURE 10.6 Effect of a commitment strategy on preference between a smaller sooner reward (SSR) and a larger later reward (LLR). The commitment response needs to be made before the SSR becomes imminent. It will be effective to the extent that it reduces the value of the SSR, even when it is imminent, to below the value of the LLR.

effectively competes with the value of studying and the larger later reward of obtaining a good mark.

Behavioral contracting, in which a person formally arranges to attain certain rewards for resisting temptation or receive certain punishers for yielding to temptation, essentially operates on this principle. The contract is negotiated with the therapist at an early point in time, before encountering the temptation. The contingencies outlined in the contract serve to reduce the attractiveness of the tempting alternative. Of course, in some circumstances, it might even be possible to completely eliminate the tempting alternative. A student who is spending too much time playing a computer game rather than studying might solve the problem by simply wiping the game off his hard drive and giving the software disk to a friend for the rest of the semester.

Although the use of a commitment strategy might be seen as one that requires a certain amount of intelligence and foresight, experiments have shown that even pigeons can learn to make commitment responses. Rachlin and Green (1972) presented pigeons with a choice between a smaller sooner food reward and a larger later food reward. The pigeons invariably chose the SSR over the LLR. The pigeons were then given the option, several seconds before being presented with this choice, of pecking another key that would eliminate the SSR as one of the choices and leave the LLR as the only alternative. Many of the pigeons selected this option, thereby essentially removing the temptation ahead of time. The pigeons did the equivalent of giving away the computer game in the morning so that, when evening came around, they would be more likely to study.

1. A _____ response is designed to either eliminate or reduce the value of an upcoming temptation.

2. Such a response is most likely to be carried out at an (early/later) _____ point in time when the temptation is quite (near/distant) _____.

3. Gary would love to go running each evening but always feels so tired after work that he just plumps down in his favorite chair when he gets home and has a glass of wine. If Gary wishes to make a commitment to go running, such as arranging to go running with a neighbor, he is most likely to make this commitment (the day before/immediately before) _____ the run is supposed to take place.

The Small-But-Cumulative Effects Model

The basic delay of gratification paradigm, which both Mischel's early research and the original Ainslie–Rachlin model are built upon, involves a simple choice between a single SSR and a single LLR. This is, however, an extreme simplification of the full set of contingencies that we often face when trying to control our behavior. As mentioned earlier, many situations involve choosing between a combination of rewarding and punishing outcomes that vary not only in their value and delay but also in the certainty with which they are likely to occur. More importantly, in relation to the issue of certainty, many of the most difficult self-control issues cannot be resolved by a single choice; rather, they require an ongoing (often never-ending) series of choices, with any single choice having relatively little effect. Thus, according to this *small-but-cumulative effects model,* each individual choice on a self-control task has only a small but cumulative effect on our likelihood of obtaining the desired long-term outcome (e.g., Malott, 1989; see also Ainslie, 2001, and Rachlin, 2000).

Imagine, for example, that you have been following a program of healthy eating, but then find yourself choosing between a restaurant's world famous Greaze-Burger and their far healthier, but much less appetizing, Tofu Salad Supreme. In terms of achieving the larger later reward of good health, the choice might seem obvious. But is it obvious? That one Greaze-Burger, *by itself,* is very unlikely to make any significant difference in your quest to become healthy; in the same way, a single Tofu Salad Supreme will not, by itself, make you healthy. It is only by repeatedly selecting tofu salads over Greaze-Burgers that you will realize any significant, long-term effects on your health. So it is relatively easy, on any particular occasion, to talk yourself into making an exception to your healthy eating plan: "Hey, it's been a tough day, so why not indulge just this once?" The problem, of course, is that this same logic applies each time you encounter a tasty treat. Each single treat that you encounter will not, in and of itself, significantly affect your health. But to the extent that you are thereby seduced into frequently consuming those treats (and we very often are), you undermine the possibility of achieving good health.

This small-but-cumulative effects approach can be incorporated into the basic Ainslie–Rachlin model that we discussed earlier. The fact that each single choice of a smaller sooner reward has such little effect in the long run helps allow its value, when it becomes imminent, to rise above the value of the larger later reward. After all, would you really be tempted to eat a Greaze-Burger if you knew that one burger would, like a slow-acting poison, give you a heart attack in 20 or 30 years? Would you really smoke a cigarette if you knew that one cigarette would some day give you cancer? And would you really watch TV tonight rather than study if you knew that not studying tonight would result in obtaining a low grade in the course and completely ruin your chances of getting into law school? Not likely. It is only because that one burger, one cigarette, or one TV night is unlikely, by itself, to result in such punishing outcomes that its value can rise so sharply when it becomes imminent.

Each choice of an SSR versus LLR has only a small but cumulative effect, which helps explain why self-control is, for many of us, such a difficult task. Fortunately, the small-but-cumulative effects model also suggests ways to improve self-control. For example, it clarifies the importance of having a plan in place to handle occasional lapses (i.e., a relapse prevention plan; e.g., Marlatt & Gordon, 1985; Watson & Tharp, 2002), given that we will very likely be faced with an ongoing series of highly seductive temptations that we may not always be able to resist. This model also indicates the importance of establishing rules that clearly distinguish between acceptable and unacceptable behaviors, since the actual point when an impulsive behavior becomes harmful is often not clear. For some people or in some circumstances, the clearest rule might be total abstinence from a tempting event. For example, the Alcoholics Anonymous' rule of never, ever consuming alcohol seems to be an effective boundary for some recovered alcoholics. For other people or in other circumstances, it may be that total abstinence is too severe and one may do better to occasionally indulge oneself within clearly specified limits. For example, a flexible study plan that allows for some level of indulgence or interruptions may be more effective than a highly rigid plan that is difficult to maintain (see Ainslie, 2001).

We will return again to the issue of self-control, and especially the importance of establishing clear rules for our behavior, when we discuss rule-governed behavior in Chapter 12.

1. According to the _____ model, self-control is a difficult task because each temptation has only a _____ but _____ effect on our likelihood of obtaining the long-term goal.

2. This model highlights the potential usefulness of establishing clear r_____ for distinguishing between acceptable and unacceptable behaviors, since the point at which impulsive behavior becomes harmful (is/is not) _____ clear.

QUICK QUIZ N

And Furthermore

But Why Do I Sometimes Just Give Up?

The small-but-cumulative effects model readily explains how a self-control program can gradually deteriorate. Because each temptation has only an insignificant effect on our long-term goal, we are repeatedly tempted to indulge ourselves "just this once," and may easily indulge ourselves so often that we forgo attaining our long-term goal. Thus, Julie might embark on a stringent exercise plan for the fall semester but, by Christmas, realize she's missed so many exercise sessions that she is essentially back to her old habit of being a couch potato. But what happens when a self-control program just seems to collapse? For example, Tracie, who embarked on a healthy eating program, might pig out on junk food one evening and then abandon any attempt at healthy eating over the next several days. Why didn't she at least try to hop back on the wagon, since that one evening of junk food is actually insignificant in the overall scheme of things?

Well, here is one possible explanation for this pattern. Because each choice between healthy and unhealthy eating has only a small but cumulative effect, a healthy eating program makes sense only if Tracie sticks with it for a long time. That means that each time she makes a healthy choice, she is essentially betting that she will continue to make healthy choices in the future (Ainslie, 2001). This also means that if, for some reason, Tracie comes to predict that she is unlikely to make healthy choices in the future, it will no longer make sense for her to follow the program. Why should she deprive herself now if the program is likely to fail anyway? This may be what happened in Tracie's case. Indulging in junk food that one evening was a cue signaling for her the likelihood of not eating healthy in the future. Therefore, why persist with the program? Why not instead acknowledge that the program is not working, indulge herself over the next several days (which will be a nice reinforcer for making such a decision), and then hop back on the wagon at some point in the future?

This scenario again indicates why planning what to do in the event of an unexpected lapse can be helpful. If unexpected lapses are incorporated into your overall plan, they no longer strongly indicate a low likelihood of carrying on with your program in the future. In Tracie's case, her relapse prevention plan might include calling a supportive friend whenever she significantly violates her healthy eating program or feels on the verge of abandoning the program altogether. She and her friend could have an arrangement that at such times they will go for a run or a swim together, followed by a relaxing meal at a restaurant that specializes in healthy and appetizing meals. When combined with other tactics, such as engaging in specific relaxation exercises whenever she feels stressed (stress being a high risk situation for becoming impulsive), such a relapse prevention plan could greatly increase Tracie's likelihood of maintaining her healthy eating program over the long haul.

SUMMARY

On a concurrent schedule of reinforcement, the subject responds on two or more independent schedules of reinforcement that are simultaneously available. Choice behavior in such situations often obeys the matching law, which predicts that the proportion of responses emitted on an alternative will match the proportion of reinforcers received on that alternative. The matching law has been shown to have real-world applicability, ranging from predicting communication patterns in humans to foraging behavior in animals.

Researchers have also discovered certain deviations from matching. In undermatching, the difference in proportion of responses on the richer versus poorer schedules is less than that predicted by matching. In overmatching, the difference in proportion of responses on the richer versus poorer schedules is greater than that predicted by matching. Bias from matching occurs when one alternative receives more responses than would be predicted by matching, both when it contains the poorer schedule and when it contains the richer schedule.

According to melioration theory, matching results from the subject's tendency to shift behavior toward a better-paying alternative. This tendency can sometimes reduce the overall amount of reinforcement. For example, more behavior may be directed to a better-paying alternative than is needed to obtain the available reinforcers. Furthermore, overindulgence in a highly reinforcing alternative can result in long-term habituation to that alternative, so that it is no longer as enjoyable as it once was. Melioration also results in a tendency to be overly attracted to immediate reinforcers as opposed to delayed reinforcers.

Skinner viewed self-control as involving a choice between conflicting outcomes. He believed that self-control is facilitated by emitting a controlling response that then alters the probability of a controlled response. Specific techniques of self-control include physical self-restraint, self-deprivation or self-satiation, and self-reinforcement and self-punishment. A major problem with the latter is that one can easily short-circuit such self-directed consequences.

Others have noted that self-control involves a choice between immediate outcomes, which are relatively powerful, and delayed outcomes, which are relatively weak. From this delay-of-gratification perspective, self-control can be defined as choosing a larger later reward (LLR) over a smaller sooner reward (SSR), while impulsiveness can be defined as choosing an SSR over an LLR.

Research has shown that children who are good at resisting temptation in a delay of gratification task try to distract themselves from the tempting reward. As well, children are better able to resist temptation when they think of the reward in terms of its abstract rather than concrete properties. Follow-up research has revealed that children who are successful in such delay of gratification tasks are, in later years, more academically and socially competent.

The Ainslie–Rachlin model of self-control is based on the assumption that the delay function for a reward is often deeply scalloped, so that its value increases sharply as it becomes imminent. This explains why preferences for LLRs and SSRs tend to shift over time. When both rewards are far away, the value of the LLR outweighs the value of the SSR. As the SSR becomes imminent, however, its value rises sharply, possibly exceeding the value of the LLR at that time.

Thus, one means for facilitating self-control is flattening the delay function for the LLR so that its value remains fairly high even at long delays. Factors that may affect the shape of a delay function include biological variables (including differences between species and between individuals within a species), age, experience with responding for delayed rewards, the presence of other sources of reinforcement, and the attainment of subgoals relating to the LLR. Another means for facilitating self-control is by making a commitment to the LLR at an early point in time, before the SSR becomes imminent. A commitment response is a response that serves to reduce the value of the SSR so that its value remains below the value of the LLR.

According to the small-but-cumulative effects model, each individual choice on a self-control task has only a small but cumulative effect on our likelihood of obtaining the desired long-term outcome. It is largely because of this factor that we are frequently tempted to make an exception to a self-control program insofar as each individual temptation has only an insignificant effect on our long-term goal. However, repeated violations of our program can eventually result in the collapse of the program. It is for this reason that relapse prevention programs, in which we create a plan for coping with the possibility of occasional lapses, are so important.

SUGGESTED READINGS

Epstein, R. (1997). Skinner as self-manager. *Journal of Applied Behavior Analysis*, 30, 545–568. An interesting discussion of Skinner's use of behavioral techniques to manage his own behavior.

Herrnstein, R. J. (1997). *The matching law: Papers in psychology and economics.* Cambridge, MA: Harvard University Press. For the serious student who wishes to acquire a more in-depth understanding of matching, melioration, and the behavioral approach to economics.

Watson, D. L., & Tharp, R. G. (2002). *Self-directed behavior: Self-modification for personal adjustment* (8th ed.). Pacific Grove, CA: Brooks/Cole. A good source book on various tactics of self-control for a wide range of everyday behavior problems.

STUDY QUESTIONS

1. What is a concurrent schedule? Diagram an example of a concurrent schedule that might be used in an operant conditioning experiment with pigeons.
2. Define the matching law. State the matching law as an equation, and define each of its terms.
3. Using the matching equation, show what the matching law predicts concerning the distribution of behavior displayed on a concurrent VI 10-sec

VI 30-sec schedule of reinforcement. (Hint: What is the expected distribution of reinforcers on this schedule?)

4. What is a changeover delay (COD)? In what sense is a COD similar to a foraging situation with animals?

5. What is overmatching? Give an example of overmatching (with hypothetical proportions) that might occur on a concurrent VI 20-sec VI 30-sec schedule.

6. What is undermatching? Give an example of undermatching (with hypothetical proportions) that might occur on a concurrent VI 20-sec VI 30-sec schedule.

7. What is bias from matching? Give an example of bias (with hypothetical proportions) that might occur on a concurrent VI 20-sec VI 30-sec schedule.

8. Describe melioration theory. Briefly describe three ways in which the tendency to meliorate can reduce the overall level of reinforcement.

9. Describe the major difficulty with the use of self-reinforcement and self-punishment.

10. What are the definitions of self-control and impulsiveness within the context of a delay-of-gratification task? Describe some of the strategies children use to facilitate success in a delay-of-gratification task.

11. With the help of a graph, describe the general effect of delay on reward value.

12. With the help of a graph, describe how the Ainslie–Rachlin model accounts for preference reversal between a smaller sooner reward and a larger later reward.

13. List four of the variables that can affect the shape of the delay function and hence the extent to which a person or animal is likely to display self-control.

14. With the help of a graph, describe how a commitment response serves to facilitate self-control.

15. Describe the small-but-cumulative effects model of self-control and impulsiveness. Explain how this accounts for the difficulty people often have in following an exercise program.

CONCEPT REVIEW

bias from matching. A deviation from matching in which one alternative attracts a higher proportion of responses than would be predicted by matching, regardless of whether that alternative contains the richer versus poorer schedule.

commitment response. An action carried out at an early point in time that serves to either eliminate or reduce the value of an upcoming temptation.

concurrent schedule of reinforcement. A complex schedule consisting of the simultaneous presentation of two or more independent schedules, each leading to a reinforcer.

impulsiveness. With respect to choice between two rewards, selecting a smaller sooner reward over a larger later reward.

matching law. The principle that the *proportion* of responses emitted on a particular schedule matches the *proportion* of reinforcers obtained on that schedule.

melioration theory. A theory of matching that holds that the distribution of behavior in a choice situation shifts toward those alternatives that have higher value regardless of the long-term effect on overall amount of reinforcement.

overmatching. A deviation from matching in which the proportion of responses on the richer schedule versus poorer schedule is more different than would be predicted by matching.

self-control. With respect to choice between two rewards, selecting a larger later reward over a smaller sooner reward.

small-but-cumulative effects model. Each individual choice on a self-control task has only a small but cumulative effect on our likelihood of obtaining the desired long-term outcome.

undermatching. A deviation from matching in which the proportion of responses on the richer schedule versus poorer schedule is less different than would be predicted by matching.

CHAPTER TEST

12. According to the _____ law, if 25% of reinforcers are obtained on one of two simultaneously available schedules, then _____ of responses are likely to be emitted on that schedule.

6. The Ainslie–Rachlin model is based on the assumption that the value of a reward increases more and more sharply as delay _____ and attainment of the reward becomes _____.

17. The matching law predicts that on a concurrent VI 15-sec VI 60-sec schedule, 80% of responses should be emitted on the VI 15-sec schedule and 20% on the VI 60-sec schedule. In reality, you obtain 65% on the VI 15-sec schedule and 35% on the VI 60-sec schedule. This is an example of _____matching.

9. A _____ schedule of reinforcement consists of the simultaneous presentation of two or more independent schedules, each of which leads to a _____.

13. The _____ law holds that the _____ of responses emitted on a particular schedule matches the _____ of reinforcers obtained on that schedule.

31. Hoa sometimes feels well and sometimes feels sick. If feeling healthy is a form of reinforcement, we would expect Hoa to be most impulsive when she is feeling (healthy/sick) _____.

18. The matching law predicts that on a concurrent VI 10-sec VI 30-sec schedule, 25% of responses should be emitted on the VI 30-sec schedule

and 75% on the VI 10-sec schedule. In reality, you obtain 15% on the VI 30-sec schedule and 85% on the VI 10-sec schedule. This is an example of _____ matching.

3. From a temporal perspective, lack of self-control arises from the fact that our behavior is more heavily influenced by _____ consequences as opposed to _____ consequences.

20. When the cost of switching between schedules is quite high, then _____ matching is likely to occur. When the cost of switching is extremely low, then _____ matching is likely to occur.

30. Exposure to rewards that are presented at gradually increasing delays is likely to result in a(n) (increase/decrease) _____ in impulsiveness, which also means that the reward delay curve for these individuals has become (more/less) _____ deeply scalloped.

1. You always eat a full meal before going shopping, so that you will not be tempted (through hunger) to buy those chocolate cookies you are addicted to. From the perspective of self-control, Skinner would refer to the act of eating the meal as the _____ response and the subsequent decreased tendency to buy cookies as the _____ response.

27. In general, melioration is often the result of behavior being too strongly governed by _____ consequences as opposed to _____ consequences.

10. Given a choice between a VR 140 schedule and a VR 40 schedule of reinforcement, a rat is likely to show (exclusive/partial) _____ preference for the _____ schedule.

35. Given a choice between a VI 60-sec schedule and a VI 20-sec schedule, a pigeon is likely to emit _____% of its responses to the VI 20-sec alternative.

23. According to _____ theory, the distribution of behavior in a choice situation shifts toward those alternatives that have _____ value regardless of the effect on the overall amount of reinforcement.

14. Given a choice between a VI 40-sec schedule and a VI 20-sec schedule, a rat is likely to emit _____% of its responses to the VI 40-sec alternative.

5. From a behavioral perspective, self-control consists of preference for a _____ reward over a _____ reward, while the opposite of self-control, known as _____, consists of preference for a _____ reward over a _____ reward.

26. As soon as Mario retired, he moved to Florida and went for walks on the beach every day. Unfortunately, although going for walks continued to be his most enjoyable activity, it soon became less enjoyable than it used to be. This appears to be an example of how the tendency to _____ can result in long-term _____.

33. A commitment response is most likely to be made at a(n) (early/later) _____ point in time before the (smaller sooner/larger later) _____ reward becomes imminent.

16. As Sal and his wife converse with the neighbor one evening, Sal is three times more responsive to the neighbor's comments than his wife is. Research

evidence suggests that the neighbor will direct his conversation toward Sal, as opposed to his wife, (three times as often/exclusively) _____.

28. In general, humans have a (more/less) _____ deeply scalloped delay function than chickens. As well, a person who is very impulsive is likely to have a (more/less) _____ deeply scalloped delay function than a person who is very patient.

7. In keeping with the Ainslie–Rachlin model of self-control, I am most likely to choose $50 over $100 when the choice is between (A) $50 now versus $100 a year from now, or (B) $50 a year from now versus $100 two years from now. The answer is alternative _____, which means that I tend to become impulsive when the smaller sooner reward is (imminent/delayed) _____.

11. According to the matching law, the proportion of _____ emitted on a certain schedule will roughly equal the proportion of _____ obtained on that schedule.

4. To the extent that Romano decides to get up early to study for that math test next week, as opposed to lying in bed for an extra hour, he is displaying self-_____. To the extent that he chooses to lie in bed, he is displaying _____.

19. As Sal and his wife converse with the neighbor one day, Sal is three times more responsive to the neighbor's comments than his wife is. The neighbor, however, looks at Sal's wife about as often as he looks at Sal. During the next day's conversation, Sal's wife is three times more responsive to the neighbor's comments than Sal is. This time the neighbor looks at Sal's wife five times as often as he looks at Sal. This appears to be an example of the deviation from matching known as _____, which also suggests that the neighbor finds Sal's wife _____.

32. Maria announces to her parents that she is going to study all weekend, knowing that they will severely chastise her if she does not live up to her promise. Given that Maria hates being chastised by her parents, her announcement can be seen as a _____ response that will lower the value of any alternate activity that might interfere with studying during the weekend.

21. You tend to shop at two favorite clothing stores, Madison's Fine Fashions and Mike's Grubbies. Over time, you have learned that Mike's is twice as likely to have something in stock that you wish to buy. If the two stores are side by side, then you are likely to visit Mike's (twice/equally) _____ as often as Madison's. This is an example of _____ matching.

8. According to the Ainslie–Rachlin model, one way to enhance self-control would be to raise the delay curve for the (smaller sooner/larger later) _____ reward.

24. On a concurrent VR 50 VI 10-sec schedule, a pigeon is likely to _____ the number of responses emitted on each schedule to the number of reinforcers obtained. By doing so, it (will/will not) _____ maximize the amount of reinforcement it obtains during the session. Such results support the _____ theory of matching.

2. You decide to do your housework each evening at 7:00 P.M., and then reward yourself with 1 hour of playing your favorite computer game. A major problem with this kind of self-reinforcement procedure is that you might _____.
This problem is known as _____.

25. Professor Huynh spends a lot of time reading articles, which she enjoys, but little time in the lab doing research, which she does not enjoy. Insofar as she needs to do research to maintain her position at the university, this appears to be an example of how _____ can lead to suboptimal patterns of behavior.

34. The _____ effects model of self-control helps emphasize the importance of establishing rules that clearly distinguish between acceptable and unacceptable behavior. It also makes clear the importance of having a _____ prevention plan to cope with situations in which we might violate our self-control program.

15. According to the _____ effects model, a student will often have difficulty studying on a particular night because the consequences for not studying that night are (aversively significant/ largely insignificant) _____.

22. You tend to shop at two favorite clothing stores, Madison's Fine Fashions and Mike's Grubbies. Over time, you have learned that Mike's is twice as likely to have something in stock that you wish to buy. If the two stores are separated by a long and difficult drive, then you are likely to demonstrate _____ matching in your visits to Mike's versus Madison's, which means that you are (twice/more than twice) _____ as likely to visit Mike's than Madison's.

29. In general, as people grow from childhood into adulthood, their delay curves will likely become (more/less) _____ deeply scalloped.

Visit the book companion Web site at <http://www.academic.cengage.com/ psychology/powell> for additional practice questions, answers to the Quick Quizzes, practice review exams, and additional exercises and information.

ANSWERS TO CHAPTER TEST

1. controlling; controlled
2. play the game and not do the housework; short-circuiting
3. immediate; delayed
4. control; impulsiveness
5. larger later; smaller sooner; impulsiveness; smaller sooner; larger later
6. decreases; imminent
7. A; imminent
8. larger later
9. concurrent; reinforcer
10. exclusive; VR 40
11. responses; reinforcers
12. matching; 25%
13. matching; proportion; proportion
14. 33%
15. small-but-cumulative; largely insignificant
16. three times as often
17. under

18. over
19. bias; attractive
20. over; under
21. equally; under
22. over; more than twice
23. melioration; higher
24. match; will not; melioration
25. melioration
26. meliorate; habituation
27. immediate; delayed
28. less; more
29. less
30. decrease; less
31. sick
32. commitment
33. early; smaller sooner
34. small-but-cumulative; relapse
35. 75%

CHAPTER 11

Biological Dispositions in Learning

CHAPTER OUTLINE

Ken was worried about his girlfriend, Chantal, who had lost a lot of weight in recent months. As one of his friends noted, she was starting to look like a "hockey stick with hair." Nevertheless, Chantal maintained that she was still overweight and needed to lose a few more pounds. Ken had heard that anorexia is characterized by a distorted body image, in which people deny how thin they are. He wondered if Chantal was suffering from this type of denial. He had also heard that anorexia often results from growing up in an overcontrolling family—though on the surface, it seemed like her family was pretty nice.

Other than his concerns about her weight, Ken thought Chantal was terrific. He particularly loved the fact that she shared his enthusiasm for long-distance running. In fact, she was more addicted to running than he was.

By this time, you probably realize that the basic principles of conditioning have a surprising degree of generality and apply to a wide range of species and behaviors. But you may also recall how, at certain points in this text, we have noted some limitations in this regard. For example, people more readily learn to be afraid of events that have some type of evolutionary association with danger, such as encountering snakes and spiders, than they do of modern-day events, such as encounters with cars and electrical outlets. It is possible then that we have inherited a biological tendency to learn certain types of fears more readily than others. This innate tendency for an organism to more easily learn certain types of behaviors or to associate certain types of events with each other is known as *preparedness.* In this chapter, we further explore the role of biological preparedness in conditioning, as well as the manner in which such preparedness seems to produce an overlap between processes of classical conditioning and operant conditioning.

Preparedness and Conditioning

Preparedness in Classical Conditioning

Fear conditioning is one form of classical conditioning in which preparedness seems to play an important role. Another is *taste aversion conditioning,* a form of classical conditioning in which a food item that has been paired with gastrointestinal illness becomes a conditioned aversive stimulus. Simply put, an animal that becomes sick after ingesting a food item associates the food with the illness and subsequently finds it distasteful.

Conditioned taste aversions are quite common. In one survey of undergraduate students, 65% reported developing a taste aversion at some point in their lives (Logue, Ophir, & Strauss, 1981). Interestingly, and perhaps not surprisingly, many of these aversions involved an alcoholic drink of some sort.

Most taste aversions are quite rational because the person believes that the food item was actually the cause of the illness. In some cases, however, the person knows that the food did not cause the illness and that the illness was instead caused by some other factor (such as the flu) with which the food was only coincidentally associated. Nevertheless, the person still finds the food item highly aversive—a convincing testament to the strength of this type of conditioning.

In a typical experiment on taste aversion conditioning, rats are first given some type of preferred food or drink to ingest, such as sweet-tasting (saccharin-flavored) water. The animal is then made to feel sick, either by injecting a nausea-inducing drug directly into the gut or through exposure to X-ray irradiation. After the rat recovers, it is given a choice of either sweet water or normal water. Although a rat typically prefers sweet water over normal water, it now strongly prefers the normal water. This indicates that the sweet water has become an aversive conditioned stimulus (CS) through its association with illness. This procedure can be diagrammed as follows:

Sweet water: X-ray irradiation → *Nausea*
     NS   **US**   **UR**
Sweet water → *Nausea* (as indicated by avoidance of the sweet water)
    CS   **CR**

Taste aversion conditioning involves many of the same processes used in other forms of classical conditioning (Schafe & Bernstein, 1996). For example, *stimulus generalization* often occurs when the food items that taste similar to the aversive item are also perceived as aversive. Thus, a conditioned aversion to one type of fish might generalize to other types of fish. A conditioned taste aversion can also be *extinguished* if the aversive food item is repeatedly ingested without further illness. As well, *overshadowing* can occur in that we are more likely to develop an aversion to a stronger-tasting food item, such as onions, than to a milder-tasting item, such as potatoes, that was consumed at the same meal. And the presence of a food item that already has aversive associations can *block* the development of aversive associations to other food items. If you have already acquired a taste aversion to peas, but force yourself to eat them anyway, and then get sick because of some spoiled fish that was served at the same meal, you will *not* develop an aversion to the fish. The presence of the peas (already a CS for nausea) will block any conditioning occurring to the fish.

Of particular importance in taste aversion conditioning is the phenomenon of *latent inhibition*. We are more likely to associate a relatively novel item, such as an unusual liqueur, with sickness than we would a more familiar item such as beer (Kalat, 1974). Latent inhibition helps explain why it is often difficult to poison a rat. When a rat encounters a novel food item, such as rat bait, it will most likely eat only a small amount of the item before moving on to other, more familiar items. If the rat later becomes ill, it will associate the illness with the novel item rather than with any of the familiar items. The rat also has a high probability of recovering from the illness because it will have eaten only a small amount of the poisoned item.[1]

1. The term p_____ refers to an innate tendency for an organism to more easily learn certain types of behaviors or to associate certain types of events with each other.

2. After recovering from a bad case of the flu, Robbie could not bring himself to eat oatmeal, which he had tried to eat during his illness. In all likelihood, Robbie has developed a t_____ a_____ to the oatmeal.

3. Robbie now dislikes other types of porridge as well, which appears to be an example of s_____ g_____.

4. Robbie's aversion to porridge would likely be e_____ if he repeatedly ate it without experiencing any further illness.

5. According to the o_____ effect, the strongest-tasting item in a meal is most likely to become associated with a subsequent illness. As well, a food item that was previously associated with illness will b_____ the development of aversive associations to other items in a meal.

6. In keeping with the process of l_____ i_____, Robbie would have been less likely to develop a taste aversion to oatmeal porridge if he had frequently eaten oatmeal before his illness.

Although taste aversion conditioning is in many ways similar to other forms of classical conditioning, there are also some major differences.

1. **The Formation of Associations Over Long Delays.** In most classical conditioning procedures, the neutral stimulus (NS) and unconditioned stimulus (US) must occur in close temporal proximity, separated by no more than a few seconds. By contrast, taste aversions can develop when food items are consumed several hours before the sickness develops. For example, Etscorn and Stephens (1973) found that rats could develop taste aversions to flavored water that had been ingested up to 24 hours before they were injected with an illness-inducing drug. The ability to associate food with illness after lengthy periods of time is highly adaptive in that poisonous substances often have a delayed effect. If animals

---

[1]This tendency to be wary of new food items, which is also present in humans and is especially strong in children, is known as *dietary neophobia* (a *neophobia* is a fear of something new). Neophobia is particularly important for rats, which are physically incapable of vomiting to purge toxins from the stomach. More generally, however, neophobia is an especially adaptive tendency for small animals and the young of most species because the dose–response relationships for many toxins are body-weight dependent. Simply put, small animals are more susceptible to food poisoning than large animals and have therefore evolved to be especially wary of food poisoning.

were unable to form such delayed associations, they would be at great risk of repeatedly consuming a poisonous food item and eventually perishing.

2. **One-Trial Conditioning.** Strong conditioned taste aversions can usually be achieved with only a single pairing of food with illness, particularly when the food item is novel (Riley & Clarke, 1977). One-trial conditioning sometimes occurs in other forms of conditioning, especially fear conditioning, but not as consistently as it does in taste aversion conditioning. As with the ability to form associations over long delays, one-trial conditioning of taste aversions is highly adaptive insofar as it minimizes the possibility of a repeat, possibly fatal, experience with a poisonous substance.

3. **Specificity of Associations.** When you feel nauseous following a meal, do you associate the nausea with that episode of *American Idol* you are watching (even though, given the quality of some of the singing, that might seem appropriate), or with the meal? Fortunately for the broadcast networks, you are more likely to associate the nausea with the meal. Similarly, the rat that receives an injection of a nausea-inducing drug several hours after drinking a sweet water solution does not associate the illness with the injection; it instead associates the illness with the sweet water. In other words, there seems to be a strong, inherited tendency to associate a gastrointestinal illness with food or drink rather than with any other kind of item (Garcia & Koelling, 1966). This type of preparedness is sometimes referred to as **CS-US relevance**, an innate tendency to more readily associate certain types of stimuli with each other.

An excellent example of the role of CS-US relevance in taste aversion conditioning was provided by Garcia and Koelling (1966) in their initial demonstration of this type of conditioning. In this experiment, the rats initially drank sweet water that was paired with a light and a noise (each time they licked the water tube, they heard a click and saw a light flash). This compound stimulus can therefore be described as "bright, noisy, sweet water." After consuming the water, some of the rats received a slight foot shock that elicited a fear reaction, while other rats received a dose of X-ray irradiation that made them nauseous. Finally, all of the rats were given a choice between two water bottles, one containing only "bright, noisy" water (i.e., regular water associated with the light and click) and the other containing only sweet water. Can you guess the results?

The rats that had been made nauseous by the X-ray irradiation avoided the sweet water and drank the bright, noisy water, which is consistent with the basic notion that nausea is more readily associated with taste than with other kinds of stimuli.

Conditioning trial:
Bright, noisy, sweet water: X-ray irradiation → *Nausea*
        NS   **US**   **UR**

Test trials:
Sweet water → *Nausea*
      CS   **CR**
Bright, noisy water → **No nausea**
       NS   —

But what about the rats that received a foot shock? It turns out that they avoided the bright, noisy water but not the sweet water. In other words, they developed a fear of the noise and lights associated with the water, but not the taste, and were quite willing to drink the sweet water.

Conditioning trial:
Bright, noisy, sweet water: Foot shock → *Fear*
          NS   **US**   **UR**

Test trials:
Bright, noisy water → *Fear*
       CS   **CR**
Sweet water → **No fear**
      NS   —

Thus, not only do rats have a predisposition to readily associate nausea with taste, they also have a predisposition to associate tactually painful events with visual and auditory stimuli. This makes sense from an evolutionary perspective in that tactile pain is more likely to result from something "out there" that a rat can see and hear, whereas nausea is more likely to result from something a rat ingests and can be tasted. Thus, for a rat to evolve in such a way that it could readily make such associations would facilitate its survival.

Further evidence for the role of biological dispositions in taste aversion conditioning has been revealed by comparative research on between-species differences in the types of stimuli that can be associated. In one experiment, both quail and rats drank dark blue, sour-tasting water before being made ill (Wilcoxon, Dragoin, & Kral, 1971). The animals were then given a choice between dark blue water and sour-tasting water. As expected, the rats naturally avoided the sour-tasting water and strongly preferred the dark blue water. They associated the taste of the water with the nausea. The quail, however, were more likely to avoid the dark blue water than the sour-tasting water. This suggests that quail, which are daytime feeders and rely heavily on vision for identifying food, are more disposed to associate the visual aspects (rather than the taste aspects) of food with nausea. Rats, however, being nighttime feeders, rely more heavily on taste (and smell) than vision and are therefore generally disposed to associate the taste (and smell) aspects of food with nausea. (This is not to say that rats cannot learn to associate the visual aspects of food with nausea. They can, but additional conditioning trials are required to form such associations.)

In addition to between-species differences, there are often sex differences in taste aversion learning, which can be related to differences in sensory and perceptual processing. In humans, females are better than males at detecting odors and discriminating among odors. Because of this ability, women are more reactive to odors associated with the experience of nausea and are more prone to developing taste aversions (Chambers et al., 1997). As well, most women report that their sense of smell and taste is enhanced during the early stages of pregnancy, which often leads to the development of taste aversions (Nordin, Broman, Olafsson, & Wulff, 2004). Although experiencing these kinds of symptoms during early pregnancy might seem counterproductive, it is actually a highly adaptive mechanism. Fetal organ systems are developing during the first few months of pregnancy and are highly vulnerable to damage by toxins at this stage. A dislike of certain foods (especially bitter foods) and a propensity to taste aversions might prevent a woman from ingesting foods that contain dangerous bacteria (bitterness can indicate the presence of bacteria).

It should be noted that research on taste aversion conditioning has some practical applications. For example, cancer patients sometimes develop aversions to food items that have been inadvertently associated with the nausea resulting from chemotherapy (Bernstein, 1991). Because cancer patients often suffer from severe weight loss anyway, the development of taste aversions that lead to avoidance of certain food items could be serious. Fortunately, research has suggested ways to minimize this problem. One way is to serve meals that consist of highly familiar foods. In keeping with the latent inhibition effect, such familiar foods will be less likely to become associated with nausea. Along the same lines, the patient can be served a highly novel, yet trivial, food item just before a chemotherapy session. This novel item will then be associated with the nausea, preventing the development of taste aversions to other, more essential food items. For example, in one study, children about to undergo chemotherapy were given coconut- or root-beer-flavored candies following a regular meal. Compared to children who had not been given these candies, the children in the study later developed fewer aversions to their regular food items (Broberg & Bernstein, 1987).

QUICK QUIZ B

1. Distinctive features of taste aversion conditioning, compared to other types of classical conditioning, include the fact that the associations can be formed over (short/long) _____ delays, typically require (one/several) _____ pairing(s) of the NS and US, and (are/are not) _____ specific to certain types of stimuli.

2. In the classic experiment by Garcia and Koelling, the rats that had been made ill avoided the (sweet/bright, noisy) _____ water, while the rats that had been shocked avoided the _____ water.

3. In the experiment on taste aversions in quail and rats, the rats avoided the (blue/sour) _____ water, while the quail avoided the _____ water.

4. To counter the possibility that chemotherapy-induced nausea will result in the development of taste aversions, patients should be fed meals that consist mostly of highly (familiar/unfamiliar) _____ foods. As well, just before the chemotherapy session, they can be given some trivial type of (familiar/unfamiliar) _____ food item, which will attract most of the aversive associations.

5. According to the concept of _____-_____ rel_____, certain types of stimuli are more easily associated with each other.

And Furthermore

Conditioned Food Preferences

Just as conditioning processes sometimes make foods aversive, such processes can also make foods more appetitive. For example, a powerful way to increase our preference for a disliked food is to mix it with some food item or sweetener that we strongly prefer. This may be how some people grow to like black coffee: They first drink it with cream and sugar and then gradually eliminate the extra ingredients as the taste of the coffee itself becomes pleasurable. Similarly, in one study, college students developed increased preference for broccoli or cauliflower after eating it a few times with sugar (E. D. Capaldi, 1996). Unfortunately, few parents use such a method to improve their children's eating habits, possibly because they perceive sugar to be unhealthy and do not realize that the sugar can later be withdrawn (Casey & Rozin, 1989). Instead, parents often try to entice their children to eat a disliked food by offering dessert as a reward—a strategy that easily backfires in that the contrast between the disliked food and the subsequent dessert might result in the former becoming even more disliked. (See E. D. Capaldi, 1996, for other ways in which food preferences can be conditioned.)

Preparedness in Operant Conditioning

Biological preparedness also seems to play a role in some forms of operant conditioning. For example, Stevenson-Hinde (1973) found that the sound of recorded chaffinch songs (chaffinches are a type of bird) was an effective reinforcer for training chaffinches to perch in a certain spot, but not for training them to key-peck. Conversely, food was an effective reinforcer for training them to key-peck but not training them to perch in a certain spot. Chaffinches seem to be biologically prepared to associate perching in a certain spot with the consequence of hearing songs, and to associate pecking with the consequence of obtaining food.

In a similar manner, rats will more readily learn to press a lever to obtain food pellets than to avoid shock (Bolles, 1970). But they readily learn to freeze or run to avoid shock. Once more, the explanation for these differences may reside in the animals' evolutionary history. Rats have evolved dexterous forepaws that are often used for eating; thus, pressing a lever for food is not far removed from the type of food-gathering behavior they display in the natural environment. However, avoiding painful events is, for a rat, more naturally related to the response of freezing or running than it is to manipulating objects with its forepaws.

Biological dispositions for certain types of avoidance responses have also been found in pigeons. Bedford and Anger (cited in Bolles, 1979) found that pigeons will quickly learn to fly from one perch to another to avoid shock, but they will not learn to peck a response key to avoid shock. As with rats, the typical behavior pigeons use when fleeing danger provides an explanation: Flying is the usual way a pigeon escapes danger, while pecking is not. Thus pigeons, like rats, seem predisposed to learn certain types of avoidance responses more readily than others.

It may have occurred to you from the preceding examples that preparedness seems to play a particularly strong role in avoidance behavior. This observation has led Bolles (1970, 1979) to propose that some avoidance responses are actually not operants (in the sense of being controlled by their consequences) but are instead elicited behaviors (that are controlled by the stimuli that precede them). More specifically, he contends that aversive stimulation elicits a *species-specific defense reaction* (SSDR), which in the natural environment is often effective in countering danger. For this reason, a rat easily learns to run or freeze to avoid painful stimulation, simply because running and freezing are behaviors that are naturally *elicited* in dangerous situations. Indeed, a rat's tendency to freeze is so strong that it will sometimes freeze even when doing so *results* in shock rather than avoids shock. (Humans also have a tendency to freeze when feeling threatened, even when it is counterproductive to do so—as when giving a speech to a large audience or when being ordered about by a gunman.)

1. Chaffinches easily learn to associate (perching/pecking) _____ with the consequence of hearing a song and _____ with the consequence of obtaining food.

2. Rats are biologically prepared to learn to avoid a painful stimulus by (lever pressing/running) _____, while pigeons are biologically prepared to learn to avoid a painful stimulus by (pecking/flying) _____.

3. According to Bolles, these types of avoidance responses are s_____-s_____ defense reactions that are naturally e_____ by the aversive stimulus.

QUICK QUIZ C

Operant–Respondent Interactions

Bolles's concept of the SSDR is one example of how it is sometimes difficult to distinguish between operant behaviors and respondent (or elicited) behaviors. In this section, we discuss two further examples of the overlap between operants and respondents: instinctive drift and sign tracking.

Instinctive Drift

It was once assumed that an animal could be trained to perform just about any behavior it was physically capable of performing. Indeed, considering the remarkable array of behaviors that animals can be trained to display, this assumption does not seem all that unreasonable. There are, however, limits to such training, as two of Skinner's students discovered in the course of training animals for show business.

Marian and Keller Breland were former students of Skinner's who decided to put their knowledge of operant conditioning to commercial use. They established a business of training animals to perform unusual behaviors for television commercials and movies. In this endeavor, they were usually quite successful. Occasionally, however, they encountered some rather interesting limitations in what certain animals could be taught (Breland & Breland, 1961). For example, they once attempted to train a pig to deposit a wooden coin in a piggy bank. Using processes of shaping and chaining, the training initially proceeded quite smoothly. As time passed, however, a strange thing began to happen. The pig no longer simply deposited the coin in the bank, but started tossing the coin in the air and then rooting at it on the ground. Eventually, the tossing and rooting became so frequent that the coin never made its way to the bank. The Brelands also attempted to use a raccoon for this trick, but here too they ran into difficulties. As training progressed, the raccoon began rubbing the coin back and forth in its paws rather than dropping it into the bank. This stereotyped action sequence eventually became so dominant that this attempt too had to be abandoned.

Although these results were originally regarded as a strange anomaly and a serious blow to the generality of operant conditioning, it is now recognized that they merely represented situations in which a classically conditioned, fixed action pattern had gradually emerged to interfere with the operant behavior that was being shaped. With both the pig and the raccoon, the coin had become so strongly associated with food that it began to elicit species-specific behavior patterns associated with feeding. In the case of the pig, this meant that the coin was subjected to the type of rooting behavior pigs often display when feeding. In the case of the raccoon, the coin was repeatedly rubbed and washed in the way raccoons normally rub and wash their food (often shellfish). In both cases, the coin had become a CS that elicited a conditioned response (CR) in the form of a food-related, fixed action pattern.

Thus, in the case of the pig, the Brelands intended this:

> **Coin:** *Deposit coin in bank* → **Food**
> S^D ⠀⠀⠀⠀⠀ **R** ⠀⠀⠀⠀⠀⠀⠀ S^R

which is an operant conditioning procedure. Initially, this worked quite well, but as the coin became more and more strongly associated with food, what happened instead was this:

> **Coin: Food** → *Rooting*
> ⠀NS⠀⠀US⠀⠀⠀⠀UR
> **Coin** → *Rooting*
> ⠀CS⠀⠀⠀⠀CR

Which is a classical conditioning procedure. And as the classically conditioned response increased in strength, it eventually overrode the operantly conditioned response of depositing the coin in the bank. Thus, ***instinctive drift*** is an instance of classical conditioning in which a genetically based, fixed action pattern gradually emerges and displaces the behavior that is being operantly conditioned.

QUICK QUIZ D

1. In the phenomenon known as i_____ d_____, a genetically based f_____ a_____ pattern gradually emerges and displaces the behavior being shaped.

2. In the experiment with the raccoon, the coin became a (CS/S^D) _____ that elicited a (R/CR/UR) _____ of washing and rubbing.

Sign Tracking

Pavlov once reported that one of his dogs, during a classical conditioning experiment, approached a light that had signaled the delivery of food and licked it (Pavlov, 1941). It seemed as though the light not only signaled food, but had acquired some of its appetitive properties. Little attention was paid to this finding, however, until recently. This phenomenon is now known as sign tracking.

In *sign tracking*, an organism approaches a stimulus that signals the presentation of an appetitive event (Tomie, Brooks, & Zito, 1989). The approach behavior seems very much like an operant behavior because it appears to be quite goal directed, yet the procedure that produces it is more closely akin to classical conditioning. Thus, sign tracking is yet another way in which classical and operant conditioning appear to overlap.

Take, for example, a hungry dog that has been trained to sit on a mat to receive food presented in a dish at the far side of the room. Suppose, too, that a light is presented just before the food, such that this light becomes a cue for food delivery (see Figure 11.1). A couple of things are liable to happen because

FIGURE 11.1 Experimental setting for a sign-tracking experiment. The dog first learns to sit on the mat to receive food. A light is then presented before each food delivery.

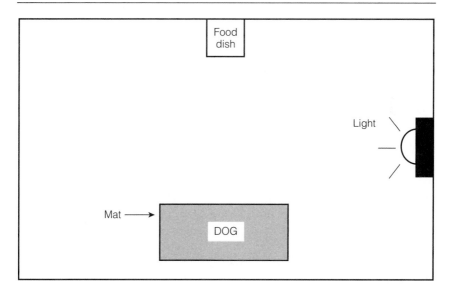

of this arrangement. One is that the dog will probably start salivating whenever the light is presented. Through classical conditioning, the light will have become a CS for the conditioned response of salivation. But that is not all that will happen. Logically, when the light appears (which is a signal for food delivery), the dog should immediately walk over to the food dish and wait for the food. What happens instead is that the dog *walks over to the light* and starts displaying food-related behaviors toward it, such as licking it or even barking at it as though soliciting food from it. These behaviors are of course entirely unnecessary and have no effect on whether the food will appear. It seems as though the light has become so strongly associated with food that it is now a CS that elicits innate food-related behavior patterns (see Jenkins, Barrera, Ireland, & Woodside, 1978, for a description of a similar experiment).

Sign tracking has also been found in pigeons, and in fact it helps to account for the ease with which pigeons learn to peck a response key for food. Brown and Jenkins (1968) presented pigeons with a key light for 8 seconds followed by the *noncontingent* delivery of food. Although the pigeons did not have to peck the key to obtain the food, they soon began doing so anyway. It was as though the pigeons automatically pecked the key, simply because it was associated with food. The pecking therefore seemed to be an elicited response, with the key light functioning as a CS through its association with food:

Key light: Food → *Peck*
　　NS　　　US　　　UR
Key light → *Peck*
　　CS　　　　CR

This procedure is known as ***autoshaping***, a type of sign tracking in which a pigeon comes to automatically peck at a key because the key light has been associated with the response-independent delivery of food. Rather than trying to deliberately shape the behavior of key pecking, the researcher merely has to put the pigeon in the chamber, program the equipment to present light and food in the appropriate order, and presto, within an hour or so, out pops a key-pecking pigeon. Once the pecking response has been established this way, the food can then be made *contingent* upon pecking (i.e., food appears only when the key has been pecked), at which point the pecking begins functioning as an operant:

Key light: *Peck* → Food
　　S^D　　　R　　　S^R

Thus, a behavior that starts off as an elicited behavior (controlled by the stimulus that precedes it) becomes transformed into an operant behavior (controlled by its consequence). In other words, the pigeon initially pecks the key because the key light predicts the free delivery of food; later, it pecks the key because it has to do so to obtain food.

Autoshaping is one type of classical conditioning that fits well with Pavlov's stimulus-substitution theory (discussed in Chapter 5). Because of its association with food, the key light appears to become a substitute for food, with the bird attempting to consume it. Further evidence for this stimulus-substitution

ADVICE FOR THE LOVELORN

Dear Dr. Dee,

My old girlfriend, to whom I was very attached, recently moved away. I am now trying to get over her, but I still find myself going to our favorite restaurant, our favorite beach, and so on. Why do I torture myself like this?

What a Birdbrain

Dear Birdbrain,

Think of your behavior as similar to sign tracking. Your girlfriend was a powerful appetitive stimulus, with the result that you now approach stimuli that have been strongly associated with her. In fact (and somewhat in keeping with your signature), researchers have found similar behavior patterns in Japanese quail. Burns and Domjan (1996) found that if they lowered a block of wood into a chamber just before opening a door that allowed access to a female quail, male quail had a strong tendency to approach and stand near the block of wood rather than near the door. The block of wood had become a CS that elicited what was essentially a sexual sign-tracking response. In similar fashion, we may have a tendency to approach settings that are strongly associated with a person with whom we have had an intimate relationship. In any event, your "birdbrained" tendency to approach these settings should eventually extinguish.

Behaviorally yours,

Dr. Dee

interpretation comes from an experiment that compared autoshaped key pecks toward a key light signaling water delivery versus a key light signaling food delivery (Jenkins & Moore, 1973). When the bird pecked a key associated with water, it did so with its eyes open and its beak almost closed—the standard pattern of behavior when pigeons drink water. But when the bird pecked a key associated with food delivery, it did so with its eyes closed and its beak open, which is the standard pattern of behavior when a pigeon pecks at food. (The eyes are closed possibly because, in the natural environment, pecking at food sometimes results in dust or pebbles being thrown upward.) In other words, it seemed as though the bird was attempting to drink the key that was associated with water and eat the key that was associated with food.

Autoshaping procedures have powerful effects on behavior. For example, pigeons will peck a key associated with food even when doing so *prevents* the delivery of food (Williams & Williams, 1969). In other words, although the contingency requires the pigeons to refrain from pecking to actually obtain the food (they should simply wait for the food when the key light appears), they will nevertheless compulsively peck at the key. The key light exerts such strong control over the behavior that it essentially overrides the negative punishment (loss of food) associated with pecking. This phenomenon, in which sign tracking persists despite the resultant loss of a reinforcer, is known as *negative automaintenance*.

QUICK QUIZ E

1. In s_____ t_____, an organism approaches a stimulus that signals the availability of food. In such circumstances, the stimulus is best defined as a(n) (CS/US/S^D) _____, while the approach behavior is best defined as a(n) (CR/UR/operant) _____.

2. In au_____, a pigeon will begin to peck a lit response key that is presented for 8 seconds before the non_____ delivery of food. The peck in this situation appears to be functioning as a(n) (elicited/operant) _____ behavior. Later, when a peck is required for the food to be delivered, the peck becomes a(n) _____.

3. In n_____ aut_____, pigeons will peck a lit response key that signals food delivery even when the act of pecking (prevents/facilitates) _____ the delivery of food.

Adjunctive Behavior

Instinctive drift and sign tracking represent two types of anomalous (unexpected) behavior patterns that can develop during an operant conditioning procedure. Yet another type of anomaly is adjunctive behavior. *Adjunctive behavior* is an excessive pattern of behavior that emerges as a by-product of an intermittent schedule of reinforcement for some other behavior. In other words, as one behavior is being strengthened through intermittent reinforcement, another quite different behavior emerges as a side effect of that procedure. Adjunctive behavior is sometimes referred to as *schedule-induced behavior*, and the two terms will be used interchangeably in this discussion.

Basic Procedure and Defining Characteristics

Falk (1961) was the first person to systematically investigate adjunctive behavior in animals. He found that when rats were trained to press a lever for food on an intermittent schedule of reinforcement, they also began drinking excessive amounts of water. During a 3-hour session, the rats drank almost three-and-a-half times the amount they would normally drink in an entire day. (To get a handle on this, imagine that a person who typically drinks 8 glasses of water a day instead drinks 28 glasses of water in a 3-hour period!) In fact, some of the rats drank up to half their body weight in water. These numbers are all the more remarkable because the rats were food deprived, not water deprived; and food deprivation typically produces a decrease, not an increase, in water intake. This pattern of excessive drinking—called *schedule-induced polydipsia (polydipsia* means "excessive thirst")—developed quite rapidly, usually beginning in the first session and becoming firmly established by the second session.

Studies of adjunctive behavior typically employ fixed interval (FI) or fixed time (FT) schedules of reinforcement (Falk, 1971). On such schedules, the delivery of each reinforcer is followed by a period of time during which another reinforcer is not available. It is during such *interreinforcement intervals* that adjunctive behavior occurs. For example, when schedule-induced polydipsia is generated by exposure to an FI schedule of food reinforcement, the rat usually drinks during the postreinforcement pause that is typical of such schedules. Thus, a short period of time during which there is a low probability or zero probability of reinforcement seems to be a critical factor in the development of adjunctive behavior.

Researchers soon discovered that schedule-induced polydipsia could be generated in other species, including mice, pigeons, and chimpanzees. They also discovered that it was possible to generate other types of adjunctive behaviors, such as chewing on wood shavings, licking at an air stream (presumably because of the sensory stimulation it provides), and aggression. In the latter case, it was found that pigeons exposed to an FI or FT schedule of food delivery soon began attacking a nearby target pigeon—or, more commonly, a picture or stuffed model of a pigeon—following each reinforcer (e.g., Flory & Ellis, 1973). Unlike extinction-induced aggression, which often grows weaker over time, this type of schedule-induced aggression tends to remain strong and persistent. (See Falk, 1971, 1977, and Staddon, 1977, for overviews of the findings on adjunctive behavior.)

Researchers also found that adjunctive behavior could be generated using reinforcers other than food delivery. For example, rats were found to eat excessive amounts of food (that is, they engaged in schedule-induced eating) when exposed to an intermittent schedule of electrical stimulation to the pleasure centers in the brain (J. F. Wilson & Cantor, 1987). Thus, rather than using food as a reinforcer to produce some other type of adjunctive behavior, these researchers used electrical stimulation of the pleasure centers as a reinforcer to produce an adjunctive pattern of eating. Interestingly, these rats gained considerable weight due to their compulsive tendency to snack between reinforcers, suggesting that schedule-induced eating may play a role in the development of obesity.

1. Adjunctive behavior is an excessive pattern of behavior that emerges as a _____ of an _____ schedule of reinforcement for (that behavior/a different behavior) _____.

2. Adjunctive behavior is also referred to as s_____-_____ behavior.

3. An excessive pattern of drinking that is produced by exposure to an intermittent schedule of food reinforcement is called s_____-_____ p_____.

4. Studies of adjunctive behavior typically use (fixed interval/variable interval) _____ or (fixed time/variable time) _____ schedules of food reinforcement. This is because adjunctive behavior tends to occur when there is a (high/low) _____ probability of reinforcement.

QUICK QUIZ F

According to Falk (1971, 1977), adjunctive behavior has several distinguishing features. These include the following:

1. As previously noted, **adjunctive behavior typically occurs in the period immediately following consumption of an intermittent reinforcer.** For example, in schedule-induced polydipsia, the rat will quickly eat each food pellet as soon as it is delivered and then immediately move over to the drinking tube for a quick bout of drinking. The start of the interval between food pellets, therefore, tends to be dominated by drinking. The end of the interval, however, as the next pellet becomes imminent, tends to be dominated by food-related behaviors, such as lever pressing for the food (Staddon, 1977).

2. **Adjunctive behavior is affected by the level of deprivation for the scheduled reinforcer.** The greater the level of deprivation for the reinforcer, the stronger the adjunctive behavior that emerges as a by-product. For example, with schedule-induced polydipsia, greater food deprivation not only produces a higher rate of lever pressing for food pellets, it also produces a higher rate of drinking between food pellets.

3. **Adjunctive behaviors can function as reinforcers for other behaviors.** This is in keeping with the Premack principle, which holds that high-probability behaviors can often serve as effective reinforcers for low-probability behaviors. Thus, with schedule-induced polydipsia, the rat will not only press a lever to obtain access to food pellets but, during the interval between food pellets, it will also press a lever to gain access to water so that it can engage in adjunctive drinking.

4. **There is an optimal interval between reinforcers for the development of adjunctive behavior.** For example, rats will engage in little drinking with an interreinforcement interval of 5 seconds between food pellets, more drinking as the interval is lengthened to 180 seconds, and then less drinking as the interval is lengthened beyond that. At an interreinforcement interval of 300 seconds, one again finds little drinking. The optimal interreinforcement intervals for other types of adjunctive behaviors tend to be similar, often in the range of 1 to 3 minutes.

1. Adjunctive behavior tends to occur (just before/just after) _____ delivery of a reinforcer.

2. As the deprivation level for the scheduled reinforcer increases, the strength of the adjunctive behavior associated with it tends to (increase/decrease) _____.

3. The opportunity to engage in an adjunctive behavior can serve as a (reinforcer/ punisher) _____ for some other behavior. This is in keeping with the P_____ principle.

4. The optimal interreinforcement interval for the production of adjunctive behavior is often in the range of (a few seconds/a few minutes/several minutes) _____.

Adjunctive Behavior in Humans

The preceding discussion probably has you wondering about the extent to which adjunctive behaviors occur in humans. On an anecdotal level, Falk (1977) noted that a diverse range of human behaviors, from nail biting and talkativeness to snacking and coffee drinking, are commonly associated with periods of enforced waiting. Falk (1998) also noted that drug and alcohol abuse is frequently found in environments that provide sparse levels of economic and social reinforcement, suggesting that adjunctive processes (in addition to the physiological effects of the drug) contribute to the development of drug and alcohol abuse. This is supported by the fact that schedule-induced polydipsia has been used to induce rats to drink excessive amounts of water containing alcohol or other drugs. In other words, schedule-induced polydipsia can be used to create an animal analogue of drug and alcohol abuse (Falk, 1993; Riley & Wetherington, 1989).

On an experimental level, humans have produced adjunctive-type behavior patterns that are similar to, though not as extreme as, those found in animals. For example, Doyle and Samson (1988) found that human subjects exposed to FI schedules of monetary reinforcement for game playing displayed an increased tendency to drink water following each reinforcer. Similar to schedule-induced polydipsia in animals, the length of the interval between reinforcers was an important variable, with nearly twice as much drinking occurring on an FI 90-sec schedule as on an FI 30-sec schedule.

Experimental evidence for adjunctive drug use in humans has also been obtained. Cherek (1982) found high rates of cigarette smoking when monetary payment for button pushing was presented on an FI 120-sec schedule as opposed to FI 30-sec, 60-sec, or 240-sec schedules. And Doyle and Samson (1988) found high rates of beer sipping when monetary payment for playing a game was presented on an FI 90-sec schedule as opposed to an FI 30-sec schedule. In both cases, the drug-related behavior (smoking or beer sipping) was most likely to occur during the period immediately following delivery of the reinforcer, which is consistent with the notion that it was functioning as an adjunctive behavior. Studies such as these support the notion that adjunctive processes may play a significant role in the development of substance abuse in humans. Especially in the early phases of an addiction, adjunctive processes may encourage an individual to frequently consume an addictive substance, with the result that the person eventually becomes addicted to it (Falk, 1998).

1. Evidence that humans engage in adjunctive behavior includes the fact that studies of adjunctive-type behavior patterns in human subjects usually (find/do not find) _____ an optimal time interval between reinforcers for producing such behaviors.

2. Certain behavior patterns in humans, such as smoking and nail biting, are often associated with periods of (extreme activity/enforced waiting) _____ _____, which (agrees with/contradicts) _____ the notion that these may be adjunctive behaviors.

QUICK QUIZ H

And Furthermore

Extreme Polydipsia: Not Just a "Rat Thing"

Schedule-induced polydipsia is a bizarre behavior pattern in which rats ingest enormous amounts of water in a short time. Experimental studies of schedule-induced drinking in humans have typically produced much lower rates of drinking, suggesting that rats and humans are quite different in their susceptibility to polydipsia (Klein, 1996). But extreme polydipsia does sometimes occur in humans. In fact, as a psychiatric label, the term *polydipsia* refers to a rare condition in which patients drink incessantly—so much so that they sometimes die from the disruption of electrolytes in their bodies. Although there are no doubt major differences between this psychiatric form of polydipsia in humans and schedule-induced polydipsia in rats, there might also be some similarities. If nothing else, schedule-induced polydipsia—and other adjunctive behaviors—are compulsive-type patterns of behavior and might therefore provide insight into the behavioral and neurological processes that maintain compulsive behaviors in humans. Psychiatrists have therefore shown considerable interest in schedule-induced polydipsia, in sorting out the neurological processes that underlie it, and in determining the effects of psychiatric drugs on alleviating it (Wallace & Singer, 1976). Research on adjunctive behavior could therefore have implications for furthering our understanding and treatment of some serious psychiatric conditions in humans.

3. It has also been noted that alcohol and drug abuse is most likely to develop in environments in which economic and social reinforcers are (frequently/infrequently) _____ available, which (agrees with/contradicts) _____ the notion that these may be adjunctive behaviors.

4. Adjunctive processes may play a particularly important role in the development of an addiction during the (early/later) _____ stages of the addiction.

Adjunctive Behavior as Displacement Activity

Why would a tendency to develop adjunctive behaviors ever have evolved? What purpose do such activities serve, especially given how self-destructive they sometimes are? For example, it requires a considerable amount of energy for a rat to process and excrete the huge amounts of water ingested during a session of schedule-induced polydipsia. And drug and alcohol abuse is decidedly counterproductive for both rats and humans.

In this regard, Falk (1977) has proposed that adjunctive behaviors represent a type of *displacement activity*, an apparently irrelevant activity sometimes displayed by animals when confronted by conflict or thwarted from attaining a goal. For example, a bird that is unable to reach an insect hidden between some rocks might begin pecking at some nearby twigs. This behavior seems completely unrelated to the goal of capturing the insect, which led early investigators to propose that displacement activities like this serve simply as a means of releasing pent-up energy (Tinbergen, 1951).

In contrast to this energy release model, Falk (1977) proposes that displacement activities serve two purposes. First, they provide for a more diversified range of behaviors in a particular setting, and a diverse range of behavior is often beneficial. Consider, for example, a bird that has a tendency to peck at twigs while waiting for an insect to emerge from its hiding place. By doing so, the bird may uncover another source of food or may even stumble upon using a twig as a tool for rooting out the insect. In fact, some species of birds do use twigs to root out insects—an evolved pattern of behavior that may have begun as a displacement activity. In similar fashion, an employee who grows restless and busies herself with some paperwork while waiting for an important phone call is apt to be a more productive employee than one who simply stares at the phone until the phone call arrives.

A second benefit of displacement activities is that they help the animal remain in a situation where a significant reinforcer might eventually become available. Periods of little or no reinforcement can be aversive—as any student knows when buckling down to study a boring subject matter—and anything that can alleviate the aversiveness of these intervals will heighten the probability of attaining the delayed reinforcer. Thus, pecking the ground gives the bird "something to do" while waiting for an insect to emerge from its hiding place, just as whittling a stick allows a hunter to patiently wait for a moose, and munching on licorice enables a student to sit still and study patiently throughout a study session.

Adjunctive behavior can therefore be seen as a natural tendency to do something else while waiting for a reinforcer. To the extent that it enhances the individual's ability to wait out the delay period, it thus constitutes a sort of built-in self-control device. This is a paradoxical notion in that adjunctive behaviors, such as smoking and drinking, are usually the kinds of behaviors that are viewed as indicating a *lack of self-control* (Tomie, 1996). But this depends on the specific consequence to which one is referring. Smoking is an impulsive behavior in terms of providing short-term pleasure at the risk of undermining one's long-term health, but it can also enhance self-control in terms of helping an individual work long hours so as to obtain a promotion. For this reason, students often find it particularly difficult to quit smoking during the academic year. Quitting smoking not only results in the temporary onset of withdrawal symptoms, it also undermines the student's ability to study for long periods of time.[2] Congruent with this notion, it has been shown

---

[2]As Freud once complained, if he could not smoke, then he could not work. Interestingly, Freud was famous for his ability to work long hours, which is often attributed to his "self-discipline." Yet this self-discipline seems to have been at least partially dependent on the availability of an adjunctive activity in the form of smoking. Unfortunately, his 20-cigars-a-day habit resulted in cancer of the jaw, from which he eventually died (Gay, 1988).

that people who successfully overcome an addiction (such as alcoholism) are more likely to seek out a replacement for the addictive activity (such as coffee drinking) than those who are not successful in overcoming their addiction (Brown, Stetson, & Beatty, 1989). The moral of the story is that adjunctive behaviors sometimes serve a purpose, and we might do well to acknowledge that purpose and find other ways to fulfill it.

1. According to Falk, adjunctive behavior may be a type of d_____ activity, which is an irrelevant activity displayed by animals when confronted by c_____ or when they are (able/unable) _____ to achieve a goal.

2. One benefit of such activities is that it is often useful to engage in (just one type/a diverse range) _____ of behavior(s) in a situation.

3. The second benefit derived from such activities is that they may facilitate (moving away from/remaining near) _____ a potential reinforcer.

4. To the extent that adjunctive activities facilitate waiting for, or working toward, a(n) (immediate/delayed) _____ reinforcer, such activities may (facilitate/impede) _____ efforts at self-control.

Activity Anorexia

One type of behavior that can be generated as an adjunctive behavior is wheel running. When exposed to an intermittent schedule of food reinforcement for lever pressing, rats will run in a wheel for several seconds during the interval between reinforcers (Levitsky & Collier, 1968). A related type of procedure, however, produces even more extreme running. Known as *activity anorexia*, it has some important implications for people who are undertaking a diet and exercise program to lose weight.[3]

Basic Procedure and Defining Characteristics

The procedure for creating activity anorexia is as follows: If rats are allowed to access food for only a single 1.5-hour feeding period each day, and if they have access to a running wheel during the 22.5-hour interval between meals, they will begin to spend increasing amounts of time running during that interval. Not only that, the more they run, the less they eat, and the less they eat, the more they run. In other words, a sort of negative feedback cycle develops in which the two behavioral tendencies, increased running and decreased eating,

---

[3]Activity anorexia is considered by some researchers to be a type of adjunctive or schedule-induced behavior (e.g., Falk, 1994), and by other researchers to be a separate class of behaviors involving distinctly different processes (e.g., Beneke, Schulte, & Vander Tuig, 1995). For purposes of this discussion, we will adopt the latter position.

reciprocally strengthen each other. Within a week or so, the rats are running enormous distances—up to 20,000 revolutions of the wheel per day (equivalent to about 12 miles!)—and eating nothing. If the process is allowed to continue (for humane reasons, the experiment is usually terminated before this), the rats will become completely emaciated and die (e.g., Routtenberg & Kuznesof, 1967).

Thus, *activity anorexia* is an abnormally high level of activity and low level of food intake generated by exposure to a restricted schedule of feeding (Epling & Pierce, 1991). It is important to note that rats that are given restricted access to food, but with *no* wheel available, do just fine—they easily ingest enough food during the 1.5-hour meal period to maintain body weight. Rats that have access to a wheel, but without food restriction, also do just fine—they display only moderate levels of running and no tendency toward self-starvation. It is the combination of food restriction and the opportunity to run that is so devastating.

1. The basic procedure for the development of ac_____ an_____ in rats is the presentation of (one/several) _____ meal period(s) each day along with access to a running wheel during the (meal/between-meal) _____ period.

2. Thus, _____ _____ is an abnormally (low/high) _____ level of _____ and a (low/high) _____ level of food intake generated by exposure to a r_____ schedule of feeding.

QUICK QUIZ J

Comparisons With Anorexia Nervosa

Activity anorexia was first investigated by Routtenberg and Kuznesof (1967). Two other researchers, Epling and Pierce (e.g., 1988), later noted its similarity to *anorexia nervosa* in humans. Anorexia nervosa is a psychiatric disorder in which patients refuse to eat adequate amounts of food and as a result lose extreme amounts of weight. People with this disorder often require hospitalization; and of those who do become hospitalized, more than 10% eventually die from the disorder or from complications associated with it (such as from a disruption of the body's electrolyte balance; American Psychological Association, *Diagnostic and Statistical Manual IV,* 2000).

Epling and Pierce (1991) contend that there are several similarities between activity anorexia in rats and anorexia nervosa in humans. For example, just as activity anorexia in rats can be precipitated by imposing a restricted schedule of feeding, so too anorexia nervosa in humans usually begins when the person deliberately undertakes a diet to lose weight. Even more significant, anorexia in humans, as with anorexia in rats, is often accompanied by very high levels of activity (Davis, Katzman, & Kirsh, 1999; Katz, 1996). This may consist of a deliberate exercise program designed to facilitate weight loss, or it may be displayed as a severe sort of restlessness. Although clinicians have typically regarded such high activity as a secondary characteristic of the disorder (e.g., Bruch, 1978), Epling and Pierce (1996) suggest that it is more fundamental than that. Thus, as with activity anorexia in rats, many cases of anorexia nervosa in humans might result from the combined effects of a stringent diet and high activity levels.

The importance of high activity levels in the development of anorexia nervosa is supported by several lines of evidence. First, even in humans who do not have anorexia, a sudden increase in activity is usually followed by a decrease in food intake, and a decrease in food intake is usually followed by an increase in activity (Epling & Pierce, 1996). Second, individuals who engage in high levels of activity appear to be at high risk for becoming anorexic. For example, ballet dancers, who are under constant pressure to remain thin and are extremely active, show a higher incidence of the disorder than do fashion models who are under pressure only to remain thin (Garner & Garfinkel, 1980). Likewise, a surprising number of athletes develop symptoms of anorexia (Katz, 1986; Wheeler, 1996) or an "overtraining syndrome" that bears many similarities to anorexia (Yates, 1996).

In addition to high activity levels, there are other interesting parallels between anorexia in rats and humans. For example, just as anorexia nervosa in humans is more common among adolescents (*DSM IV*, 2000), activity anorexia is more easily induced in adolescent rats than in older rats (Woods & Routtenberg, 1971). Another similarity concerns the manner in which anorexics approach food. Although human anorexics eat little, they nevertheless remain quite interested in food (Bruch, 1978). For example, they often enjoy preparing food for others. As well, when they do eat, they often spend considerable time arranging the food on their plates, cutting it into pieces, and slowly savoring each bite. Anecdotal evidence suggests that anorexic rats might sometimes behave similarly (D. P. Boer, 2000, personal communication). Although the rats eat little or no food during each meal period, they do spend considerable time shredding the food with their teeth and spitting it out. And if allowed to do so, they will carry food with them when they are allowed to reenter the wheel following the meal period. In other words, like humans, rats seem to remain quite interested in food, even if they are not eating it.

Thus, activity anorexia in rats appears to be a rather close analogue of anorexia nervosa in humans. As with most analogues, however, the similarity is less than perfect. For example, the anorexic rat is physically restricted from accessing food except during the meal period, whereas the anorexic human is on a self-imposed diet with food still freely available. Epling and Pierce (1991) argue, however, that the free availability of food may be more apparent than real. Just as the researcher physically restricts the rat's supply of food, societal pressures to become thin may psychologically restrict a person's access to food. Women, of course, are more commonly subjected to such pressures; thus, it is not surprising that anorexia is more commonly diagnosed in women than it is in men (although medical biases toward viewing thin women as anorexic and thin males as, well, just thin, probably also play a role).

A more substantial difference between humans and rats is that anorexia in humans is often accompanied by bulimia: a tendency to binge on food and then purge oneself by vomiting or taking laxatives. In fact, psychiatrists distinguish between two types of anorexia: the *restricting type*, which is characterized by simple food restriction, and the *binge-eating/purging type*, in which dieting is combined with episodes of binging and purging (*DSM IV*, 2000). Of course, anorexic rats do not binge and purge; indeed, it would be difficult for them to do so because rats are physically incapable of vomiting. Thus, activity anorexia in rats is most relevant to the restricting type of anorexia in humans. And, in fact, the restricting type of anorexia is most strongly associated with high activity levels (Katz, 1996).

1. As with the development of activity anorexia in rats, most instances of human anorexia begin with the person undertaking a d_____. As well, human anorexics tend to display (high/low) _____ levels of activity.

2. A sharp increase in activity is usually associated with a (decrease/increase) _____ in food intake, which in turn can result in a(n) (decrease/increase) _____ in activity.

3. Anecdotal evidence suggests that, as with human anorexics, anorexic rats are often quite (interested/uninterested) _____ in food.

4. Similar to anorexia nervosa in humans, activity anorexia in rats is more easily induced in (adolescent/adult) _____ rats.

5. Activity anorexia in rats is most similar to the r_____ type of anorexia in humans rather than the b_____-p_____ type of anorexia.

QUICK QUIZ K

Underlying Mechanisms

Given the self-destructive nature of activity anorexia, what are the mechanisms underlying it? On a neurophysiological level, the processes involved are probably complex, involving several classes of hormones and neurotransmitters (Pierce & Epling, 1996). Evidence, however, suggests that endorphins may play a particularly important role. Endorphins are a class of morphine-like substances in the brain that have been implicated in pain reduction. They have also been implicated in the feeling of pleasure that sometimes accompanies prolonged exercise, which is commonly known as "runner's high" (Wheeler, 1996). Significantly, drugs that block the effect of endorphins will temporarily lower the rate of wheel running in food-deprived rats (Boer, Epling, Pierce, & Russell, 1990).

Such evidence suggests that both activity anorexia in rats and anorexia nervosa in humans might be maintained by what is essentially an addiction to an endorphin high (Marrazzi & Luby, 1986). In support of this notion, anorexic patients often report that the experience of anorexia is quite similar to a drug-induced high. To quote three patients: "[O]ne feels intoxicated, literally how I think alcoholism works" (Bruch, 1978, p. 73); "being hungry has the same effect as a drug, and you feel outside your body" (p. 118); and perhaps most disturbing, "I enjoy having this disease and I want it" (p. 2).

From an evolutionary perspective, Epling and Pierce (1988, 1991) have suggested that a tendency toward activity anorexia might have survival value. An animal that becomes highly active when food supplies are scarce is more likely to travel great distances and encounter new food supplies. Under extreme circumstances, the animal might even do well to ignore small amounts of food encountered along the way—the gathering of which could be costly in terms of time and energy spent relative to the amount of energy gained—and cease traveling only when an adequate food supply has been reached. In support of this notion, research has shown that activity anorexia can be halted by suddenly providing access to a continuous supply of food (Epling & Pierce, 1991). When confronted with a plentiful food source, the rats cease running and begin eating.

QUICK QUIZ L

1. Endorphins are a class of morphine-like substances in the brain that are associated with p_____ reduction.

2. Congruent with the possibility that endorphins may be involved in activity anorexia, endorphins have been implicated in the feeling of p_____ that is sometimes experienced following prolonged exercise.

3. This finding suggests that both activity anorexia in rats and anorexia nervosa in humans may be maintained by an _____ high.

4. From an evolutionary perspective, increased activity in response to decreased food intake could (interfere with/facilitate) _____ contacting a new food supply.

5. This evolutionary perspective is supported by evidence that the activity anorexia cycle can be broken by suddenly providing (intermittent/continuous) _____ access to food.

Clinical Implications

The activity anorexia model has several clinical implications. From a treatment perspective, the model suggests that behavioral treatments for anorexia nervosa should focus as much on establishing normal patterns of activity as they do on establishing normal patterns of eating. As well, research into the biochemistry underlying this phenomenon could facilitate the development of drugs for treating anorexia. For example, it may be possible to develop long-lasting endorphin blockers that will effectively reduce the feelings of pleasure that help maintain the anorexic process.

The activity anorexia model also has implications for prevention. First and foremost, people should be warned that combining a stringent exercise program with severe dieting places them at risk for developing this disorder. The model thus calls into question those disciplines that traditionally combine dieting with intense activity. As already noted, one such discipline is ballet; another is amateur wrestling. Wrestlers are traditionally expected to lose several pounds before competition so as to compete in the lightest weight category possible. Many of the physical and psychological changes accompanying this process are similar to those found in anorexia nervosa—an indication that these athletes are at risk for developing symptoms of the disorder (Symbaluk, 1996).

The activity anorexia model also suggests that people who are dieting should eat several small meals per day as opposed to a single large meal, insofar as rats do not become anorexic when the 1.5-hour meal period is broken up into

And Furthermore

The Healthy Side of the Diet–Activity Connection

We have so far discussed the negative aspect of the connection between food restriction and activity. There is also a positive side to this connection. Boer (1990) found that by adjusting the *amount of food* eaten by the rats, as opposed to the *length of the meal period,* he could precisely control the amount of wheel running. For example, rats that were given 15 grams of food once per day developed the typical activity anorexia cycle (see also Morse et al., 1995), whereas rats that were given 18 grams of food displayed only a moderate level of running (5–6 miles per day) with no tendency toward self-starvation. These rats were also quite healthy. Interestingly, the same effect was found using rats that had a genetic predisposition toward obesity (J. C. Russell et al., 1989). Raised on a regime of diet and exercise, these "genetically fat" rats remained incredibly lean and fit—an impressive demonstration of the healthy effects of a healthy lifestyle, even in subjects whose genetics are working against them.

It is also worth repeating that, as noted in Chapter 2, calorie restriction is currently the most reliable means known for slowing the aging process, at least in nonhuman animals (Weindruch, 1996). Lest the reader imagine, however, that this might be a good excuse for eating like a person with anorexia and quickly losing a lot of weight, the health-enhancing effects of low-calorie diets demand regular meals composed of highly nutritious foods—a far cry from the "two carrots and a cookie" diet of many people with anorexia. (See Masoro, 2005, for an overview of recent findings and theories concerning calorie restriction and longevity.)

several shorter meal periods (Epling & Pierce, 1991). As well, people who are attempting to increase their exercise levels should do so slowly, because rats that become anorexic display the greatest reduction in food intake following a sharp increase in activity (Pierce & Epling, 1996). (Interestingly, the sharp increase in activity also has been shown to be most clearly associated with appetite suppression in humans.) And, finally, dieters should ensure that their meals are well balanced nutritionally. Research has shown that activity anorexia is more easily induced in rats that are on a low-protein diet as opposed to a normal diet (Beneke & Vander Tuig, 1996).

Of course, further research is needed to confirm the usefulness of these suggestions for preventing anorexia nervosa in humans. What is clear, however, is that a combination of severe dieting and exercise can have serious consequences and should not be undertaken lightly.

1. The activity anorexia model suggests that therapists should focus as much on establishing normal a_____ levels as they presently do on establishing normal eating patterns.

2. Specific suggestions (derived from activity anorexia research) for minimizing the risk of anorexia in humans include eating (several/one) _____ meal(s) per day, increasing exercise levels (rapidly/slowly) _____, and eating a diet that is (imbalanced/well balanced) _____.

QUICK QUIZ M

Behavior Systems Theory

As seen throughout this chapter, biological dispositions appear to play a strong role in many aspects of conditioning. Needless to say, this evidence has led several researchers to propose various theories to explain these findings. The most comprehensive of these is behavior systems theory (e.g., Timberlake, 1993; Timberlake & Lucas, 1989). According to *behavior systems theory,* an animal's behavior is organized into various motivational systems, such as feeding, mating, avoiding predators, and so forth. Each of these systems encompasses a set of relevant responses, each of which, in turn, can be activated by particular cues. (The theory is actually more complex than this, but a simplified version will suffice for now.) Note that some of these responses may be very rigid, in the form of a reflex or fixed action pattern, whereas others may be more flexible and sensitive to the consequences of the response. Different systems may also overlap such that a response that is typically associated with one system may sometimes be instigated by another system.

As an example, let us consider the *feeding system* in the rat. When a rat is hungry, it becomes predisposed to engage in various food-related responses, such as salivating, chewing, food handling (with its paws), searching for food, and so on. Thus, during a period of hunger, all of these responses become primed, meaning that they can easily be set in motion. Which response is actually set in motion, however, will depend on the situation. For example, in a situation in which the delivery and consumption of food is imminent, behaviors such as salivating and food handling will occur. When food is slightly more distant than that, a focused search pattern will emerge, such as sniffing and looking about. When food is still more distant, a more general search pattern may dominate, such as running and exploring.

Interestingly, this theory helps explain the types of experimental procedures that have evolved to study learning in animals. It is no accident that the favorite methods for studying learning in rats have been maze running and lever pressing. These methods have become widely adopted because they work so well, and they work so well because they are congruent with the types of behaviors that rats are naturally predisposed to display in food-related situations. Thus, rats are great at running through mazes because they have evolved to run along narrow, enclosed spaces—such as through tunnels in a burrow—to find food. Similarly, rats have evolved dexterous forepaws that they use to pick up food and manipulate it. Therefore, manipulating something with their forepaws, such as pressing a lever, is for them a natural response associated with feeding.

Behavior systems theory also provides a comprehensive explanation for many of the unusual behavior patterns described in this chapter. For example, consider a sign-tracking experiment in which dogs approach a light that predicts food and begin to beg and whine as though they are soliciting food from it. Dogs are pack animals for which feeding is a social event; and subordinate animals often have to solicit food from the dominant leader who controls that food. Thus, the feeding situation that was set up in these experiments, in which a light strongly predicted the delivery of food, essentially elicited this social component of the dog's feeding system.

Although behavior systems theory assigns an important role to innate patterns of behavior, it assigns an equally important role to the environmental cues that determine which behavior will be activated. An illustration can be found in sign-tracking studies with rats. Timberlake and Grant (1975) devised a chamber in which a *stimulus rat* could be mechanically inserted and withdrawn (see Figure 11.2). When the stimulus rat was inserted just before the delivery of food, thus becoming a CS for food, the participant rat would approach the stimulus rat and engage in various forms of social behavior, including sniffing the mouth, pawing, and grooming. This behavior pattern becomes understandable when we consider that rats have evolved to pay close attention to what other rats are eating and will even steal food from the mouths of other rats. The stimulus rat that predicted the delivery of food therefore seemed to elicit this social component of the feeding system in the participant rat. By contrast, a wooden block that predicted the delivery of food did not elicit social contact, with the participant rat merely orienting toward it. Likewise, in a different study, a rolling marble that predicted food delivery elicited a pattern of clawing, grasping, and gnawing, as though the rat was attempting to capture and consume the marble (Timberlake, 1983). Presumably, the moving marble activated the predatory component of the rat's feeding system, such as would naturally be activated by a small, moving insect (rats often hunt and devour insects). Such predatory behavior was not elicited, however, when the moving marble predicted the delivery of water.

FIGURE 11.2   Illustration of the apparatus used by Timberlake and Grant (1975). The stimulus rat became a CS when it was inserted on a movable platform into the experimental chamber just before the delivery of food.

And Furthermore

The Intelligence of Dogs

Domesticated animals differ from other species in several ways. First, they have evolved as a result of artificial selection, rather than natural selection. Second, as a result of artificial selection, significant differences can be found across different "breeds" of the same species. If you consider the differences in appearance alone that exist across the different breeds of domesticated dogs (*Canis familiaris*), you can appreciate how there might be significant differences in behavior as well. In fact, breeds can vary significantly in instinctive tendencies, temperament, and in what could be called "intelligence."

Stanley Coren is a psychologist who has spent decades studying the behavior of dogs. As a result, he has proposed a Canine IQ Test (Coren, 1994) that assesses how well a dog will perform certain tasks requiring learning, memory, and problem solving. (Search the web for "Coren" and "canine IQ" and you can quickly find the test, which is relatively short and can be lots of fun to try with your dog.) Although Coren has gathered data on the extent to which certain breeds outperform others, the test can be used on dogs of any breed or mix of breeds.

A major aspect of Coren's notion of canine intelligence is trainability and obedience, which he calls "working intelligence." In assessing differences between breeds for this trait, Coren surveyed approximately 200 judges from both the American and Canadian Kennel Clubs. Based on their input, he created a list that rank-orders breeds from 1 (very easy to train) to 79 (very difficult to train). Although Coren and the surveyed judges acknowledged that there are significant individual differences in trainability between dogs (regardless of breed), they also concluded that there are substantial differences across breeds. More than 90% of the judges agreed that the border collie was one of the most intelligent breeds, and nearly as many identified poodles and Shetland sheepdogs as ranking near the top. There was less agreement on which breeds were the least bright, but about 60% ranked

The extent to which behavior systems theory provides a comprehensive explanation for animal behavior has yet to be determined. According to Mazur (2002), neither does this theory undermine the importance of basic principles of conditioning, such as reinforcement and punishment, as powerful factors in learning and behavior. Behavior systems theory does, however, remind us of the need to pay attention to an animal's innate tendencies when attempting to modify its behavior. For example, the dog that habitually nips at your hand when you attempt to touch its food is not simply displaying a behavior that has been negatively reinforced by the removal of your hand. Rather, it might also indicate that the dog has assumed a position of dominance within the household, a naturally evolved pattern of behavior that is highly adaptive within a pack but rather a nuisance among humans. In a sense, the dog's tendency to be food aggressive reflects both the social component of its feeding system as well as the feeding component of its social system. Thus, a comprehensive attempt to modify this behavior might need to include strategies for signaling to the dog its subordinate status within the family—such as feeding the dog by hand rather than providing free food throughout the day (thereby clearly the Afghan hound (which was bred for running) at the bottom of the list, and basenjis and bulldogs earned less than honorable mentions. Coren comments that although his own dogs (relatively "dull" breeds, including a Cavalier King Charles spaniel, ranked 44th, and a cairn terrier, ranked 35th) are well trained and perform well in obedience competitions, he has found them more difficult to train than high-ranked breeds:

> a woman with a Labrador retriever (ranked 7) was once enrolled in one of our beginners dog obedience classes . . . in the hope that I might 'do something with it'. After the regular class, I spent some time with the dog. In one hour of work, this dog had learned the basics of the entire set of seven beginning commands—something that my cairn terrier had only achieved after ten weeks of intensive training. (Coren, 1994, p. 187)

Coren's canine IQ test is at best a rough measure of doggy intelligence and suffers from many of the same difficulties that hound (pun intended) even well-researched measures of human intelligence. One particular difficulty lies in the behaviors used to define doggy intelligence, which could vary depending upon the behaviors one considers desirable. For example, it may be relatively easy to teach a "bright" dog, like a miniature schnauzer, all sorts of tricks, but teaching that same dog *not* to bark may be considerably more difficult. Like most small terriers, the miniature schnauzer will bark vigorously at any stimulus that seems novel or unexpected, and this barking can be extremely difficult to eliminate. If you want a quiet dog, you might do better with a "low-IQ," but also less-vocal, English bulldog.

Finally, we do well to remember the critical importance of training. Read again the above quotation, and note the owner's opinion of her Labrador retriever before Coren worked with it. In the same way that a seemingly "dull" child is often a victim of exposure to poorly managed contingencies of reinforcement, so too a "dumb" dog is more often the result of exposure to improper training methods than of any inherited limitation in its overall intelligence. The main benefit of understanding a dog's inherited tendencies is that it allows one to optimize the selection and training of a dog; it should never be an excuse to quickly give up on a dog.

indicating to the dog that humans control the food supply). Fortunately, just as shaping is becoming a well-established technique among pet owners, so too is an appreciation of the need to understand a pet's innate tendencies (e.g., Coren, 1994; McConnell, 2003; see also "The Intelligence of Dogs" in the And Furthermore box).

QUICK QUIZ N

1. According to _____ _____ theory, an animal's behavior is organized into a number of mo_____ systems, such as feeding and mating. Each of these systems is connected to a set of relevant responses, each of which can be activated by situational c_____.

2. In terms of behavior systems theory, Bolles' notion of sp_____-sp_____ d_____ reactions (SSDR) is concerned with responses that are driven by the defense-against-predators system.

3. In the sign-tracking experiment with dogs, the light that predicted food seemed to activate the (predatory/consumatory/social) _____ component of the dog's feeding system.

SUMMARY

Animals appear to be biologically prepared to learn some things more readily than others. For example, in taste aversion conditioning, a food item that has been paired with nausea quickly becomes conditioned as an aversive CS. This type of conditioning is similar to other forms of classical conditioning in that processes such as stimulus generalization, extinction, and overshadowing can be found. It differs from other forms of classical conditioning in that strong associations can be formed over long delays and require only a single conditioning trial. As well, the nausea is specifically associated with a food item rather than some other stimulus.

Examples of preparedness in operant conditioning include how easily food can be used to reinforce pecking but not perching in chaffinches, while the sound of a chaffinch song can be used to reinforce perching but not pecking. As well, rats more easily learn to run or freeze to escape shock than press a lever to escape shock. The latter example suggests that many escape behaviors may be species-specific defense reactions elicited by the aversive stimulus.

Instinctive drift is a genetically based, fixed action pattern that gradually emerges to displace a behavior that is being operantly conditioned. Sign tracking is a tendency to approach (and perhaps make contact with) a stimulus that signals the presentation of an appetitive event. In both cases, the behavior superficially appears to be a goal-directed operant behavior, yet the procedures that produce it suggest it is actually an elicited (or respondent) behavior.

Adjunctive behavior, also known as schedule-induced behavior, is an excessive pattern of behavior that emerges as a by-product of an intermittent schedule of reinforcement. In schedule-induced polydipsia, for example, rats drink extreme amounts of water during the interval between food reinforcers that are delivered on an FI or FT schedule. Adjunctive behavior typically occurs in the period immediately following the delivery of the scheduled reinforcer, varies directly with the level of deprivation for the scheduled reinforcer, can function as a reinforcer for another behavior, and is most likely to occur when the interreinforcement interval is a few minutes in length. Examples of possible adjunctive behaviors in humans include smoking cigarettes, drinking alcohol, and using drugs. Adjunctive behavior may be a type of displacement activity that functions to ensure a diverse range of activities in a setting and to facilitate waiting for a delayed reinforcer.

Activity anorexia is a pattern of excessive activity and low food intake in animals as a result of exposure to a restricted food supply. It bears many similarities to certain forms of anorexia nervosa in humans, which is characterized by severe dieting and high activity levels. Evidence suggests that activity anorexia in animals as well as anorexia nervosa in humans may be maintained by an endorphin high that accompanies the process. From an evolutionary perspective, a tendency toward activity anorexia might induce an animal to travel long distances, thereby increasing the likelihood of encountering a new food supply. Clinical implications that have grown out of this research include the possibility of developing long-lasting endorphin blockers that could break the anorexic cycle. These findings also suggest that people should be cautious about combining a stringent diet with severe exercise.

According to behavior systems theory, an animal's behavior is organized into several motivational systems. Each of these systems encompasses a set of relevant responses; and in turn, each response can be activated by situational cues. This theory accounts for many of the unusual behavior patterns, including sign tracking, described in this chapter. It also accounts for the particular kinds of tasks that researchers have used to study animal learning.

SUGGESTED READINGS

Garcia, J. (1981). Tilting at the paper mills of academe. *American Psychologist, 36,* 149–158. Garcia's fascinating account of the difficulties he encountered in attempting to publish his early results on taste aversion conditioning simply because they violated certain assumptions of classical conditioning that were widely held at that time.

Epling, W. F., & Pierce, W. D. (1991). *Solving the anorexia puzzle: A scientific approach.* Toronto, Canada: Hogrefe & Huber. Epling and Pierce's overview of activity anorexia and its applicability to understanding anorexia nervosa in humans.

Timberlake, W. (1993). Behavior systems and reinforcement: An integrative approach. *Journal of the Experimental Analysis of Behavior, 60,* 105–128. For the serious student, a discussion of behavior systems theory and its applicability to operant behavior.

Coren, S. (1995). *The intelligence of dogs: A guide to the thoughts, emotions, and inner lives of our canine companions.* New York: Bantam Books. A fun and interesting guide for helping us better understand our canine companions.

STUDY QUESTIONS

1. Define preparedness and CS-US relevance.
2. Define taste aversion conditioning and diagram an experimental example.
3. Outline three ways in which taste aversion conditioning differs from most other forms of classical conditioning.
4. Describe (or diagram) the results of the experiment by Garcia and Koelling that illustrates the role of biological preparedness in classical conditioning.
5. Describe two examples of the role of preparedness in operant conditioning.
6. What is instinctive drift? Describe (or diagram) one of the Brelands's examples of instinctive drift.
7. What is sign tracking? Describe the experimental example of sign tracking in dogs.

8. Define autoshaping and describe the procedure used to produce it. Describe the research result that seems particularly supportive of a stimulus-substitution interpretation of autoshaping.
9. Define adjunctive behavior. What other term is used to refer to this class of behaviors?
10. What is schedule-induced polydipsia, and what is the typical procedure for inducing it in rats?
11. List four characteristics of adjunctive behaviors.
12. What are displacement activities? What are two benefits that may be derived from such activities?
13. Define activity anorexia. What is the basic procedure for inducing this behavior pattern?
14. List three similarities (other than low food intake) between activity anorexia in rats and anorexia nervosa in humans.
15. What type of chemical substance in the brain seems to play a role in the development of anorexia? Briefly describe Epling and Pierce's evolutionary explanation for the occurrence of activity anorexia.
16. List two implications for treatment and four implications for prevention that have grown out of activity anorexia research.
17. Define behavior systems theory. Describe the results of sign-tracking studies in rats that indicate the importance of environmental cues.

CONCEPT REVIEW

activity anorexia. An abnormally high level of activity and low level of food intake generated by exposure to a restricted schedule of feeding.

adjunctive behavior. An excessive pattern of behavior that emerges as a by-product of an intermittent schedule of reinforcement for some other behavior.

autoshaping. A type of sign tracking in which a pigeon comes to automatically peck at a response key because the key light has been associated with the response-independent delivery of food.

behavior systems theory. A theory proposing that an animal's behavior is organized into various motivational systems; each of these systems encompasses a set of relevant responses, each of which, in turn, can be activated by particular cues.

CS-US relevance. An innate tendency to easily associate certain types of stimuli with each other.

displacement activity. An apparently irrelevant activity sometimes displayed by animals when confronted by conflict or thwarted from attaining a goal.

instinctive drift. An instance of classical conditioning in which a genetically based, fixed action pattern gradually emerges and displaces a behavior that is being operantly conditioned.

preparedness. An innate tendency for an organism to more easily learn certain types of behaviors or to associate certain types of events with each other.

sign tracking. A type of elicited behavior in which an organism approaches a stimulus that signals the presentation of an appetitive event.

taste aversion conditioning. A form of classical conditioning in which a food item that has been paired with gastrointestinal illness becomes a conditioned aversive stimulus.

CHAPTER TEST

9. To prevent the development of anorexia nervosa, humans who are dieting might do well to eat (several small/one large) _____ meal(s) per day. And if they are exercising, they should increase the level of exercise (quickly/slowly) _____.

20. Taste aversion conditioning differs from other forms of conditioning in that associations can be formed over _____ delays, and in (many/a single) _____ trial(s).

2. According to the phenomenon of negative _____, a pigeon will compulsively peck at a key light that precedes the delivery of food even though the key peck _____ the delivery of food.

28. Displacement activities, including certain types of adjunctive behaviors, may serve as a type of self-_____ device in that they facilitate the act of waiting for a _____ reinforcer.

11. In general, a pigeon that is (more/less) _____ food deprived will display a greater tendency to engage in schedule-induced aggression.

1. When a key light is presented just before the noncontingent delivery of food, the pigeon will begin pecking at the key. This phenomenon is known as _____.

24. When a pig receives reinforcement for carrying a napkin from one table to another, it eventually starts dropping it and rooting at it on the ground. This is an example of a phenomenon known as _____ in which a _____ pattern gradually emerges and replaces the operant behavior that one is attempting to condition.

4. An excessive pattern of behavior that emerges as a by-product of an intermittent schedule of reinforcement for some other behavior is called _____ behavior.

12. In schedule-induced polydipsia, a rat likely (will/will not) _____ learn to press a lever to gain access to a (drinking tube/running wheel) _____ during the interval between food pellets.

19. Angie became sick to her stomach when she and her new boyfriend, Gerald, were on their way home after dining at an exotic restaurant. Fortunately for (Gerald/the restaurant) _____, Angie is most likely to form an aversion to (Gerald/the food) _____.

33. According to behavior _____ theory, the motivation to acquire a mate would constitute a _____, whereas spreading one's tail feathers to attract a female would constitute a relevant _____ within that system.

26. A _____ activity is a (highly relevant/seemingly irrelevant) _____ activity sometimes displayed by animals when confronted by conflict or blocked from attaining a goal.

16. Following a turkey dinner in which, for the first time, Paul also tasted some caviar, he became quite nauseous. As a result, he may acquire a conditioned _____, most likely to the (turkey/caviar) _____.

31. Activity anorexia is more easily induced among relatively (young/old) _____ rats, which is (similar to/different from) _____ the pattern found with human who suffer from anorexia.

8. Whenever a person combines a stringent exercise program with a severe diet, he or she may be at risk for developing symptoms of _____.

13. For the development of adjunctive behaviors, the optimal interval between the delivery of reinforcers is often about (3/6/9) ____ minutes.

22. My canary likes the sound of my whistling. Research suggests that my whistling will be a more effective reinforcer if I am attempting to train the bird to (perch in a certain spot/peck at the floor) _____.

29. An abnormally high level of activity and low level of food intake generated by restricted access to food is called _____.

6. From an evolutionary perspective, a tendency toward activity anorexia could (increase/decrease) _____ the likelihood of the animal encountering a new food supply. Indirect evidence for this includes the fact that the activity anorexia cycle can often be (stopped/greatly enhanced) _____ by suddenly presenting the animal with a continuous supply of food.

18. When Selma was eating oatmeal porridge one morning, she broke a tooth on a small pebble that accidentally had been mixed in with it. The next morning, after eating some bran flakes, she became terribly ill. If she develops aversions as a result of these experiences, chances are that they will be an aversion to the (look/taste) _____ of oatmeal and the _____ of bran flakes.

10. Adjunctive behavior tends to develop when a behavior is being reinforced on a _____ or_____ schedule of reinforcement. Also, adjunctive behavior is most likely to occur in the interval immediately (following/preceding) _____ the presentation of each reinforcer.

23. When a rat is shocked, it easily learns to run to the other side of the chamber to escape. According to Bolles, this is because the running is actually a(n) (operant/respondent) _____ that is (elicited/negatively reinforced) _____ by the (application/removal) _____ of shock.

7. The activity anorexia model suggests that behavioral treatments for anorexia nervosa should focus as much on establishing normal patterns of _____ as they do on establishing normal patterns of eating.

14. The tendency for many people to smoke while waiting in traffic can be viewed as an example of an _____ behavior in humans.
 3. Adjunctive behavior is also known as _____ behavior.
27. One advantage of displacement activities is that they allow for a more (diverse/focused) _____ pattern of behavior, which is often advantageous.
32. According to _____ theory, an animal's behavior is organized into a number of motivational systems, with each system encompassing a set of relevant responses.
21. An innate tendency to more readily associate certain types of stimuli with each other is a type of preparedness that is known as _____.
17. Taste aversion conditioning most readily occurs to (familiar/unfamiliar) _____ food items, as well as to the (strongest/mildest) _____ tasting item in the meal. The latter can be seen as an example of the _____ effect in classical conditioning.
 5. A class of brain chemicals that may play a particularly important role in the development of anorexia in both rats and humans is _____. Evidence for this includes the fact that people suffering from anorexia often report that the feeling that accompanies the disorder is quite (unpleasant/pleasant) _____.
25. A behavior pattern in which an organism approaches a stimulus that signals the presentation of an appetitive event is known as _____.
30. As with the development of anorexia in rats, many cases of anorexia in humans might be the result of the combined effects of _____ restriction and high _____ levels.
15. Despite getting a shock when he plugged in his toaster one day, Antonio feels only slight anxiety when using it. On the other hand, he is deathly afraid of spiders, ever since one jumped on him when he tried to swat it. The difference in how easily Antonio learned to fear these two events seems to be an illustration of the effect of _____ on conditioning.

Visit the book companion Web site at <http://www.academic.cengage.com/psychology/powell> for additional practice questions, answers to the Quick Quizzes, practice review exams, and additional exercises and information.

ANSWERS TO CHAPTER TEST

1. autoshaping
2. automaintenance; prevents
3. schedule-induced
4. adjunctive
5. endorphins; pleasant
6. increase; stopped
7. activity
8. anorexia nervosa
9. several small; slowly
10. FT; FI; following
11. more
12. will; drinking tube
13. 3
14. adjunctive
15. preparedness
16. taste aversion; caviar

17. unfamiliar; strongest;
    overshadowing
18. look; taste
19. Gerald; the food
20. long; a single
21. CS-US relevance
22. perch in a certain spot
23. respondent; elicited; application
24. instinctive drift; fixed action

25. sign tracking
26. displacement; seemingly irrelevant
27. diverse
28. control; delayed
29. activity anorexia
30. food; activity
31. young; similar to
32. behavior systems
33. systems; system; response

CHAPTER 12

Observational Learning, Language, and Rule-Governed Behavior

CHAPTER OUTLINE

"I don't care what Dr. Dee says!" Gina shouted in exasperation when Steve again pronounced judgment on some aspect of their relationship. "I am starting to wish you had never enrolled in that stupid course. Why don't you just listen to what I'm saying rather than acting like 'Mr. Behaviorist' all the time?"

Much of this text has been concerned with basic processes of conditioning in which new patterns of behavior are acquired through direct exposure to the relevant events. Ming fears dogs because she was once bitten by a dog, and Kyle goes to a particular restaurant because in the past he received good food there. However, not all behavior patterns are acquired this directly. Some people acquire a fear of dogs without ever being attacked by a dog, or they eagerly head off to a restaurant despite never having been there before. Such behaviors have somehow been acquired in the absence of any direct exposure to the relevant events.

In this chapter, we focus on processes that allow us to acquire new behavior patterns through indirect means. We begin with observational learning (a process that was touched on in previous chapters), which plays a strong role in human learning but is also found in animals. We then discuss language, which enables us to transmit and receive large amounts of information. Although language has traditionally been considered a uniquely human form of behavior, research on language training in animals is, according to some, now challenging that view. Finally, we outline the way we use language to generate rules (or instructions) to control behavior, including the implications of such "rule-governed behavior" for understanding and enhancing self-control.

Observational or Social Learning

Do you remember your first day of school? If so, you probably remember being a little afraid and unsure about what to do when you first arrived—where to stand, who to talk to, even where to go to the bathroom. After a while, though, it all became much clearer because you could watch what other people did and follow them. This type of learning is called *observational learning*.

In *observational learning,* the behavior of a *model* is witnessed by an *observer,* and the observer's behavior is subsequently altered. Because observational learning is essentially a social process, and humans are social beings, we can quickly acquire new behavior patterns in this way (Bandura, 1986). In fact, observational learning is *often* referred to as *social learning* and, as discussed in Chapter 1, constitutes a significant aspect of Bandura's social learning theory. There is considerable evidence that people can improve their performance on many tasks, including sports, simply by *watching* others perform (e.g., Blandin, Lhuisset, & Proteau, 1999; Shea, Wright, Wulf, & Whitacre, 2000). In fact, this type of learning can occur without our even being aware that our behavior has been influenced in this way. For example, we may see television commercials showing attractive people modeling new, even undesirable, behaviors such as driving too fast in a new car. This subtle form of modeling might then affect our behavior when we find ourselves in a similar situation. Conversely, models need not be aware that their behavior is being observed, which means that we do not have to "teach'" someone for them to learn from us. This is another reason the term *social learning* is often used. Being in a social situation can change behavior, even if no one in the group realizes it.

Observational learning can be involved in both classical and operant conditioning. We begin, however, with two rudimentary forms of social influence, known as *contagious behavior* and *stimulus enhancement*, that are often confused with more sophisticated forms of observational learning.

Contagious Behavior and Stimulus Enhancement

Contagious behavior is a more-or-less instinctive or reflexive behavior triggered by the occurrence of the same behavior in another individual. For example, suppose you and your friends are sitting around a table in the library, studying for a quiz. You start to yawn. One by one, each of your classmates also yawns. Not a good sign for how your study session will progress, but it is an excellent example of contagious behavior.

Although yawning is one of the best-documented examples of contagious behavior in humans (see Provine, 1996, for a review), other behaviors in both humans and other animals are potentially contagious. All it takes to get a flock of ducks off and flying is one startled duck. The rest flee even if they do not detect any real threat. Fear responses of all kinds are quite contagious, which makes good adaptive sense. In a dangerous environment, you are more likely to survive and reproduce if you flee when you notice that someone else is fleeing, as opposed to taking the time to look around and ask a lot of questions such as "Hey Burt, why are you running from that bear?"

Behaviors that are important for social interaction and bonding are also often contagious. Have you ever noticed that you rarely laugh when you are alone? Even when watching a funny movie or reading a humorous novel (which, as media, could be considered quasi-social events), we laugh more in the presence of others than when we are by ourselves (Provine, 1996). Television producers know this, so they include laugh tracks or live (laughing) audiences in most comedy programs. Most of us have had the experience of starting to laugh with a friend and being unable to stop. Even when the laughing dies down, and even if you don't remember why you started in the first place, if the other person chuckles just a bit it will set you off for another bout of side-splitting laughter. A particularly powerful example of this type of emotional contagion can be seen in a case documented in Tanganyika, from a boarding school for 12- to 18-year-old girls (Rankin & Philip, 1963). The girls one day began to laugh uncontrollably, which subsequently spread through the entire district. Officials even had to temporarily close the school in order to contain the "epidemic!"

Orienting responses can also be contagious. Not only do we orient ourselves toward stimuli we have just sensed (like a sudden noise or movement in our peripheral visual field), but we also orient ourselves in the direction that *others* have oriented. For example, infants as young as 4 months of age will follow the gaze of others (Farroni, Johnson, Brockbank, & Simion, 2000), and adults will do likewise. To test this response, simply have a conversation with someone, and then shift your gaze over his or her shoulder and widen your eyes a bit. See how quickly the other person turns to look. Interestingly, this effect also occurs across species. If you have a pet, you may have found yourself orienting in the direction of your pet's gaze, and becoming frustrated when you did not see anything! Because dogs and cats have somewhat different perceptual systems than humans, they can often hear, see, or smell things that we cannot detect. *(Question: Can you think of an evolutionary explanation for why orienting should be contagious, even across species?)*

Another rudimentary form of social influence, which is related to contagious orienting, is **stimulus enhancement,** in which the probability of a behavior is changed because an individual's attention is drawn to a particular item or location by the behavior of another individual. For example, imagine that you are sitting in a waiting room, reading a very old magazine, when a father and his daughter walk in. The girl emits a giggle of delight, so you look up and see that she is running toward a large bowl of candy in the corner that you had not previously noticed. Five minutes later, you help yourself to some candy. You do so, however, not because she took some candy (which as you will see would be an example of observational learning of an operant response), but simply because her behavior made you aware of the candy.

Stimulus enhancement is particularly effective for increasing the probability of a behavior associated with eating, drinking, or mating (although it can also be effective for other behaviors). These behaviors often have strong instinctive components; and in the presence of the appropriate triggers, the behaviors are highly likely to occur. Stimulus enhancement simply allows the triggers to be noticed. In the example of the candy, once your attention is directed toward the candy, the incentive value of the candy is sufficient to lead to its consumption whether or not the little girl actually took some candy (e.g., her father might have actually stopped her from having candy, but you would have taken some of it anyway).

A wide variety of cues can lead to stimulus enhancement. Animals will often use scent marking at food sites. When a conspecific (another animal of the same species) comes across the scent mark, that scent is sufficient to cause the animal to pay close attention to the location and find the food. The behavior of the model could happen hours or even days before the observer arrived, but the resulting stimulus enhancement of the location of food was a result of an observer utilizing a social cue to direct its behavior. Stimulus enhancement effects can also be generated by using learned symbols. One of the authors recalls an incident from her undergraduate days, when a classmate put up large orange arrow signs in the hallway, pointing toward an empty classroom where he waited. Within an hour, more than a dozen students and two professors wandered into the empty classroom to ask what was happening there. (It would likely be no surprise to you that the classmate was also a psychology major.)

FIGURE 12.1 Young children learn many behaviors through observation. (Unfortunately for parents, this particular behavior pattern occurs much less readily when children reach their teens.)

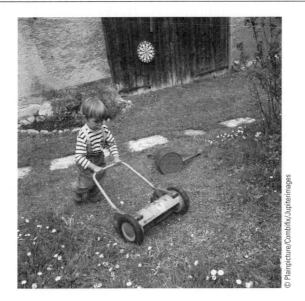

© Plainpicture/Combifix/Jupiterimages

Behavioral contagion and stimulus enhancement are clearly examples of social influence. But it can be argued that they are at best rudimentary forms of social influence in that they may result in only a momentary change in behavior (though subsequent processes, like being rewarded by candy for going to the candy bowl, could result in a more lasting change). More substantial forms of learning occur when observation of a model is involved in classical and operant conditioning (see Figure 12.1).

Observational Learning in Classical Conditioning

As mentioned earlier, observational learning is often involved in the development of classically conditioned responses. In such cases, the stimuli involved are usually *emotional* in nature. For example, imagine a young child walking into a daycare center. She sees other children laughing and smiling while playing with a new toy. The smiles and laughter of the other children can act as stimuli that elicit similar emotional responses in the observer. Such emotions, called *vicarious emotional responses,* are classically conditioned emotional responses that result from seeing those emotional responses exhibited by others. This type of conditioning is therefore called *vicarious emotional conditioning.*

Vicarious emotional conditioning can take place in two ways. First, as noted in Chapter 5, expressions of fear in others may act as unconditioned stimuli (USs) that elicit the emotion of fear in ourselves (Mineka, 1987). In other words, because we quickly need to learn which events are dangerous, we may have an inherited tendency to react fearfully whenever we see someone else looking fearful. For example, a young child could learn to fear jellyfish in the following way:

Jellyfish: Look of fear in others → *Fear in oneself*
     NS   US   UR
Jellyfish → *Fear in oneself*
     CS   CR

The more traditional way of viewing the process of vicarious emotional conditioning, however, is to construe it as a form of higher-order conditioning. In this case, the emotional reactions of others serve as conditioned stimuli (CSs) rather than USs. For example, because fearful looks in others are often associated with frightening events, they come to serve as CSs for the emotion of fear in ourselves:

Look of fear in others: Frightening events → *Fear in oneself*
          NS_1 US   UR
Look of fear in others → *Fear in oneself*
          CS_1 CR

This look of fear in others can now function as a CS in the higher-order conditioning of a fear response to a previously neutral stimulus (NS), such as a jellyfish:

Jellyfish: Look of fear in others → *Fear in oneself*
     NS_2 CS_1 CR
Jellyfish → *Fear in oneself*
     CS_2 CR

Thus, with respect to fear conditioning, the look of fear in others may function as either a US or a CS. Of course, it is also possible that both processes are involved, and they may even combine to produce a stronger fear reaction.

Higher-order conditioning no doubt plays a major role in the conditioning of other, subtler emotions. For example, because smiles are usually associated with pleasurable events—such as when a smiling mother feeds a baby—they quickly become conditioned to elicit pleasurable emotions. In diagram form:

Smiles in others: Pleasurable events → *Pleasant emotions in oneself*
          NS_1 US   UR
Smiles in others → *Pleasant emotions in oneself*
          CS_1 CR

As a result, through observing others' reactions to a novel event, we may now acquire the same type of emotional response through a process of higher-order conditioning:

Raw oysters: Smiles in others → *Pleasant emotions in oneself*
          NS_2 CS_1 CR
Raw oysters → *Pleasant emotions in oneself*
          CS_2 CR

Needless to say, vicarious emotional responses, once acquired, can motivate other types of new behavior patterns (e.g., Eisenberg, McCreath, & Ahn, 1988; Gold, Fultz, Burke, & Prisco, 1992). After watching happy children playing with a toy, the observing child may be eager to play with the toy herself. And once we have seen someone else react fearfully to a particular type of spider, we may go out of our way to avoid any encounter with that type of spider (Mineka & Cook, 1993). Also, as noted in Chapter 4, many advertisers use emotional conditioning to influence our view of their products. When we see a television family reunited by a long-distance phone call, with tears of joy flowing freely, the vicarious emotions elicited by the joy of the models can cause us to associate the phone company with that emotion. Thus, the phone company becomes a positive CS, and the likelihood of our subscribing to its service increases. (See "It's an Acquired Taste . . ." in the And Furthermore box.)

1. In observational learning, the person performing a behavior is the m_____;
the person watching the behavior is the o_____.

2. From a classical conditioning perspective, smiles, giggles, and laughs are _____s
that can elicit v_____ e_____ r_____ in observers.

3. In fear conditioning, the expressions of fear in other people may function as (CSs/
USs/both CSs and USs) _____ that elicit the same emotional response in
ourselves.

4. David watches a television infomercial about a new product guaranteed to promote weight loss. The audience members are smiling, laughing, and enthusiastic in
their praise for the product. Later, David decides that he will buy the product, even
though he initially viewed it with skepticism. David's buying decision is probably
motivated by v_____ e_____ conditioning that occurred
during exposure to the infomercial.

QUICK QUIZ A

Observational Learning in Operant Conditioning

Just as the observation of a model can influence the development of classically conditioned responses, it can also influence the development of operant
responses. Descriptions of this process traditionally emphasize the distinction between *acquisition* and *performance* of a behavior. For example, you may
have watched your parents driving a car for years, and you may have thereby
acquired most of the basic information needed to drive the car—how to start it,
how to shift gears, how to use the signal lights, and so on. However, until you
reached legal driving age, you were not permitted to translate that acquired
knowledge into the actual *performance* of driving.

Acquisition Acquisition of an operant response (or, for that matter, a classically conditioned response) through observational learning first requires that
the observer pay attention to the behavior of the model. After all, you cannot
learn from someone unless you actually watch what that person does. So, what
makes us attend to a model?

And Furthermore

It's An Acquired Taste . . .

In this chapter, we describe some of the ways we learn from those around us. One area of social learning that has been studied extensively is how we learn to eat and drink. Of course, eating and drinking are behaviors that occur very naturally, so we do not have to learn *to* eat and drink, but we do seem to learn *what* to eat and drink. Across the world, there are dramatic differences in flavor preferences, foods that are considered edible, and various practices associated with preparing and consuming food. Many North Americans, for example, have a hard time imagining how someone would enjoy the flavor and texture of various bugs, how it would feel to sit down to a dinner of dog or horse, or why anyone would eat something like haggis.

Much social learning about food and flavor preference is related to stimulus enhancement and social referencing, through which individuals (especially young children) attend to those things that others are attending to, and look to others for emotional cues about how to behave. If your niece is watching you eat a slice of pizza and sees the expression of pure joy on your face, she will be inclined to try the pizza as well. In general, children tend to eat the foods that are eaten around them, and these culturally or socially mediated preferences are strengthened over time, even for flavors that are very strong (see Rozin, Fischler, Imada, Sarubin, & Wrzesniewski, 1999, for a cross-cultural comparison of food preferences and attitudes).

In addition to food preferences, there is evidence for socially learned preferences for alcohol. In humans, it has been demonstrated that children like the smell of alcohol if they have been raised by parents who drink heavily (Mennella & Garcia, 2000). In fact, according to a longitudinal study that has been ongoing since 1974, exposure to alcohol early in life is a risk factor for alcohol use by adolescents (Streissguth, Barr, Bookstein, Samson, & Carmichael Olson, 1999). This socially mediated preference for alcohol can even be found in animals. Rats that are raised with alcohol available, but that do not observe alcohol consumption by their

First, we are very sensitive to the *consequences of the model's behavior*. If a model's behavior is reinforced, an observer is more likely to attend to the behavior. For example, if you see a television commercial featuring a husband receiving lavish praise and affection for sending flowers to his wife, you are likely to learn that sending flowers may result in positive reinforcement.

A second factor that influences attention is whether the *observer receives reinforcement for the behavior of attending to a model* (e.g., Pepperberg & Sherman, 2000). Teaching is often based on this principle. Teachers demonstrate desired behaviors—something as basic as reading or as complex as writing a college essay—and reinforce their students' attention to their demonstrations. They may also use various techniques for drawing attention to their behaviors, including prompting ("Look here. See what I'm doing?") and physical modeling ("Hold the football like this, with one hand behind the other"). Teachers then provide verbal reinforcers when students pay attention mother or foster mother, drink very little alcohol when they are adolescents. In fact, most laboratory rats will not drink plain alcohol when it is available unless the concentration is very low. However, if they do observe their mother or foster mother drinking alcohol, those young rats will drink twice as much alcohol when they are adolescents (Honey & Galef, 2003; Honey, Varley, & Galef, 2004). This type of social learning is fairly powerful and long-lasting. With only a week of exposure and a delay of 1 month before having an opportunity to drink alcohol, young rats will still demonstrate an enhanced preference for alcohol (Honey & Galef, 2004). In fact, Hunt and Hallmark (2001) found that even as little as 30 minutes of exposure to an adolescent (rather than adult) rat can also lead to alcohol use.

We do not usually think of alcohol as an "odd" thing to consume; but alcohol is actually a relatively unpalatable substance, especially without the addition of various sugars and flavorings. Most people and animals initially dislike the flavor and smell of high concentrations of alcohol. However, once the rewarding, intoxicating aspects of alcohol have been experienced, it becomes more enjoyable. Observational learning is one way to enhance the likelihood that someone will try alcohol in the first place, which can then lead to a preference for alcohol and the possibility of alcohol abuse.

So here is something to think about: If we acquire all sorts of complex behaviors through social learning, is it not likely that we also learn *how* to drink from those around us? And just as some individuals might be learning maladaptive patterns of drinking from their families or peers, might others be learning to drink in a controlled or "responsible" way? Certainly there are multiple factors involved in the development of uncontrolled drinking, including genetic predisposition and one's ability to delay gratification as well as processes of social learning. But the next time you are in a bar or at some social event where alcohol is served, take a moment to watch the people around you and consider the roles of emotional contagion, stimulus enhancement, and observational learning in the drinking behavior you observe.

("Good!"). Reinforcing observer attention in these ways can greatly increase the amount of knowledge that an observer can acquire from a model.

A third determinant of whether we attend to a model depends on *whether the observer has sufficient skills to benefit from the modeling*. For example, if a model plays "Chopsticks" on the piano, even a musically inexperienced observer may be able to pick up the tune quickly and, with appropriate help, play it herself. However, if a model plays a complex Beethoven sonata, the observer may give up all hope of ever being able to play the piano. If you play computer video games, you have probably felt this way. Watching expert players in a video arcade is a humbling experience and may keep observers from trying the games themselves. Modeling works only when observers have the skills necessary to learn the behavior.

Finally, *the personal characteristics of a model can strongly influence the extent to which we will attend to their behavior*. We are much more likely to attend to models who resemble us—for example, if they are roughly the same age, dress similarly, and have similar interests (e.g., Bussey & Bandura, 1984; Dowling, 1984). We also attend to models we respect or admire, or who are noted authorities in that realm of activity. If the coach of your junior hockey team is a former NHL player and teammate of Wayne Gretzky's, you pay much more attention to what he tells you than if he is the local high school football coach who got pushed into coaching hockey because no one else is available.

Of course, you can acquire information about a behavior without ever translating that information into performance. Television exposes viewers to thousands of hours of violent scenes, yet only a few people ever "act out" those violent behaviors. How we move from knowledge to performance is the topic of the next section.

1. You may watch cooking shows on television and learn how to perform complex culinary feats. Translating that knowledge into a gourmet meal is the difference between a_____ and p_____.

2. An important aspect of gaining information about a modeled behavior is the extent to which we a_____ to the model.

3. Teachers often directly reinforce the behavior of paying a_____, sometimes accompanied by the use of pr_____, such as "Look at what I'm doing."

4. The average person is unlikely to pay much attention to the precise moves of a grand master in chess simply because the average person does not have the sk_____ to benefit from that type of modeling.

5. You are more likely to pay attention to a model whose behavior is (reinforced/not reinforced) _____, who is (similar/dissimilar) _____to you, who is (admired/hated) _____, and who is a noted au_____ in that activity.

Performance   How does observational learning translate into behavior? As you might expect, it involves those familiar processes of reinforcement and punishment (e.g., Carroll & Bandura, 1987). Reinforcement and punishment work to modify our behavior in modeling situations in three ways. First, *we are more likely (or less likely) to perform a modeled behavior when we have observed the model experience reinforcement (or punishment) for that behavior* (e.g., Bandura & McDonald, 1994; G. R. Fouts & Click, 1979). The effect of such consequences on our behavior is technically known as *vicarious reinforcement* (or *vicarious punishment*). For example, when a model is seen using a fragrance that appears to attract members of the opposite sex to her like flies to honey, that increases the likelihood that an observer will try that fragrance herself (assuming she desires the same effect!). And if you watch a comedian telling a joke that gets a big laugh, you may repeat that same joke to your friends. Conversely, if you see a comedian tell a joke that bombs, you are not likely to repeat it.

A second factor that influences performance is the consequence for the *observer* of performing the modeled behavior. *We are more (or less) likely to perform a modeled behavior when we ourselves will experience reinforcement (or punishment) for performing that behavior.* If you tell the same joke that got the comedian a big laugh and your friends love it, then you will continue to tell it; if you tell the joke and everyone frowns, then you probably will not tell it again. In general, the reinforcement or punishment of the *observer's* behavior ultimately determines whether a modeled behavior will be performed (e.g., Weiss, Suckow, & Rakestraw, 1999).

A third factor that influences our performance is *our own history of reinforcement or punishment for performing modeled behaviors.* Throughout our lives, we learn when it is appropriate to perform modeled behaviors as well as who is an appropriate model. Chances are that behavior modeled after that of teachers, coaches, and parents has been explicitly reinforced while behavior modeled after that of less exemplary individuals has been explicitly punished ("Don't be like that awful boy next door!"). As well, performance of a modeled behavior can be differentially reinforced in different contexts. The performance of some modeled behaviors—such as smoking or swearing—may be reinforced in the presence of your close friends but punished in the presence of your parents. Thus, over the years we gradually learn, through our own unique history of reinforcement and punishment, when it is appropriate to perform behaviors that have been modeled by others. (See also the discussion of *generalized imitation* in the next section.)

1. Not only are you more likely to a_____ to a model's behavior if you see the model's behavior reinforced, you are also more likely to p_____ that behavior.

2. A second factor that influences whether we will perform a modeled behavior is the c_____ we receive for performing the behavior.

3. A third factor that influences our performance of a modeled behavior is our h_____ of r_____ for performing modeled behaviors.

4. When you repeat an off-color joke to your friends, they laugh heartily; but when you tell the same jokes to your parents, you are met with frowns. Due to dif_____ reinforcement, you soon learn to tell such jokes only when you are with your friends.

QUICK QUIZ C

Imitation

Imitation is a term that is often used interchangeably with observational learning. *True imitation,* however, is a form of observational learning that involves the close duplication of a novel behavior (or sequence of behaviors). For example, imagine that Chelsea is standing in a line outside an exclusive club when she sees a woman walk to the front of the line and begin flirting with the doorman. The doorman allows the woman to enter without standing in line. Chelsea gets out of line, walks up to the doorman, and also begins flirting with him. If she flirts in a different way from the other woman (using her own "flirting style"), this would be an example of observational learning but not true imitation. But if she flirts in virtually the same way as the other woman, which also happens to be quite different from the way Chelsea normally flirts (so it is a novel behavior pattern for her), then we would say that true imitation has taken place.

Children have a strong tendency to imitate the behaviors of those around them, hence the popularity of games like "Simon says." Interestingly, operant conditioning appears to play a major role in the development of this ability. In the earliest study along these lines, Baer and Sherman (1964) reinforced children's behavior of imitating certain behavior patterns that were displayed by a puppet. The researchers found that this process resulted in an increase not only in the frequency of the behaviors that had been reinforced but also in the frequency of other behaviors that had been displayed by the model but for which the children had never received reinforcement. In other words, the children had acquired a generalized tendency to imitate the model.

Generalized imitation is therefore a tendency to imitate a new modeled behavior with no specific reinforcement for doing so. This process has considerable real-world application. Applied behavior analysts make use of it when working with children who are developmentally delayed or autistic and who are often deficient in their ability to learn through observation (e.g., Baer, Peterson, & Sherman, 1967; Lovaas, 1987; Lynch, 1998). By deliberately reinforcing the imitation of some behaviors, therapists can produce in these children a generalized tendency to imitate, that then greatly facilitates subsequent training.

Can Animals Imitate? Although it is clear that humans are capable of true imitation, there has been considerable debate over the extent to which animals are capable of it (e.g., Galef, 1988; Tomasello, 1996). This is actually an old issue; early animal behaviorists and learning theorists, like Romanes (1884), Morgan (1900), and Thorndike (1911), debated whether animals could "intentionally" imitate (which could be construed as indicative of higher-level cognitive functioning) or whether any appearance of imitation was due to some lower-level, perhaps instinctive, mechanism. Now the controversy has again arisen, with a wealth of experimental studies examining the issue.

Most of these studies have examined the ability of animals, usually monkeys and apes, to solve novel problems such as how to obtain food locked away in a box. In a typical experiment, the animals watch a model perform a complex series of behaviors—such as getting a key, opening a lock, pulling a lever, and then using a stick to pull food out of a hole that has now been revealed in the side of the box. The observer animal is then given a chance to try opening the box. If the animal can imitate, it should be able to duplicate the actions performed by the model to obtain the food. What often happens, though, is that the animals do *not* copy the actions of the model exactly—they may pull the lever, for example, but not use the key; or they may turn the box over and shake it to remove the food rather than use the stick (e.g., Call, 1999; Call & Tomasello, 1995; Nagel, Olguin, & Tomasello, 1993; Whiten, 1998).

Further, when animals do show evidence of imitation in these types of studies, it is often not clear that the effects of stimulus enhancement and other potential confounds have been ruled out. For example, Chesler (1969) demonstrated that kittens more quickly learn to press a lever for food if they had observed their mothers pressing a lever than if they had observed a strange female cat pressing the lever. Although this study has been widely cited as providing evidence of imitation, Galef (1988) points out that the study might simply demonstrate that mothers are better stimulus enhancers than strangers are! Kittens are likely to pay more attention to their mother than to a stranger, and to attend to any item that she manipulates. This in turn makes it more likely that the kittens would themselves manipulate the lever and, through trial and error, receive food. Thus, simple stimulus enhancement could result in a duplication of behavior that looks a lot like imitation. Due to these kinds of difficulties, some researchers have suggested that nonhuman animals are incapable of true imitation (e.g., Tomasello, 1996).

Other researchers, however, have argued that sufficient evidence now exists, gathered from well-controlled studies, to indicate that at least some animals (especially birds and great apes) are capable of true imitation (see Zentall, 2006, for a review). For example, in a study by Nguyen, Klein, and Zentall (2005), demonstrator pigeons were trained either to peck at or step on a treadle and then push a screen either to the left or to the right to obtain food. Observer pigeons were significantly more likely to demonstrate the sequence they had observed (e.g., treadle step and screen push right) as opposed to a sequence they had not observed (treadle peck and screen push left).

It has also been argued that past research on this issue has sometimes utilized inappropriate criteria for judging imitative ability in animals. Horowitz (2003), for example, replicated a study using a task that had previously revealed greater evidence of true imitation in children than in chimpanzees, except that Horowitz also gave the task to human adults. He found that the adults' level of imitation was more similar to that of the chimpanzees than the children's level was! In other words, both human adults and chimpanzees displayed more flexible behavior patterns in solving the problem—as compared to the children, who had a stronger tendency simply to do what the model had demonstrated. The lower rate of imitation that had been shown by chimpanzees compared to the children in the previous study therefore seems like a poor basis for drawing inferences about their lack of imitative ability, insofar as one can hardly argue that human adults are also incapable of true imitation.

Finally, researchers have uncovered some impressive anecdotal evidence of true imitation. Russon and Galdikas (1993, 1995) observed orangutans living with humans in a camp designed to reintroduce the animals to the wild. They found that the orangutans regularly copied the complex actions of the humans with whom they interacted, including learning to hang hammocks, build bridges, and use boats. In one case, an orangutan even learned how to start a fire—something that the researchers did not expect and

And Furthermore

Can Animals Teach?

We have so far discussed whether animals can learn by observing a model. An even more interesting question, perhaps, is whether animals can "deliberately" act as models for teaching another animal. This is not an easy question to answer, because people usually assume that teaching requires a "conscious intention" to demonstrate, or transfer knowledge from one individual to another, that is obviously difficult to assess in nonhuman animals. For example, consider an ape that seems to be calling her offspring's attention toward her tool use. By simply observing her actions, we may find it difficult to determine if she is trying to teach her young to use a tool to get food or simply trying to get food while at the same time keeping her offspring nearby. If her offspring do learn to use the same tool in the same way, were they intentionally taught by the mother? Or, did the offspring simply pick up the behavior on their own through observational learning or stimulus enhancement?

As with true imitation, some researchers have argued that teaching is a behavior performed only by humans (King, 1991). They contend that evidence that does suggest teaching by animals is often anecdotal and subject to *anthropomorphism* (assuming human motives or characteristics when observing animal behavior). Nevertheless, evidence has been gathered suggesting that at least some nonhuman animals, especially chimpanzees (Boesch, 1991) and bonobos (also known as pygmy chimpanzees; de Waal, 2005) do behave as teachers. A few anecdotes, in particular, are difficult to ignore. For example:

> At the Georgia State University Language Research Center in Atlanta, a bonobo called Kanzi has been trained to communicate with people. He has become a bonobo celebrity, known for his fabulous understanding of spoken English. Realizing that some of his fellow apes do not have the same training, Kanzi occasionally adopts the role of teacher. He once sat next to Tamuli, a younger sister who has had minimal exposure to human speech, while a researcher tried to get Tamuli to respond

certainly did not demonstrate on purpose! (See "Can Animals Teach?" in the And Furthermore box.)

QUICK QUIZ D

1. If a young gorilla learns to gather tasty wild ginger plants by watching his mother forage, we can say that he has demonstrated o_____ learning.

2. Copying a new behavior to achieve a particular result is (true imitation/stimulus enhancement) _____; having one's attention drawn to a particular place or thing is (true imitation/stimulus enhancement) _____.

3. Jessica has just purchased a new computer and is trying to learn how to use the modem to access the Internet. She asks her friend Jill to show her how to do it. Jill performs a complicated series of clicks and keystrokes, and Jessica watches closely. If Jessica then connects to the Internet on her own using the same actions as Jill, Jessica's behavior is best described as an example of (true imitation/stimulus enhancement) _____.

to simple verbal requests; the untrained bonobo didn't respond. As the researcher addressed Tamuli, it was Kanzi who began to act out the meanings. When Tamuli was asked to groom Kanzi, he took her hand and placed it under his chin, squeezing it between his chin and chest. In this position, Kanzi stared into Tamuli's eyes with what people interpreted as a questioning gaze. When Kanzi repeated the action, the young female rested her fingers on his chest as if wondering what to do. (de Waal, 2005, pp. 6–7)

In the quote, you may have noticed that several assumptions, which may or may not be warranted, were made about Kanzi's and Tamuli's motives. On the other hand, the behaviors Kanzi displayed are very much the types of behaviors that, with humans, we often use to infer the existence of an "intention." It is difficult, therefore, to witness a behavior like this and not assume that Kanzi is making some humanlike attempt at teaching or coaching. But it should also be noted that Kanzi is somewhat unique among bonobos in his demonstrated language and problem-solving abilities, and he may have skills that are not typical of other apes. (You will read more about Kanzi later in this chapter.)

Kanzi with his trainer, Sue Savage-Rumbaugh.

Courtesy of www.GreatApeTrust.org

4. Joe has also purchased a new computer and is trying to access the Internet. He watches his friend Daryl as he accesses the Internet and notices that he uses a couple of applications to do so. Joe opens those applications himself and then plays around with the settings until he figures it out. Joe's behavior is best described as an example of (true imitation/stimulus enhancement) _____.

Social Learning and Aggression

Bandura is well known for his studies on aggression, and he is particularly famous for what are now known as the "Bobo doll studies" (e.g., Bandura, 1965). In those studies, children observed adult models behaving aggressively toward a Bobo doll (an inflatable toy doll that pops back up when pushed over). The children were then tested to determine whether they also had learned to behave aggressively. The research involved various types of models,

Two images from Albert Bandura's famous Bobo doll study. The image on the left is from the film of the aggressive adult model that was shown to the children (the Bobo doll has bounced into the air from the force of the attack). The image on the right shows one of the children later attacking the Bobo doll.

Courtesy of Albert Bandura

various forms of demonstrated aggression, and children of varying ages. In these studies, Bandura found some *striking* evidence concerning the social learning of aggression (pun intended).

First, children who observed a model behaving aggressively toward the Bobo doll and other targets tended to replicate the same behaviors when they were allowed into the same room that the model had previously occupied (Bandura, Ross, & Ross, 1961; Bandura, Ross, & Ross, 1963; Bandura 1965). By *replicate*, we do not just mean that the children demonstrated an increase in general aggression (although that also occurred). The children in Bandura's studies were very precise in some of their aggressive behavior, performing many of the same motor movements toward the same targets, using the same weapons, and uttering the same hostile statements. In other words, these children demonstrated true imitation of the model's aggressive behavior.

The children were also influenced by the consequences that the model experienced while behaving aggressively. Although simply witnessing the aggressive adult often resulted in aggressive behavior in the child, the effect was even stronger if the child had observed reinforcement of the adult's aggression. Likewise, children who had observed models' aggressive behavior being punished were somewhat *less* likely to reproduce the behaviors spontaneously. However, if the researchers then offered the children incentives to behave aggressively, the level of aggression went back up; the children showed that they had in fact learned the behaviors very well (Bandura, 1965).

In a related study, children watched a televised fight in the presence of an adult male. The adult watched the film with the children and responded approvingly, disapprovingly, or made no comment. Children who had heard the disapproving comments produced far fewer aggressive behaviors upon testing compared to the other two groups—*but only when the disapproving adult was present.* In the absence of the disapproving adult, these children exhibited an increase in aggression (Hicks, 1968).

1. The aggressive behavior of children in Bandura's studies was so similar to the model's behavior that it can be considered as an example of t_____ i_____.

2. Watching a model demonstrate violent behavior has been shown to lead to an (increase/decrease) _____ in violence by observers; observing the reinforcement of violent behavior further (increased/decreased) _____ the amount of violence displayed by observers.

3. Although children in Bandura's study exhibited somewhat less violent behavior if the model's behavior had been p_____, their levels of violence increased again if they were later offered an i_____ for behaving violently.

Social Learning and Media Violence: From Bobo Doll to Grand Theft Auto   In his research, Bandura found that filmed violence was as effective as live violence for inducing violent behavior in observers (Bandura, Ross, & Ross, 1963). Although this research was conducted before the extreme proliferation of mass media in the late 20th century, these preliminary findings foreshadowed the concerns of modern researchers who examine the impact of violent media on the behavior of children and adolescents.

Children have always had opportunities to learn about violence, by observing violence at home and in the community. Children are often exposed to warfare and are sometimes even trained as soldiers. Social learning of violence by children is therefore nothing new, but the constant availability of aggressive or violent models is new and pervasive. Between 1950, when approximately 9% of American homes contained a television, and 2000, when virtually all North American families owned a television (Federal Trade Commission, 2000), there has been a substantial change in children's exposure to violent media. In addition to television, which is an essentially passive medium (one simply watches it), children are increasingly exposed to violent or aggressive video games that allow for a high degree of interaction and participation. Indeed, when looking at the hyperrealistic violent games now available— including the Grand Theft Auto™ series of games that depict violent criminal behavior such as theft, murder, and rape—it's hard to believe that in the 1980s, some parents complained that Pac-Man was too violent because Pac-Man went around eating the other characters!

Longitudinal studies and prospective studies are especially useful for isolating critical factors in violent behavior. Eron and his colleagues have studied a large sample of boys from 1960 until the present day. They have found that the amount of violent media viewed in childhood is significantly correlated with aggressive and antisocial behavior 10 years later, even after controlling for variables such as initial aggressiveness, social class, and education (Eron, Huesmann, Lefkowitz, & Walder, 1972). This early viewing of violence, and early aggression, has also been shown to be significantly related to adult criminality (Huesmann, 1986), although the relationship is weaker. More recently, Johnson and his colleagues have summarized the results of another 17-year study, in which they determined that the amount of television watched in childhood is positively correlated with amount of aggressive or violent behavior toward others (Johnson, Cohen, Kasen, & Brook, 2007). Although Johnson's team found a bidirectional relationship between viewing violence and aggressive behavior (in which those who are aggressive also tend to seek out violent media), the effect of violent media on later aggressive behavior was still robust.

Are there sex differences in the effects of media violence? Most studies find that males are more likely to express the effects of exposure to violent video games. C. A. Anderson and Dill report that male video-game players have a more hostile view of the world than do females (2000), and some longitudinal studies suggest that males are more aggressive than females after exposure to violent media (Eron et al., 1972; Huesmann, Moise-Titus, Podolski, & Eron, 2003; Lefkowitz, Eron, Walder, & Huesmann, 1977). This conforms to results described by Bandura (1965) in his early Bobo doll studies. For example, he found that boys tended to produce more spontaneous acts of aggression than girls did. He also found that girls inhibited their aggression to a greater degree if the model had been punished. Once an incentive was provided for reproducing the aggressive acts, however, the sex differences disappeared. It appears therefore that girls learn violence as well as boys do, but girls have a greater tendency to inhibit violence unless there is an incentive for violence. Girls will also demonstrate a higher frequency of aggressive acts when the aggressive model is female as opposed to male (see review by Bandura, 1973). Since most violent models in the media and on computer games are male, this could account for some of the sex differences that we observe.

One troubling possibility is that, although exposure to violent media does not predispose females toward behaving aggressively as much as it does males, it might make females more vulnerable to being *victims* of aggression. Desensitization to violence may allow females to feel that violence and aggression are normal aspects of life, which could lead them to enter violent relationships. This may be related to the fact that, whereas most models of violent behavior are male, a high proportion of victims are female. Thus, in the same way that exposure to spousal violence in childhood increases the likelihood of becoming a victim of spousal abuse in adulthood (Ehrensaft et al., 2003), it is possible that females who watch violent media are more likely to become victims of violence.

Given all the evidence for the damaging effects of media violence, from both experimental and correlational studies, why do we rarely see this evidence clearly reported in the newspapers and other aspects of the popular press? Bushman and Anderson (2001) have proposed several reasons for why this is the case. For one thing, media sources are often interlinked. Thus, if the film or television industry wants to promote (or suppress) a particular viewpoint, they are likely to have connections at the level of newspapers and magazines that enable them to do so. Media outlets also tend to take a "balanced" approach to the topic of media violence by frequently including comments from researchers who believe that the effects of media violence have been overstated. On the surface, this appears to be a fair approach, since both sides of the debate are given equal representation. However, insofar as the vast majority of researchers agree that media violence is dangerous, then the "equal air time" given to the few naysayers tends to mislead the public into believing that the evidence linking media violence and aggression is much weaker than it is. Finally, researchers themselves have not been forceful enough in presenting their findings to the public. For example, media executives have sometimes argued that the correlations between media violence and aggression are so small as to be of little real significance, whereas in fact they are almost as high as the correlations between cigarette smoking and lung cancer—and they are higher than the correlations between passive smoking and lung cancer, exposure to asbestos and laryngeal cancer, and even condom use and sexually transmitted HIV! No one argues that these correlations are so small as to be of little real significance.

The comparison to lung cancer is particularly instructive. Smoking is an important cause of lung cancer—but it is not the only cause, and many people who smoke will never get lung cancer. On average, however, the risk of developing lung cancer if you are a smoker is substantially higher than if you are a nonsmoker. The same logic holds true for the effects of media violence on violent behavior. Watching violent TV is not the only contributing factor to personal violence. Some individuals who watch violent films or play violent video games will never demonstrate an increase in violent behavior. On average, however, those who view or interact with violent media have an increased risk of becoming violent themselves. As noted earlier, the possibility also exists that exposure to media violence can increase the likelihood of becoming a victim of violence. Therefore, although further research is warranted, it appears that media violence is very likely a significant contributor to violence in society.

QUICK QUIZ F

1. Longitudinal studies have shown that exposure to violent media is (strongly/weakly) _____ correlated with ag_____ and antis_____ behavior.

2. One troubling aspect of sex differences in response to media violence is that while (males/females) _____ are more likely to become violent as a result of such exposure, (males/females) _____ may be more likely to become _____ of violence.

3. The problem with the media giving equal air time to those who are (convinced/skeptical) _____ about the effects of media violence on violent behavior is that the public is then misled into thinking that the evidence for such effects is (stronger/weaker) _____ than it actually is.

Language

Since you have managed to make it this far in this book, it is a pretty safe bet that you understand language, and not only *written* language but *spoken* language and *symbolic* language—like road signs, gestures, and "body language"—as well. Language has often been used as the defining feature of human beings—the thing that makes our species unique. We use language, whether written, spoken, or symbolic, to communicate everything—meaning, motives, feelings, and beliefs. In fact, it is difficult to imagine how humans could exist without language.

If language is so basic to the human condition, you may wonder why we even discuss a topic like language in a textbook on learning. After all, many people believe language is not learned like other behaviors but rather is largely innate (e.g., Chomsky, 1988; Pinker, 1994). According to this view, humans are born with a "black box" that helps them to quickly acquire language, an ability not shared by other species. However, from an evolutionary viewpoint, humans and animals share many common features, including basic learning processes and cognitive abilities. Is it possible, then, that animals can use language? Behaviorists have expended considerable effort in attempting to answer this question, and in this section we summarize some of what they have discovered.

There are, in fact, many examples of animal species that have evolved complex communication systems of their own. One of the best examples is vervet monkeys, small primates that live in Africa. Unfortunately for vervets, they are preyed upon by a wide variety of other species, including snakes, leopards, and eagles, each of which attacks the monkeys in a different way. This means that the monkeys have to be constantly on guard against predators. Because of that, they have evolved a communication system of alarm calls to warn fellow vervets that a predator has been spotted in the area. Alarm calling is not unique to vervets; many other animal species use alarm calls too. What *is* unique is that vervets have different calls for different predator types, and the different calls elicit different behavioral responses from the rest of the group. Thus, if a vervet monkey spots an eagle flying overhead, she sounds the "eagle" alarm, and they all dive for cover in the dense underbrush of the forest. If one of the monkeys sees a leopard, a different call is given, and the monkeys climb into the nearest tall tree (Seyfarth, Cheney, & Marler, 1980). This communication system (which seems extremely logical to us language-using humans) is very special, because it illustrates that animals can use arbitrary symbols to symbolically refer to objects that exist in the world. This ability to use arbitrary symbols, which is called ***reference,*** is one of the important features of any language (e.g., Savage-Rumbaugh, 1993). We take reference for granted because human languages are based on the idea that a combination of arbitrary sounds can stand for actual objects. For example, if I use the word *apple*, you know what I am talking about. And when I learn a new language, such as French, I have to learn that the word *pomme* means the same thing as *apple* and that they both refer to the tasty, round object found on trees.

In addition to reference, there are other important characteristics that define a communication system as language (e.g., Hockett, 1960). One feature of any language is grammar, which you might remember spending tedious hours learning as a child in school. ***Grammar*** is simply a set of rules that control the meaning of a string of words. For example, if I ask you

"Who is that?" you know that the appropriate response to my question is a proper name ("Joe") rather than an object ("Apple") or location ("There"). You know how to answer my question because you understand the rules—the grammar—of the English language. There are a finite number of rules for any language, and once those rules are learned, an infinite number of expressions can be generated to express novel or creative ideas. This feature is called ***productivity***, and it is yet another important characteristic of language. Related to that is the idea of ***situational freedom***, which means that language can be used in a variety of contexts and is not fixed to a particular situation. Accordingly, you can discuss things that are not currently present, such as the fact that you went to a movie last weekend or that you will soon be going on a vacation.

1. Humans communicate through several forms of language, including wr_____, sp_____, and sym_____ forms.

2. Vervet monkeys give different alarm calls when they see different predators. This illustrates that vervet monkey communication has an important feature of language, called r_____.

3. You are taking a fascinating psychology course on behaviorism and are learning all sorts of exciting new terms, such as stimulus enhancement. You find yourself using these new words at the dinner table to describe behaviors you have observed that day. You have just illustrated the sit_____ fr_____ aspect of language.

4. The fact that you understand that "John likes Sarah" means something entirely different than "Sarah likes John" suggests that you know the gr_____ of the English language.

5. Your young nephew asks you to make up a story and tell it to him. Much to his delight, you are able to create a story that portrays him as a prince in a fabulous kingdom. This illustrates the pr_____ aspect of language.

Can Animals "Talk?"

Now that we know a few important characteristics of language (reference, grammar, productivity, and situational freedom), we can go back to our original question: Can animals use language? This question has intrigued people for generations. After all, who has not wished that a pet dog or cat could talk and wondered what the pet might say if it could? The most comprehensive research programs aimed at this question have attempted to teach animals a humanlike language. Unlike Dr. Doolittle, who talked *to* the animals, many researchers have tried to teach the animals to talk to *us*.

The best-known research on language learning in animals involves our closest relatives, the great apes, including chimpanzees, gorillas, orangutans, and bonobos (that is, pygmy chimpanzees). The great apes share many characteristics in common with humans, from anatomy, blood chemistry, and DNA all the way to social behavior and cognitive skills (e.g., Begun, 1999). Since chimpanzees in particular are closely related to humans, the early experiments in this area focused on them. The first attempts to teach chimps language were based on the idea that wild chimpanzees did not use language simply because they had no motivation or encouragement to do so. This fits nicely with the *empiricist* approach described in Chapter 1. It was assumed that, with proper training, chimpanzees could learn and use human language. The first researchers, therefore, tried to train chimps to speak by raising infant chimps in a home environment reminiscent of that in which infant children are reared (e.g., Hayes & Hayes, 1951; Kellogg & Kellogg, 1933). Such studies are called *cross-fostering* experiments because the chimpanzees were raised in human foster homes. This research received considerable public interest; and one of the chimps, named Viki, became quite a celebrity. However, even though the chimpanzees thrived in the home environment, they never learned to talk. In fact, Viki learned to produce only four words: *cup*, *up*, *mama*, and *papa*. In watching old films of Viki, it is obvious that "speaking" is not something that chimps do naturally. Viki had to tortuously manipulate her mouth with her hand to produce those four short words.

Sign Language Experiments

Although chimps lacked the vocal apparatus to produce comprehensible speech, language experiments with chimpanzees eventually revealed that they might be capable of producing and understanding other forms of language. Thus, the next approach was to teach chimpanzees a different kind of language, one that relied on gestures instead of spoken words. In the wild, chimpanzees do communicate with each other using gestures—pointing, arm waving, and so on—so it seemed logical to assume that they might be able to learn a language that relied on hand gestures such as American Sign Language (ASL). Sign languages have been used by deaf people for many years, and there are many different such languages. ASL has existed for more than 100 years and is commonly used in North America. Contrary to popular belief, sign languages are not simply "finger spelling" of English words. They are complex, rich languages that share all the important features of any language, including reference and grammar. Each signed "word" can convey different meanings, depending on the inflection, and some words can represent entire phrases. Sign languages are also learned in the same way that spoken languages are learned—through modeling, correction by adults, and learning the rules of grammar.

Experimenters conducted cross-fostering studies on chimps' ability to learn ASL in a natural home environment, thereby simulating the way human children learn language. This meant that the chimps were not taught by rote memorization or language drills but learned in day-to-day activities in a family group. Of course, the prospect of raising chimps like humans was a daunting one. The researchers had to devote years of their lives to the project because language acquisition is a long-term effort. The researchers also had to become fluent in ASL and to use only signs, not spoken English, in the presence of their foster "children." The first ASL cross-fostering study was named Project Washoe, after Washoe County in Reno, Nevada. An infant chimp named Washoe was raised by two scientists, Beatrix and Allen Gardner (e.g., Gardner & Gardner, 1969). Since Washoe, other chimps have been cross-fostered to replicate the findings of Project Washoe—and to give Washoe other chimps to "talk" to (Gardner, Gardner, & Van Cantfort, 1989).

The researchers discovered that the best way to teach apes sign language is to use modeling—demonstrating the sign while performing the action that the sign refers to, such as signing "open" while opening a door. They also used a technique called *molding*, which involves placing the ape's hands in the correct signing position and associating that position with the object being "talked" about. Using these techniques, most ASL-trained chimps ended up with vocabularies of well over 100 signs. Both these procedures worked better than standard operant conditioning, which paired a food reward with correct signing. The researchers found that rewarding each sign with food resulted in a very automatic or "reflexive" type of behavior that was oriented to the food reward. Interestingly, this process seems similar to the process of undermining intrinsic motivation through extrinsic rewards, which was briefly discussed in Chapter 6. Food rewards seemed to focus the chimps on producing the signs rather than on communicating with the researchers. Interestingly, Washoe (and other language-trained chimpanzees) often signed spontaneously, even when she was alone, which suggests that the signing behavior was rewarding in and of itself.

Strictly controlled tests of language use were performed with many of the chimpanzees trained in sign language (e.g., Fouts, 1973). All the chimps seemed to pass the test of *reference;* that is, they could all use the arbitrary ASL signals to refer to objects and could easily categorize novel objects using signs. For example, if Washoe was shown a photo of a kitten that she had never seen before, she immediately applied the (correct) sign for "cat." Whether the ASL-trained chimps exhibited the other features of language—grammar, productivity, and situational freedom—is much less clear. There is some evidence that Washoe did follow the grammatical rules of ASL. She responded to questions such as "What is that?" with, for example, "That apple" rather than simply "Apple" (Gardner & Gardner, 1975). However, there is only anecdotal evidence that Washoe and other language-trained chimps used signs in novel contexts or produced novel signs for unfamiliar objects. Further, ASL is not a rigid language. The syntax (or ordering of words) is relatively loose, so ASL speakers are not required to follow strict sequences of words. It is therefore extremely difficult to systematically assess chimpanzees' use of language when the language is a fluid, gestural language like ASL.

1. Our closest relatives are chimpanzees, orangutans, and gorillas, known as the g_____ a_____.

2. Early attempts to teach chimpanzees to speak failed miserably, probably because chimps (have/do not have) _____ the v_____ apparatus to produce speech.

3. Studies by the Gardners and others looked at whether chimpanzees could learn a symbolic, gestural language called A_____ S_____ L_____.

4. In c_____-f_____ experiments, apes are raised in human environments.

5. W_____ was the first chimpanzee trained in ASL.

6. Researchers found that mod_____ was the easiest way to teach sign language to the chimpanzees. They also found mol_____, which involves physically placing the ape's hands in the correct position, to be an effective method.

7. On the other hand, simply rewarding correct signs with f_____ tended to produce ref_____-type behavior that was oriented more toward producing signs than communicating with the researchers.

8. Almost all apes that have been trained in ASL can demonstrate r_____, the ability to associate particular signs with particular objects or actions.

Artificial Language Experiments

To get around the difficulties posed by the sign language cross-fostering studies, the next series of experiments designed to determine whether animals could use language were conducted in laboratory situations, using artificially constructed languages. These languages did not consist of spoken words or physical gestures; rather, they consisted of visual symbols, either plastic tokens placed on a magnetic board (Premack, 1971b; 1976) or symbols on a computer keyboard (Rumbaugh, 1977; Savage-Rumbaugh, McDonald, Sevcik, Hopkins, & Rubert, 1986). The chimps that participated in these experiments were not raised in human-like environments and did not interact with their caretakers in the same way that Washoe and the other ASL-trained chimps did. They lived in laboratories, and they conversed via the artificial language. A typical sentence in one of these languages—called "Yerkish" after the Yerkes Primate Research Center where it was created—is? WHAT NAME OF THIS. You may notice that Yerkish grammar is *not* the same as English grammar. The question mark is placed at the beginning of the sentence, and there are words missing. Nonetheless, it has its own grammar and is a language. The chimps that learned Yerkish could respond to questions and ask for objects (e.g., PLEASE MACHINE GIVE BANANA). Although this type of language may seem restricted compared to ASL—and indeed it is, with a much smaller vocabulary and very rigid grammatical rules—it is constructed that way purposefully. The idea was to discover, once and for all, whether chimps could learn and use all the basic features of language. Also, the artificial and highly controlled surroundings made systematic assessment relatively easy. Everything the chimps "said" was displayed and recorded by a computer, so the way the chimps were using language was much clearer than in the ASL studies, which could often be interpreted differently by different observers.

Unfortunately, the artificial language experiments did not give the unequivocal answers that scientists were hoping for. The chimps in these experiments, like those in the ASL studies, did appear to use symbols to represent or categorize objects, so they seemed to have the ability to *reference* objects. However, whether the chimps had mastered the artificial *grammar* was less clear. Most of the chimps' sentences were of the form PLEASE MACHINE GIVE "X" (where "X" was usually a preferred food item, such as apples, bananas, or M&M candies). It can be argued that learning to produce a sequence of symbols like PLEASE MACHINE GIVE X is not the same as learning the underlying rules governing language production. In fact, pigeons can be readily trained to peck a sequence of four symbols to receive a food reward (Terrace, 1985), and very few people would say that those pigeons had learned language. It is clear, though, that the chimps in the artificial language experiments generally did not have much to talk about except obtaining food, so perhaps this type of study was not a fair test of their language ability after all. And although recent studies of ape language ability claim to have produced stronger evidence of language capacity (e.g., Benson, Greaves, O'Donnell, & Taglialatela, 2002; Savage-Rumbaugh, Shanker, & Taylor, 1998), some language specialists remain unimpressed (e.g., Pinker, 1994).

In considering the results of the cross-fostering ASL studies and the artificial language experiments together, it is difficult to draw a firm conclusion. Chimpanzees definitely can learn to use symbols to refer to objects, but they just as definitely do not use those symbols in the same way that adult humans do (Terrace, 1979; Terrace, Petitio, Sanders, & Bever, 1979). But how do other animals fare in this regard?

QUICK QUIZ 1

1. Studies of animals' ability to use symbolic languages created by researchers in a laboratory setting are known as (artificial/cross-fostering) _____ language experiments.

2. These studies allowed researchers to systematically assess the language abilities of chimpanzees in a (more/less) _____ controlled setting than was the case with the sign language cross-fostering studies.

3. One of the first artificial languages created was called "Yer_____."

4. Results of the artificial language experiments strongly suggest that many of the chimpanzees mastered (reference/grammar) _____, but there is less evidence that they mastered (reference/grammar) _____.

Although the language studies with chimpanzees received the most public attention, other researchers have focused on training other species—ranging from parrots (Pepperberg, 1999) to gorillas (Patterson & Linden, 1981) to dolphins (Herman, Pack, & Morrel-Samuels, 1993)—to use language. That list of species might seem completely random to you; but in fact, animals that have been language-trained share some important features. First, they have relatively large, complex brains, which makes it likely that they have the cognitive capacity to represent concepts. Second, they are usually species that are extremely social. Social species, such as humans, generally evolve more complicated communication abilities simply because they have more neighbors to "talk" to and about. Dolphins are a good example of that because they have large brains as well as a social system in which they regularly interact with members of their own and other species. In fact, although dolphins are far removed from primates in an evolutionary sense, they are often thought of as similar to primates in terms of cognitive abilities. (The alleged "mystical" qualities of dolphin–human interactions that have been reported also added to their cachet as potential language users.)

For almost 20 years, Louis Herman and his colleagues have been training dolphins to use a symbolic language (Roitblat, Herman, & Nachtigall, 1993). These researchers have worked with two dolphins, each trained with a different artificial language. One dolphin, called Akeakamai, has learned a gestural language, similar to ASL. The other dolphin, called Phoenix, has learned a computer-generated language of acoustic signals, similar to Yerkish. Both dolphins "work" on their language training in large tanks at the University of Hawaii (nice work if you can get it!). Although the languages are limited to describing things that the dolphins can see and do underwater, it is clear that the animals have learned a vocabulary of symbols—ball, pipe, surfboard, spit, fetch, bottom, and so on—that *refer* to objects and actions (Herman & Forestell, 1985; Shyan & Herman, 1987). It is also clear that the dolphins understand rudimentary *grammatical* rules. For example, when given a sentence like FRISBEE FETCH BASKET, Phoenix knows to take the Frisbee and put it in the basket. When the sentence is given in the opposite order—BASKET FETCH FRISBEE—she takes the basket to the Frisbee. Both dolphins also show very accurate performance on novel sentences, using new "words" (e.g., Herman, Kuczaj, & Holder, 1993; Herman, Morrel-Samuels, & Pack, 1990). Interestingly, California sea lions, another sea mammal species, have also learned symbolic gestures and can respond accurately to three-word sentences like those used with the dolphins (Schusterman & Gisiner, 1988).

So, back to our original question: Can animals use language? As you now know, this is not a simple question, and it certainly does not have a simple answer. It depends on how you define language, and whom you ask. Some animal species are clearly capable of learning some aspects of language and of using symbols in a variety of situations. Teaching animals to use language has also expanded the types of questions that researchers are asking about the way animals think. Although we may never be able to sit down with a chimpanzee and have a deep discussion about the meaning of life, we have been able to study complex phenomena such as concept discrimination and categorization (Savage-Rumbaugh, Rumbaugh, Smith, & Lawson, 1980) and logical reasoning (Premack & Woodruff, 1978), which are very difficult to study without "words" of some kind. (See also "Talking to the Animals" in the And Furthermore box.)

And Furthermore

Talking to the Animals (by Suzanne MacDonald)

What is it like to "talk" to animals that have been trained to use sign language? Chantek, a famous language-trained orangutan, has worked with researcher Lyn Miles for many years (Miles, 1990, 1994, 1999). Lyn Miles has trained Chantek, with a combination of modeling and explicit reinforcement, to use hundreds of ASL signs. Chantek signs all day long—in fact, he is pretty chatty! On a recent visit, I (Suzanne MacDonald) watched delightedly as Chantek talked about what he wanted for lunch

Chantek, the orangutan, is one of the most capable ape communicators through the use of American Sign Language.

(yogurt, which he eats with a spoon). Eventually, Chantek asked Lyn who I was. She made up a new ASL sign for my name, which Chantek promptly used, inviting me to put a jigsaw puzzle together with him. Although Chantek does not discuss the meaning of life—focusing instead on more practical matters like food—it is an amazing experience to see him forming his huge, hairy hands into the familiar ASL signs, communicating his moods and desires.

The ultimate "ape communicator," though, has to be the bonobo chimpanzee known as Kanzi. Kanzi lives and works with Sue Savage-Rumbaugh at a special research facility outside of Atlanta (for a detailed description, see Savage-Rumbaugh & Lewin, 1994; Savage-Rumbaugh et al., 1998). Kanzi understands spoken English, but because he cannot actually produce speech he uses a special computer keyboard to "talk." The various keys represent hundreds of different concepts, ranging from simple food items like blueberries to complex ideas like love. If you are not yet convinced that observational learning works, you will be less skeptical when you hear that Kanzi learned this very sophisticated symbolic language as an infant, simply by watching his mother while she was being trained to use the keyboard. Kanzi has also provided some of the strongest evidence of a nonhuman animal understanding the rules of grammar.

When I met Kanzi I was very impressed by his obvious grasp of the computer symbols and by his strong desire to communicate with his human visitors. When I left Kanzi for the day, I asked him what he would like me to bring him the next day when I returned. Using his keyboard, he quickly replied, "celery." Naturally, I brought celery with me the next morning. However, I did not go to visit Kanzi right away, stopping off in the lab first to work on a computer program. Soon after, the phone rang in the lab; it was Kanzi's keeper, calling to let me know that Kanzi had been using his keyboard to insist that she call me and ask where his celery was! The keeper, who had not been there the day before, was very apologetic, because she had no idea what Kanzi was "talking" about. Needless to say, I brought Kanzi his celery. And I will never forget the day I got a phone call from an ape.

QUICK QUIZ J

1. Dolphins, gorillas, and parrots are all (social/solitary) _____ species that have relatively (complex/simple) _____ brains, which makes them good candidates for studying language acquisition.

2. Dolphins have been taught to communicate acoustically as well as gesturally, evidence that they may be able to use sym_____ language.

3. Results of the dolphin language experiments clearly indicate that the dolphins mastered the (reference/productivity) _____ aspect of language.

4. BALL FETCH BASKET means the opposite of BASKET FETCH BALL to language-trained dolphins. This suggests that, unlike many of the language-trained chimps, these dolphins can understand the rules of a language, or gr_____.

Rule-Governed Behavior

Although determining whether animals are capable of using language is a complex issue, it is obvious that humans are capable of using language. It is also obvious that our use of language greatly enhances our ability to interact with one another and to adapt to the world around us. A prime example of this is the manner in which language ability allows us to influence each other, and ourselves, through the presentation of rules.

Definitions and Characteristics

A *rule* can be defined as a verbal description of a contingency. In other words, it is a statement telling us that in a certain setting, if we perform a certain behavior, then a certain consequence will follow: "If you drive through a red light, you will get a ticket"; "If you study hard throughout the semester, you will get a good grade"; and "If you are pleasant to others, they will be pleasant to you" are all examples of rules. Likewise, the course syllabus you receive at the start of a course is a set of rules about what you need to do to pass the course, and a guidebook to Paris is a set of rules about how best to find and enjoy the sites of Paris. Behavior that has been generated through exposure to rules, such as doing what the course outline tells you to do or touring Paris in the manner suggested by the guidebook, is known as *rule-governed behavior* (Skinner, 1969).

In its purest form, a rule is simply a statement about a contingency; it does not say anything about how we should respond with respect to that contingency. If it does say something about how we should respond, then it can also be called an *instruction* (Malott, Malott, & Trojan, 2000). Thus, "If you drive through a red light, you will get a ticket" is simply a rule, whereas "Don't drive through a red light, or you will get a ticket" (or "Don't drive through a red light!" in which case the consequence is implied) is an instruction. In this discussion, however, we will use the terms *rule* and *instruction* interchangeably given that many of the rules that concern us are offered in the form of instructions. (See Baldwin & Baldwin, 1998, for a further discussion of different types of rules.)

Rules (or instructions) are extremely useful for rapidly establishing appropriate patterns of behavior. As with observational learning, we can learn how to behave effectively in a certain setting before we have any direct experience with the contingencies operating in that setting. We do not have to repeatedly drive through red lights to find out what happens if we do, and we do not have to fail a course repeatedly to figure out how to pass the course. We simply have to follow the rules that we have been given in order to behave effectively in those settings.

To illustrate the effectiveness of using rules to modify behavior, consider the task of teaching a rat to press a lever for food whenever it hears a tone. First, you have to shape the behavior of lever pressing by reinforcing closer and closer approximations to it. Then, once lever pressing is well established, you reinforce lever presses that occur only in the presence of a tone and not those that occur in the absence of the tone. Eventually, the rat learns to press the lever only when the tone is sounding. Now consider the task of teaching a person to press a button to earn money whenever a light is turned on (a common task in operant conditioning experiments with humans). All you have to do is sit the person down in front of the panel and provide the following instructions: "Whenever the light is on, you can earn money by pressing this button." Instantly, you have a button-pushing, money-earning human on your hands. What may require several hours of training with a rat requires only a few seconds of instruction with a verbally proficient human.

Learning to follow rules is so beneficial and important that parents devote considerable time to training this ability in young children. When Billie, for example, complies with his mother's request to pick up his toys, his mother praises him for doing so. Billie soon learns that people are pleased when he complies with their instructions, and he is therefore more likely to comply in the future. Billie later learns that following instructions can also be useful for completing a task. When, for example, he ignores the instructions that accompany a model airplane kit, he makes a complete mess of things; when he follows the instructions, he produces a great-looking model. Billie therefore learns that good things happen when he follows instructions; consequently, he acquires a generalized tendency to follow instructions. Of course, if bad things had happened when Billie followed instructions, or if good things happened when he did not follow instructions, he might instead have acquired a generalized tendency not to follow instructions and to be noncompliant. Thus, the extent to which we follow instructions—as well as the specific instructions we choose to follow—depends largely on the consequences we have received for following instructions (Baldwin & Baldwin, 1998).

1. A rule can be defined as a v_____ d_____ of a c_____.

2. Behavior that is generated through exposure to rules is known as r_____-g_____ behavior.

3. A rule that includes a statement about how you should behave with respect to a contingency is an i_____.

4. Rules are extremely useful in that they allow us to learn about appropriate patterns of behavior in a setting (with/without) _____ direct exposure to the contingencies operating in that setting.

5. Children learn to follow instructions because they are often (praised/ ignored) _____ for following instructions. As well, they learn that following instructions is usually a (good/poor) _____ way to actually accomplish a task.

6. The result is that most children acquire a (generalized/localized) _____ tendency to follow instructions.

7. In general, the extent to which we follow instructions—as well as the specific instructions we choose to follow—depends largely on the c_____ we have received for following instructions.

Some Disadvantages of Rule-Governed Behavior

As you can see, rules can be very useful. Unfortunately, they also have their drawbacks. One drawback is that rule-governed behavior is often less efficient than behavior that has been directly shaped by natural contingencies. For example, no matter how many books you read on how to play golf, you will undoubtedly be a poor golfer unless you devote considerable time to actually playing and practicing the game (see Figure 12.2). Instructions can give us only a rudimentary knowledge of how to play, and while this may be useful for

FIGURE 12.2 Although golf lessons are a great way to get started in the game, the rules learned are, at best, general pointers that must then be modified through the actual experience of hitting the ball and seeing where it goes.

© Michael S. Yamashita/CORBIS

A good example of how the inflexible application of rules can get in the way of organizational efficiency.

getting started or for modifying certain aspects of an established game, nothing can replace the actual experience of hitting a golf ball and seeing where it goes (Baldwin & Baldwin, 1998).

A second drawback of rule-governed behavior is that such behavior is sometimes surprisingly insensitive to the actual contingencies of reinforcement operating in a particular setting. This phenomenon has been demonstrated experimentally. For example, when human participants are told they can earn money by pressing a button, they will indeed begin pressing the button. Their button pressing may not, however, be very efficient given the schedule of reinforcement that is in effect. For instance, on an FI schedule of reinforcement, human subjects often do not display the scalloped pattern of responding that is typical of FI performance in rats and pigeons. Some subjects, for example, respond rapidly throughout the interval—as though continuous, rapid responding is necessary to produce the reinforcer (Lowe, 1979). Focusing only upon the rule they have been given—"Push the button to earn money"—some subjects never slow down enough to realize that such a high rate of response is unnecessary.[1] (See also Bentall, Lowe, & Beasty, 1985; Lowe, Beasty, & Bentall, 1983).

Likewise, a person who is taught to swing a golf club a certain way may persist with that swing for several years despite the fact that it is inappropriate for her build and level of flexibility. Because she is locked into the notion that she must follow the instructions she has been given, her golf game may

---

[1]The first author of this text directly experienced this phenomenon when, as a graduate student, he was conducting just such a button-pushing study. Because each session in the study lasted a couple of hours (and because the task was excruciatingly boring), subjects were given 10-minute breaks at regular intervals throughout each session. One subject, however, began spending almost all of her breaks in the washroom. Asked if she was okay, she explained that she was going to the washroom to run her arm under cold water to reduce the pain. As it turns out, having been told that pushing buttons would produce money, she assumed that faster button pushing produced more money. She therefore pushed the button at a blistering pace throughout each session, so much so that her arm muscles had begun to cramp. In fact, the money was being delivered on variable interval (VI) schedules of reinforcement, and she could have earned the full amount each session with a quite leisurely rate of response.

never evolve to a more effective level. Similarly, a veteran businessman who has acquired a set of rules about how best to conduct business may have difficulty modifying his business practices to compete effectively in the new global economy. As the world of business changes, his old rules, highly effective in the old economy, are now an impediment. Thus, although rules are often extremely beneficial, we do well to recognize that they have their limitations and often require modification according to the particular circumstances in which we find ourselves.

1. One problem with rule-governed behavior is that it is often (less/more) _____ efficient than behavior that has been shaped by the natural c_____.

2. A second problem with rule-governed behavior is that such behavior is sometimes surprisingly i_____ to the actual contingencies of reinforcement in a particular setting.

3. As an example of the above, experimental subjects who are told to press a button to earn money sometimes display a (scalloped pattern/high rate) _____ of responding on an FI schedule of reinforcement, which is (the same as/different from) _____ the type of responding typically shown on such schedules by animals.

Personal Rules in Self-Regulation

Although rules have their drawbacks, their advantages obviously outweigh their disadvantages. For this reason, we use rules not only to influence the behavior of others but also to influence our own behavior. In other words, we often give ourselves instructions as to how we should behave: "I should study in the library rather than at home, because it is much quieter in the library"; "I should work out each day if I want to remain fit and healthy"; and "If I am polite to others, they will be polite to me." Such statements can be called *personal rules (or self-instructions),* which can be defined as verbal descriptions of contingencies that we present to ourselves to influence our behavior (Ainslie, 1992).

Many of the personal rules that we use to regulate our behavior exert their effect as a function of "say–do correspondence." *Say–do correspondence* occurs when there is a close match between what we say we are going to do and what we actually do at a later time. If I say that I will go running at 4:00 in the afternoon and then actually go running at that time, my statement of what I intend to do matches the actual behavior that I later perform. As with rule-governed behavior in general, parents play a critical role in the development of this correspondence. If Billie promises that he will put his toys away when he is finished playing with them, and later he does put his toys away, his parents are quite pleased and praise him for carrying through on his promise. But when he does not carry through on his promise, they are annoyed. To the extent that Billie's parents apply these

ADVICE FOR THE LOVELORN

Dear Dr. Dee,

My boyfriend and I very much enjoy reading your columns. Unfortunately, Steve (my boyfriend) has begun using the ideas in these columns to analyze each and every aspect of our relationship. I know he means well, but it is starting to drive me nuts. Furthermore, I think his conclusions about our relationship are usually dead wrong. What is your opinion on this?

Going Nutty

Dear Going,

At the start of this book, we explicitly warned against taking these columns too seriously. For one thing, the advice given is usually quite speculative; it is not grounded in scientific research, nor is it based on a careful assessment of the relationship being discussed (which, in any case, is just a fictional relationship). Thus, our purpose in presenting these columns was simply to give students a sense of the *potential* ways in which behavioral principles *might* be applicable to some important aspects of human behavior.

It is also important to recognize that each relationship is unique, meaning there's no guarantee that advice that is appropriate for one relationship is relevant to another relationship. In fact, you can think of such advice as a rule for how to improve your relationship—and the act of following that advice as a form of rule-governed behavior. As we discuss in this chapter, such rules may not accurately reflect the actual contingencies that are in effect, and the person following the rule may become insensitive to the actual contingencies. This may be what has happened in your boyfriend's case. He seems to have concluded that the advice given in these columns is relevant to your own situation, which it might not be.

Tell him to lighten up a bit, pay less attention to what's being said in these advice columns (or, for that matter, anyone else's advice column), and pay more attention to what's going on in your relationship. And if you do need advice, there is often nothing better than some plain old common sense from one's close friends and family. After all, these people usually have a better knowledge of the type of person you are and the actual contingencies surrounding your relationship than any advice columnist could ever have.

Behaviorally yours,

Dr. Dee

consequences consistently, Billie will likely grow up to display a strong level of say–do correspondence. He will become known as a reliable individual who can be trusted to carry through on his promises to others. Not only that, he may concurrently develop an ability to carry through on his promises to himself, which means that he will be able to use such promises as personal rules to guide his own behavior (Guevremont, Osnes, & Stokes, 1986).

Although personal rules can be useful in helping us manage our behavior, not all personal rules are equally effective. Ainslie (1986), for example, has proposed that personal rules are most effective when they establish a "bright boundary" between acceptable and unacceptable patterns of behavior. A bright boundary is a strategic concept stating that military leaders should make use of clearly specified landmarks, such as rivers, streams, or roads, to mark the limits of their territory. Such boundaries are easier to defend because they allow one to clearly determine when the enemy has intruded into one's territory. Similarly, in trying to carry through on rules for our own behavior, we are more likely to succeed when the rule specifically sets out the conditions under which it has been obeyed or violated. For example, the statement "I will study today" is so vaguely worded that we are at high risk for delaying the act of studying until it is too late to study. The point at which the rule has been violated is not easily determined until we have, in a sense, been overrun and lost the battle. By contrast, the statement "I will study from 7:00 P.M. to 9:00 P.M. this evening" is so specific that any violation of the rule—for example, it is now 7:10 P.M. and we are still watching television—will be readily apparent. This is related to the notion, discussed in Chapter 10, that each choice in a self-control situation often has only a small but cumulative effect upon the overall outcome. Each Greaze-Burger that we eat will not, by itself, undermine our efforts at attaining good health; rather, it is only the repeated consumption of unhealthy foods like Greaze-Burgers that undermines our health. If we wish to occasionally indulge in such treats, it will help to clearly specify the level at which we will do so, since there is no natural boundary indicating the point at which further indulgence will significantly undermine our health.

The importance of clear, specific rules has been empirically supported. For example, Gollwitzer and Brandstätter (1997) asked college students to name two projects they intended to complete during Christmas break, one of which would be easy to accomplish (e.g., go skating) and the other of which would be difficult to accomplish (e.g., complete an English assignment). Students were also asked if they had made a decision about when and where the activity would be carried out. Following the Christmas break, the same students were asked if they had completed the project. For activities that were easy to implement, about 80% of the students said they had indeed completed them. With such easy projects, it seemed to make little difference if the students had also decided upon a time and place for implementing them. For difficult projects, however, students who had decided when and where their project would be carried out were significantly more likely to have completed it compared to those who had not made such a decision. In other research, participants who specified when and where they would take a vitamin supplement were significantly more consistent in taking the supplement than were those who merely intended to take the supplement (Sheeran & Orbell, 1999); likewise, patients who specified when, where, and how they would make a cervical cancer screening appointment were more likely to obtain such screening than were those who had not made such plans (Sheeran & Orbell, 2000).

More recently, Luszczynska, Sobczyk, and Abraham (2007) asked a group of Weight Watchers participants to formulate specific food and exercise plans for each day throughout the week (e.g., "This is my plan concerning the consumption of sweets for the next 7 days. I plan to eat . . . [listing type and amount of sweets] at . . . [indicating time at which it would be eaten] at . . . [indicating place at which it would be eaten]"). The participants also made specific relapse prevention plans for how they would cope with temptations that might arise ("If someone offers me my favorite unhealthy food, then I will . . ."). Compared to a control group of Weight Watchers participants who did not formulate such plans, those who did lost twice as much weight during a 2-month period.

Thus, the act of specifying when, where, and how a goal is to be accomplished can significantly affect the probability of accomplishing that goal. Gollwitzer (1999) refers to such when-where-and-how statements as *implementation intentions*. However, to be more consistent with Ainslie's (1992) terminology, they could also be called ***personal process rules***, insofar as they are personal rules that indicate the specific process by which a task is to be accomplished. And a possible reason such rules are effective is that they establish a bright boundary between actions that conform to the rule and those that do not.

QUICK QUIZ M

1. A p_____ rule is a description of a contingency that we verbalize to ourselves to influence our own behavior.

2. A close match between what we say we are going to do and what we actually do at a later point in time is called a _____-_____ c_____.

3. People who have been trained to display a high level of _____-_____ correspondence can more effectively use personal rules (or self-instructions) to influence their behavior.

4. P_____ p_____ rules indicate the specific process by which a task is to be carried out. The formulation of such rules tends to (increase/decrease) _____ the likelihood that the task will be accomplished. Such rules have also been called im_____ i_____.

And Furthermore

Say–Do Correspondence and Willpower

Using personal rules to regulate one's behavior represents a form of say–do correspondence. Moreover, to the extent that one displays a strong level of say–do correspondence, such personal rules might even function as a type of *commitment* response. As you may recall from Chapter 10, a commitment response is any response made at an early point in time that so reduces the value of a smaller sooner reward that it no longer serves as a temptation when it becomes imminent. One is therefore able to ignore the temptation and carry on working toward a larger later reward. Thus, handing your sister $10 with the understanding that she will return it only if you have completed a certain amount of studying that evening will reduce the value of any nonstudy activity to a level where you will in fact be quite likely to study (because any activity that interferes with studying will be associated with the loss of $10). Perhaps, however, people who display a very strong level of say–do correspondence do not require such artificial consequences to control their behavior; perhaps for them the mere act of promising to do something is by itself a sufficient form of commitment.

To what extent can self-promises serve as a strong form of commitment? Consider the following passage from a letter quoted by William James (1907) in his classic article, "The Energies of Men":

> My device [Prince Pueckler-Muskau writes to his wife] is this: I give my word of honour most solemnly to myself to do or to leave undone this or that. I am of course extremely cautious in the use of this expedient, but when once the word is given, even though I afterwards think I have been precipitate or mistaken, I hold it to be perfectly irrevocable, whatever inconveniences I foresee likely to result. If I were capable of breaking my word after such mature consideration, I should lose all respect for myself—and what man of sense would not prefer death to such an alternative? (p. 16)

The prince describes how, once he has vowed to perform or not perform an activity, he feels duty bound to carry out this vow. As a result, he is able to use this device to accomplish tasks that would otherwise be very difficult. He is also extremely careful in using this device, recognizing that its potency lies in the fact that he *always* keeps his word in such matters. In other words, a major consequence motivating adherence to his verbal commitments is that he always keeps these commitments, and to the extent that he does so they will remain a valuable tool (see also Ainslie, 1992). Note, too, how the prince pronounces these verbal commitments in a "most solemn" manner, thereby establishing a *bright boundary* between statements of intention that must be fulfilled ("I swear most solemnly that I shall complete this project by the weekend") and more ordinary statements of intention, which do not represent a commitment ("I should really try to complete this project by the weekend").

Another example of the power of verbal commitments can be found in the life of Mohandas K. (Mahatma) Gandhi, the famous statesman who led India to independence and whose philosophy of passive resistance strongly influenced Martin Luther King Jr. In his autobiography (1927/1957), Gandhi reveals that he made frequent use of verbal commitments to control his behavior and that the effectiveness of these commitments lay partly in the fact that breaking a commitment produced within him a tremendous feeling of guilt. At one point, for example, he was severely ill and was strongly urged by his doctors to drink milk (as a needed source of protein). As a committed vegetarian, he refused, maintaining that he would rather die than break his vow never to eat animal products. Only when his advisors pointed out to him that he had probably been thinking of cow's milk when he made his vow and not goat's milk did he acquiesce and drink goat's milk. He recovered from his illness but nevertheless felt considerable guilt over violating the spirit, if not the precise intention, of the vow he had made.

The great Indian statesman, Mahatma Gandhi, displayed a considerable degree of "say–do correspondence" during his illustrious life.

© Bettmann/CORBIS

The strength of Gandhi's verbal commitments is also illustrated by the effect of his vow to remain sexually abstinent (despite being married). Before making the vow—and believing that it should be possible to practice abstinence without a vow—he had found the task extremely difficult. Making the vow, however, immediately resolved these difficulties. As he later wrote:

> As I look back on the twenty years of the vow, I am filled with pleasure and wonderment. The more or less successful practice of self-control had been going on since 1901. But the freedom and joy that came to me after taking the vow had never been experienced before 1906. Before the vow I had been open to being overcome by temptation at any moment. Now the vow was a sure shield against temptation. (Gandhi, 1927/1957, p. 208)

Gandhi's description indicates that the vow was such a strong form of commitment that it essentially eliminated the temptation to engage in sexual intercourse, thereby removing any sense of conflict.

You may remember how, in our discussion of self-control in Chapter 10, we rejected the concept of willpower as useful, arguing instead that it was often no more than a descriptive term for the fact that a person had in fact been able to resist a temptation. Perhaps, however, the concept of willpower is useful if what it refers to is an individual's ability to make use of a verbal commitment—derived in turn from a history of training in strong say–do correspondence—to exert control over his or her behavior. In this sense, some individuals may indeed have a considerable amount of willpower. Thus, as often happens when we examine traditional concepts from a behavioral perspective, the examination results not so much in a rejection of the concept but in a new and possibly useful way of understanding it.

Finally, are there lessons in this for those of us who wish that we could more often carry through on our own verbal commitments? Although we may not be capable of acquiring the same ability as Gandhi (nor perhaps would many of us even desire such

(Continued)

an ability), most of us would probably agree that we are too often lacking in our level of say–do correspondence. In this regard, we might do well to close with yet another passage from William James (1890/1983), who wrote often on the concept of will (bracketed comments are ours):

> As a final practical maxim, relative to these habits of the will, we may, then, offer something like this: *Keep the faculty of effort alive in you by a little gratuitous effort every day.* That is, be systematically ascetic or heroic in little unnecessary points, do every day or two something for no other reason than that you would rather not do it [*and because you promised yourself you would do it*], so that when the hour of dire need draws nigh, it may find you not unnerved and untrained to stand the test. Asceticism of this sort is like the insurance which a man pays on his house and goods. The tax does him no good at the time, and possibly may never bring him a return. But if the fire *does* come, his having paid it will be his salvation from ruin. So with the man who has daily inured himself to habits of concentrated attention, energetic volition, and self-denial in unnecessary things. He will stand like a tower when everything rocks around him, and when his softer fellow-mortals are winnowed like chaff in the blast. (p. 130; see also Barrett, 1931, and Assagioli, 1974; see Oaten and Cheng, 2006, for evidence concerning the extent to which repeated practice at self-control on one task can generalize to other tasks.)

SUMMARY

In observational learning, an observer's behavior is altered as a result of socially interacting with or observing the behavior of a model. Two simple forms of observational influence are contagious behavior and stimulus enhancement. In the classical conditioning aspect of observational learning, the emotional cues exhibited by a model serve as CSs that elicit conditioned responses, called vicarious emotional responses, in an observer. The operant conditioning aspect of observational learning concerns the manner in which a model's operant behavior is translated into the behavior of an observer. First, the observer must acquire information from the model. Such acquisition depends on the consequences of the model's behavior, the personal characteristics of the model, whether the observer is capable of understanding and duplicating the modeled behavior, and whether the observer is explicitly reinforced for attending to the modeled behavior. Translating acquired knowledge into performance in turn depends on whether the observer's performance of the behavior is reinforced or punished.

Animals also learn by observation. However, unlike humans, many animal species appear to be unable to truly imitate the actions of another individual. Apparent examples of imitation can often be explained as examples of stimulus enhancement, which involves directing an animal's attention to a particular place or object, thereby making it more likely that the animal will approach that place or object. There is evidence, however, of true imitation in some species, and perhaps even intentional teaching.

Although much social learning is beneficial and positive, social learning of violent behavior is more controversial, especially in the context of exposure to violence through mass media and interactive games. Bandura (1965) initially warned of the power of social learning of violent behavior in his classic "Bobo doll studies." More recent correlational and experimental evidence suggests that exposure to media violence increases the likelihood that a person will behave violently, or perhaps become a victim of violence.

Defining characteristics of language include reference, grammar, situational freedom, and productivity. Research programs have attempted to teach animals, mostly chimpanzees, a human-like language. The first studies in this area attempted, unsuccessfully, to teach chimpanzees to speak. Later studies focused on teaching them to use gestural (sign) language. The chimps learned to use dozens of signs, although systematic assessment of their abilities was difficult. To obtain more experimental control, later studies were conducted in laboratory situations with artificially constructed languages. The chimpanzees participating in these experiments readily used the symbols to refer to food items and behaviors, but evidence of grammatical ability was again less clear. Other species, most notably dolphins, have also demonstrated that they can learn that symbols can be used to represent and categorize objects and actions. They have also shown some evidence of grammatical ability.

A rule is a verbal description of a contingency, and behavior that is generated as a result of such rules is known as rule-governed behavior. A rule that also includes information about how we should behave in a setting is an instruction. Rules are tremendously adaptive in that they allow us to learn about contingencies without having to directly experience those contingencies. Parents spend considerable effort training their children to follow rules, and children learn that following rules not only leads to praise but also facilitates accomplishing a task.

Nevertheless, rules have their drawbacks. First, rule-governed behavior is often less efficient than behavior that has been shaped by actual contingencies. Second, rule-governed behavior is sometimes surprisingly insensitive to contingencies. A personal rule (or self-instruction) is a description of a contingency that we verbalize to ourselves to influence our own behavior. The use of personal rules to regulate behavior is dependent on training in say–do correspondence, which occurs when there is a close match between what we say we are going to do and what we actually do at a later time. Personal rules tend to be most effective when they are stated in such a way that there is a clear distinction (a bright boundary) between when the rule has been followed and when it has not. In support of this, researchers have shown that specifying personal process rules (or implementation intentions) indicating the specific manner in which a project is to be carried out increases the likelihood that the project will be accomplished.

SUGGESTED READINGS

Savage-Rumbaugh, E. S., Shanker, S. G., & Taylor, T. J. (1998). *Apes, language and the human mind.* New York: Oxford University Press. The evidence for language learning in apes, presented by one of the premiere researchers in the field.

Bushman, B. J., & Anderson, C. A. (2001). Media violence and the American public: Scientific facts versus media information. *American Psychologist, 56,* 477–489. A fascinating presentation of just how strong the evidence is for the harmful effects of media violence on viewers, and how this finding has remained hidden from the general public.

STUDY QUESTIONS

1. Define observational learning, and give an example. Be sure to clearly differentiate the model from the observer.
2. Define contagious behavior and stimulus enhancement, and give an example of each.
3. Define vicarious emotional responses. Diagram the conditioning process by which a smile can become a conditioned stimulus for pleasant emotions.
4. Distinguish the roles of classical and operant conditioning in observational learning.
5. List three important features that determine whether an observer will attend to a model's behavior.
6. List three ways in which acquisition of information through observational learning translates into performance of the behavior.
7. Define true imitation. Describe evidence that some animals are capable of imitation.
8. Define stimulus enhancement. How does it differ from true imitation?
9. Use examples to illustrate the difference between stimulus enhancement and true imitation.
10. Describe Bandura's Bobo doll studies. What were the main conclusions from those studies?
11. Describe research which indicates that interaction with violent media increases the risk of violent behavior.
12. What are the sex differences associated with exposure to violent media and subsequent violent behavior?
13. Why has evidence about the relationship between violent media and violent behavior been underestimated or ignored?
14. List four main features of language, and provide an example of each.
15. Distinguish between ASL and artificial language studies. What was the reasoning behind each type of study?
16. Provide at least two examples of evidence supporting the notion that animals can use rudimentary language.
17. Define the terms *rule* and *rule-governed behavior*. What is the distinction between a rule and an instruction?

18. Describe the main advantage of rule-governed behavior over contingency-shaped behavior. What are two disadvantages of rule-governed behavior?
19. What is a personal rule? What is say–do correspondence, and how is it related to the effectiveness of personal rules for controlling behavior?
20. What is a personal process rule (or implementation intention)? Why (in terms of bright boundaries) are personal process rules particularly effective?

CONCEPT REVIEW

contagious behavior. A more-or-less instinctive or reflexive behavior triggered by the occurrence of the same behavior in another individual.

generalized imitation. The tendency to imitate a new modeled behavior in the absence of any specific reinforcement for doing so.

grammar. The rules that control the meaning of a sequence of language symbols.

observational learning. The process whereby the behavior of a model is witnessed by an observer, and the observer's behavior is subsequently altered.

personal process rule. A personal rule that indicates the specific process by which a task is to be accomplished. (Also referred to as an *implementation intention.*)

personal rule (or self-instruction). A verbal description of a contingency that we present to ourselves to influence our behavior.

productivity. The ability of language users to combine language symbols in new and creative ways.

reference. The ability to associate arbitrary symbols with objects or events.

rule. A verbal description of a contingency.

rule-governed behavior. Behavior that has been generated through exposure to rules.

say–do correspondence. A close match between what we say we are going to do and what we actually do at a later time.

situational freedom. Language can be used in a variety of contexts and is not fixed in a particular situation.

stimulus enhancement. Directing attention to a particular place or object, making it more likely that the observer will approach that place or object.

true imitation. Duplicating a novel behavior (or sequence of behaviors) to achieve a specific goal.

vicarious emotional response. A classically conditioned emotional response resulting from seeing that emotional response exhibited by others.

CHAPTER TEST

11. Many animal species, when shown a sequence of actions designed to extract food from a locked box, (do/do not) _____ duplicate the sequence exactly. This suggests that few species exhibit true _____.

28. The name of the first artificial language employed in language-learning studies with apes is _____.

1. Improving your golf game by watching a video of an excellent golf player is a form of _____ learning.

20. Knowing that the phrase "dog bites man" means the opposite of "man bites dog" suggests that you know the _____ of the English language.

26. Artificial language experiments taught (laboratory-constructed/ASL) _____ languages to apes.

25. At the start of each day, Victoria carefully plans out her studying for the day, writing down what she will study as well as when and where she will study. Although she is not always successful in fulfilling these plans, she usually accomplishes most of what she sets out to do. Her success is likely due to the fact that she is making use of personal _____ rules that establish a(n) _____ boundary between acceptable and unacceptable patterns of behavior.

6. If Claire observes her friend David laughing while enjoying a game of table tennis, she is (more/less) _____ likely to try the game herself. If Claire observes David frowning while he struggles over a math problem, she is (more/less) _____ likely to tackle the problem herself.

32. A rule that includes information about how we should respond is called a(n) _____.

38. "I should sit straight while working on the computer if I wish to prevent back problems." This is an example of a(n) _____ rule (or self-_____).

12. If a dog sees another dog eating at a particular location, it is more likely to visit that location later. This is an example of _____.

21. Your ability to discuss plans for an upcoming vacation means that language has the feature of _____.

27. Cross-fostering studies taught (laboratory-constructed/gestural) _____ languages (such as ASL) to apes.

5. The stimuli involved in the classical conditioning aspect of observational learning are often (emotional/rational) _____ in nature.

10. Tina tells herself each day that she will study, but she rarely succeeds in doing so. This illustrates a lack of _____ correspondence, which also means that, in general, she may have difficulty using _____ rules to control her behavior.

24. American Sign Language is a (spoken/written/symbolic) _____ language.

3. Smiling, yawning, laughing, and orienting when others do so are all examples of _____.

33. A big advantage of rules is that one (has to/does not have to) _____ directly experience a set of contingencies to behave appropriately with respect to those contingencies.

14. Bandura demonstrated that children who observed violent models were (more/less) _____ likely to behave violently themselves. Further, the behavior of the observers was so (similar/dissimilar) _____ to that of the models, it could be considered _____.

2. Observational learning can be involved in both _____ and _____ conditioning.

18. A belief that language in humans is (innate/learned) _____ also implies that animals may be able to learn and use language.

16. Longitudinal studies have demonstrated that exposure to violent media is _____ with violent behavior and criminality by observers.

35. Joel is very noncompliant. Chances are that he has received reinforcement for (following/not following) _____ instructions and/or punished for (following/not following) _____ instructions.

13. Directing a person's or animal's attention to an object or place is called _____; duplicating the actions of a model to obtain a goal is called _____.

4. Contagion of orienting responses is closely related to the process of s_____ e_____.

29. Results of artificial language experiments (do/do not) _____ provide strong support for the notion that most apes can master the rules of grammar.

23. Although chimpanzees cannot (speak/use sign language) _____, they have been taught to successfully (speak/use sign language) _____.

36. When Salima's mom became ill with a neurological disorder, Salima was assigned the task of giving her a daily massage to loosen up her tense muscles. By contrast, Byron has taken several massage workshops. Interestingly, Byron is much less skillful at massage than Salima, which may reflect the fact that _____ behavior is sometimes less efficient than behavior that has been shaped through direct exposure to the natural _____.

17. Exposure to violent media may increase observers' violent behavior; it may also make some observers more likely to become _____ of violence. This is especially likely with (males/females) _____.

8. After training her daughter to imitate the manner in which she eats food with a knife and fork, Ashley noticed her daughter spontaneously imitating the manner in which Ashley uses a spoon to eat soup. This is an example of a process known as _____.

19. The word *cat* stands for "four-legged, furry animals that meow." This illustrates the language characteristic of _____.

34. Children receive reinforcement for following instructions, both by their caretakers and by the fact that instructions can help them accomplish a task. As a result, most children acquire a (generalized/specific) _____ tendency to follow instructions.

9. If a juvenile rat watches its mother eat a novel food, like chocolate chips, the young rat is (more/less/neither more nor less) _____ likely to try the chocolate chips.

31. A(n) _____ can be defined as a verbal description of a contingency, while _____ behavior is the behavior that is generated by such verbal descriptions.

15. Bandura determined that children were affected both by live violence and _____ violence. Thus, Bandura was the first to demonstrate the potential influence of the mass m_____ on violent behavior.

37. Kent read somewhere that women are very attracted to a man who acts strong and dominant. Despite his efforts to appear strong and dominant, he is eventually dumped by every woman he meets. He nevertheless assumes that there must be something wrong with these women and persists in cultivating his heroic image. Kent's problem may reflect the fact that _____ behavior is sometimes surprisingly insensitive to the actual contingencies of reinforcement.

22. Your ability to write a short story for your creative writing class illustrates the _____ characteristic of language.

 7. If a model receives reinforcement for performing a behavior, an observer is (more/less) _____ likely to perform the same behavior; if a model receives punishment for performing a behavior, an observer is (more/less) _____ likely to perform the same behavior.

30. Results of artificial language experiments suggest that dolphins (can/cannot) _____ master the rules of grammar.

Visit the book companion Web site at <http://www.academic.cengage.com/ psychology/powell> for additional practice questions, answers to the Quick Quizzes, practice review exams, and additional exercises and information.

ANSWERS TO CHAPTER TEST

 1. observational
 2. classical; operant
 3. contagious behaviors
 4. stimulus enhancement
 5. emotional
 6. more; less
 7. more; less
 8. generalized imitation
 9. more
10. say–do; personal
11. do not; imitation
12. stimulus enhancement
13. stimulus enhancement; true imitation
14. more; similar; true imitation
15. filmed; media
16. strongly (positively) correlated
17. victims; female
18. learned
19. reference

20. grammar
21. situational freedom
22. productivity
23. speak; use sign language
24. symbolic
25. process; bright
26. laboratory-constructed
27. gestural
28. Yerkish
29. do not
30. can
31. rule; rule-governed
32. instruction
33. does not have to
34. generalized
35. not following; following
36. rule-governed; contingencies
37. rule-governed
38. personal; instruction

Glossary

acquisition. The process of developing and strengthening a conditioned response through repeated pairings of an NS (or CS) with a US.

activity anorexia. An abnormally high level of activity and low level of food intake generated by exposure to a restricted schedule of feeding.

adjunctive behavior. An excessive pattern of behavior that emerges as a by-product of an intermittent schedule of reinforcement for some other behavior.

adjusting schedule. A schedule in which the response requirement changes as a function of the organism's performance while responding for the previous reinforcer.

anticipatory contrast. The process whereby the rate of response varies inversely with an upcoming ("anticipated") change in the rate of reinforcement.

appetitive conditioning. Conditioning procedure in which the US is an event that is usually considered pleasant and that an organism seeks out.

appetitive stimulus. An event that an organism will seek out.

applied behavior analysis. A technology of behavior in which basic principles of behavior are applied to real-world issues.

autoshaping. A type of sign tracking in which a pigeon comes to automatically peck at a response key because the key light has been associated with the response-independent delivery of food.

aversion therapy. A form of behavior therapy that attempts to reduce the attractiveness of a desired event by associating it with an aversive stimulus.

aversive conditioning. Conditioning procedure in which the US is an event that is usually considered unpleasant and that an organism avoids.

aversive stimulus. An event that an organism will avoid.

avoidance behavior. Behavior that occurs before the aversive stimulus is presented and therefore prevents its delivery.

avoidance theory of punishment. The theory that punishment involves a type of avoidance conditioning in which the avoidance response consists of any behavior other than the behavior being punished.

backward conditioning. Conditioning procedure in which the onset of the NS follows the onset of the US.

baseline. The normal frequency of a behavior before some intervention.

behavior. Any activity of an organism that can be observed or somehow measured.

behavior analysis (or experimental analysis of behavior). The behavioral science that grew out of Skinner's philosophy of radical behaviorism.

behavior systems theory. A theory proposing that an animal's behavior is organized into various motivational systems; each of these systems encompasses a set of relevant responses, each of which, in turn, can be activated by particular cues.

behavioral bliss point approach. The theory that an organism with free access to alternative activities will distribute its behavior in such a way as to maximize overall reinforcement.

behavioral contrast. A change in the rate of *reinforcement* on one component of a multiple schedule produces an opposite change in the rate of *response* on another component.

behaviorism. A natural science approach to psychology that traditionally focuses on the study of environmental influences on observable behavior.

bias from matching. A deviation from matching in which one alternative attracts a higher proportion of responses than would be predicted by matching, regardless of whether that alternative contains the richer versus poorer schedule.

blocking. The phenomenon whereby the presence of an established CS interferes with conditioning of a new CS.

British empiricism. A philosophical school of thought (of which John Locke was a member) maintaining that almost all knowledge is a function of experience.

case study approach. A descriptive research approach that involves intensive examination of one or a few individuals.

chained schedule. A schedule consisting of a sequence of two or more simple schedules, each with its own S^D and the last of which results in a terminal reinforcer.

changing-criterion design. A type of single-subject design in which the effect of the treatment is demonstrated by how closely the behavior matches a criterion that is systematically altered.

classical conditioning. A process whereby one stimulus that does not elicit a certain response is associated with a second stimulus that does; as a result, the first stimulus also comes to elicit a response.

cognitive behaviorism. A brand of behaviorism that utilizes intervening variables, usually in the form of hypothesized cognitive processes, to help explain behavior. Sometimes called "purposive behaviorism."

cognitive map. The mental representation of one's spatial surroundings.

commitment response. An action carried out at an early point in time that serves to either eliminate or reduce the value of an upcoming temptation.

comparative design. A type of control group design in which different species constitute one of the independent variables.

compensatory-response model. A model of conditioning in which a CS that has been repeatedly associated with the primary response (a-process) to a US will eventually come to elicit a compensatory response (b-process).

complex schedule. A schedule consisting of a combination of two or more simple schedules.

compound stimulus. A complex stimulus that consists of the simultaneous presentation of two or more individual stimuli.

concurrent schedule of reinforcement. A complex schedule consisting of the simultaneous presentation of two or more independent schedules, each leading to a reinforcer.

conditioned response (CR). The response, often similar to the unconditioned response, that is elicited by the conditioned stimulus.

conditioned stimulus (CS). Any stimulus that, although initially neutral, comes to elicit a response because it has been associated with an unconditioned stimulus.

conditioned suppression theory of punishment. The assumption that punishment does not weaken a behavior, but instead produces an emotional response that interferes with the occurrence of the behavior.

conjunctive schedule. A type of complex schedule in which the requirements of two or more simple schedules must be met before a reinforcer is delivered.

contagious behavior. A more-or-less instinctive or reflexive behavior triggered by the occurrence of the same behavior in another individual.

contingency. A predictive relationship between two events such that the occurrence of one event predicts the probable occurrence of the other.

continuous reinforcement schedule. A schedule in which each specified response is reinforced.

contrived reinforcers. Reinforcers that have been deliberately arranged to modify a behavior; they are not a typical consequence of the behavior in that setting.

control group design. A type of experiment in which, at its simplest, subjects are randomly assigned to either an experimental (or treatment) group or a control group; subjects assigned to the experimental group are exposed to a certain manipulation or treatment, while those assigned to the control group are not.

counterconditioning. The procedure whereby a CS that elicits one type of response is associated with an event that elicits an incompatible response.

countercontrol. The deliberate manipulation of environmental events to alter their impact on our behavior.

covert behavior. Behavior that can be *subjectively* perceived only by the person performing the behavior. Thoughts and feelings are covert behaviors.

CS–US relevance. An innate tendency to easily associate certain types of stimuli with each other.

cumulative recorder. A device that measures total number of responses over time and provides a graphic depiction of the rate of behavior.

delayed conditioning. Conditioning procedure in which the onset of the NS precedes the onset of the US, and the two stimuli overlap.

delayed matching-to-sample. An experimental procedure in which the animal is first shown a sample stimulus and then, following some delay, is required to select that stimulus out of a group of alternative stimuli.

dependent variable. That aspect of an experiment that is allowed to freely vary to determine if it is affected by changes in the independent variable.

deprivation. The prolonged absence of an event that tends to increase the appetitiveness of that event.

descriptive research. Research that focuses on describing the behavior and the situation within which it occurs.

differential reinforcement of high rates (DRH). A schedule in which reinforcement is contingent upon emitting at least a certain number of responses in a certain period of time—or, more generally, reinforcement is provided for responding at a fast rate.

differential reinforcement of low rates (DRL). A schedule in which a minimum amount of time must pass between each response before the reinforcer will be delivered—or, more generally, reinforcement is provided for responding at a slow rate.

differential reinforcement of other behavior (DRO). Reinforcement of any behavior other than a target behavior that is being extinguished. One variant of this is called differential reinforcement of incompatible behavior (DRI), in which the behavior that is being reinforced is specifically incompatible with the behavior being extinguished.

differential reinforcement of paced responding (DRP). A schedule in which reinforcement is contingent upon emitting a series of responses at a set rate—or, more generally, reinforcement is provided for responding neither too fast nor too slow.

discrimination training. As applied to operant conditioning, the differential reinforcement of responding in the presence of one stimulus (the S^D) and not another.

discriminative stimulus (S^D). A stimulus in the presence of which responses are reinforced and in the absence of which they are not reinforced.

discriminative stimulus for extinction (S^{Δ}). A stimulus that signals the absence of reinforcement.

discriminative stimulus for punishment. A stimulus that signals that a response will be punished.

dishabituation. The reappearance of a habituated response following the presentation of a seemingly irrelevant novel stimulus.

disinhibition. The sudden recovery of a response during an extinction procedure when a novel stimulus is introduced.

displacement activity. An apparently irrelevant activity sometimes displayed by animals when confronted by conflict or thwarted from attaining a goal.

drive reduction theory. According to this theory, an event is reinforcing to the extent that it is associated with a reduction in some type of physiological drive.

duration. The length of time that an individual repeatedly or continuously performs a certain behavior.

empiricism. In psychology, the assumption that behavior patterns are mostly learned rather than inherited. Also known as the *nurture* perspective (or, more rarely, as *nurturism*).

errorless discrimination training. A discrimination training procedure that minimizes the number of errors (i.e., nonreinforced responses to the S^Δ) and reduces many of the adverse effects associated with discrimination training.

escape behavior. A behavior that results in the termination of an aversive stimulus.

establishing operation. A procedure that affects the appetitiveness or aversiveness of a stimulus.

evolutionary adaptation. An inherited trait (physical or behavioral) that has been shaped through natural selection.

excitatory conditioning. Conditioning procedure in which the NS is associated with the *presentation* of a US.

experimental neurosis. An experimentally produced disorder in which animals exposed to unpredictable events develop neurotic-like symptoms.

exposure and response prevention (ERP). A method of treating obsessive-compulsive behavior that involves prolonged exposure to anxiety-arousing events while not engaging in the compulsive behavior pattern that reduces the anxiety.

external inhibition. A decrease in the strength of the conditioned response due to the presentation of a novel stimulus at the same time as the conditioned stimulus.

extinction. In classical conditioning, the repeated presentation of the CS in the absence of the US, the result of which is a decrease in the strength of the CR; in operant conditioning, the nonreinforcement of a previously reinforced response, the result of which is a decrease in the strength of that response. Note that extinction can be both a procedure and a process. The procedure of extinction is the manner in which extinction is carried out, for example, in operant conditioning the nonreinforcement of a previously reinforced response. The process of extinction is the subsequent decrease in the strength of the response.

extinction burst. A temporary increase in the frequency and intensity of responding when extinction is first implemented.

extrinsic punishment. Punishment that is not an inherent aspect of the behavior being punished but that simply follows the behavior.

extrinsic reinforcement. The reinforcement provided by a consequence that is external to the behavior, that is, an extrinsic reinforcer.

fading. The process of gradually altering the intensity of a stimulus.

fixed action pattern. A fixed sequence of responses elicited by a specific stimulus.

fixed duration (FD) schedule. A schedule in which reinforcement is contingent upon continuous performance of a behavior for a fixed, predictable period of time.

fixed interval (FI) schedule. A schedule in which reinforcement is contingent upon the first response after a fixed, predictable period of time.

fixed ratio (FR) schedule. A schedule in which reinforcement is contingent upon a fixed, predictable number of responses.

fixed time (FT) schedule. A schedule in which the reinforcer is delivered following a fixed, predictable period of time, regardless of the organism's behavior.

flexion response. The automatic response of jerking one's hand or foot away from a hot or sharp object.

flooding therapy. A behavioral treatment for phobias that involves prolonged exposure to a feared stimulus, thereby providing maximal opportunity for the conditioned fear response to extinguish.

functional relationship. The relationship between changes in an independent variable and changes in a dependent variable; a cause-and-effect relationship.

functionalism. An approach to psychology holding that the mind evolved to help us adapt to the world around us, and that the focus of psychology should be the study of those adaptive processes.

generalization gradient. A graphic description of the strength of responding in the presence of stimuli that are similar to the S^D and vary along a continuum.

generalized imitation. The tendency to imitate a new modeled behavior in the absence of any specific reinforcement for doing so.

generalized (or generalized secondary) punisher. An event that has become punishing because it has in the past been associated with many other punishers.

generalized (or generalized secondary) reinforcer. A type of secondary reinforcer that has been associated with several other reinforcers.

goal gradient effect. An increase in the strength and/or efficiency of responding as one draws near to the goal.

grammar. The rules that control the meaning of a sequence of language symbols.

habituation. A decrease in the strength of an elicited behavior following repeated presentations of the eliciting stimulus.

higher-order conditioning. The process whereby a stimulus that is associated with a CS also becomes a CS.

impulsiveness. With respect to choice between two rewards, selecting a smaller sooner reward over a larger later reward.

incentive motivation. Motivation derived from some property of the reinforcer, as opposed to an internal drive state.

incubation. The strengthening of a conditioned fear response as a result of brief exposures to the aversive CS.

independent variable. That aspect of an experiment that is made to systematically vary across the different conditions in an experiment.

inhibitory conditioning. Conditioning procedure in which the NS is associated with the *absence* or *removal* of a US.

instinctive drift. An instance of classical conditioning in which a genetically based, fixed action pattern gradually emerges and displaces a behavior that is being operantly conditioned.

intensity. The force or magnitude of a behavior.

intermittent (or partial) reinforcement schedule. A schedule in which only some responses are reinforced.

interval recording. The measurement of whether or not a behavior occurs within a series of continuous intervals. (The number of times that it occurs within each interval is irrelevant.)

intrinsic punishment. Punishment that is an inherent aspect of the behavior being punished.

intrinsic reinforcement. Reinforcement provided by the mere act of performing the behavior; the performance of the behavior is inherently reinforcing.

introspection. The attempt to accurately describe one's conscious thoughts, emotions, and sensory experiences.

latency. The length of time required for a behavior to begin.

latent inhibition. The phenomenon whereby a familiar stimulus is more difficult to condition as a CS than is an unfamiliar (novel) stimulus.

latent learning. Learning that occurs in the absence of any observable demonstration of learning and only becomes apparent under a different set of conditions.

law of contiguity. A law of association holding that events that occur in close proximity to each other in time or space are readily associated with each other.

law of contrast. A law of association holding that events that are opposite from each other are readily associated.

law of effect. As stated by Thorndike, the proposition that behaviors that lead to a satisfying state of affairs are strengthened or "stamped in," while behaviors that lead to an unsatisfying or annoying state of affairs are weakened or "stamped out."

law of frequency. A law of association holding that the more frequently two items occur together, the more strongly they are associated.

law of parsimony. The assumption that simpler explanations for a phenomenon are generally preferable to more complex explanations.

law of similarity. A law of association holding that events that are similar to each other are readily associated.

learned helplessness. A decrement in learning ability that results from repeated exposure to uncontrollable aversive events.

learning. A relatively permanent change in behavior that results from some type of experience.

matching law. The principle that the *proportion* of responses emitted on a particular schedule matches the *proportion* of reinforcers obtained on that schedule.

melioration theory. A theory of matching that holds that the distribution of behavior in a choice situation shifts toward those alternatives that have higher value regardless of the long-term effect on overall amount of reinforcement.

methodological behaviorism. A brand of behaviorism that asserts that, for methodological reasons, psychologists should study only those behaviors that can be directly observed.

mind–body dualism. Descartes' philosophical assumption that some human behaviors are bodily reflexes that are automatically elicited by external stimulation, while other behaviors are freely chosen and controlled by the mind.

multiple-baseline design. A type of single-subject design in which a treatment is instituted at successive points in time for two or more persons, settings, or behaviors.

multiple schedule. A complex schedule consisting of two or more independent schedules presented in sequence, each resulting in reinforcement and each having a distinctive S^D.

nativism. The assumption that a person's characteristics are largely inborn. Also known as the *nature* perspective.

natural reinforcers. Reinforcers that are naturally provided for a certain behavior; that is, they are a typical consequence of the behavior within that setting.

natural selection. The evolutionary principle according to which organisms that are better able to adapt to environmental pressures are more likely to survive and reproduce than those that cannot adapt.

naturalistic observation. A descriptive research approach that involves the systematic observation and recording of behavior in its natural environment.

negative contrast effect. The process whereby an increase in the rate of *reinforcement* on one component of a multiple schedule produces a decrease in the rate of *response* on the other component.

negative punishment. The removal of a stimulus (one that is usually considered pleasant or rewarding) following a response, which then leads to a decrease in the future strength of that response.

negative reinforcement. The removal of a stimulus (one that is usually considered unpleasant or aversive) following a response, which then leads to an increase in the future strength of that response.

neobehaviorism. A brand of behaviorism that utilizes intervening variables, in the form of hypothesized physiological processes, to help explain behavior.

noncontingent schedule of reinforcement. A schedule in which the reinforcer is delivered independently of any response.

observational learning. The process whereby the behavior of a model is witnessed by an observer, and the observer's behavior is subsequently altered.

occasion setting. A procedure in which a stimulus (known as an *occasion setter*) signals that a CS is likely to be followed by the US with which it is associated.

operant behavior. A class of emitted responses that result in certain consequences; these consequences, in turn, affect the future probability or strength of those responses.

operant conditioning. A type of learning in which the future probability of a behavior is affected by its consequences.

opponent-process theory. A theory proposing that an emotional event elicits two competing processes: (1) an a-process (or primary process) directly elicited by the event, and (2) a b-process (or opponent process) that is elicited by the a-process and serves to counteract the a-process.

orienting response. The automatic positioning of oneself to facilitate attending to a stimulus.

overexpectation effect. The decrease in the conditioned response that occurs when two separately conditioned CSs are combined into a compound stimulus for further pairings with the US.

overmatching. A deviation from matching in which the proportion of responses on the richer schedule versus poorer schedule is more different than would be predicted by matching.

overshadowing. The phenomenon whereby the most salient member of a compound stimulus is more readily conditioned as a CS and thereby interferes with conditioning of the less salient member.

overt behavior. Behavior that has the potential for being directly observed by an individual other than the one performing the behavior.

partial reinforcement effect. The process whereby behavior that has been maintained on an intermittent (partial) schedule of reinforcement extinguishes more slowly than behavior that has been maintained on a continuous schedule.

peak shift effect. Following discrimination training, the peak of a generalization gradient will shift from the S^D to a stimulus that is further removed from the S^Δ.

personal process rule. A personal rule that indicates the specific process by which a task is to be accomplished. (Also referred to as an *implementation intention*.)

personal rule (or self-instruction). A verbal description of a contingency that we present to ourselves to influence our behavior.

positive behavioral contrast. The process whereby a decrease in rate of reinforcement on one component of a multiple schedule produces an increase in the rate of response on the other component.

positive punishment. The presentation of a stimulus (one that is usually considered unpleasant or aversive) following a response, which then leads to a decrease in the future strength of that response.

positive reinforcement. The presentation of a stimulus (one that is usually considered pleasant or rewarding) following a response, which then leads to an increase in the future strength of that response.

Premack principle. The notion that a high-probability behavior can be used to reinforce a low-probability behavior.

Premack principle of punishment. The notion that a low-probability behavior (LPB) can be used to punish a high-probability behavior (HPB).

preparatory-response theory. A theory of classical conditioning that proposes that the purpose of the CR is to prepare the organism for the presentation of the US.

preparedness. An innate tendency for an organism to more easily learn certain types of behaviors or to associate certain types of events with each other.

primary (or unconditioned) punisher. Any event that is innately punishing.

primary reinforcer (or unconditioned reinforcer). An event that is innately reinforcing.

productivity. The ability of language users to combine language symbols in new and creative ways.

pseudoconditioning. A situation in which an elicited response that appears to be a CR is actually the result of sensitization rather than conditioning.

punisher. An event that (1) follows a behavior and (2) decreases the future probability of that behavior.

radical behaviorism. A brand of behaviorism that emphasizes the influence of the environment on overt behavior, rejects the use of internal events to explain behavior, and views thoughts and feelings as behaviors that themselves need to be explained.

rate of response. The frequency with which a response occurs in a certain period of time.

ratio strain. A disruption in responding due to an overly demanding response requirement.

reciprocal determinism. The assumption that environmental events, observable behavior, and "person variables" (including internal events) reciprocally influence each other.

reciprocal inhibition. The process whereby certain responses are incompatible with each other, and the occurrence of one response necessarily inhibits the other.

reference. The ability to associate arbitrary symbols with objects or events.

reflex. A relatively simple, involuntary response to a stimulus.

reflex arc. A neural structure that underlies many reflexes and consists of a sensory neuron, an interneuron, and a motor neuron.

reinforcer. An event that (1) follows a behavior and (2) increases the future probability of that behavior.

Rescorla-Wagner theory. A theory of classical conditioning that proposes that a given US can support only so much conditioning and that this amount of conditioning must be distributed among the various CSs available.

resistance to extinction. The extent to which responding persists after an extinction procedure has been implemented.

response. A particular instance of a behavior.

response cost. A form of negative punishment involving the removal of a specific reinforcer following the occurrence of a behavior.

response deprivation hypothesis. The notion that a behavior can serve as a reinforcer when (1) access to the behavior is restricted and (2) its frequency thereby falls below its preferred level of occurrence.

response-rate schedule. A schedule in which reinforcement is directly contingent upon the organism's rate of response.

resurgence. The reappearance during extinction of other behaviors that had once been effective in obtaining reinforcement.

reversal design. A type of single-subject design that involves repeated alternations between a baseline period and a treatment period.

rule. A verbal description of a contingency.

rule-governed behavior. Behavior that has been generated through exposure to rules.

satiation. The prolonged exposure to (or consumption of) an event that tends to decrease the appetitiveness of that event.

say–do correspondence. A close match between what we say we are going to do and what we actually do at a later time.

schedule of reinforcement. The response requirement that must be met to obtain reinforcement.

secondary (or conditioned) punisher. An event that has become punishing because it has in the past been associated with some other punisher.

secondary reinforcer (or conditioned reinforcer). An event that is reinforcing because it has been associated with some other reinforcer.

selective sensitization. An increase in one's reactivity to a potentially fearful stimulus following exposure to an unrelated stressful event.

self-control. With respect to choice between two rewards, selecting a larger later reward over a smaller sooner reward.

semantic generalization. The generalization of a conditioned response to verbal stimuli that are similar in meaning to the CS.

sensitization. An increase in the strength of an elicited behavior following repeated presentations of the eliciting stimulus.

sensory preconditioning. In this phenomenon, when one stimulus is conditioned as a CS, another stimulus it was previously associated with can also become a CS.

shaping. The gradual creation of new operant behavior through reinforcement of successive approximations to that behavior.

sign stimulus (or releaser). A specific stimulus that elicits a fixed action pattern.

sign tracking. A type of elicited behavior in which an organism approaches a stimulus that signals the presentation of an appetitive event.

simple-comparison design. A type of single-subject design in which behavior in a baseline condition is compared to behavior in a treatment condition.

simultaneous conditioning. Conditioning procedure in which the onset of the NS and the onset of the US are simultaneous.

single-subject design. A research design requiring only one or a few subjects in order to conduct an entire experiment.

situational freedom. Language can be used in a variety of contexts and is not fixed in a particular situation.

small-but-cumulative effects model. Each individual choice on a self-control task has only a small but cumulative effect on our likelihood of obtaining the desired long-term outcome.

social learning theory. A brand of behaviorism that strongly emphasizes the importance of observational learning and cognitive variables in explaining human behavior. It has more recently been referred to as "social-cognitive theory."

spatial contiguity. The extent to which events are situated close to each other in space.

speed. The amount of time required to perform a complete episode of a behavior from start to finish.

spontaneous recovery (in classical conditioning). The reappearance of the conditioned response following a rest period after extinction.

spontaneous recovery (in operant conditioning). The reappearance of the operant response following a rest period after extinction.

S-R (stimulus-response) model. As applied to classical conditioning, this model assumes that the NS becomes directly associated with the UR and therefore comes to elicit the same response as the UR.

S-R theory. The theory that learning involves the establishment of a connection between a specific stimulus (S) and a specific response (R).

S-S (stimulus-stimulus) model. A model of classical conditioning that assumes that the NS becomes directly associated with the US, and therefore comes to elicit a response related to that US.

startle response. A defensive reaction to a sudden, unexpected stimulus, which involves automatic tightening of skeletal muscles and various hormonal and visceral changes.

stimulus. Any event that can potentially influence behavior. (The plural for stimulus is *stimuli.*)

stimulus control. A situation in which the presence of a discriminative stimulus reliably affects the probability of a behavior.

stimulus discrimination. In classical conditioning, the tendency for a response to be elicited more by one stimulus than another; in operant conditioning, the tendency for an operant response to be emitted more in the presence of one stimulus than another.

stimulus enhancement. Directing attention to a particular place or object, making it more likely that the observer will approach that place or object.

stimulus generalization. In classical conditioning, the tendency for a CR to be elicited by a stimulus that is similar to the CS; in operant conditioning, the tendency for an operant response to be emitted in the presence of a stimulus that is similar to an S^D.

stimulus-substitution theory. A theory of classical conditioning that proposes that the CS acts as a substitute for the US.

structuralism. An approach to psychology holding that it is possible to determine the structure of the mind by identifying the basic elements that compose it.

systematic desensitization. A behavioral treatment for phobias that involves pairing relaxation with a succession of stimuli that elicit increasing levels of fear.

taste aversion conditioning. A form of classical conditioning in which a food item that has been paired with gastrointestinal illness becomes a conditioned aversive stimulus.

temperament. An individual's base level of emotionality and reactivity to stimulation that, to a large extent, is genetically determined.

temporal conditioning. A form of classical conditioning in which the CS is the passage of time.

temporal contiguity. The extent to which events occur close together in time.

three-term contingency. The relationship between a discriminative stimulus, an operant behavior, and a reinforcer or punisher.

time-out. A form of negative punishment involving the loss of access to positive reinforcers for a brief period of time following the occurrence of a problem behavior.

time-sample recording. The measurement of whether or not a behavior occurs within a series of discontinuous intervals. (The number of times that it occurs within each interval is irrelevant.)

topography. The physical form of a behavior.

trace conditioning. Conditioning procedure in which the onset and offset of the NS precede the onset of the US.

true imitation. Duplicating a novel behavior (or sequence of behaviors) to achieve a specific goal.

two-process theory of avoidance. The theory that avoidance behavior is the result of two distinct processes: (1) classical conditioning, in which a fear response comes to be elicited by a CS, and (2) operant conditioning, in which moving away from the CS is negatively reinforced by a reduction in fear.

unconditioned response (UR). The response that is naturally elicited by the unconditioned stimulus.

unconditioned stimulus (US). A stimulus that naturally elicits a response.

undermatching. A deviation from matching in which the proportion of responses on the richer schedule versus poorer schedule is less different than would be predicted by matching.

US revaluation. A process that involves the postconditioning presentation of the US at a different level of intensity, thereby altering the strength of response to the previously conditioned CS.

variable. A characteristic of a person, place, or thing that can change (vary) over time or from one situation to another.

variable duration (VD) schedule. A schedule in which reinforcement is contingent upon continuous performance of a behavior for a varying, unpredictable period of time.

variable interval (VI) schedule. A schedule in which reinforcement is contingent upon the first response after a varying, unpredictable period of time.

variable ratio (VR) schedule. A schedule in which reinforcement is contingent upon a varying, unpredictable number of responses.

variable time (VT) schedule. A schedule in which the reinforcer is delivered following a varying, unpredictable period of time, regardless of the organism's behavior.

vicarious emotional response. A classically conditioned emotional response resulting from seeing that emotional response exhibited by others.

References

Adams, L. A., & Rickert, V. I. (1989). Reducing bedtime tantrums: Comparison between positive routines and graduated extinction. *Pediatrics, 84*, 585–588.

Ader, R. (2003). Conditioned immunomodulation: Research needs and directions. *Brain, Behavior, and Immunity, 17*, 51–57.

Ader, R., & Cohen, N. (1975). Behaviorally conditioned immunosuppression. *Psychosomatic Medicine, 37*, 333–340.

Ainslie, G. (1975). Specious reward: A behavioral theory of impulsiveness and impulse control. *Psychological Bulletin, 82*, 463–496.

Ainslie, G. (1986). Beyond microeconomics: Conflict among interests in a multiple self as a determinant of value. In J. Elster (Ed.), *The multiple self.* Cambridge, UK: Cambridge University Press.

Ainslie, G. (1992). *Picoeconomics: The strategic intervention of successive motivational states within the person.* Cambridge, UK: Cambridge University Press.

Ainslie, G. (2001). *The breakdown of will.* Cambridge, UK: Cambridge University Press.

Ainslie, G., & Haendel, V. (1983). The motives of the will. In E. Gottheil, A. T. McLellan, & K. Druley (Eds.), *Etiologic aspects of alcohol and drug abuse.* Springfield, IL: Charles C. Thomas.

Allison, J. (1983). *Behavioral economics.* New York: Praeger.

Amabile, T. M., Hennessey, B. A., & Grossman, B. S. (1986). Social influences on creativity: The effects of contracted-for reward. *Journal of Personality and Social Psychology, 50*, 14–23.

American Psychiatric Association. (2000). *Diagnostic and statistical manual of mental disorders* (4th ed., text revision). Washington, DC: Author.

Anderson, C. M., Hawkins, R. P., Freeman, K. A., & Scotti, J. R. (2000). Private events: Do they belong in a science of human behavior? *The Behavior Analyst, 23*, 1–10.

Anderson, C. A., & Dill, K. E. (2000). Video games and aggressive thoughts, feelings, and behavior in the laboratory and in life. *Journal of Personality and Social Psychology, 78*, 772–790.

Antonitis, J. J. (1951). Response variability in the white rat during conditioning, extinction, and reconditioning. *Journal of Experimental Psychology, 42*, 273–281.

Assagioli, R. (1974). *The act of will.* New York: Penguin.

Axelrod, S., & Apsche, J. (Eds.). (1983). *The effects of punishment on human behavior.* New York: Academic Press.

Axelrod, S., Hall, R. V., Weiss, L., & Rohrer, S. (1974). Use of self-imposed contingencies to reduce the frequency of smoking behavior. In M. J. Mahoney & C. E. Carlson (Eds.), *Self-control: Power to the person.* Monterey, CA: Brooks/Cole.

Azrin, N. H., & Holz, W. C. (1966). Punishment. In W. K. Honig (Ed.), *Operant behavior: Areas of research and application.* New York: Appleton.

Azrin, N. H., Hutchinson, R. R., & Hake, D. F. (1966). Extinction-induced aggression. *Journal of the Experimental Analysis of Behavior, 9*, 191–204.

Baeninger, R., & Ulm, R. R. (1969). Overcoming the effects of prior punishment on inter-species aggression in the rat. *Journal of Comparative and Physiological Psychology, 69*, 628–635.

Baer, D. M., Peterson, R. F., & Sherman, J. A. (1967). The development of imitation by reinforcing behavioral similarity to a model. *Journal of the Experimental Analysis of Behavior, 10*, 405–416.

Baer, D. M., & Sherman, J. A. (1964). Reinforcement control of generalized imitation in young children. *Journal of Experimental Child Psychology. 1*, 37–49.

Baker, T. B., & Cannon, D. S. (1979). Taste aversion therapy with alcoholics: Techniques and evidence of a conditioned response. *Behaviour Research and Therapy, 17,* 229–242.

Balderston, J. L. (1924). *A morality play for the leisured class.* New York: Appleton.

Baldwin, J. D., & Baldwin, J. I. (1998). *Behavior principles in everyday life* (3rd ed.). Upper Saddle River, NJ: Prentice-Hall.

Bandura, A. (1965). Influence of models' reinforcement contingencies on the acquisition of imitative response. *Journal of Personality and Social Psychology, 1,* 589–595.

Bandura, A. (1973). *Aggression: A social learning analysis.* Englewood Cliffs, NJ: Prentice-Hall.

Bandura, A. (1975). Effecting change through participant modeling. In J. D. Krumboltz & C. E. Thoresen (Eds.), *Counseling methods.* New York: Holt, Rinehart & Winston.

Bandura, A. (1976). Self-reinforcement: Theoretical and methodological considerations. *Behaviorism, 4,* 135–155.

Bandura, A. (1977). *Social learning theory.* Englewood Cliffs, NJ: Prentice-Hall.

Bandura, A. (1986). *Social foundations of thought and action: A social cognitive theory.* Upper Saddle River, NJ: Prentice-Hall.

Bandura, A. (1997). *Self-efficacy: The exercise of self-control.* New York: W. H. Freeman.

Bandura, A., Blanchard, E. B., & Ritter, B. (1969). The relative efficacy of desensitization and modeling approaches for inducing behavioral, affective, and attitudinal changes. *Journal of Personality and Social Psychology, 13,* 173–199.

Bandura, A., & McDonald, F. J. (1994). Influence of social reinforcement and the behavior of models in shaping children's moral judgments. In B. Puka (Ed.), *Defining perspectives in moral development. Moral development: A compendium* (Vol. 1). New York: Garland.

Bandura, A., Ross, D., & Ross, S. A. (1961). Transmission of aggression through imitation of aggressive models. *Journal of Abnormal and Social Psychology, 63,* 575–582.

Bandura, A., Ross, D., & Ross, S. A. (1963). Imitation of film-mediated aggressive models. *Journal of Abnormal and Social Psychology, 66,* 3–11.

Barlow, D. H. (1988). *Anxiety and its disorders: The nature and treatment of anxiety and panic.* New York: Guilford.

Barlow, D. H., & Hersen, M. (1984). *Single-case experimental designs: Strategies for studying behavior change* (2nd ed.). New York: Pergamon.

Baron, R. A., & Byrne, D. (1997). *Social psychology* (8th ed.). Boston: Allyn & Bacon.

Barrett, B. (1931). *The strength of will and how to develop it.* New York: R. R. Smith.

Baum, W. M. (1974). On two types of deviation from the matching law: Bias and undermatching. *Journal of the Experimental Analysis of Behavior, 22,* 231–242.

Baum, W. M. (1979). Matching, undermatching, and overmatching in studies of choice. *Journal of the Experimental Analysis of Behavior, 32,* 269–281.

Begun, D. R. (1999). Hominid family values: Morphological and molecular data on relations among the great apes and humans. In S. T. Parker, R. W. Mitchell, & H. L. Miles (Eds.), *The mentalities of gorillas and orangutans: Comparative perspectives.* Cambridge, UK: Cambridge University Press.

Beneke, W. M., Schulte, S. E., & Vander Tuig, J. G. (1995). An analysis of excessive running in the development of activity anorexia. *Physiology and Behavior, 58,* 451–457.

Beneke, W. M., & Vander Tuig, J. G. (1996). Effects of dietary protein and food restriction on voluntary running of rats living in activity wheels. In W. F. Epling & W. D. Pierce (Eds.), *Activity anorexia: Theory, research, and treatment.* Mahwah, NJ: Erlbaum.

Benjamin L. T., Jr., Whitaker, J. L., Ramsey, R. M., & Zeve, D. R. (2007). John B. Watson's alleged sex research: An appraisal of the evidence. *American Psychologist, 62,* 131–139.

Bennett, R. H., & Samson, H. H. (1991). Ethanol-related cues and behavioral tolerance to ethanol in humans. *Psychological Record, 41,* 429–437.

Benson, J., Greaves, W., O'Donnell, M., & Taglialatela, J. (2002). Evidence for symbolic language processing in a Bonobo (*Pan paniscus*). *Journal of Consciousness Studies, 9,* 33–56.

Bentall, R. P., Lowe, C. F., & Beasty, A. (1985). The role of verbal behavior in human learning: II. Developmental differences. *Journal of the Experimental Analysis of Behavior, 43,* 165–180.

Bernstein, I. L. (1991). Aversion conditioning in response to cancer and cancer treatment. *Clinical Psychology Review, 11,* 185–191.

Billet, E. A., Richter, M. A., & Kennedy, J. L. (1998). Genetics of obsessive-compulsive disorder. In R. P. Swinson, M. M. Antony, S. Rachman, & M. A. Richter (Eds.), *Obsessive-compulsive disorder: Theory, research, and treatment.* New York: Guilford.

Bjork, D. W. (1993). *B. F. Skinner: A life.* New York: Basic Books.

Blandin, Y., Lhuisset, L., & Proteau, L. (1999). Cognitive processes underlying observational learning of motor skills. *Quarterly Journal of Experimental Psychology: Human Experimental Psychology, 52A,* 957–979.

Boer, D. P. (1990). Determinants of excessive running in activity-anorexia. *Dissertation Abstracts International. 50(11-B),* 5351.

Boer, D. P., Epling, W. F., Pierce, W. D., & Russell, J. C. (1990). Suppression of food deprivation-induced high-rate wheel running in rats. *Physiology and Behavior, 48,* 339–342.

Boesch, C. (1991). Teaching among wild chimpanzees. *Animal Behaviour, 41,* 530–532.

Boice, R. (1989). Procrastination, business and bingeing. *Behaviour Research and Therapy, 27,* 605–611.

Boice, R. (1996). *Procrastination and blocking: A novel, practical approach.* Westport, CT: Praeger.

Bolla-Wilson, K., Wilson, R. J., & Bleecker, M. L. (1988). Conditioning of physical symptoms after neurotoxic exposure. *Journal of Occupational Medicine, 30,* 684–686.

Bolles, R. C. (1970). Species-specific defense reactions and avoidance learning. *Psychological Review, 77,* 32–48.

Bolles, R. C. (1979). *Learning theory* (2nd ed.). New York: Holt, Rinehart & Winston.

Bootzin, R. R., Epstein, D., & Wood, J. M. (1991). Stimulus control instructions. In P. J. Hauri (Ed.), *Case studies in insomnia.* New York: Plenum Press.

Bouvier, K. A., & Powell, R. A. (2008, June). *A driven versus balanced approach to studying: The importance of rest and recuperation in academic performance.* Poster presented at the Annual Convention of the Canadian Psychological Association, Halifax, Nova Scotia.

Bovbjerg, D. H., Redd, W. H., Maier, L. A., Holland, J. C., Lesko L. M., Niedzwiecki, D., Rubin, S. C., & Hakes, T. B. (1990). Anticipatory immune suppression and nausea in women receiving cyclic chemotherapy for ovarian cancer. *Journal of Consulting and Clinical Psychology, 58,* 153–157.

Braun, B. G. (1980). Hypnosis for multiple personalities. In H. J. Wain (Ed.), *Clinical hypnosis in medicine.* Chicago: Yearbook Medical.

Breland, K., & Breland, M. (1961). The misbehavior of organisms. *American Psychologist, 16,* 681–684.

Brethower, D. M., & Reynolds, G. S. (1962). A facilitative effect of punishment on unpunished responding. *Journal of the Experimental Analysis of Behavior, 5,* 191–199.

Breuer, E., & Freud, S. (1955). Studies on hysteria. In J. Strachey (Ed. and Trans.), *The standard edition of the complete psychological works of Sigmund Freud* (Vol. 2). London: Hogarth Press. (Original work published 1895)

Brigham, T. A. (1978). Self-control. In A. C. Catania & T. A. Brigham (Eds.), *Handbook of Applied Behavior Analysis.* New York: Irvington.

Broberg, D. J., & Bernstein, I. L. (1987). Candy as a scapegoat in the prevention of food aversions in children receiving chemotherapy. *Cancer, 60,* 2344–2347.

Brogden, W. J. (1939). Sensory pre-conditioning. *Journal of Experimental Psychology, 25,* 323–332.

Brown, P. L., & Jenkins, H. M. (1968). Autoshaping of the pigeon's key-peck. *Journal of the Experimental Analysis of Behavior, 11*, 1–8.

Brown, S. A., Stetson, B. A., & Beatty, P. A. (1989). Cognitive and behavioral features of adolescent coping in high-risk drinking situations. *Addictive Behaviors, 14*, 43–52.

Bruch, H. (1978). *The golden cage: The enigma of anorexia nervosa.* Cambridge, MA: Harvard University Press.

Buckley, K. W. (1989). *Mechanical man: John Broadus Watson and the beginnings of behaviorism.* New York: Guilford.

Bullock, D. H., & Smith, W. C. (1953). An effect of repeated conditioning-extinction upon operant strength. *Journal of Experimental Psychology, 46*, 349–352.

Burns, M., & Domjan, M. (1996). Sign tracking versus goal tracking in the sexual conditioning of male Japanese quail (*Coturnix japonica*). *Journal of Experimental Psychology: Animal Behavior Processes, 22*, 297–306.

Bushman, B. J., & Anderson, C. A. (2001). Media violence and the American public: Scientific facts versus media misinformation. *American Psychologist, 56*, 477–489.

Buske-Kirschbaum, A., Kirschbaum, C., Stierle, H., Jabaij, L., & Hellhammer, D. (1994). Conditioned manipulation of natural killer (NK) cells in humans using a discriminative learning protocol. *Biological Psychology, 38*, 143–155.

Bussey, K., & Bandura, A. (1984). Influence of gender constancy and social power on sex-linked modeling. *Journal of Personality and Social Psychology, 47*, 1292–1302.

Byrne, D., & Clore, G. L. (1970). A reinforcement model of evaluative responses. *Personality: An International Journal, 1*, 103–128.

Call, J. (1999). Levels of imitation and cognitive mechanisms in orangutans. In S. T. Parker, R. W. Mitchell, & H. L. Miles (Eds.), *The mentalities of gorillas and orangutans: Comparative perspectives.* Cambridge, UK: Cambridge University Press.

Call, J., & Tomasello, M. (1995). The use of social information in the problem-solving of orangutans (*Pongo pygmaeus*) and human children (*Homo sapiens*). *Journal of Comparative Psychology, 109*, 308–320.

Cameron, J. (2001). Negative effects of reward on intrinsic motivation—A limited phenomenon: Comment on Deci, Koestner, and Ryan (2001). *Review of Educational Research, 71*, 29–42.

Cameron, J., Banko, K. M., & Pierce, W. D. (2001). Pervasive negative effects of rewards on intrinsic motivation: The myth continues. *The Behavior Analyst, 24*, 1–44.

Cameron, J., & Pierce, W. D. (1994). Reinforcement, reward, and intrinsic motivation: A meta-analysis. *Review of Educational Research, 64*, 363–423.

Cameron, J., & Pierce, W. D. (2002). *Rewards and intrinsic motivation: Resolving the controversy.* Westport, CT: Bergin & Garvey.

Capaldi, E. D. (1996). Conditioned food preferences. In E. D. Capaldi (Ed.), *Why we eat what we eat: The psychology of eating.* Washington, DC: American Psychological Association.

Capaldi, E. J. (1966). Partial reinforcement: A hypothesis of sequential effects. *Psychological Review, 73*, 459–477.

Capaldi, E. J., Miller, D. J., & Alptekin, S. (1989). Multiple-food-unit-incentive effect: Nonconservation of weight of food reward by rats. *Journal of Experimental Psychology: Animal Behavior Processes, 15*, 75–80.

Carroll, W. R., & Bandura, A. (1987). Translating cognition into action: The role of visual guidance in observational learning. *Journal of Motor Behavior, 19*, 385–398.

Casey, R., & Rozin, P. (1989). Changing children's food preferences: Parent opinions. *Appetite, 12*, 171–182.

Catania, A. C. (1975). The myth of self-reinforcement. *Behaviorism, 3*, 192–199.

Catania, A. C. (1988). The operant behaviorism of B. F. Skinner. In A. C. Catania & S. Harnad (Eds.), *The selection of behavior: The operant behaviorism of B. F. Skinner: Comments and consequences.* New York: Cambridge University Press.

Chambers, K. C., Yuan, D., Brownson, E. A., & Wang, Y. (1997). Sexual dimorphisms in conditioned taste aversions: Mechanism and function. In M. E. Bouton & M. S. Fanselow (Eds.), *Learning, motivation, and cognition: The functional behaviorism of Robert C. Bolles.* Washington, DC: American Psychological Association.

Chance, P. (1994). *Learning and behavior* (3rd ed.). Pacific Grove, CA: Brooks/Cole.

Cherek, D. R. (1982). Schedule-induced cigarette self-administration. *Pharmacology, Biochemistry, and Behavior, 17,* 523–527.

Chesler, P. (1969). Maternal influence in learning by observation in kittens. *Science, 166,* 901–903.

Chomsky, N. (1988). *Language and problems of knowledge.* Cambridge, MA: MIT Press.

Cialdini, R. B. (1993). *Influence: Science and practice* (3rd ed.). New York: HarperCollins.

Clark, H. B., Rowbury, T., Baer, A. M., & Baer, D. M. (1973). Timeout as a punishing stimulus in continuous and intermittent schedules. *Journal of Applied Behavior Analysis, 6,* 443–455.

Clark, L. A., Watson, D., & Mineka, S. (1994). Temperament, personality, and the mood and anxiety disorders. *Journal of Abnormal Psychology, 103,* 103–116.

Conger, R., & Killeen, P. (1974). Use of concurrent operants in small group research. *Pacific Sociological Review, 17,* 399–416.

Cook, M., & Mineka, S. (1989). Observational conditioning of fear to fear-relevant versus fear-irrelevant stimuli in rhesus monkeys. *Journal of Abnormal Psychology, 98,* 448–459.

Coon, D. J. (1994). "Not a creature of reason": The alleged impact of Watsonian behaviorism on advertising in the 1920s. In J. T. Todd & E. K. Morris (Eds.), *Modern perspectives on John B. Watson and classical behaviorism.* Westport, CT: Greenwood Press.

Coon, D. (1998). *Introduction to psychology: Exploration and application* (8th ed.). Pacific Grove, CA: Brooks/Cole.

Coren, S. (1994). *The intelligence of dogs: A Guide to the thoughts, emotions, and inner lives of our canine companions.* New York: Free Press.

Corsini, R. (2002). *The dictionary of psychology.* New York: Brunner-Routledge.

Craig, G. J., Kermis, M. D., & Digdon, N. L. (1998). *Children today* (Canadian ed.). Scarborough, Canada: Prentice-Hall.

Crespi, L. P. (1942). Quantitative variation of incentive and performance in the white rat. *American Journal of Psychology, 55,* 467–517.

Critchfield, T. S., & Kollins, S. H. (2001). Temporal discounting: Basic research and the analysis of socially important behavior. *Journal of Applied Behavior Analysis, 34,* 101–122.

Danaher, B. G. (1977). Rapid smoking and self-control in the modification of smoking behavior. *Journal of Consulting and Clinical Psychology, 45,* 1068–1075.

Darwin, C. R. (1859). *On the origin of species by means of natural selection.* London: Murray.

Davey, G. C. L. (1992). Classical conditioning and the acquisition of human fears and phobias: A review and synthesis of the literature. *Advances in Behaviour Research & Therapy, 14,* 29–66.

Davey, G. C. L., De Jong, P., & Tallis, F. (1993). UCS Inflation in the aetiology of a variety of anxiety disorders: Some case histories. *Behaviour Research and Therapy, 31,* 495–498.

Davis, C., Katzman, D. K., & Kirsh, C. (1999). Compulsive physical activity in adolescents with anorexia nervosa: A psychobehavioral spiral of pathology. *Journal of Nervous and Mental Disease, 187,* 336–342.

de Waal, F. (2005). *Our inner ape: A leading primatologist explains why we are who we are.* New York: Penguin.

Deci, E. L., Koestner, R., & Ryan, R. M. (2001a). Extrinsic rewards and intrinsic motivation: Reconsidered once again. *Review of Educational Research, 71,* 1–27.

Deci, E. L., Koestner, R., & Ryan, R. M. (2001b). The pervasive negative effects of rewards on intrinsic motivation: Response to Cameron (2001). *Review of Educational Research, 71,* 43–51.

Deci, E. L., & Ryan, R. M. (1985). *Intrinsic motivation and self-determination in human behavior.* New York: Plenum Press.

Delk, J. L. (1980). High-risk sports as indirect self-destructive behavior. In N. L. Farberow (Ed.), *The many faces of suicide: Indirect self-destructive behavior.* New York: McGraw-Hill.

Dinsmoor, J. A. (1954). Punishment: I. The avoidance hypothesis. *Psychological Review, 61,* 34–46.

Domjan, M. (2000). *The essentials of conditioning and learning* (2nd ed.). Belmont, CA: Wadsworth.

Domjan, M. (2003). *The principles of learning and behavior* (5th ed.). Belmont, CA: Wadsworth.

Dowling, J. E. (1984). Modeling effectiveness as a function of learner-model similarity and the learner's attitude toward women. *Dissertation Abstracts International, 45*(1-A), 121.

Doyle, T. F., & Samson, H. H. (1988). Adjunctive alcohol drinking in humans. *Physiology and Behavior, 44,* 775–779.

Durand, V. M. (1990). *Severe behavior problems: A functional communication training approach.* New York: Guilford.

Dweck, C. S., & Reppucci, N. D. (1973). Learned helplessness and reinforcement responsibility in children. *Journal of Personality & Social Psychology, 25,* 109–116.

Ehrensaft, M. K., Cohen, P., Brown, J., Smailes, E., Chen, H., & Johnson, J. G. (2003). Intergenerational transmission of partner violence: A 20-year prospective study. *Journal of Consulting and Clinical Psychology, 71,* 741–753.

Eikelboom, R., & Stewart, J. (1982). Conditioning of drug-induced physiological responses. *Psychological Review, 89,* 507–528.

Eisenberg, N., McCreath, H., & Ahn, R. (1988). Vicarious emotional responsiveness and prosocial behavior: Their interrelations in young children. *Personality and Social Psychology Bulletin, 14,* 298–311.

Eisenberger, R. (1992). Learned industriousness. *Psychological Review, 99,* 248–267.

Eisenberger, R., Carlson, J., Guile, M., & Shapiro, N. (1979). Transfer of effort across behaviors. *Learning and Motivation, 10,* 178–197.

Eisenberger, R., Masterson, F. A., & McDermitt, M. (1982). Effects of task variety on generalized effort. *Journal of Educational Psychology, 74,* 499–505.

Eisenstein, E. M., Eisenstein, D., & Smith, J. C. (2001). The evolutionary significance of habituation and sensitization across phylogeny: A behavioral homeostasis model. *Integrative Physiological and Behavioral Science, 36,* 251–265.

Ellenberger, H. F. (1970). *The discovery of the unconscious: The history and evolution of dynamic psychiatry.* New York: Basic Books.

Ellis, N. R. (1962). Amount of reward and operant behavior in mental defectives. *American Journal of Mental Deficiency, 66,* 595–599.

Epling, W. F., & Pierce, W. D. (1988). Activity-based anorexia: A biobehavioral perspective. *International Journal of Eating Disorders, 7,* 475–485.

Epling, W. F., & Pierce, W. D. (1991). *Solving the anorexia puzzle: A scientific approach.* Toronto, Canada: Hogrefe & Huber.

Epling, W. F., & Pierce, W. D. (1996). An overview of activity anorexia. In W. F. Epling & W. D. Pierce (Eds.), *Activity anorexia: Theory, research, and treatment.* Mahwah, NJ: Erlbaum.

Epstein, R. (1985). Extinction-induced resurgence: Preliminary investigations and possible applications. *Psychological Record, 35,* 143–153.

Epstein, R. (1997). Skinner as self-manager. *Journal of Applied Behavior Analysis, 30,* 545–568.

Epstein, S. M. (1967). Toward a unified theory of anxiety. In B. A. Maher (Ed.), *Progress in experimental personality research* (Vol. 4). New York: Academic Press.

Ericsson, K. A., & Charness, N. (1994). Expert performance: Its structure and acquisition. *American Psychologist, 49,* 725–747.

Ericsson, K. A., Charness, N., Feltovich, P. J., & Hoffman, R. R. (Eds.). (2006). *The Cambridge handbook of expertise and expert performance.* New York: Cambridge University Press.

Ericsson, K. A., Krampe, R. Th., & Tesch-Römer, C. (1993). The role of deliberate practice in the acquisition of expert performance. *Psychological Review, 100,* 363–406.

Eron, L. D., Huesmann, L. R., Lefkowitz, M. M., & Walder, L. O. (1972). Does television violence cause aggression? *American Psychologist, 27,* 253–263.

Esterson, A. (1993). *Seductive mirage: An exploration of the work of Sigmund Freud.* Chicago: Open Court.

Estes, W. K., & Skinner, B. F. (1941). Some quantitative properties of anxiety. *Journal of Experimental Psychology, 29,* 390–400.

Etscorn, F., & Stephens, R. (1973). Establishment of conditioned taste aversions with a 24-hour CS-US interval. *Physiological Psychology, 1,* 251–259.

Exton, M. S., von Auer, A. K., Buske-Kirschbaum, A., Stockhorst, U., Gobel, U., & Schedlowski, M. (2000). Pavlovian conditioning of immune function: Animal investigation and the challenge of human application. *Behavioural Brain Research, 110,* 129–141.

Eysenck, H. J. (1957). *The dynamics of anxiety and hysteria: An experimental application of modern learning theory to psychiatry.* London: Routledge & Kegan Paul.

Eysenck, H. J. (1967). *The biological basis of personality.* Springfield, IL: Charles C. Thomas.

Eysenck, H. J. (1968). A theory of the incubation of anxiety/fear response. *Behaviour Research and Therapy, 6,* 63–65.

Eysenck, H. J. (1976). The learning theory model of neurosis—A new approach. *Behaviour Research and Therapy, 14,* 251–267.

Falk, J. L. (1961). Production of polydipsia in normal rats by an intermittent food schedule. *Science, 133,* 195–196.

Falk, J. L. (1971). The nature and determinants of adjunctive behavior. *Physiology and Behavior, 6,* 577–588.

Falk, J. L. (1977). The origin and functions of adjunctive behavior. *Animal Learning and Behavior, 5,* 325–335.

Falk, J. L. (1993). Schedule-induced drug self-administration. In F. van Haaren (Ed.), *Methods in behavioral pharmacology.* Amsterdam: Elsevier.

Falk, J. L. (1994). Schedule-induced behavior occurs in humans: A reply to Overskeid. *Psychological Record, 44,* 45–62.

Falk, J. L. (1998). Drug abuse as an adjunctive behavior. *Drug and Alcohol Dependence, 52,* 91–98.

Fanselow, M. S., DeCola, J. P., & Young, S. L. (1993). Mechanisms responsible for reduced contextual conditioning with massed unsignaled unconditional stimuli. *Journal of Experimental Psychology: Animal Behavior Processes, 19,* 121–137.

Farroni, T., Johnson, M. H., Brockbank, M., & Simion, F. (2000). Infants' use of gaze direction to cue attention: The importance of perceived motion. *Visual Cognition, 7,* 705–718.

Federal Trade Commission. (2000). *Marketing violent entertainment to children: A review of self-regulation and industry practices in the motion picture, music recording, and electronic game industries.* Washington, DC: Author.

Ferguson, E., & Cassaday, H. J. (1999). The gulf war and illness by association. *British Journal of Psychology, 90,* 459–475.

Ferster, C. B., & Skinner, B. F. (1957). *Schedules of reinforcement.* New York: Appleton-Century-Crofts.

Flory, R. K., & Ellis, B. B. (1973). Schedule-induced aggression against a slide-image target. *Bulletin of the Psychonomic Society, 2,* 287–290.

Foa, E. B., Franklin, M. E., & Kozak, M. J. (1998). Psychosocial treatments for obsessive-compulsive disorder: Literature review. In R. P. Swinson, M. M. Antony, S. Rachman, & M. A. Richter (Eds.), *Obsessive-compulsive disorder: Theory, research, and treatment.* New York: Guilford.

Foa, E. B., Zinbarg, R., & Rothbaum, B. O. (1992). Uncontrollability and unpredictability in post-traumatic stress disorder: An animal model. *Psychological Bulletin, 112,* 218–238.

Fouts, G. R., & Click, M. (1979). Effects of live and TV models on observational learning in introverted and extroverted children. *Perceptual and Motor Skills, 48,* 863–867.

Fouts, R. S. (1973). Acquisition and testing of gestural signs in four young chimpanzees. *Science, 180,* 978–980.

Fox, L. (1962). Effecting the use of efficient study habits. *Journal of Mathematics, 1,* 75–86.

Franks, C. M. (1963). Behavior therapy, the principles of conditioning and the treatment of the alcoholic. *Quarterly Journal of Studies on Alcohol, 24,* 511–529.

Freud, S. (1955). Lines of advance in psychoanalytic therapy. In J. Strachey (Ed. and Trans.), *The Standard Edition of the Complete Psychological Works of Sigmund Freud* (Vol. 17, pp. 159–168). London: Hogarth Press. (Original work published 1919)

Furomoto, L. (1971). Extinction in the pigeon after continuous reinforcement: Effects of number of reinforced responses. *Psychological Reports, 28,* 331–338.

Galef, B. G., Jr. (1988). Imitation in animals: History, definition and interpretation of data from the psychological laboratory. In T. R. Zentall & B. G. Galef, Jr. (Eds.), *Social learning: Psychological and biological perspectives.* Hillsdale, NJ: Erlbaum.

Gandhi, M. K. (1957). *An autobiography: The story of my experiments with truth.* Boston: Beacon Press. (Original work published 1927)

Garcia, J., & Koelling, R. A. (1966). Relation of cue to consequence in avoidance learning. *Psychonomic Science, 4,* 123–124.

Gardner, H. (1993). *Multiple intelligences: The theory in practice.* New York: Basic Books.

Gardner, R. A., & Gardner, B. T. (1969). Teaching sign language to a chimpanzee. *Science, 165,* 664–672.

Gardner, R. A., & Gardner, B. T. (1975). Evidence for sentence constituents in the early utterances of child and chimpanzee. *Journal of Experimental Psychology: General, 104,* 244–267.

Gardner, R. A., Gardner, B. T., & Van Cantfort, T. E. (1989). *Teaching sign language to chimpanzees.* New York: State University of New York Press.

Garner, D. M., & Garfinkel, P. E. (1980). Socio-cultural factors in the development of anorexia nervosa. *Psychological Medicine, 10,* 647–656.

Gay, P. (1988). *Freud: A life for our time.* New York: Norton.

Gibson, B. M., & Kamil, A. C. (2001). Search for a hidden goal by Clark's nutcrackers (*Nucifraga columbiana*) is more accurate inside than outside a landmark array. *Animal Learning & Behavior, 29,* 234–249.

Gleaves, D. H. (1996). The sociocognitive model of dissociative identity disorder: A reexamination of the evidence. *Psychological Bulletin, 120,* 42–59.

Gold, S. R., Fultz, J., Burke, C. H., & Prisco, A. G. (1992). Vicarious emotional responses of macho college males. *Journal of Interpersonal Violence, 7,* 165–174.

Gollwitzer, P. M. (1999). Implementation intentions: Strong effects of simple plans. *American Psychologist, 54,* 493–503.

Gollwitzer, P. M., & Brandstätter, V. (1997). Implementation intentions and effective goal pursuit. *Journal of Personality and Social Psychology, 73,* 186–199.

Goodall, J. (1990). *Through a window: My thirty years with the chimpanzees of Gombe.* Boston: Houghton Mifflin.

Goodwin, C. J. (2005). *A history of modern psychology* (2nd ed.). Hoboken, NJ: Wiley.

Gottman, J. (1994). *Why marriages succeed or fail: And how you can make yours last.* New York: Simon & Schuster.

Gray, J. (1999). Ivan Petrovich Pavlov and the conditioned reflex. *Brain Research Bulletin, 50,* 433.

Green, L., Fisher, E. B., Perlow, S., & Sherman, L. (1981). Preference reversal and self control: Choice as a function of reward amount and delay. *Behaviour Analysis Letters, 1,* 43–51.

Grice, G. R. (1948). The relation of secondary reinforcement to delayed reward in visual discrimination learning. *Journal of Experimental Psychology, 38,* 1–16.

Grosskurth, P. (1991). *The secret ring: Freud's inner circle and the politics of psychoanalysis.* London: Jonathan Cape.

Guevremont, D. C., Osnes, P. G., & Stokes, T. F. (1986). Preparation for effective self-regulation: The development of generalized verbal control. *Journal of Applied Behavior Analysis, 19,* 99–104.

Guthrie, E. R. (1952). *The psychology of learning* (Rev. ed.). New York: Harper & Row. (Original work published 1935)

Hagopian, L. P., Fisher, W. W., & Legacy, S. M. (1994). Schedule effects of noncontingent reinforcement on attention-maintained destructive behavior in identical quadruplets. *Journal of Applied Behavior Analysis, 27,* 317–325.

Haggbloom, S. J., Warnick, R., Warnick, J. E., Jones, V. K., Yarbrough, G. L., Russell, T. M., Borecky, C. M., McGahhey, R., Powell III, J. L., Beavers, J., & Monte, E. (2002). The 100 most eminent psychologists of the 20th century. *Review of General Psychology, 6,* 139–152.

Hall, G. C. N., Shondrick, D. D., & Hirschman, R. (1993). Conceptually derived treatments for sexual aggressors. *Professional Psychology: Research and Practice, 24,* 62–69.

Hanson, H. M. (1959). Effects of discrimination training on stimulus generalization. *Journal of Experimental Psychology, 58,* 321–334.

Harackiewicz, J. M., Manderlink, G., & Sansone, C. (1984). Rewarding pinball wizardry: Effects of evaluation and cue value on intrinsic interest. *Journal of Personality and Social Psychology, 47,* 287–300.

Harlow, H. F., Harlow, M. K., & Meyer, D. R. (1950). Learning motivated by a manipulative drive. *Journal of Experimental Psychology, 40,* 228–234.

Haupt, E. J., Van Kirk, M. J., & Terraciano, T. (1975). An inexpensive fading procedure to decrease errors and increase retention of number facts. In E. Ramp & G. Semb (Eds.), *Behavior analysis: Areas of research and application.* Englewood Cliffs, NJ: Prentice-Hall.

Hayes, K. J., & Hayes, C. (1951). The intellectual development of a home-raised chimpanzee. *Proceedings of the American Philosophical Society, 95,* 105–109.

Hayes, S. C., Rosenfarb, I., Wulfert, E., Munt, E. D., Korn, Z., & Zettle, R. D. (1985). Self-reinforcement effects: An artifact of social standard setting? *Journal of Applied Behavior Analysis, 18,* 201–214.

Heffernan, T., & Richards, C. S. (1981). Self-control of study behavior: Identification and evaluation of natural methods. *Journal of Counseling Psychology, 28,* 361–364.

Hergenhahn, B. R. (1988). *An introduction to theories of learning* (3rd ed.). Englewood Cliffs, NJ: Prentice-Hall.

Herman, J. L. (1992). *Trauma and recovery.* New York: Basic Books.

Herman, L. M., & Forestell, P. H. (1985). Reporting presence or absence of named objects by a language-trained dolphin. *Neuroscience and Biobehavioral Reviews, 9,* 667–681.

Herman, L. M., Kuczaj, S. A., & Holder, M. D. (1993). Responses to anomalous gestural sequences by a language-trained dolphin: Evidence for processing of semantic relations and syntactic information. *Journal of Experimental Psychology: General, 122,* 184–194.

Herman, L. M., Morrel-Samuels, P., & Pack, A. A. (1990). Bottlenosed dolphin and human recognition of veridical and degraded video displays of an artificial gestural language. *Journal of Experimental Psychology: General, 119,* 215–230.

Herman, L. M., Pack, A. A., & Morrel-Samuels, P. (1993). Representational and conceptual skills of dolphins. In H. L. Roitblat, L. M. Herman, and P. E. Nachtigall (Eds.), *Language and communication: Comparative perspectives.* Hillsdale, NJ: Erlbaum.

Herrnstein, R. J. (1961). Relative and absolute strength of response as a function of frequency of reinforcement. *Journal of the Experimental Analysis of Behavior, 4,* 267–272.

Herrnstein, R. J. (1966). Superstition: A corollary of the principle of operant conditioning. In W. K. Honig (Ed.), *Operant behavior: Areas of research and application*. New York: Appleton-Century-Crofts.

Herrnstein, R. J. (1969). Method and theory in the study of avoidance. *Psychological Review, 76,* 49–69.

Herrnstein, R. J. (1981). Self-control as response strength. In C. M. Bradshaw, E. Szabadi, & C. F. Lowe (Eds.), *Recent developments in the quantification of steady-state operant behavior.* Amsterdam: Elsevier/North Holland Biomedical Press.

Herrnstein, R. J. (1990). Rational choice theory: Necessary but not sufficient. *American Psychologist, 45,* 356–367.

Herrnstein, R. J. (1997). *The matching law: Papers in psychology and economics.* Cambridge, MA: Harvard University Press.

Herrnstein, R. J., & Heyman, G. M. (1979). Is matching compatible with reinforcement maximization on concurrent variable interval, variable ratio? *Journal of the Experimental Analysis of Behavior, 31,* 209–223.

Herrnstein, R. J., & Hineline, P. N. (1966). Negative reinforcement as shock-frequency reduction. *Journal of the Experimental Analysis of Behavior, 9,* 421–430.

Herrnstein, R. J., & Loveland, D. H. (1975). Maximizing and matching on concurrent ratio schedules. *Journal of the Experimental Analysis of Behavior, 24,* 107–116.

Hicks, J. (1968). Effects of co-observers' sanctions and adult presence on imitative aggression. *Child Development, 39,* 303–309.

Hinson, R. E., & Poulos, C. X. (1981). Sensitization to the behavioral effects of cocaine: Modification by Pavlovian conditioning. *Pharmacology, Biochemistry, and Behavior, 15,* 559–562.

Hockett, C. D. (1960). The origin of speech. *Scientific American, 203,* 88–96.

Honey, P. L., & Galef, B. G., Jr. (2003). Ethanol consumption by rat dams during gestation, lactation and weaning increases ethanol consumption by their adolescent young. *Developmental Psychobiology, 42,* 252–260.

Honey, P. L., & Galef, B. G., Jr. (2004). Long lasting effects of rearing by an ethanol-consuming dam on voluntary ethanol consumption by rats. *Appetite, 43,* 261–268.

Honey, P. L., Varley, K. R., & Galef, B. G., Jr. (2004). Effects of ethanol consumption by adult female rats on subsequent consumption by adolescents. *Appetite, 42,* 299–306.

Horowitz, A. C. (2003). Do humans ape? Or do apes human? Imitation and intention in humans (*Homo sapiens*) and other animals. *Journal of Comparative Psychology, 3,* 325–336.

Hothersall, D. (1984). *History of psychology.* New York: Random House.

Houston, A. (1986). The matching law applies to wagtails foraging in the wild. *Journal of the Experimental Analysis of Behavior, 45,* 15–18.

Huesmann, L. R. (1986). Psychological processes promoting the relation between exposure to media violence and aggressive behavior by the viewer. *Journal of Social Issues, 42,* 125–139.

Huesmann, L. R., Moise-Titus, J., Podolski, C.-L., & Eron, L. D. (2003). Longitudinal relations between children's exposure to TV violence and their aggressive and violent behavior in young adulthood: 1977–1992. *Developmental Psychology, 39,* 201–221.

Hull, C. L. (1932). The goal gradient hypothesis and maze learning. *Psychological Review, 39,* 25–43.

Hull, C. L. (1934). The rat's speed-of-locomotion gradient in the approach to food. *Journal of Comparative Psychology, 17,* 393–422.

Hull, C. L. (1943). *Principles of behavior.* New York: Appleton-Century-Crofts.

Hunt, P. S., & Hallmark, R. A. (2001). Increases in ethanol ingestion by young rats following interaction with intoxicated siblings: A review. *Integrative Psychological and Behavioral Science, 36,* 239–248.

Jacobson, E. (1938). *Progressive relaxation* (2nd ed.). Chicago: University of Chicago Press.

James, W. (1907). The energies of men. *The Philosophical Review, 16,* 1–20.

James, W. (1983). *The principles of psychology.* Cambridge, MA: Harvard University Press. (Original work published 1890)

Jenkins, H. M., Barrera, F. J., Ireland, C., & Woodside, B. (1978). Signal-centered action patterns of dogs in appetitive classical conditioning. *Learning and Motivation, 9,* 272–296.

Jenkins, H. M., & Moore, B. R. (1973). The form of the autoshaped response with food or water reinforcers. *Journal of the Experimental Analysis of Behavior, 20,* 163–181.

Jensen, R. (2006). Behaviorism, latent learning, and cognitive maps: Needed revisions in introductory psychology textbooks. *The Behavior Analyst, 29,* 187–209.

Johnson, J. G., Cohen, P., Kasen, S., & Brook, J. S. (2007). Extensive television viewing and the development of attention and learning difficulties during adolescence. *Archives of Pediatric and Adolescent Medicine, 161,* 480–486.

Jones, M. C. (1924). The elimination of children's fears. *Journal of Experimental Psychology, 7,* 382–390.

Kaiser, D. H., Sherburne, L. M., & Zentall, T. R. (1997). Directed forgetting in pigeons resulting from reallocation of memory-maintaining processes on forget-cue trials. *Psychonomic Bulletin & Review, 4,* 559–565.

Kalat, J. W. (1974). Taste salience depends on novelty, not concentration, in taste-aversion learning in the rat. *Journal of Comparative and Physiological Psychology, 86,* 47–50.

Kamin, L. J. (1969). Predictability, surprise, attention and conditioning. In B. A. Campbell & R. M. Church (Eds.), *Punishment and aversive behavior.* New York: Appleton-Century-Crofts.

Kantor, T. G., Sunshine, A., Laska, E., Meisner, M., & Hopper, M. (1966). Oral analgesic studies: Penzocine hydrochloride, codeine, aspirin, and placebo and their influence on response to placebo. *Clinical Pharmacology and Therapeutics, 7,* 447–454.

Kaplan, H. I., Sadock, B. J., & Grebb, J. A. (1994). *Kaplan and Sadock's synopsis of psychiatry* (7th ed.). Baltimore: Williams & Wilkins.

Katcher, A. H., Solomon, R. L., Turner, L. H., LoLordo, V. M., Overmier, J. B., & Rescorla, R. A. (1969). Heart-rate and blood pressure responses to signaled and unsignaled shocks: Effects of cardiac sympathectomy. *Journal of Comparative and Physiological Psychology, 68,* 163–174.

Katz, J. L. (1986). Long-distance running, anorexia nervosa, and bulimia: A report of two cases. *Comprehensive Psychiatry, 27,* 74–78.

Katz, J. L. (1996). Clinical observations on the physical activity of anorexia nervosa. In W. F. Epling & W. D. Pierce (Eds.), *Activity anorexia: Theory, research, and treatment.* Mahwah, NJ: Erlbaum.

Kawamura, S. (1963). The process of sub-cultural propagation among Japanese macaques. In C. H. Southwick (Ed.), *Primate social behavior.* New York: Van Nostrand.

Kazdin, A. E. (1994). *Behavior modification in applied settings* (5th ed.). Pacific Grove, CA: Brooks/Cole.

Keesey, R. (1964). Intracranial reward delay and the acquisition rate of a brightness discrimination. *Science, 143,* 702.

Keith-Lucas, T., & Guttman, N. (1975). Robust single-trial delayed backward conditioning. *Journal of Comparative and Physiological Psychology, 88,* 468–476.

Kelleher, R. T., & Fry, W. (1962). Stimulus functions in chained fixed-interval schedules. *Journal of the Experimental Analysis of Behavior, 5,* 167–173.

Kellogg, W. N., & Kellogg, L. A. (1933). *The ape and the child.* New York: McGraw-Hill.

Kimble, G. A. (1961). *Hilgard and Marquis' conditioning and learning* (Rev. ed.). New York: Appleton-Century-Crofts.

Kimble, G. A. (1967). *Foundations of conditioning and learning.* New York: Appleton-Century-Crofts.

King, B. J. (1991). Social information transfer in monkeys, apes, and hominids. *Yearbook of Physical Anthropology, 34,* 97–115.

Kirsch, L. G., & Becker, J. V. (2006). Sexual offending: Theory of problem, theory of change, and implications for treatment effectiveness. *Aggression and Violent Behavior, 11,* 208–224.

Klein, S. B. (1996). *Learning: Principles and applications* (3rd ed.). New York: McGraw-Hill.

Kleinke, C. L., Meeker, G. B., & Staneske, R. A. (1986). Preference for opening lines: Comparing ratings by men and women. *Sex Roles, 15,* 585–600.

Klinger, E. (1975). Consequences of commitment to and disengagement from incentives. *Psychological Review, 82,* 1–25.

Klinger, E., Barta, S. G., & Kemble, E. D. (1974). Cyclic activity changes during extinction in rats: A potential model for depression. *Animal Learning and Behavior, 2,* 313–316.

Kluft, R. P. (1998). The argument for the reality of delayed recall of trauma. In P. S. Appelbaum, L. A. Uyehara, & M. R. Elin (Eds.), *Trauma and memory: Clinical and legal controversies.* New York: Oxford University Press.

Kohlenberg, R. J. (1973). Behavioristic approach to multiple personality: A case study. *Behavior Therapy, 4,* 137–140.

Kohlenberg, R. J., & Tsai, M. (1991). *Functional analytic psychotherapy: Creating intense and curative therapeutic relationships.* New York: Plenum Press.

Kohler, W. (1939). Simple structural function in the chimpanzee and the chicken. In W. D. Ellis (Ed.), *A course book of gestalt psychology.* New York: Harcourt Brace. (Original work published 1918)

Kohler, W. (1947). *Gestalt psychology: An introduction to new concepts in modern psychology.* New York: Liveright.

Kohn, A. (1993). *Punished by rewards.* Boston: Houghton Mifflin.

Kossoff, M. J. (1999, March/April). Gary Player: Swinging hard on life's course. *Psychology Today, 32,* 58–61, 78, 82.

Koubova, J. (2003). How does calorie restriction work? *Genes & Development, 17,* 313–321.

Lakein, A. (1973). *How to get control of your time and your life.* New York: New American Library.

Lang, W. J., Ross, P., & Glover, A. (1967). Conditional responses induced by hypotensive drugs. *European Journal of Pharmacology, 2,* 169–174.

LaRowe, S. D., Patrick, C. J., Curtin, J. J., & Kline, J. P. (2006). Personality correlates of startle habituation. *Biological Psychology, 72,* 257–264.

Lasagna, L., Mosteller, F., von Felsinger, J. M., & Beecher, H. K. (1954). A study of the placebo response. *American Journal of Medicine, 16,* 770–779.

Lefkowitz, M. M., Eron, L. D., Walder, L. O., & Huesmann, L. R. (1977). *Growing up to be violent: A longitudinal study of the development of aggression.* Oxford, MA: Pergamon.

Lepper, M. R., Green, D., & Nisbett, R. E. (1973). Undermining children's intrinsic interest with extrinsic reward: A test of the "overjustification" hypothesis. *Journal of Personality and Social Psychology, 28,* 129–137.

Lerman, D. C., & Iwata, B. A. (1996). Developing a technology for the use of operant extinction in clinical settings: An examination of basic and applied research. *Journal of Applied Behavior Analysis, 29,* 345–382.

Levis, D. J. (1988). Observation and experience from clinical practice: A critical ingredient for advancing behavioral theory and therapy. *Behavior Therapist, 11,* 95–99.

Levis, D. J. (1989). The case for a return to a two-factor theory of avoidance: The failure of non-fear interpretations. In S. B. Klein & R. R. Mowrer (Eds.), *Contemporary learning theories: Pavlovian conditioning and the status of learning theory.* Hillsdale, NJ: Erlbaum.

Levis, D. J. (1995). Decoding traumatic memory: Implosive theory of psychopathology. In W. O'Donohue & L. Krasner (Eds.), *Theories of behavior therapy: Exploring behavior change.* Washington, DC: American Psychological Association.

Levis, D. J., & Boyd, T. L. (1979). Symptom maintenance: An infrahuman analysis and extension of the conservation of anxiety principle. *Journal of Abnormal Psychology, 88,* 107–120.

Levis, D. J., & Brewer, K. E. (2001). The neurotic paradox: Attempts by two-factor fear theory and alternative avoidance models to resolve the issues associated with sustained avoidance responding in extinction. In R. R. Mowrer & S. B. Klein (Eds.), *Handbook of contemporary learning theories.* Mahwah, NJ: Erlbaum.

Levitsky, D., & Collier, G. (1968). Schedule-induced wheel running. *Physiology and Behavior, 3,* 571–573.

Lewes, G. H. (1965). *The life of Goethe.* New York: Frederick Ungar.

Lewinsohn, P. M. (1974). A behavioral approach to depression. In R. J. Friedman & M. M. Katz (Eds.), *The psychology of depression: Contemporary theory and research.* New York: Winston/ Wiley.

Lichstein, K. L., & Riedel, B. W. (1994). Behavioral assessment and treatment of insomnia: A review with an emphasis on clinical application. *Behavior Therapy, 25,* 659–688.

Lichtenstein, E., & Glasgow, R. E. (1977). Rapid smoking: Side effects and safeguards. *Journal of Consulting and Clinical Psychology, 45,* 815–821.

Lieberman, D. A. (2000). *Learning: Behavior and cognition* (3rd ed.). Belmont, CA: Wadsworth.

Lilienfeld, S. O., Kirsch, I., Sarbin, T. R., Lynn, S. J., Chaves, J. F., Ganaway, G. K., & Powell, R. A. (1999). Dissociative identity disorder and the sociocognitive model: Recalling the lessons of the past. *Psychological Bulletin, 125,* 507–523.

Linnoila, M., Stapleton, J. M., Lister, R., Guthrie, S., & Eckhardt, M. (1986). Effects of alcohol on accident risk. *Pathologist, 40,* 36–41.

Loftus, E. F. (1993). The reality of repressed memories. *American Psychologist, 48,* 518–537.

Logue, A. W. (1995). *Self-control: Waiting until tomorrow for what you want today.* Upper Saddle River, NJ: Prentice-Hall.

Logue, A. W., Ophir, I., & Strauss, K. E. (1981). The acquisition of taste aversions in humans. *Behaviour Research and Therapy, 19,* 319–333.

Lovaas, O. I. (1987). Behavioral treatment and normal educational and intellectual functioning in young autistic children. *Journal of Consulting and Clinical Psychology, 55,* 3–9.

Lowe, C. F. (1979). Determinants of human operant behavior. In M. D. Zeller & P. Harzem (Eds.), *Reinforcement and the organization of behavior.* New York: Wiley.

Lowe, C. F., Beasty, A., & Bentall, R. P. (1983). The role of verbal behavior in human learning: Infant performance on fixed-interval schedules. *Journal of the Experimental Analysis of Behavior, 39,* 157–164.

Lubow, R. E., & Gewirtz, J. C. (1995). Latent inhibition in humans: Data, theory, and implications for schizophrenia. *Psychological Bulletin, 117,* 87–103.

Luszczynska, A., Sobczyk, A., & Abraham, C. (2007). Planning to lose weight: Randomized controlled trial of an implementation intention prompt to enhance weight reduction among overweight and obese women. *Health Psychology, 26,* 507–512.

Lynch, S. (1998). Intensive behavioural intervention with a 7-year-old girl with autism. *Autism, 2,* 181–197.

Maier, S. F., Jackson, R. L., & Tomie, A. (1987). Potentiation, overshadowing, and prior exposure to inescapable shock. *Journal of Experimental Psychology: Animal Behavior Processes, 13,* 260–270.

Maki, W. S., & Hegvik, D. K. (1980). Directed forgetting in pigeons. *Animal Learning and Behavior, 8,* 567–574.

Malone, J. C. (1990). *Theories of learning: A historical approach.* Belmont, CA: Wadsworth.

Malott, R. W. (1989). Achievement of evasive goals: Control by rules describing contingencies that are not direct acting. In S. C. Hayes (Ed.), *Rule-governed behavior: Cognition, contingencies, and instructional control.* New York: Plenum Press.

Malott, R. W., Malott, M. E., & Trojan, E. A. (2000). *Elementary principles of behavior* (4th ed.). Upper Saddle River, NJ: Prentice-Hall.

Malott, R. W., & Suarez, E. A. T. (2004). *Principles of behavior.* Upper Saddle River, NJ: Pearson.

Marks, I. M. (1969). *Fears and phobias.* New York: Academic Press.

Marlatt, G. A., & Gordon, J. R. (Eds.). (1985). *Relapse prevention: Maintenance strategies in addictive behavior change.* New York: Guilford.

Marrazzi, M. A., & Luby, E. D. (1986). An auto-addiction opioid model of chronic anorexia nervosa. *International Journal of Eating Disorders, 5,* 191–208.

Marsh, G., & Johnson, R. (1968). Discrimination reversal following learning without "errors." *Psychonomic Science, 10,* 261–262.

Martin, G., & Pear, J. (1999). *Behavior modification: What it is and how to do it* (6th ed.). Upper Saddle River, NJ: Prentice-Hall.

Maslow, A. H. (1971). *The farther reaches of human nature.* New York: Viking Press.

Masoro, E. J. (2005). Overview of caloric restriction and ageing. *Mechanisms of Ageing and Development, 126,* 913–922.

Masserman, J. H. (1943). *Behavior and neurosis: An experimental psychoanalytic approach to psychobiologic principles.* Chicago: University of Chicago Press.

Masters, J. C., Burish, T. G., Hollon, S. D., & Rimm, D. C. (1987). *Behavior therapy: Techniques and empirical findings* (3rd ed.). New York: Harcourt Brace Jovanovich.

Mayou, R. A., & Ehlers, A. (2000). Three-year follow-up of a randomized controlled trial: Psychological debriefing for road accident victims. *British Journal of Psychiatry, 176,* 589–593.

Mazur, J. E. (2002). *Learning and behavior* (5th ed.). Upper Saddle River, NJ: Prentice-Hall.

Mazur, J. E., & Logue, A. W. (1978). Choice in a self-control paradigm: Effects of a fading procedure. *Journal of the Experimental Analysis of Behavior, 30,* 11–17.

McConnell, P. B. (2003). *The other end of the leash.* New York: Ballantine Books.

McCusker, C. G., & Brown, K. (1990). Alcohol-predictive cues enhance tolerance to and precipitate "craving" for alcohol in social drinkers. *Journal of Studies on Alcohol, 51,* 494–499.

Melvin, K. B. (1985). Attack/display as a reinforcer in *Betta splendens. Bulletin of the Psychonomic Society, 23,* 350–352.

Mennella, J. A., & Garcia, P. L. (2000). Children's hedonic response to the smell of alcohol: Effects of parental drinking habits. *Alcoholism: Clinical and Experimental Research, 24,* 1167–1171.

Michael, J. (1982). Distinguishing between discriminative and motivational functions of stimuli. *Journal of the Experimental Analysis of Behavior, 37,* 149–155.

Miles, H. L. W. (1990). The cognitive foundations for reference in a signing orangutan. In S. T. Parker & K. R. Gibson (Eds.), *"Language" and intelligence in monkeys and apes.* Cambridge, UK: Cambridge University Press.

Miles, H. L. W. (1994). ME CHANTEK: The development of self-awareness in a signing orangutan. In S. T. Parker, R. W. Mitchell, & M. L. Boccia (Eds.), *Self-awareness in animals and humans: Developmental perspectives.* Cambridge, UK: Cambridge University Press.

Miles, H. L. W. (1999). Symbolic communication with and by great apes. In S. T. Parker, R. W. Mitchell, & H. L. Miles (Eds.), *The mentalities of gorillas and orangutans: Comparative perspectives.* Cambridge, UK: Cambridge University Press.

Miller, H. L. (1976). Matching-based hedonic scaling in the pigeon. *Journal of the Experimental Analysis of Behavior, 26,* 335–347.

Miller, L. K. (1997). *Principles of everyday behavior analysis* (3rd ed.). Pacific Grove, CA: Brooks/Cole.

Miller, N. E. (1960). Learning resistance to pain and fear: Effects of overlearning, exposure, and rewarded exposure in context. *Journal of Experimental Psychology, 60*, 137–145.

Miller, N. E., & Dollard, J. (1941). *Social learning and imitation.* New Haven, CT: Yale University Press.

Miltenberger, R. G. (1997). *Behavior modification: Principles and procedures.* Pacific Grove, CA: Brooks/Cole.

Mindell, J. A. (1999). Empirically supported treatments in pediatric psychology: Bedtime refusal and night wakings in young children. *Journal of Pediatric Psychology, 24*, 465–481.

Mineka, S. (1985). Animal models of anxiety-based disorder: Their usefulness and limitations. In A. H. Tuma & J. Maser (Eds.), *Anxiety and the anxiety disorders.* Hillsdale, NJ: Erlbaum.

Mineka, S. (1987). A primate model of phobic fears. In H. Eysenck & I. Martin (Eds.), *Theoretical foundations of behavior therapy.* New York: Plenum Press.

Mineka, S., & Cook, M. (1993). Mechanisms involved in the observational conditioning of fear. *Journal of Experimental Psychology: General, 122*, 23–38.

Mineka, S., Gunnar, M., & Champoux, M. (1986). Control and early socio-emotional development: Infant rhesus monkeys reared in controllable versus uncontrollable environments. *Child Development, 57*, 1241–1256.

Mischel, W. (1966). Theory and research on the antecedents of self-imposed delay of reward. In B. A. Maher (Ed.), *Progress in experimental personality research* (Vol. 3). New York: Academic Press.

Mischel, W. (1974). Processes in delay of gratification. In L. Berkowitz (Ed.), *Advances in experimental social psychology* (Vol. 7). New York: Academic Press.

Monte, C. F. (1999). *Beneath the mask: An introduction to theories of personality* (6th ed.). New York: Harcourt Brace.

Morgan, C. L. (1894). *An introduction to comparative psychology.* London: W. Scott.

Morgan, C. L. (1900). *Animal behaviour.* London: Arnold.

Morse, A. D., Russell, J. C., Hunt, T. W., Wood, G. O., Epling, W. F., & Pierce, W. D. (1995). Diurnal variation of intensive running in food-deprived rats. *Canadian Journal of Physiology and Pharmacology, 73*, 1519–1523.

Mowrer, O. H. (1947). On the dual nature of learning: A reinterpretation of "conditioning" and "problem-solving." *Harvard Educational Review, 17*, 102–150.

Mowrer, O. H. (1960). *Learning theory and behavior.* New York: Wiley.

Mowrer, O. H., & Jones, H. (1945). Habit strength as a result of the pattern of reinforcement. *Journal of Experimental Psychology, 35*, 293–311.

Mukerjee, M. (1997, February). Trends in animal research. *Scientific American, 272*, 86–93.

Nagel, K., Olguin, K., & Tomasello, M. (1993). Processes of social learning in the tool use of chimpanzees (*Pan troglodytes*) and human children (*Homo sapiens*). *Journal of Comparative Psychology, 107*, 174–186.

Nairne, J. S. (2000). *Psychology: The adaptive mind* (2nd ed.). Pacific Grove, CA: Brooks/Cole.

Newman, A., & Kanfer, F. H. (1976). Delay of gratification in children: The effects of training under fixed, decreasing and increasing delay of reward. *Journal of Experimental Child Psychology, 21*, 12–24.

Newman, L. S., & Baumeister, R. F. (1996). Toward an explanation of the UFO abduction phenomenon: Hypnotic elaboration, extraterrestrial sadomasochism, and spurious memories. *Psychological Inquiry, 7*, 99–126.

Newsom, C., Favell, J., & Rincover, A. (1983). The side effects of punishment. In S. Axelrod & J. Apsche (Eds.), *The effects of punishment on human behavior.* New York: Academic Press.

Nguyen, N. H., Klein, E. D., & Zentall, T. R. (2005). Imitation of a two-action sequence by pigeons. *Psychonomic Bulletin & Review, 12*, 514–518.

Nordin, S., Broman, D. A., Olafsson, J. K., & Wulff, M. (2004). A longitudinal descriptive study of self-reported abnormal smell and taste perception in pregnant women. *Chemical Senses, 29,* 391–402.

O'Brien, R. M., Figlerski, R. W., Howard, S. R., & Caggiano, J. (1981, August). *The effects of multi-year, guaranteed contracts on the performance of pitchers in major league baseball.* Paper presented at the annual meeting of the American Psychological Association, Los Angeles, CA.

Oaten, M., & Cheng, K. (2006). Improved self-control: The benefits of a regular program of academic study. *Basic and Applied Social Psychology, 28,* 1–16.

O'Donohue, W., & Ferguson, K. E. (2001). *The psychology of B. F. Skinner.* Thousand Oaks, CA: Sage.

Ono, K. (1987). Superstitious behavior in humans. *Journal of the Experimental Analysis of Behavior, 47,* 261–271.

Öst, L. (1989). One-session treatment for specific phobias. *Behaviour Research and Therapy, 27,* 1–7.

Patterson, F. G., & Linden, E. (1981). *The education of Koko.* New York: Holt, Rinehart & Winston.

Pavlov, I. P. (1927). *Conditioned reflexes* (G. V. Anrep, Trans.). London: Oxford University Press.

Pavlov, I. P. (1928). *Lectures on conditioned reflexes.* (W. H. Gantt, Trans.). New York: International Publishers.

Pavlov, I. P. (1941). *Conditioned reflexes and psychiatry.* New York: International Publishers.

Pendergrast, M. (1995). *Victims of memory: Incest accusations and shattered lives.* Hinesburg, VT: Upper Access.

Pepperberg, I. M. (1999). *The Alex studies: Cognitive and communicative abilities of grey parrots.* Cambridge, MA: Harvard University Press.

Pepperberg, I. M., & Sherman, D. (2000). Proposed use of two-part interactive modeling as a means to increase functional skills in children with a variety of disabilities. *Teaching and Learning in Medicine, 12,* 213–220.

Perin, C. T. (1942). Behavior potentiality as a joint function of the amount of training and the degree of hunger at the time of extinction. *Journal of Experimental Psychology, 30,* 93–113.

Phelps, B. J. (2000). Dissociative identity disorder: The relevance of behavior analysis. *Psychological Record, 50,* 235–249.

Pierce, W. D., & Epling, W. F. (1995). *Behavior analysis and learning.* Englewood Cliffs, NJ: Prentice-Hall.

Pierce, W. D., & Epling, W. F. (1996). Theoretical developments in activity anorexia. In W. F. Epling & W. D. Pierce (Eds.), *Activity anorexia: Theory, research, and treatment.* Mahwah, NJ: Erlbaum.

Pierce, W. D., & Epling, W. F. (1999). *Behavior analysis and learning* (2nd ed.). Upper Saddle River, NJ: Prentice-Hall.

Pinker, S. (1994). *The language instinct: How the mind creates language.* New York: William Morrow.

Plant, E. A., Ericsson, K. A., Hill, L., & Asberg, K. (2005). Why study time does not predict grade point average across college students: Implications of deliberate practice for academic performance. *Contemporary Educational Psychology, 30,* 96–116.

Pliskoff, S. S. (1963). Rate change effects with equal potential reinforcements during the "warning" stimulus. *Journal of the Experimental Analysis of Behavior, 6,* 557–562.

Poling, A., Nickel, M., & Alling, K. (1990). Free birds aren't fat: Weight gain in captured wild pigeons maintained under laboratory conditions. *Journal of the Experimental Analysis of Behavior, 53,* 423–424.

Powell, R. A., & Gee, T. L. (1999). The effects of hypnosis on dissociative identity disorder: A reexamination of the evidence. *Canadian Journal of Psychiatry, 44,* 914–916.

Premack, D. (1965). Reinforcement theory. In D. Levine (Ed.), *Nebraska symposium on motivation* (Vol. 13). Lincoln, NE: University of Nebraska Press.

Premack, D. (1971a). Catching up with common sense or two sides of a generalization: Reinforcement and punishment. In R. Glaser (Ed.), *The nature of reinforcement.* New York: Academic Press.

Premack, D. (1971b). Language in a chimpanzee? *Science, 172,* 808–822.

Premack, D. (1976). *Intelligence in ape and man.* Hillsdale, NJ: Erlbaum.

Premack, D., & Woodruff, G. (1978). Chimpanzee problem-solving: A test for comprehension. *Science, 202,* 532–535.

Provine, R. R. (1996). Contagious yawning and laughter: Significance for sensory feature detection, motor pattern generation, imitation, and the evolution of social behavior. In C. M. Heyes & B. G. Galef. Jr. (Eds.), *Social learning in animals: The roots of culture.* San Diego, CA: Academic Press.

Provine, R.R. (2004). Laughing, tickling and the evolution of speech and self. *Current Directions in Psychological Science, 13,* 215–218.

Pryor, K. (1975). *Lads before the wind: Adventures in porpoise training.* New York: Harper & Row.

Pryor, K. (1999). *Don't shoot the dog: The new art of teaching and training* (Rev. ed.). New York: Bantam Books.

Rachlin, H. (1974). Self-control. *Behaviorism, 2,* 94–107.

Rachlin, H. (1978). A molar theory of reinforcement schedules. *Journal of the Experimental Analysis of Behavior, 30,* 345–360.

Rachlin, H. (1991). *Introduction to modern behaviorism* (3rd ed.). New York: W. H. Freeman.

Rachlin, H. (2000). *The science of self-control.* Cambridge, MA: Harvard University Press.

Rachlin, H., & Baum, W. M. (1972). Effects of alternative reinforcement: Does the source matter? *Journal of the Experimental Analysis of Behavior, 18,* 231–241.

Rachlin, H., & Green, L. (1972). Commitment, choice and self-control. *Journal of the Experimental Analysis of Behavior, 17,* 15–22.

Rachman, S. (1977). The conditioning theory of fear-acquisition: A critical examination. *Behaviour Research and Therapy, 15,* 375–387.

Rachman, S., & Hodgson, R. J. (1968). Experimentally induced "sexual fetishism": Replication and development. *Psychological Record, 18,* 25–27.

Rachman, S., & Hodgson, R. J. (1980). *Obsessions and compulsions.* Englewood Cliffs, NJ: Prentice-Hall.

Rankin, A. M., & Philip, P. J. (1963). An epidemic of laughing in the Bukoba District of Tanganyika. *Central African Journal of Medicine, 9,* 167–170.

Rathus, S. A., Nevid, J. S., & Fichner-Rathus, L. (2000). *Human sexuality in a world of diversity* (4th ed.). Boston: Allyn & Bacon.

Reed, D. D., Critchfield, T. S., & Martens, B. K. (2006). The generalized matching law in elite sport competition: Football play calling as operant choice. *Journal of Applied Behavior Analysis, 39,* 281–297.

Remington, B., Roberts, P., & Glautier, S. (1997). The effect of drink familiarity on tolerance. *Addictive Behaviors, 22,* 45–53.

Rescorla, R. A. (1980). Simultaneous and successive associations in sensory preconditioning. *Journal of Experimental Psychology: Animal Behavior Processes, 6,* 207–216.

Rescorla, R. A., & Wagner, A. R. (1972). A theory of Pavlovian conditioning: Variations in the effectiveness of reinforcement and nonreinforcement. In A. H. Black & W. F. Prokasy (Eds.), *Classical conditioning II: Current research and theory.* New York: Appleton-Century-Crofts.

Reynolds, G. S. (1961). Behavioral contrast. *Journal of the Experimental Analysis of Behavior, 4,* 57–71.

Reynolds, G. S. (1975). *A primer of operant conditioning* (2nd ed.). Glenview, IL: Scott, Foresman.

Rickert, V. I., & Johnson, C. M. (1988). Reducing nocturnal awakening and crying episodes in infants and young children: A comparison between scheduled awakenings and systematic ignoring. *Pediatrics, 81,* 203–212.

Riley, A. L., & Clarke, C. M. (1977). Conditioned taste aversions: A bibliography. In L. M. Barker, M. R. Best, & M. Domjan (Eds.), *Learning mechanisms in food selection.* Waco, TX: Baylor University Press.

Riley, A. L., & Wetherington, C. L. (1989). Schedule-induced polydipsia: Is the rat a small furry human? (An analysis of an animal model of human alcoholism). In S. B. Klein & R. R. Mowrer (Eds.), *Contemporary learning theories: Instrumental conditioning theory and the impact of biological constraints on learning.* Hillsdale, NJ: Erlbaum.

Robins, L. N. (1974). A follow-up study of Vietnam veterans' drug use. *Journal of Drug Issues, 4,* 61–63.

Rogers, C. R. (1959). A theory of therapy, personality, and interpersonal relationships, as developed in the client-centered framework. In S. Koch (Ed.), *Psychology: A study of a science* (Vol. 3). New York: McGraw-Hill.

Roitblat, H. L., Herman, L. M., & Nachtigall, P. E. (Eds.). (1993). *Language and communication: Comparative perspectives.* Hillsdale, NJ: Erlbaum.

Romanes, G. J. (1884). *Animal intelligence.* New York: Appleton.

Romanes, G. J. (1888/1989). *Mental evolution in man: Origin of human faculty.* London: Kegan Paul.

Ross, C. A. (1997). *Dissociative identity disorder: Diagnosis, clinical features, and treatment of multiple personality* (2nd ed.). New York: Wiley.

Ross, C. A., & Norton, G. R. (1989). Effects of hypnosis on the features of multiple personality disorder. *American Journal of Clinical Hypnosis, 32,* 99–106.

Routtenberg, A., & Kuznesof, A. W. (1967). Self-starvation of rats living in activity wheels on a restricted food schedule. *Journal of Comparative and Physiological Psychology, 64,* 414–421.

Rozen, P., Reff, D., Mark, M., & Schull, J. (1984). Conditioned opponent processes in human tolerance to caffeine. *Bulletin of the Psychonomic Society, 22,* 117–120.

Rozin, P., Fischler, C., Imada, S., Sarubin, A., & Wrzesniewski, A. (1999). Attitudes to food and the role of food in life: Comparisons of Flemish Belgium, France, Japan and the United States. *Appetite, 33,* 163–180.

Rumbaugh, D. M. (Ed.). (1977). *Language learning by a chimpanzee: The LANA project.* San Diego, CA: Academic Press.

Russell, J. C., Amy, R. M., Manickavel, V., Dolphin, P. J., Epling, W. F., Pierce, W. D., & Boer, D. P. (1989). Prevention of myocardial disease in JCR:LA-corpulent rats by running. *Journal of Applied Physiology, 66,* 1649–1655.

Russell, M., Dark, K. A., Cummins, R. W., Ellman, G., Callaway, E., & Peeke, H. V. S. (1984). Learned histamine release. *Science, 225,* 733–734.

Russon, A. E., & Galdikas, B. M. F. (1993). Imitation in ex-captive orangutans. *Journal of Comparative Psychology, 107,* 147–161.

Russon, A. E., & Galdikas, B. M. F. (1995). Constraints on great apes' imitation: Model and action selectivity in rehabilitant orangutan (*Pongo pygmaeus*) imitation. *Journal of Comparative Psychology, 109,* 5–17.

Salkovskis, P. M. (1998). Psychological approaches to the understanding of obsessional problems. In R. P. Swinson, M. M. Antony, S. Rachman, & M. A. Richter (Eds.), *Obsessive-compulsive disorder: Theory, research, and treatment.* New York: Guilford.

Savage-Rumbaugh, E. S. (1993). Language learnability in man, ape and dolphin. In H. L. Roitblat, L. M. Herman, & P. E. Nachtigall (Eds.), *Language and communication: Comparative perspectives.* Hillsdale, NJ: Erlbaum.

Savage-Rumbaugh, E. S., & Lewin, R. (1994). *Kanzi: The ape at the brink of the human mind.* New York: Wiley.

Savage-Rumbaugh, E. S., McDonald, K., Sevcik, R. A., Hopkins, W. D., & Rubert, E. (1986). Spontaneous symbol acquisition and communicative use by pygmy chimpanzees (*Pan paniscus*). *Journal of Comparative Psychology, 115,* 211–235.

Savage-Rumbaugh, E. S., Rumbaugh, D. M., Smith, S. T., & Lawson, J. (1980). Reference: The linguistic essential. *Science, 210,* 922–925.

Savage-Rumbaugh, E. S., Shanker, S. G., & Taylor, T. J. (1998). *Apes, language and the human mind.* New York: Oxford University Press.

Schafe, G. E., & Bernstein, I. L. (1996). Taste aversion learning. In E. D. Capaldi (Ed.), *Why we eat what we eat: The psychology of eating.* Washington, DC: American Psychological Association.

Schmidt, R. A., & Bjork, R. A. (1992). New conceptualizations of practice: Common principles in three paradigms suggest new concepts for training. *Psychological Science, 3,* 207–217.

Schreiber, F. R. (1973). *Sybil.* Chicago: Henry Regnery.

Schusterman, R. J., & Gisiner, R. (1988). Artificial language comprehension in dolphins and sea lions: The essential cognitive skills. *Psychological Record, 38,* 311–348.

Seligman, M. E. P. (1971). Phobias and preparedness. *Behavior Therapy, 2,* 307–320.

Seligman, M. E. P. (1975). *Helplessness: On depression, development, and death.* San Francisco: Freeman.

Seligman, M. E. P., & Maier, S. (1967). Failure to escape traumatic shock. *Journal of Experimental Psychology, 74,* 1–9.

Seligman, M. E. P., Rosellini, R. A., & Kozak, M. J. (1975). Learned helplessness in the rat: Time course, immunization, and reversibility. *Journal of Comparative and Physiological Psychology, 88,* 542–547.

Seyfarth, R. M., Cheney, D. L., & Marler, P. (1980). Monkey responses to three different alarm calls: Evidence for predator classification and semantic communication. *Science, 210,* 801–803.

Shea, C. H., Wright, D. L., Wulf, G., & Whitacre, C. (2000). Physical and observational practice afford unique learning opportunities. *Journal of Motor Behavior, 32,* 27–36.

Sheeran, P., & Orbell, S. (1999). Implementation intentions and repeated behaviour: Augmenting the predictive validity of the theory of planned behaviour. *European Journal of Social Psychology, 29,* 349–369.

Sheeran, P., & Orbell, S. (2000). Using implementation intentions to increase attendance for cervical cancer screening. *Health Psychology, 19,* 283–289.

Shoda, Y., Mischel, W., & Peake, P. K. (1990). Predicting adolescent cognitive and self-regulatory competencies from preschool delay of gratification: Identifying diagnostic conditions. *Developmental Psychology, 26,* 978–986.

Shyan, M. R., & Herman, L. M. (1987). Determinants of recognition of gestural signs in an artificial language by Atlantic bottle-nosed dolphins (*Tursiops truncatus*) and humans (*Homo sapiens*). *Journal of Comparative Psychology, 101,* 112–125.

Sidman, M. (1960). *Tactics of scientific research: Evaluating experimental data in psychology.* New York: Basic Books.

Siegel, S. (1983). Classical conditioning, drug tolerance, and drug dependence. In R. G. Smart, F. B. Glaser, Y. Israel, H. Kalant, R. E. Popham, & W. Schmidt (Eds.), *Research advances in alcohol and drug problems* (Vol. 7). New York: Plenum Press.

Siegel, S. (1984). Pavlovian conditioning and heroin overdose: Reports by overdose victims. *Bulletin of the Psychonomic Society, 22,* 428–430.

Siegel, S. (1989). Pharmacological conditioning and drug effects. In A. J. Goudie & M. W. Emmett-Oglesby (Eds.), *Psychoactive drugs: Tolerance and sensitization.* Clifton, NJ: Humana Press.

Siegel, S. (2002). Explanatory mechanisms for placebo effects: Pavlovian conditioning. In H. A. Guess, A. Kleinman, J. W. Kusek, & L. W. Engel (Eds.), *The science of the placebo: Toward an interdisciplinary research agenda.* New York: BMJ Books.

Siegel, S. (2005). Drug tolerance, drug addiction, and drug anticipation. *Current Directions in Psychological Science, 14,* 296–300.

Siegel, S., Hinson, R. E., Krank, M. D., & McCully, J. (1982). Heroin "overdose" death: The contribution of drug-associated environmental cues. *Science, 216,* 436–437.

Sijbrandij, M., Olff, M., Reitsma, J. B., Carlier, I. V. E., & Gersons, B. P. R. (2006). Emotional or educational debriefing after psychological trauma: Randomised control trial. *British Journal of Psychiatry, 189,* 150–155.

Skinner, B. F. (1938). *The behavior of organisms: An experimental analysis.* Acton, MA: Copley.

Skinner, B. F. (1948a). *Walden II.* New York: Macmillan.

Skinner, B. F. (1948b). "Superstition" in the pigeon. *Journal of Experimental Psychology, 38,* 168–172.

Skinner, B. F. (1950). Are theories of learning necessary? *Psychological Review, 57,* 193–216.

Skinner, B. F. (1953). *Science and human behavior.* New York: Macmillan.

Skinner, B. F. (1956). A case history in scientific method. *American Psychologist, 11,* 221–233.

Skinner, B. F. (1967). B. F. Skinner. In E. G. Boring & G. Lindzey (Eds.), *A history of psychology in autobiography: Vol. 5.* New York: Appleton-Century-Crofts.

Skinner, B. F. (1969). *Contingencies of reinforcement: A theoretical analysis.* New York: Appleton-Century-Crofts.

Skinner, B. F. (1971). *Beyond freedom and dignity.* New York: Vintage Books.

Skinner, B. F. (1974). *About behaviorism.* New York: Knopf.

Skinner, B. F. (1983). *A matter of consequences.* New York: Knopf.

Skinner, B. F. (1987). *Upon further reflection.* Englewood Cliffs, NJ: Prentice-Hall.

Skinner, B. F. (1989). *Recent issues in the analysis of behavior.* Columbus, OH: Merrill.

Skinner, B. F., & Vaughan, M. E. (1983). *Enjoy old age: A program of self-management.* New York: Norton.

Skinner-Buzan, D. (2004, March 12). I was not a lab rat. *The Guardian.*

Slater, L. (2004). *Opening Skinner's box: Great Psychological Experiments of the Twentieth Century.* New York: Norton.

Soares, J. J., & Öhman, A. (1993). Backward masking and skin conductance responses after conditioning to nonfeared but fear-relevant stimuli in fearful subjects. *Psychophysiology, 30,* 460–466.

Sokolowska, M., Siegel, S., & Kim, J. A. (2002). Intraadministration associations: Conditional hyperalgesia elicited by morphine onset. *Journal of Experimental Psychology: Animal Behavior Processes, 28,* 309–320.

Solomon, L. J., & Rothblum, E. D. (1984). Academic procrastination: Frequency and cognitive-behavioral correlates. *Journal of Counseling Psychology, 31,* 503–509.

Solomon, R. L. (1980). The opponent-process theory of motivation: The costs of pleasure and the benefits of pain. *American Psychologist, 35,* 691–712.

Solomon, R. L., & Corbit, J. D. (1974). The opponent-process theory of motivation: I. Temporal dynamics of affect. *Psychological Review, 81,* 119–145.

Solomon, R. L., & Wynne, L. C. (1953). Traumatic avoidance learning: Acquisition in normal dogs. *Psychological Monographs, 67* (4, Whole No. 354).

Solomon, R. L., & Wynne, L. C. (1954). Traumatic avoidance learning: The principles of anxiety conservation and partial irreversibility. *Psychological Review, 61,* 353–385.

Solomon, R. L., Kamin, L. J., & Wynne, L. C. (1953). Traumatic avoidance learning: The outcomes of several extinction procedures with dogs. *Journal of Abnormal and Social Psychology, 48,* 291–302.

Solvason, H. B., Ghanta, V. K., & Hiramoto, R. N. (1988). Conditioned augmentation of natural killer cell activity: Independence from nociceptive effects and dependence on interferon-beta. *Journal of Immunology, 140,* 661–665.

Spanos, N. P. (1994). Multiple identity enactments and multiple personality disorder: A socio-cognitive perspective. *Psychological Bulletin, 116,* 143–165.

Spanos, N. P. (1996). *Multiple identities & false memories: A sociocognitive perspective.* Washington, DC: American Psychological Association.

Spence, K. W. (1937). The differential response in animals to stimuli varying within a single dimension. *Psychological Review, 44,* 430–444.

Spiegler, M. D., & Guevremont, D. C. (1998). *Contemporary behavior therapy* (3rd ed.). Pacific Grove, CA: Brooks/Cole.

Staddon, J. E. R. (1977). Schedule-induced behavior. In W. K. Honig & J. E. R. Staddon (Eds.), *Handbook of operant behavior.* Englewood Cliffs, NJ: Prentice-Hall.

Staddon, J. E. R., & Simmelhag, V. L. (1971). The "superstition" experiment: A reexamination of its implications for the principles of adaptive behavior. *Psychological Review, 78,* 3–43.

Stampfl, T. G. (1987). Theoretical implications of the neurotic paradox as a problem in behavior theory: An experimental resolution. *The Behavior Analyst, 10,* 161–173.

Starkes, J. L., & Ericsson, K. A. (Eds.). (2003). *Expert performance in sports: Advances in research on sport expertise.* Champagne, IL: Human Kinetics.

Steketee, G., & Foa, E. B. (1985). Obsessive-compulsive disorder. In D. H. Barlow (Ed.), *Clinical handbook of psychological disorders: A step-by-step treatment manual.* New York: Guilford.

Stevenson-Hinde, J. (1973). Constraints on reinforcement. In R. A. Hinde & J. Stevenson-Hinde (Eds.), *Constraints on learning.* New York: Academic Press.

Streissguth, A. P., Barr, H. M., Bookstein, F. L., Samson, P. D., & Olson, H. C. (1999). The long-term neurocognitive consequences of prenatal alcohol exposure. A 14-year study. *Psychological Science, 10,* 186–190.

Sulzer-Azaroff, B., & Mayer, G. R. (1991). *Behavior analysis for lasting change.* Fort Worth, TX: Holt, Rinehart, & Winston.

Symbaluk, D. G. (1996). The effects of food restriction and training on male athletes. In W. F. Epling & W. D. Pierce (Eds.), *Activity anorexia: Theory, research, and treatment.* Mahwah, NJ: Erlbaum.

Tacitus (Trans. 1956). *Annals of imperial Rome* (M. Grant, Trans.). New York: Penguin.

Task Force on Promotion and Dissemination of Psychological Procedures. (1995). Training in and dissemination of empirically-validated psychological treatments. Report and recommendations. *The Clinical Psychologist, 48,* 3–24.

Terrace, H. S. (1963a). Discrimination learning with and without "errors." *Journal of the Experimental Analysis of Behavior, 6,* 1–27.

Terrace, H. S. (1963b). Errorless transfer of a discrimination across two continua. *Journal of the Experimental Analysis of Behavior, 6,* 223–232.

Terrace, H. S. (1979). *Nim.* New York: Knopf.

Terrace, H. S. (1985). On the nature of animal thinking. *Neuroscience and Biobehavioral Reviews, 9,* 643–652.

Terrace, H. S., Petitio, L. A., Sanders, R. J., & Bever, T. G. (1979). Can an ape create a sentence? *Science, 206,* 891–902.

Thigpen, C. H., & Cleckley, H. M. (1957). *The three faces of Eve.* New York: McGraw-Hill.

Thompson, R. F. (1972). Sensory preconditioning. In R. F. Thompson & J. F. Voss (Eds.), *Topics in learning and performance.* New York: Academic Press.

Thompson, T. (1963). Visual reinforcement in Siamese fighting fish. *Science, 141,* 55–57.

Thorndike, E. L. (1898). Animal intelligence: An experimental study of the associative processes in animals. *Psychological Review Monograph Supplement, 2,* 1–109.

Thorndike, E. L. (1911/1965). *Animal intelligence*. New York: Hafner.

Thyer, B. A. (1999). Was Carl Jung a behavior analyst? *Journal of Applied Behavior Analysis, 32,* 533.

Timberlake, W. (1983). Rats' responses to a moving object related to food or water: A behavior systems analysis. *Animal Learning and Behavior, 11,* 309–320.

Timberlake, W. (1993). Behavior systems and reinforcement: An integrative approach. *Journal of the Experimental Analysis of Behavior, 60,* 105–128.

Timberlake, W., & Allison, J. (1974). Response deprivation: An empirical approach to instrumental performance. *Psychological Review, 81,* 146–164.

Timberlake, W., & Grant, D. S. (1975). Autoshaping in rats to the presentation of another rat predicting food. *Science, 190,* 690–692.

Timberlake, W., & Lucas, G. A. (1989). Behavior systems and learning: From misbehavior to general principles. In S. B. Klein & R. R. Mowrer (Eds.), *Contemporary learning theories: Instrumental conditioning theory and the impact of biological constraints on learning.* Hillsdale, NJ: Erlbaum.

Tinbergen, N. (1951). *The study of instinct.* Oxford: Clarendon Press.

Tolin, D. F., & Steketee, G. (2007). General issues in psychological treatment for obsessive-compulsive disorder. In M. M. Antony, C. Purdon, & L. J. Summerfeldt (Eds.), *Psychological treatment of obsessive-compulsive disorder: Fundamentals and beyond.* Washington, DC: American Psychological Association.

Tolman, E. C. (1932). *Purposive behavior in animals and men.* New York: Appleton-Century-Crofts.

Tolman, E. C. (1948). Cognitive maps in rats and men. *Psychological Review, 55,* 189–208.

Tolman, E. C., & Honzik, C. H. (1930). Degrees of hunger, reward and nonreward, and maze learning in rats. *University of California Publications in Psychology, 4,* 241–275.

Tomasello, M. (1996). Do apes ape? In B. G. Galef, Jr., & C. M. Heyes (Eds.), *Social learning in animals: The roots of culture.* New York: Academic Press.

Tomie, A. (1996). Self-regulation and animal behavior. *Psychological Inquiry, 7,* 83–85.

Tomie, A., Brooks, W., & Zito, B. (1989). Sign-tracking: The search for reward. In S. B. Klein & R. R. Mowrer (Eds.), *Contemporary learning theories: Pavlovian conditioning and the status of traditional learning theory.* Hillsdale, NJ: Erlbaum.

Ulrich, R. E., & Azrin, N. A. (1962). Reflexive fighting in response to aversive stimuli. *Journal of the Experimental Analysis of Behavior, 5,* 511–520.

Valentine, C. W. (1930). The innate bases of fear. *Journal of Genetic Psychology, 37,* 394–420.

Van der Kolk, B. A. (1989). The compulsion to repeat the trauma: Re-enactment, revictimization, and masochism. *Psychiatric Clinics of North America, 12,* 389–411.

Van Houten, R. (1983). Punishment from the animal laboratory to the applied setting. In S. Axelrod & J. Apsche (Eds.), *The effects of punishment on human behavior.* New York: Academic Press.

Vander Wall, S. B. (1982). An experimental analysis of cache recovery in Clarke's nutcracker. *Animal Behavior, 30,* 84–94.

Vargas, J. S. (1990). B. F. Skinner—The last few days. *Journal of Applied Behavior Analysis, 23,* 409–410.

Vollmer, T. R., & Bourret, J. (2000). An application of the matching law to evaluate the allocation of two- and three-point shots by college basketball players. *Journal of Applied Behavior Analysis, 33,* 137–150.

Wallace, I., & Pear, J. J. (1977). Self-control techniques of famous novelists. *Journal of Applied Behavior Analysis, 10,* 515–525.

Wallace, M., & Singer, G. (1976). Schedule induced behavior: A review of its generality, determinants and pharmacological data. *Pharmacology, Biochemistry, and Behavior, 5,* 483–490.

Wasserman, E. A., & Zentall, T. R. (Eds.). (2006). *Comparative cognition: Experimental explorations of animal intelligence.* New York: Oxford University Press.

Watson, D. L., & Tharp, R. G. (2002). *Self-directed behavior: Self-modification for personal adjustment* (7th ed.). Pacific Grove, CA: Brooks/Cole.

Watson, J. B. (1913). Psychology as the behaviorist views it. *Psychological Review, 20,* 154–177.

Watson, J. B. (1930). *Behaviorism.* New York: Norton.

Watson, J. B., & Rayner, R. (1920). Conditioned emotional reactions. *Journal of Experimental Child Psychology, 3,* 1–14.

Webster, R. (1995). *Why Freud was wrong: Sin, science and psychoanalysis.* New York: Basic Books.

Weindruch, R. (1996, January). Caloric restriction and aging. *Scientific American, 274,* 46–52.

Weiss, H. M., Suckow, K., & Rakestraw, T. L., Jr. (1999). Influence of modeling on self-set goals: Direct and mediated effects. *Human Performance, 12,* 89–114.

Welker, R. L. (1976). Acquisition of a free-operant-appetitive response in pigeons as a function of prior experience with response-independent food. *Learning and Motivation, 7,* 394–405.

Wells, A., & Papageorgiou, C. (1995). Worry and the incubation of intrusive images following stress. *Behaviour Research and Therapy, 33,* 579–583.

Wheatley, K. L., Welker, R. L., & Miles, R. C. (1977). Acquisition of barpressing in rats following experience with response-independent food. *Animal Learning and Behavior, 5,* 236–242.

Wheeler, G. (1996). Exercise, sports, and anorexia. In W. F. Epling & W. D. Pierce (Eds.), *Activity anorexia: Theory, research, and treatment.* Mahwah, NJ: Erlbaum.

Whiten, A. (1998). Imitation of the sequential structure of actions by chimpanzees (*Pan troglodytes*). *Journal of Comparative Psychology, 112,* 270–281.

Wicks, S. R., & Rankin, C. H. (1997). Effects of tap withdrawal response habituation on other withdrawal behaviors: The localization of habituation in the nematode *Caenorhabditis elegans. Behavioral Neuroscience, 111,* 342–353.

Wilcoxon, H. C., Dragoin, W. B., & Kral, P. A. (1971). Illness-induced aversions in rat and quail: Relative salience of visual and gustatory cues. *Science, 171,* 826–828.

Williams, B. A. (1981). The following schedule of reinforcement as a fundamental determinant of steady state contrast in multiple schedules. *Journal of the Experimental Analysis of Behavior, 35,* 293–310.

Williams, D. R., & Williams, H. (1969). Automaintenance in the pigeon: Sustained pecking despite contingent nonreinforcement. *Journal of the Experimental Analysis of Behavior, 12,* 511–520.

Williams, J. L. (1973). *Operant learning: Procedures for changing behavior.* Monterey, CA: Brooks/Cole.

Wilson, C. (1972). *New pathways in psychology: Maslow and the post-Freudian revolution.* New York: Taplinger.

Wilson, G. T. (1997). Behavior therapy at century close. *Behavior Therapy, 28,* 449–457.

Wilson, J. F., & Cantor, M. B. (1987). An animal model of excessive eating: Schedule-induced hyperphagia in food-satiated rats. *Journal of the Experimental Analysis of Behavior, 47,* 335–346.

Wolfe, J. B., & Kaplon, M. D. (1941). Effect of amount of reward and consummative activity on learning in chickens. *Journal of Comparative Psychology, 31,* 353–361.

Wolpe, J. (1958). *Psychotherapy by reciprocal inhibition.* Stanford, CA: Stanford University Press.

Wolpe, J. (1995). Reciprocal inhibition: Major agent of behavior change. In W. O'Donohue & L. Krasner (Eds.), *Theories of behavior therapy: Exploring behavior change.* Washington, DC: American Psychological Association.

Woods, D. J., & Routtenberg, A. (1971). "Self-starvation" in activity wheels: Developmental and chlorpromazine interactions. *Journal of Comparative and Physiological Psychology, 76,* 84–93.

Worthington, E. L. (1979). Behavioral self-control and the contract problem. *Teaching of Psychology, 6,* 91–94.

Yates, A. (1996). Athletes, eating disorders, and the overtraining syndrome. In W. F. Epling & W. D. Pierce (Eds.), *Activity anorexia: Theory, research, and treatment*. Mahwah, NJ: Erlbaum.

Zeiler, M. D. (1971). Eliminating behavior with reinforcement. *Journal of the Experimental Analysis of Behavior, 16*, 401–405.

Zelman, D. C., Brandon, T. H., Jorenby, D. E., & Baker, T. B. (1992). Measures of affect and nicotine dependence predict differential response to smoking cessation treatments. *Journal of Consulting and Clinical Psychology, 60*, 943–952.

Zentall, T. R. (2006). Imitation: Definitions, evidence, and mechanisms. *Animal Cognition, 9*, 335–353.

Index